The Rise and Development of FinTech

This comprehensive guide serves to illuminate the rise and development of FinTech in Sweden, with the Internet as the key underlying driver. The multiple case studies examine topics such as: the adoption of online banking in Sweden; the identification and classification of different FinTech categories; process innovation developments within the traditional banking industry; and the Venture Capital (VC) landscape in Sweden, as shown through interviews with VC representatives, mainly from Sweden but also from the US and Germany, as well as offering insight into the companies that are currently operating in the FinTech arena in Sweden. The authors address questions such as: How will the regulatory landscape shape the future of FinTech companies? What are the factors that will likely drive the adoption of FinTech services in the future? What is the future role of banks in the context of FinTech and digitalization? What are the policies and government initiatives that aim to support the FinTech ecosystem in Sweden? Complex concepts and ideas are rendered in an easily digestible yet thought-provoking way.

The book was initiated by the IIS (the Internet Foundation in Sweden), an independent organization promoting the positive development of the Internet in the country. It is also responsible for the Internet's Swedish top-level domain .se, including the registration of domain names, and the administration and technical maintenance of the national domain name registry. The book illustrates how Sweden acts (or does not act) as a competitive player in the global FinTech arena, and is a vital addition to students and practitioners in the field.

Robin Teigland is Professor of Business Administration with a specialization in Strategic Information Systems Management and Co-director of the Center for Strategy and Competitiveness at the Stockholm School of Economics (SSE), Sweden.

Shahryar Siri is a Researcher and Project Manager at the Stockholm School of Economics Institute for Research (SIR), Sweden, where he is responsible for the three-year research project "The Innovative Internet" in collaboration with the Internet Foundation in Sweden (IIS). Prior to his role at SIR, he worked as a Consumer Insights Researcher at Ericsson and on a freelance basis.

Anthony Larsson is a Doctoral Candidate of Medical Science at Karolinska Institutet (KI), Sweden, and a Researcher at the Stockholm School of Economics Institute of Research (SIR), Sweden. He holds a MSc in Business & Economics, an MBA in Business, a MSc in Political Science, a MSc in Anthropology and an A.S. in Psychology. His research interests include management, organization studies, entrepreneurship, innovation studies, customer loyalty, digitalization, branding, stakeholder analysis, political science, anthropology, and qualitative research methods.

Alejandro Moreno Puertas is a MSc finance student at the Stockholm School of Economics (SSE), Sweden. He has previously worked in Shanghai as a representative of *Sociedad Española de Negocios en Asia y America SL* for their Chinese business development. He graduated from Tilburg University with a BSc in economics.

Claire Ingram Bogusz is a Researcher at the Stockholm School of Economics (SSE), Sweden. Her research interests are in how code-based technologies affect entrepreneurship and organizational change. Her PhD thesis examined FinTech entrepreneurship reliant on peer-to-peer technologies.

Routledge International Studies in Money and Banking

For a full list of titles in this series, please visit www.routledge.com/series/SE0403

86 Wages, Bonuses and Appropriation of Profit in the Financial Industry
The Working Rich
Olivier Godechot

87 Banking and Monetary Policies in a Changing Financial Environment
A Regulatory Approach
Wassim Shahin and Elias El-Achkar

88 Modern Monetary Theory and European Macroeconomics
Dirk H. Ehnts

89 Capital Flows, Financial Markets and Banking Crises
Chia-Ying Chang

90 Banking and Economic Rent in Asia
Rent Effects, Financial Fragility and Economic Development
Edited by Yasushi Suzuki, Mohammad Dulal Miah, Manjula K. Wanniarachchige, and S.M. Sohrab Uddin

91 Finance at Work
Edited by Valérie Boussard

92 The Development of International Monetary Policy
Christopher Warburton

93 Pension Fund Economics and Finance
Efficiency, Investments and Risk-Taking
Edited by Jacob A. Bikker

94 The Rise and Development of FinTech
Accounts of Disruption from Sweden and Beyond
Edited by Robin Teigland, Shahryar Siri, Anthony Larsson, Alejandro Moreno Puertas, and Claire Ingram Bogusz

The Rise and Development of FinTech

Accounts of Disruption from Sweden and Beyond

Edited by Robin Teigland, Shahryar Siri, Anthony Larsson, Alejandro Moreno Puertas, and Claire Ingram Bogusz

Routledge
Taylor & Francis Group
LONDON AND NEW YORK

First published 2018
by Routledge
2 Park Square, Milton Park, Abingdon, Oxon OX14 4RN

and by Routledge
605 Third Avenue, New York, NY 10017

First issued in paperback 2020

Routledge is an imprint of the Taylor & Francis Group, an informa business

British Library Cataloguing-in-Publication Data
A catalogue record for this book is available from the British Library

Library of Congress Cataloging-in-Publication Data
Names: Teigland, Robin, 1964- editor.
Title: The rise and development of fintech : accounts of disruption from Sweden and beyond / [edited by] Robin Teigland [and four others].
Description: Abingdon, Oxon ; New York, NY : Routledge, 2017. | Includes bibliographical references and index.
Identifiers: LCCN 2017045736 (print) | LCCN 2017051503 (ebook) | ISBN 9781351183628 (eBook) | ISBN 9780815378501 (hardback : alk. paper)
Subjects: LCSH: Finance—Technological innovations—Sweden. | Internet banking—Sweden.
Classification: LCC HG186.S85 (ebook) | LCC HG186.S85 R57 2017 (print) | DDC 332.10285/4678—dc23
LC record available at https://lccn.loc.gov/2017045736

ISBN 13: 978-0-367-73518-0 (pbk)
ISBN 13: 978-0-8153-7850-1 (hbk)

Typeset in Times New Roman
by Swales & Willis Ltd, Exeter, Devon, UK

Contents

Figures

Tables

Contributors

Niklas Arvidsson is Associate Professor in Industrial Dynamics at the Royal Institute of Technology, and holds a PhD from the Stockholm School of Economics. He is published in *Organization Science, Management Science*, and *Scandinavian Journal of Management*, as well as by Cambridge University Press, John Wiley & Sons, Earthscan, and Oxford University Press. His research focuses on innovation and change in payments via projects studying: merchants' views on cash; merchants' strategies for payments and omnichannel platforms; disruptive innovation in payments; the cashless society; and turbulence in the field of payments. He is teaching strategy, innovation, knowledge formation, and leadership.

Michael Björn is Head of Research at Ericsson ConsumerLab. In his role, he is studying global consumer trends, as well as the process of assimilation of ICT into everyday consumer life. Professionally, he is most well known as the author of the Ericsson ConsumerLab *10 Hot Consumer Trends* report that has been published annually for six years and gained much international media coverage, including interviews with BBC World News and CNN. Between 2000 and 2002, Michael Björn was responsible for mobile Internet applications at Ericsson in Japan. He joined Ericsson in 1997 as an analyst, after having completed his PhD in Data Modeling at the University of Tsukuba in Japan. Michael is also Adjunct Professor at the Lund University School of Economics and Management, a novelist with two works of fiction, and a journalist regularly contributing to Tokyo-based rock music magazine *Strange Days*.

Catharina Burenstam Linder is Head of Investor Relations at the Swedish cleantech company Climeon. She has been in the consulting business for the past ten years focusing on operational strategy and change management. She has an academic background from Stockholm University, where she graduated with an MSc in Molecular Biology.

Alexandre Dubois' research has led him to investigate entrepreneurship and globalization processes in rural regions, and more specifically how actors in geographically peripheral parts of Europe are engaged in multiple streams of relations that extend both locally and internationally.

Anna Felländer has extensive experience in analyzing how digitalization is changing society, business, and the economy. She has published a number of reports on the subject, one of which describes opportunities and challenges of the sharing economy. Felländer has been working with the Swedish government for 10 years, and is currently an advisor to the Swedish Minister of Digitalization. Also, she is a visiting fellow to the Swedish House of Finance at SSE. She is also a senior advisor to the Boston Consulting Group, as well as a board member and expert advisor to AI companies. In addition to her work with the Digitalization Commission, she was an expert advisor in the government's official report on taxi and car sharing in 2016. From 2013 to 2016, she held positions as Chief Economist and Digital Economist at Swedbank. Felländer has a Master of Science in International Economics from the Stockholm School of Economics.

Åke Freij is a researcher with focus on innovation, business models and regulations. He earned his PhD in 2017 at the Stockholm School of Economics. In his thesis Åke reported on what companies do to master the impact of regulatory change. He is currently Managing Principal at Capco, where he advises clients on the future of regulatory management and RegTech. In his research Åke wants to increase understanding of the interplay between regulatory compliance and digitalization to create innovation.

Michal Gromek is a researcher on FinTech at the Center for Strategy and Competitiveness at the Stockholm School of Economics (SSE). As a former executive of Rocket Internet and FundedByMe, he is a rare breed in European academia. Recognized by both CrowdfundingHub and the European Equity Crowdfunding Association as an expert in the field of FinTech, he is the co-author of the Pan-European Crowdfunding Report. Michal has launched digital financing platforms on three continents and seven countries, and performed a FinTech training session with the Malaysian Securities Commission in Kuala Lumpur. Currently halfway through his PhD in Business Administration, he has authored or co-authored four chapters in this book, and coordinates the Stockholm FinTech Report, which will be published by the end of 2017.

Mattias Hallberg's passions are economics and education policy, preferable both at the same time. He is currently working as a political advisor for the ranking member of the Committee on Finance at the Swedish parliament. Before that, he was studying economics at Stockholm University and works as a research assistant at IIES. Previously, he was the President of the Swedish Federation of Student Unions; the largest youth organization in Sweden. His latest publication was a policy report on higher education, research, and innovation in Sweden, commissioned by the Arvid Lindman Foundation.

Håkan Holmberg is a data scientist specializing in the fields of psychometrics and blockchain technology. He is presently involved in projects at Uppsala University as well as the National Board of Health and Welfare. He has previously published on the topic of blockchain technology in *Europaperspektiv 2017*. Håkan holds a master's degree in Mathematics from Stockholm University.

Claire Ingram Bogusz is a researcher at the Stockholm School of Economics (SSE), Sweden. Her research interests are in how code-based technologies affect entrepreneurship and organizational change. Her PhD thesis examined FinTech entrepreneurship reliant on peer-to-peer technologies.

Katarzyna Jereczek is an entrepreneur, project manager, and speaker, focusing on the global disruption of the finance industry. As a project manager, she worked at the world's largest company builder to develop and launch the first P2P lending platform in Poland. In recent years, she helped and worked with numerous companies implementing mobile banking solutions, cryptocurrency exchange platforms, and establishing global compliance and regulatory guidelines. Katarzyna holds a master's degree in Project Management from Warsaw School of Economics, and dedicates her current research work to topics grouped around the development of FinTech globally, and regulatory changes and adjustments.

Georgios Kryparos is an IT and information security specialist with more than 13 years of experience in the industry. He has an MSc in Information and Communication Systems Security from the Royal Institute of Technology (KTH) in Stockholm, as well as several IT and information security industry certifications. He currently works at Klarna as a lead security engineer, focusing on implementing and assessing the security architecture of products and services, as well as testing the security of internal and external applications and systems. He also frequently gives talks and presentations in internal and external events with the purpose of raising awareness around security among his colleagues and the general public.

Anthony Larsson is a Doctoral Candidate of Medical Science at Karolinska Institutet (KI), Sweden, and a Researcher at the Stockholm School of Economics Institute of Research (SIR), Sweden. He holds a MSc in Business & Economics, an MBA in Business, a MSc in Political Science, a MSc in Anthropology, and an A.S. in Psychology. His research interests include management, organization studies, entrepreneurship, innovation studies, customer loyalty, digitalization, branding, stakeholder analysis, political science, anthropology, and qualitative research methods.

Mats Lewan is an author, international keynote speaker, futurist, consultant, journalist, and research analyst focused on future and technology. He has been working for more than 15 years as a technology reporter for the leading Swedish technology magazine *Ny Teknik*. He also started the forward-looking Swedish digital magazine *Next Magasin*, for which he was Managing Editor. Previously, Mats worked internationally as a freelance journalist, and as a reporter for CBS CNET News in San Francisco while attending the Innovation Journalism program at Stanford University. Mats holds an MSc degree in Engineering Physics from the Royal Institute of Technology in Stockholm, Sweden.

Agnė Mačijauskaitė is currently a Master in Finance student at the Stockholm School of Economics (Stockholm) and a private equity analyst at Nordic Real Estate Partners (NREP). She has two years' experience in investment banking, and has worked on international projects within technology, pharma, and infrastructure. Agnė holds a BSc in Business Administration with a finance specialization from the Norwegian Business School (Oslo), as well as a BSc in economics with a political specialization from ISM University of Management and Economics (Vilnius). Her main research focus is on FinTech and behavioral and household finance.

Timotheos Mavropoulos (Lic.) did his PhD in Finance studies at the Swedish House of Finance, Stockholm School of Economics and is a corporate finance researcher at Pinq Mango Capital Partners, the world's first Behavioural Investment Bank. His research interests include real estate finance, behavioral finance, social finance, and FinTech. He has worked as a research assistant for Sweden's Central Bank during its inquiry into the risks in the Swedish housing market, and has participated in completing the "Household Finance" chapter in the *Handbook of the Economics of Finance*. He has performed teaching assignments for corporate finance, behavioral finance, international financial management, corporate transition, and degree projects in finance courses.

Alejandro Moreno Puertas is a MSc finance student at the Stockholm School of Economics (SSE), Sweden. He has previously worked in Shanghai as a representative of *Sociedad Española de Negocios en Asia y America SL* for their Chinese business development. He graduated from Tilburg University with a BSc in economics.

Björn Olsson is a passionate economist currently working at the Swedish Bankers' Association. Previously he has worked for the party leader of the Moderate party. He completed his MSc in Economics at the University of Lund and has studied Business and Finance at Cass Business School in London.

Claudia Olsson is an innovation leader and speaker in the field of digital transformation. She is the founder and CEO of Exponential AB, a global consultancy specialized in providing strategic advice, analysis, and professional development related to the digital transformation. Her work focuses on the impact of new technologies on citizens, society, and global markets. In 2016, Claudia authored the *Sweden 2030* future scenario for the Digitalization Commission at the Government of Sweden, focused on the digital, integrated, smart, and competitive society. She also co-authored the acclaimed report "Blockchain-Decentralized Trust" for the Entrepreneurship Forum. Claudia has served as Associate Faculty at Singularity University as well as Senior Advisor to the Office of Strategic Analysis at the Ministry for Foreign Affairs in Sweden. Claudia previously set up and managed the policy think tank ACCESS Health International in Singapore following her work for ACCESS in India and her assignment with the United Nations Economic and Social Council (ECOSOC).

Elizabeth Press is the founder of D3M Labs, a consultancy focused on data monetization and creation of data-as-a-service products. Elizabeth has also worked as a consultant for federal ministries. As an intrapreneur at Dell, Elizabeth built up and managed advanced analytics functions globally. Before Dell, she worked in top-tier strategy consulting and quantitative finance. She has a BA in International Relations from Tufts University and an MSc in International Economics and Business from the Stockholm School of Economics. She has published numerous blogs and white papers on the topic of strategic uses of data and organizational transformation.

Shahryar Siri is a Researcher and Project Manager at the Stockholm School of Economics Institute for Research (SIR), Sweden, where he is responsible for the three-year research project "The Innovative Internet" in collaboration with the Internet Foundation in Sweden (IIS). Prior to his role at SIR, he worked as a Consumer Insights Researcher at Ericsson and on a freelance basis.

Robin Teigland is Professor of Business Administration with a specialization in Strategic Information Systems Management and Co-director of the Center for Strategy and Competitiveness at the Stockholm School of Economics (SSE), Sweden.

Jochem van der Zande will finish his CEMS Master in International Management at the Rotterdam School of Management in February 2018. He also holds a BSc in International Business Administration from RSM and went on exchanges to the Stockholm School of Economics and BI Norwegian Business School. Before starting his Masters, Jochem spent a year doing internships at EY Transaction Advisory Services and AkzoNobel. From March onward, he will work at Danske Bank in Copenhagen as a strategy consultant. His research interests are mergers & acquisitions and technology. He is currently writing his Master thesis on the role of external advisors during the acquisition process. Outside of his studies, Jochem is a passionate badminton player.

Acknowledgments

This edited volume constitutes the third and penultimate phase of the three-year project 'The Innovative Internet,' which is funded by the Internet Foundation in Sweden (IIS—Internetstiftelsen i Sverige). The editorial team, together with our co-authors, would like to extend our deepest gratitude to IIS, and in particular Danny Aerts and Jannike Tillå, who have supported and guided us throughout the project but equally allowed us the full freedom to take ownership and to keep an open and explorative approach to our research. We would also like to thank the Marianne and Marcus Wallenberg Foundation for funding research within the FinTech area by one of the Editors and some of the authors, which served as a catalyst for this volume.

Furthermore, this volume would not have been possible without the dedicated team of co-authors, practitioners, and industry experts who, during the course of the year, researched, interviewed, and analyzed the Swedish FinTech ecosystem and its numerous interlocking parts. We would also like to thank Johan Söderholm at the Stockholm Institute of Research, as well as Kristina Abbots and Laura Hussey, along with the rest of the assisting staff at Routledge for their help and support throughout every step in the making of this volume. Last but not least, we would also like to extend special gratitude to our families and friends for their unwavering and invaluable moral support throughout this process.

We on the editorial team welcome feedback of any kind on the volume as we believe that transparency and cooperation outside our research team is paramount to ensuring that our research is conveyed as thoroughly as possible. Feel free to reach out to us should you like to discuss any of the topics raised in this book or if you would like to discuss prospects for future collaborations. As this is an Open Access volume, we welcome you to freely spread it to any and all interested parties you may encounter. On this final note, we hope that you will enjoy reading this volume as much as we enjoyed working on it.

The Editorial Team: Robin Teigland, Shahryar Siri,
Anthony Larsson, Alejandro Moreno Puertas, and Claire Ingram Bogusz
Stockholm, January 2018

Foreword

The past decade has seen a global surge in the development of new financial technologies, both as a response to the financial crisis of 2008 and as a consequence of rapid advances in digitalization. Democratization of technology has enabled new market entrants and grassroots innovators to disrupt traditional industries and practices through decentralized financial solutions, increased transparency, and a higher degree of automation. These forces are in the process of revolutionizing the user experience while at the same time increasing the efficiency in the financial system.

Sweden has taken an active role in the development of breakthrough financial technologies, in line with the country's long history of embracing technological innovations. In 1968, Sweden launched the world's first online ATM, and in 2003 a national system for electronic identification was introduced (BankID), which laid an important foundation for a rapid deployment of new FinTech and digital services ventures. Over the past decades, companies such as Klarna and iZettle have helped strengthen Sweden's position as an influential player in the field of financial technologies. Following the larger successes, a beneficial ecosystem for FinTech startups is taking form, and several areas of the financial industry present opportunities going forward.

Globally, Sweden is one of the few countries that has become a nearly cashless economy. Transaction fees have gone down and many banks no longer offer cash services nor ATMs, some stores and cafés do not even accept cash. The Riksbank, Sweden's Central Bank, contributed to this development by eliminating the country's highest denomination bill, the SEK 10,000 bill, in 1991. The implementation of this mobile payment system, Swish, in 2012, which enables frictionless, instant and free transactions for individuals to Swedish bank accounts, has been another important factor. Furthermore, many public services, such as buses and trains, no longer accept cash payments in favor of digital alternatives. As digital trust continues to grow, and the Millennials, mostly a "digital native" population, play a larger role in the economy, these trends are expected to continue.

We are seeing the beginning of what some refer to as the Fourth Industrial Revolution, where exponential technology development is impacting a wide range of sectors. Digital, physical, and even biological areas are merging, and in the wake of the innovations, data are becoming an abundant and exponentially increasing asset. For FinTech innovators, the data that can be accessed and analyzed constitute the base for new products and services related to financial transactions. As the Internet of Things further develops—with 5G enabling a smart and highly connected society—we can expect this trend to further accelerate.

The value of data, which are continually identified, created, and stored in connection to the financial system, can largely be unlocked through automated and algorithm-driven services. Through advancements in artificial intelligence and related machine learning, automated systems will be able to actively help customers plan and invest their assets, taking over a role traditionally held by human brokers. By eliminating the human factor, the costs of trades will continue to decrease, and services previously only accessible to high net-worth investors will become increasingly available to the population at large. The new financial technologies have the potential to support a safer and more sound personal finance planning. This will become increasingly in focus as retirement saving schemes are being updated and shaped to meet the needs of the new global workforce as the number of freelancers and independent contractors continues to grow.

One of the developments in financial technologies that is currently attracting the most attention is blockchain-based systems and related distributed ledger technologies. These technologies are expected to both have an impact within regulated financial markets, where they can provide a secure system for handling and tracking financial assets, and also outside regulated financial markets, where they can provide transparent and global decentralized financial mechanisms as well as digital alternative currencies. Swedish banks and other financial institutions are exploring the potential of applying blockchain technology within existing legal frameworks.

The development of peer-to-peer computing globally has also given rise to platforms that connect borrowers directly to lenders and where the "crowd" is engaged to fund new entrepreneurial initiatives. The trend has gained momentum as it grants access to borrowers or entrepreneurs who would otherwise not be able to obtain investments from banks or traditional credit institutions. Further peer-to-peer innovations are expected in FinTech in the years to come.

The establishment of the FinTech space is still in its early days, and further advancements are anticipated as artificial intelligence and abundant data shape the financial landscape. Some developments may be initiated by governments and central banks. One such possibility is the launch of the e-krona, a Swedish national digital currency that has been proposed and is under consideration by the Riksbank. Other developments will come from outside the traditional centralized financial system, for example through the expansion of public blockchain-based currencies and applications that enable direct peer-to-peer transactions on a global scale without intermediaries. Looking ahead, the adoption of financial technologies will also be further enabled by the European Union's banking legislation, enabling open banking or the opening up of sets of customer data for third-party integration.

As FinTech evolves, we can expect the role of traditional players in the financial markets as well as financial institutions to be affected, and many will have to change or modify their customer offerings and even their business models. The advancement of a cashless society, with decentralized financial mechanisms for transactions, lending, borrowing, and fundraising, may require new legislation and mechanisms for oversight.

FinTech developments in Sweden are contributing to the formation of technological expertise, know-how, and experience that can be of significant importance for the growth of other Internet-related industries in Sweden. Many sectors will be able to learn from the innovations in FinTech, for example from the security and cryptographic solutions that the financial systems require. These can become of use in a variety of fields, ranging from supply chain management and property rights to the educational sector.

The main developments and insights in the history and future potential of FinTech are presented in this book, *The Rise and Development of FinTech: Accounts of Disruption from Sweden and Beyond*. This book provides guidance for entrepreneurs, established actors, and policymakers both within the financial services sector as well as in other sectors both in Sweden and abroad on how to leverage the potential of the latest and future technological progress within FinTech. The collection of insightful articles and cases provides an important understanding for one of the fastest-developing technological fields, with significant impact on society at large.

Claudia Olsson
CEO Exponential AB
Young Global Leader World Economic Forum
Associate Faculty Singularity University

Introduction

FinTech and shifting financial system institutions

Robin Teigland, Shahryar Siri, Anthony Larsson, Alejandro Moreno Puertas, and Claire Ingram Bogusz

Introduction

It is, today, widely known that the financial system as we knew it was shaken to the core by the 2008 global financial crisis. Not only did consumers lose their homes and savings due to bankers' disreputable—and sometimes illegal—practices, but governments also cracked down on this risk-taking. They did this by raising capital requirements, and in some cases requiring banks to ring-fence capital—a measure used by banks to protect assets from less favorable conditions and regulations in particularly hard-hit and high-risk countries.

Therefore, it is not too surprising that financial system actors came to be viewed suspiciously by consumers, firms, and governments. Combined with advances in new technologies and commonplace digital tools such as smartphones, this lack of trust in established financial actors paved the way for new financial technologies, firms, and practices.

The scale of this change, both in Sweden and globally, has been so large that one might say that what was once "taken for granted" in finance has changed. What consumers, bankers, and governments today consider to be normal is not what it once was.

Studies of activities that are "taken for granted," what are known as institutionalized activities, have long been conducted by institutional theorists. However, their starting point is that institutional change is difficult. Incumbents in a field, such as the financial services industry, benefit from things staying the same, and they often have the most power and resources at their disposal to prevent changes to the *status quo* (Scott, 1995). Moreover, all actors in a particular institutional field are influenced by sets of established norms, ways of thinking, and regulations. They therefore tend to gravitate toward similar business models and practices (DiMaggio and Powell, 1983). In so doing, they reinforce existing norms, ways of thinking, and regulations.

Changes are therefore curious when they do occur. The "paradox of embedded agency" suggests that agents, or actors, operating in an established field can only exercise agency within the framework of existing norms, ways of thinking, and regulations (Greenwood and Suddaby, 2006). Institutional theorists are thus intrigued by how institutional-level changes occur, as has clearly been the case with the emergence of FinTech.

Institutional theory not only demonstrates why it is that entrepreneurs and other change agents have to fight against the tide in order to become accepted, but it also gives us some insight into what the mechanisms are whereby changes may occur, and what initiates these changes in the first place. In this chapter, we introduce modern institutional theory as a lens with which to understand and investigate the shifts that the financial services industry has undergone during the past 10 years. Below, we first provide a background to modern institutional theory as an umbrella lens for this book on FinTech before turning to a discussion on each of the four forces that lie at the heart of the institutional shifts in the industry. In presenting these forces, we also relate to the chapters of this book, while intertwining them with each of the chapters.

A modern institutional theory lens on FinTech

The building of new ways of doing things—or the maintenance and perpetuation of old ways—has long been studied through the lens of institutional theory. The first wave of institutional theorists argued that organizing, and thus business, was performed by rational bureaucracies. These rational bureaucracies would, as rational actors, come to the same conclusions about how—and why—businesses should be run in certain ways (Weber, 1978; Selznick, 1996). The introduction of any beneficial new technology under this conception would therefore be adopted and spread through all organizations like wildfire. As a result, there would be little or no room for entrepreneurship as existing organizations would adopt any potentially groundbreaking technologies quickly and efficiently. The reality of organizations, however, is not only that the people who run them are not perfectly rational, but that the technologies—particularly as the advantages that they confer are often uncertain—may also take time to be adopted.

A second wave of institutional theorists, or neo-institutional theorists, therefore began to examine institutionalization through a new lens: one that focused on an actor's cognition and the effects of micro-, meso-, and macro-level norms on both individuals and organizations (DiMaggio and Powell, 1983). These theorists pointed to the importance of cognitive processes, most notably those around norms and informal interactions, in shaping organizations (DiMaggio and Powell, 1983, 1991).

Ultimately, these new institutional theorists outlined three sources of influence when it came to perpetuating—and even potentially reshaping—institutionalized activities. These included not only the all-important *regulations*, but also *cognition* and *norms*. Furthermore, these theorists emphasized the role of the different actors driving the changes in the field. Initial studies pointed to the importance of *peripheral* actors in forcing change within an institutional field (e.g., Battilana, Leca, and Boxenbaum, 2009), while more recent studies have shown how, particularly when it comes to economic activities, *incumbent* actors might be the ones to initiate change (e.g., Greenwood and Suddaby, 2006; Smets, Morris, and Greenwood, 2012). Together, these four forces—regulations, cognition, norms, and external and internal actors—can be used to understand and explore institutional change and how industries transform.

Indeed, it can sometimes be hard to tease apart the effects of different forces. Smets, Morris and Greenwood (2012), in a study of a merger between a British and German law firm, point out that new behaviors are typically embedded in old ones. Moreover, just as incumbent firms do not immediately leave the field when there has been a new innovation, institutional legacies are visible in a field long after firms and businesses have moved on.

The four forces driving change in financial services

Turning to the subject of this book, FinTech and the transformation of the financial services industry, we find evidence of these sources of influence at work within the financial services industry in Sweden.

Regulations: explicit and implicit drivers of change

When one thinks of regulations, one typically thinks of explicit regulations, for instance laws and policies that come from the state. However, when institutional theorists talk about regulations, they refer to the rules in a field that are both explicit and implicit (Thornton and Ocasio, 2008). Explicit regulations remain the simplest to nail down and to closely examine, while implicit rules tend not to change decisively and abruptly in the same way that explicit regulations do. When regulations are explicit and clear, change can potentially be expedited as startups and incumbents do not waste valuable resources on understanding how "things get done around here," but instead invest in activities building their venture. In the case of FinTech, one of the reasons that Sweden may have been more successful than other European countries, such as Italy, is the fact that regulations are clear (Lewan, Chapter 10, this volume).

Past studies of changes in regulations have shown how they have swiftly filtered down to businesses and their economic activities. For instance, in the finance industry in the 1990s, deregulation led to changes in the whole environment in which financial activities were conducted. This deregulation led to a change in consumer expectations, and the market feedback that followed these changes drove firms to change their business models and activities. This response to market feedback shows how it can be in actors' best interests to respond to institutional shifts (Lounsbury, 2002). Thus, market feedback not only promotes change through new activities and organizational forms, but it also deinstitutionalized old forms, leading to their demise (Lee and Pennings, 2002).

Turning to the current wave of change within financial services in Sweden, it is necessary to go back 20 years to the 1990s to understand some of the first regulatory drivers. To promote the early adoption of computers and the Internet across the country, the Swedish government designed a set of subsidies and tax breaks for home PC use, effectively deregulated the telecom market in 1998 (Swedish Competition Authority, 1998), and promoted the development of a physical infrastructure for the Internet. These visionary policy actions were instrumental in paving the way for the emergence of FinTech (Lewan, Chapter 10, this volume).

Computer penetration in Swedish households grew from 28 percent in 1995 to 76 percent in 2000, thereby encouraging the use of computers and the Internet not only by adults, but also by children, who perhaps preferred to stay inside and play with them as opposed to going outside during the cold and dark winters (Skog et al., 2016).

Many of these children have now entered the workforce, and as a result of early computer use are leading the way in developing innovations across a number of sectors (Skog et al., 2016). For example, Sebastian Siemiatkowski, CEO and one of the founders of Klarna, stated in an interview in *The Independent*: "When I was young, my family couldn't afford a computer. But because of this subsidy we could, and from the age of 10 I was always playing around with it. [It] was very visionary of the politicians back then" (Benwell, 2014). Today, Klarna is perhaps the largest FinTech in Europe in terms of customers, with over 60 million end customers facilitating 650,000 transactions daily, and it just recently received its banking license (Klarna, 2017).

Moving forward to the 2008 financial crisis, one of the outcomes from this was an increase in regulations. Since 2008, the banking sector in Europe has undergone one of the most extensive periods of regulatory change in modern history. For example, the United Kingdom's Financial Conduct Authority (FCA), as well as the European Commission, has introduced more than 80 regulations and rules to the domestic market (British Banking Association, 2016).

Regulatory change is a most pressing challenge for firms in numerous industries, for example automobiles and life sciences, yet the difficulty in successfully handling regulatory requirements is most challenging for financial services companies (Freij, Chapter 1, this volume). Thus, while regulatory compliance had enabled incumbents for years to maintain their position due to resulting high barriers to entry, this increase in regulations led to a reverse effect in terms of innovation in the market in the first phase of FinTech (Felländer et al., Chapter 8, this volume). First, the incumbent banks were forced to expend considerably more resources to ensure their compliance with national, regional, and global regulations across all four core areas of banking activities, thereby reducing their available resources to spend on innovation. In general, since the turn of the century, not only have the complexity and volume of each single regulation increased, but there are variations depending on the local jurisdiction, as well as different implications for different business units, for example insurance, retail banking, and investment management. The end result is that today, a major financial services company can have well over 100 regulatory implementation projects currently in progress (Freij, Chapter 1, this volume).

However, niche FinTech startups, initially in the area of payments such as Klarna and iZettle, were able to take advantage of this situation, having only to ensure a relatively limited compliance. Numerous new entrants appeared, and by 2016 around 217 companies had licenses to compete in Sweden in the payment service markets (Arvidsson, Chapter 13, this volume), Second, these stricter regulations hampered the supply of credit from banks, while the creation of new legislation led to increased risk aversion among other traditional financial providers, and as a result new forms of lending emerged. In Sweden, FundedByMe, CrowdCube, CrowdCulture, and Toborrow entered the crowdfunding segment, thereby offering consumers access to all four kinds of crowdfunding: donation, reward, equity, and lending (Felländer et al., Chapter 8, this volume; Gromek and Dubois, Chapter 12, this volume). As these platforms were merely acting as a platform for transactions and not directly holding financial assets, they were not bound to comply with the same regulations as traditional banks.

Thus, regulatory forces can both directly hamper as well as hasten institutional changes. Within Sweden and abroad, FinTech moved into a second phase in the middle of 2016, in which the industry and government began to understand that "FinTech" was here to stay. Realizing that FinTech solutions have the potential to improve the financial system for the benefit of consumers, regulators and politicians have started several actions to investigate how to best regulate FinTech startups such that these innovative initiatives are not stifled (Felländer et al., Chapter 8, this volume). Due to rigid regulations, the lead time in the financial sector is long, which can be a deal breaker for early-stage startups with little or no investments (Burenstam Linder, Chapter 20, this volume). To improve conditions for startups—although not in Sweden—the FCA in the UK has implemented a "regulatory sandbox." This sandbox is a restricted environment in which FinTech startups and industry incumbents can build and test their FinTech products and services without expending resources on interpreting and attempting to comply with potentially non-relevant regulations (Olsson and Hallberg, Chapter 3, this volume). Furthermore, within this second phase, industry incumbents also began to see that they needed to become more innovative as niche FinTech startups began chipping away at their customer base. Some are now proactively approaching changing regulations not as a threat, but as a platform for innovation instead, for instance through PSD2 (Payment Services Directive II) (Freij, Chapter 1, this volume).

When it comes to these changing rules, many entrepreneurs have treated changes in rules as opportunities for innovation. Indeed, changes in regulations have been seen to drive institutional changes, whether directly or indirectly (Lounsbury, 2002). Sometimes these rules might be implicit. For instance, it is clear that a digital presence is now vital for most modern-day businesses to reach their customers. While no explicit rule has led to this state of affairs, technological progress has made a digital presence an implicit rule—or norm—in modern commerce (DiMaggio et al., 2001).

As these changes lead to changing patterns, new regulatory responses often follow. This is often a consequence of political and social pressure. Indeed, political pressures have been widely observed to impact the legitimacy of existing institutional arrangements by shifting power arrangements in a field (Oliver, 1992). These kinds of power shifts have, in the past, come from crises of performance, changes in an environment, and compelling evidence that the taken-for-granted way of doing things is no longer effective.

The rise in digital businesses, for instance, has necessitated new rules around the collection and use of individuals' data. In Europe, the General Data Protection

Regulation (GDPR) will shortly become national law in European states; these regulations are seen as necessary to ensure that individuals are comfortable sharing their data, and protects those individuals who are less data-savvy (Felländer et al., Chapter 8, this volume; Ingram Bogusz, Chapter 11, this volume).

Cognition: legitimacy and changing beliefs

When it comes to another force driving institutional change—cognition, or how individuals think about and understand the actors and activities within an institutional field—one of the strongest influences within the current financial services transformation concerns the issue of legitimacy. Legitimacy is the degree to which an actor has the right to perform a certain activity, and the legitimacy of institutionalized activities is known to sometimes wax and wane over time (Dacin, Goodstein, and Scott, 2002). When legitimacy is at a low point, this provides opportunities for other activities to emerge and to spread.

In the aftermath of the 2008 financial crisis, it became clear that the field of finance could no longer carry on as it had. Instead, both consumers and governments began to question financial actors' activities—a classic instance in which powerful actors call legitimacy into question. Trust in banking institutions fell to new lows, with financial institutions "consistently at or near the bottom of any survey of public trust" (Flint, 2014, p.1), thereby opening the door for new actors to emerge.

Within Sweden prior to the financial crisis, the financial industry was characterized by high barriers to entry due to not only regulations, but also a high level of trust in existing players, which prevented startups from entering the market. However, the 2008 financial crisis revealed significant inefficiencies within the Swedish financial industry and considerably decreased the level of trust by society in incumbent actors (Felländer et al., Chapter 8, this volume). As a result, the number of Swedish FinTech startups has grown exponentially since 2008. Today, Stockholm boasts a vibrant FinTech startup ecosystem, with the number of FinTech companies numbering well over 100 (Stockholm FinTech Hub, 2017), while Stockholm ranks among the top five cities when it comes to FinTech investment (Gromek, Chapter 9, this volume).

While the loss of legitimacy in existing institutions enabled FinTech startups to enter the scene, these startups, like any startup, often lack the necessary legitimacy to successfully grow their business by attracting and retaining investors and customers. Within the Swedish FinTech startup scene, entrepreneurs have been employing a variety of ways to gain legitimacy, such as appointing well-known key persons to the board, starting collaborations with established actors, and aiming for appearance in relevant media—and in a longer perspective, always taking care of the customers and being reliable for them (Lewan, Chapter 6, this volume). For example, the cryptocurrency exchange Safello focused on ensuring regulatory compliance, with half of its staff working with such issues, while Dreams, the mobile savings app, partnered with an existing bank—Ålandsbanken—in order to leverage Ålandsbanken's reputation.

Recently, as noted above, the payment services unicorn Klarna received its banking license, further cementing its legitimacy in the market.

Furthermore, an initiative to bring legitimacy to the FinTech sector as a whole within Sweden is the creation of the Stockholm FinTech Hub in early 2017. This FinTech hub is an accelerator and coworking space that brings together Swedish FinTech startups, large financial institutions, and regulators to improve communication among these actors and facilitate innovation. Within the first half year from its inception in early 2017, the hub has managed to attract more than 50 members to the physical space, with many more in the virtual community.

Incumbent actors often have the most to gain by supporting the status quo (and often driving out, or ignoring, sources of change). However, when incumbent organizations face decreased legitimacy in the eyes of customers and others, they may be forced to change. In a study of the electric power industry, for instance, a shift away from a belief in regulated monopolies forced incumbent power firms to change their business models—and organizational forms (Sine and David, 2003). In Sweden, as new FinTech startups appeared, established banks endeavored to regain their legitimacy by building trust within Swedish society (Felländer et al., Chapter 8, this volume). However, trust is a dynamic concept. As changes in cognition occur, so do changes in the narrative to maintain and acquire investors and customers in an industry. Thus, established actors need to adjust to fit this emerging narrative, and one means is to mimic successful organizations (or elements of their strategies and managerial actions). This is not only how institutions change, but how organizations ensure their survival—at least until the next shift comes along. Thus, one means to gain back legitimacy that Sweden's established banks employed was to mimic the FinTech startups and develop their own innovative FinTech solutions. Two of the greater success stories are Swish, a peer-to-peer mobile payment system, and BankID, a digital identification app, both of which were created by the traditional banks joining forces, thereby putting Sweden on the map globally for its collaborative, innovative environment. From its inception in December 2012 to November 2016, Swish reached 5 million users, equaling over 50 percent of the Swedish population (Swish, 2016), with 84 percent of all Swedes ages 20–40 using BankID (IIS, 2017) (Felländer et al., Chapter 8, this volume).

Additionally, studies have shown that market feedback can be an invaluable way for incumbent firms to ascertain when norms have changed and how to respond to them (Lee and Pennings, 2002). Within Sweden, we found that the perception among bank managers from various established major Swedish banks was affected by FinTech startups in an unconventional way. This is exemplified by an inversion of what is known as the *Bell Doctrine*, which conventionally states that a dominant actor in a regulated industry can extend into, and dominate, a non-regulated industry. In this case, however, the growth of FinTech startups has prompted the incumbent, traditional banks to adapt and expedite their digital transformation in order to match their competition in order to safeguard sustainability and customer loyalty, thus effectively inverting the concept of the *Bell Doctrine*. Nevertheless, the incumbent, traditional banks' ability to compete effectively is still challenged and impeded by an asymmetrical regulatory system that has the traditional banks at a disadvantage (Larsson, Chapter 7, this volume).

As an industry transforms, one of the main areas of changes in cognition relates to the definition and understanding of the core value-creation activities within the industry. Traditional core banking activities fall under four subcategories: lending, payments, insurance, and savings. While these categories are well accepted across the globe, the emergence of FinTech and what exactly constitutes a FinTech company has led to a state of confusion. For example, Citibank has extended the four categories to seven categories: lending, payments, blockchain, insurance, wealth management, enterprise finance, and RegTech. Furthermore, two recent reports on British FinTech differed in the size of investment rounds in FinTech ventures by USD 80 million, and two reports on Stockholm FinTech 2015 investments displayed a discrepancy of USD 50 million, or 20 percent of the total investment. The reasons for such a variety of outputs are traced back to a lack of unified definition of FinTech and clarification of what branches of business can or cannot be counted as parts of FinTech industry (Gromek, Chapter 9, this volume).

Recently, a joint effort by representatives from the leading FinTech actors in Stockholm—Stockholm FinTech Hub, the Nordic Tech List, NFT Ventures, PA Consulting, and researchers from the Stockholm School of Economics—led to a classification of FinTech firms within Sweden into four categories for retail banking: wealth and cash management; payments and transfers; capital, debt, and equity; and InsurTech, as well as five categories for corporate banking: wealth and cash management; payments and transfers; capital, debt, and equity; InsurTech; and trading and exchange. In total, 69 subcategories were also developed (Gromek, Chapter 9, this volume).

Moving forward, while regulations are put in place to ensure a safe business environment and provide protection for customers, information security remains an integral part of the operations of a financial service provider, regardless of its size, to ensure customer trust and loyalty (Kryparos, Chapter 2, this volume).

New norms enabled by new technologies and standards

How—and from where—sources of influence come to change institutions varies. New technologies and standards can serve to challenge existing norms related to how "things are done around here" by enabling new value-creating activities. New technologies in particular are often championed by outsiders of a field, and thus can be considered to be an exogenous force that coerces organizations to change.

For example, in a study of Sun Microsystems' commercialization of the software Java, the open-source technology destroyed existing "taken-for-granted" standards and enabled new norms to emerge when it came to developing software for the Internet (Garud, Jain, and Kumaraswamy, 2002). This shift in norms, however, was not smooth. Existing software developers and the sponsors of other technological standards fought back, forcing the new open-source standard and associated new rules to compete with established standards for supremacy. Yet over time, the momentum behind open-source software not only initiated institutional change, but also started a chain of events that would lead to institutional changes for years to come.

A parallel to this can be seen in the phenomenon of crowdfunding. One of the earliest areas for FinTech startups, crowdfunding platforms enable entrepreneurs to obtain funds through the Internet from a wider variety of individual investors. As noted above, four forms of crowdfunding have emerged: donation, reward, lending, and equity, thereby creating an additional source of funding beyond the traditional sources of business angels, venture capitalists, banks, and pension funds (Gromek and Dubois, Chapter 12, this volume).

Furthermore, the nascent robo-advisory industry has emerged to tackle investors' demand for a more transparent wealth management service with low commission fees. Robo-advisors replace traditional human investors with algorithm-based platforms to provide personalized financial advice on financial instruments, reducing its expenses, and thus associated commission fees (Mačijauskaitė, Chapter 14, this volume).

The speed with which new technologies influence norms differs across countries. For the adoption and uptake of online banking services, Sweden may not be the most technologically advanced; however, Sweden does have the largest population share that actively uses online banking services. This is due to Swedish consumers being quick to adopt new technologies and standards, thereby creating a test bed for new products and services (Björn, Chapter 5, this volume).

Sociologists have pointed to the fact that it is not just the creation of a new technology that can prompt institutional change, but also its diffusion and utilization by new actors within and across new fields. The importance of smartphones, for instance, lies not just in the fact that they were invented, but in the fact that the possibilities that they afford have varied across fields. Gaming, for instance, has not been affected by mobiles in the same way as finance has (although, of course, it too has been revolutionized). One norm that is being challenged is the use of credit cards and cash in society as mobile payments are rapidly overtaking as the standard form of payment in Sweden (Arvidsson, Chapter 4, this volume). This can also be described by the relatively early and swift uptake of mobile banking by Swedes (Björn, Chapter 5, this volume).

The diffusion of technologies, such as big data analytics enabled by digital traces and blockchain, has therefore meant that these technologies have affected different actors in finance. Digital traces have opened doors for data analysts to map human behavior and offer tailor-made services. These tailor-made services, based on user behavior, have proven to be successful and revolutionized the advertising industry. Currently, the same methods are being applied to a wider variety of businesses, such as credit scoring, fraud detection, asset management, and insurance, and they are taking a bigger role in our society.

As their diffusion and adoption increase, they will continue to be important drivers of change. For example, the blockchain technologies that were previously known and used only by a small fraction of the population in 2007 are now being piloted by some of the leading international banks, for example, to facilitate settlement processes, payment transactions, enable electronic shareholder voting systems, and corporate governance (Moreno Puertas and Teigland, Chapter 15, this volume; Holmberg, Chapter 16, this volume).

A view of the actors

One key element that affects how changes occur is whether the changes are driven by endogenous or exogenous forces. While exogenous forces, particularly actors—such as entrepreneurs—that are completely new to a field, are commonly associated with institutional changes (Battilana, Leca, and Boxenbaum, 2009), incumbent firms have also been known to drive changes when they see this as necessary. The changes that result may therefore be completely different in different locations or in different organizations; the activities could be hybrids of one another, variations on the same, or new activities entirely.

Within Sweden, FinTech startups have been the initial drivers of transformation. Not only have changes in regulations and changing customer beliefs and behaviors enabled the emergence of FinTech startups, but also an exponential decrease in the financial resources required to start up a business has occurred. Today, there are more than 100 FinTech startups in the Stockholm area, with well over 240 in Sweden as a whole (Gromek, Chapter 9, this volume).

As noted above, many incumbent banks have started to realize the potential threat that inaction in the wake of these new entrants could hold. However, as heads-on competition with the new entrants is proving to be an expensive endeavor due to the relative advantage of the new entrants in terms of smaller organizational size and speed of innovation, the banks have started to look for alternative ways to approach these new companies and technologies (van der Zande, Chapter 17, this volume).

In addition to incumbent actors and startups, one other set of actors that has been found to play a vital role in the transformation of the financial services industry is that of business angels and venture capitalists (Press, Chapter 18, this volume). For example, the number of Swedish angel investments in FinTech in Sweden more than doubled from 2015 to 2016, from around 200 to 400. This group of investors began to notice the potential of high return in the industry, and many of these investors were from the traditional financial services industry and were looking to find the next disruptor. Additionally, many incumbent firms developed their own VC activities investing in FinTech startups in order to develop their businesses and better understand the disruptive forces in the industry. Even foreign actors have influenced the transformation as the amount of foreign investment in Sweden's FinTech has increased. As FinTech startups enter their expansion phase, foreign investors have in many instances joined domestic investors on the investor roster of a FinTech startup. These foreign actors provide not only money for growth, but they also enable cross-pollination across their many global locations, thus further accelerating the rate of change (Press, Chapter 18, this volume).

One example of a geographic shift that has implications for institutions lies in the UK's exit from the European Union. "Brexit," as it has been called, and the potential exodus of financial institutions and firms from the UK, could be a boon for continental Europe, as well as for the Nordics (Gromek and Mavropoulos, Chapter 22, this volume).

Lastly, although these drivers have been catalysts for change, the resulting changes are unlikely to be identical everywhere in the world—nor even identical in different parts of a country as small as Sweden. Instead, institutional theorists have highlighted that differences in environment, namely through different societies, fields, and organizations, lead to a diversity in activities. As Dacin, Goodstein, and Scott (2002) point out, "organizations and managers are not sponges or pawns, but actors responding to challenges under the guidance of existing institutions."

When it comes to crowdfunding, for instance, proximity has been seen to be of lasting importance: even with the advent of the Internet, investors are more likely to engage with local actors when it comes to investment and financing opportunities (Dubois and Gromek, Chapter 19, this volume). Moreover, there are both opportunities and costs to being located in a hub of economic activity, for instance inside or outside a cluster such as Stockholm (Jerezcek, Chapter 21, this volume).

Having examined in detail some of the extant theory around institutional changes and how these lead to change in the field of FinTech, we turn now to presenting summaries of the chapters contained in this book.

Chapter summaries

Part 1: New regulations

1. *Åke Freij*: Successful FinTech innovation is dependent on a number of key factors that comprise the financial services industry ecosystem, such as customer demand and new technologies. However, a less explored driver for FinTech innovation is the role of regulatory change. In the chapter "A Regulatory Innovation Framework: How Regulatory Change Leads to Innovation Outcomes for FinTechs," Åke Freij explores six strategies for realizing the benefits from regulatory change both for incumbents and FinTechs, and exemplifies an innovation opportunity by discussing the upcoming PSD2 directive (the Second Payment Services Directive).
2. *Georgios Kryparos*: While regulations are put in place to ensure a safe business environment and provide protection for customers, information security remains an integral part of the operations of a financial service provider, regardless of its size, to ensure customer trust and loyalty. In the chapter "Information Security in the Realm of FinTech," Georgios Kryparos examines the current landscape for FinTechs with regard to the relationship between information security and customer trust, and further looks into recent trends and developments that can pose as either threats or opportunities, and associated response recommendations.

3 *Björn Olsson and Mattias Hallberg*: Another key component of a successful FinTech ecosystem, arguably supporting the above-mentioned key drivers, such as customer demand, technological leadership, and an effective regulatory landscape, stems from innovation policy. In the chapter "FinTech in Sweden: Will Policymakers' (In)action Nurture or Starve Its Growth?" Björn Olsson and Mattias Hallberg explore the current policy landscape that is fueling the FinTech ecosystem in Sweden, and look at future threats and opportunities for Sweden to remain a competitive location for FinTechs to start, develop, and thrive.

4 *Niklas Arvidsson*: After the bankruptcy of the first Swedish bank, Banco Stockholm, in 1664, the Swedish government took a prominent role by establishing the first central bank in the world, in 1668, and issuing the first state-supported bills and coins. Today, Sweden is on track to becoming the first cashless society in the world. In the chapter "The Future of Cash," Niklas Arvidsson tracks the development of the Swedish monetary system over the centuries, discusses the proposed changes in legislations, and offers an insightful perspective on how Swedish cash may evolve over time.

5 *Michael Björn*: As discussed previously in the chapter, a key driver for innovation is customer demand. Sweden has a reputation for being a test bed for new products and services, and this is arguably due to the fact that Swedish consumers are quick to adopt new technologies and standards. In the chapter "The Adoption of Online Banking in Sweden," Michael Björn contrasts the adoption and uptake of online banking services compared to that of a selection of other developed countries, and argues that while Sweden may not be the most technologically advanced of them, Sweden has the largest population share that actively use online banking services.

Part 2: Cognition: legitimacy and views

6 *Mats Lewan*: Trust plays an essential role in the functioning of a capitalistic society (Hosking, 2014). However, trust is a dynamic concept that is perceived differently across cultures, industries, and time. Firms need to permanently adjust to fit the narrative in order to maintain and gain investors and clients. The narrative has been changing over time, and our introductory chapter aims to answer the question of what the current narrative is: how firms build trust as of 2017 and what the narrative of tomorrow could be. In the chapter "The Role of Trust in Emerging Technologies," Mats Lewan interviews some of the key players in the financial sector, the Scandinavian tech and startup community, to gain insights on how people perceive trust across different industries. Then he briefly investigates the new technologies that are changing the role of trust, such as the blockchain and the Trustnet.

7 *Anthony Larsson*: The Internet has changed the classical interaction between financial firms and their clients. In the past, firms needed to invest in subsidiaries in order to gain access to new clients. The reason was that consumers valued spatial convenience, and banks competed by establishing nearby

subsidiaries. However, the Internet has allowed consumers to interact with financial institutions directly through their computer or smartphone. As a result, the spatial competition transitioned toward a digital one. The digitalization of financial services also enabled a new wave of FinTech startups to compete against the established financial institutions. In the chapter "Responding to the FinTech Challenge: A Study of Swedish Bank Managers' Perceptions of FinTech's Effects on Digitalization and Customer e-Loyalty," Anthony Larsson explores the key challenges that FinTech firms have posed to Swedish banks in terms of securing customer loyalty through a series of interviews with managers representing different banks. The chapter also investigates the Bell Doctrine, in which large firms (traditional banks) in regulated industries are able to dominate non-regulated industries (FinTech).

8 *Anna Felländer, Shahryar Siri, and Robin Teigland*: The financial industry used to be characterized by high entry costs and required a high level of trust, which prevented other newly established companies from entering the market. However, the 2008 financial crisis revealed inefficiencies within the financial industry and decreased the level of trust deposited in them. This, combined with faster Internet, smartphones, and big data, allowed entrepreneurs to enter the market and challenge the established financial firms. In the chapter "The Three Phases of FinTech," Anna Fellander, Shahryar Siri, and Robin Teigland explain the redistribution of power from larger, established banks to FinTech firms. The chapter is divided into three phases, starting from 2008 and ending with a forecast of the relationship between the financial industry and FinTech startups in 2020.

9 *Michal Gromek*: The term "FinTech" is widely used in the media, yet there is no clear framework on what can be considered as FinTech. In the chapter "Clarifying the Blurry Lines of FinTech: Opening the Pandora's Box of FinTech categorization," Michal Gromek attempts to create a comprehensive guide for categorizing FinTech firms and provides a visualization of companies adopting a model from the area of social sciences to FinTech industry needs.

10 *Mats Lewan*: The FinTech revolution in Sweden wouldn't have happened without a specific set of conditions and innovations that allowed entrepreneurs to enter financial markets. The Swedish government played an important role in the early introduction of the Internet by designing the right incentives and effectively deregulating the telecom market in 1998 (Konkurrensverket, 1998). The resulting infrastructure also allowed mobile Internet to be introduced rapidly across the country. The early introduction of both the Internet and mobile Internet was essential to create a comfortable environment for FinTech startups to offer their services. The BankID, which was developed by Finansiell ID-Teknik BID AB, also played an important role, allowing third parties—FinTech startups—to use their system in exchange for a small fee. In the chapter "The Internet as an Enabler of FinTech," Mats Lewan aims to discover the key enablers of FinTech in Sweden by conducting a series of interviews with renowned people in the Scandinavian tech community.

Part 3: New norms enabled by new technologies and standards

11 *Claire Ingram Bogusz*: Digital traces have opened doors for data analysts to map human behavior and offer tailor-made services. These tailor-made services, based on user behavior, have proven to be successful and revolutionized the advertising industry. Currently, the same methods are being applied to a wider variety of businesses, such as credit scoring, fraud detection, asset management, and insurance, and they are taking a bigger role in our society. As the collection of data increases and the methods become more accurate, a new legal framework is necessary to ensure that we are comfortable sharing our data. In the chapter "Digital Traces, Ethics, and Insight: Data-Driven Services in FinTech," Claire Ingram Bogusz explores the ethical implications of collecting such data, and provides a detailed overview of the data-gathering industry and the data-driven services within the FinTech and banking landscape.

12 *Michal Gromek and Alexandre Dubois*: The revolution of the Internet has enabled entrepreneurs to obtain funds from a wider variety of investors. This has given rise to a new type of fundraising called crowdfunding. The chapter "Digital Meetings: Real Growth, Better Funding? An Introduction to Swedish Crowdfunding" describes the development of crowdfunding platforms with a focus on Sweden, gives a detailed view of the different types of crowdfunding, summarizes its key benefits and challenges, and proposes future scenarios for this industry.

13 *Niklas Arvidsson*: Sweden was the first country to issue central bank state-backed bills and coins. However, it is experimenting a transition toward a cashless society. A new wave of entrepreneurs are offering cash payment services that provide the simplicity and convenience that most users demand. The chapter "The Payment Landscape in Sweden" offers an overview of the current trends in payment systems in Sweden and promotes a payment landscape that is characterized by innovation and competition.

14 *Agnė Mačijauskaitė*: The financial crisis in 2008 revealed inefficiencies and a lack of transparency in the financial industry. As a result, the nascent robo-advisory industry has emerged to tackle the investors' demand for a more transparent wealth management service with low commission fees. Robo-advisors use algorithm-based platforms to provide personalized financial advice on financial instruments, reducing its expenses, and thus its associated commission fees. The chapter "Introduction to the Robo-Advisory Industry in Sweden" describes the development of the young robo-advisory industry, provides a qualitative analysis of the Swedish market, and offers insights into future trends.

15 *Alejandro Moreno Puertas and Robin Teigland*: Peer-to-peer networks were popularized by the famous, and now defunct, file-sharing service called Napster. The same concept was combined with cryptographic proof to create a new type of (crypto)currency called Bitcoin. The infrastructure of Bitcoin has proved to be efficient as it deals with over USD 1 billion in transactions per day without a clear centralized oversight. The chapter "Blockchain: The

Internet of Value" describes the history of Bitcoin, explains the key concepts of its underlying infrastructure and of other similar cryptocurrencies, such as Ethereum, Ripple, Hyperledger, and RSCoin, provides an overview of blockchain applications, and examines the wider discussion on the principles of blockchain technology.

16 *Håkan Holmberg*: As of 2017, bitcoin is the leading cryptocurrency in terms of market value. The original idea was to provide a decentralized electronic cash system with low transaction costs. However, the network was designed to only accept two to seven transactions per second. As the demand for transactions has grown over the last years, the network cannot process transactions in time. This has increased the transaction costs and the processing time, diminishing Bitcoin's advantages. In the chapter "How to Scale Bitcoin: A Payment Network That No One Controls," Håkan Holmberg explores the current challenges that the Bitcoin community is facing, and describes the two alternatives proposed by Bitcoin Unlimited and SegWit to solve the scalability problem.

Part 4: A view of the actors

17 *Jochem van der Zande*: A case in point of exogenous forces impacting the financial services sector, slowly but steadily capturing more of the traditional banks' customers and activities, many incumbent banks have started to realize the potential threat that inaction in the wake of these new entrants could result in. However, as head-on competition with the new entrants is proving to be an expensive endeavor due to the relative advantage of the new entrants in terms of smaller organizational size and speed of innovation, the banks have started to look for alternative ways to approach these new companies and technologies. In the chapter "Banks and Digitalization," Jochem van der Zande engages with the four major banks in Sweden to illustrate different strategies to respond to organizational change resulting from these exogenous change forces.

18 *Elizabeth Press*: A key enabling factor for new entrants is access to financing and willingness of these financiers to take risk in ventures that in many, if not most, cases do not turn profitable over their lifetime. In the chapter "The Role of Venture Capital in the Success of the Swedish FinTech Industry," Elizabeth Press discusses the role of venture capital in the Swedish FinTech landscape, and also looks at some of the future threats and opportunities for Swedish FinTech investments.

19 *Alexandre Dubois and Michal Gromek*: As argued previously, the resulting changes from an industry transformation are not evenly distributed across organizations, users, and geographies. In the chapter "How Distance Comes into Play in Equity Crowdfunding," Michal Gromek and Alexandre Dubois exemplify the discrepancy by looking at the continued importance of proximity in equity crowdfunding. Thus, pointing to the fact that even

with the advent of the Internet enabling us to communicate over great distances, we are still more likely to engage with our local communities, particularly with regard to investment and financing opportunities.

20 *Catharina Burenstam Linder*: While the rise of the FinTech sector can be seen both as a threat and an opportunity to the traditional banking sector, the fact that the industry, as a whole, is undergoing a transformation remains. In order for the ecosystem to be able to come together, discuss, plan, and collaborate for the continued success of the Stockholm FinTech cluster, and championing Sweden in the global FinTech community, a common space was needed. In the chapter "The Stockholm FinTech Hub," Catharina Burenstam Linder discusses the recently launched Stockholm FinTech Hub and how the hub works to assist and accommodate the continued growth of the local ecosystem, as well as develop the potential of Stockholm within the global finance ecosystem.

21 *Katarzyna Jereczek*: Referring to the above chapter on the importance of distance in crowdfunding, and the establishment of a physical hub for the growth of the Stockholm ecosystem, it becomes more evident that being close to the ecosystem is likely to increase the chances for success of a new FinTech startup. However, in the chapter "Geographic Decentralization of FinTech Companies in Sweden," Kata Jereczek looks into the rising FinTech activity in smaller cities in Sweden, and contrasts the advantages and disadvantages of starting up inside or outside a cluster such as Stockholm.

22 *Michal Gromek and Timotheos Mavropoulos*: Again, as Dacin, Goodstein, and Scott (2002, p.50) note, organizations are "actors responding to challenges under the guidance of existing institutions." In the wake of the 2016 UK referendum on leaving the EU, many have debated the future prospects for London remaining the world's strongest financial center, and arguably also the world's leading hub for FinTech and financial innovation. In the chapter "When Britain Leaves the EU, Will FinTechs Turn to the Vikings?" Michal Gromek and Timotheos Mavropoulos look at the arguments put forth for and against an exodus of financial institutions and firms from the UK to continental Europe, to the Nordics, and particularly to Stockholm.

Bibliography

Battilana, J., Leca, B., and Boxenbaum, E., 2009. How actors change institutions: Towards a theory of institutional entrepreneurship. *Academy of Management Annals*, 3(1), p.65 LP-107.

Benwell, M., 2014. Stockholm is rivalling Silicon Valley with a hotbed of technology start-ups. *The Independent*. [online] Available at: www.independent.co.uk/life-style/gadgets-and-tech/features/stockholm-is-rivalling-silicon-valley-with-a-hotbed-of-technology-start-ups-9931876.html [Accessed January 16, 2018].

British Banking Association, 2016. *BBA briefing: Reforms since the financial crisis*. [online] Available at: www.bba.org.uk/news/reports/bba-briefing-reforms-since-the-financial-crisis/#.WbFTrNOg-_B [Accessed January 16, 2018].

Dacin, M.T., Goodstein, J., and Scott, W.R., 2002. Institutional theory and institutional change: Introduction to the special research forum. *Academy of Management Journal*, 45(1), pp.45–57.

DiMaggio, P.J. and Powell, W.W., 1983. The iron cage revisited: Institutional isomorphism and collective rationality in organizational fields. *American Sociological Review*, 48(2), pp.147–160.

DiMaggio, P.J. and Powell, W.W., 1991. Introduction. In: W.W. Powell and P.J. DiMaggio, eds. *The new institutionalism in organizational analysis*. Chicago, IL: University of Chicago Press, pp.1–40.

DiMaggio, P.J., Hargittai, E., Neuman, W.R., and Robinson, J.P., 2001. Social implications of the Internet. *Annual Review of Sociology*, 27, pp.307–336.

Flint, D., 2014. *Business ethics in banking: Time for a second chance?* [online] Available at: www.hsbc.com/news-and-insight/media-resources/speeches/2014/business-ethics-in-banking [Accessed January 16, 2018].

Garud, R., Jain, S., and Kumaraswamy, A., 2002. Institutional entrepreneurship in the sponsorship of common technological standards: The case of Sun Microsystems and Java. *Academy of Management Journal*, 45(1), pp.196–214.

Greenwood, R. and Suddaby, R., 2006. *Professional service firms*. Oxford: Elsevier JAI.

Hosking, G., 2014. Trust and financial markets. *European Financial Review*. [online] Available at: www.europeanfinancialreview.com/?p=3523 [Accessed September 7, 2017].

IIS, 2017. *E-handel, betaltjänster och delningsekonomi* [E-purchase, payment services and shared economy]. [online] Available at: www.soi2016.se/e-handel-internetbank-och-betaltjanster/mobilt-bankid-och-swish/ [Accessed January 16, 2018].

Klarna, 2017. *Klarna statistics*. [online] Available at: www.klarna.com/uk/about-us/klarna-statistics [Accessed January 16, 2018].

Konkurrensverket, 1998. *Deregulated markets in Sweden: A follow-up study*. [online] Available at: www.konkurrensverket.se/globalassets/english/publications-and-decisions/deregulated-markets-in-sweden.pdf [Accessed January 16, 2018].

Lee, K. and Pennings, J.M., 2002. Mimicry and the market: Adoption of a new organizational form. *Academy of Management Journal*, 45(1), pp.144–162.

Lounsbury, M., 2002. Institutional transformation and status mobility: The professionalization of the field of finance. *Academy of Management Journal*, 45(1), pp.255–266.

Oliver, C., 1992. The antecedents of deinstitutionalization. *Organization Studies*, 13(4), pp.563–588.

Scott, W.R., 1995. *Institutions and organizations*. Thousand Oaks, CA: Sage.

Selznick, P., 1996. Institutionalism "old" and "new." *Administrative Science Quarterly*, 41(2), pp.270 277.

Sine, W.D. and David, R.J., 2003. Environmental jolts, institutional change, and the creation of entrepreneurial opportunity in the US electric power industry. *Research Policy*, 32(2), pp.185–207.

Skog, A., Lewan, M., Karlström, M., Morgulis-Yakushev, S., Lu, Y., and Teigland, R., 2016. *Chasing the tale of the unicorn: A study of Sweden's misty meadows*. [online] Available at: https://www.hhs.se/en/about-us/news/2016/new-research-explores-the-success-of-swedish-high-tech-startup-companies [Accessed January 16, 2018].

Smets, M., Morris, T., and Greenwood, R., 2012. From practice to field: A multilevel model of practice-driven institutional change. *Academy of Management Journal*, 55(4), pp.877–904.

Stockholm FinTech Hub, 2017. *Swedish FinTech in numbers*. [online] Available at: http://data.stockholmfin.tech/ [Accessed January 16, 2018].

Swedish Competition Authority, 1998. Deregulated markets in Sweden: A follow-up study. *Distribution*, [online] pp.1–157. Available at: www.konkurrensverket.se/globalassets/english/publications-and-decisions/deregulated-markets-in-sweden.pdf [Accessed January 16, 2018].

Swish, 2016. *Fem miljoner svenskar swishar!* [online] Available at: https://www.getswish.se/oldsite/getswish/wp-content/uploads/2016/10/20161121_Pressmeddelande_5milj.pdf [Accessed January 16, 2018].

Thornton, P.H. and Ocasio, W., 2008. Institutional logics. In: R. Greenwood, C. Oliver, R. Suddaby, and K. Sahlin, eds. *The Sage handbook of organizational institutionalism*. Los Angeles, CA: Sage, pp.99–128.

Weber, M., 1978. *Economy and society: An outline of interpretive sociology*. Berkeley, CA: University of California Press.

Part 1

New regulations

1 A regulatory innovation framework

How regulatory change leads to innovation outcomes for FinTechs

Åke Freij

Introduction

While regulatory change is a most pressing challenge for firms in numerous industries, for example automobiles (Liker, 2015; Schrage, 2015) and life sciences, the difficulty in successfully handling regulatory requirements is most challenging for financial services companies (Wessel, 2012; Moreno, 2014). The difficulty is present both for incumbent players as well as for FinTech startups. Regulatory requirements are seldom seen as an engine for innovation, but rather as an obstacle to creativity and customer satisfaction. At the same time as pressure for digital transformation continues to increase, regulatory changes should be seen as an opportunity for FinTech startups and incumbents alike.

In this chapter, my aim is to present a framework that enables both FinTechs and incumbents to consider an innovation strategy that leverages regulations. To do so, I first present four areas where regulatory changes have been found to influence a firm: product design, service processes, customer relationships, and technology platforms, illustrating each with an example of a regulatory change. I then present the four opportunities that I have found emerge in connection with these regulatory changes: dominant designs, firm collaboration, technical requirements, and legal protection. Combining the four areas of regulatory changes with the four opportunities builds the basis for my regulatory innovation framework through which I have identified six innovation strategies for dealing with any given regulatory change and corresponding opportunities. To illustrate the strategies, I provide examples of how both incumbents and FinTech startups have implemented innovation as a result of a regulatory change.

In addition, I further articulate the helpfulness of the framework by relating it to the FinTech industry. First, I discuss the relevant sets of activities emerging within FinTech: peer-to-peer, customer intimacy, payments, personal financial management, and underbanked innovation. I then apply the framework to a current regulatory change with a potentially strong influence on the FinTech sector, PSD2 (the Second Payment Services Directive), before positioning selected FinTech startups within the framework based on their business model. I then conclude with recommendations for FinTechs, incumbents, and regulators.

About the research

The research behind this chapter was performed over a time span of six years as part of my PhD thesis research project and includes empirical data from the Swedish financial services industry. Fifty personal interviews were performed concerning one regulatory change over the time period 1990–2005, and a study of 10 regulations in the Swedish life insurance industry with a historical perspective from 1903 until today was based on archival data and additional interviews (Freij, 2017). These data were supplemented with studies of firms implementing 10 other global financial services regulations. In addition, an analysis of 100 academic innovation articles plus 20 industry trade publications was performed. Extensive source data analysis was made to find the reported patterns and strategies. Data about FinTech firms were collected with a focus on the Swedish entrepreneurial ecosystem by listing all available FinTechs and categorizing them relative to a regulatory innovation framework. FinTechs with the most relevance for one selected regulatory change were identified along with innovation opportunities connected to each FinTech.

Regulatory change drives the evolution of financial services

In the financial services industry, there is no single issue that currently takes so much attention, time, investment, and management energy as the changes in regulations. There is no indication that this development will slow down at any point in the future, but rather it could escalate further. Regulations (together with technology) have been identified as a significant source for radical innovation in the industry (Bieck and Freij, 2010). Hence, I argue that actions connected to these changes are the best way to develop a competitive advantage, in opposition to seeing them as a burden of mandatory compliance. The argument is based on and guided by tangible research findings and analysis, as well as from business practice experience. Applying a more positive strategy toward regulations is of benefit for both existing firms but also for the growing FinTech population.

Regulations are exponentially increasing in frequency and impact

In the beginning of the twentieth century, regulations were introduced with slow intervals. A new regulation was considered a long time before implementation, and the industry was generally well prepared for the implications of this change. Currently, entering the twenty-first century, the pure number of regulations to be implemented within the near future by any financial institution is approaching 50. Not only is the complexity and volume of each single regulation increasing, but there are also variations depending on local jurisdiction, as well as different implications for different business units, for example insurance, retail banking, and investment management. The end result is that a major financial services company can have well over 100 regulatory implementation projects currently in progress. These implementation projects for regulatory changes are seldom seen as a source of innovation. Rather, businesses tend to have a negative view at the outset. A new entrant that pursues a strategy to embrace rather than avoid or minimize regulations may have opportunities to establish a strong position in the evolving market.

Business managers are usually (very) negative toward new regulations

Executives act relative to changes in regulations in a conservative way and make more effort to avoid these changes rather than to embrace them (Levitt, 1968). This approach stands in stark contrast to the progressive and innovative approach taken by businesses when it comes to "regular" business innovation activities that are driven by internal ideas or customer requirements. Firms that adopt their strategies in a proactive way when regulations change are likely to experience more success than those firms that do not adapt (Smith and Grimm, 1987). On the other hand, negligence to adapt to regulatory change can lead to increased risk that organizations fail.

Implementations of regulatory change are not efficient

Due to the increasing frequency, volume, and complexity of regulatory changes, there is a practical approach of implementing these changes in a less than efficient way. Implementations are made in silos (i.e., both concerning individual regulations and for each organizational unit), which leads to a multitude of tasks performed by uncoordinated resources. The implementations are almost always reactive in mindset, meaning that the approach taken is to do the minimal effort possible to just pass the compliance threshold. Many times, the solutions implemented are "tick-box"-oriented or "forms-centered." The main purpose is to deliver a set of information to a corresponding regulator without much thought of the value of the information contained. In addition, there is a weak connection between the compliance organization responsible for the projects and the capabilities concerning acquisition of technology solutions. When adding these circumstances together, the picture is that of limited innovation and considerable investments.

Four areas of regulatory change impact

Based on my empirical data and analysis, four different areas of impact from regulatory change emerged. Asking firms what they did after a regulatory change derived the picture of impact. The four areas signify the main impact from any single regulation, but any regulations in addition also influence the other three areas over time. Below, I briefly illustrate the four impact areas of product design, service processes, customer relationships, and technology platforms, and how they influence companies when a regulatory change occurs.

Product design

The products designed and sold by financial services firms are an important area of impact from regulatory change. Regulators can target transparency of products by demanding improved disclosure (Richard and Devinney, 2005). Products are designed to define firms' offerings to the market and customers (Fixson and Park, 2008). A regulatory change can present requirements for new products, as in the cars developed toward zero-emission rules (Dyerson and Pilkington, 2000). The company needs to understand the regulatory change and how it creates demand for new products, and also how it influences the existing products.

> One example of a regulation affecting product design is the fund-based life insurance introduced in Sweden in 1990 and in several other countries in the late 1900s. The regulation presented requirements for new components to be assembled into innovative products with a higher degree of flexibility than before.
>
> A second example is the regulations concerning securities funds (Undertakings in Collective Investments in Tradable Securities, UCITS). This regulation defines the role of the financial product called "investment fund." When the UCITS regulation was updated to version 5 in 2016, products were influenced due to changes in the ability to remunerate providers of funds.

Service processes

Service processes are necessary to deliver the promise of functionality offered in products. Due to the visibility of processes, regulators target them to increase efficiency in an industry. Processes are required over the entire life cycle of the product (Jacobides, 2005). A change in regulations influences how firms modify their internal processes (Cabigiosu and Camuffo, 2012). A proactive company can offer services to customers whereby the requirements from regulations are supported as a process delivered to the market.

> An example of a regulation influencing service processes is Foreign Account Tax Compliance Act (FATCA) for reporting on US tax status for customers in non-US banks. The regulation implied that new information was captured in the process of establishing a customer account.
>
> A second is the implementation of "best execution" regulations concerning trading of securities in the EU regulation Markets in Financial Instruments Directive (MiFID). New processes were required to analyze the consequence of buying and selling specific securities across multiple markets.

Customer relationships

A key rationale for regulators to address regulatory change is to strengthen the protection of customers. Regulations can contain requirements for increased transparency, and clarification of roles in connection with the customers. Such regulations are prominent in, for example, the building industry (Cacciatori and Jacobides, 2005) and in the airline engine industry (Brusoni, Prencipe, and Pavitt, 2001). Thereby, the roles of actors interfacing the customer, across the processes of sales, advice, distribution, and maintenance, are often changed as a result of new regulations.

One example of a regulation influencing the customer relationship is the European Union directive MiFID2 (the second Markets in Financial Instruments Directive), including requirements for Know Your Customer (KYC). Demands are presented in this new regulation of how the advisory relationship with the customer is to be documented. In addition, there are instructions for the use of external intermediaries, and how such partners are remunerated. Numerous variations of regulations concerning financial advice exist in different countries.

Another example of a regulatory change that will alter customer relationships is PSD2, which will be addressed later in the chapter.

Technology platforms

Regulatory changes with impact on technology can be either technical specifications, where requirements are infused to certify a new technology (Teece, 1986), or a broad regulation, which puts entirely new obligations onto the platforms of an industry (Tee and Gawer, 2009). Technology also plays a role in addressing the requirements of regulations across products and processes. The use of platforms to manage regulatory requirements has proven viable in the financial services industry (Meyer and Dalal, 2002).

The Payment Card Industry Data Security Standard (PCI DSS) is an example of a detailed and specific requirement for technology. Even if it is formally not a government regulation, it can be regarded as a de facto regulation for payment cards.

An example of regulatory change with impact on technology is Solvency 2 for insurance. This regulation covers capital requirements, risk management, and reporting, and thereby drives new technical foundations for information management. A corresponding regulation is the existing Basel 2 rules for banks, which is currently superseded by the Basel 3 framework.

Opportunities when regulations change

Discontinuities due to an external source, such as regulatory changes, can lead to significant changes in how an industry organizes itself, with important implications for the control or profitability of a firm. The results of regulatory evolution can lead to different outcomes in the ownership of assets (Tee and Gawer, 2009). Evidence of the innovation effects from regulations has been presented by contributions from previous research (see e.g. Ferraro and Gurses, 2009). For example, firms that are in possession of production assets, such as platforms, can leverage these to create new services that support common regulatory compliance processes across different business units. Four main areas (as depicted in Figure 1.1) have been found where firms can achieve innovation, representing clear windows of entrepreneurial opportunity. The first area is dominant design, or the evolution of well-defined approaches to the design of products and services, such as through standards. The second area is that regulatory demands can change conditions for how firms collaborate due to challenges with requirements in the interface between actors. A third area is the modification to technical requirements arising from regulatory change. Finally, in the fourth area, firms can explore the expiry of legal protections. I discuss each of these in turn below.

Establish advantages from dominant designs

As industries evolve, there are certain ways of performing business and designing products and services that become dominant. Such practices are called dominant designs, and they emerge as widely adopted ways to configure products and systems (Anderson and Tushman, 1990). These designs emerge as a trial-and-error process after breakthrough innovations, as manufacturers, suppliers, customers, and regulatory agencies compete to decrease the uncertainty in a market that is related to a significant variation in products, processes, customer relationships, and technology. Dominant designs evolve in a process that includes social, political, technological, and economic aspects (Abernathy and Utterback, 1978). One particular type of dominant design is standards. Standards contribute to the establishment of stable industry conditions. Government regulation often compels the adoption of standards, and firms could contribute to the development of these standards. From another perspective, the lack of agreement of a dominant design can hinder innovation evolving in a market. For example, in a market such as the mobile payments segment, innovation investments will be made under unclear criteria, and hence may hamper business innovation as resources are spent

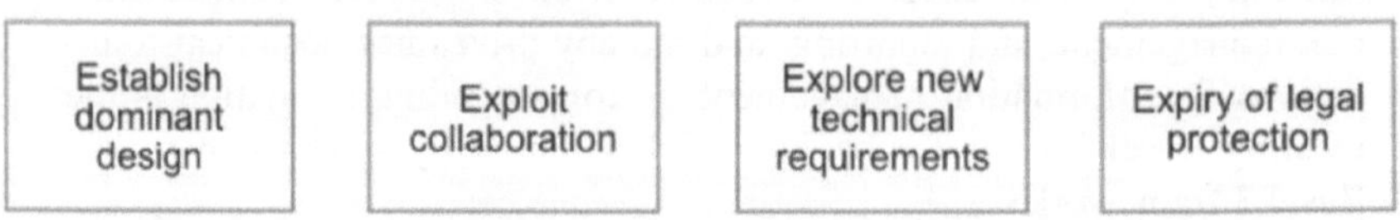

Figure 1.1 Four innovation opportunities when regulations change

inefficiently (Ozcan and Santos, 2015). Firms that can interpret and implement such unclear requirements can become winners in the emerging market.

Exploit changed conditions for firm collaboration

Regulations can limit the conditions for collaboration between firms. Such collaboration involves interaction through interfaces between the firms, and the regulatory forces can create requirements to those interfaces that may constrain the innovative activities of firms. Certain actors might be concerned about security and reliability imposed by regulations when collaborating with other firms. These concerns arise since violations of specific regulations might risk hurting the trustworthy image of a company. Such regulations may limit the combination of complementary resources and capabilities, especially in cases of collaboration across industry boundaries (Jaspers, Prencipe, and Ende, 2012). The cooperation between firms has benefits against which coordination costs, including legal circumstances that mandate governance structure, have to be offset.

Understand the modification to technical requirements

New regulations imposed on an existing industry may establish new technical requirements or demand changes in performance standards that favor revolutionary or architectural strategic development (Abernathy and Clark, 1985). Deregulation may have the same effect. Industry incumbents, constrained by regulatory and institutional logics, react to external events such as new technical requirements, and their actions (or lack thereof) create a space for newcomers to acquire mispriced resources (Ferraro & Gurses, 2009). Government or regulators can influence the development of market infrastructure, and thereby affect the role of firms and generate innovation for some actors (Jacobides, 2005). Changes in regulations might escalate or kick-start the diffusion of a technical requirement under development.

Utilize the expiry of legal protection

Over time, products and processes become well understood as the technology supporting them becomes widely available through the diffusion of knowledge and as legal and regulatory protections such as patents expire (Teece, 1986). The integration of regulatory compliance into product offerings can expand the role of a firm. The interpretation of regulatory requirements can as a result be moved from the firm's internal processes to outside vendors and partners. This could mean that regulatory frameworks enable new markets between private firms to emerge, and as such prompt the development of a new mode of organizing (Teece, 2006). Regulation tends to either institute or legitimize new rules, such as vertically co-specialized arrangements. As players in each part of an industry try to lobby for their interests, they promote an industry structure that is maximally profitable for them. Deregulation is freeing companies to divide the market in new ways. In the financial services industry, previously integrated sectors have been taken apart, partly as a result of changed regulations.

Based on the above observations, it could be argued that actions related to regulatory change will impact the position of firms vis-à-vis other firms, customers, and regulators, and thereby create significant opportunities to benefit from innovation. The relevant ecosystem for this innovation process includes not just firms, but also regulators, educational institutions, standard-setting bodies, and the courts. Regulations can be seen as a type of technology, and therefore new regulations could be positioned as a new technology, especially in services industries (Rogers, 1995).

A regulatory innovation framework

Below, I present the regulatory innovation framework used to understand the impact of changes in regulations. The framework is developed from my research combining theoretical and empirical findings from studying what actions firms take to implement regulatory change requirements. First, I present the six strategies that emerged in my research before presenting a "checklist" of actions to help guide firms in executing this strategy.

Strategies for regulatory innovation

In order to determine how to focus the work with innovation in connection with regulatory change, the four areas of impact are juxtaposed with the four areas of opportunities. When merging this juxtaposition with theory, six innovation strategies emerged from a detailed analysis of the concepts and themes inherent in the respective dimensions (see Figure 1.2). One conclusion from my research is that the impact of regulatory change can benefit both established financial companies (incumbents) and FinTechs. Thus, below, I discuss each of these strategies in turn and illustrate them with an example from both an incumbent and FinTech startup.

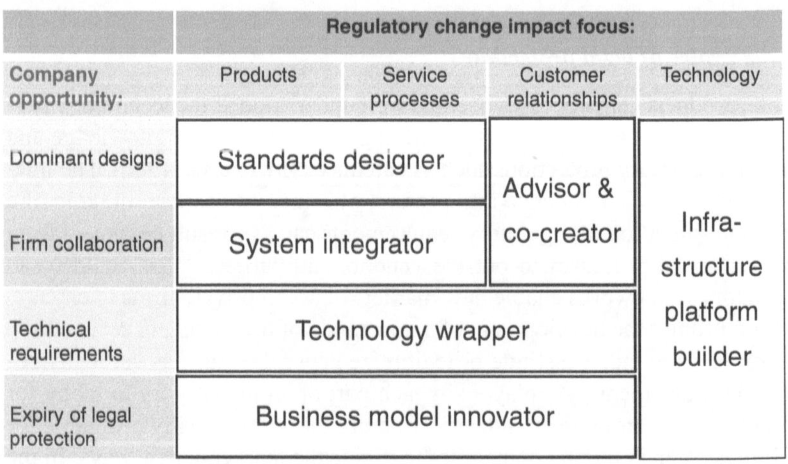

Figure 1.2 Regulatory innovation strategies

Standards designer

This strategy involves using regulations as a way to determine the forms for doing business in the industry. Large firms could even push for higher regulatory demands in order to define intricate criteria for the establishment for new entrants. This strategy needs careful work with architecture (for both products and processes), reference models, and common standards (internal and external).

Examples of successful standards designers

Incumbent: SWIFT My Standards

By establishing the unit My Standards, the global payments network organization SWIFT has taken a proactive stance in the process of defining the standards for transactions. The active consideration of new standards connected to new regulations has proven valuable for the actors in the industry. The developed solution claims to support current and emerging regulations impacting the payments industry.

FinTech: Ant Financial

Ant Financial, the spin-off from Alipay providing online payment services, is a good example of a standards designer that has established a secure platform for processing payments (and analyzing credit scores) for large volumes of transactions. In the wake of the upcoming regulation for payment services in the EU, this company can claim account information from incumbent banks and payment providers.

System integrator

A system integrator applies practices to enable ecosystem constellations across firm products and service processes boundaries. This strategy involves the use of automated processes, API design, and concepts covering the "systems of engagement" (i.e., processes where different actors meet across boundaries in an ecosystem).

Examples of successful system integrators

Incumbent: Skandia

In the wake of several major regulatory changes, the company Skandia has shown capabilities of system integration. The most prominent example is the introduction of the new regulation for fund-based life insurance.

(continued)

(continued)

Here, Skandia was the only firm that introduced externally managed funds and combined this with the use of external sales and service providers.

FinTech: Tink

The personal finance aggregator Tink has established processes that support system integration. This strategy is beneficial considering existing and new regulations such as PSD2, AMLD4, and MiFID2, which both require extended insight into the data and behavior of customers (a concept often described as Know Your Customer, KYC).

Advisor and co-creator

This strategy calls for a proactive stance toward customers and ecosystem partners. It is essential to establish processes to co-create solutions with customers, as well as internal assembly of combined solutions that meet customer needs.

Examples of successful advisors and co-creators

Incumbents: large banks arranging "hackathons"

Several large financial institutions attempt to leverage their customer relationships, experience of collaboration arrangements, and their dominant position in the industry. They do this by collaborating with entrepreneurs in so-called "hackathons." Examples of such events are those hosted by Nordea and CitiBank. When partnerships are established between existing and new actors, the result could be new solutions that support requirements introduced by changed regulations.

FinTech: Sparplatsen/Insurance Simplified

Several interesting examples of FinTechs applying this strategy exist. Two cases from the insurance industry in Sweden are Sparplatsen and Insurance Simplified. The first is focusing on life insurance and the balance to give advice without incurring high costs for assuring quality and compliance with regulations related to transparency of advice (such as MiFID2). The second focuses on transparency in the property insurance segment. This can prove to be a valuable solution in the wake of the new EU directive for insurance distribution (Insurance Distribution Directive, IDD).

Infrastructure platform builder

The foundation for innovation in connection with regulatory change is a solid infrastructure platform. This platform contains flexible delivery of infrastructure capabilities and the functions needed to understand regulatory change and to deliver solutions in production. This strategy will include approaches toward the opening of APIs[1] for internal and external consumers.

Examples of successful infrastructure platform builders

Incumbents: Swedish bank collaborations

The joint work of the banking industry in Sweden has over recent years resulted in widely adopted solutions for infrastructure. Two examples are the "peer-to-peer" payments solution Swish, and the security and identification foundation technology BankID. As a result of the above two projects, the incumbent banks have kept a central position in the industry, despite the emergence of FinTech challengers. The solutions developed will also support change required due to upcoming regulations concerning payments transactions and treatment of individual security online (such as the emerging EU data privacy regulation GDPR).

FinTech: Betalo/PayPal

A Swedish FinTech venture with the potential to establish a platform in the wake of upcoming changes in the payment industry is Betalo, which is focused on simplified and cheaper global payments. The requirements for open APIs in the wake of the PSD2 regulation can influence this venture. A global example that has established an infrastructure platform is PayPal.

Technology wrapper

There is an opportunity to integrate the changing requirements for regulatory compliance into products and services. This can save the trouble for the bank and insurance company's end customer to consider these requirements. Niche challengers that enter the market with a specific solution for a regulatory requirement can also take this role.

Examples of successful technology wrappers

Incumbent: cyber insurance (Swiss Re)

The increasing risks (and associated compliance demands) with cyberthreats have promoted firms to support their customers with processes concerning risk and compliance in the form of insurance products. Such solutions have been designed and marketed by Swiss Re as Cyber Solutions, in collaboration with the technology provider IBM. Extended solutions for insurance

(continued)

(continued)

coverage can be relevant when companies struggle to support the technical requirements inherent in the EU data privacy regulation GDPR.

FinTech: iZettle

The solutions from the FinTech company iZettle are an example of a technology wrapper. The new requirements from regulations in payments and data privacy can drive demand for products and services that influence customer relationships where iZettle can mitigate difficulties for incumbents to be compliant.

Business model innovator

The change in conditions for achieving value from innovation calls for new business models to emerge. This strategy incorporates models for defining the constituting parts of the business, as well as approaches to defining how these parts belong together and relate to the existing business of the company.

Examples of successful business model innovators

Incumbents: European Multilateral Clearing Facility (EMCF)

The establishment of the clearing facility EMCF by the two Dutch banks Fortis and ABN Amro was a radical approach to capturing value in the changed industry structure around securities settlements. This change was driven by the implementation of the MiFID directive and specific regulations concerning "best execution" of securities trading transactions.

FinTech: M-PESA

Introduced in several African countries by a group of telecommunications providers, this company changed the business models in the payments industry by applying existing mobile networks to channel transactions. Since M-PESA is not a fully regulated financial institution, they can avoid certain details concerning regulations such as KYC but also gain detailed insight into customer behavior needed to support regulations.

Checklist for developing a regulatory innovation strategy

In addition to developing six innovation strategies, I have also developed a "master list" of 160 action steps that can be divided across the six innovation strategies (this is 10 per cell in the framework). The action steps are found by combining the four

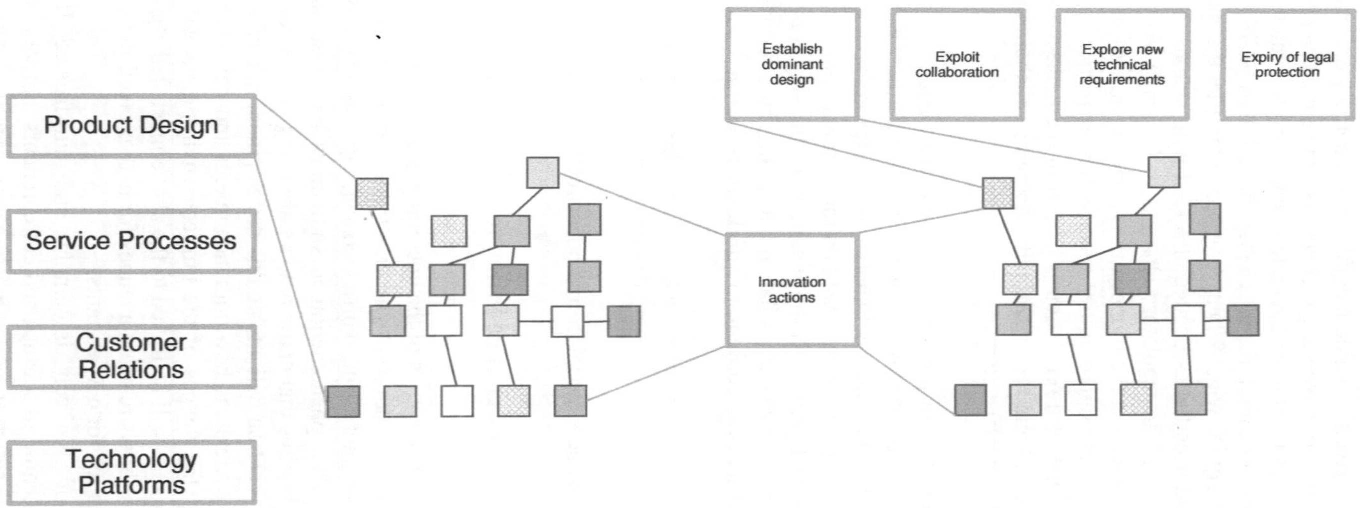

Figure 1.3 Innovation action list derived from the regulatory innovation framework

impact areas with the four innovation opportunities (as outlined in Figure 1.3). These actions are derived to guide tangible and specific work that both incumbents and new actors can pursue to gain benefits from a regulatory change.

Using the framework with an integrated checklist may enable firms to better manage the impact of a regulatory change since it may enable them to better understand potential quick wins. When a company identifies the appropriate innovation strategy, and uses the associated checklist with actions, a more efficient and innovative response to regulatory changes will emerge. Also, one or more regulations can be placed in the framework (in one or more of the 16 cells) as a basis for a deep dive into opportunities specific for the particular regulation. As an illustrative example, if a regulation is placed in the intersection between the impact area "products" and the opportunity "explore collaboration," this "cell" prescribes the following 10 actions:

1. Partners are selected for products on a component level.
2. The complementarity of knowledge with product partners is mapped.
3. Network models for product collaboration are explored.
4. Product portfolio governance is defined for partners.
5. The role of product partners in the customer relationship is investigated.
6. Product architecture considers collaboration arrangements (current and future).
7. Value of information content in products is defined for collaboration arrangements.
8. Complementary assets are mapped to each collaboration/product arrangement.
9. Integration points are defined and designed toward the collaboration partner on a product level.
10. Influences on business model from product-related collaboration are outlined.

Understand regulatory change influence on "FinTech" innovation

The press is filled with accounts of the upcoming death of the legacy incumbents in the financial services industry. The existing actors in the financial services industry are showing increasing worries concerning new entrants attacking the existing business. This phenomenon is sometimes packaged under the term "FinTech," which implies that entrepreneurs are using new technology to start a new business. This section will situate this development related to the evolution of regulations, and understand how both incumbents and startups could act in this environment. First, the themes of the FinTech environment will be identified. After that, these themes will be linked to the above presented regulatory innovation strategies. This shows relevant avenues for both protection by incumbents as well as attack scenarios for new entrants.

The landscape of "FinTech" is complex and multifaceted. It is mistakenly sometimes seen as equal to startups and entrepreneurs, but ventures in this area come from both new actors as well as existing companies in the industry and large firms from other industries, such as telecommunications operators and technology providers. A condensed summary of the activities inherent in this market shows five main areas: peer-to-peer, customer intimacy, payments, personal financial management, and underbanked innovation.

Peer-to-peer is a collection of business models where consumers are connected directly to each other without intermediation from a traditional financial services institution. This could be in terms of lending (with examples such as Lending Club, Zopa, and Toborrow), global money transfer (Betalo), and securities investing (Nutmeg). This area is concerned with the process of development of relationships in networks.

Customer intimacy is underpinned by technology such as predictive services that leverage the recent advances in systems that adapt and learn from information patterns (this includes emerging cognitive systems and artificial intelligence). This area includes related technologies such as predictive analytics. Examples here are Betterment, as well as firms such as Alpha Modus, applying cognitive technologies in automated securities trading. The main process here is to understand patterns of behavior.

The area of payments is a functional domain that covers both direct payment solutions but also the domain of transactions over the Internet and mobile networks. Examples in this area are numerous, including iZettle, Square, and PayPal. These actors all provide solutions for cutting out the legacy bank settlement system in transactions over new technology platforms. The main process here is related to transactions.

Personal financial management providers work with the aggregation and advice around the full picture of the financial situation. Examples include Mint, WiseBanyan, Robin Hood, and Tink. Common for these actors is that they make efforts to gather and aggregate personal financial information from existing providers. They then present this information to the customer and present advice on prospective actions for the individual. The key process focus here is aggregation.

A final under-explored area with high innovation potential is underbanked innovation. This is a domain where business models are exploited to find value in the "long tail" of customers who do not pay high fees for investment management. Examples include Currency Fair, Wipit, and Xfers. The emerging firms here present offerings for free or at a very low price for small but frequent transactions. The central process focus in this area is disruption.

The relationship between the above FinTech activities to the previously depicted regulatory innovation strategies and the underlying technologies is summarized in Table 1.1.

Understanding the strategies applied by "FinTech" actors to attack the existing financial services actors should be related to the evolution of regulations. Thereby, any FinTech can understand which regulations (current and emerging) could influence their ability to succeed. This analysis displays a combination of the two most important innovation drivers for the industry: technology and regulations. Below, I give life to the arguments outlined above by applying the framework in part to a current regulatory change. Selected actions will be compared to FinTechs identified to have a business opportunity with the PSD2 regulatory change.

Table 1.1 Relating regulatory innovation strategies to FinTech themes and underlying technologies

Regulatory innovation strategy	*FinTech theme*	*Solution focus*	*Underlying technology*
Standards designer	Payments	Transactions	API management
System integrator	Peer-to-peer	Relationships	Social network analysis
Advisor and co-creator	Personal financial management	Aggregation	Big data analytics
Technology wrapper	Customer intimacy	Pattern understanding	Predictive analytics
Business model innovation	Underbanked innovation	Disruption	Platforms
Infrastructure platform provider	Reaches across all above themes	Efficiency and flexibility	Cloud, artificial intelligence (platform enablers)

A current example: the Second Payment Services Directive (PSD2)

The PSD2 regulation is predicted to considerably change the structure of the payment services industry (Derebail et al., 2016). New actors will emerge, such as third-party providers (TPPs), account information service providers (AISPs), and payment initiation service providers (PISPs) (Finextra and CA Technologies, 2016). These actors will change the industry and drive the adoption of new business models, integration arrangements, and the use of new technology (Valcke, Vandezande, and Van de Velde, 2015). When considering the impact by applying the regulatory innovation framework, one suitable place is the area of system integrator. Selected innovation actions behind this strategy (covering two selected cells of the framework) are compared to a list of examples of FinTechs in Table 1.2. In addition, two examples of innovative actions from incumbent players are discussed below.

The above finding that regulatory changes can present opportunities to both incumbents and FinTechs calls for a brief illustration of entrepreneurial actions of an incumbent. One example is the recently launched collaboration between Visa and IBM, with the goal to turn every device into a potential point of sale. In addition, the Nordic bank Nordea has recently presented a solution where APIs are available for consumption in an "open banking" environment. Related to the innovation actions for the selected cell in the framework, these actions by incumbents address, for example, the following innovation actions:

- Services are designed to enable collaboration.
- Business model innovation is explored on an industry level.
- The role of product partners in the customer relationship is investigated.

Table 1.2 Examples of FinTechs that could take advantage of PSD2 changes and link to selected innovation actions from the framework

	Business characteristics and innovation focus	*Relation to selected innovation actions for PSD2*
Bambora	Card payments and resolution via store, mobile, and web. Link physical and digital business model.	Services are designed to enable collaboration.
Betalo	Global payments and bill settlement. Eight times cheaper than the bank. Global model.	New sourcing arrangements are explored for "back office" processes.
Billhop	Pay invoices with credit card. Interesting collaborations and alliances.	Network models for product collaboration are explored.
Dreams	Goal-based savings and collaboration. Link to peers for savings. Collaboration with Ålandsbanken.	The role of product partners in the customer relationship is investigated.
Fidesmo	Consolidate use of plastic cards to one. Merge of different technologies on one hardware device.	Interfaces for services are well defined toward internal and external providers.
iZettle	Payment solutions for stores, physical terminals. Link between old and new dominant designs (credit card and mobile).	Product architecture considers collaboration arrangements (current and future).
Klarna	E-business payments solutions. Simplified credit rating process. Convenience for customers and merchants.	Service processes are modularized (service architecture is decomposed).
Klirr	Savings as rounding up at purchase. Link between retail and fund savings business.	Business model innovation is explored on an industry level.
Mondido	Payment solutions to be integrated in e-commerce platforms. Link different technologies.	Integration points are defined and designed toward the collaboration partner on a product level.
PayAir	Mobile payments and digital wallets. Focus on security, simplified processes for shopping.	Differences in regulatory view are mitigated in service collaborations.
Tink	Personal financial management aggregation. Collaborations with incumbent banks.	Distribution (sales and advice) is managed across firm boundaries.

PSD2 is a prominent and visible regulatory change that most actors understand will impact the industry value chain. Therefore, initiatives for implementation are underway to position companies for the payments market change in 2018. As a contrast, there are also other (and more mundane) regulatory changes that might well alter the competitive conditions and relationships between incumbents and FinTechs. Such examples are emerging accounting standards in the form of International Financial Reporting Standards (IFRS), the data privacy regulation GDPR (General Data Privacy Regulation), and regulations that increase transparency in advisory and distribution processes, such as IDD and MiFID2. Within a seemingly mundane regulation can hide important messages from the market and the customers, telling the firms to behave in a new way. All firms active in and around the financial services industry should consider the role of regulatory change relative to their strategies and plans for products, solutions, processes, and customer relationships, and also the role of current and future technology.

Recommendations and conclusion

As a conclusion, below I present recommendations for FinTechs, incumbents, and regulators. First, FinTechs should take an analytical approach to consider regulations and regulatory changes as a vital element of their expansion strategy, asking the following questions: Which regulations are potential drivers of our business? Where do threats lie in terms of innovation restrictions? How are the incumbents in the industry we are attacking expected to act?

For incumbents, a recommendation is to select one regulatory innovation strategy (from the six in the framework above), and from there determine partnerships and proactive actions. Incumbents should review all listed (20–40) innovation actions in scope for any one strategy to assess their capability to be innovative in connection with future regulatory changes, asking the following question: Which partnerships can we arrange with FinTechs to improve our capability?

A tangible recommendation to regulators is to use the framework for understanding the impact of regulations to entrepreneurs by creating a sandbox environment. Through analyzing the innovations by FinTech startups and relating those to the respective regulations, the correct slack from the existing regulatory regime can be given, and not just a random statement that "entrepreneurs should have less regulatory pressure."

If nothing is done to change the behavior of new and existing firms, a vicious circle of negativity toward regulations will continue. Firms will be more reactive, implement the new requirements less efficiently, spend more on regulatory maintenance, and then be even more reactive once a new regulation comes. The above recommendations are the basis for organizations to create an environment in which incumbent companies may look at regulations with a more positive view, and FinTechs can be given balanced freedom and also align with the incumbents. Finally, the regulators will have a tool at hand to better understand the impact of their new regulatory initiatives for innovation from both incumbents and FinTechs. This can be the basis for environments that nurture joint innovation rather than actors playing a "zero-sum game."

Note

1 The regulatory evolution concerning APIs is under intensive debate in the UK, where the government looks at mandating banks to provide interfaces. Aspects of open APIs are also inherent in the new regulations concerning EU payments called the Second Payment Services Directive (PSD2).

Bibliography

Abernathy, W.J. and Clark, K.B., 1985. Innovation: Mapping the winds of creative destruction. *Research Policy*, 14(1), pp.3–22.

Abernathy, W.J. and Utterback, J.M., 1978. Patterns of industrial innovation. *Technology Review*, 80(7), pp.40–47.

Anderson, P. and Tushman, M., 1990. Technological discontinuities and dominant designs: A cyclical model of technological change. *Administrative Science Quarterly*, 35(4), pp.604–633.

Bieck, C. and Freij, Å., 2010. *Solving the innovation puzzle: A framework for consistent innovation in banking and insurance*. [online] Available at: www-935.ibm.com/services/us/gbs/thoughtleadership/ibv-banking-insurance-innovation.html [Accessed January 6, 2018].

Brusoni, S., Prencipe, A., and Pavitt, K., 2001. Knowledge specialization, organizational coupling, and the boundaries of the firm: Why do firms know more than they make? *Administrative Science*, 46(4), pp.597–621.

Cabigiosu, A. and Camuffo, A., 2012. Beyond the "mirroring" hypothesis: Product modularity and interorganizational relations in the air conditioning industry. *Organization Science*, 22(3), pp.686–703.

Cacciatori, E. and Jacobides, M., 2005. The dynamic limits of specialization: Vertical integration reconsidered. *Organization Studies*, 26(12), pp.1851–1883.

Derebail, A., Bhushan, B., Gamblin, R., and van Oijen, A., 2016. *European Payment Services Directive 2: Address new requirements and capitalize on emerging opportunities*. [online] Available at: https://www-01.ibm.com/events/wwe/grp/grp308.nsf/vLookupPDFs/PSD2%20Whitepaper/$file/PSD2%20Whitepaper.pdf [Accessed January 6, 2018].

Dyerson, R. and Pilkington, A., 2000. Innovation in complex systems: Regulation and technology towards the electric vehicle. *International Journal of Innovation*, 4(1), pp.33–49.

Ferraro, F. and Gurses, K., 2009. Building architectural advantage in the US motion picture industry: Lew Wasserman and the Music Corporation of America. *European Management Review*, 6(4), pp.233–249.

Finextra and CA Technologies, 2016. *Preparing for PSD2: Exploring the business and technology implications of the new payment services directive*. [online] Available at: https://www.finextra.com/surveys/survey.aspx?surveyguid=162c6191-d287-4eae-ab5f-0e023368d05a [Accessed January 6, 2018].

Fixson, S. and Park, J., 2008. The power of integrality: Linkages between product architecture, innovation, and industry structure. *Research Policy*, 37(8), pp.1296–1316.

Freij, Å., 2017. *Mastering the impact of regulatory change: The capability of financial services firms to manage interfaces*. [online] Stockholm: Stockholm School of Economics.

Available at: www.hhs.se/contentassets/574f17c1efcf48daa6c6974a4dad5740/disscover_ake-freij-master-file-161231_korredit_3.pdf [Accessed January 6, 2018].

Jacobides, M., 2005. Industry change through vertical disintegration: How and why markets emerged in mortgage banking. *Academy of Management Journal*, 48(3), pp.465–498.

Jaspers, F., Prencipe, A., and Ende, J., 2012. Organizing interindustry architectural innovations: Evidence from mobile communication applications *Journal of Product Innovation*, 29(3), pp.419–431.

Levitt, T., 1968. Why business always loses. *Harvard Business Review*, 46(2), pp.81–89.

Liker, J., 2015. Assessing the sins of Volkswagen, Toyota, and General Motors. *Harvard Business Review*. [online] Available at: https://hbr.org/2015/09/assessing-the-sins-of-volkswagen-toyota-and-general-motors [Accessed January 6, 2018].

Meyer, M. and Dalal, D., 2002. Managing platform architectures and manufacturing processes for nonassembled products. *Journal of Product Innovation*, 19(4), pp.277–293.

Moreno, K., 2014. For the financial sector, regulations are here to stay—time to make the best of them. *Forbes*. [online] Available at: www.forbes.com/sites/forbesinsights/2014/10/09/for-the-financial-sector-regulations-are-here-to-stay-time-to-make-the-best-of-them/#38713693cc73 [Accessed January 6, 2018].

Ozcan, P. and Santos, F., 2015. The market that never was: Turf wars and failed alliances in mobile payments. *Strategic Management Journal*, 36(10), pp.1486–1512.

Richard, P.J. and Devinney, T.M., 2005. Modular strategies: B2B technology and architectural knowledge. *California Management Review*, 47(4), pp.86–113.

Rogers, E.M., 1995. *Diffusion of innovations*. 4th ed. New York: Free Press.

Schrage, M., 2015. Is VW's fraud the end of large-scale corporate deception? *Harvard Business Review*. [online] Available at: https://hbr.org/2015/09/is-vws-fraud-the-end-of-large-scale-corporate-deception [Accessed January 6, 2018].

Smith, K. and Grimm, C., 1987. Environmental variation, strategic change and firm performance: A study of railroad deregulation. *Strategic Management Journal*, 8(4), pp.363–376.

Tee, R. and Gawer, A., 2009. Industry architecture as a determinant of successful platform strategies: A case study of the i-mode mobile Internet service. *European Management Review*, 6(4), pp.217–232.

Teece, D., 1986. Profiting from technological innovation: Implications for integration, collaboration, licensing and public policy. *Research Policy*, 15(6), pp.285–305.

Teece, D., 2006. Reflections on "profiting from innovation." *Research Policy*, 35(8), pp.1131–1146.

Valcke, P., Vandezande, N., and Van de Velde, N., 2015. *The evolution of third party payment providers and cryptocurrencies under the EU's upcoming PSD2 and AMLD4*. [online] Available at: www.swiftinstitute.org/papers/the-evolution-of-third-party-payment-providers-and-cryptocurrencies-under-the-eus-upcoming-psd2-and-amld4/ [Accessed January 6, 2018].

Wessel, D. (2012). Bank balance: Regulation and innovation. *The Wall Street Journal*. [online] Available at: www.wsj.com/articles/SB10001424052702304072004577323500303451074 [Accessed January 6, 2018].

List of regulations included in the text

AMLD4 (the Fourth Anti Money Laundry Directive): In order to limit the use of the financial system for criminal activities, there have been regulations established to prevent such use. AMLD4 is the recent extension of regulations, and rules such as Counter Terrorist Financing (CTF) and Politically Exposed Persons (PEP) are included in the regulation.

Basel 2 and 3: The need for banks to understand the level of capital needed to support their business, as well as the processes in place to manage risk, are developed over time to be more stringent. The reason is to avoid support by society once the company is in trouble.

FATCA (Foreign Account Tax Compliance Act): A regulation introduced by the US to track the flow of funds by US citizens with accounts in other jurisdictions.

GDPR (General Data Protection Regulation): A major strengthening of the rights of individuals against the firms that collect and process personal data. Requirements include right to erasure, notification of breach, and the balance of data collected relative to the purpose of use.

IDD (Insurance Distribution Directive): This regulation is increasing demands on insurance companies to be transparent about relationships with distributors and sales channels. The transparency includes conflicts of interest, bundles of products, and remuneration schemes.

IFRS (International Financial Reporting Standards): A series of rules for how to compile financial statements. Current projects of relevance for the financial industry are IFRS9 (reporting of financial instruments) and IFRS4 (accounting for insurance contracts).

KYC (Know Your Customer): This is not a specific regulation, but a term used in connection with regulations dealing with customer relationships, such as MiFID2 and AMLD4.

MiFID2 (the Second Markets in Financial Instruments Directive): The extension of the first MiFID increases demand for documenting financial advice and increases transparency of relationships around the financial institution.

PCI DSS (Payment Card Industry Data Security Standard): This standard applies to companies of any size that accept credit card payments. If your company intends to accept card payment, and store, process, and transmit cardholder data, you need to host your data securely with a PCI-compliant hosting provider.

PSD2 (the Second Payment Services Directive): A major change to the payment services industry that will drive requirements for (so-called) open APIs where account data can be accessed, and also better control over levels of fees included in products and solutions.

Solvency 2: A major regulatory change to the insurance industry. The EU regulation consists of three pillars. The first contains demands on capital required to run the business, the second instructs the firm how to manage risk, and the third is related to processes and data to be reported to regulators.

UCITS (Undertakings in Collective Investments in Tradable Securities): With focus on investment funds, this regulation increases requirements of transparency and control over management of the capital in such funds.

2 Information security in the realm of FinTech

Georgios Kryparos

Introduction

Two of the most easily demonstrated advantages of FinTech companies comparing to traditional financial institutions, such as banks, are their focus on simplifying the customer experience of existing or new financial products and their responsiveness with regard to addressing customer needs. It is this very customer focus combined with the broad adoption of the Internet by the general public that has been the driver for their business success (International Telecommunication Union, 2016). However, for this success to be capitalized to its full potential, retention and expansion of this customer base is a key factor. Research has shown that even a mere 5 percent increase in customer retention can increase profits by 25 to 95 percent (Reichheld and Schefter, 2000). What is essential for this to be achieved is customer loyalty, and therefore trust in the company, its products, and its commitment to prioritize and safeguard these customer needs.

Given how receptive customers are to experimentation today, and businesses eagerness to challenge the established status quo, it seems very possible that an innovative new concept or solution can rather easily have a positive or even enthusiastic first response from customers. Achieving such an emotional reaction to a product or service is an essential step for every business, albeit one that mainly focuses on attracting the customer. In order to retain that customer, though, loyalty and trust are needed—values built over years of consistency to a company's vision and its ability to deliver on this vision and its promises. Most FinTech companies have not existed for 10 years, so it is self-evident in most cases that they have not reached this point yet. By trust in this case, we refer to the confidence that customers show to FinTech companies in their ability to ensure the integrity of their customers' assets in case the customers decide to use their services. On the other hand, trust in traditional banks has been declining steadily since the financial crisis of 2008 (IBM, 2012). By trust in this case, we refer to the confidence the bank customers have to their banks that they have their customers' best interest as a priority. There are obviously different types of trust. In this chapter, we will focus on the first type since this is what FinTech companies currently miss, and this is what prevents most of these customers from fully abandoning the traditional financial institutions, no matter how dissatisfied they might be with them.

With the exception of the Asian markets due to their different social and political circumstances, even customers who are considered as fully embracing digitalization have a hard time completely disengaging from their relationship with traditional financial institutions—banks and such (KPMG, 2016).

One aspect of this trust is the assurance that customers require for their financial assets to always remain both secure and private. Customers do not want their personal and financial data to leak into the public domain, be abused by different threat actors, or, even worse, get lost. Historically, the business domain that has been dealing with these issues is information security. As defined by ISO 27001 (ISO and IEC, 2013), "the purpose of information security is to protect and preserve the confidentiality, integrity, and availability of information." In other words, this means that information must remain secret and unaltered by unauthorized parties, and that it must be available to those who need to consume it at all times, though this is easier said than done in the current hyperconnected society, where almost anything is accessible via the keyboard and screen of a computer without the restrictions of physical access.

Even though customers cannot always translate their desire for security and privacy into specific information security requirements, they can always verbalize their desire to know that the company they entrust their data with is trustworthy and safe from attackers. So even if customers may not be aware that what they demand is better security for their data by the FinTech companies, they are well aware that they demand trust. Therefore, any FinTech that prides itself in being customer-focused needs to have the ability to translate these demands into concrete technical and organizational security assurance requirements.

Current state of affairs

After the Snowden revelations in 2013, information security has become a topic of increasing interest and importance (Greenwald, MacAskill, and Poitras, 2013). The extensive coverage that security incidents and breaches receive in online and offline media, and the consequences of these events, have turned information security into one of the top business priorities, especially for companies in the financial sector (Newman, 2016a; Perez, 2016). This has been a growing trend in the past few years, and 2016 has been no exception, most recently with the allegations of the 2016 US elections having been influenced by illegal hacking.

New stories of large-scale attacks and high-profile breaches of computer networks and systems surged during 2016 on a monthly basis, revealing the compromise of sensitive customer and corporate information by unauthorized parties, resulting in direct and indirect financial losses of millions of dollars for the corporations involved. The frequency of such events has increased comparing to previous years, but it is not the increase that is the most noteworthy event of 2016 (PwC, 2016). What changed during 2016 is the scale of these network attacks and the medium that was used to deliver them.

The most prominent example is the attack against the personal website of technology journalist Brian Krebs on September 20, 2016 (Krebs, 2016c). One single individual, going by the nickname "Anna-senpai," initiated and executed the largest distributed denial of service (DDoS) cyberattack seen to date (Krebs, 2016d). A Denial of Service (DoS) attack is a type of cyberattack where the attacker or attackers manage to render a computer machine or network unavailable due to an overload of its computing resources. This is usually achieved by "flooding" the target with an excessive amount of network connection requests. When such an overload occurs, legitimate user requests cannot be "served" by the machine or the network, rendering the service unavailable. A DDoS attack is based on the same concept, with the difference that the source of the excessive and illegitimate requests is not a single attack launch point, but multiple, controlled by the attacker or attackers (hence "distributed"). The reason Krebs became the target of such an attack was that he had recently exposed criminals who were offering such attacks as a service to their illegal clientele (Krebs, 2016b; see also Krebs 2016a, 2016c). What made this attack exceptional and particularly interesting were two things.

First of all, the "launch points" were not hacked servers on the Internet or even personal computers of unsuspecting customers who clicked on an email link or mistakenly installed a malicious program, as is usually the case in these types of scenarios. Anna-senpai succeeded in this attack by taking control of possibly hundreds of thousands of misconfigured Internet-connected devices such as IP cameras, home routers, digital video recorders, or even baby monitors—the ones that anyone can buy and install in their home (Krebs, 2016d). These devices are nowadays commonly referred to as the Internet of Things (IoT). The misconfiguration was the simple fact that these devices had default passwords for their remote administration that their owners had not changed, and therefore allowed access to the computing resources of these devices to anyone on the Internet. The sophistication of this attack method is quite low and definitely not requiring advanced skills to exploit. At the same time, the capabilities required by these devices are absolutely minimal. All they need to be able to do is transmit very little network traffic toward their target—the equivalent of much less than what is required to download a very poor-quality image from the Internet via a web browser. Despite the simplicity of the attack method, it is actually difficult to defend against it since the only way to mitigate this risk is for all the different users who own such devices to actively change their passwords. Unfortunately, the reality is that most people who buy such devices are not aware that there are such features and definitely cannot imagine or even know that their devices are used as part of an illegal network of attacking devices used against different targets upon request of an attacker, commonly referred to as botnets. This specific botnet became known as the "Mirai botnet," named after a Japanese manga TV series (The Future Diary, 2010).

The second interesting point with this attack was the fact that a few days after, either in fear of being discovered or for whatever other unknown reasons, the attacker decided to publish the tools that were used on the Internet, making it possible for anyone to download, adapt, and use them (Krebs, 2016d). Consequently, anyone now has the power to control and command an "army" of unprotected IoT devices without necessarily having the technical skills that are usually required.

The motivation for Anna-senpai is that the noise generated by multiple people possibly performing such attacks can help him/her remain undetected during the current and future investigations.

But how is this relevant for FinTechs? How can a few baby monitors affect the financial industry? This question can be addressed if we imagine that an "army" of devices and the associated attackers who hide behind them were not interested only in simply taking revenge against a single individual. What if instead they were collectively and in an automated fashion exploiting software vulnerabilities of payment systems, causing money to change hands or get lost in the process? What if every baby monitor was shifting a few cents of payment transactions to different bank accounts, and doing that constantly in a way that remains undetected by fraud monitoring systems? Such an attack would probably stay under the radar of detection, it would happen extremely fast due to its scale, and it would also be impossible to stop due to its geographically distributed nature, without blocking all transactions or even closing down the FinTech service until the problem is resolved.

This is not a concern only for companies in the financial sector. All industry sectors can be affected by the same type of attacks if adopted to the business context of every industry. It is understandable, though, that an attacker has a higher incentive to focus his/her energy on targets on the financial sector. According to the 2017 Verizon Data Breach Investigations Report (DBIR), the industry with the most security data breaches during 2016 has been that of the financial services (471 breaches), even though it was not the industry with the highest number of security incidents (998 incidents) (Verizon, 2017). This shows that the attacks against financial services are more organized, and therefore more successful (circa 47 percent success rate). As a comparison, companies in the public sector seemed to have been the primary target during 2016, with 21,239 incidents but only 239 confirmed breaches (circa 1 percent success rate). The entertainment industry had the second biggest number of incidents (5,534), but with only 11 confirmed breaches (circa 0.2 percent success rate). These statistics show that when there is money to be gained, there is always a higher incentive.

The traditional solution to software vulnerabilities of financial systems was to limit access to the potentially vulnerable systems in the first place. The easiest way to defend a system is to make it unreachable for the attacker. A lot of established financial institutions relied on creating isolated silos where these business-sensitive systems would be available only to a very small number of employees. These employees would either execute transactions on behalf of customers or perform other types of maintenance and administration activities by using proprietary technology in most cases, reassuring the security of the system by the secrecy surrounding the technology used. This approach is often referred to among the circle of information security specialists as "security through obscurity"; instead of ensuring the security of a system based on the defending technical controls, its monitoring procedures and the appropriate access policies, companies relied, and in some cases still do, on the illusion of "others not knowing how the system works or where it is."

With the rise of the Internet and the recent usage explosion of open network protocols and web technologies, this is not feasible anymore. FinTechs have correctly embraced the principles of "always on" and "open standards design," and in their case this old-fashioned mentality of silos and technological secrecy is simply not an option. Services and products always have to be available, they have to be on the Internet because this is where their customers are, but at the same time they have to be resilient and secure by design, expecting and assuming that anyone who can use them can also abuse them. The concept of trust therefore reappears, but in this case on the customer side. Just because someone can reach a service or a website, it does not mean that this person can be trusted at face value. His/her access rights have to be assessed by the service and granted only if their validity is proven. Traditional institutions have understood this business requirement, but they are facing a philosophy transition where they need to embrace a new way of working and at the same time retain the same level of assurance. Unfortunately, in many cases, they do not know how to reach that compromise, either by being too conservative or by being too optimistic that things will be as safe in the new way of working, simply because they have been safe for them in the past. FinTechs, on the other hand, have learned to live with these risky realities of "always on" and potentially "always under attack." This reality makes them by definition more vulnerable, but without necessarily making them less or more secure. It is true, though, that by doing so, they have acquired the ability to adapt faster to a changing landscape where in many cases they are not in full control.

The question is not who has been in the past or is currently more secure, FinTechs or the traditional banks. The question is who will be more secure in the financial landscape that is being shaped now with the penetration of new technologies and the rise of customer demands. And the solution now is not to hide; the solution is to be highly available and highly responsive, but at the same time highly secure, in order to also be highly successful.

Drivers

Different business functions are concerned about different business risks. Information security is concerned with the way the information of a company and its customers is safeguarded from misuse or abuse, and the risks that the company is willing to take while dealing with this information. Information security helps businesses make informed and risk-based decisions as early as possible, and this is the reason why it is important for the business sustainability of any company, and even more for financial institutions. Some arguments have already been briefly discussed about why this will become even more crucial in the coming years, but in this section we will further explore the business needs and market expectations that drive investments in information security.

First of all, the main driver for implementing information security tools and processes in FinTechs is the ever-increasing need for trust, both from the customer and the company's perspective. Due to the very nature of the business, customers require a very high level of assurance in knowing that their personal and financial information is safeguarded at all times. A potential leak or unintentional change in their accounts will harm the company's reputation not only in the eyes of the affected customers, but also the prospect ones. There is no point for a customer to use a financial service that might be innovative and easy to use if he/she cannot trust the outcome of their financial transactions and the potential monetary loss. At the same time, the FinTech company needs to be able to trust that the customer intentionally used its services in the intended way without impersonating someone else or denying that he/she executed a certain transaction. The need for integrity of the transactions, privacy of the customer's personal and financial information, and traceability of every performed action is of vital importance. These requirements can only be fulfilled with the use of information security processes such as access control, encryption, and authentication, just to name a few.

A lot of these requirements usually stem from the need for legal compliance. Demonstration of compliance to the requirements of regulatory bodies has always been an issue of great concern for financial institutions. The risk of losing the business right to operate in the regulated environment of financial services often creates uncertainty, fear, and discomfort to business owners. Information security is used as the tool to bridge the gaps between how business operates and what the regulatory authorities require from them. During 2017 and 2018, one of the main focus areas for all businesses operating in the financial services realm within the European Union, FinTechs or not, will be to implement the requirements imposed on them by new regulations such as the Second Payment Services Directive (PSD2) (European Commission, 2007) and the General Data Protection Regulation (GDPR) (European Commission, 2016). Both regulations have a strong focus on protecting customers within the EU and helping them safeguard and even take control of their data. The technicalities of how this is done from the financial services side (with requirements such as the one for strong user authentication and open but secure communication between companies) falls very much under the domain of information security. Especially for FinTechs, security expertise will be key in order to implement these requirements in a scalable way that the business fulfills its regulatory obligations and at the same time strengthens its security posture without making the wrong investments and stifling innovation. If done correctly and promptly, these obligations might very well turn into a competitive advantage for many FinTechs.

One of the reasons why the regulations, and especially GDPR, are of particular concern is because the penalties in case of a security breach will be dramatically increased. In case of customer data being leaked or having their privacy violated, the fines for the involved company will be up to 4 percent of its annual global turnover or EUR 20 million, whichever is greater. By many, this requirement alone is considered a game changer that will prompt a lot of businesses to pay much closer attention to how they design and implement their internal processes and tools so that the customer's security and privacy are always assured.

Costs can be imposed not only as a result of noncompliance to laws and regulations, but also as a result of a security attack against a company's infrastructure. In case of a security incident during which a threat actor compromises the system and starts manipulating its information, the impact of taking this system offline for any FinTech will be potentially damaging not only to the reputation and brand of the company, but also to its revenue. For a FinTech company, being always online and offering its services 24/7 is the very reason for its existence. In this sense, the availability of the service is directly correlated to the revenue of its business. On the other hand, and in case of such an incident, keeping the system online might also not be the best course of action either. If the attack is focused on stealing information or even money, the longer it goes on, the greater the monetary loss for the business. Therefore, a decision to keep the system running during a security breach might generate more cost than profit. It is easy to argue about these direct costs, but what is often overseen are the indirect costs. As outlined in the 2016 Verizon DBIR, the majority of money spent during and after a security breach is for legal guidance and forensics investigations (Verizon, 2016). Not to mention the brand reputation damage and the potential loss of customer base. The obvious solution is never getting in that situation in the first place, and this is where information security helps. Nevertheless, no matter how strong, strict, and enforcing your security program is, you cannot mitigate all risks from all possible threats, but what information security can and should cater for is the speed in which a risk is remediated, and business returns to being fully operational.

The motivations for a cyberattack can be numerous and diverse: profit, reputation damage, industrial espionage, cyberterrorism or simple cyberbullying (Verizon, 2016). The threat actors can be equally diverse. As mentioned earlier, the wide adoption of the Internet and its democratization created the conditions where every person in the world, regardless of their economic situation, geographical location, and social status, has access to the nearly unlimited resources of the Internet and the companies that conduct business over it. The benefits of this democratization are obviously vast, but one cannot forget the challenges that come along with the created opportunities. Every person has the right to access, but not every person conducts him/herself under the legal boundaries that the current legal frameworks provide. This makes tracing and identifying the source of a cyberattack a technically difficult problem to solve, especially if the right investment in security monitoring, incident management, and forensic investigations has not been made.

The democratization of technology and its advancements have contributed to an ever-growing number of new business ventures and at the same time of consumer demands. These demands dramatically impact the need for businesses to continuously innovate and do it at a pace that the competition is outrun. "Time to market" is the number-one requirement for most businesses, including those in the FinTech world (Kahn, 2005). A product or service has to be innovative, useful, and solve a real-world problem, but it also has to be launched onto the market as fast as possible, before any other competitors capitalize on being first in solving that problem. In any aspect of our life, when trying to go fast, there is always the risk of an "accident," and this is true for business as well. Going fast is important, but too fast might actually lead to the opposite results, especially when considering that this usually means "cutting corners." Cutting corners on any feature has undesirable consequences, but cutting corners in developing a secure product or service inadvertently damages its long-term sustainability. Even if nothing happens right away, this does not mean that it will not happen later. The parallelism with race car driving is often one that graphically explains this argument. The fastest race cars have the greatest need for the best brakes. Brakes, if used correctly, are not there to slow the driver down during the entire course of the race, but in order to give the driver the assurance he/she needs that they will not fail him/her when he/she needs them the most. In other words, the brakes are there not to slow down the car, but to enable the car and the driver to go as fast as they can, as are information security and its principles.

The last but definitely not least driver for information security derives from the previous one (i.e., the need for speed). All financial services and products, whether delivered by FinTechs or traditional banks, heavily rely on technology these days, and software in particular. The main differentiation between FinTechs and banks is not how they transform the financial product itself, but how they transform the technology and the software behind it, making it possible to improve the product in turn. One of the key aspects in this is the ability to deliver new software at a very fast pace and in a way that adds value to the customer from the very beginning and keeps on improving that value as time progresses with small but continuous improvements. This need has given birth to a software development movement called agile software development, commonly known as agile. The *Agile Manifesto* outlines 12 principles for this software development methodology, where working software that meets customer needs is delivered in frequent intervals by self-organizing teams that value communication and continuous improvement more than rigid planning (Beck et al., 2001). In principle, this is a great way to deliver value to customers fast while empowering a company's employees to work autonomously, and eventually grow and profit the business. Unfortunately, in some cases, the people involved focus more on the practicalities and tools of agile development while losing track of the bigger picture. They interpret these 12 principles in a way that fits their personal interests and keeps their workload manageable by avoiding performing tasks for which they themselves cannot see the direct impact, such as business sustainability, legal compliance, and security. It must be emphasized that information security is not a blocker in agile development, but it should not be excluded either. Given the popularity of agile, the traditional information security processes, procedures, and tools need to be adapted to the new business reality. It is true that information security must reinvent itself in order to remain relevant and demonstrate its real business value. At the same time, it must be noted that the lack of security in many organizations who have fully embraced agile development is daily hurting the business, and even putting it at risk as a whole. Agile development is therefore not making security irrelevant. Information security can and should be adopted by companies in a more inclusive way as part of the development process, and not as an afterthought, because of the need for agile development.

Challenges

What often drives success or evolution in an industry are the problems or challenges which that industry faces. Such is the case of information security too. According to the 2016 Verizon DBIR, the industry with the most security incidents was the financial services one, which means that banks and FinTechs are the primary targets for hackers (Verizon, 2016). According to the same report, what the attackers mainly aim for is monetary profit, since 95 percent of the confirmed breaches due to insecure web applications were financially motivated. There are currently no statistics separating the verified incidents between traditional banking institutions and FinTechs, so we cannot conclusively have a crystal-clear picture of the risks and threats targeted specifically toward FinTechs. What we can probably conclude, though, is that they will not be identical given their significantly different modi operandi.

Every time a new technical security vulnerability is released, the general public is advised to update the software on their mobile devices or personal computers. Many see the technical deficiencies of the software that led to vulnerabilities as the root cause of the security problem, while in reality it is just a symptom. The same is true when media reports stories of companies or organizations leaking the passwords or personal information of their customers (Hackett, 2015). It is not the specific system, platform, or piece of software that handles the passwords or the particular type of leaked customer information that is of concern; it is the processes, tools, and people who are behind it. In this section, we will focus on the root causes, and specifically those that mostly affect FinTechs.

The biggest driver and at the same time challenge in today's business landscape is the need for speed—the ever-more aggressive "time to market" business plans. This requirement has contributed wildly to the adoption of the agile development principles that were mentioned in the previous section. Unfortunately, in many cases, this desire for team autonomy, constant change, and minimal planning has become the excuse for delivering undocumented, untested, and poor-quality software that suffers from software deficiencies. It is important to make clear that the problem is not the methodology itself, but its misinterpretation by people who either lack the experience or the desire to deliver products that cater for anything more than the surface features of the developed product. In these scenarios, the development team down-prioritizes almost anything else apart from the features of an application or service that are visible to the customer. This means that the solution is not robust enough, secure enough, and without the necessary solid infrastructure behind it to make it resilient to potential attackers. The overall software design and system architecture is not considered, making it not only less secure, but also more difficult to maintain and scale in the future. Having this mindset, it is possible that the same development team (or the next one that will inherit the software in question) will be forced to completely refactor the entire application, and maybe even its supporting systems, when a new business feature will be required. This short-term thinking, apart from hurting the business in the long run, also hurts the security of the product, since security features and requirements are usually overseen. Therefore, the impact of such decisions needs to be clearly communicated early in the development process; going fast for business reasons (such as time to market) without considering the future sustainability of a product might end up slowing its development at a later stage. In other words, when business will require the next feature, it should not come as a surprise when it recognizes that it will require more work than initially planned, due to what is commonly referred to as "technical debt." Technical debt concerns problems that are repeatedly not addressed and eventually become the basis on top of which future versions of software are built, making it particularly difficult to correct. In the fast-moving world of FinTech, this should be a primary concern for everyone involved. It might make sense to go fast at certain points in time, but one must always be aware of the consequences and consider the time, effort, and planning capacity that will need to be invested later on to address any identified issues. The challenge with security incidents is that when they occur (based on software defects that were intentionally introduced), a response plan with corrective actions will also need to be put in place as an emergency measure. When operating under such pressure, it becomes even riskier to correct a problem without potentially risking the operations and availability of the product or service. For example, if a security incident affects a banking application, the recommended course of action is for the application to be taken offline. This is done in order to block potential attackers from stealing information or funds from the banking systems, as well as for the incident management processes to take place in a forensically sound way. Additionally, if this banking application processes payment orders, rendering this application unavailable for the public has a dire business impact. Finally, if the incident occurs toward the end of the month, which is when most payments typically take place, then the security incident may have major business significance.

Another challenge for information security, and similar in nature to the need for speed, is the attention to superficiality. Appearance and looks are crucial for everything in order to attract any person to anything, in the real and online world. What is important, though, due to its long-lasting effect, is substance. During the recent years, there has been a sharp focus on design and customer experience, which is exactly what is needed in order for a product to be successful. Businesses who embrace this to the fullest prove its criticality through their results and success. Unfortunately, this very important principle is also being misunderstood and abused. In the words of Steve Jobs, "Design is not just what it looks like and feels like. Design is how it works" (Walker, 2003). A correctly composed color palette, functional and non-obstructive visual effects, beautiful images, and professionally shot videos are a vital part of design, but not the only one. Making sure that the application is responsive to customer actions and system-triggered events, that it is structured in a simple format but without being overly simplistic or unrealistic, that it is resistant to unexpected faults or at least tolerant to them, and of course that it always delivers the correct and accurate data to all involved parties are critical elements of the design and the overall user experience. A system should have the exact same requirements of responsiveness, correctness, simplicity, and fault tolerance in order to be considered secure. The very essence of information security is ensuring that both the customer and the involved systems stay assured that the correct data are being transferred to the correct party, unaltered and in a secure manner, and therefore making it very difficult, if not impossible, for a threat actor to intervene and manipulate them. Complexity should also be avoided since it usually leads to difficulty in system maintenance, as well as difficulty in detecting and correcting security vulnerabilities. What needs to be noted about complexity, though, is that it can never fully be eliminated; it can only be transferred. The simpler a product is for the customer, the more complex it is when building the behind-the-scenes processes and tools. For all the reasons above, design and security should be tightly coupled in order to deliver the best possible customer experience.

Another long-standing challenge for information security specialists is cloud services and how they are used by companies. There are four main use cases for cloud services in the corporate world, and FinTech companies take advantage of all of these options. The first is the usage of cloud services directly as part of the FinTech product, such as data center and data hosting providers. The second is for business-specific online solutions, such as credit card processors in the case of financial companies. The third is for enabling or fully operating supporting business functions, such as human resources, sales, marketing, accounting, etc. Finally, the fourth is the usage of cloud services as a means for the employees to work and collaborate more efficiently, such as email providers, project management tools, or monitoring services. Cloud services have revolutionized the world of information technology (IT), giving the ability to companies to build, deploy, and scale their services faster, offload mundane or noncore parts of their business and cut costs. They are therefore ideal for startups or for companies that operate like startups since they can help them save a lot of upfront costs and investments when exploring their business ideas and the viability of their products. However, even after these companies become successful, cloud services can still be proven relevant in terms of cost-efficiency and speed, which is why they are widely used. On the other hand, every time a company outsources any part of its operations to a cloud provider, they lose at least some level of control over the data they collect, produce, or store via this service. There are different categories of cloud services that define different levels of control, but what needs to be clear is that the cloud is not an invisible entity, all-powerful and capable of anything that one can desire. The cloud is simply a third party's computer system, or set of systems, software that someone else owns, controls, and maintains, and people that operate them who will remain anonymous to the company. Given these conditions, one can simply never know if a cloud provider will manipulate, steal, or lose a company's entrusted data. What any company should be aware of is that the cloud provider can potentially do all this if they choose to. There is usually nothing stopping them from technically doing that. The only thing preventing them from doing so are the legal boundaries of agreements put in place between the company and the cloud provider, either in the form of signed contractual agreements, or as part of the terms and conditions of the cloud service. However, if something is legally binding, it does not automatically mean that it is also secure. Losing control over your data by trusting a third party with your business-critical or secret information, usually without being able to hold them accountable if something happens, is a risk that is difficult to manage. How should a company control and monitor the way cloud providers work with the data that are entrusted to them? How should a company control which cloud services their employees use and whether or not it is for company purposes or not? These are questions that commonly concern both business owners and information security specialists, and rarely have straightforward and "one-size-fits-all" answers.

The explosion of cloud services has put the definition of the classification of information to the test. What is internal and what is not? What is secret and what is not? What is business-critical and what is not? What can be shared online and where? Finally, where do the boundaries of the IT environment of a company start and end? In the past, an employee needed to be physically inside the walls of the company and in close proximity to his/her colleagues in order to be able to work. Nowadays, all this person needs is access to the Internet. Most of the tools required to do his/her work are hosted on cloud services. Even for internal applications hosted in the company's internal computer infrastructure, remote access technologies such as virtual private networks (VPNs) make it possible for the employee to be physically located anywhere in the world and still have authorized access to anything that is needed for performing his/her duties. Giving access to a company's network from a remote location means that you also trust the network in that remote location, partly or completely depending on the security controls put in place for managing that remote access. This demonstrates how "elastic" the perimeter of company networks has become. The physical boundaries and security controls of a building cannot cover most of the information security needs of a company, as was the case until the recent past. This is particularly true for FinTechs, where the working climate often resembles that of dynamically growing startups whose employees cannot or do not want to be limited by access restrictions. It is difficult to imagine an employer not allowing their employees to work from home if they need to or to not be able to browse any website they see fit while using company resources (e.g., company computers or smartphones). The elasticity of the network perimeter is therefore one more point of concern for information security professionals. A company needs to make its resources available from anywhere, but at the same time make sure that only authorized people have access to them, and only after they have properly been identified and authenticated. It also needs to educate its employees about using company resources and equipment (such as the computer network and systems) in a responsible manner in order to avoid leaking information to places that do not fulfill the company's security, legal, and compliance requirements.

Employees have always been a central piece in the puzzle of business. They can make all the difference, either in a positive or negative way, in any working environment. The prerequisite for them to thrive is trust and empowerment from the company's side. Power, though, comes with responsibility. When employees have access to information and resources such as those given to them by their working environment, it is important for them to be aware of the risks that the company faces and be able to tackle them. Therefore, awareness and accountability are equally crucial nowadays. In the majority of the security incidents across all the different industry segments, the actions performed by attackers are opportunistic (Verizon, 2017). Very few attacks are highly targeted and persistent. Most of them are least-effort driven hoping to find the weakest link in the chain of information security. And usually that weakest link is the human. Not all risks of the spectrum can be managed or mitigated by technical controls and restrictions. There will always be humans behind every machine that are susceptible to falling victims to an email asking them to click on a link, or a malicious website urging them to supply their personal information, or a phone call from a fake technician asking them to grant remote access to their computer files. This category of attack is commonly known as social engineering, the most prominent of them being the various spam emails that employees receive daily. Some of them might simply be sales and marketing material from vendors trying to attract customers, but some of them might be focusing on stealing information or money out of the company that the employee is working in. During 2016, such spam emails have become a recurring theme (Krebs, 2016a). An example commonly seen in the FinTech world is when someone could be impersonating the CEO of a company by using a fake email account similar to the real one, and requesting in an authoritative and urgent tone from one or several employees, especially someone working in the finance department, to transfer company funds to an external bank account for business reasons (Butler, 2014). This seems like a known trick that should be common knowledge by now to most, but since emails such as these still circulate, we can safely assume that they are successful to some degree. Maybe the reason is the fact that smaller companies are eager to complete business deals as fast as possible and that they do not invest in security awareness programs in the early stages of their business journey due to their small size and limited resources. The challenge for these companies and their employees is to continue being vigilant and particularly careful because the attackers will always find socially exploitable and technically sound techniques to deceive their victims.

There are more security challenges to be identified in the FinTech world, but under the scope of this document we will mention only one more: the insufficient and sometimes incorrect performance of security testing. After a product has been developed, but before becoming available to the customers, it has to be tested that it fulfills the business requirements. It also has to be tested for security vulnerabilities that might have been unintentionally introduced during the development life cycle. The scope of security testing involves not only the correct functionality of the delivered product features, but the product as a whole. It also involves testing the security of its supporting infrastructure, since this infrastructure can be used by attackers as the stepping stone for further exploitation of the product itself, other internal systems, and eventually the entirety of the company. Security testing is hard, and therefore often ignored, because it focuses on the negative ways of how a product could be used. It is first of all difficult to identify all the different abuse and misuse cases, either based on the functionality the product was designed to offer or the functionality that can be revealed due to misconfiguration of other supporting components. Furthermore, even if most of the abuse cases can be identified, performing the tests usually requires specialized tools, trained security professionals, and a significant amount of time due to the numerous combinations of tests that need to be performed before ensuring that the product does not work in a way that it was not designed for. As Albert Einstein once said, "No amount of experimentation can ever prove me right; a single experiment can prove me wrong" (Calaprice and Einstein, 2005, p.291). For these reasons, companies avoid security testing, or perform the absolute minimum required by authorities for compliance reasons, though the value that security testing offers is underestimated. The first step for a security tester to successfully identify abuse cases is to know how the product works, which means that functional testing is also included, even if not explicitly mentioned. This also implies that some documentation or design description is also given as part of the initial discussion. While doing so, it is not uncommon for the product owners and software developers to identify problems themselves simply as part of the need to describe their product to someone external. This documentation work is therefore adding value by itself. Finally, security testing prevents identifying problems at a later time, saving valuable time and money. Research has shown that the cost of fixing a software deficiency early in the development phase, or at least during testing, is significantly less than fixing it after it has been released to the public (Morana, 2006; Grossman, 2009; Cornell, 2012). The cost savings are even greater if one considers the possibility of this security deficiency becoming a security incident—monetary loss, branding damage, incident handling costs, operational costs, disaster recovery costs, etc.

Solutions

Every business faces challenges daily. It is the response to these challenges that defines their success or failure. The challenges are always greater when never faced before, having no predetermined path of how to deal with them. This is the situation that most FinTechs find themselves today. By breaking ground in business and technology, FinTechs end up having to deal with problems that are not common and require creative thinking in order to find solutions. In this chapter, we will look into ways of dealing with the challenges mentioned previously, and propose solutions that usually address more than one of them at a time, given that most of the challenges are tightly coupled.

The most important thing that any startup should keep in mind regarding information security is that it is not an add-on; it is not a patch that can be applied when something goes wrong. If there is one thing that will contribute the most to FinTechs' security, it is to adapt a company culture that includes information security at its core. Processes, documentation, and tools are important, but nothing beats a company culture that understands the risks and works in a proactive and systematic way toward addressing them. First, both employees and executives have to be aware of the risks and threats that exist and have a mindset that takes security into consideration every step of the way. Considering the risk scenarios while building a system or creating a business partnership will increase the chances for success of such a system or partnership, instead of doing so as an afterthought. For example, a development team should not wait for the security personnel to intervene at the end of the development life cycle to test the final product; they should consider the most frequent abuse cases while building the product, and prevent it from being built in an insecure way, or at least take an informed decision that has the support of the business if an introduced feature will knowingly increase the security risk exposure. Moreover, an executive should always consider the regulatory and security requirements that might need to be considered while signing a business partnership, in order to avoid putting customer data at risk. Usually, a security culture such as this is fostered only after a severe security incident has taken place and the importance of security is vividly demonstrated to all involved parties (Associated Press, 2014). However, the remaining question is why companies should have to wait until an incident such as that takes place. In many cases, this might be the last incident they will ever have to deal with, as the impact can be disastrous for the company's reputation and even existence. Security culture is usually built not with the purchase of tools and systems. It is built by people who can be trusted promoting and applying this mindset in daily business tasks without becoming blockers, but rather educators. This can be achieved either with awareness and hands-on training or documentation regarding the accepted policies, instructions, and guidelines, or both. There is no right or wrong. Every company will have to choose their preferred method. Both can be done correctly and both can be done wrongly. This is why having security personnel and top-level management with a direct understanding, interest, and responsibility in security is of key importance.

The second recommended solution is having a high level of preparedness for security incidents. The maturity and responsiveness of an organization to such an event defines its potential to handle it successfully and remediate it correctly, efficiently, and with the least possible impact. FinTechs, like all companies, must learn to respond to an incident, not react. This is easier said than done when the human factor is involved. Different people react differently in moments of stress, depending on their character, emotional status, or knowledge of the subject. The solution to this is to have a well-communicated and rehearsed incident response plan. An incident plan helps in different types of incidents, but there are some things that are particular with security incidents which may require more careful handling due to the sensitivity of the situation; for example, someone might need to involve the authorities or make sure to collect forensic evidence before informing the involved parties. This is why the presence of people trained in such operational tasks is important, but most important of all is the ability for upper management to correctly weigh the criticality of incidents without downplaying their significance, be open about them to the organization when possible, and communicate correctly without ever creating an environment where scapegoats are sought. People make mistakes and systems sometimes fail. This is the reality in the world of technology, and what needs to be done is to learn to adapt to it instead of trying to eliminate it completely, as this is simply impossible.

In order to be able to respond to incidents and at the same time be able to demonstrate compliance toward nearly any regulatory standards, monitoring is of vital importance. If you do not know what happens in your company, your networks, your systems, and your assets, it would be impossible to detect an incident. Not knowing what is happening at any given moment in your company, even if nothing bad happens, is worse than something bad actually happening while monitoring the situation. Monitoring is essential but it has to be done correctly. It should not violate in any way the privacy and integrity of the employees or the customers. Any collected information should be accessible only by those on a need-to-know basis, and this information should, if possible, be anonymized. Monitoring systems should be centralized, receiving data from as many collecting points as possible and maintained by dedicated personnel so that important events can raise alarms when needed and not get lost in the "noise" of excessive information. Monitoring is arguably even more important than prevention (Hanson et al., 2015). FinTechs can accept the risk of allowing risky behavior in their products, systems, or networks, but in this case they must have good compensating monitoring processes that allow them to respond accurately and fast when something happens, instead of blocking every possible risk just in case something happens. This might be more expensive since it requires a high level of automation and competence in dedicated personnel, but it might be worth the price that a company needs to pay in order to allow experimentation and exploration of different technologies, without being blockers of human behavior. Freedom might eventually boost productivity and also creativity, but of course it always has to be combined with accountability and a sense of responsibility. As noted earlier, awareness and the presence of a strong security culture is of strategic importance.

The discussion about monitoring brings to light the issue of automation. In modern agile environments, this is absolutely critical. Automation is encouraged and sought after in every part of agile development, and it should therefore also be adopted when it comes to security processes. Speed and continuous delivery of new software, features, and products is the *raison d'être* of agile development, and information security cannot become the inhibitor to it. For this reason, auto-generated security alarms, automated and closely embedded security testing as part of the development life cycle, and continuous security auditing of access to systems are some of the procedures and tools that FinTechs could employ in order to be able to handle information security in an effective and efficient manner without needing to continuously scale up their security personnel as time progresses. More transactions, more software, more systems, and more employees should not necessarily lead to a proportional increase of security personnel. One more benefit to point out here is that the existence of automated and continuous testing as part of the delivery pipeline of software can dramatically reduce or eliminate both the time needed for security testing before the launch of a product as well as the unintentional and unknown exposure to security risks after its launch (Humble and Farley, 2010).

Finally, a subject of high sensitivity among security professionals is that of access. Who can access what data and from where? Where do we set up the perimeter? For decades, people have been relying on the physical barriers of systems—on locked rooms, secure buildings with tall walls and cameras, etc. All these measures are still relevant, but more so for data center hosting facilities and top secret government agencies, not so much for FinTech companies. The expansion of cloud services, the outsourcing to server hosting providers, and the need for employee mobility have made the need for a network perimeter almost irrelevant. What is more important instead is a more granular level of access control, where each employee gets access to the services and information needed to perform his/her work tasks based on the job function that person serves, and not the geographical location or the type of device that access is requested from. Access should be given based on an employee's identity and current job function, and not based on which system that person has been granted access in the past (who they know and under which branch of the organizational chart they belong). Access should be granted on a need-to-know basis, it should be time-limited, and preferably transparent. These requirements are technically possible, but do require some more upfront investment in order to ensure secure and at the same time simple access to the information needed. What also needs to be considered are the benefits in terms of administration of granting and revoking access, boosting productivity, and reducing friction and annoyance from the employee's side.

2018 trends

Up to this point, we focused our attention on existing problems and existing solutions. In a fast-moving world, though, this is not enough. In order to advance and evolve, one must always look ahead and try to anticipate what lies ahead. Change is inevitable, and one must prepare for it instead of worrying about it. The best tools for someone to use so that the anticipation does not lead to unpleasant and unexpected surprises are the facts of the present and the experiences of the past. The information security challenges that the FinTech industry has been experiencing until today, and the solutions that have been implemented up to now, can give signs of where things might be going. So when one wishes to understand what the future might be holding for FinTech companies during 2018, there is no need for a crystal ball. The facts of the present, if interpreted correctly, can lead to safe estimations. The order in which the suggested trends are presented in this chapter are not indicative of their priority or importance.

It is expected that 2018 will be the year influenced the most by regulations. PSD2 and GDPR will have an indisputable impact on FinTechs for better or worse. Regardless of their objective, whether it is to better protect customers' data and privacy, or to foster innovation and competition among payments, they impose stricter security and privacy requirements toward FinTech companies. Most requirements under the scope of information security are for the best, but that does not mean that some of them might not be possible to be challenged either in the political arena or by introducing innovative solutions that take advantage of the frequent ambiguity and non-descriptive nature of the law. What is to be expected, though, is a drive toward multi-factor authentication for customer-facing applications, the need for an established and structured information security framework inside FinTechs, and finally the enforcement of better data protection mechanisms, even inside the virtual network boundaries of a company, for example with the use of encryption or more granular access control to data. Information security improvements might also take place as a matter of competition between FinTechs and traditional financial institutions. Under the scope of PSD2, financial service providers are expected to cooperate so that they can exchange data for the benefit of their customers. The issue of trust will become relevant, and how financial service providers can better safeguard these data. For example, if the originating party A needs to make its data available to the receiving party B, then it is in the best interest of A to demonstrate that it uses secure technologies to sufficiently verify the identity of B, so that it protects these data before they are accessed, as well as to make sure that their transmission is secure. On the other hand, B will probably want to demonstrate compliance with the new regulations and market itself to the customers of A as a secure and trustworthy alternative.

Given that FinTechs get deeper and deeper into the most technically challenging products of traditional financial services, some of the traditional regulatory requirements such as those of bank secrecy, "know your customer" (KYC) and "anti-money laundering" (AML) will become more relevant for them. FinTechs have always focused their business models by being available only in the digital world for reasons of cost-efficiency, accessibility, and convenience (European Commission, 2015). One of the best features of the Internet from a customer perspective, but not from a business perspective, is the anonymity it offers, despite the recent technological advancements against it, as well as the different scandals that concern state-sponsored surveillance activities of citizens around the world. Anonymity makes the job of FinTechs to fulfill their legal obligations for KYC and AML harder. One solution would be to take the step that banks have been following for years: a customer must first go to a local bank branch, prove his/her identity by showing some sort of legal document identification, and then get access to the financial services offered by the bank. But this would decrease FinTechs' competitive advantages of cost-efficiency, customer convenience, and speed. The solution might come from two different sides: either from the side of the corporate world, where online identification technologies might innovate the way a customer can prove his/her real identity without leaving the convenience of his/her computer, or from the side of the national governments stepping in and granting virtual identity credentials that could be used by a variety of online services, including financial ones. Examples of the first option could be online document scanning or biometric identification technologies with the help of artificial intelligence and machine learning. Examples of the second option could be the issuing of an electronic national identity, such as the one promoted by the eIDAS regulations of the European Union (European Commission, 2014), or the equivalent of a financial identity issued by consortiums of banks, such as the BankID initiative in

Sweden (BankID, 2003). Such eID solutions will obviously increase the level of trust toward the customer, making it possible for FinTechs to offer more advanced services with less risk. In this case, secure identification, which is a vital part of the information security domain, becomes the business enabler and the competitive advantage for a company that decides to implement it. Initiatives such as the eIDAS might bring an end to the potentially insecure, untrustworthy, and error-prone process of account sign-ups with a username and password.

Driven by regulations again, it is very possible that 2018 will bring the proliferation of cybersecurity insurances (The Economist, 2014). GDPR, for example, introduces much higher fees toward financial institutions in case of a security breach; a business may be held liable for up to EUR 20 million or 4 percent of their global turnover. In most cases, such a breach, and therefore the associated fee, will have a great financial impact on the affected FinTech company. The mitigation measures for the company are either to increase the level of their information security posture or purchase a cybersecurity insurance, which might help cover the costs in such a scenario. One, of course, does not exclude the other, and it is up to the FinTechs to evaluate which option best fits their needs and establish a business continuity plan. What one needs to be aware of and careful with in terms of cybersecurity insurances is the same as with any type of insurances. The contractual details might have conditions that imply either a very limited liability or a requirement for an already tightened information security posture. Undoubtedly, though, there are business opportunities in the insurance sector to cooperate and find synergies with the finance sector, even more than before.

Finally, any 2018 prediction would be incomplete if we did not take into consideration the big story of 2016 and 2017: IoT devices. The DDoS attack against Brian Krebs on September 2016 revealed the explosion of IoT devices in the world and how they can easily be abused to launch attacks. The Mirai botnet was not the first of its kind, but it was the first where its author published the software's source code publicly for anyone to copy, edit, and improve (US-CERT, 2016). It is therefore very probable to come across clones of the Mirai botnet. We have actually already seen the same or similar vulnerable devices being used to mine bitcoins, attack critical national infrastructure, become money mules, so why not target FinTechs for financial profit (Newman, 2016b)? Not all FinTechs have the same level of information security posture as banks do, but they might have the same type of wealth. Therefore, they qualify themselves as a very lucrative target for an attacker. Monetization of IoT attacks should consequently come as no surprise to anyone in the near future. Every random or opaque software vulnerability, which would normally attract limited attention, should be evaluated from a different risk exposure perspective.

Summary

FinTechs are building and launching a wide range of new products that significantly improve the customer experience, accessibility, and reach of financial services by leveraging the capabilities of modern technology. This brings progress in a conservative sector dominated for years by a very small, closed group of individuals and companies, and thus democratizes the financial services to the benefit of the end customer. The future looks bright for FinTechs, but one of the few potential threats to this aggressive expansion is neglecting the importance of information security.

The technological benefits and the road to progress usually outweigh the security risks, but right now FinTech companies are in a position where they can make informed decisions and find the right balance between speed and security. They cannot afford to ignore that opportunity since the impact can be detrimental to those who choose to do so. Threats cannot be controlled; they will always be there, lurking for a window of opportunity. Risks, on the other hand, can be managed, and in the case of software vulnerabilities of FinTech services, they can also be treated. The difficulty in this is to find the right balance between the possibility of such threats becoming tangible risks, and the cost and complexity that the mitigating solutions might potentially generate. The answer can usually be found by bringing together the technology, the people, and the processes so that all aspects of a problem can be considered when seeking solutions.

It is important for FinTech companies to embrace a risk-based approach where the identified risks are not understated or remain unhandled. It is also equally important for information security professionals to stop relying on scare tactics, and instead provide concrete advice to businesses by finding smart, or at least smarter than before, solutions. Continuous monitoring and testing with the use of automation, a security culture of inclusiveness without blaming or shaming, a tested plan of business continuity, and technologies that embrace and adapt to a more decentralized IT environment can be tools that empower that change. Information security professionals should not be there to fulfill a compliance requirement or to simply be assigned the responsibility for information security. Information security is after all the responsibility of everyone in any company, and information security professionals should eventually be there so that a company will never really need to use them.

Conclusively, not every risk can be prevented, and for every such risk there is always an exposure window that cannot be avoided. What matters the most is how fast and successfully we work in decreasing that window and remediating the risk by simultaneously improving the security of the company and the product itself. Ensuring that any implemented defenses work in accordance with the business needs of agility and speed, and not hamper innovation or creativity by becoming blockers or "speed bumps," is of essence here. This is where information security can become the differentiating factor, and even the competitive advantage for a FinTech, by helping to build trust toward its customers and partners.

Bibliography

Associated Press, 2014. *Companies tightening up data security after Sony Pictures hack.* [online] Gadgets 360. Available at: http://gadgets.ndtv.com/internet/news/companies-tightening-up-data-security-after-sony-pictures-hack-636877 [Accessed August 27, 2017].

BankID, 2003. *This is BankID.* [online] Available at: www.bankid.com/en/om-bankid/detta-ar-bankid [Accessed August 27, 2017].

Beck, K., Beedle, M., van Bennekum, A., Cockburn, A., Cunningham, W., Fowler, M., et al., 2001. *Manifesto for agile software development.* [online] Available at: http://agilemanifesto.org/ [Accessed August 27, 2017].

Butler, S., 2014. *Scammers pose as company execs in wire transfer spam campaign.* [online] Symantec Official Blog. Available at: www.symantec.com/connect/blogs/scammers-pose-company-execs-wire-transfer-spam-campaign [Accessed August 27, 2017].

Calaprice, A. and Einstein, A., 2005. *The new quotable Einstein.* Princeton, NJ: Princeton University Press.

Cornell, D., 2012. *Remediation statistics: What does fixing application vulnerabilities cost?* [online] RSA Conference 2012. Available at: www.rsaconference.com/writable/presentations/file_upload/asec-302.pdf [Accessed August 27, 2017].

European Commission, 2007. *Directive 2007/64/EC of the European Parliament and the Council.* [online] Available at: https://ec.europa.eu/info/business-economy-euro/banking-and-finance/consumer-finance-and-payments/payment-services_en [Accessed August 27, 2017].

European Commission, 2014. Regulation (EU) No 910/2014 of the European Parliament and of the Council. *Official Journal of the European Union.* [online] Available at: http://eur-lex.europa.eu/legal-content/EN/TXT/HTML/?uri=CELEX:32014R0910&from=EN [Accessed August 27, 2017].

European Commission, 2015. Directive (EU) 2015/849 of the European Parliament and of the Council. *Official Journal of the European Union.* [online] Available at: http://eur-lex.europa.eu/legal-content/EN/TXT/PDF/?uri=OJ:JOL_2015_141_R_0003&from=EN [Accessed August 27, 2017].

European Commission, 2016. *European Commission – press release – capital markets union: Commission supports crowdfunding as alternative source of finance for Europe's start-ups.* [online] Available at: http://europa.eu/rapid/press-release_IP-16-1647_en.htm [Accessed August 25, 2017].

Greenwald, G., MacAskill, E., and Poitras, L., 2013. Edward Snowden: the whistleblower behind the NSA surveillance revelations. *The Guardian*, [online] p.1. Available at: www.theguardian.com/world/2013/jun/09/edward-snowden-nsa-whistleblower-surveillance [Accessed August 23, 2017].

Grossman, J., 2009. *Mythbusting: Secure code is less expensive to develop.* [online] Jeremiah Grossman Blog. Available at: http://blog.jeremiahgrossman.com/2009/05/mythbusting-secure-code-is-less.htm [Accessed August 27, 2017].

Hackett, R., 2015. What to know about the Ashley Madison hack. *Fortune.* [online] Available at: http://fortune.com/2015/08/26/ashley-madison-hack/ [Accessed August 27, 2017].

Hanson, M., Johansson, T., Lindgren, C., and Oehme, R., 2015. *Information security – trends 2015: A Swedish perspective.* [online] Stockholm: Myndigheten för samhällsskydd och beredskap (MSB) [Swedish Civil Contingencies Agency]. Available at: www.msb.se/RibData/Filer/pdf/27584.pdf [Accessed August 27, 2017].

Humble, J. and Farley, D., 2010. *Continuous delivery: Reliable software releases through build, test, and deployment automation.* Upper Saddle River, NJ: Addison-Wesley Professional.

IBM, 2012. *Rebuilding customer trust in retail banking.* [online] IBM Financial Sector: Thought Leadership White Paper. Available at: www-935.ibm.com/services/multimedia/IBM1049_Trust_White_Paper_05.pdf [Accessed August 27, 2017].

International Telecommunication Union, 2016. *Measuring the Information Society Report*. [online] Geneva: ITU. Available at: www.itu.int/en/ITU-D/Statistics/Documents/publications/misr2016/MISR2016-w4.pdf [Accessed August 27, 2017].

ISO and IEC, 2013. *ISO/IEC 27001:2013, information technology – security techniques – information security management systems – requirements*. [online] Geneva: ISO and IEC. Available at: www.iso.org/standard/54534.html [Accessed August 27, 2017].

Kahn, K.B., 2005. Approaches to new product forecasting. In: K.B. Kahn, G. Castellion, and A. Griffin, eds.*The PDMA handbook of new product development*. 2nd ed. Chichester: Wiley, pp.173–187.

KPMG, 2016. *The pulse of FinTech, Q3 2016: Global analysis of FinTech venture funding*. [online] KPMG Insights. Available at: https://home.kpmg.com/xx/en/home/insights/2016/03/the-pulse-of-fintech-q1-2016.html [Accessed August 27, 2017].

Krebs, B., 2016a. *DDoS mitigation firm has history of hijacks*. [online] Krebs on Security. Available at: https://krebsonsecurity.com/2016/09/ddos-mitigation-firm-has-history-of-hijacks/ [Accessed August 27, 2017].

Krebs, B., 2016b. *FBI: $2.3 billion lost to CEO email scams*. [online] Krebs on Security. Available at: https://krebsonsecurity.com/2016/04/fbi-2-3-billion-lost-to-ceo-email-scams/ [Accessed August 27, 2017].

Krebs, B., 2016c. *KrebsOnSecurity hit with record DDoS*. [online] Krebs on Security. Available at: https://krebsonsecurity.com/2016/09/krebsonsecurity-hit-with-record-ddos/ [Accessed August 27, 2017].

Krebs, B., 2016d. *Source code for IoT botnet "Mirai."* [online] Krebs on Security. Available at: https://krebsonsecurity.com/2016/10/source-code-for-iot-botnet-mirai-released/ [Accessed August 27, 2017].

Morana, M.M., 2006. *Building security into the software life cycle: A business case*. [online] Black Hat, USA. Available at: www.blackhat.com/presentations/bh-usa-06/bh-us-06-Morana-R3.0.pdf [Accessed August 27, 2017].

Newman, L.H., 2016a. Hack brief: Hackers breach a billion Yahoo accounts. A billion. *Wired*, [online] December 14. Available at: www.wired.com/2016/12/yahoo-hack-billion-users [Accessed August 27, 2017].

Newman, L.H., 2016b. The botnet that broke the Internet isn't going away. *Wired*, [online] December 9. Available at: www.wired.com/2016/12/botnet-broke-internet-isnt-going-away [Accessed August 27, 2017].

Perez, S., 2016. 117 million LinkedIn emails and passwords from a 2012 hack just got posted online. [online] TechCrunch. Available at: https://techcrunch.com/2016/05/18/117-million-linkedin-emails-and-passwords-from-a-2012-hack-just-got-posted-online [Accessed August 27, 2017].

PwC, 2016. *Toward new possibilities in threat management: How businesses are embracing a modern approach to threat management and information sharing*. [online] The Global State of Information Security Survey 2017. Available at: www.pwc.com/gsiss [Accessed August 27, 2017].

Reichheld, F.F. and Schefter, P., 2000. E-loyalty: your secret weapon on the web. *Harvard Business Review*, 78(1), pp.105–113.

The Economist, 2014. Defending the digital frontier: Special report on Cyber security. *The Economist*. [online] Available at: www.economist.com/news/special-report/21606416-companies-markets-and-countries-are-increasingly-under-attack-cyber-criminals [Accessed August 27, 2017].

The Future Diary, 2010. *Mirai Nikki*. [online] Available at: www.future-diary.tv [Accessed August 27, 2017].

US-CERT, 2016. *Alert (TA16-288A): Heightened DDoS threat posed by Mirai and other botnets*. [online] *United States Computer Emergency Readiness Team*. Available at: www.us-cert.gov/ncas/alerts/TA16-288A [Accessed August 27, 2017].
Verizon, 2016. *2016 Data Breach Investigations Report: 89% of breaches had a financial or espionage motive*. [online] Available at: www.verizonenterprise.com/resources/reports/rp_DBIR_2016_Report_en_xg.pdf [Accessed August 27, 2017].
Verizon, 2017. *2017 Data Breach Investigations Report*. [online] Available at: www.verizonenterprise.com/verizon-insights-lab/dbir/2017/ [Accessed August 27, 2017].
Walker, R., 2003. The guts of a new machine. *The New York Times Magazine*. [online] Available at: www.nytimes.com/2003/11/30/magazine/the-guts-of-a-new-machine.html [Accessed August 27, 2017].

3 FinTech in Sweden

Will policymakers' (in)action nurture or starve its growth?

Björn Olsson and Mattias Hallberg

Introduction

Sweden has the potential to be successful in the globalized digital economy. We typically score among the top 10 in various "most innovative country" lists. In the 2017 Bloomberg Innovation Index, Sweden finished second only to South Korea (Jamrisko and Lu, 2017). The index listed seven indicators;[1] however, Sweden never scored higher than fifth on any individual indicator. We were, so to say, *not exceptionally bad or good* at anything; thus, Sweden achieved its position in a very "Swedish" way.

Our country's favorable position of today is of course perceived in a positive manner, but a clever politician cares less about the current position and more about the direction in which the country is heading. A fundamental truism for policymakers is that the initiatives that made us successful yesterday do not necessarily make us successful tomorrow. If we have learned anything from history, it is that catching up is easy, while true groundbreaking innovation is difficult and consumes a lot of resources. Maintaining a leadership position for a prolonged period of time is very demanding. That is why crafting growth-generating policies is a challenge for policymakers. It entails creating a fertile ground for researchers, innovators, entrepreneurs, and investors to meet and form connections that will lead to new ideas and business opportunities. In our experience, the part that is hardest to solve is to coordinate policy that ranges across the entire spectrum of education, research, and business, so that they all pull in the same direction. This is the humble task we will try to surmount in this chapter. In this quest, we will focus on several topics where actions or inactions from policymakers can have a pivotal impact on the FinTech ecosystem in Sweden. Those include primarily innovation and education policy. The policy recommended is then categorized into different stages of a FinTech firm's growth process.

To understand how the FinTech environment is affected and limited by public policy in Sweden, we would like to separate between two channels. First, there are general structural malfunctions and inefficiencies related to Swedish policy that affect the larger economy. Second, there are also FinTech-specific problems with the current policy regime. We will analyze and propose solutions to both from a sequential perspective. However, first, we will make a brief recap of what we mean by FinTech and the state of the sector in Sweden.

The Swedish FinTech market is rapidly growing and becoming diversified, with new companies and technologies being created and discovered almost every day. The rise of leading actors, such as Klarna and iZettle, has helped turn Sweden into the second largest FinTech community in Europe (second only to the UK) (Wesley-James et al., 2015). Between 2014 and 2016, 89 FinTech investments totaling EUR 474.4 million took place in the Nordic region (Jonsdottir et al., 2017). Sweden took the lion's share, with 50 out of 89 FinTech investments (see Figure 3.1).

Two explanations of the rapid success of Swedish FinTech are that Sweden has been quick to embrace digital banking and electronic payments, placing the country among the least cash-dependent societies in the world. The Internet was made available to large parts of society early, and IT usage is among the highest in the world. Sweden has the second highest smartphone penetration in the world at 72 percent, and 90 percent of its population used the Internet in 2015 (Newzoo, 2017). Sweden also has a powerful history of building global brands, such as IKEA and Volvo, inspiring today's young entrepreneurs to think globally. Recent success stories such as Spotify, King, and Klarna have made it more acceptable to be an entrepreneur, but there are still challenges, as we will see later in the chapter. Stories such as these have also attracted interest from policymakers who are now intrigued to listen to the FinTech community and try to set up both university entrepreneurship programs and support mechanisms across Sweden (Jonsdottir et al., 2017).

The dominance of Sweden in the Nordics also stems from the long history of education and innovation within high-skilled areas, but as we all know, a glorious history can both be an asset and a drag, depending on how it is treated.

Many companies are now at a critical stage in their development, and the ecosystem as such is still frail. One could compare the FinTech landscape with the very vibrant scene of social networking sites in Sweden in the early 2000s. We were ahead of most countries, and it was a sort of breeding ground for this new way of interacting with friends and acquaintances. Still, the Swedish companies

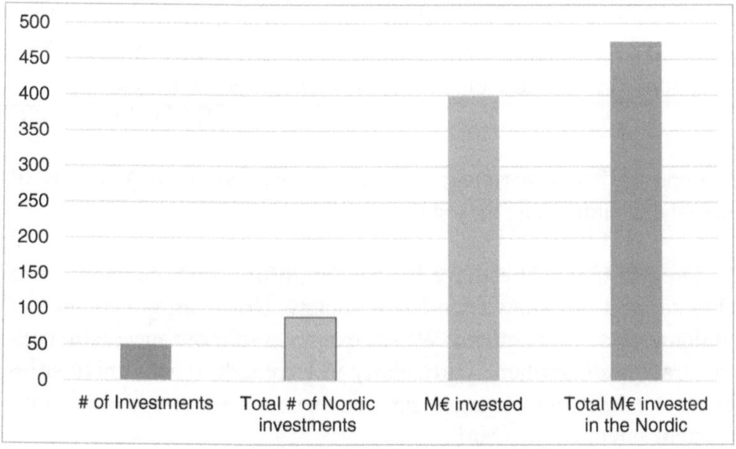

Figure 3.1 Swedish FinTech investments since 2014

did not have the strength to go global and were killed almost immediately after Facebook captured the market in the Western world. There is a clear risk that the Swedish FinTech sector could face the same destiny. The right policy, however, is not the only solution; FinTech must be able to compete on its merits, and not as a sector taken under the wings of a benevolent government.

Innovation policy in Sweden

Sweden is a world-leading country in innovation, but there are signs indicating that our progress has stagnated in the last 5–10 years. For instance, the Swedish research community has not kept pace with Denmark and Singapore—to mention two countries that have similar prerequisites or market conditions to Sweden. Even though the startup scene in Stockholm has been attracting a lot of new investments, we can see that more established technologically advanced companies such as Ericsson, ABB, and AstraZeneca are pulling R&D investments from Sweden and placing them elsewhere (Görnerup, 2015).

In 2016, the OECD (2016c) made a thorough review of the Swedish innovation policy, in which they made some interesting and unfortunately rather discouraging observations. They began by noting that Sweden does not in general suffer from a shortage of resources for research and innovation. This confirms the picture described previously where Swedish FinTech has been attracting large investments for the last couple of years. On the contrary, Sweden spends a relatively large portion of GDP on R&D—slightly above 3 percent on average. However, the public share has been increasing while the private share has gone down. What the OECD critiques is the governance structure of the innovation system. They conclude that:

> the greatest challenge lies in the overall system level. Swedish policy makers, together with relevant stakeholders, should devise and implement a national visioning mechanism that can build greater consensus around majority priorities without excluding other research and innovation efforts that are necessary in a well-functioning innovation system. Research and innovation policy, governance and co-coordination mechanisms should be transformed to effectively link public research and innovation and address societal challenges.
>
> (OECD, 2016c, p.17)

They are not alone in their assessment. When the Royal Swedish Academy of Science evaluated the same issue, they stated that:

> In effect, Swedish universities have become multifunctional conglomerates designed to support our knowledge-based society. However, governance of these conglomerates is not optimal. We see examples of more successful conglomerate strategies elsewhere, particularly in Denmark, where universities have seen an extension of their organizational mandate but remained committed to stringent scientific standards.
>
> (Öquist and Benner, 2012, p.24)

Policy goals have simply been too numerous and varied over time in the Swedish system, and do not form a coherent system of research governance. Rather, there is an opportunistic mixture of goals that direct the research system in too many directions at the same time. As we understand from these two testimonies, Sweden lacks the proper governance structures that a robust innovation system needs. This is not a new phenomenon; the relatively weak academic and political leadership in this area has been known for quite some time. How can Sweden then still be a leading innovation economy? For a starter, Sweden has had a very good foundation to build upon. Our primary and secondary education system was for a long time one of the best in the world (especially in science and literacy), and the free access to higher education enabled talents to grow independent of social background (Gustafsson and Yang Hansen, 2009).

The second important factor in Sweden's success story has been its strong and research-heavy large corporations. They have served as the visionary leaders for Swedish innovation that have attracted both domestic and foreign talent. Traditionally, private companies have accounted for 75 percent of total Swedish R&D. It has both been applied science, close to commercial application and product development, and basic research where commercialization is far off in the future. The Wallenberg foundation is probably the best example—a private foundation that funded basic research for a total of EUR 250 million in 2015 (Government Offices of Sweden, 2015).

Human capital and FinTech

Education

FinTechs, just like most "new economy" sector companies, are in great need of human capital. This is probably the area where policymakers can play the most active role in delivering on the needs of the sector. In most welfare states, the public sector stands for the clear majority of investments in education (i.e., human capital). According to the OECD, 97 percent of all resources spent on education in Sweden were publicly funded, a rather extreme position in comparison to the OECD average at 84 percent (OECD, 2016b). Though clearly, the government is the largest actor in the education landscape in any developed economy. This public commitment to foot the bill for training the workers that different sectors and industries will hire, however, comes with some consequences. It arguably creates inefficiencies and over-/underinvestments in some skills versus others. Overall, it tends to lead to overinvestments in education due to various political considerations, but in all these developed economies, there are disparities between the skills produced by the predominantly public education system and the skills needed by the private sector.

In Sweden, there are systemic problems, such as high unemployment insurance and low incentives for higher education institutions (HEIs) to meet the needs of businesses, which in turn creates this skill gap causing a mismatch on the labor market. This is something that the government has been aware of for a long time (Löfbom and Sonnerby, 2015), but it does not seem to act in solving the fundamental problem. However, the government will not solve the issue by itself. What is needed is higher engagement from the private sector. This starts in primary school, where business leaders should be more engaged in advising and directing the curriculum to make sure that the skills taught in classrooms are compatible with the skills needed in the modern workplace. More importantly, however, are the contacts needed between businesses and HEIs.

Talent availability

We have been inspired by an analytical framework that the British government commissioned to investigate the competitiveness of its FinTech sector (EY, 2016). Unfortunately, no Nordic country was included in their analysis, so we have applied the same framework to the Swedish setting.

A favorable talent environment includes both a good availability today and a developed pipeline that makes sure that there is growth potential. We begin by analyzing the availability of the three key talents that the FinTech industry arguably needs (see Figure 3.2).

Tech skills

On the tech side, Sweden has a long tradition of a high technological skill level, especially digital skills (European e-Skills, 2014). This also shows the potential importance of progressive government policies. A driving force behind both the dotcom era and our current digital miracle was early investments in Internet access to all and a policy that effectively made it deductible to buy a PC (known as "hem PC," translated as "home PC").

In terms of technical skills, the two primary recruitment grounds for FinTechs today are (1) tech giants; and (2) technological HEIs. In Sweden, the Royal Institute of Technology (KTH) in Stockholm and Chalmers in Gothenburg are two examples of the latter. Thus, Sweden's ability to attract and keep both global and European headquarters for large tech corporations is essential if it is to remain an attractive FinTech hub.

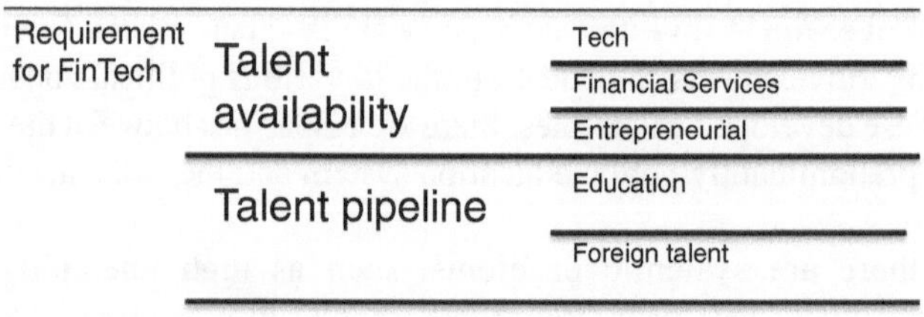

Figure 3.2 Talent: requirement for FinTech

Skills in financial services (FS)

The financial services (FS) sector is a large part of the Swedish economy; it makes up 4.7 percent of GDP and employs 85,000 people annually (Swedish Bankers' Association, 2017b). There are lots of good pathways via business schools into the sector. However, the relative proximity, both culturally and geographically, to London creates something of a brain drain. Policymakers have been two-faced toward the sector, such that it creates a catch-22 of "not being able to live with or without it." The sector is too important for the Swedish economy to dispose of. According to Beck-Friis (2014), it has been a sport for politicians, from both left and right, to pick on the banks in tough times. Arguably, if Sweden is to become a leading FinTech nation, this "love–hate" relationship must end, and policymakers should make it clear that they are committed to creating long-lasting, fair policies for the FS sector.

FS talent is essential for a vibrant FinTech scene, and Sweden, and in particular Stockholm, has a long way to go. Even though we have some large financial institutions such as the multinational bank Nordea, operating in 19 countries with 11 million customers (Nordea, 2017), we struggle to compete with cities such as New York, London, Frankfurt, or even Paris in terms of industry size. Stockholm had, and still has, the opportunity to attract parts of the financial sector that surely will leave the UK after Brexit, as discussed in Chapter 22 in this volume. However, the prospects for this have been hampered by the restrictive policy that the current government has considered, such as the potential levying of even higher resolution fees on banks (Government Offices of Sweden, 2017a). As a result of the proposed policy, Nordea announced that they would consider relocating their global headquarters to either Copenhagen or Helsinki (Kellberg, 2017). It is in this context pertinent to compare it to the Swedish government's effort to attract the European Medicine Agency (EMA) to Sweden following Brexit. A fully staffed office with lobbyists and bureaucrats works to win the political bidding over other EU states (Government Offices of Sweden, 2016). The potential upside, besides the political prestige, is to create approximately 900 jobs. In contrast, the entire FS sector in the UK employs 1.2 million people (EY, 2016). This raises several questions: Why have no banks or other financial institutions been invited to Sweden? Why have there been no proposals on targeted legislation? Based on the above, one could argue that it is currently unlikely that UK banks will move their operations to Stockholm. Notwithstanding the prospects of attracting UK financial institutions, it is arguably important to signal to domestic FS actors that Sweden values their contribution to the economy.

Entrepreneurial skills

Another important driver for the growth of FinTech is the availability of entrepreneurial talent. This is where Sweden has the potential to stand out and be a winner. According to the 2017 Global Entrepreneurship Index, Sweden ranks fourth in the world after the US, Canada, and Switzerland, respectively (Ács, Szerb, and Lloyd, 2017). If we dig deeper in the indicators that make up the index, we realize that even though we outperform most countries in the world, we have some obvious areas where we can improve. Startup skills, human capital, and high growth[2] are the most important. The fact that we score below the European average on startup skills is surprising, considering our favorable position on the Global Entrepreneurship Index (Ács, Szerb, and Lloyd, 2017). The indicator is defined as the share of the able-bodied population claiming to possess the required knowledge/skills to start a business. As evidenced by the World Bank Group's (2017) *Doing Business* reports, starting a business in Sweden has become significantly easier in the last decade. Today, Sweden is among the best nations in terms of ease of starting a business (see Figure 3.3). Our conclusion is that the proportion of the self-employed population needs to increase to make entrepreneurship more visible in society. Educational programs such as *Ung Företagsamhet* (*Junior Achievement Sweden*), where high school students get a hands-on experience in starting a business, should thus be expanded (Nykvist, 2017).

In our experience, most people perceive employment as the chief indicating factor of job security and economic stability. In a welfare system such as Sweden, where the social safety net is built around employment and negotiated via large collective bargaining processes, self-employment and SME ownership is regarded as very risky. However, the economy is changing, and the social welfare system that most Swedes cherish and want to keep must develop to stay up to date.

At various "career opportunity" theme days on campuses all over Sweden, the aim is to match students with the right employer, and the possibility of entrepreneurship is mostly overlooked (Drivhuset, 2013). This practice is effectively discouraging educational aspirations from an education policy point of view. As we can see from the above analysis, the Swedish ecosystem for entrepreneurs is

Opportunity perception	1,00
Start-up skills	0,51
Risk acceptance	0,75
Networking	0,74
Cultural support	0,90
Opportunity start-up	0,95
Technology absorption	1,00
Human capital	0,63
Competition	0,83
Product innovation	0,81
Process innovation	1,00
High growth	0,61
Internationalization	0,87
Risk capital	0,62

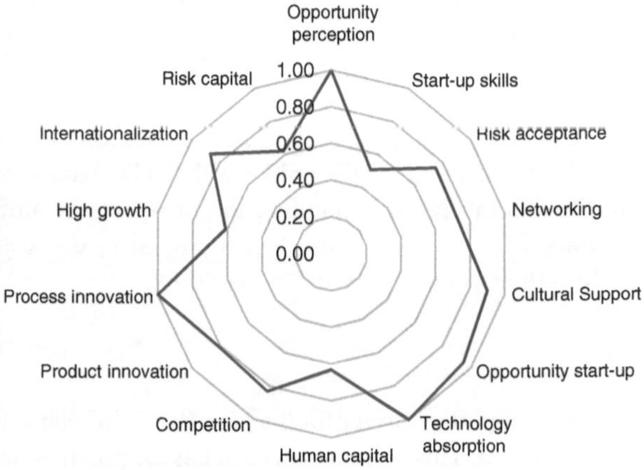

Figure 3.3 Entrepreneurship score profile for Sweden

comparatively good, but we make a poor job of selling it to our own population, possibly due to our labor laws having made it too comfortable to be employed.

Talent pipeline

Education and academic networks

The next segment is the talent pipeline. For the FinTech sector to grow, there must be effective channels to foster employees and entrepreneurs with all those talents described above. Here, the outlook is far from perfect. Today, there are no master's programs at universities that explicitly combine the three key talents needed in FinTech. Even though there is something called the Stockholm School of Entrepreneurship, a joint project for all major HEIs in Stockholm, it cannot compete with, for instance, the Copenhagen Business School's strong commitment to entrepreneurship, which was ranked fifth best in the world according to the Eduniversal (2017) masters ranking of 2017.

Further up in the pipeline, we have problems with STEM skills in Sweden. Our position in the international PISA assessment, which measures and monitors 15-year-olds' skills in STEM, math, and reading, has been declining for years. In 2016, Sweden was below the OECD average in STEM (OECD, 2016a). This has led to a shortage of students with the right skills to attend more advanced tech programs at universities.

Foreign talent

In a global world where specialization is one key aspect of success in most sectors, no country can be a completely self-sustaining ecosystem. To be able to import talent from abroad is just as important as fostering your own talents. We could even take it one step further by claiming that it is critical to mix domestic and foreign influences to achieve a creative melting pot of innovation. Since the liberalization of labor force migration policies in Sweden in 2007, the number of high-skilled laborers from outside the EU permitted residency in Sweden has increased. This is potentially a very important aspect of the Swedish regulatory landscape. The most common position among the high-skill labor migrants is computer scientist (Swedish Migration Agency, 2017). At a time when right-wing populism and neo-nationalism is on the rise in most Western countries, it is more important than ever to keep our liberal system for labor migration. However, after the refugee crisis that befell Sweden in the fall of 2015, multiple tech companies have complained that the migration agency has become stricter in its application of the law and that the waiting time has been prolonged (Wisterberg, 2016).

When it comes to international mobility, it is safe to say that Sweden probably is a net contributor of talent in all the three key areas. Sweden struggles to attract enough young people with high potential and large aspirations. An eye-opener for this development was an open letter written by the Spotify co-founders Daniel Ek and Martin Lorentzon in the spring of 2016. They warned that they would have no choice but to quit Sweden if politicians did not act to address the Stockholm housing shortage, the limitations of the education system, and tax laws. As they wrote in the letter:

> Today we have employees from 48 countries working in Stockholm. To demand that young people coming to a new country immediately buy expensive apartments decreases our attractiveness and is no longer sustainable. Compare this to cities like New York, London and Singapore where rental apartments are cheap. There is, unlike Stockholm, flexibility. There are among experts and decision-makers a broad insight that factors like rental control, the tax structure and current regulations result in a shortage of rentals being built and that the market basically is not working.
>
> (Ek and Lorentzon, 2016)

Since then, Spotify has been expanding in New York rather than in Stockholm. Other entrepreneurs witness the same thing. Henrik Bergqvist, CEO and co-founder of Pickit, stated in an interview that "Swedes grew up with the Internet, meaning we're a digitally savvy nation. However, it will be difficult for companies to remain in Sweden in the long run, particularly with skilled employees moving to the US" (Sheffield, 2016).

Retaining and attracting talent is one crucial challenge that businesses and government have in common, and there should therefore be joint initiatives in this area. We should not just preserve our liberal rules, but instead expand them and make it easier for foreign nationals to contribute to our economy and culture.

Policy recommendations

First of all, as shown by both the FinTech investment data and the OECD, access to capital does not seem to be a major issue for Swedish FinTech firms. Interest rates are low and the latest years have shown that investors dare to invest in often abstract and low-security ideas (Riminton, 2016).

However, as described above, Sweden has some potential problems down the road. The declining performance of the primary and secondary school system is influencing the skill level in the young adult population, as confirmed by the OECD's PIAAC studies (Bussi and Pareliussen, 2015). The decline in skills that students get from primary school has decreased across the board, but most dramatically in both ends of the skill distribution. For instance, Sweden had fewer high-performing students in 2016 compared to 2006 (Henrekson and Jävervall, 2016). Combine this with the fact that the large corporations that have guided R&D in Sweden are divesting, and a structural problem emerges.

What is then needed to counteract these macro-trends to revitalize the innovation landscape? Our main conclusion is that Sweden has spread itself too thin and now needs to focus its ambition of world-class positions into fewer fields in terms of research, innovation, and business.

From a FinTech perspective, R&D is a core activity of their work. FinTechs are heavily reliant on skilled workers and must be able to apply innovations fast and continuously. But R&D looks different in a tech startup compared to a multinational corporation with large teams of researchers. R&D is much more collaborative in the tech world. Patents are becoming less important since in a world of infinite scalability, the first mover advantage is more important. R&D also relies heavier on human capital, and not machines or physical investments in research facilities.

The policy recommendations that we make in this chapter are presented from a sequential perspective. We have, first, the startup phase, implementing the business idea and gaining proof of concept; next, the talent phase, where it is crucial to find the right people to develop the product; then, the growth stage, where the firm solidifies its market position; and last, the global phase, where the firm has a chance of gaining world leader status.

Startups

A Swedish sandbox model

To lower barriers for FinTech startups, we suggest that regulatory bodies change their mindset from just being an administrator of the regulation to working proactively with innovators to help them navigate existing regulation. This approach has already been implemented in the UK with the FCA's regulatory sandboxes (Jonsdottir et al., 2017).

London is today the biggest FinTech hub in the world. The explanation is not one-sided, but the development of the "sandbox model" might well be a key factor. The Financial Conduct Authority (FCA) has implemented a "regulatory sandbox," which is a limited environment enabling FinTechs and incumbents to build and test their products and services in a less restricted environment. If the outcome is positive, then the firms can apply for full licenses and grants. Since it started, the FCA has received over 600 requests, and over 50 percent have so far been accepted as a part of the sandbox model (Jonsdottir et al., 2017). The process can be described as in Figure 3.4.

The sandbox model is effectively a way to signal to highly skilled entrepreneurs that the UK is willing to help them succeed with their projects. Through this model, the UK government attracts a lot of talent.

On a practical level, the Swedish sandbox model would have to be based on different legislative systems than in the UK. The FCA does not only monitor the market participants' compliance with regulation; it also serves to legislate the market. The sandbox model is based on this dual role, as the FCA can permit exceptions from the regulation for a certain limited time (Jonsdottir et al., 2017).

Enhanced know-your-customer process

Know-your-customer (KYC) schemes enable customers to choose which banks can gain access to their credit information. This allows customers to easily apply

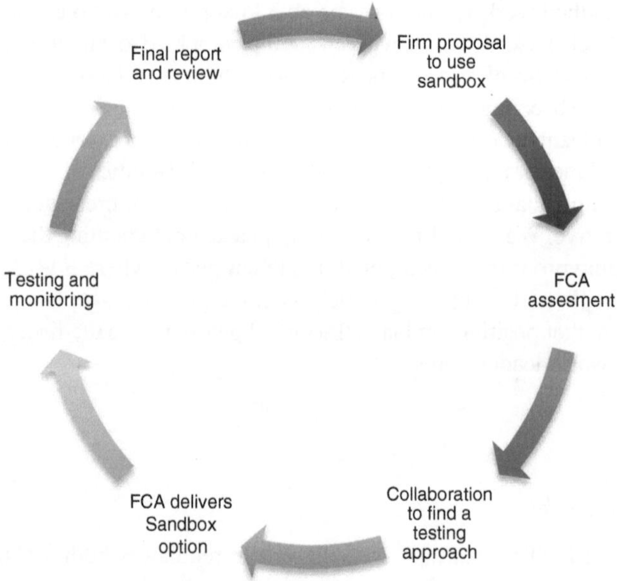

Figure 3.4 The regulatory sandbox model, as used in the UK

for loans at banks that have no previous information on the specific customer's creditworthiness. Today, the Swedish Bankers' Association is investigating the possibility of enhanced KYC norms (Swedish Bankers' Association, 2017a). It is essential that such a system is available not only to established banks, but also to small FinTech firms. If KYC norms are relaxed, arguably the financial intermediaries could focus on what they are best at—financial innovation.

Programming in school

To increase the labor skills and make IT and FinTech a field for vision and entrepreneurship for all, programming should be taught as one of the basic mandatory languages in school. It is indeed a large commitment to ensure that future generations have access to opportunities.

Policymakers have an ambivalent approach to digital skills and digital literacy in the national curriculum. As Asp (2016) shows, digital skills were introduced as early as 1980, but then removed in 1994, to enter again in the early 2000s. Now, with the new curriculum from 2011, schools and teachers have a pronounced task to teach digital skills; however, we are far from teaching code to every school child. It is rather something picked up in one's pastime, should one have the passion and interest. This means a lot of young people never encounter programing languages, and if they do, it might happen rather later in life. We need to capture the curiosity of children and youth, and show them that there are endless opportunities in this field. This especially applies to girls, since the "computer nerd" personality has traditionally been a male stereotype (Cheryan et al., 2013).

In her study, Asp (2016) also showed that teachers requested more concrete guidance from the government and more opportunities for professional development in this field. The problem for Sweden is not access to machines; our schools are well equipped with computers and tablets. What is lacking is the pedagogical and technological skills among the educators (Swedish National Agency for Education, 2015). Here, the municipalities in Sweden who oversee primary and secondary education must take their responsibility and invest in the skills needed by their staff.

Incentivize company-founded higher education

In general, the higher up in the education hierarchy you move, the more advanced and applied skills are taught. The idea is that those skills will be directly applied in the business sector to create growth and prosperity. It is our opinion that a larger economic commitment to higher education from the business community is needed to bridge the skill gap we see today. In the US, 83 percent of organizations surveyed by the International Foundation of Employee Benefit Plans (2015) offered some sort of educational assistance or tuition reimbursement to their employees. It is not unusual for employers in the US or UK to sponsor their promising employees' graduate school education, but then they are heavily involved in ensuring that the skills taught match the skills needed. This is exactly what is missing in the Nordic "government pays all" education environment. The government should try to take a step aside and allow the markets equivalent to the professional master's degree develop. This could be accomplished within the existing HEI framework, or alternatively within a completely new framework. The crowding out and matching problem that the current funding system causes is poorly understood today, and deserves more attention from both academia and politicians.

A master's degree in FinTech

Today, there are no master's programs that explicitly combine the three key talents needed in FinTech. In Sweden, universities have tended to train students to study entrepreneurship rather than training them to become entrepreneurs. Why can there not be a joint program involving KTH and the Stockholm School of Economics (SSE), the two leading HEIs in FS and tech in Stockholm? Just as Swedish universities began early on to educate a combination of business and engineering, they could again take such a new, innovative step.

Lowered government tax

The Swedish tax rate on high incomes today is among the highest in the world (OECD, 2017). Over time, this has caused talents and high performers to relocate to other countries where the tax system rewards rather than punishes high-skilled labor. Throughout the years, different governments have sought to soften these taxes by reducing and imposing different deductions and loopholes. Such have been the different tax rules, including a tax relief for entrepreneurs, and today staff stock options are debated, particularly to the benefit of young startups that often do not have enough capital to take on full-time employees. Yet these are arguably mere excuses to avoid the structural problem. Recent research has even shown that an abolishment of the temporary austerity levy, an additional surtax on high-income earners known as "värnskatt," would not only be fully financed in itself, but result in an increase in government revenue by around EUR 0.3 billion (Lundberg, 2016). Such a reform would send a strong signal that talent will be rewarded in Sweden in the future. Hanushek et al. (2015) showed that Sweden has the lowest return to skills in the whole OECD.

Increased housing

As Ek and Lorentzon (2016) have cautioned, the lack of affordable rental property in Sweden, and particularly in Stockholm, makes it difficult to attract new talent from overseas, and results in Swedish talent moving abroad to cities such as Berlin, London, and Prague. Although housing today is one of the major topics up for debate in Sweden, little is being done. From an economist's perspective, the dynamics of the housing market are easy to explain. A high demand and low supply result in a substantial increase in real estate prices. In a well-functioning economy, this encourages and increases housing investments, as more companies want to sell expensive homes. However, in Sweden, this has not been the case, as regulations and standards have caused a structural deficit in housing investment, resulting in even higher housing prices.

The solution is technical yet simple: regulators and local politicians need to not only encourage housing, but also enable it. This means both a reduction in regulations on environmental issues and the rights to appeal. But it also means that each and every housing project should aim for greater height and a larger number of apartments.

As pointed out by others (e.g., Ek and Lorentzon, 2016), the market for rental apartments is dysfunctional in Stockholm, mostly due to an outdated rent control scheme. In May 2017, the Swedish Fiscal Policy Council endorsed a move to a more market-based approach to prices for rental apartments in Stockholm. We support their recommendation.

Growth

Swedish FinTech council within the FSA

The Swedish government has ordered the Swedish financial services authority to conduct, overview, and evaluate its organization and to facilitate the growth and development of FinTech firms (Government Offices of Sweden, 2017b).

However, there is an impending risk that it is not taken seriously, as such government products tend to lack necessary political backing.

Instead, the FSA should implement a special FinTech council where stakeholders from the regulatory bodies, startups, and large banks can discuss together how existing regulations might need to be adapted to fit with future innovative technology. Stockholm FinTech is obviously a natural partner in such an enterprise. This approach has already been implemented in the UK with the FCA's Project Innovate.

Moderation of compliance processes

A major difficulty of running a financial company is often the tight compliance processes that have been mandated by the regulators. The FinTech sector increases rapidly, as will regulation and compliance. It is essential that this is done in a controlled and cooperative manner where the new regulations are presented easily and in harmony with the industry—without resulting in further obstacles for new business models and innovation.

Global

Free enterprise zone for FinTech

Hong Kong and London are two of the world's most successful examples of free enterprise zones (FEZs). In today's hard international competition for talent and successful companies, Sweden must play an active role. Just recently, when Spotify moved into their new office in New York, expanding from 900 to 1,900 employees, the rent was reduced because of a decision by the state of New York (New York State, 2017). This type of government-led competition for fast-growing companies will most likely increase. In this competition, Sweden needs to play an active role. Therefore, Sweden should consider establishing a special FinTech-focused FEZ, which was already considered in 2013 by the previous government. An FEZ could take the Swedish FinTech sector to the next level.

Scandinavian FinTech council

Realistically speaking, Sweden is not particularly big, and faces global competition for talent. However, the Scandinavian countries combined would equal the world's eleventh largest economy in terms of GDP (World Bank, 2017). The differing policy and regulatory environments across the Nordics have made cross-border collaboration very difficult. In fact, little to no communication occurs between the Nordic financial authorities. Fostering this dialogue and striving for regulatory interoperability across the Nordics would not only reduce barriers for innovation, but also make it easier for FinTech startups to scale across borders. This is especially important in Nordic countries, which are by default small markets.

If Scandinavia would cooperate and ease access to each other's markets, it could be the largest FinTech hub in the world. Offering a proof of concept that a firm's product works under different countries' regulatory frameworks and that it can attract different consumers enables firms to expand more quickly and internationalize.

Regulatory improvements

The new Second Payment Services Directive (PSD2) legislation, as previously described in Chapter 1 in this volume, forces banks to open their infrastructure for payment initiations, as well as for requests for customer account information by third parties. It is intended to increase competition and innovation within the payments area. It is crucial that this new directive, like similar regulations ahead, is reviewed, meets its objective, and does not discriminate against the often smaller third parties. Such a review process is especially important in countries where cases of banks discriminating against smaller FinTech firms have been witnessed.

Conclusion

Right now, there is a momentum for FinTech in Sweden. This is not the only part of the economy where things are happening and new profitable ideas are generated, but it is surely one of the most exciting. The sector combines many of the aspects of Swedish society that can be transformed into competitive advantages in relation to other countries and markets. Even though this chapter is aimed specifically toward policymakers, we are in general pessimistic about governments' capacity to "create" business opportunities. In terms of supporting the business sector, the government must understand what is moving. Which sectors are catching speed and which are dying? Policy cannot stop or reverse the inherent process of creative destruction that capitalism brings with it, but it can be a midwife for the new economy.

We have tried to make the case that Swedish FinTechs are ready to take the next step and go global, but that they cannot do it without support from policymakers. Fortunately, many of the policy recommendations that we have outlined are not FinTech-specific; rather, they are sound policies that many aspects of Swedish society would benefit from. In our mind, the cost–benefit analysis weighs over in the direction of reform. Sure, there are risks involved, but the pathway down a spiral of stagnation and lost dynamism is a very unattractive alternative.

The beauty of the beast is that Sweden is filled with potential areas to reform. Programming skills should be taught at a young age and developed in a master's degree. Talent should view Sweden as a country of low taxes and cheap apartments. Regulation should enhance rather than discourage innovation and entrepreneurship. In conclusion, we would like to reform the way we produce, incentivize, and reward human capital all the way from primary school to business and bonuses. With such a policy agenda, FinTech in Sweden can progress to become outstanding.

Notes

1 R&D intensity, manufacturing value-added, productivity, high-tech density, tertiary efficiency, researcher concentration, and patent activity.
2 The high growth indicator is a combined measure of: (1) the percentage of high-growth businesses that intend to employ at least 10 people and plan to grow more than 50 percent in five years; (2) the availability of venture capital; and (3) business strategy sophistication (Ács, Szerb, and Lloyd, 2017, p.79).

Bibliography

Ács, Z.J., Szerb, L., and Lloyd, A., 2017. *Global Entrepreneurship Index 2017*. Washington, DC: CreateSpace Independent Publishing Platform.

Asp, L., 2016. *Digital litteracitet i svensk grundskola Digital litteracitet enligt svenska styrdokument och lärares praktik [Digital literacies in Swedish Schools: Digital literacies in the Swedish curriculum and the teachers' perspective of the assignment]*. [online] University of Gothenburg. Available at: http://hdl.handle.net/2077/48089 [Accessed August 30, 2017].

Beck-Friis, U., 2014. *Val utan skiljelinjer [Choice without demarcation lines]*. [online] Finansliv. Available at: http://beck-friis.net/wp-content/uploads/2014/04/andersson-o-borg.pdf [Accessed August 30, 2017].

Bussi, M. and Pareliussen, J.K., 2015. *Skills and labour market performance in Sweden*. [online] OECD Economics Department Working Papers. Paris: OECD. Available at: www.oecd-ilibrary.org/economics/skills-and-labour-market-performance-in-sweden_5js0cqvnzx9v-en [Accessed August 30, 2017].

Cheryan, S., Plaut, V.C., Handron, C., and Hudson, L., 2013. The stereotypical computer scientist: Gendered media representations as a barrier to inclusion for women. *Sex Roles*, 69(1–2), pp.58–71.

Drivhuset, 2013. *Studenter är framtidens entreprenörer [Students are the entrepreneurs of the future]*. [online] Attityd 12/13. Available at: www.drivhuset.se/aktuellt/studenter-ar-framtidens-entreprenorer [Accessed August 30, 2017].

Eduniversal, 2017. *Top 100 2017 Eduniveral Best Masters Ranking: Entrepreneurship*. [online] Available at: www.best-masters.com/ranking-master-entrepreneurship.html [Accessed August 30, 2017].

Ek, D. and Lorentzon, M., 2016. *Vi måste agera eller bli omsprungna! [We have to act or be outrun!]*. [online] Medium. Available at: https://medium.com/@SpotifySE/vi-måste-agera-eller-bli-omsprungna-383bb0b808eb [Accessed August 30, 2017].

European e-Skills, 2014. *e-Skills in Europe: Sweden – country report*. [online] Available at: http://eskills-monitor2013.eu/fileadmin/monitor2013/documents/country_reports/country_report_sweden.pdf [Accessed August 30, 2017].

EY, 2016. *UK FinTech: On the cutting edge*. [online] Available at: www.ey.com/Publication/vwLUAssets/EY-UK-FinTech-On-the-cutting-edge-Executive-summary/$FILE/EY-UK-FinTech-On-the-cutting-edge-exec-summary.pdf [Accessed August 30, 2017].

Görnerup, E., 2015. *Kunskapsekonomi på sluttande plan? En undersökning av företagens FoU i Sverige [A slippery slope for the knowledge economics? An investigation of the corporations' R&D in Sweden]*. [online] Available at: www.svensktnaringsliv.se/fragor/forskning/kunskapsekonomi-pa-sluttande-plan-en-undersokning-av-foretagens-f_616081.html [Accessed August 30, 2017].

Government Offices of Sweden, 2015. *Finansiering av forskning i Sverige [Financing higher education in Sweden]*. [online] Available at: www.regeringen.se/regeringens-politik/hogskola-och-forskning/finansiering-av-forskning-i-sverige [Accessed August 30, 2017].

Government Offices of Sweden, 2016. *Ambassadör Christer Asp leder EMA-sekretariatet [Ambassador Christer Asp to lead the EMA-secretariat]*. [online] Press Statement. Available at: www.regeringen.se/pressmeddelanden/2016/12/ambassador-christer-asp-leder-ema-sekretariatet/ [Accessed August 30, 2017].

Government Offices of Sweden, 2017a. *Ett ökat avgiftsuttag till resolutionsreserven [Increased resolution fees]*. [online] Available at: www.regeringen.se/rattsdokument/departementsserien-och-promemorior/2017/02/ett-okat-avgiftsuttag-till-resolutions reserven/ [Accessed August 30, 2017].

Government Offices of Sweden, 2017b. *Uppdrag till Finansinspektionen om innovation av finansiella tjänster [Order to FSA on innovation of financial services]*. [online] Press Statement. Available at: www.regeringen.se/pressmeddelanden/2017/03/uppdrag-till-finansinspektionen-om-innovation-av-finansiella-tjanster [Accessed August 30, 2017].

Gustafsson, J.-E. and Yang Hansen, K., 2009. Resultatförändringar i svensk grundskola [Changes in results in Swedish elementary school]. In: Skolverket, ed. *Vad påverkar resultaten i svensk grundskola?: Kunskaps-översikt om betydelsen av olika faktorer [What affects the results in the Swedish elementary school: Knowledge overview of the significance of different factors]*. Stockholm: Skolverket, pp.40–85.

Hanushek, E.A., Schwerdt, G., Wiederhold, S., and Woessmann, L., 2015. Returns to skills around the world: Evidence from PIAAC. *European Economic Review*, 73, pp.103–130.

Henrekson, M. and Jävervall, S., 2016. *Svenska skolresultat rasar – vad vet vi? [Swedish school results are plummeting – what do we know?]*. [online] Available at: www.iva.se/globalassets/info-trycksaker/iva/201609-iva-henrekson-javervall-i.pdf [Accessed August 30, 2017].

International Foundation of Employee Benefit Plans, 2015. *Educational assistance benefits: 2015 survey results*. [online] Available at: www.ifebp.org/bookstore/educational-assistance-benefits-2015-survey-results/Pages/default.aspx [Accessed August 30, 2017].

Jamrisko, M. and Lu, W., 2017. *These are the world's most innovative economies*. [online] *Bloomberg Markets*. Available at: www.bloomberg.com/news/articles/2017-01-17/sweden-gains-south-korea-reigns-as-world-s-most-innovative-economies [Accessed August 30, 2017].

Jonsdottir, F., Toivonen, O., Jaatinen, V., Utti, A., and Lindqvist, R., 2017. *FinTech in the Nordics: A Deloitte review*. [online] Available at: www2.deloitte.com/content/dam/Deloitte/se/Documents/financial-services/FinTech_Publikation_A4_WEB_FINAL.PDF [Accessed August 30, 2017].

Kellberg, A., 2017. Nordea hotar med flytt [Nordea is threatening to move]. *Dagens Industri*. [online] Available at: www.di.se/nyheter/nordea-hotar-med-flytt/ [Accessed August 30, 2017].

Löfbom, E. and Sonnerby, P., 2015. *Utbildning för framtidens arbetsmarknad [Education for the future labor market]*. [online] Available at: www.regeringen.se/rattsdokument/statens-offentliga-utredningar/2015/10/sou-201590/ [Accessed August 30, 2017].

Lundberg, J., 2016. *Den kostsamma värnskatten [The costly temporary austerity levy]*. [online] *Timbro's Briefing Paper*. Available at: https://timbro.se/app/uploads/2016/08/3_varnskatt.pdf [Accessed August 30, 2017].

New York State, 2017. *Governor Cuomo announces Spotify to relocate and expand its US headquarters at 4 World Trade Center*. [online] *Governor Andrew M. Cuomo*. Available at: www.governor.ny.gov/news/governor-cuomo-announces-spotify-relocate-and-expand-its-us-headquarters-4-world-trade-center [Accessed August 30, 2017].

Newzoo, 2017. *Global Mobile Market Report 2017*. [online] Available at: https://newzoo.com/insights/trend-reports/ [Accessed August 30, 2017].

Nordea, 2017. *Våra marknader [Our markets]*. [online] Available at: www.nordea.com/sv/om-nordea/var-vi-finns/vara-marknader/ [Accessed August 30, 2017].

Nykvist, C., 2017. *Junior Achievement Sweden official website*. [online] Available at: http://ungforetagsamhet.se/om-oss/junior-achievement-sweden [Accessed August 30, 2017].

OECD, 2016a. *Country note: Results from PISA 2015*. [online] Paris: OECD. Available at: www.oecd.org/pisa/PISA-2015-Sweden.pdf [Accessed August 30, 2017].

OECD, 2016b. *Education at a glance 2016: OECD indicators*. Paris: OECD.

OECD, 2016c. *OECD reviews of innovation policy: Sweden 2016*. Paris: OECD.

OECD, 2017. *Taxing wages: Comparative tables – average tax wedge – single person at 100% of average earnings, no child*. [online] Available at: http://stats.oecd.org/viewhtml.aspx?datasetcode=AWCOMP&lang=en# [Accessed August 30, 2017].

Öquist, G. and Benner, M., 2012. *Fostering breakthrough research: A comparative study*. [online] Available at: https://knaw.nl/shared/resources/actueel/bestanden/Akademiskrapport_KVA_DEC20122kopia.pdf [Accessed August 30, 2017].

Riminton, H., 2016. *The Swedish Tech Funding Report*. [online] Available at: www.nordictechlist.com/assets/swe_report_16.aed55b0f5492aec14e7e250471050c6b.pdf [Accessed August 30, 2017].

Sheffield, H., 2016. Spotify's threats to leave Sweden spur startup protest in Stockholm. *The Independent*. [online] Available at: www.independent.co.uk/news/business/news/spotifys-threats-to-leave-sweden-spur-startup-protest-in-stockholm-a6986431.html [Accessed August 30, 2017].

Swedish Bankers' Association, 2017a. *Penningtvätt [Money laundering]*. [online] Available at: www.swedishbankers.se/foer-bankkunder/penningtvaett/kaenn-din-kund/ [Accessed August 30, 2017].

Swedish Bankers' Association, 2017b. *Stoppa straffskatten: Påjobben inom bank, finans och försäkring [Stop the penal taxes: For the jobs within bank, finance and insurance]*. [online] Available at: www.swedishbankers.se/media/3061/1701_stoppastraffskatten_2017.pdf [Accessed August 30, 2017].

Swedish Migration Agency, 2017. *Arbetstagare: Beviljade uppehållstillstånd för arbetstagare 2010-01-2017-07 [Employees: Approved residence permit to employees 2010-01-2017-07]*. [online] Available at: www.migrationsverket.se/Om-Migrationsverket/Statistik/Arbetstagare---de-storsta-yrkesgrupperna.html [Accessed August 30, 2017].

Swedish National Agency for Education, 2015. *IT-användning och IT-kompetens i skolan: Skolverkets IT-uppföljning 2015 [IT use and IT competence in the school: The Swedish National Agency for Education IT follow-up 2015]*. [online] Available at: www.skolverket.se/om-skolverket/publikationer/visa-enskild-publikation?_xurl_=http%3A%2F%2Fwww5.skolverket.se%2Fwtpub%2Fws%2Fskolbok%2Fwpubext%2Ftrycksak%2FBlob%2Fpdf3617.pdf%3Fk%3D3617 [Accessed August 30, 2017].

Wesley-James, N., Ingram, C., Källstrand, C., and Teigland, R., 2015. *Stockholm FinTech: An overview of the FinTech sector in the greater Stockholm region*. [online] Stockholm

School of Economics. Available at: www.hhs.se/contentassets/b5823453b8fe4290828fcc81189b6561/stockholm-fintech---june-2015.pdf [Accessed January 16, 2018].

Wisterberg, E., 2016. *Svenska techstjärnornas vädjan – låt kodarna få komma in i Sverige [Swedish tech stars plead – let the coders enter Sweden]*. [online] Breakit. Available at: www.breakit.se/artikel/5061/svenska-techstjarnornas-vadjan-lat-kodarna-fa-komma-in-i-sverige [Accessed August 30, 2017].

World Bank, 2017. *GDP Ranking Table*. [online] Available at: https://data.worldbank.org/data-catalog/GDP-ranking-table [Accessed August 30, 2017].

World Bank Group, 2017. *Doing Business 2017: Equal opportunities for all*. 14th ed. Washington, DC: World Bank Group.

4 The future of cash

Niklas Arvidsson

Introduction

Payments have been at the center of trade and business since the birth of mankind (Ferguson, 2008). Unless favors are based entirely on charity or on perpetual reciprocation, some sort of payment system is needed to stimulate trade, and thereby enable specialization and prosperity. It is much more convenient if an economic system has a general way to define value—such as a coin—that then can be used to settle trade between, for instance, a farmer selling olives and a carpenter building houses. Deciding how to barter olives for a house is a tedious and risky transaction. Money enables each of them to focus on their specialized skills without having to worry about their welfare. Receiving money instead of bartering goods and services will give merchants opportunities to pursue their skills and then use received money to buy whatever they want on the market. But even an economic system entirely based on non-pecuniary trade needs trade term agreements. For instance, how to make a fair trade between rice and milk would in essence lay the foundation of one important feature of money (i.e., unit of account). If one kilogram of rice can be exchanged for two liters of milk, the system has set a value on both products, and this value can then be accounted for via a monetary system. Such monetary systems have proven to be important for economic development throughout the history of mankind.

Money has a long history dating back several thousand years. One of the early uses of money was discovered in the economic system of Mesopotamia over 3,600 years ago. Historians have found clay coins issued by the king Ammi-Ditana, who ruled Mesopotamia in the period 1683–1647 BC. The coins had inscriptions stating that they could be exchanged for a certain amount of corn, and this exchange was guaranteed by the king (Ferguson, 2008). This monetary foundation is the same as we have today, with central banks (and ultimately national governments) guaranteeing the value of money. There have also been other ways to guarantee the value of money, such as with metal-based coins. The Tang Dynasty in China was one of the first governments to use bills. The bill represented a deposit of coins or metal that was state-proven via a paper-based receipt. This paper-based receipt became a promissory note that could be used as a means of payment between other parties. The low weight and the possibility to make high-value payments in an efficient manner made such notes attractive to merchants. Ultimately, the idea of paper-based money became increasingly popular.

Today, the value of state-backed bills and coins is based on the economic performance of the state and the credibility behind the promise that money has a certain value. Sweden was one of the first countries to launch government-supported cash in its current form, and may now become one of the first countries to stop issuing government-supported cash. This chapter aims to point out critical aspects of the process in which cash is being replaced by electronic payments, thereby possibly leading to a cashless society.

The origins of cash payments in Sweden

The birth and growth of the Swedish payment system took a long time. It started in AD 995, when the town of Sigtuna issued minted coins as a response to the increasing trade between European merchants (Wetterberg, 2009a). The first banks were not created until the beginning of the seventeenth century when the chancellor of the realm, Axel Oxenstierna, spoke about the need for banks that could create a better connection between savings and lending in Sweden.

The King of Sweden, Karl X Gustav, was fighting wars in Poland in the mid-seventeenth century, and needed new financing mechanisms for the war. As a result, in 1656, he awarded the first rights to start a Swedish bank, which came in the form of Stockholm Banco in 1656 (Wetterberg, 2009d). The bank was privately owned by Johan Palmstruch but strongly regulated by the monarch. Stockholm Banco launched their own credit notes and quickly ran into problems as they printed too many bills for which they did not have coverage. This led to a bank run that forced the bank to close down in 1664. A bank run is a situation in which the clients, who have deposited their money in the bank, become uncertain of the bank's ability to repay, and all withdraw their savings at the same time, causing a liquidity crisis (Kärrlander, 2011). Johan Palmstruch was sentenced to death for the mismanagement of the bank, but was later reprieved. In 1668, the Swedish parliament decided to re-establish Stockholm Banco under a new name—Riksens Ständers Bank—and under the ownership and control of the state (Wetterberg, 2009c). This is the first central bank in the world, which later changed its name to the Riksbank—the Central Bank of Sweden—and also the first bank to issue state-supported bills and coins.

The next centuries saw a slow move toward a single currency based on a uniform standard in Sweden, but it was not until the 1897 Central Banking Law through which the Sveriges Riksbank was granted a monopoly on issuing bank notes in Sweden that we saw a single supplier of cash in Sweden. The monopoly started to operate in 1904. This laid the foundation for a modern banking system with a central bank as the key central part. The Swedish crown was then pegged in different ways—to gold, to the British pound, to the US dollar, and then to the Bretton Woods system (Wetterberg, 2009b)—during the first parts of the twentieth century. The crown was also devalued several times in the 1970s, and eventually became fully convertible and floating.

Cash in the Swedish payment system today

There is a long tradition of increasing digitalization of payments in Sweden that started in the middle of the twentieth century but has been increasing significantly in speed and coverage in the last decade. The success of substitutes to cash—such as mobile payment services like Swish and iZettle—combined with other drivers of change, such as unions acting to limit the use of cash in Sweden, an interest among merchants and consumers to use electronic payment services, costs and problems related to cash, as well as other factors, has meant that the last non-digital part of the system—cash—is facing a rapid decline in utility/popularity, and is potentially becoming marginalized. Swedish cash was launched as state-supported bills and coins in 1668, and can be said to have peaked in the end of 2007, when the value of cash in circulation reached its highest level. The decrease of the use of cash has been substantial during the last 10 years (especially in 2017), and it seems to be continuing to decrease in a stable pattern (see Table 4.1).

We should note that the strong declining trend of cash use in Sweden, as well as in neighboring countries such as Denmark, Norway, and Finland during the 2010s, is not representative of the global average (Capgemini and BNP Paribas, 2016). Still, this development naturally leads to the question: Is it possible to foresee a cash-free society?

Is a cash-free society possible?

Is it then likely that we will see a process of evolution leading to an entirely cashless society? That is to say, a society wherein cash issued and backed up by national or supranational governmental bodies does not exist, where central banks are no longer assigned the task to issue cash, and where cash is not legal tender. Well, there are signs that it is theoretically possible.

Table 4.1 Value of cash in circulation

	2005	*2006*	*2007*	*2008*	*2009*	*2010*	*2011*	*2012*	*2013*	*2014*	*2015*	*2016*	*2017**
Nominal value (SEK billion)**	96.3	96.5	97.0	96.7	96.6	95.5	90.7	86.8	84.4	78.2	73.5	65.0	48.8
Nominal value as share of GDP (%)	3.3	3.1	2.9	2.9	2.9	2.7	2.5	2.4	2.2	2.0	1.8	1.3	n/a

Source: Riksbank (2017a).

Notes

* As of November 30, 2017.

** Annual average, excluding banks' holdings.

The US economist Kenneth Rogoff has tackled the issue of cash for many years, and not only discusses, but actually advocates a motion toward, a cashless society in his book *The Curse of Cash* (Rogoff, 2016). As an economist, he addresses the question with a focus on economic and financial policies. His two main arguments behind a move toward less cash include benefits as discouragement of tax evasion and crime, as well as enabling governments and central banks to more effectively handle economic crises by abolishing the "zero lower bound" interest rates that the existence of cash ensures. In addition, he argues that the existence of cash and the ability to pay wages and salaries to unemployed people for temporary jobs is one factor that stimulates illegal immigration and consequential social challenges. This must be weighed against the risk of financial exclusion of people that are dependent on cash and will have problems accessing electronic payment services, as well as the loss of *seignorage*[1] by central banks when cash is not issued to the market.

Rogoff (2016, p.81) defines seignorage as "the difference between the face value of coins minted by the government and the cost of inputs, including both materials and production costs." It thus constitutes the profit a central bank receives when selling cash to the market for the nominal value of bills and coins, while the production cost of those bills and coins are rather small compared to the nominal value. The level of seignorage differs substantially between countries, depending on how much cash is used. In countries such as Sweden, Mexico, Norway, and Denmark, it is close to zero, while in countries such as Hong Kong and Russia, it can amount to well over 1 percent of GDP (Rogoff, 2016). Sweden actually had a negative seignorage during the period 2006–2016 (Rogoff, 2016). The existence of seignorage is seen to ensure a stream of revenues to a central bank, and therefore enable the central bank to pursue its tasks independently from the government (Rogoff, 2016). If a central bank was entirely dependent on finances from the government, some fear it would lose its independence. This statement is heavily debated, however. Rogoff (2016) also shows that even if the outstanding share of US dollars fell by 50 percent, the seignorage for the US Federal Reserve would still by far cover its operating budget. In addition, central banks can still make money on margins between lending and borrowing, and thereby ensure its independence from governmental funding. All in all, even if a reduced seignorage will harm the financial independence of central banks, it would not disable them to run open market operations, perform independent analysis, and pursue independent research.

Researchers at the Swedish Central Bank—the Riksbank—argue that it is reasonable to address the issue of whether cash should be legal tender or not. In an economic commentary, Segendorf and Wilbe (2014, p.7) ask the question if cash has a future as legal tender, and conclude that given the small use of cash in Sweden:

> it would be wise if the legislator begins to investigate now whether a new and technology neutral regulation is needed to determine the method of payment when there are no agreements on this and if there are situations in which it will continue to be necessary to pay in cash.

There is a review of the Central Bank Law, where the issue of cash is one of several other issues to be reviewed during 2017–2019 (Government Offices of Sweden, 2016).

Segendorf and Wilbe (2014) contrast two alternatives:

1 to strengthen the obligation by market actors to accept cash; and
2 to abolish the status of cash as legal tender.

The first alternative—to strengthen the obligations by banks, merchants, and other actors to accept cash—would mean that the market actors would be pushed to follow the current Central Bank Law stating that cash is legal tender. This would have strong positive effects for those that are dependent on cash, even if that group is not large and other actions—such as the legal right to a bank account—are aiming to handle this problem (Segendorf and Wilbe, 2014). The disadvantages of this alternative are that it is not technology-neutral, but rather locks the system in a cash-related technological path instead of stimulating innovation. This in turn could become costly from a socioeconomic perspective (see Segendorf and Jansson, 2012a, 2012b) if the decreased use of cash continues.

Segendorf and Wilbe (2014) argue that the second alternative—to abolish the status of cash as legal tender in Sweden—offers two advantages: (1) the legislation would better reflect the actual use of payment services; and (2) market actors would be able to more freely decide which payment services they prefer to accept and use. The authors also note that this is a long-term process. Hence, such change in the legislation would need to be complemented by measures that help the groups facing negative effects should cash disappear. This includes categories as people with physical and/or cognitive disabilities, the elderly, immigrants/refugees, small cash-dependent companies in rural areas, and smaller organizations (Ehrenberg and Jansson, 2016).

In my previous study of whether or not Sweden may become a cash-free society (Arvidsson, 2013), I concluded that a cash-free society is possible. There are, of course, many factors that influence this development, and the development is therefore difficult to predict. The report concludes that Sweden may become a cash-free society, but not before 2030 (Arvidsson, 2013). The main determinant if Sweden will stop issuing cash in krona is of a political nature. Even if the Riksbank researchers conclude that it is possible to envision that Sweden will stop issuing cash (Segendorf and Wilbe, 2014), there are no signs of Swedish politicians and political parties arguing in this direction. In fact, we are now seeing an opposite development, as one of the parties in the Swedish parliament—the Center Party—contends that the Riksbank ought to be given a formal and official duty to ensure that all companies and households throughout Sweden have access to cash withdrawal and cash deposit services (Dagens Nyheter, 2014; Centerpartiet, 2017a, 2017b). The party argues that the legal cash regulations in the *Sveriges Riksbank Act* (1988:1385), subject to new review during 2017–2019 (Government Offices of Sweden, 2016), must be changed to provide for these stipulations.

Other critical factors affecting or indicating the use of cash in Sweden include:

- Demographical changes since cash tends to be preferred more by elderly and less by young people.
- New companies, technologies, and services that can replace cash payments, such as iZettle, PayPal, Swish, WyWallet, and services from, for example, Kivra, Klarna, Seamless, and Trustly (Arvidsson, 2016).
- The continued growth of card payments (see Chapter 13 in this volume).
- An increase of stores that do not accept cash, as well as an increased use of e- and m-commerce, instead of shopping in traditional retail stores. This means fewer outlets accepting cash, while access to ATMs will continue to be stable, albeit with a reduced number of transactions (Swedish Bankers' Association, 2016). At the same time, the bank offices offering cash-handling services were around 40 percent of all retail banks, with increased fees for cash-handling services and a remaining fear of robberies by merchants, etc. (Ehrenberg and Jansson, 2016).

One other interesting factor affecting the use of cash in Sweden was the introduction of new bills and coins in krona. In 2010, the Riksbank motioned to launch new bills and coins in Sweden throughout the period 2015–2017 (Riksbank, 2010). The process (Riksbank, 2017b) was organized in a way that new bills in the denominations of SEK 20, 50, 200, and 1,000 were introduced October 1, 2015, and new bills in the denominations of SEK 100 and 500, as well as coins denominated in SEK 1, 2, and 5, were introduced on October 3, 2016. The older SEK 20, 50, and 1,000 bills were invalidated by June 30, 2016, while the older SEK 100 and 500 bills, as well as the coins denominated in SEK 1, 2, and 5, were declared invalid as of June 30, 2017. The decision to launch the new cash made sense, as it was taken before the rapid decline of cash had started and was motivated by the ambition to decrease the risk of forged cash. The paradox is that the introduction of new cash seems to have motivated different actors to actually stop accepting and/or using cash before the new bills and coins are introduced. Even if this is somewhat speculative, one may wonder why so many bank offices no longer offer cash-handling services and why an increasing number of merchants have stopped accepting cash. One reason could be that the introduction of new cash has led decision-makers in banks and merchants to address the strategic decision whether to stop accepting cash or not, and that companies such as Telia, Tele2, KungSängen Digital Inn, and the Abba museum, among others, came to the conclusion that it is wise to stop accepting cash and/or offering cash-handling services. Paradoxically, it is not unlikely that instead of stimulating a renewed interest in cash, the new bills and coins may have led to a decreased interest in cash.

The potential route toward a cash-free society

A top-down driven plan

In Chapter 7 of his book, Rogoff (2016) outlines a plan for how central banks and governments can address the move toward a cash-free society. The first part involves phasing out paper currency in different steps, where the large bills are the first to be phased out, which is then followed by lower and lower denominations until only small bills remain. In this phase, it is even a possibility to replace small bills with coins to limit the benefits of using cash. The second part involves a political scheme for universal financial inclusion to ensure that the most cash-dependent people and companies do not suffer when cash is phased out. This could be based on universal access to electronic accounts operated by the central bank or commercial banks, as well as debit cards for all—perhaps even via governmental subsidies. In addition, all forms of state-based payments, such as unemployment benefits, welfare, pensions, child provision, and other forms, would be paid directly to these electronic accounts. The third part is to enforce strong regulations and laws to protect privacy and integrity for people making electronic payments. This aims to ensure consumers trust the systems behind payments. The last part is to build clearing and settlement systems that realize real-time payments—or close to real-time payments—in order to create a functionality of electronic payments that is close to the functionality of cash payments. It should be noted that Rogoff sees this as a gradual and long-term process where the definite end date of cash—where it is not legal tender anymore—is not defined. The slow process will also enable the system to deal with challenges as they occur.

Given Rogoff's plan, it is interesting to note that the parliament (Finansutskottet, 2014) or the Riksbank did not decide to stop the largest bill—the SEK 1,000 bill—when they decided to launch new cash in Sweden. This is not in line with what Rogoff argues. Had the politicians in fact been driven by a political ambition to get rid of cash in Sweden, they would have been likely to decide not to launch a SEK 1,000 bill, but instead withdraw it totally. This is a strong sign that the reduced use of cash in Sweden is primarily driven by market actors such as banks, other technology and service providers, merchants, and consumers. Still, it should be noted that the Riksbank has issued commentaries on the future status of cash as legal tender. The Central Bank Law stipulates that cash is legal tender (The Riksbank Act (1988:1385)), but—as discussed above—this is, as of 2017, being reviewed. Researchers from the Central Bank of Sweden have also acknowledged the need to review the law, and do not exclude the possibility that the law is changed in a way so that cash is not legal tender anymore (Segendorf and Wilbe, 2014).

A sociotechnical development of the cash system

In addition to a top-down approach, we need to understand other factors such as technologies, demand, societal values, business strategies and interest, and other issues to get a complete picture. It is clearly the case that Rogoff discusses the route toward a cash-free society from a macroeconomic and central bank perspective, and consequently does not discuss other relevant dimensions.

In a study of the sociotechnical system behind cash payments and how this is likely to affect the use of cash in Sweden (Arvidsson, 2016), several critical factors deciding the development were identified. The strongest factors moving the system toward less use of cash included technological solutions that can replace cash (such as Swish), the debate in society on how to understand cash and its implications (where both see an increasing campaign saying that cash is needed and others arguing we should get rid of cash), the development of interoperable platforms for new payment services (including platforms for identification, processing, clearing, and settlement), demographical development (since elderly people generally are the most cash-intensive group), and political and societal efforts to detect and handle crimes related to cash.

The same study (Arvidsson, 2016) also identified factors that will lead to a continued use of cash. These were:

- The time it takes for consumers to change habits and values related to payments.
- The strategic games between banks, FinTech, telcos, and others that sometimes make the development more connected to strategic ambitions of providers than to the actual value for payers and payees.
- That different payment services (e.g., cash, cards, invoicing, mobile payments) compete in radically different ways in terms of fees, and that the actual use of services is somewhat biased toward services not having clear consumer fees.
- The role that politicians and lawmakers take in this issue, and the public debate that it creates.

In this scenario, factors related to competition and to the public debate are the most important ones.

It is also interesting to discuss the process from a value-in-use perspective. The value of a payment service is highly dependent on network effects and interoperability, where the value of the service as such, both for payers and payees (i.e., payment receivers), depends on the number of users in the system (Economides, 1996; Hagiu and Wright, 2015). A service with few payers and/or few payees is naturally less useful than a service with many payers and many payees. The international card payment systems are good examples of this. A Visa or Mastercard payment can be made in a large number of stores globally and by a large number of consumers. Interoperability is very high, and the value of the service is therefore high. The development in Sweden for cash during the last decade is characterized by a gradual reduction of interoperability, and the value of the service is therefore decreasing. One can then speculate if there is some point—a "tipping point" (Gladwell, 2000)—at which a slow gradual decline leads to a situation where more and more payers as well as payees stop using or accepting cash since the network value is too low in relation to the costs of continuing to use or accept cash. It is not unlikely that Sweden is nearing the tipping point when it comes to the use of cash.[2]

We should also acknowledge that there are opponents to the reduction of cash-based services in Sweden. There are initiatives such as "Kontantupproret" (Cash Uprising) and several Swedish senior citizen interest organizations such as PRO and SPF[3] that perform lobbying with the aim of keeping cash services in Sweden (Eriksson, 2015). "Kontantupproret" was, as of 2015, led by former national police chief Björn Eriksson, and can be understood as an interest organization for the industry providing services related to protection and handling cash, while PRO and SPF are consumer organizations focusing on senior citizens. "Kontantupproret" has also lobbied for the government to take the concept of access to cash more seriously as the reduction of cash services has impeded many consumers and business owners (Eriksson, 2015). PRO has also acted in this matter by collecting names of people that want to keep cash in Sweden (PRO, 2017).

Even if I have not discussed all factors affecting the use of cash in Sweden, we can conclude that there are a number of factors leading the payment system toward less use of cash, but there are also factors that work in the opposite direction. Having weighed these together, we can predict a development where the use of cash continues to decrease and eventually becomes less important for the payment system as such. Fewer merchants are likely to accept cash[4] and fewer consumers are likely to use cash. The rapid decrease of the use of cash in Sweden may lead to a situation where Sweden has become a cash-free society within five years (i.e., one where cash is legal tender but where few payers and payees use and accept cash).

The role of a central bank in a cash-free society

An interesting question concerns which role a central bank should have in a cashless society. As discussed by Rogoff (2016) and others, the role of a central bank will also be central in a cashless society, even if the task of issuing money may change drastically. Should governments decide to continue to issue money with the backing of a nation or a supranational body such as the European Union, be it in the form of traditional cash or not, the central banks will continue to have a critical role in the payment system. Central banks—for instance, from Canada, Sweden, and the UK—are studying whether and how they may provide "electronic cash" (i.e., electronic money that is supported by the national state). This is called central bank digital currencies (CBDCs), and is seen being similar to traditional cash in a legal and functional sense, even if it is electronic. The idea is to launch electronic money that in concept resembles and functions like cash. The Riksbank of Sweden has studied the possibility of launching an "e-crown," while the Bank of England and the Bank of Canada have been looking into the possibility of introducing a central bank-issued digital currency. The discussion of CBDC focuses on its relation to payments, but there are in addition studies indicating positive macroeconomic gains if a central bank introduces a "central bank digital currency" (Barrdear and Kumhof, 2016).

The Bank of England has been running a program focusing on the implications for a central bank should it issue a digital currency (Bank of England, 2017b). To this point, the Bank of England has been studying the role of digital currencies in challenges related to macroeconomic effects that such a shift may have on the economy as a whole. The Bank of England has also studied how it could affect the financial system, how it could affect policies related to monetary and financial stability, and how it will be realized. One particular question concerns whether a blockchain-based system may function jointly with the existing infrastructure (Bank of England, 2017a). To conclude, the Bank of England, which was one of the first central banks to launch cash, is also one of the first to address the possibility of launching digital cash. To this end, the bank has also put extra effort into understanding how blockchain technology can be used in this endeavor.

The Bank of Canada has also been pursuing the question of whether or not they should issue a digital currency. To this extent, they have developed several arguments as to why this may be a good idea (Bank of Canada, 2017; Engert and Fung, 2017). In a discussion paper by two researchers at the Bank of Canada (Fung and Halaburda, 2016), it is argued that the three main reasons behind introducing a digital currency by a central bank are: (1) it may improve the efficiency of issuing money; (2) it may improve the efficiency and safety of both retail and large-value payments; and (3), it may also give a possibility to handle monetary policy goals and to promote financial stability better in a digitalized payment system. The report also proposes a framework to be used to evaluate desirable properties of such a digital currency (Fung and Halaburda, 2016). They first outline some characteristics that are predetermined or seen as nonnegotiable. These include:

- the fact that the unit of account is the national currency;
- that the central bank continues to issue bank notes and to provide settlement balance or reserve accounts to banks;
- that the central bank offers the possibility to exchange the digital currency to paper currency at par; and
- that the supply of digital currency is decided by the central bank and is consistent with its monetary policy framework.[5]

Other important properties include high efficiency in handling transactions, wide adoption or high interoperability, efficient markets and allocation of resources in the technology and business system, as well as the need to comply with legal requirements such as anti-money laundering (AML) and counterterrorist funding (CTF) requirements.[6]

The Riksbank in Sweden has also been looking at the possibility of introducing a digital currency, or an "e-crown" (Riksbank, 2016). The bank has communicated that it is studying this challenge, and that the development in Sweden with the rapid decline in use and access to cash has led to a need for the Riksbank to address the challenge now. They have outlined three different areas in which they need to make decisions. The first concerns which technologies—both centralized and decentralized—as well as devices may be used. The second concerns which policies—including areas such as the Central Bank Law, the payment system as such, financial policies, financial stability, and other policies—need to be in place when a digital currency is issued. The third concerns which legal requirements must be addressed. The Riksbank has clearly stated that this has been a challenging project, and that it will take time before it can reach a decision in the matter. However, the Riksbank has also pointed out that similar changes have been made previously. An example of which was when paper-based archives for registering ownership of shares were digitalized. As such, there is deep experience and competence that can be deployed in order to meet this challenge.

Concluding remarks and summary

There has been a swift decline in the use of cash in Sweden that does not appear to have lost its momentum. We can therefore foresee a development where the value of cash-based payments—both for payers and for payees—continues to decrease as the interoperability of cash is reduced. In addition, the demographic development will continue to put pressure on cash in favor of electronic and mobile payments. We can expect a future where a decreasing number of payers as well as payees use and accept cash, whereas specific groups in society, such as the elderly, physically and/or cognitively impaired people, etc., still depend on cash. In addition, there may be regions with unreliable telecommunication systems and Internet access, prompting these regions to favor cash. One critical role and responsibility for the state and its agencies is therefore to make sure these groups are helped in this transition.

Another task for the state, as well as for market actors, is of course to develop and supply electronic payment services that create value for payers as well as payees in the situations where cash dominates today. The technological development and digitalization cannot—and should not—be stopped, but there are actions that can be taken to reduce negative effects for certain groups during this transformation. Perhaps an e-crown—or a central bank digital currency (CBDC)—can become another way to enable people to benefit from digitalization and development in the payment industry. One thing that is very apparent is that central banks are continuously searching for and learning to understand their future role should cash disappear.

Notes

1 Seignorage is, in short, the difference between the nominal value of cash—let's say SEK 100—and the production costs of that bill. Seignorage is therefore a windfall gain a state receives when issuing new bills and coins.
2 To receive an answer on this, a consortium of researchers from the Royal Institute of Technology (KTH), Copenhagen Business School, and the Riksbank are, in 2017, conducting a large study of Swedish merchants' views on accepting cash.
3 Such as Pensionärernas Riksorganisation (www.pro.se) and SPF (www.spfseniorerna.se).
4 We are currently pursuing a study, due for publication in 2018, on when Swedish merchants will stop accepting cash.
5 This last requirement is very different from most cryptocurrencies, where the supply is—for natural reasons—not at all connected to a nation's monetary policies.
6 The list of relevant properties that must be handled is long, and includes, for instance, level of anonymity, limits on accounts and spending, fees, technological interface, access devices, distribution channels, verification systems, speed of settlement and reversibility, and ecosystem management, including business models.

Bibliography

Arvidsson, N., 2013. *Det kontantlösa samhället: Rapport från ett forskningsprojekt [The cash-free society: Report from a research project]*. Stockholm: Kungliga Tekniska högskolan.

Arvidsson, N., 2016. *Framväxten av mobila, elektroniska betalningstjänster i Sverige: n studie av förändring inom betalsystemet [The growth of mobile, electronic payment solutions in Sweden: A study on the change within the payment system].* [online] Konkurrensverket [Swedish Competition Authority]. Available at: www.konkurrens verket.se/globalassets/publikationer/uppdragsforskning/forsk-rapport_2016-4.pdf [Accessed August 27, 2017].

Bank of Canada, 2017. *Bank of Canada.* [online] Available at: www.bankofcanada.ca [Accessed August 27, 2017].

Bank of England, 2017a. *Bank of England.* [online] Available at: https://www.bankofengland.co.uk/research [Accessed January 9, 2018].

Bank of England, 2017b. *Digital currencies.* [online] Available at: https://www.bankofengland.co.uk/research/digital-currencies [Accessed January 9, 2018].

Barrdear, J. and Kumhof, M., 2016. *The macroeconomics of central bank issued digital currencies.* [online] Staff Working Paper. Available at: https://www.bankofengland.co.uk/working-paper/2016/the-macroeconomics-of-central-bank-issued-digital-currencies [Accessed January 9, 2018].

Capgemini and BNP Paribas, 2016. *World Payments Report 2016.* [online] Available at: www.capgemini.com/service/world-payments-report-2017-from-capgemini-and-bnp-paribas [Accessed January 9, 2018].

Centerpartiet, 2017a. *Centerpartiet: Riksbanken måste se till att kontanter finns [The Center Party: The central bank must ensure the availability of cash].* [online] Available at: www.centerpartiet.se/lokal/fyrbodal/uddevalla/startsida/nyheter/nyheter/2017-01-28-center partiet-riksbanken-maste-se-till-att-kontanter-finns.html [Accessed August 27, 2017].

Centerpartiet, 2017b. *Så får fler tillgång till kontanter [How to make cash more accessible to people].* [online] Available at: www.centerpartiet.se/media/nyhetsarkiv-2017/2017-01-26-sa-far-fler-tillgang-till-kontanter.html [Accessed August 27, 2017].

Dagens Nyheter, 2014. Centerpartiet: Riksbanken måste se till att kontanter finns [The Center Party: The Central Bank must ensure the availability of cash]. *Dagens Nyheter.* [online] Available at: www.dn.se/ekonomi/centerpartiet-riksbanken-maste-se-till-att-kontanter-finns/ [Accessed August 27, 2017].

Economides, N., 1996. The economics of networks. *International Journal of Industrial Organization*, 14(6), pp.673–699.

Ehrenberg, S. and Jansson, J., 2016. *Bevakning av grundläggande betaltjänster 2016 [Monitoring the basic payment solutions 2016].* [online] Available at: www.lans styrelsen.se/Dalarna/Sv/publikationer/rapporter-2016/Pages/Betaltjanster-2016.aspx [Accessed August 28, 2017].

Engert, W. and Fung, B.S.C., 2017. Central bank digital currency: Motivations and implications. Staff Discussion Paper 2017–16, Bank of Canada. [online] Available at: http://www.bankofcanada.ca/wp-content/uploads/2017/11/sdp2017-16.pdf [Accessed January 9, 2018].

Eriksson, B., 2015. *Yrkande om att Riksbanksfullmäktige markerar mot bankernas agerande i kontantfrågan [Request to the Riksbank General Council to denounce the banks' actions in regards to the cash question].* [online] Kontantupproret. Available at: www.kontantupproret.se/wp-content/uploads/2014/11/Skrivelse-till-Riksbanksfullmäktige-från-Kontantupproret-dec-2015.pdf [Accessed August 28, 2017].

Ferguson, N., 2008. *The ascent of money: A financial history of the world.* New York: Penguin Press.

Finansutskottet, 2014. *Ogiltigförklarande av vissa sedlar och mynt [Invalidation of certain banknotes and coins].* [online] Available at: www.riksbank.se/Documents/

Protokollsbilagor/Fullmaktige/2014/probil_fullm_bilaga_B2_140822.pdf [Accessed August 28, 2017].

Fung, B.S.C. and Halaburda, H., 2016. *Central bank digital currencies: A framework for assessing why and how.* [online] Staff Discussion Paper. Available at: www.bank-banque-canada.ca [Accessed August 27, 2017].

Gladwell, M., 2000. *The tipping point: How little things can make a big difference.* Boston, MA: Little, Brown.

Government Offices of Sweden, 2016. *Översyn av det penningpolitiska ramverket och riksbankslagen [Review of the monetary framework and the Riksbank Act].* [online] Kommittédirektiv [Committee Directive]. Government Offices of Sweden. Available at: www.regeringen.se/rattsdokument/kommittedirektiv/2016/12/dir.-2016114 [Accessed August 28, 2017].

Hagiu, A. and Wright, J., 2015. Multi-sided platforms. *International Journal of Industrial Organization*, 43, pp.162–174.

Kärrlander, T., 2011. *Malmö Diskont – En institutionell analys av en bankkris [Malmö Diskont: An institutional analysis of a bank crisis].* [online] Doctoral Dissertation. Kungliga Tekniska Högskolan. Available at: www.diva-portal.org/smash/get/diva2:443847/FULLTEXT01.pdf [Accessed August 28, 2017].

PRO, 2017. *Kontanter behövs [Cash is needed].* [online] Available at: www.pro.se/pension/Nyhetsarkiv/Kontanter-behovs/ [Accessed August 28, 2017].

Riksbank, 2010. *Riksbanken förnyar sedel- och myntserien [The Riksbank renews the banknote and coin series].* [online] Available at: www.riksbank.se/sv/Press-och-publicerat/Pressmeddelanden/2010/Riksbanken-fornyar-sedel--och-myntserien/ [Accessed August 28, 2017].

Riksbank, 2016. *Skingsley: Borde Riksbanken ge ut e-kronor? [Should the Riksbank distribute e-crowns?].* [online] Available at: www.riksbank.se/sv/Press-och-publicerat/Riksbanken-Play/Skingsley-Borde-Riksbanken-ge-ut-e-kronor [Accessed August 28, 2017].

Riksbank, 2017a. *Statistik [Statistics].* [online] Available at: www.riksbank.se/sv/Sedlar--mynt/Statistik/ [Accessed August 28, 2017].

Riksbank, 2017b. *Tidplan för sedel- och myntutbytet [Time plan for the banknote and coin exchange].* [online] Available at: www.riksbank.se/sv/Sedlar--mynt/Sedlar/Tidplan/ [Accessed August 28, 2017].

Rogoff, K.S., 2016. *The curse of cash.* Princeton, NJ: Princeton University Press.

Segendorf, B. and Jansson, T., 2012a. Cards or cash: How should we pay? *Sveriges Riksbank Economic Review*, [online] 3, pp.1–17. Available at: www.riksbank.se/Documents/Rapporter/POV/2012/rap_pov_artikel_5_121017_eng.pdf [Accessed August 28, 2017].

Segendorf, B. and Jansson, T., 2012b. The cost of consumer payments in Sweden. *Sveriges Riksbank Working Paper Series.* [online] Available at: www.riksbank.se/documents/rapporter/working_papers/2012/rap_wp262_120619.pdf [Accessed August 28, 2017].

Segendorf, B. and Wilbe, A., 2014. Does cash have any future as legal tender? *Economic Commentaries*, [online] 9, pp.1–8. Available at: www.riksbank.se/Documents/Rapporter/Ekonomiska_kommentarer/2014/rap_ek_kom_nr09_141125_eng.pdf [Accessed August 28, 2017].

Swedish Bankers' Association, 2016. *Bank and finance statistics 2015.* [online] Available at: https://bf-swedishbankers.azurewebsites.net/media/2661/2015_bankfinans_eng_.pdf [Accessed August 28, 2017].

The Riksbank Act (1988:1385). [online] Available at: www.riksdagen.se/sv/dokument-lagar/dokument/svensk-forfattningssamling/lag-19881385-om-sveriges-riksbank_sfs-1988-1385 [Accessed August 28, 2017].

Wetterberg, G., 2009a. Förspelet [Foreplay]. In: G. Wetterberg, ed. *Pengarna och makten: Riksbankens historia [The money and the power: The history of the Swedish Riksbank]*. Stockholm: Atlantis, pp.15–22.

Wetterberg, G., 2009b. Från kris till norm [From crisis to norm]. In: G. Wetterberg, ed. *Pengarna och makten: Riksbankens historia [The money and the power: The history of the Swedish Riksbank]*. Stockholm: Atlantis, pp.397–461.

Wetterberg, G., 2009c. Frihetstiden [Age of Freedom]. In: G. Wetterberg, ed. *Pengarna och makten: Riksbankens historia [The money and the power: The history of the Swedish Riksbank]*. Stockholm: Atlantis, pp.75–110.

Wetterberg, G., 2009d. Stockholms Banco. In: G. Wetterberg, ed. *Pengarna och makten: Riksbankens historia [The money and the power: The history of the Swedish Riksbank]*. Stockholm: Atlantis, pp.25–45.

5 The adoption of online banking in Sweden

Michael Björn

Swedish Internet users in international comparison

Sweden is commonly thought of as a very advanced country when it comes to Internet usage. Among other things, the Swedish government has been very active in promoting the use of computers and the Internet. For example, Sweden enacted the "hem PC" (home PC) initiatives, in which companies could offer employees PCs for their homes on a pre-tax basis, and the 3G licensing process, in which licenses were not auctioned for money, but instead given to those operators who could present the best plans for nationwide coverage, in the early 2000s to promote computer and Internet usage (Swedish Post and Telecom Authority, 2006).

However, although Internet usage in Sweden is at a relatively high level, it is not necessarily exceptional compared to other developed countries. While there are many reports on Internet usage, the Ericsson ConsumerLab has surveyed consumers in several countries for more than 20 years. One quantitative questionnaire-based consumer study performed by Ericsson ConsumerLab across 31 countries during 2015–2016 revealed that Sweden does not rank first in measures related to general Internet usage (Ericsson ConsumerLab, 2016). Rather, the country tends to fall somewhere within the medium to high range.

In the aforementioned Ericsson ConsumerLab survey, we can see the differences between Sweden and other countries in terms of time spent on the Internet. On average, South Korea spent the most time on the Internet, while Sweden was #7. For time spent on the Internet at home, Canada ranked #1, Sweden was #7, and South Korea fell to #14. When it comes to time spent on the Internet at work, South Korea was back to #1 and Sweden ranked #6.

From the perspective of devices used for Internet access, Sweden was #17 for time spent on mobile phones. This follows a general trend in which most industrialized countries are far down the list and emerging markets take the top positions. The notable exception here again is South Korea, which ranked #5. Sweden fares better when it comes to time spent on PCs, where it was ranked #12, with Japan ranking #1, and on tablets, where Sweden ranked #6, with the US ranking #1.

A similar pattern follows when looking at time spent using various services, with Sweden ranking #3 on general browsing, #9 on email use, #6 on time spent viewing video, and #5 on music. Again, on applications, where industrialized countries in general are ranked lower, Sweden also ranks lower, with a #20 rank on instant messaging and a #15 rank on time spent on social networking services.

However, when we look at the share of the population conducting online banking and the time spent on this activity (regardless of Internet device), we find that Sweden has actually led the way over the last decade. For this reason, this chapter aims to give a fuller picture of the adoption process itself, rather than just a simple ranking exercise.

A four-phase model of online banking adoption

In order to take a deeper look at the adoption of online banking in Sweden relative to other countries, we turn to the diffusion of innovation literature. Rogers (1962) initially proposed the diffusion of innovation model to describe the penetration of a new product or service in a market by using different categories of users: innovators, early adopters, early majority, late majority, and laggards (see Figure 5.1).

While the above model may be well known and widely used, it focuses specifically on market penetration. In order to provide more insight on the differences between markets, we will focus on the intensity (measured as average daily time spent or average daily frequency of use) of the actual usage of a new technology while still acknowledging the underlying influence of the diffusion of innovation model. Here, we propose that the average time spent per user using the innovation goes through four phases related to the different categories of users.

Before we can show these phases, we must first establish a connection between early adoption and time spent using a specific service. In Ericsson ConsumerLab, we use an advanced segmentation model based on values, attitudes, and life stages in order to determine what category in the diffusion

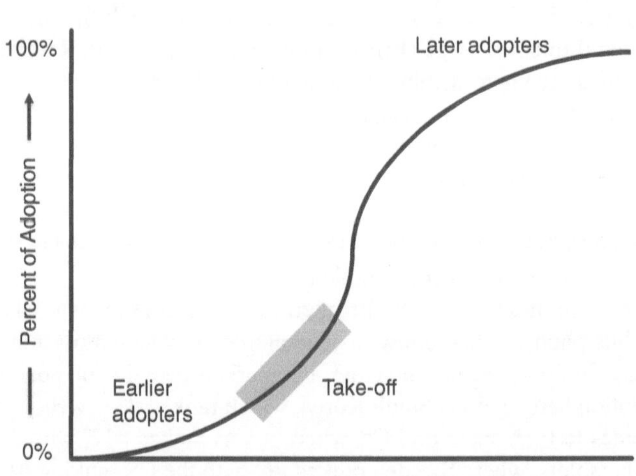

Figure 5.1 Diffusion of innovation
Source: Adapted from Rogers (1962).

of innovation curve a particular person belongs to. Using this segmentation model, it becomes quite clear that early adopters have higher use intensity of services, and that this use intensity falls the closer one gets to the laggards group. However, given that we do not have the space to explain such a model here, we will instead use the straightforward attitudinal question "I always look for advanced technology products" that respondents were asked to answer on a seven-point agree/disagree Lichert scale as a proxy for early adoption. In Figure 5.2, we show the results for six countries in 2015, where we asked for time spent on online banking as well as frequency of use of mobile banking. As can be clearly seen, the self-reported early adopters show a higher use both in time and in frequency of the services toward the top of the scale and lower toward the bottom of the scale. Thus, we can conclude that in a market where there are relatively many early adopters, we could expect higher average use times and use frequencies than in a market where there are relatively fewer early adopters. In this way, adoption of a specific service goes through a number of phases that are shaped not only by increasing market penetration, but also by fluctuations in average intensity of use of the service.

In the first phase, innovators and early adopters, who are sometimes referred to as "power users" as they not only are early out, but their use is often quite intensive, lead to an increasingly high average usage time per person. However, in the second phase, as the early majority begins to use the innovation, the average time spent by each user decreases as the innovators and early adopters are increasingly

I always look for advanced technology products

7 point Lichert-scale: Agree – Disagree

Use of online banking

Avg minutes/day	Brazil	China	Japan	Sweden	UK	USA
Agree (top 2 boxes)	9.0	5.9	10.1	20.2	18.9	16.4
MID 3	6.8	5.8	7.5	15.0	15.2	13.8
Disagree (bottom 2 boxes)	4.2	4.3	5.7	12.3	10.7	9.9

Use of mobile banking

Avg frequency/day	Brazil	China	Japan	Sweden	UK	USA
Agree (top 2 boxes)	2.3	1.1	1.4	3.4	2.9	2.8
MID 3	1.4	0.8	0.6	1.8	1.5	1.9
Disagree (bottom 2 boxes)	1.0	0.5	0.3	1.0	0.6	1.1

Base: Respondents aged 15–69; Sample size 1,500–2,500 respondents per country

Figure 5.2 Early adopters have higher use time/frequency

outnumbered by increasingly more casual users, perhaps an unexpected result. As the innovation becomes mainstream with the early majority, it gradually becomes the socially normative way of doing things, and the average usage time per person starts to increase again in the third phase. Finally, in the fourth phase, as the late majority and some of the laggards enter, the increase in average usage per person slows as these groups of users may remain skeptical to using the innovation to the same degree as the early majority.

Schematically, this four-phase model of adoption in relation to average time spent per person can be illustrated as in Figure 5.3.

We illustrate this four-phase approach to diffusion with online banking. As with any technology, we can expect that the diffusion of innovation model is valid, and market penetration will go from innovators across the different groups until finally laggards enter the market. However, the process becomes more interesting if we try to imagine the intensity of use of the service as well. Then we would expect that initially when only innovators and early adopters are conducting banking services on the Internet, they are using the service quite actively—potentially even substituting all physical banking services with online ones. In a second phase, the average usage of online banking per person decreases as an early majority starts conducting some basic online banking, such as checking the status of their bank accounts. However, they continue to conduct the majority of their financial

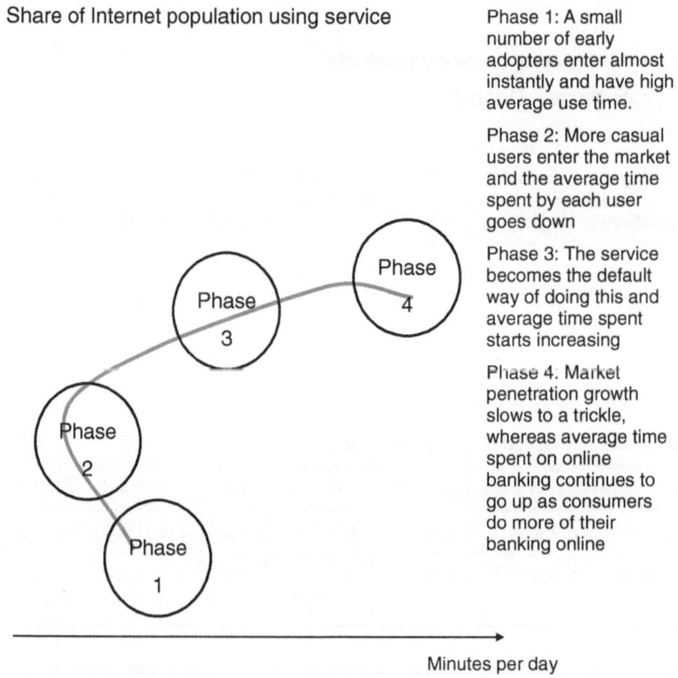

Figure 5.3 Four adoption phases

transactions offline, such as going to the bank in person or sending payments by mail. In a third phase, the average time spent on online banking might start rising as the early majority increasingly substitutes offline banking services with online ones and online banking becomes the social norm among Internet users as more than 50 percent use the service. Finally, in a fourth phase, the late majority along with some of the laggards begin adopting limited online banking behavior, whereas others may refuse to do so. In this phase, market penetration growth continues; however, the growth of the average time spent on online banking slows to a trickle, even though more consumers conduct banking online than offline.

This type of approach should be quite illuminating when trying to understand how an Internet service such as online banking penetrates a market. In a market characterized by a high level of Internet penetration, regardless of device and interest in testing new services, one would expect a new Internet service such as online banking to show a different adoption pattern than in a less mature market with a low level of Internet penetration and interest in trying new services. For example, we would expect that in a mature market, the "knee" inflection point between phase 2 and phase 3 should be higher, with the subsequent slope in phase 3 flatter than in a less mature market due to the broader base of active Internet users interested in adopting the service.

Diffusion of online banking in Sweden relative to other countries

As Ericsson ConsumerLab surveys have collected data on a number of measures on at least a biannual basis, we have the opportunity to follow the adoption of Internet services, such as online banking, over time. Figure 5.4 shows the evolution of online banking average minutes of use for Sweden along with three of the leading industrialized markets, the US, the UK, and Japan. Figure 5.5 shows the evolution for the emerging markets of Brazil and China. Unfortunately, we only have data for all countries from 2000, and not from the mid-1990s, when the first Internet banks appeared, and therefore we missed some data on the first phase of the model.

At first glance, the US and UK graphs in Figure 5.4 look similar to the point of being interchangeable. But at a closer look, it becomes apparent that the left sides of the curves are actually quite different. The "knee" is higher up in the UK as the part of the curve below this inflection point is much longer. Whereas the size of the phase 1 innovator/early adopter group seems to have been significantly larger in the US back in the year 2000, the UK quickly catches up during the next four years, and by 2004 online banking in the UK has already become slightly more mainstream, with more than one-third of Internet users engaging at least once a month in the activity. In comparison, online banking has only reached just over one-quarter of Internet users in the US in the same time period.

A graph that sticks out starkly from the others is that of Japan in Figure 5.4. This pattern is created by the fact that after 2004, online banking in Japan developed only to a small degree. Although the start looked promising, and as many

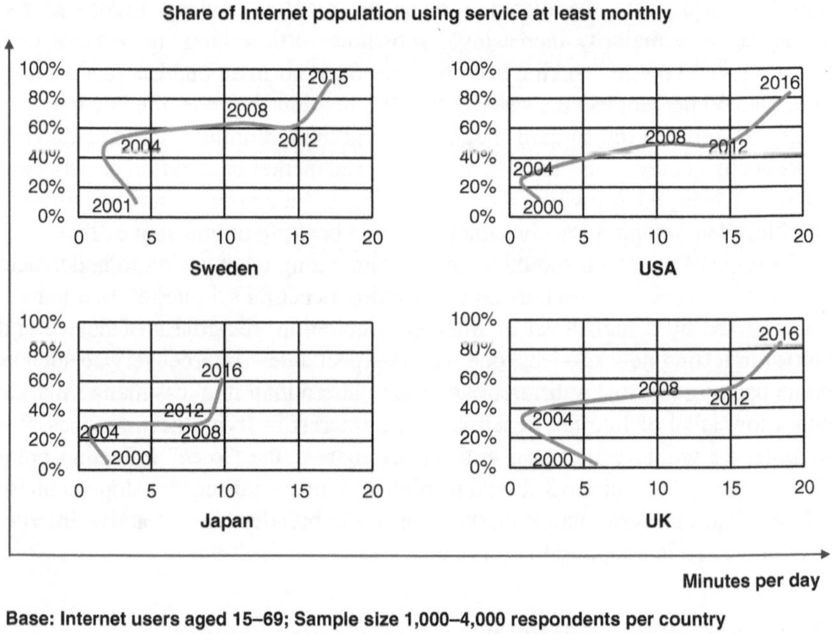

Figure 5.4 Online banking

as 29 percent of Internet users were doing online banking by 2004, it took Japan around 10 years to reach phase 3 when 50 percent of the population were already using the service at least once a month. To this day, banking in Japan is still conducted primarily through traditional offline channels by a large share of its inhabitants. One obvious reason for this is the well-documented aging population issue, and the lack of Internet penetration and resistance to Internet services by this demographic, but there may also be other reasons.

Finally, although the Sweden line might not be as "eye-popping" as the Japanese one, it provides some interesting insight into the Swedish market. By the 2004 time frame, the "knee" between phases 2 and 3 had already reached 50 percent of the population. Although the incline of the curve is not very steep for the next few years, this indicates that online banking is already the default way of banking as the majority of the population is engaging in this activity after 2004 and onwards. By the time that both the UK and the US manage to reach approximately the same population share and approximately the same daily time spent doing online banking (15–20 minutes) as Sweden, the majority of Swedes had been doing this for the previous 12 years.

In other words, online banking in Sweden reached phase 3 with a stable majority user base already in early 2005, whereas a similar situation was not reached in the UK or the US until 2008. That suggests that Swedish consumers, by and large, were forerunners when it came to the use of online banking, a trend that has been continued as new FinTech services have been introduced.

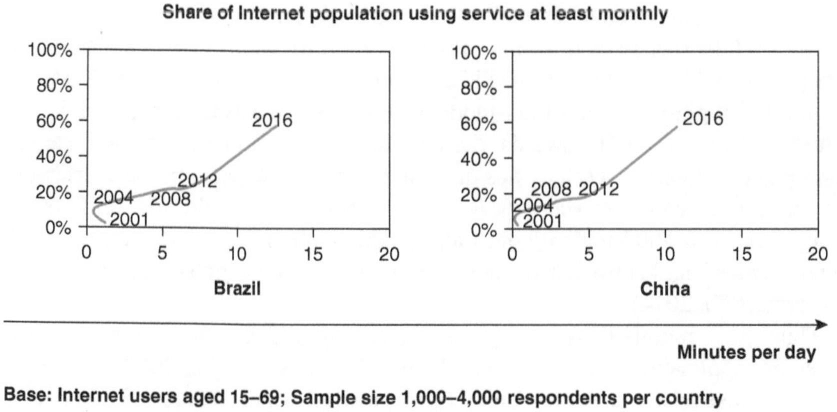

Figure 5.5 Online banking in emerging markets

Turning to the emerging markets of Brazil and China in Figure 5.5, we find significantly different-looking lines than in Figure 5.4, with the knee between phases 2 and 3 considerably lower. Our interpretation is that the underlying Internet penetration was evolving so quickly during these years that the uptake of specific services becomes overshadowed by the market evolution of Internet access overall.

The effect of mobile phone usage on online banking

In each of these markets, there is a sharp upward turn in penetration of the service between 2012 and 2016. The sharpness of this line is not something that could be expected from the approach outlined above. Instead, this shows the effect of a new base technology entering the market. In this case, the new technology is of course the smartphone.

As it happens, financial technology and the smartphone actually have a long prehistory worth noting. As documented in Mari Matsunaga's book *i-Mode Jiken*, the precursor to the smartphone was introduced in Japan already in February 1999 by NTT DoCoMo and was called i-mode (Matsunaga, 2000). The first "app" that was developed for that phone was a banking app; however, it failed miserably.

In 2001, the i-mode creator Mari Matsunaga revealed to me in a discussion that the whole purpose of starting with a banking app was actually not to create a mass market application. Instead, there was something of a hidden agenda. By getting a bank on board, it was possible for the i-mode team to go to other companies and show them that their system was so safe and secure that even banks were creating applications. Thereby, there would be no risk involved for anyone else to join either. The strategy worked. The first app to be a smash hit on i-mode and the first one to top a million downloads during the first year was not the banking app, but a character screen app called "Chara-pa" by the toy company Bandai.

In Europe and elsewhere, however, WAP phones were struggling to get off the ground, and although banking applications were also part of the initial phase, they had just as little success as in Japan—although it is difficult to say how much of that was part of WAP itself failing to build a sustainable user base (Palomäki, 2004).

In 2007, eight years after the i-mode, a new i-device was launched, the Apple iPhone. From that point onwards, the mobile phone's influence on the creation and uptake of Internet services was quick and massive. As shown in the Ericsson ConsumerLab report *Interactivity Beyond the Screen*, it would take only about four years from 2007 until iPhones and Android phones created sharp upward trends in mass market uses of various Internet services on a global scale (Ericsson ConsumerLab, 2014).

Thus, since mobile banking was not in any way different than a host of other consumer applications, and was more the result of a maturing mobile technology than the cause of it, our interpretation of the upwards slant in Figure 5.3 between 2012 and 2016 is that this is the result of the mass market effect of mobile banking on overall online banking. Smartphones enabled the late majority to begin using online banking. However, they limited their use to simple transactions, similar to when the early majority began using online banking in phase 2, thereby reducing the average time used per person.

Mobile banking in Sweden

Turning to mobile banking in Sweden as an example, as recently as in 2012 only about one-third of Internet users were using mobile banking. Furthermore, they only used it 1.9 times a week on average, as can be seen in Figure 5.6. Three years later, the situation looked quite different. At this point, more than half of the population was using mobile banking—and at the same time, they were doing it almost twice as frequently, or 3.6 times every week according to the Ericsson ConsumerLab survey results. In terms of the diffusion of innovation model extension introduced earlier, it appears that penetration has skipped over phase 2 and moved directly into phase 3 with market growth slowing down, whereas average time spent on the activity is still increasing. Currently, mobile banking has become part of the socially normative way of doing bank-related activities. One explanation might be that mobile banking penetrated society so quickly that a more fine-grained analysis should be performed (i.e., using monthly instead of biannual data).

Although Sweden exhibits a high penetration in terms of the percentage of users doing mobile banking at least once a month, Sweden lags behind the US when it comes to the average frequency of use, which might be surprising given the high level mobile usage. One factor may be that recent mobile payment solutions have been driven as much by IT companies and mobile handset manufacturers as by banks and credit card companies—and that such players have focused more on extending their services in the US than in Sweden. Another contributing reason is that our biannual data sets include only 2015 for Sweden, whereas the US data are for 2016. Mobile banking is still very much developing as we speak!

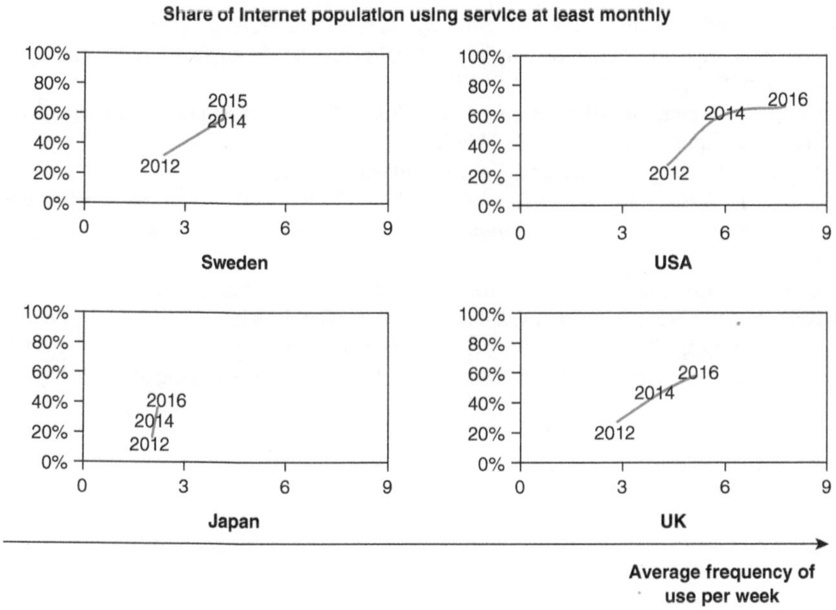

Base: Internet users aged 15–69; Sample size 1,500–4,000 respondents per country

Figure 5.6 Mobile banking

Conclusion

In summary, what does this maturity imply for the future of FinTech services in Sweden? There are probably at the very least two important conclusions to draw from this.

On the one hand, the fact that such a broad share of the Swedish consumer base has been engaging with online banking for such a long time implies that their online financial literacy is high and that their corresponding ability to judge the relevance and applicability of new financial technology will be quite advanced. In other words, they may not jump at just any new service, but they could be expected to be reasonably able to separate the useful services from those that are more of technology experiments.

On the other hand, online banking does not exist in a vacuum, and neither will new FinTech services. Given that Sweden—as has been argued in this chapter—is relatively mature across a broad range of Internet usage perspectives, and not just banking, Swedish consumers are already engaging in a broad range of other online or Internet-related activities where those services can be tried out and potentially also used on a mass market scale. In other words, new financial services will naturally become part of a plethora of ecosystems that are already evolving as we speak, and those services that are good enough will not only become successful, but in their own turn continue to feed the ongoing maturation process in the market.

Bibliography

Ericsson ConsumerLab, 2014. *Interactivity beyond the screen.* [online] Ericsson. Available at: www.ericsson.com/assets/local/news/2014/6/interactivity-beyond-the-screen.pdf [Accessed August 27, 2017].

Ericsson ConsumerLab, 2016. *Primary data from 2000–2016 Ericsson ConsumerLab surveys* [Unpublished report]. Stockholm.

Matsunaga, M., 2000. *I-mode Jiken*. Tokyo: Kadokawa Shoten.

Palomäki, J., 2004. Case WAP: Reasons for failure. In: S. Luukainen, ed. *Innovation dynamics in mobile communications*. Espoo: Helsinki University of Technology, pp.98–101.

Rogers, E.M., 1962. *Diffusion of innovations*. New York: Free Press.

Swedish Post and Telecom Authority, 2006. *Fact sheet: 3G in Sweden PTS-F-2005:5*. [online] Swedish Post and Telecom Authority (PTS). Available at: www.pts.se/en-GB/Documents/Fact-sheet/2005/Fact-sheet-3G-in-Sweden-PTS-F-20055/ [Accessed August 27, 2017].

Part 2

Cognition

Legitimacy and views

6 The role of trust in emerging technologies

Mats Lewan

Introduction

The scope of this chapter is to investigate the role of trust in emerging technologies, particularly with regard to FinTech.

The concept of trust is often defined in terms of reliability and truth, for example "firm belief in the reliability, truth, or ability of someone or something" (Oxford University Press, 2017). But ultimately, from a functional point of view, particularly in business, you could also define trust in terms of predictability, for example as discussed in the piece *The Power of Predictability* (Stevenson and Moldoveanu, 1995), where the authors note that "predictability built the trust that allowed people to synchronize their actions in mutually productive ways." One such definition of trust could also be "possibility to predict a desirable outcome from interactions with someone or something," where high trust equals "high possibility to . . ."

Given that the financial industry deals with people's money, and presuming that people and organizations want to be able to predict what a financial service will do with their money, the definitions of trust above would imply that trust has a particular importance in the financial industry and also for FinTech startups. This is the first hypothesis that I aim to investigate.

The second hypothesis is that ways of building trust might be subject to change due to Internet-based and digital technologies that fundamentally change the conditions for doing business, for interacting, for communicating, and for analyzing information.

Method

The aim of this study was to gain knowledge on the views on trust from people with understanding and experience of various functions with regard to the Swedish FinTech industry—regulation, startups, funding, and infrastructure.

In order to gain this knowledge, interviews were conducted with a group of renowned people selected to represent players having these functions.

Interviews were semi-structured and focused on a limited number of questions: the importance of trust in the financial industry; how startups are building trust toward the market and toward customers; how trust depends on security; how Internet-based technologies are affecting trust; what kind of players users have trust in today compared to before; and new ways of building trust by using digital technology such as blockchain.

Interviews were conducted during February through April 2017, with the following individuals:

Cecilia Skingsley, Deputy Governor of Sweden's Central Bank, the Riksbank

Henrik Rosvall, CEO of the savings app Dreams

Johan Lundberg, co-founder at the FinTech-focused VC firm NFT Ventures

Daniel Kjellén, CEO at the integrated bank information app Tink

Ulf Ahrner, CEO at the investment digital advising company Primepilot

Danny Aerts, CEO at Internetstiftelsen (IIS)

Lan-Ling Fredell, Head of Operations at Stockholm FinTech Hub

Sofie Blakstad, CEO and founder at the financial trust platform Hiveonline

Frank Schuil, CEO and co-founder at the Bitcoin-focused startup Safello

Jonathan Jogenfors, researcher at the University of Linköping

Most interviews were recorded, but two of them, with Kjellén and with Lundberg, were not. In those cases, uncertain quotes have been controlled by the interviewees at a later occasion.

Report from the interviews

The different aspects of trust brought up by the interviewees are not easily divided into separate parts, but rather reflect each individual's experiences and views on the topic. The following interview report will therefore be divided by person.

Cecilia Skingsley, Deputy Governor of the Riksbank

Skingsley discussed how FinTech startups manage to build trust in a short time frame, operating on a digital market where everything moves at a very high pace:

> How come people willingly provide credit card numbers and other information to companies that they have never heard of or that they know very little about? I've been thinking about this, because it doesn't say Volvo or Ericsson or Astra Zeneca or any other well-known company name. And I think it's a combination; you don't hear that much about casualties—if you're exposed to fraud on the Internet, you're most often compensated.

> And you don't hear bad stories about people buying things on the Internet. The security measures seem to be secure, and I think that's important for the perception that there's trust.
>
> Then there's the aspect of integrity. It's possible that there's a different view on integrity in the young generation than in the older ones—that they are less worried about others being able to follow your consumption behavior, or even how you move geographically in the country or abroad. Perhaps younger people are as fond of their integrity online as their older peers, but nevertheless think it is worth giving some of it up in return for the ability to buy and sell and do banking errands wherever and whenever they want. A necessary evil, if you will.

Skingsley also gave her view on blockchain technology:

> That's one of the examples of technological change that we at the Riksbank have to understand and follow for several reasons. So far, however, it's difficult to draw any extensive conclusions on which advances blockchain technology can contribute to. I think you need to be humble about that. But potentially you could build a kind of trust machine, and that's of course interesting to follow.

Daniel Kjellén, CEO at the integrated bank information app Tink

Kjellén explained how Tink addressed the issue of building trust with users:

> First, we asked who we would like to have as angel investors. Our analysis was in short that we couldn't just say, "Welcome to Tink, we're secure," and then invite people to seminars, explaining our security solutions. Instead, we had to find markers, communicating trust. For example, our chairman of the board is Nicklas Storåkers, and people understand that he cannot take that position if he's not comfortable with the company. I definitely believe that such factors have an influence.
>
> We also hired a consultancy firm, Cybercom, that assessed our security level, and we tried to get exposure in important media outlets. That's also a marker: "Journalists have met them and they seem clean, intact, and professional." If there were a silver bullet for making people trust you, it would be to remain clean, intact, and professional every day. Now, four or five years later, we are perceived as trustworthy and secure in our groups—external parties, the public, journalists, the finance industry, etc.
>
> Also, Mobile BankID, which doesn't influence our security at all, has significance—there are both false and true markers. We use BankID only to allow you to log in at your Internet bank, but Tink's security has very little to do with Mobile BankID.
>
> Another marker was to get an ISO 27001 certification, which is the highest-level standardization certification we could possibly achieve. But

in the end, I think that the most important aspect is that you trust your friends as a user. We know that about 80 percent of all users have arrived organically—somebody has told them that the app is really good, and that's extremely important for building trust.

Yesterday, as an example, we released a feature that allows users to change bank loans, and within 30 minutes there was a user who had moved his loan. The user hadn't read about it and we didn't do any PR but just released the feature the night before. And without any external support or validation, this user must have observed, "Well, now here's this feature," and then entered and performed the move. That requires a certain level of trust.

I believe that the users care much less than we do. Let's say that 1 out of 100 is capable of assessing Tink's security from the outside. If we make him happy, he won't say anything but will just continue as before. However, if he wouldn't be satisfied, things would start going downhill fast. He would tell 10 friends, who would then tell 10 friends . . . So it's more important than you think.

What's happening today is that we're going from trusting our bank to a distributed trust system—I have more trust in my 10 best friends, or in Instagram profiles I follow, than I do in my bank. An example is the website Trustpilot [provides user-generated reviews of businesses] where in five minutes you can get a very good picture of a business/service.

Henrik Rosvall, CEO of the savings app Dreams

For me, there are two different kinds of trust. The first one pertains to if someone will steal your money. If I put my money in an account with SEB, will a thief be able to steal it? Security is close to trust, and the security [in banks] is perceived as very high, even though I don't always agree that it is as high as it is perceived to be. The second kind of trust regards those who manage my money. Do I trust the culture of the bank? Do I trust its brand and that it can advise me on my private economy? And I think that the first kind of trust is still high, whereas the second one is decreasing rapidly for traditional banks.

We still think that the banks have a clear role in the value chain. We don't think that they are good at everything. Different banks are good at different things—some are good at building systems and infrastructure, others at managing customers' assets and making them grow, while very few are good at user experience. But there's almost none, if any, which is good at everything. And I think it's in this way that the value chain is being split—you have to choose where you can add value and focus on being the best somewhere in the value chain—be it infrastructure, risk and compliance, building smart products, or taking care of the customers.

We believe that banks have the security aspect in their DNA. Their entire organizations are built to take as little risk as possible, and that's also why they're so bad at product development, because product development is about taking risk. And those two cultures don't go well together. But they still have power greed and control issues, wanting to own the whole value chain. Rather than buying services, they would rather acquire companies that they can control inside their structure.

That's where I think we will have a position, together with them, using them for what they are good at—security, being risk-averse, and taking care of our customers' money and their identities—while we will run the customer experience.

Rosvall discussed how Dreams was building trust with customers:

> At the beginning, you have to take extremely good care of customers in all situations, building trust as a serious partner. Then you can find a strategy of ingredient branding to strengthen certain attributes such as security (e.g., with the Ålandsbanken, Mobile BankID, and Touch ID on the iPhone).

Rosvall also agreed with Skingsley that banks and payment card providers over time have contributed to building trust for e-commerce. And he shared the view with Kjellén on the importance of users' personal network:

> Everything goes faster since the adoption time [for new services] has become shorter. And I think word of mouth has greatly influences trust. If I use a service and it works well, then my family and friends will know that it works well, fairly quickly. But above all, they will also know if it doesn't work. So today, trust can be demolished much faster than before when Internet penetration was not as high. I believe that the most important influence factor on trust is what your peers have experienced.
>
> I think that if you ask Millennials who they believe they will do banking business with in the future, then 50 percent would say that banks will not be involved at all. They have high trust in Google, in Facebook, and in Spotify—another kind of trust that these companies have built through their digital services. It doesn't have to be associated with a banking license, but rather with how a brand takes care of its customers over time.

Discussing future players and future infrastructure, Rosvall said:

> If Facebook or Google would start to manage money and loans, they will need a banking license and they then will become banks or financial institutions. But if you look at blockchain, that's a very unregulated market today, working on completely different premises. We don't know what will happen, but I believe there will be a lot more transactions made through other technologies, which is what banks have always done, aiming at decreasing the risk of all transactions. However, many banks have not been willing to decrease their position in the value chain.

I believe that this is the first part of a banking revolution showing that you can do things in a different way. Blockchain is a fantastic possibility if you can get it going. But it would cut half the body of all banks, everything from investment funds, stock trade, and insurance, to money transfer and security transfer—half the banking business in short.

Johan Lundberg, co-founder at the FinTech-focused VC firm NFT Ventures

Trust is one of the most fundamental topics we discuss with our companies all the time. It's extremely important and it's the basis for growth. That's what we keep telling our customers. If you want to be in business 10 years from now, you'll have to build trust.

One part of it is compliance, overseen by Finansinpsektionen. You cannot have errors in your systems, and you need extremely good controls to prevent fraud, hacking, and attacks.

Another part of trust is towards users and it regards operation reliability. The most important thing is to do what you have promised your customers.

For example, I would say that the flows and the information management of Nordkap [a web-based treasury platform] has gained more trust than banks have.

When asked about his view on alternative infrastructure technologies such as blockchain, Lundberg said:

It's too early to know how it will look for blockchain. I think banks will have to decide first what kind of infrastructure they will use, and then others can follow. But as of today, I would say that the trust in the traditional banking system is higher than in blockchain technology.

Swish is a good example of a service that has exploded in terms of users, and Mobile BankID too. They have gained trust very quickly and new perspectives have been opened up in the last year. No one has doubts about using Mobile BankID or Swish today.

You have to translate trust with functionality. If a service does what it should, then you have trust. If you provide what you are supposed to provide, then you build trust.

Lan-Ling Fredell, Head of Operations at Stockholm FinTech Hub

Fredell mentioned the importance of the government's role in building trust:

Because the government has backed Internet usage so strongly here in Sweden, that has to a certain extent driven a level of trust that maybe you don't have in other economies. And then you also have large players standing together here, like for example banks and BankID. You don't see that in the US—there's no BankID equivalent there that I'm aware of.

She also highlighted the role of trust in FinTech, and the role of regulation:

> I think that for FinTech, because you're dealing often with money issues, trust is extremely important. Because if you deal with money, people have to feel safe that you're not going to lose it, or misuse it.
>
> With Europe Loan [an online mortgage bank where Fredell was part of the founding team], we decided to go by regulation. We went and got a banking license. As a lender, you don't have to be a full-on bank, but we elected to be a full-on bank in order to gain trust. And to be honest, it worked beautifully.

Another aspect Fredell discussed was how FinTech companies can trust their customers:

> Trust works in both directions. You want to trust the person you're doing business with, but it's also the other way round. And for FinTechs in particular, it comes back to regulation again. For many functions, you have a lot of KYC—know your customer. There's a lot of regulation pertaining to customer knowledge—you have to know whom you're giving a loan or a service to. And often this slows down the process, because if you have to meet someone face-to-face, then the Internet didn't help you much, right? So how can you identify people without meeting them face-to-face? Again, Sweden has been very early in developing strategies for that with BankID and so forth.
>
> Even in, say, the US, people are doing algorithms where you take a photo of an ID, and then they match the ID with publicly available databases to try to verify that people are who they say they are. So the trust aspect is definitely both ways, and there's a lot of innovation going on in that space.

Fredell also answered the question on whether the time frame for building trust is shifting:

> Yes, I think people are finding trust in a shorter time. Back when Amazon was created, people were saying, "Would you ever even buy anything online? I mean, how could you trust them?" But nowadays, to buy something online, that's ubiquitous. Why would you go to a store if you didn't have to? Maybe not so much in Sweden, for infrastructure and delivery reasons, but certainly in the US—I have Amazon Prime and I never leave the house if I don't have to, in terms of shopping.
>
> So in 15 or 20 years, we have gone from completely distrusting the Internet to almost total trust. I would buy something online from a relatively unknown player at this point, partially because I'm guaranteed with the credit card, so I can trust my credit card even if I cannot trust the person I'm buying from.
>
> So I think that same thing goes with financial services, now that the idea of having financial services online seems normal rather than an odd anomaly.

> And then if you look at the next generation, at 15-year-olds and how they interact, how much they're willing to give away about their identity and information online. They have no problem with it; they see it as the norm. So I think that this is definitely a social and a cultural shift, for trusting online, or mistrusting, as the case may be, or being wary, but in a different way than people who are pre-Internet are wary.

Sofie Blakstad, CEO and founder at the financial trust platform Hiveonline

Blakstad's commenting on trust relates to her being the CEO and founder at the financial trust platform Hiveonline (www.hivenetwork.online). The aim of the platform is to offer a more objective alternative to traditional credit ratings.

Hiveonline collects digital assets such as contracts, payments, photographs, certificates, and guarantees, and then registers these assets in a vault on a blockchain—a distributed ledger accessible to all participants in the system. The assets, which are fact-based and cannot be eliminated or altered, are eventually input to an algorithm producing a credit score, which does not depend on human judgments, but on context—basically on large-scale statistics and machine learning, being the basis for the algorithm. Hiveonline also manages payments with Bitcoin.

Blakstad first answered the question whether there is a new kind of trust mechanism emerging with the Internet:

> Yes, I absolutely think so. Because we are now able to produce cheaply contextualized true trust in a way we couldn't before. The challenge with the old way of proving ourselves trustworthy is that we used systems where the data was available and relatively easy to access. And there is a small number of institutions that control that access, which I think is a problem. So your bank, or Experian [a global information services group] holds your credit record that it amalgamates up within the information that your bank holds. Your local country holds your ID record in terms of who you are, where you belong, and where you live. Those records are not contextual.
>
> Now, if you are hiring a carpenter, you're not particularly interested in whether that builder paid his bills on time and you probably don't care where he comes from. What you do care about is whether he does a good job. And neither his credit record nor his identity paper is going to tell you that, but contextualized trust does.
>
> That's why there has been this big shift towards all these Facebook reviews and other reviews, which, by the way, are very unreliable because they are subjective opinions and they are easy to manipulate. The answer is using this technology to provide contextualized trust that you cannot make up and that is not subject to opinions.
>
> I actually just read a paper from 2009 about how you can analyze interactions to provide a stronger trust signature, rather than opinions. And interactions

are something that we have got huge amounts of data on because everything on a platform makes those.

An example would be how customers of a platform search for each other, form connections with each other, and then behave within the context of those relationships. There have been behavioral analyses made by phone companies in Africa where you can tell more about an individual, whether they're trustworthy or not, from their interaction behavior, than you can from their credit record—how many contacts they've got, how often they speak to them, where they go, etc.

In our case, the data collection is automatic. As people are using the system to manage their jobs, we record the contracts and the payments and the electronic assets so that we can see whether terms have been met, whether payments have been made, whether there are any issues with quality, which we measure with the number of projections and repeat activities, and then that just builds the trust score. So none of this is done by hand.

And one of the reasons I use blockchain for my customers is that my customers don't have to trust me. They just have to trust the blockchain.

Blakstad then continued to explain how you could make sure that you can trust the algorithm calculating the trust record:

> Partly through the research you put into it, partly through the learning that your system does as it is being used. So you could answer that you keep testing it. And these things are largely driven by customers as well, because as customers learn that an algorithm is fair or not, their behavior will alter, and you can use that in order to refine the algorithm and make sure that it is fair.

Blakstad also gave her view on what the implications could be of an increased use of contextualized trust:

> In the developed economies, contextualized trust will rebalance power between large corporations and microbusinesses. In less developed economies, it may have a much more significant implication, because of the 2 billion people without bank accounts, every one of whom could have a trust signature based on these disintermediated approaches, and that means that if you are a microbusiness who can't open a bank account because you have no credit history, because your key interactions are managed over the phone, you can still build a trust record, which now means that you can go to that bank and get a loan and build your business. You can actually prove not only that you do work and get paid for it, which is your trust signature, but you can also prove things like your identity. 1.5 billion people have no formal identification documentation, no birth certificate, no passport, nothing.
>
> So I think it's going to revolutionize particularly developing countries. And I'm not the only one—phone companies are all working with developing these things.

Another perspective on the use of contextual trust that Blakstad brought up was with regard to fake news and fake information on the Internet:

> People do trust a critical mass of information, whether it's true or not. But if you bring contextual records that are based on facts, my belief is that people will trust those as well, if not more, knowing that they are based on facts. I think the reason that people trust fake news is obviously because it confirms their personal biases, but also because there's a vacuum of contextual trust. How can I validate that what I'm being asked to believe is true? If there's no fact-based validation for it, you reach for whatever sources that are available.

Ulf Ahrner, CEO at the investment digital advising company Primepilot

Ahrner discussed the conditions for new companies gaining trust:

> Trust is an issue for all new companies, regardless of the Internet. But for the finance industry, this issue is larger for two reasons. The first is that you deal with people's money; the second that there are many individuals pretending to be part of the finance industry but who in fact are imposters. And that's a problem, of course, because firms that steal money do not belong to the finance industry, they are simply criminals. But often media describe them as "finance companies fooling people," which is a strange confusion. Unfortunately, this means that the trust in new companies in this industry is low.
>
> The way we address this is appointing key persons to the board, start collaborations with established companies—everything that our customers deposit with us, for example, is kept on accounts at our bank [the SEB bank]. Initially, you have to build on collaborations with well-known brands and on individuals considered to be trustworthy in the board, in our case the chairman of the board.
>
> After having operated for a few years, it's more about the fact that you're still in the business, that you haven't been reported, and maybe also how many customers you have.

Ahrner also answered the question on how trust can be built more quickly today:

> For example, in the App Store, when our app is published there, it has to be approved by Apple. People know this, and therefore they trust that if it's approved, it's probably also good to use since Apple has checked the background, that the company is real, that there's no malware, no phishing or other problems. And it will continue to be like that as long as Apple and Google manage to maintain that track record.
>
> This is specific for the app economy. On the Internet, which is not controlled, you don't have the same level of trust. And this was the business idea behind Klarna, to bridge the lack of trust between the consumer and e-commerce websites by taking the credit risk and guaranteeing delivery to the customer. In this way, you could have a web shop with no history, and if

> you managed the payments through Klarna or another established payment provider, you knew that there would be no problem, because they would take the risk. And now it's so accepted that people don't even care any longer.
>
> Transactions today are managed by fairly large and established brands, and you won't provide your card details to just anyone. Then if there's no delivery, you will go to the bank and say that you have been defrauded and they will give you the money back. So there's a security built on larger companies that you have trust in.

On a question regarding the possibilities of building trust with blockchain-based applications, Ahrner answered:

> There's a substantial hype around blockchain, unfortunately making it a bit overrated. The problem with blockchain is that it is designed to be the technology supporting cryptocurrencies. And what many people don't understand is that the basis of the technology is being a currency. Thus, they are the same thing, and you cannot just take blockchain and apply it to something else. Because blockchain is an ordinary distributed database solution, which is something that has existed for 15 years, but with the only difference that it has a unique time stamp [on each block] that you have achieved by awarding a little bit of the currency to who puts the time stamp on the next block [in the database]. The problem is what you should award if you use the blockchain for shares in an incorporated company. Should you award new shares in this company every 10 minutes? Maybe theoretically, but I have never heard anyone discuss this issue [about how those putting on the time stamp should be awarded if the blockchain application is not a cryptocurrency].
>
> Blockchain is designed for currencies, not for, let's say, deed letters. You could put a distributed database on a secret computer somewhere, but then it's not blockchain. In blockchain, you don't have any secret computer, and the data is not encrypted. As soon as you encrypt the data, it's no longer blockchain. So if you can make a distributed share register without encryption, that would be blockchain, but I don't think anyone will do that, because then you have to reward shares every 10 minutes to who puts on the time stamp [which requires a difficult computation].

Ahrner then discussed if another financial infrastructure could emerge, beyond the existing traditional infrastructure:

> Yes, certainly. You have Swift—I don't even remember when it was built—and Euroclear and other centralized database solutions that the banks, through banking licenses, have exclusive rights to manage and to use for transferring money and assets. Klarna, by becoming a bank, can now access these systems directly. So the first wave of FinTech would be that companies grow and get banking licenses, and in that way can circumvent the need for using the banks as a basis. That's mostly an economic issue.

A second wave would be that we replace Swift and Euroclear, and of course that will happen. Those systems are ancient so I'm convinced that it will happen, but it will probably take another 20 years, I think. Because I'm not convinced that blockchain is the solution that will replace those systems. But something will do it. It's too deep-seated. It will take a very long time, because it's so incredibly complicated.

It's difficult to explain. I've been working with so many parts of it and I have seen it live. Swift is a system which makes it possible to transfer money between every single bank account in the whole world, several times a day. To replace that, you need to achieve a network effect.[1] For a long time, Facebook was alone having achieved a network effect. And the problem is that this kind of network effect exists for the payment infrastructure—Swift and the card infrastructure have an incredibly strong network effect, and replacing them will take a very long time, or will have to be completely ingenious.

The thing is Bitcoin doesn't go well with political control of the economy. Then you can claim that it will prevail anyway. No, it's not like that. If countries make something prohibited, it won't exist. You just need a stroke of a pen by policymakers and it's gone.

Danny Aerts, CEO at Internetstiftelsen (IIS)

Aerts' take on trust was particularly focused on security:

I think that the field that people talk the least about but that will emerge more and more is security—can I trust that my money is still there? It has become so easy and cheap to hack almost anything. In my position, I see lots of attacks, and it's just a question of time before we have really nice examples of things going radically wrong.

Banks today have a philosophy that they know they're not secure, they know that they get hacked, but it's too expensive to solve, so they prefer to compensate those who have been exposed. Theft of ID is one example. Banks know that they are not secure, and that BankID or Swish leads to large-scale fraud. The solution would then be a stronger ID, with cryptography plus pin code and biometrics, for example, but they do not want to give up the strong position with the current BankID solution. Another problem is the banks' limited interest in DNSSEC[2]—without it, a man-in-the-middle attack is possible, and thus theft of the customer's ID. But if you want to support the trend with new players, new technology, new ways to produce your services, then you cannot afford large security problems. As I assess the market now, there's a significant probability that we're going to have fairly large security holes where your money and my money will disappear.

I think it's an underestimated issue. There's too much focus on front-end app development and too little on fundamental information security activity to protect user data.

And this will affect trust. It can influence a whole industry in a negative way since there might be large-scale effects. If you manage to enter a database, you can bring a lot with you. Recently, it became known that the NSA was able to read files and transactions in the Swift system,[3] and my guess is that they can also make changes. Who says that others cannot do that too? Here we are talking about large-scale effects. What if banks cannot trust each other and clearing does not work? And there's a fundamental issue—what is money today? It doesn't exist. It's just a number.

Aerts did not agree that it's easier and quicker to build trust today:

No, I don't think so. It goes up and down. There's much inertia, and I would say that you trusted new services more 10 years ago than you do today. We're a bit wounded today, too much has happened. Ten years ago, there were many optimistic people, a bit naïve, thinking that everything with the Internet was just positive. But we hadn't yet been hit by what we know now—Snowden hadn't reported everything that the US does behind the curtains, and we feel that there's more surveillance today than there was 10 years ago. So I would say that there's a steeper uphill today regarding trust.

And if you get a situation where you remain longer with established players, then it will become more difficult for new players to get started.

Personally, I believe that established brands such as Amazon and Facebook have built so many practices with their customers that it will be easier for them to integrate new services than it would be for a new player that arrives from outside to build and introduce new service, even if their service is better and more user-friendly. The large global players didn't have that power 10 years ago. It was more open in one way.

Aerts then discussed what would happen if a real security crisis arrives:

People will be lost. They won't know what to do. You don't have any money in your wallet and you can't trust that the money is in the bank, so you will become insecure. And how will people behave then—I don't know. It might be that you will try to have several currencies at home. And the banking system might fail.

Therefore, I'm positive about Bitcoin, and about blockchain technology too. From a security point of view, it's more robust. If you want a technological solution that is difficult to attack, then that technology is better, since you don't have any single point of failure, you have lots of instances controlling and calculating, being able to see if something is happening. And you can already see it—as soon as something happens, if there's unrest on the market, the Bitcoin value increases. I think people use it as a last resort. Therefore, it's only a question of time before it becomes more accepted too. Then I don't know if there will be other kinds of cryptocurrencies—it doesn't have to be Bitcoin. I think it's fully possible that Amazon, Google, or Facebook provide their own cryptocurrency that would offer customers advantages over Bitcoin—a modern customer loyalty program that becomes an independent currency.

Frank Schuil, CEO and co-founder at the Bitcoin-focused startup Safello

As a CEO and co-founder of the Bitcoin-focused company Safello, Schuil discussed the topic of trust related to Safello's business field:

> We realized from day one that trust was going to be the most important part of our business, hence the name "Safe Fellow—Safello." And particularly, it related to our industry in 2013 when we started—there were a lot of hacks and scams, and headlines were centered on the negative aspects of cryptocurrencies. So the whole premise of our company was that we wanted to do it by the book and cooperate with existing financial institutions instead of fighting them.
>
> We chose to incorporate the company in Sweden since Sweden is a trusted country around the world, and we registered as a financial institution. We were able to get cooperation with one of the top four banks, Handelsbanken, and we then looked at the biggest failures in our industry, which regarded erosion of trust, typically when people were losing their money, their bitcoins.
>
> Therefore, we set up our company so that we'd never store our customers' funds, but instead connect them to third-party suppliers for storage. So unlike pretty much all other players in the market, we have never lost any of our customers' bitcoins, we have never been breached, and we have never been scammed.

Schuil explained the dilemma with registering as a financial institution or not:

> On the one hand, registering as a financial institution gives you trust, but on the other it makes it harder to move in a certain direction and to be a global company. Our position and our strategic choice to be "the trusted company," doing everything by the book, also meant that we are not able to compete in a lot of local geographies around us, where other companies are doing only fraud prevention to make sure that they don't have losses on the book that could bankrupt them. And it's fundamentally different following the European anti-money laundry legislation, doing the ID verification, doing the sanction list screening, doing the politically exposed person screening, the know your customer questionnaires, and all the checks and balances on the behavior of the customer, or just doing an implementation of fraud prevention.

Schuil then discussed the importance of identity:

> Identity is going to be the most important thing going forward. Because the core of my ability to move around freely is identity and all the information that I have attached to my identity. Putting your information on the blockchain, making it decentralized, and giving partial access to relevant parties where you are in control, allows for a global ID, a global citizenship if you will.

> This empowers the customer, or the citizen, to independently move around the world—which could then become a borderless world. Bringing that back to something as simple as Mobile BankID, it's geographically restricted in Sweden, it's a collaboration between the banks, so it makes sense to them, but ultimately you need to have a global system for this. So I don't know for the Nordics how they would transition to that, it's kind of hard to see. Now it's a great trust mechanism and it's a new type of social login, a Facebook login but for financial institutions. But if you look at identity as a whole, it's so much more.

Discussion

Cultural differences

The concept of trust is a wide field, involving subtle human reactions and observations, which may vary not only between individuals, but also more significantly between different cultures. A good and thoughtworthy overview of such cultural differences is reported in the piece *Getting to Si, Ja, Oui, Hai, and Da* (Meyer, 2015), covering how different approaches with regard to trust in various parts of the world make negotiations and agreements between people from different countries more complicated.

One fundamental distinction that Meyer makes is between *cognitive* and *affective* trust, where cognitive trust is based on the confidence you feel in someone's accomplishments, skills, and reliability, whereas affective trust arises from feelings of emotional closeness, empathy, or friendship:

> In most emerging or newly emerged markets, from BRIC to Southeast Asia and Africa, negotiators are unlikely to trust their counterparts until an affective connection has been made. The same is true for most Middle Eastern and Mediterranean cultures. That may make negotiations challenging for task-oriented Americans, Australians, Brits, or Germans.
>
> (Meyer, 2015)

He also notes that "Americans draw a sharp line between cognitive and affective trust. (. . .) Mixing the two risks conflict of interest and is viewed as unprofessional" (Meyer, 2015).

Another aspect of trust reported in the article is that Americans often rely heavily on written contracts, making it possible to do business with people that you otherwise maybe would not trust, whereas in countries where the legal system is traditionally less reliable, and relationships carry more weight in business, written contracts are less frequent, and pushing a written contract could even be seen as a lack of trust.

While the interviews reported in this paper show that our way of building trust is under influence from a strong technological shift brought by the Internet, and while visions of new Internet-based and automated mechanisms for building trust are explored, it is probably wise to keep in mind the cultural and geographical differences with regard to trust mentioned above. This should be particularly important since Internet-based solutions by their nature aim for global reach.

The Trustnet

One such global vision that has not been mentioned in the interviews is the concept of what could be called the *Trustnet*. The idea is touched upon in the book *The Inevitable: Understanding The 12 Technological Forces That Will Shape Our Future* by Kevin Kelly (2016). Kelly discusses the issue with tracking or surveillance, and comes to the conclusion that it is pointless to try to stop tracking since the Internet by its nature is a surveillance machine. Instead, he argues, we should embrace it, while trying to address what he sees as the main problem with today's surveillance—asymmetry. Kelly notes that in a small village, everyone often knows everything about everybody, which makes surveillance less threatening—it is symmetric. And one way of achieving symmetry at a global scale in the highly effective detailed and continuous surveillance made possible by the Internet would be to create a Trustnet—a part of the Internet that you can only access if you publicly identify yourself electronically through a distributed system not controlled by any entity, state, or government. Since everyone has to be identified, individuals working for governmental agencies and authorities will also be identified, and the Trustnet thereby becomes symmetric, meaning that if anyone is tracking you, you will know who it is (and vice versa).

The open question would then be if people would "vote with their feet" and move some of their online activities to the Trustnet or not, a movement that governments could not influence since the identification system is independent. One possible outcome is that people would spend their time online divided between the Trustnet, where people are identified, and the Internet, where people can be anonymous, depending on the character of their activities. At the other end of the identification scale, you could also consider the "Darknet," for people wanting to be both anonymous and invisible.

A little-discussed security issue with blockchain and the Internet

There is an important security issue with blockchain technology, and actually with security on the Internet as a whole, which is surprisingly little discussed.

Several of the interviewees in this report refer to blockchain technology as a potential framework for an independent platform for trust, and as such, blockchain applications could also be imagined for the independent identification system, which would be fundamental for the "Trustnet" discussed above.

However, any such application must be designed with the existence of the following fundamental cryptographic issue in mind.

Blockchain, as well as a vast majority of all secure applications on the Internet, such as online banking, encrypted connections to email services, and digital signatures, make use of asymmetric cryptography, which essentially means that encryption and decryption is made with two different keys, one of which might be public, as in public key cryptography.

Asymmetric cryptography is based on the huge difficulty to solve certain mathematical problems with conventional computers, such as finding the prime factors of large integers. But in 1994, the American mathematician Peter Shor showed that such problems could be effectively solved by large quantum computers, using an algorithm now called Shor's algorithm.

The algorithm does not yet present any immediate security threat on the Internet since development of actual quantum computers is still in its infancy, but the discovery of Shor's algorithm is generally considered to have increased the efforts for building quantum computers significantly.

"Shor's algorithm struck down like a bomb in the crypto world because in principle, it makes all today's asymmetric cryptography insecure," says Jonathan Jogenfors, researcher on quantum computing, blockchain, and Bitcoin at the University of Linköping, Sweden. Jogenfors continues:

> The impact on Bitcoin and on blockchains is that one of the cornerstones of the system—the digital signatures that guarantee the authenticity of the transactions—is falling apart. Anyone will be able to initiate transactions from any account and the system collapses.
>
> But you have to see this from an even bigger perspective. If [the public key cryptography systems] ECC and RSA fail, we will basically lose the Internet. We will not be able to guarantee secrecy and accuracy in encrypted communication, mobile phones can be hacked, healthcare data becomes public, etc. etc.
>
> Me and my colleagues here at LiU, and our partner in this field, Sectra, are worried about the future. Almost worse is the almost total lack of interest from society at large. Quantum computers are not available today; however, there is an incredible development currently going on, both in terms of excellence and width, in the efforts to building quantum computers.

As an example, it can be noted that the European Commission is preparing the ground for the launch in 2018 of a EUR 1 billion flagship initiative on quantum technologies (European Commission, 2016).

Jogenfors also pointed out that there is research going on at LiU on quantum resistant algorithms for asymmetric cryptography (disclaimer: after concluding his PhD in 2017, Jogenfors will start working as a research director at Sectra).

Ownership of personal data

Finally, one important aspect of trust that has been mentioned only briefly is about who has access to our personal data, and who controls it. In one part of his interview, which is not reported above, Danny Aerts gave his view on this topic.

Aerts answered the question on what kind of regulation he thought will be important in the coming years: "What I find most interesting is regulation that would make you own your personal data, which would be good both for privacy reasons and for data protection, giving you the possibility to move your data where you want."

Aerts noted that personal data have a value, and that this value should benefit the user. He described a situation where a user brings his or her personal data to a kind of a membership service, or a broker, that will then continuously negotiate insurances, banking deals, transportation subscriptions, and other services with service providers, receiving an economic value from the service providers based on the richness of the user's data, a value that would be given back to the user.

"The regulation has to make it possible for me not to get locked in, but to keep my bubble of data and bring it with me. Then we can design enormously exciting services," Aerts said.

Conclusions

There are good reasons to believe that the two hypotheses—that trust has a particular importance in the financial industry and also for FinTech startups, and that ways of building trust might be transformed due to Internet-based and digital technologies—are valid.

The interviewees agreed that trust was fundamental in the financial industry and for FinTech startups. They also agreed on a number of seemingly natural steps to build initial trust—appointing well-known key persons to the board, starting collaborations with established brands, and aiming for appearance in relevant media—and in a longer perspective, always taking care of the customers and being reliable to them.

Today, trust also depends increasingly on people's friends and personal network, according to many of the interviewees.

Some of them also made a distinction between different kinds of trust, such as trust in security and trust in institutions' ability to give good advice, where banks, at least according to one of the interviewees, still enjoy much of the first kind and maybe less of the second.

In contrast, Internet giants such as Amazon and Facebook were considered by the interviewees to enjoy high trust among young users, and some expected new financial services to be successfully introduced by those companies.

Blockchain was highlighted as an interesting technology for building a neutral and independent infrastructure, but the divergent opinions among the interviewees on blockchain's potential was significant and noteworthy.

In a discussion, the cultural aspects of trust, the fundamental security issue with the entire Internet if large quantum computers can be built, and the concept of a *Trustnet*—a part of the Internet only accessible for users publicly identifying themselves, making anonymous tracking and surveillance impossible—were brought up.

Lastly, another interview mentioned the importance of letting users own their personal data, bring it with them, and benefit from its value.

Notes

1 Network effect—a phenomenon whereby a product or service gains additional value as more people use it.
2 DNSSEC is a suit of specifications to make the DNS system, which translates between ordinary web addresses and IP numbers, more secure.
3 SWIFT provides a network that enables financial institutions worldwide to make transactions between bank accounts.

Bibliography

European Commission, 2016. *European Commission will launch €1 billion quantum technologies flagship*. [online] Available at: https://ec.europa.eu/digital-single-market/en/news/european-commission-will-launch-eu1-billion-quantum-technologies-flagship [Accessed August 25, 2017].

Kelly, K., 2016. *The inevitable: Understanding the 12 technological forces that will shape our future*. [online] Available at: www.worldcat.org/title/inevitable-understanding-the-12-technological-forces-that-will-shape-our-future/oclc/925398078?referer=di&ht=edition [Accessed August 25, 2017].

Meyer, E., 2015. Getting to si, ja, oui, hai, and da. *Harvard Business Review*. [online] Available at: https://hbr.org/2015/12/getting-to-si-ja-oui-hai-and-da [Accessed August 25, 2017].

Oxford University Press, 2017. *Trust – definition of trust in English*. [online] Oxford Dictionaries. Available at: https://en.oxforddictionaries.com/definition/trust [Accessed August 25, 2017].

Stevenson, H.H. and Moldoveanu, M.C., 1995. The power of predictability. *Harvard Business Review*. [online] Available at: https://hbr.org/1995/07/the-power-of-predictability [Accessed August 25, 2017].

7 Responding to the FinTech challenge

A study of Swedish bank managers' perceptions of FinTech's effects on digitalization and customer e-loyalty

Anthony Larsson

Introduction

As the fast-paced technological changes of the twenty-first century continue to develop, payment services are no longer considered to be part of the banks' monopoly/oligopoly (Araujo and Urizar, 2016). Instead, non-bank entities are steadily gaining ground (Rajan, 2016). The greatest competition is seen in retail banking, where competition is expected to increase even more so within the coming years (Green, 2013). The Internet's continuing expansion and development has provided companies and customers with more easily accessible means of communication. New forms of online communication offer a wide array of innovative and cost-effective possibilities for customer retention, while simultaneously intensifying competition (Vatanasombut, Stylianou, and Igbaria, 2004). This has impacted the financial service industry as customers now have the ability to follow transactions in real time (Peppard, 2000). Traditional banks have long been the vanguard of online banking channel development, and still control the lion's share of the total market (Pikkarainen et al., 2004; Zahir and Gharleghi, 2014). However, the technological advancements have given rise to further developments in the financial service industry.

FinTech has traditionally denoted startup firms attempting to replace incumbent financial systems, services, processes, products, and/or business models with a more effective digital alternative (Arner, Barberis, and Buckley, 2015; Landers, 2016). This while challenging traditional corporations that rely on analogue or outdated digital functions (Alt and Puschmann, 2012; Lee, 2015). The fastest-growing FinTech service is the proliferation of the mobile payment market, as it provides easy payment services (Kim et al., 2016). Also, the increased use of social media has profoundly affected business processes, prompting companies to adapt new procedures and operations (Hennig-Thurau, Hofacker, and Bloching, 2013). Moreover, social networks provide an additional channel of communication between the company and its customers (Oberhofer et al., 2015). For this reason, the ability to successfully engage with one's customers via digital channels (also known as "omnichannels") can be a game changer. This includes being able to deliver relevant and appropriate information to customers in a swift manner (Odden, 2012; Nasir, 2015). Still, it is important to remember that the digital process also incurs many challenges to the industry as well (Kaplan and Haenlein, 2010). One of the most prominent challenges is the asymmetrical information flow between the retailer and its customers. That is to say that it is not always possible for the company to accurately predict the customers' knowledgeability (Sharpe, 1990; Pedraja and Yagüe, 2001).

By and large, the FinTech environment is far less regulated than the traditional banking sector and is still under much development (Arner, Barberis, and Buckley, 2015). An MIT FinTech report suggests the end of traditional banking is near due to the lack of innovation in the banking sector (Lipton, Shrier, and Pentland, 2016). This urgency is accentuated by the fact that the FinTech sector is growing. McKinsey has estimated that there are approximately 12,000 FinTechs worldwide, with FinTech ventures tripling in value to USD 12.21 billion in 2014 (Accenture, 2015b; Dietz et al., 2016). This development caused EY to issue a report calling for traditional banks to respond to the FinTech challenge by managing the digital risks and improving the customer experience (Webster and Pizzala, 2015). This has added pressure to the traditional banks to conform and adopt digitalization initiatives in order to meet customer demands. A study by Accenture (2015a) showed that bank customers of today yearn for personal relationships with their banks in addition to a greater sense of control as to how, when, and where they can conduct their bank affairs. A bank customer may in this context be defined as an individual who possesses a bank account and/or utilizes the bank's services regularly or irregularly (Ryder, Griffiths, and Singh, 2012). A reason customers wish to build relationships with their bank supplier is because they feel a close relationship increases the sense of security. The customer tends to feel safer in buying goods (especially complex products) if they have a good relationship with their supplier (Buttle and Maklan, 2015).

To this end, the impact of FinTech has ushered banks into pursuing digitalization more aggressively than before (Ferrari, 2016; Kotarba, 2016). As such, digitalization has provided more autonomy to the customers while also giving the tools to educate themselves about the products they desire. Thus, digitalization itself is often seen as an inevitable and unrelenting process (Bauer, Grether, and Leach, 2002). It is quintessential for bank managers to comprehend how relationships are built and identify the factors that ensure loyalty, as these are the key ingredients to profitability and sustainability (Sheth and Parvatiyar, 1995; Srinivasan, Anderson, and Ponnavolu, 2002; Heffernan et al., 2008). In turn, the digitalization process deeply affects the banks' ability to nurture customer loyalty (Milkau and Bott, 2015). Yet it is at this point important to distinguish *digitalization* from *digitization*. The former refers to a process where an actor's use of digital technology is adopted or increased, such as using mobile applications (Wachal, 1971; Castells, 2010; Van Dijk, 2012; Meige and Schmitt, 2015). The latter, on the other hand, suggests conversion of analogue material (e.g., images, video, and/or text, etc.) into a digital format (Feldman, 1997; Verhulst, 2002; Brynjolfsson and McAfee, 2014).

Sweden has been particularly prolific in FinTech development, which is illustrated by the fact that Stockholm has been the second highest funded FinTech city (after London) in the European Union since 2015 (Teigland et al., 2015; Wewege, 2017). Moreover, in June 2017, it was reported that the leading Swedish FinTech company Klarna had acquired a banking license, making it one of the largest FinTech companies to do so (Milne, 2017). This is indicative of the formidability of the FinTech companies' ability to seriously challenge the hegemony of the traditional banks. The foundation of this study expands upon the author's previous research into digitalization and customer loyalty (Larsson and Viitaoja, 2017). Similar to the preceding study, the point of departure for this chapter has been to investigate the perceptions of ten bank managers representing different major Swedish banks. However, this time, the study's premise seeks to understand how the FinTechs have prompted digitalization and how, in turn, this may affect customer loyalty from a bank managerial perspective.

The practical problem is that banks risk losing loyalty to the FinTech firms in the event that they are unable to fulfill customers' expectations (Harvey, 2016). If the banks fail to secure credibility, the customers may view digital solutions in a negative manner rather than as something aiding their everyday life (Jayaram, Manrai, and Manrai, 2015).

An academic problem is the scarcity of research in the area of how digital solutions are perceived by customers in a time where traditional bank offices are rapidly closing down (Ryals, 2005; Küng, Picard, and Towse, 2008). Admittedly, previous research has been conducted on bank customer relations; however, these have chiefly focused on a customer perspective (Chan and Ma, 1990; Zineldin, 1995; Nielsen, Terry, and Trayler, 1998). For this reason, this study has focused on the bank managers' perspective (Ballaine and Pellegrin, 1965; Kelly and Mohrweis, 1989; Ennew and Binks, 1996). The posed research question for this study is: *What are the most important challenges the FinTech firms have posed to the Swedish banks in terms of securing customer loyalty through the use of digital channels?*

Theoretical concepts

The Bell doctrine

The Bell doctrine (also known as *Baxter's law*) describes how a dominant actor in a regulated industry can extend into, and dominate, a non-regulated industry. This happens because there is an incentive as well as a possibility for the monopolized industry to exert its influence in a market where it is not dominant, but where its services are nevertheless in need. The ambition is thus to impose an indirect control on a market it does not currently dominate and where the market is not regulated (Nuechterlein and Weiser, 2013). In other words, a regulated monopolist tends to incur minor losses in their first monopoly level due to the existent regulation; however, it will have full gains in the new market level, and therefore it will seek to expand its monopoly (Joskow and Noll, 1999). It is argued that modern banks should be considered more in terms of oligopolies rather than strict monopolies, since there are multiple banks on the market in a formal sense, but without proffering any substantial competition to one another (Sharpe, 1990; Rajan, 1992; Parramore, 2011). However, certain rules for monopolies also hold true for oligopolies, as the dominant actors in both cases display imperfect competition while retaining some level of control over prices/supply in both structures (Belyaev, 2010). This makes the two transposable in this context in terms of assessing the Bell doctrine (Farrell and Weiser, 2003).

Banks are inherently subjected to regulation (Singh, 2007; Englund and Vihriälä, 2009; Goodheart, 2011). This subjugates the banks to certain requirements, restrictions, and guidelines. These are designed to create market transparency between banking institutions and its customers, as well as society at large (Barth, Caprio, and Levine, 2006; Siklos, 2011). Effectively, the banks have historically enjoyed a monopoly/oligopoly on various financial services. This has enabled banks to successfully utilize the Bell doctrine in various cases. For instance, banks are able to set a higher interest rate for customers by establishing a lending relationship. This is due to the fact that information asymmetry limits competition between banks. Consequently, banks can acquire monopoly rent from customers. However, it is possible for customers to use trade credit from a different financial source, thereby forgoing the bank's ability to extract monopoly rent (Tsuruta, 2008).

While Petersen and Rajan (1994) contend that information asymmetry is mitigated during the long-term relationship between the bank and the customer, other research indicates that banks tend to acquire more and more information about their customers over time, thus reinforcing the information asymmetry among long-term customers (Angelini, Di Salvo, and Ferri, 1998; D'Auria, Foglia, and Reedtz, 1999; Degryse and Van Cayseele, 2000; Berger et al., 2005). Moreover, previous studies have shown that banks may play upon information asymmetry while building up a relationship with the customer in order to cast distrust upon the non-financial firms, such as suppliers, who may offer credit to the customers instead of the banks (Tsuruta, 2008). In doing so, the banks aim to secure dominance over the less regulated scene by exerting influence over their existing customers.

Customer e-loyalty

The scientific and practical interest in relationship marketing has grown substantially along with the increased popular use of the Internet (Sheth and Parvatiyar, 2002). An integral driver of relationship marketing research is the concept of customer loyalty (Christopher, Payne, and Ballantyne, 2002). Indubitably, the ability to retain customers is crucial to any business as it affects the firm's profitability, stressing the relevance of customer loyalty (Chen and Hitt, 2002). Twenty-first-century digital technology has seen the advent of a modified form of loyalty, known as "e-loyalty" (Smith, 2000). As the name suggests, e-loyalty denotes customer loyalty in e-commerce (Reichheld and Schefter, 2000; Gommans et al., 2001; Clifford and Lang, 2012). Besides the actual medium of interaction, there is a notable conceptual difference between e-loyalty and traditional customer loyalty. The former is a distribution-driven, consumer-controlled, and technology-facilitated concept, while the latter is a product-driven, marketer-controlled concept (Schultz and Bailey, 2000). With e-loyalty, the customers have potential access to several different competing businesses online. In more specialized industries, such as the financial services, the industry's structure and available competition determines whether or not a customer is "coerced" into remaining a customer of that particular enterprise (Jones and Sasser, 1995; Carlson and Sinnappan, 2003). To this point, Salmen and Muir (2003) contend that electronic customer care tools can be used to create customer e-loyalty in the field of banking.

Bank loyalty can be identified as a biased, nonrandom, behavioral reaction articulated over a period of time by some decision-making component in regard to one bank out of a set of competitors (Bloemer, de Ruyter, and Peeters, 1998; Levy and Hino, 2016). Loyal bank customers tend to contact them more often and will more regularly enlist their services and purchase products (Tsai, Tsai, and Chang, 2010). Low loyalty tends to lower the bank's revenue and may ultimately compel the ownership to close down the bank at the given location, or move it to a different location (Mahony, Madrigal, and Howard, 2000; Bauer, Stokburger-Sauer, and Exler, 2008). Simply put, customer loyalty is most easily secured through the ability to satisfy customer needs and wants (Oliver, 1997). Bank loyalty involves repeated purchase intentions and/or behaviors at the same bank (Chen, 2012). Thus, "loyalty" can be regarded as a psychological process in which a customer adopts an attitude toward a retailer in which he/she wishes to remain a future customer (Jacoby and Kyner, 1973; Keller, 1993; Assael, 1998). Importantly, customer loyalty as well as customer satisfaction correlates positively with customer engagement, stressing the importance of successfully engaging one's customers actively (Oliver, 1999; Thakur, 2016). Online service has shown to have a particular effect on banking customers (Floh and Treiblmaier, 2006).

To this point, studies have suggested that many online consumers tend to remain more loyal than traditional consumers if they feel the service provided is of high quality (Reichheld and Schefter, 2000; Devaraj, Fan, and Kohli, 2003). The Internet per se is generally not seen as disruptive; however, online enterprises must still adhere to the conventional rules of business and economics (Howcroft, 2001). Moreover, consumers' satisfaction with Internet shopping is largely influenced by factors such as entertainment, speed, information quality, and reliability (Kim and Lim, 2001). Hence, a successful Internet strategy must ensure that the customers receive the value they expect in order to ensure their return in the future. Moreover, the cost of acquiring and retaining customers lessens considerably with each transaction (Porter, 2001). Thus, the single most important aspect in defining a successful Internet strategy is to create steadfastness as well awareness for the actor to learn that future success is contingent on the ability to change the focus and/or adjustment of the strategy to the future needs of the business (Guah, 2006).

The eight Cs

Srinivasan (2004) argues that the building of customer's trust (and thereby in extension also e-loyalty) is an ongoing process. He has previously presented a theory to identify various factors that ultimately result in e-loyalty

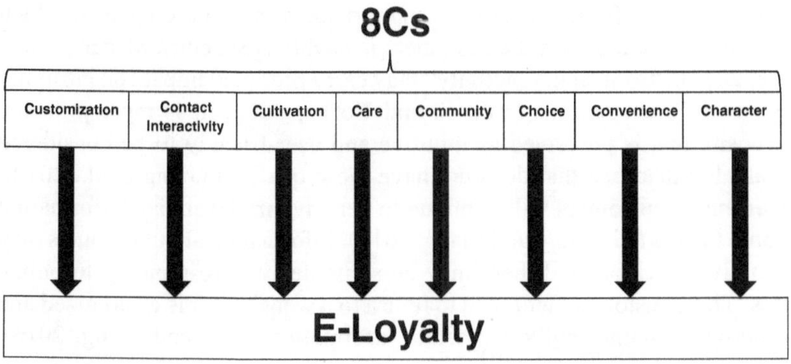

Figure 7.1 Customer loyalty model

(Srinivasan, Anderson, and Ponnavolu, 2002). These factors consider consequences and impact behind the different motivations and sensations. This is especially important when considering managerial perceptions as these perceptions can determine the strategic decision-making process (Khatri and Ng, 2000). These factors are summarized in eight different categories, known as the "eight Cs," which will seemingly affect the customer's propensity toward having a favorable opinion of the retailer (depicted in Figure 7.1).

Customization

Srinivasan, Anderson, and Ponnavolu (2002) believe that given the possibility to customize an offer, customers are more prone to finding something desirable. This, in turn, makes the transaction easier. This is by and large based on how well a website/digital system can identify customers and adapt the retailer's goods and/or services to the customer's particular needs (Semeijn et al., 2005). Loyalty is affected by "customization" as it indicates superior quality while contributing toward matching customers with products (Coelho and Henseler, 2012). Moreover, "customization" provides the perception of increased choice by placing focus on what the customer wants (Rana, Bhat, and Rani, 2015). Nevertheless, too extensive a selection is likely to exasperate customers, which may prompt them to only look for the simplest solution at their disposal (Rubio, Villaseñor, and Yagüe, 2017). In the bank sector, this could translate into the bank's ability to offer customers a customizable portfolio for investments, or payment plans adapted to the customer's needs and/or desires.

Contact interactivity

"Contact interactivity" denotes the dynamic component involving the engagement between a customer and an e-retailer via the retailer's website.

"Interactivity" in this context can be understood as a factor between accessibility, a website's efficient customer support tools, and the degree of which mutual communication with the customers is enabled (Shobeiri, Mazaheri, and Laroche, 2014). "Contact interactivity" may carry profound impact on customer loyalty for different reasons (Yüksek and Yozcu, 2016). It is more probable for a website that is perceived as intuitive and user-friendly to be considered more valuable than one that does not have these qualities (Jiang et al., 2010). However, many customers will continue to perceive irrelevant ads/information as irksome factors (Li, Yang, and Liang, 2015). Information about products may occasionally be scarce, and there may be some delay in responding to online inquiries. Thus, customers will tend to return to a website if it is customized and easily navigated with readily accessible information (Jeon and Jeong, 2016). This can designate a bank's ability to design an online platform that is responsive to the customers so that the customers can inquire about and receive the information the desire.

Cultivation

"Cultivation" signifies the extent to which a company presents relevant information and incentives to persuade the customer to purchase more (Devece, Lapiedra, and Palacios, 2014). Ultimately, the purpose of "cultivation" is to deepen and widen the retailer's comprehension of customer needs. The acquired information is then processed by databases. The ultimate intent is to equip the retailer with the tools of proactively meeting the customers' information requests. This, in turn, creates an incentive for future purchases (Mpinganjira, 2014). For the bank sector, this may manifest itself in the ability of keeping track of the customer's purchasing behavior and accommodating the products and plans accordingly.

Care

"Care" entails how a retailer handles the customer's purchasing process before and after a transaction, and/or nurtures long-term relations with their customers. Among other aspects, this involves certifying that the process proceeds without mistakes. This covers the time from when the order is placed to when it is finally delivered to the customer. Another important aspect is how swiftly and smoothly prospective problems are resolved (Jiang and Rosenbloom, 2005). Customers experiencing a positive purchasing process are more likely to return, thus increasing loyalty (Küster, Vila, and Canales, 2016). Loyal customers tend to spend more money and tend to visit their favorite website twice as often as non-loyal customers (Yun and Good, 2007). A bank might utilize this concept in terms of following up with their customers in order to see how they perceived their most recent experiences with the bank and what the bank can do to make the customer's experiences better in the future.

Community

"Community" involves the virtual surrounding where both existing and potential future customers can congregate to exchange opinions and experiences. The retailer may elect to share information regarding new offers, goods, and/or services. The modern-day IT society has played no small part in propelling the virtual surrounding, as customers have easy access to information through the Internet. This, in turn, often helps expedite the customer's decision-making process (Chen et al., 2016). "Community" can reinforce loyalty through "word of mouth" and customers' ability to exchange experiences and information with one another (Furner, Racherla, and Babb, 2016). In a bank context, this may manifest itself through the banks hosting or engaging in a platform or forum in which the bank can share news and insights with its customers, and where they can interact not only with the bank, but also with other customers if need be.

Choice

"Choice" concerns to what extent an e-retailer can offer a broad and varied selection as opposed to a traditional retailer (Pei, Wu, and Dai, 2016). The notion is that an e-retailer does not have to abide by the same constraints as traditional retailers in terms of physical storage area, localities, etc., and the cost thereof. It is thus easier for an e-retailer to become a "one-stop shop." This, in turn, increases customer loyalty since customers by and large tend to avoid seeking out too many vendors when shopping for the same items (Toufaily, Ricard, and Perrien, 2013). For banks, this may relate to the extent of the assortment of products the bank is able to offer, or if there are desired products the bank cannot, or will not, provide.

Convenience

"Convenience" entails to what degree a customer perceives a website to be useful and easy to use (Arya and Srivastava, 2014). A website's quality is of the utmost importance to an e-retailer since the website is what represents the most quintessential, perhaps even the only, market interface the customers have at their disposal (Pandey and Chawla, 2016). If a customer does not find the website logical or user-friendly, the customer might not return in the future. It should be emphasized that this is the only "eight Cs" area that Srinivasan, Anderson, and Ponnavolu (2002) believe not to significantly increase customer loyalty. For many customers, a website may be the first encounter they have with a bank, which means the bank has to ensure that it is perceived as attractive and capable to new as well as existing customers.

Character

"Character" signals how a retailer can use a website to build up awareness and recognition among its customer base. A characteristic website is articulated by the overall impression it resonates, including colors, layout, logotypes, themes, slogans, etc. (Yeap Ai Leen, Thurasamy, and Omar, 2012). Customers are then able to identify these "characters" and gain positive associations of the retailer. This may ultimately result in favorable effects on the customers' approach toward the retailer on a broader scale (Hershenson and Haber, 1965; Kim and Lennon, 2012; Levy and Hino, 2016). This in turn indicates the extent to which a bank can use its website to make itself recognizable and distinguishable in the customer's eyes as opposed to other banks.

Method

Research design

This qualitative study employed a phenomenological hermeneutic approach, meaning that the lived meaning of the respondents' basic experience is brought to light and reflected upon (Moustakas, 1994; Hesse-Biber and Leavy, 2011; Pietkiewicz and Smith, 2014). The study opted for an exploratory study approach as the intention was to probe for the mechanisms in which bank managers perceive the impact of increased FinTech services on customer relations. A systematic literature review was conducted using the PRISMA guidelines to determine the availability of research in the area (Liberati et al., 2009). Merely two relevant articles were found (Shakhsi Salim and Keramati, 2014; Wongsansukcharoen, Trimetsoontorn, and Fongsuwan, 2015). However, neither discussed the concept of e-loyalty from a bank managerial perspective, nor did they touch upon the impact of FinTech, thus highlighting the need for additional research covering this area.

Study participants

The interviewees were selected by method of purposive sampling (Johnson and Christensen, 2013). The subjects were targeted on the basis that they had managerial functions in the major Swedish bank they represented, that they were proficient in the bank's digitalization and FinTech processes, that they had extensive customer contact, and that they had insight into the bank's customer services (Chatman, 1991). Ten managers were initially contacted with an interview request via either email or equivalent electronic channel available at the bank's website. All of the contacted interviewees confirmed their competencies and accepted participation. The respondents were given complete anonymity throughout the scope of this study. Informed consent was acquired from all respondents, as the purpose of the study was communicated to all of the respondents upon contact, and once again prior to the interview. In accordance with the Declaration of Helsinki, the interviewees were given the possibility to discontinue the interview and/or withdraw participation at any given time, although no one chose to do so (Watts, 2008; Hesse-Biber and Leavy, 2011). In no instance were the respondents' actions or decisions evaluated. Table 7.1 presents an overview of the participants interviewed in this study.

Table 7.1 List of respondents representing different Swedish major banks

Interviewee	*Gender*	*Age*	*Educational background*	*Title/position*	*No. of years working in the bank*
1	F	34	Economics and finance	Bank branch manager	9
2	F	26	Economics	Manager/customer advisor	6
3	F	44	Political science	Manager/customer advisor (and business developer)	3
4	M	33	Economics	Relationship manager	6
5	F	45	Economics	Manager/business advisor	17
6	M	32	Business admin.	Product and placement manager	1
7	M	28	Business admin.	Manager/adviser	5
8	F	45	Jurist	Relationship manager	15
9	F	36	Certified marketing education	Manager/product specialist	8
10	F	31	Engineer	Business area manager	8

Data collection and analysis

Data were collected through a series of interviews with managers representing different banks. The interviews were semi-structured using open-ended questions. This gave the interviewees the opportunity to elaborate on the subject matter as they perceived them. Initially, a pilot interview was set up between a member of the research team (the interviewer) and an independent/unaffiliated senior researcher using an interview guide. This was done in order to ensure the comprehensibility of interview questions. An interview guide was devised on the basis of this pilot interview. The interview guide sought to list relevant topics and questions intended for the respondents. The questions outlined in the interview guide were all based on the "eight Cs" of customer e-loyalty (Srinivasan, Anderson, and Ponnavolu, 2002).

The interviews were conducted over the phone by interviewer during the period of April 6 to April 29, 2016. The respondents were requested to recount their perception of events and developments as they had experienced them in regard to their bank's application of digitalization, its impact on customer loyalty, and the role of FinTech. Follow-up questions were asked whenever needed in order to provide for a deeper recollection. The interviews ranged between 24 and 52 minutes in length. All interviews were digitally recorded and transcribed using the software Audacity (version 2.0.0). Additional field notes were taken during the course of the interviews in order for the interviewer to ask follow-up questions.

The data were analyzed through a phenomenological hermeneutic approach, meaning that it aims to offer insights into how individuals, in a given certain context, make sense of a given phenomenon. As the subjects all shared a common experience (bank managers), this was a suitable approach, and even more so when dealing with a fewer number of respondents (Reid, Flowers, and Larkin, 2005; Pietkiewicz and Smith, 2014). Specifically, this means data analysis was performed though a "bottom-up" approach, in that patterns were generated from the data, rather than by using an existing theory to identify patterns that might have been applicable to the data. The data extracted were then grouped into various "themes," in this case the "eight Cs" by Srinivasan, Anderson, and Ponnavolu (2002). Since the research was focused on the respondents' perceptions, the potential limitation in scope was deemed minimal. Official designations and translations of abbreviations have been used wherever possible. The author has made all other translations.

Results

Case description

The interviewees were asked semi-structured questions based on Srinivasan, Anderson, and Ponnavolu's (2002) "eight Cs" as to which area they perceived posed the most prudent challenge to their respective bank in terms of securing customer loyalty in light of FinTech's growing market shares. Each response was analyzed and grouped into the one of the "eight Cs" that appeared most in line with their perception. The following illustrates an aggregated summary of the main recurring points conveyed by the interviewees in respect to the "eight Cs."

The respondents perceived *customization* as helpful in streamlining customer solutions, in addition to opening up opportunities for more in-depth modes of interaction with the customers. Respondent 5 referred to the digital channels as a "business optimizer," inasmuch that it enabled the banks to perform a viable customer analysis in order to understand their needs. However, there were some concerns regarding the perceived threat from the FinTech firms. Respondent 4 believed there was currently an oversaturation on the market of various financial actors, and called for future collaboration with FinTech companies. Respondent 9, however, viewed customers turning to other FinTech/non-bank actors for information as "problematic," since this makes banks lose sight of what information actually reaches their customers and how it is communicated.

Contact interactivity was generally perceived favourably, with digital channels providing shorter lead times, improved feedback, and offering customers greater possibilities of gathering information. The perceived negative aspects were the complexity of the legal framework, which imposes strict limits on the banks' ability to interact with their customers and acquire information about them. Respondent 9 added that the digital meetings were perceived as "complex" as it was difficult to cater to all the different customers' needs.

Cultivation was deemed to aid the customers in their purchasing process. The respondents unanimously favored the digitalization process in this context as they felt it alleviated resource constraints while promoting additional sales, since the bank was able to use customer data in order to supply the customers with pertinent offers. Still, the respondents did agree that the lack of information regarding the customers' prior knowledge and/or competency made it difficult to meet the customers' needs. Respondent 9 added that not being able to read the customer's body language made it more difficult to establish new customer connections. Conversely, Respondent 10 argued that the digital platforms made it possible to reach out to new customers they would not have reached otherwise.

Care was seen in positive terms as it encouraged the customers to be autonomous as well as self-reliant. Care was also considered to reduce arduous bank administration. Respondent 6 articulated concerns in handling potential "gray areas," as the digitalization platform is perceived as an automated construct that does not apply data interpretation in the same way a human being would. Respondent 4 believed more niche FinTech companies could gain an upper hand in payment services. He claimed that was why his bank had elected not to compete with these, but rather opted for new business models based on more specific customers' requests instead, such as customer care and availability. Overall, the respondents voiced concern over the threat of further automatization, leading to greater redundancy of bank employees.

Community was perceived to help the banks activate their customers and guide them toward learning more about the banks' products. Notwithstanding, the respondents cited some concerns compared to the FinTech companies, namely regulations that govern the banks but that affect the FinTech companies to a much lesser extent. For instance, due to confidentiality reasons, there are limitations to how a bank can respond to complaints made in different online channels. Respondent 4 lamented that unsubstantiated "frivolous complaints issued wantonly by some users" risked creating disproportionate attention through the social media waves. Respondents 6 and 7 highlighted the risk of "astroturfing/consumer empowerment" and the "snowball effect" as social media channels may present a small number of discontent customers as being disproportionately larger in number than they actually are. Their sentiment may in turn gain traction among a broader population. A perceived drawback shared by several respondents was how certain negative publicity espoused by disgruntled customers may linger around social media sites for years after the problem has been resolved in full.

Choice was perceived in positive terms as it provided customers with a choice between different solutions, thereby seeking to reach a broader customer base. The overall negative experiences were the perceived risk of too many options confusing the customers. Respondent 8 argued that digitalization had paved the way for FinTech and startups. Respondent 3 stated that her bank had no interest in entering a partnership with a FinTech company. However, she added that the threat from the FinTech companies meant that banks by and large had been pressured into providing options to customers even though demand for that particular service is lacking, and that many banks are unable to uphold the necessary quality with a too broad selection. Respondents 6 and 10 followed similar sentiments, arguing that banks should keep manageable selections for their customers.

Convenience was perceived as an opportunity as it provided customers with availability, which encouraged them to be more self-sufficient and autonomous. The respondents' greatest concern was the customers perceiving the website/portal as too "complicated" or "inferior." If so, the customers could feel prompted

Table 7.2 Distribution of the perceived customer loyalty challenges according to the "eight Cs"

Eight Cs	*Number of respondents*	*Percent*
Customization	1	10
Contact interactivity	1	10
Cultivation	0	0
Care	0	0
Community	2	20
Choice	1	10
Convenience	5	50
Character	0	0
Total	**10**	**100**

Source: Srinivasan, Anderson, and Ponnavolu (2002).

to leave the bank for another bank or FinTech company with more advanced digital solutions. Respondent 7 even expressed apprehension of asking the customers to download updated bank software out of fear that they might perceive it as "awkward" or "complicated" and take it as a cue to leave the bank.

Character was perceived as essential as the banks desired to establish a strong online/digital presence. Respondent 10 contended that it would not have been possible to provide the same service in an analogue format. Most respondents believed the digitalization process enhanced the bank's image. Notwithstanding, Respondent 9 contended that creating a uniform bank image made it more difficult to profile its uniqueness in various local settings. Respondent 7 also argued that old transgressions/scandals the bank perpetrated years ago may continue to hurt the bank's character years later due to the continued awareness brought on by social media. Respondent 6 cautioned that the surge of FinTech companies might lead to a plethora of different companies coming to dominate future digital customer relations as customers might seek themselves to different actors for different services, complicating relationship-building with the customers.

The results from respondents regarding the greatest challenges posed by digitalization in regard to securing customer loyalty from the FinTech firms according to the "eight Cs" can be summarized in Table 7.2.

Methodological considerations

A potential limitation is the fact that this study has only interviewed 10 managers representing different Swedish banks. Nevertheless, the respondents included in this study represent a category that is an essentially homogenous cluster group (Hsieh, Hung, and Ho, 2009; Pietkiewicz and Smith, 2014). As such, a clear pattern is discernible, inasmuch that they all operate in an identical environment under comparable circumstances.

Undeniably, interviews incur a risk of "recall bias" (Riegelman, 2005). This has been handled by providing the interviewees with a clear characterization and articulation of the research question. Moreover, the application of an interview guide allowed for a standardized mode of data collection. Assuredly, each interviewee was given sufficient time before responding so that they could reflect on the situation and provide an answer in line with how they perceived the situation (Hassan, 2006).

Although the interviewees could hypothetically change their views in case a different researcher poses the same questions at a later stage, this study has employed "participant control." This means that the interviewees were able to confirm the validity of their responses after they were submitted to the interviewer. This was done by repeating the answers registered by the interviewer to the interviewees, allowing them to confirm their responses. This ensured that the respondents provided accurate accounts of their responses at the time of this study (Merriam, 1991). The possible risk of the "interviewer effect" was mitigated since all of the subjects were interviewed over the phone (Groves and Magilavy, 1986). Moreover, all interviews were prepared using precise details on exactly how the interviews would be conducted in a uniform and stringent manner throughout all the interviews conducted (David and Sutton, 2011).

As an interview was conducted, there is an inherent risk of "social desirability bias" (i.e., that the respondents could be overreporting "good behavior" or underreporting "bad behavior"). This has been remedied to the greatest possible extent by ensuring that the wording presented to the respondents was conveyed as neutral as possible. Furthermore, the respondents were all granted full anonymity, which provided for neutrality, detachment, and reassurance (McBurney and White, 2009).

Analytical summary

This study sought to research the most pressing challenges in using digital channels as a means of increasing customer loyalty in light of the emerging threat from the FinTech firms, as perceived by Swedish bank managers. The specific research question was: *What are the most important challenges the FinTech firms have posed to the Swedish banks in terms of securing customer loyalty through the use of digital channels?* The premise of the framework used was Srinivasan, Anderson, and Ponnavolu's (2002) "eight Cs." The respondents experienced several challenges, although half of the respondents (50 percent) considered *convenience* to be the most pressing challenge, followed by *community* (20 percent). *Contact interactivity, customization*, and *choice* were perceived as the most pressing challenges by 10 percent, respectively. *Character, cultivation*, and *care* were not perceived as the most pressing challenge by any of the respondents.

Convenience was perceived as the greatest challenge for different reasons depending on the respondent. Multiple interviewees believed that the customers perceived the website to be unwieldy or substandard. This, in turn, suggests a notion of a customer access problem. A few interviewees perceived information asymmetry causing rifts between the banks and the customers since it was hard to accurately predict and match suitable products to the customers. This was perceived to further widen customers' expectation gap toward the bank.

Ultimately, this was rooted in a feeling that the bank staff had failed to realize the customers' sentiments toward the digital transformation, in addition to properly assessing their level of knowledge before approaching the bank. That is to say, if the customers indicate that they know more about the product than is actually the case, there is a viable risk that they will choose an inferior product that they would not otherwise have selected. The interviewees all agreed that the current bank regulations and legal system put the traditional banks at a disadvantage compared to the FinTech firms in terms of improving customer relations. Specifically, the interviewees' dissatisfaction concerned the restrictions concerning confidentiality, as these were perceived to hamper the banks from using omnichannels to reach out to their customers directly, such as whenever they may express frustration and/or disapproval concerning their interaction with the bank.

This suggests that the traditional banks need to find ways of gaining customer understanding in a more optimal manner. The customers turn to the FinTech firms because they seek solutions that are quick and easy to use. Hence, they will turn to the actor that they perceive can best provide such a service. This actor is often a FinTech company as these are able to provide such a service without the same impediments that govern traditional banks. As the industrialized society becomes increasingly more digitalized, the simplicity of switching banks will encourage bank customers to expect the banks to deliver services to the same capacity and extent as many of the FinTech firms (Heffernan, 2016). Naturally, the banks wish to maintain a content customer stock, as it is seen to consolidate customer loyalty, and by extension profitability (Blomqvist, Dahl, and Haeger, 2004).

The respondents expressed that sustainable customer loyalty could only be secured through providing quality service and ensuring generous availability toward the customer. In an apparent paradox, however, the interviewees also stated that the banks aimed to reduce the customer's need of keeping frequent contact with the banks by making them more independent and autonomous.

By the same token, Srinivasan, Anderson, and Ponnavolu (2002) believe *convenience* to be the sole "C" to lack significant impact toward customer loyalty. In spite of this, *convenience* was understood by a majority of the interviewees as the greatest challenge toward obtaining customer loyalty. This in turn suggests that Srinivasan, Anderson, and Ponnavolu's (2002) theory in regard to *convenience* needs to be reconsidered when assessing present-day e-loyalty.

Conclusion

The findings suggest that the interviewees have felt obstructed in their digitalization endeavors by the complex regulatory bank system in a way that the FinTech companies are not. The Bell doctrine assumes that a dominant actor can extend into, and dominate, a non-regulated industry. This premise, however, indicates that the expansion of FinTech has prompted the traditional banks to expedite their digital transformation in order to meet the competition. However, due to the asymmetrical regulatory system, the bank staff fail to generate a distinct profile of their customers, which in turn makes it difficult to live up to the customers' expectations.

The primary scientific contribution of this study shows that the Bell doctrine becomes inverted, at least in terms of Swedish major traditional banks seeking to secure customer loyalty. Specifically, this is illustrated by the FinTech companies' ability to exert indirect influence on the traditional banks inasmuch as forcing them to adapt their technology (and their selections) to better match those provided by the FinTech services. The secondary scientific contribution this paper presents is the need to revise the role of *convenience* as depicted by Srinivasan, Anderson, and Ponnavolu (2002), as it is clear that it is perceived to play a much more important role today than it did at the time when the original article was written.

A possible future approach forward is to activate the customers in various co-creation processes such as informational seminars, workshops, etc. The future banks can also aim to veer toward becoming a "one-stop shop" where the banks would offer more extensive types of financial services and capitalize on the established, bona fide trust they have with their customers. At this point, it is also feasible for the traditional banks to seek collaboration with certain FinTech companies. This would not only address the perceived situation of the inverted Bell doctrine; it would also challenge the overall threat from FinTech companies at large, while also adapting and utilizing the regulatory advantages these companies have in regard to the traditional banks.

Future research

A recommendation for future research is to study similar situations in other countries around Europe and around the world in order to determine if the major bank managers share a similar perception on their situation in regard to FinTech, digitalization, and customer loyalty. A second pertinent area of scrutiny is the branding challenge toward amalgamating the FinTech industries and the traditional banks, so that it is done in a way that does not confuse the customer perception as to who the service provider is. A third and final area for future research is investigating the legal framework and how it can be updated to allow the FinTech companies and the traditional banks to operate on more equal legal terms, while at the same time ensuring that the customer's integrity and/or safety is never jeopardized.

Acknowledgments

The author gratefully acknowledges the contributions of Yamit Viitaoja (MBA) in conducting the interviews used for this study.

Bibliography

Accenture, 2015a. *Banking shaped by the customer*. [online] Available at: https://www.accenture.com/us-en/~/media/Accenture/Conversion-Assets/Microsites/Documents17/Accenture-2015-North-America-Consumer-Banking-Survey.pdf [Accessed January 16, 2018].

Accenture, 2015b. *The future of FinTech and banking: Digitally disrupted or reimagined?* [online] Available at: www.accenture.com/us-en/insight-future-fintech-banking [Accessed January 24, 2018].

Alt, R. and Puschmann, T., 2012. The rise of customer-oriented banking: electronic markets are paving the way for change in the financial industry. *Electronic Markets*, 22(4), pp.203–215.

Angelini, P., Di Salvo, R., and Ferri, G., 1998. Availability and cost of credit for small businesses: Customer relationships and credit cooperatives. *Journal of Banking & Finance*, 22(6–8), pp.925–954.

Araujo, A. and Urizar, I., 2016. 4G technology: The role of telecom carriers. In: M. Gómez-Uranga, J.M. Zabala-Iturriagagoitia and J. Barrutia, eds. *Dynamics of big Internet industry groups and future trends: A view from epigenetic economics*. New York: Springer, pp.201–242.

Arner, D.W., Barberis, J.N., and Buckley, R.P., 2015. *The evolution of FinTech: A new post-crisis paradigm?* Research Paper. [online] Hong Kong. Available at: http://ssrn.com/abstract=2676553 [Accessed January 24, 2018].

Arya, S. and Srivastava, S., 2014. E-loyalty in websites: User domain perspective. *The International Journal of Business & Management*, 2(6), pp.302–308.

Assael, H., 1998. *Consumer behavior and marketing action*. 6th ed. Cincinnati, OH: South-Western College Publications.

Ballaine, W.C. and Pellegrin, R.J., 1965. The banker's civic participation. *The Banker's Magazine*, 148(3), pp.7–12.

Barth, J.R., Caprio, G., and Levine, R., 2006. *Rethinking bank regulation: Till angels govern*. Cambridge: Cambridge University Press.

Bauer, H.H., Grether, M., and Leach, M., 2002. Building customer relations over the Internet. *Industrial Marketing Management*, 31(2), pp.155–163.

Bauer, H.H., Stokburger-Sauer, N.E., and Exler, S., 2008. Brand image and fan loyalty in professional team sport: A refined model and empirical assessment. *Journal of Sport Management*, 22(2), pp.205–226.

Belyaev, L.S., 2010. *Electricity market reforms: Economics and policy challenges*. New York: Springer.

Berger, A.N., Miller, N.H., Petersen, M.A., Rajan, R.G., and Stein, J.C., 2005. Does function follow organizational form? Evidence from the lending practices of large and small banks. *Journal of Financial Economics*, 76(2), pp.237–269.

Bloemer, J., de Ruyter, K., and Peeters, P., 1998. Investigating drivers of bank loyalty: The complex relationship between image, service quality and satisfaction. *International Journal of Bank Marketing*, 16(7), pp.276–286.

Blomqvist, R., Dahl, J., and Haeger, T., 2004. *Relationsmarknadsföring [Relationship marketing]*. 3rd ed. Gothenburg: IHM Publishing.

Brynjolfsson, E. and McAfee, A., 2014. *The second machine age: Work, progress, and prosperity in a time of brilliant technologies*. New York: W.W. Norton & Company.

Buttle, F. and Maklan, S., 2015. *Customer relationship management: Concepts and technologies*. London: Routledge.

Carlson, J. and Sinnappan, S., 2003. A framework for modelling the determinants of e-loyalty in business-to-consumer Internet commerce. In: *ACIS 2003 Proceedings 31*. [online] Perth, Australia: ACIS. Available at: http://aisel.aisnet.org/acis2003/31 [Accessed January 24, 2018].

Castells, M., 2010. *The rise of the network society: The information age—economy, society, and culture*. 2nd ed. Chichester: Wiley-Blackwell.

Chan, A.K.K. and Ma, V.S.M., 1990. Corporate banking behaviour: A survey in Hong Kong. *International Journal of Bank Marketing*, 8(2), pp.25–31.

Chatman, J.A., 1991. Matching people and organizations: Selection and socialization in public accounting firms. *Administrative Science Quarterly*, 36(3), pp.459–484.

Chen, J., Teng, L., Yu, Y., and Yu, X., 2016. The effect of online information sources on purchase intentions between consumers with high and low susceptibility to informational influence. *Journal of Business Research*, 69(2), pp.467–475.

Chen, P.-Y. (Sharon) and Hitt, L.M., 2002. Measuring switching costs and the determinants of customer retention in Internet-enabled businesses: A study of the online brokerage industry. *Information Systems Research*, 13(3), pp.255–274.

Chen, S.-C., 2012. The customer satisfaction–loyalty relation in an interactive e-service setting: The mediators. *Journal of Retailing and Consumer Services*, 19(2), pp.202–210.

Christopher, M., Payne, A., and Ballantyne, D., 2002. *Relationship marketing: Creating stakeholder value*. Oxford: Butterworth-Heinemann.

Clifford, D. and Lang, M., 2012. What determines e-loyalty? An analysis of factors affecting on-line customer retention. In: *IADIS WWW/Internet 2012 Conference*. [online] Madrid: ARAN, pp.1–8. Available at: http://hdl.handle.net/10379/3416 [Accessed January 24, 2018].

Coelho, P.S. and Henseler, J., 2012. Creating customer loyalty through service customization. *European Journal of Marketing*, 46(3/4), pp.331–356.

D'Auria, C., Foglia, A., and Reedtz, P.M., 1999. Bank interest rates and credit relationships in Italy. *Journal of Banking & Finance*, 23(7), pp.1067–1093.

David, M. and Sutton, C.D., 2011. *Social research: An introduction*. 2nd ed. London: Sage.

Degryse, H. and Van Cayseele, P., 2000. Relationship lending within a bank-based system: Evidence from European small business data. *Journal of Financial Intermediation*, 9(1), pp.90–109.

Devaraj, S., Fan, M., and Kohli, R., 2003. E-loyalty: Elusive ideal or competitive edge? *Communications of the ACM*, 46(9), pp.184–191.

Devece, C., Lapiedra, R., and Palacios, D., 2014. Website effectiveness for tourism accommodation companies. In: I. Gil-Pechuán, D. Palacios-Marqués, M.P. Peris-Ortiz, E. Vendrell, and C. Ferri-Ramirez, eds. *Strategies in e-business: Positioning and social networking in online markets*. Boston, MA: Springer, pp.55–65.

Dietz, M., Khanna, S., Olanrewaju, T., and Rajgopal, K., 2016. *Cutting through the noise around financial technology*. [online] McKinsey & Company. Available at: www.mckinsey.com/industries/financial-services/our-insights/cutting-through-the-noise-around-financial-technology [Accessed January 24, 2018].

Englund, P. and Vihriälä, V., 2009. Financial crisis in Finland and Sweden: Similar but not quite the same. In: L. Jonung, J. Kiander, and P. Vartia, eds. *The great financial crisis in Finland and Sweden: The Nordic experience of financial liberalization*. Cheltenham: Edward Elgar, pp.71–131.

Ennew, C.T. and Binks, M.R., 1996. The impact of service quality and service characteristics on customer retention: Small businesses and their banks in the UK. *British Journal of Management*, 7(3), pp.219–230.

Farrell, J. and Weiser, P.J., 2003. Modularity, vertical integration and open access policies: Towards a convergence of antitrust and regulation in the Internet age. *Harvard Journal of Law & Technology*, 17(1), pp.85–134.

Feldman, T., 1997. *An introduction to digital media*. New York: Routledge.

Ferrari, R., 2016. FinTech impact on retail banking: From a universal banking model to banking verticalization. In: S. Chishti and J. Barberis, eds. *The FinTech book: The financial technology handbook for investors, entrepreneurs and visionaries*. Chichester: John Wiley & Sons, pp.248–252.

Floh, A. and Treiblmaier, H., 2006. What keeps the e-banking customer loyal? A multigroup analysis of the moderating role of consumer characteristics on e-loyalty in the financial service industry. *Journal of Electronic Commerce Research*, 7(2), pp.97–110.

Furner, C.P., Racherla, P., and Babb, J.S., 2016. What we know and do not know about mobile app usage and stickiness: A research agenda. In: Information Resources Management Association, ed. *Geospatial research: Concepts, methodologies, tools, and applications*. Hershey, PA: IGI Global, pp.117–141.

Gommans, M., Gommans, M., Krishnan, K.S., and Scheffold, K.B., 2001. From brand loyalty to e-loyalty: A conceptual framework. *Journal of Economic and Social Research*, 3(1), pp.43–58.

Goodheart, C.A.E., 2011. Financial regulation. In: S. Eijffinger and D. Masciandaro, eds. *Handbook of central banking, financial regulation and supervision: After the financial crisis*. Cheltenham: Edward Elgar, pp.326–353.

Green, S., 2013. What banking monopoly? *Fortune*. [online] Available at: http://fortune.com/2013/09/24/what-banking-monopoly [Accessed January 24, 2018].

Groves, R.M. and Magilavy, L.J., 1986. Measuring and explaining interviewer effects in centralized telephone surveys. *Public Opinion Quarterly*, 50(2), pp.251–266.

Guah, M.W., 2006. Conclusions. In: M.W. Guah and W.L. Currie, eds. *Internet strategy: The road to web services solutions*. Hershey, PA: IRM Press, pp.227–258.

Harvey, D., 2016. Digital transformation in banks: The trials, opportunities and a guide to what is important. *Journal of Digital Banking*, 1(2), pp.136–145.

Hassan, E., 2006. Recall bias can be a threat to retrospective and prospective research designs. *The Internet Journal of Epidemiology*, 3(2), pp.339–412.

Heffernan, S.A., 2016. *Modern banking*. 2nd ed. Chichester: John Wiley & Sons.

Heffernan, T., O'Neill, G., Travaglione, T., and Droulers, M., 2008. Relationship marketing: The impact of emotional intelligence and trust on bank performance. *International Journal of Bank Marketing*, 26(3), pp.183–199.

Hennig-Thurau, T., Hofacker, C.F., and Bloching, B., 2013. Marketing the pinball way: Understanding how social media change the generation of value for consumers and companies. *Journal of Interactive Marketing*, 27(4), pp.237–241.

Hershenson, M. and Haber, R.N., 1965. Role of meaning in the perception of briefly exposed words. *Canadian Journal of Psychology*, 19(1), pp.42–46.

Hesse-Biber, S. and Leavy, P., 2011. *The practice of qualitative research*. 2nd ed. Thousand Oaks, CA: Sage.

Howcroft, D., 2001. After the goldrush: Deconstructing the myths of the dot.com market. *Journal of Information Technology*, 16(4), pp.195–204.

Hsieh, N.-C., Hung, L.-P., and Ho, C.-L., 2009. A data driven ensemble classifier for credit scoring analysis. In: T. Theeramunkong, B. Kijsirikul, N. Cercone, and T.-B. Ho, eds. *Advances in knowledge discovery and data mining: 13th Pacific-Asia Conference, PAKDD 2009 Bangkok, Thailand, April 27–30, 2009 Proceedings*. Heidelberg: Springer, pp.351–362.

Jacoby, J. and Kyner, D.B., 1973. Brand loyalty vs. repeat purchasing behavior. *Journal of Marketing Research*, 10(1), pp.1–9.

Jayaram, D., Manrai, A.K., and Manrai, L.A., 2015. Effective use of marketing technology in Eastern Europe: Web analytics, social media, customer analytics, digital campaigns and mobile applications. *Journal of Economics, Finance and Administrative Science*, 20(39), pp.118–132.

Jeon, M.M. and Jeong, M., 2016. Influence of website quality on customer perceived service quality of a lodging website. *Journal of Quality Assurance in Hospitality & Tourism*, 17(4), pp.453–470.

Jiang, P. and Rosenbloom, B., 2005. Customer intention to return online: Price perception, attribute-level performance, and satisfaction unfolding over time. *European Journal of Marketing*, 39(1/2), pp.150–174.

Jiang, Z., Chan, J., Tan, B.C.Y., and Chua, W.S., 2010. Effects of interactivity on website involvement and purchase intention. *Journal of the Association for Information Systems*, 11(1), pp.34–59.

Johnson, R.B. and Christensen, L., 2013. *Educational research: Quantitative, qualitative, and mixed approaches*. 5th ed. London: Sage.

Jones, T.O. and Sasser, W.E., 1995. Why satisfied customers defect. *Harvard Business Review*, 73(6), pp.88–99.

Joskow, P.L. and Noll, R.G., 1999. The Bell doctrine: Applications in telecommunications, electricity, and other network industries. *Stanford Law Review*, 51(5), pp.1249–1315.

Kaplan, A.M. and Haenlein, M., 2010. Users of the world, unite! The challenges and opportunities of social media. *Business Horizons*, 53(1), pp.59–68.

Keller, K.L., 1993. Conceptualizing, measuring, and managing customer-based brand equity. *Journal of Marketing*, 57(1), pp.1–22.

Kelly, A.S. and Mohrweis, L.C., 1989. Bankers' and investors' perceptions of the auditor's role in financial statement reporting: The impact of SAS No. 58. *Auditing: A Journal of Practice and Theory*, 9(9), pp.87–97.

Khatri, N. and Ng, H.A., 2000. The role of intuition in strategic decision making. *Human Relations*, 53(1), pp.57–86.

Kim, J.-H. and Lennon, S.J., 2012. Electronic retailing and service quality. In: J. Kandampully, ed. *Service management: The new paradigm in retailing*. New York: Springer, pp.97–116.

Kim, S.Y. and Lim, Y.J., 2001. Consumers' perceived importance of and satisfaction with Internet shopping. *Electronic Markets*, 11(3), pp.148–154.

Kim, Y., Choi, J., Park, Y.-J., and Yeon, J., 2016. The adoption of mobile payment services for "FinTech." *International Journal of Applied Engineering Research*, 11(2), pp.1058–1061.

Kotarba, M., 2016. New factors inducing changes in the retail banking customer relationship management (CRM) and their exploration by the FinTech industry. *Foundations of Management*, 8(1), pp.69–78.

Küng, L., Picard, R.G., and Towse, R., 2008. *The Internet and the mass media*. London: Sage.

Küster, I., Vila, N., and Canales, P., 2016. How does the online service level influence consumers' purchase intentions before a transaction? A formative approach. *European Journal of Management and Business Economics*, 25(3), pp.111–120.

Landers, R., 2016. *How FinTech is changing business (and bank accounts)*. [online] Business.com. Available at: www.business.com/finance/how-fintech-is-changing-business-and-bank-accounts [Accessed January 24, 2018].

Larsson, A. and Viitaoja, Y., 2017. Building customer loyalty in digital banking? A study of bank staff's perspectives on the challenges of digital CRM and loyalty. *International Journal of Bank Marketing*, 35(6), pp.858–877.

Lee, C., 2015. A study on FinTech (financial technology) and e-business: State of the art. *The Journal of Internet Electronic Commerce Resarch*, 15(5), pp.217–229.

Levy, S. and Hino, H., 2016. Emotional brand attachment: A factor in customer-bank relationships. *International Journal of Bank Marketing*, 34(2), pp.136–150.

Li, Y.-W., Yang, S.-M., and Liang, T.-P., 2015. Website interactivity and promotional framing on consumer attitudes toward online advertising: Functional versus symbolic brands. *Pacific Asia Journal of the Association for Information Systems*, 7(2), pp.41–58.

Liberati, A., Altman, D.G., Tetzlaff, J., Mulrow, C., Gøtzsche, P.C., Ioannidis, J.P.A., et al., 2009. The PRISMA statement for reporting systematic reviews and meta-analyses of studies that evaluate health care interventions: Explanation and elaboration. *Annals of Internal Medicine*, 151(4), p.W-65-W-94.

Lipton, A., Shrier, D., and Pentland, A., 2016. *Digital banking manifesto: The end of banks?* [online] Available at: www.getsmarter.com/career-advice/industry-advice/digital-banking-manifesto-the-end-of-banks-mit-report [Accessed January 24, 2018].

Mahony, D.F., Madrigal, R., and Howard, D.A., 2000. Using the psychological commitment to team (PCT) scale to segment sport consumers based on loyalty. *Sport Marketing Quarterly*, 9(1), pp.15–25.

McBurney, D.H. and White, T.L., 2009. *Research methods*. 8th ed. Belmont, CA: Wadsworth Cengage Learning.

Meige, A. and Schmitt, J., 2015. *Innovation intelligence. Commoditization. Digitalization. Acceleration. Major pressure on innovation drivers*. s.l.: Absans Publishing.

Merriam, S.B., 1991. *Case study research in education: A qualitative approach*. San Francisco, CA: Jossey-Bass.

Milkau, U. and Bott, J., 2015. Digitalisation in payments: From interoperability to centralised models? *Journal of Payments Strategy & Systems*, 9(3), pp.321–340.

Milne, R., 2017. Sweden's Klarna wins Europe's biggest FinTech banking licence. *Financial Times*. [online] June 19. Available at: www.ft.com/content/4351293f-82eb-3f6f-a903-4bc323ff2a2c?mhq5j=e1 [Accessed January 24, 2018].

Moustakas, C., 1994. *Phenomenological research methods*. Thousand Oakes, CA: Sage.

Mpinganjira, M., 2014. Understanding online repeat purchase intentions: A relationship marketing perspective. *Journal of Contemporary Management Issues*, 19(2), pp.117–135.

Nasir, S., 2015. *Customer relationship management strategies in the digital era*. Hershey, PA: IGI Global.

Nielsen, J.F., Terry, C., and Trayler, R.M., 1998. Business banking in Australia: A comparison of expectations. *International Journal of Bank Marketing*, 16(6), pp.253–263.

Nuechterlein, J.E. and Weiser, P.J., 2013. *Digital crossroads: Telecommunications law and policy in the Internet age*. 2nd ed. Boston, MA: MIT Press.

Oberhofer, M., Hechler, E., Milman, I., Schumacher, S., and Wolfson, D., 2015. *Beyond big data: Using social MDM to drive deep customer insight*. Upper Saddle River, NJ: IBM Press.

Odden, L., 2012. *Optimize: How to attract and engage more customers by integrating SEO, social media, and content marketing*. Hoboken, NJ: John Wiley & Sons.

Oliver, R.L., 1997. *Satisfaction: A behavioural perspective on the consumer*. New York: Irwin/McGraw-Hill.

Oliver, R.L., 1999. Whence consumer loyalty? *Journal of Marketing*, 63(3), pp.33–44.

Pandey, S. and Chawla, D., 2016. Using qualitative research for establishing content validity of e-lifestyle and website quality constructs. *Qualitative Market Research: An International Journal*, 19(3), pp.339–356.

Parramore, L.S., 2011. *Banking has become an oligopoly instead of a competitive business—and that's really bad news for us 99%.* [online] Alternet. Available at: www.alternet.org/story/152695/banking_has_become_an_oligopoly_instead_of_a_competitive_business_--_and_that's_really_bad_news_for_us_99 [Accessed January 24, 2018].

Pedraja, M. and Yagüe, J., 2001. What information do customers use when choosing a restaurant? *International Journal of Contemporary Hospitality Management*, 13(6), pp.316–318.

Pei, Y., Wu, K., and Dai, L., 2016. An empirical research on the evaluation system of cross-border e-commerce. In: *WHICEB 2016 Proceedings, Paper 40.* [online] Available at: http://aisel.aisnet.org/whiceb2016/40 [Accessed January 24, 2018].

Peppard, J., 2000. Customer relationship management (CRM) in financial services. *European Management Journal*, 18(3), pp.312–327.

Petersen, M.A. and Rajan, R.G., 1994. The benefits of lending relationships: Evidence from small business data. *The Journal of Finance*, 49(1), pp.3–37.

Pietkiewicz, I. and Smith, J.A., 2014. A practical guide to using interpretative phenomenological analysis in qualitative research psychology. *Czasopismo Psychologiczne – Psychological Journal*, 20(1), pp.7–14.

Pikkarainen, T., Pikkarainen, K., Karjaluoto, H., and Pahnila, S., 2004. Consumer acceptance of online banking: An extension of the technology acceptance model. *Internet Research*, 14(3), pp.224–235.

Porter, M.E., 2001. Strategy and the Internet. *Harvard Business Review*, 79(3), pp.62–78.

Rajan, R.G., 1992. Insiders and outsiders: The choice between informed and arm's-length debt. *The Journal of Finance*, 47(4), pp.1367–1400.

Rajan, R.G., 2016. *Payment services no longer the monopoly of banks.* [online] Business Standard. Available at: www.business-standard.com/article/opinion/payment-services-no-longer-the-monopoly-of-banks-116072300864_1.html [Accessed January 24, 2018].

Rana, A., Bhat, A., and Rani, L., 2015. A classificatory scheme for antecedents of the sources of "online brand equity." *Journal of Research in Interactive Marketing*, 9(4), pp.262–298.

Reichheld, F.F. and Schefter, P., 2000. E-loyalty: Your secret weapon on the web. *Harvard Business Review*, 78(4), pp.105–113.

Reid, K., Flowers, P., and Larkin, M., 2005. Exploring lived experience: An introduction to interpretative phenomenological analysis. *The Psychologist*, 18(1), pp.20–23.

Riegelman, R.K., 2005. *Studying a study and testing a test: How to read the medical evidence*. 5th ed. Philadelphia, PA: Lippincott Williams & Wilkins.

Rubio, N., Villaseñor, N., and Yagüe, M.J., 2017. Creation of consumer loyalty and trust in the retailer through store brands: The moderating effect of choice of store brand name. *Journal of Retailing and Consumer Services*, 34, pp.358–368.

Ryals, L., 2005. Making customer relationship management work: The measurement and profitable management of customer relationships. *Journal of Marketing*, 69(4), pp.252–261.

Ryder, N., Griffiths, M., and Singh, L., 2012. *Commercial law: Principles and policy*. Cambridge: Cambridge University Press.

Salmen, S.M. and Muir, A., 2003. Electronic customer care: The innovative path to e-loyalty. *Journal of Financial Services Marketing*, 8(2), pp.133–144.

Schultz, D.E. and Bailey, S.E., 2000. Customer/brand loyalty in an interactive marketplace. *Journal of Advertising Research*, 40(3), pp. 41–52.

Semeijn, J., van Riel, A.C.R., van Birgelen, M.J.H., and Streukens, S., 2005. E-services and offline fulfilment: How e-loyalty is created. *Managing Service Quality: An International Journal*, 15(2), pp.182–194.

Shakhsi Salim, F. and Keramati, A., 2014. How to make Iranian banks customer oriented with use of customer relationship management concepts? Methodology and comprehensive architecture. *Systemic Practice and Action Research*, 27(4), pp.377–395.

Sharpe, S.A., 1990. Asymmetric information, bank lending and implicit contracts: A stylized model of customer relationships. *The Journal of Finance*, 45(4), pp.1069–1087.

Sheth, J.N. and Parvatiyar, A., 1995. Relationship marketing in consumer markets: Antecedents and consequences. *Journal of the Academy of Marketing Science*, 23(4), pp.255–271.

Sheth, J.N. and Parvatiyar, A., 2002. Evolving relationship marketing into a discipline. *Journal of Relationship Marketing*, 1(1), pp.3–16.

Shobeiri, S., Mazaheri, E., and Laroche, M., 2014. How customers respond to the assistive intent of an e-retailer? *International Journal of Retail & Distribution Management*, 42(5), pp.369–389.

Siklos, P.L., 2011. Transparency is not enough: Central bank governance as the next frontier. In: S. Eijffinger and D. Masciandaro, eds. *Handbook of central banking, financial regulation and supervision: After the financial crisis*. Cheltenham: Edward Elgar, pp.132–157.

Singh, D., 2007. *Banking regulation of UK and US financial markets*. Aldershot: Ashgate.

Smith, E.R., 2000. *E-loyalty: How to keep customers coming back to your website*. New York: HarperBusiness.

Srinivasan, S.S., 2004. Role of trust in e-business success. *Information Management & Computer Security*, 12(1), pp.66–72.

Srinivasan, S.S., Anderson, R., and Ponnavolu, K., 2002. Customer loyalty in e-commerce: An exploration of its antecedents and consequences. *Journal of Retailing*, 78(1), pp.41–50.

Teigland, R., Ingram, C., Wesley-James, N., Bengtsson, T., and Lamberth, J., 2015. *Stockholm – Europe's No.2 FinTech city: A dynamic hub for innovative payment, funding, banking, and transaction technologies*. [online] Invest Stockholm. Available at: www.investstockholm.com/globalassets/2.-understartsidor-investment-opportunities/fintech/stockholm_fintech_report.pdf [Accessed January 24, 2018].

Thakur, R., 2016. Understanding customer engagement and loyalty: A case of mobile devices for shopping. *Journal of Retailing and Consumer Services*, 32(2), pp.151–163.

Toufaily, E., Ricard, L., and Perrien, J., 2013. Customer loyalty to a commercial website: Descriptive meta-analysis of the empirical literature and proposal of an integrative model. *Journal of Business Research*, 66(9), pp.1436–1447.

Tsai, M.-T., Tsai, C.-L., and Chang, H.-C., 2010. The effect of customer value, customer satisfaction, and switching costs on customer loyalty: An empirical study of hypermarkets in Taiwan. *Social Behavior & Personality: An International Journal*, 38(6), pp.729–740.

Tsuruta, D., 2008. Bank information monopoly and trade credit: Do only banks have information about small businesses? *Applied Economics*, 40(8), pp.981–996.

Van Dijk, J.A.G.M., 2012. *The network society: Social aspects of new media*. 3rd ed. London: Sage.

Vatanasombut, B., Stylianou, A.C., and Igbaria, M., 2004. How to retain online customers. *Communications of the ACM*, 47(6), pp.64–70.

Verhulst, S.G., 2002. About scarcities and intermediaries: The regulatory paradigm shift of digital content reviewed. In: L.A. Lievrouw and S. Livingstone, eds. *The handbook of new media*. London: Sage, pp.432–447.

Wachal, R., 1971. Humanities and computers: A personal view. *The North American Review*, 256(1), pp.30–33.

Watts, J.H., 2008. Integrity in qualitative research. In: L.M. Given, ed. *The Sage encyclopedia of qualitative research methods – volume 1*. Thousand Oaks, CA: Sage, pp.440–441.

Webster, I. and Pizzala, J., 2015. *FinTech: Are banks responding appropriately?* [online] EY Viewpoint. Available at: www.ey.com/Publication/vwLUAssets/EY-fintech-are-banks-responding-appropriately/$FILE/EY-fintech-are-banks-responding-appropriately.pdf [Accessed January 24, 2018].

Wewege, L., 2017. *The digital banking revolution: How financial technology companies are rapidly transforming retail banking industry through disruptive financial innovation*. 2nd ed. Saarbrücken: LAP Lambert Academic Publishing.

Wongsansukcharoen, J., Trimetsoontorn, J., and Fongsuwan, W., 2015. Social CRM, RMO and business strategies affecting banking performance effectiveness in B2B context. *Journal of Business & Industrial Marketing*, 30(6), pp.742–760.

Yeap Ai Leen, J., Thurasamy, R., and Omar, A., 2012. Engaging millennials in an evolving web environment: Some key points for e-retailers. *Business Strategy Series*, 13(3), pp.111–117.

Yüksek, G. and Yozcu, Ö.K., 2016. Usage of e-loyalty programs in hospitality industry. In: E. Sezgin, ed. *e-Consumers in the era of new tourism*. Singapore: Springer, pp.35–51.

Yun, Z. and Good, L.K., 2007. Developing customer loyalty from e-tail store image attributes. *Managing Service Quality: An International Journal*, 17(1), pp.4–22.

Zahir, M. and Gharleghi, B., 2014. Adoption of Internet banking in Maldives, the most important determinants. *Asian Social Science*, 11(2), pp.181–189.

Zineldin, M., 1995. Bank-company interactions and relationships: Some empirical evidence. *International Journal of Bank Marketing*, 13(2), pp.30–40.

8 The three phases of FinTech

Anna Felländer, Shahryar Siri, and Robin Teigland

Introduction

For the past several decades, a handful of large national banks have dominated the financial services industry in Sweden, offering their clients a full-scale set of financial and banking products and services (Swedish Bankers' Association, 2014). Yet segments of the banking offerings have been, and continue to be, affected by the wave of technological change. The speed of disruption in the financial sector is correlated with the falling costs, deeper client engagement, and lower entry barriers due to digitalization, a shift of trust, and regulatory changes (SKI, 2016).

Power is being redistributed from larger, slower-moving banks to FinTech actors that innovate quickly, and with lower capital investment and sometimes less regulatory burden. Economies of scale are no longer so important.

FinTech offers consumer gains through transparency, co-creation, personalization and time optimization in more decentralized networks. Yet the risks associated with the new innovations have not yet been clarified. From a government policy perspective, the gains from a more democratic, decentralized, low-cost, and consumer-friendly digital environment in the financial sector must be weighed against risks associated with asymmetric information, consumer protection, and cybersecurity, as well as a risk to the stability of the financial system.

The Swedish competitive power is strengthened both by innovation and a leading-edge robust financial sector. Adjusting the regulatory framework, attracting talent, and creating environments for test beds and collaboration between academia, risk capital, FinTech actors, regulators, and traditional banks are our recommendations to the government.

Aim

The aim of this chapter is to give an introductory overview to the Swedish FinTech landscape by first discussing the digital disruption of the financial services industry that is occurring in three phases, as we see it: (1) innovation struggle; (2) partnership and client focus; and (3) repositioning.

Within each of the three phases, case examples of Swedish FinTech startups will be presented in order to illustrate the journey toward digital disruption.

Throughout the chapter, we also highlight the importance of the regulatory shifts after the financial crisis in 2007–2008 to the current and future regulatory landscape and their effect on digital disruption.

The chapter concludes with a reiteration of the most prominent trends that we have captured, many of which will be further explored in the ensuing chapters.

The three-phase model

In order to better gauge the emergence of FinTech companies on the Swedish market, we have sought to analyze a set of events that have given rise to the disruption of the traditional financial services market. These will be presented in detail, with examples from Swedish FinTech, below.

The first phase: innovation struggle

The first phase of digital disruption in the financial and banking sector could arguably be described as an "innovation struggle"—between the large traditional Swedish banks and the FinTech startup actors. This struggle started during and after the financial crisis of 2007–2008. During this phase, which lasted until around the middle of 2016, and which many now consider to be over, traditional banks and FinTech actors saw each other as true competitors in a "zero-sum game."

In the past, the banks' core businesses—lending, payments, insurance, and savings—had been protected by high barriers to entry in the form of inhibitive regulatory compliance, infrastructure, asymmetric information, the cost of holding capital, the ability to manage large capital flows, and low transparency. However, these barriers began to fall in some core areas due to consumer-driven digital innovation. Furthermore, the traditional larger banks also suffered from a decreasing degree of trust among the new generation due to the financial crisis, a lack of transparency, and an inability to meet their demands of real-time, tailored digital offers (SKI, 2016).

Low innovative speed in the traditional banks due to compliance

For the initial part of this phase, the innovative speed of the traditional banks was relatively low compared to FinTech startups due to a number of external and internal reasons. One of the primary external reasons was the tighter regulatory environment in Europe and globally.

Following the financial crisis in 2007–2008, European policymakers began to review and update the Markets in Financial Instruments Directive (MiFID), and accompanying regulation (MiFIR), seeking to increase market confidence and bolster consumer protections. Basel 2+3 and the Capital Requirements Directive (CRD) raised the costs of holding capital on the balance sheet and involved stricter liquidity requirements. As a consequence, the resources to adjust the organization and the processes to stricter regulatory demands increased. Also, the negative policy interest rate environment led to low margins on the mortgages (reducing net interest income, their main source of earnings), which led to lower earnings. Yet the lower interest income was to a large extent offset by reductions in wholesale funding costs and higher-fee income. The stricter regulatory framework also hurt the supply of credit to corporations, leading to a credit squeeze. This was the case in almost all European countries, yet Swedish banks had been well capitalized during and after the financial crisis, and argued that it was unfair that they were "punished" anyway.

Within the traditional banks, there was a low sense of urgency to respond to the innovative challenges of the FinTech startups due to a number of organizational and cultural reasons. The banks' culture and incentive structures did not promote cross-department innovation nor "trial-and-error" approaches. Closed, non-communicative verticals and old data systems within the banks made it harder to implement any innovations that were developed. However, perhaps most importantly, the level of digitalization competence in the boardrooms of the big banks was relatively low while upper management seemed to be "resting on its laurels" due to the high entry barriers and relatively good earnings (Larsson, 2016). This was despite the negative interest rate environment leading to low margins on mortgages and lower earnings.

FinTech gaining momentum

At the same time, the FinTech cluster in Stockholm began to gain momentum, and it was especially strong in the retail banking payment segment as entry barriers began to fall. Companies such as Klarna and iZettle became significant competitors in this segment, offering user-friendly digital payment solutions. Tink, a company organizing bank clients' private economy, also grew popular.

After the turn of the financial crisis in 2009, a number of Swedish FinTech companies started to gain traction in the market, and in doing so started to attract international investors. In 2010, Klarna raised a USD 9 million Series B round led by Sequoia Capital (Schonfeld, 2011), and in the following year iZettle raised a EUR 8.2 million Series A round led by Index Ventures (iZettle, 2011). In the period between 2010 and 2011, the two companies had raised a combined EUR 135 million (Crunchbase, 2017), marking what was arguably a significant turning point for Swedish FinTech, as a number of the world's leading venture capitalists, such as Index Ventures, Accel Partners, and Greylock Partners, to name a few (Teigland et al., 2015), had started to look to Sweden for the next big financial services innovations.

Following the success within the payments sector, other FinTech sectors in Sweden started to expand. As stricter regulations after the financial crisis hampered the supply of credit from banks to companies and organizations, new forms of lending emerged to meet the demand for credit. Startups such as FundedByMe, CrowdCube, CrowdCulture, and ToBorrow entered the crowdfunding segment, thereby offering consumers access to all four kinds of crowdfunding—donation, reward, equity, and lending—which are described in more detail later in the book. Cryptocurrency and Bitcoin startups such as Safello, KnCMiner, and CryEx emerged.

During the period 2010–2014, Stockholm-based FinTech companies had raised a combined USD 532 million in 31 investment rounds, making up 18.3 percent of the total European FinTech investment during the period. In 2015, the Swedish FinTech sector employed more than 5,800 people, and the revenue of the sector was surpassing SEK 14 billion. Stockholm was ranked as one of the leading FinTech hubs in the world, ranked second only to London in Europe (Wesley-James et al., 2015).

A shift of trust under an unclear regulatory framework

A shift of trust was emerging, both due to new technology and skepticism toward the traditional banks. Trust was occurring between peers on the digital platform, replacing the traditional middle hand, the bank. Managing asymmetric information among peers by digitalizing trust was, from a political perspective, highly questionable, and a discussion about adaptable regulatory framework began. Politicians started to identify that the democratization and decentralization of banking services that FinTech actors offer, as well as the lowering of costs in the financial sector, are valuable both from a societal and economic perspective. Yet the fear of an overly expansive credit supply and lowered demands on risk assessments, which could potentially cause systematical risks in the financial infrastructure, were dominating. By this time, regulators in general had a skeptical approach, underestimating both the FinTech actors' ability to meet banking clients' needs and an emerging shift in trust.

As a consequence, FinTech startups were during this phase acting under an unclear regulatory framework, which they argued was in favor of the traditional banks, and which could have somewhat hampered innovation during this phase. Since the FinTech actors were addressing one banking segment separately, they argued that they should not act under the same regulatory framework as a full-service traditional bank. On the other hand, FinTech was sometimes described as the new "Uber"—the world's largest taxi company without owning any cars. The comparison with FinTech to Uber was that FinTech actors were offering banking services without being a bank, without the fixed cost of holding capital, while simultaneously being regulated as a full-service bank. For example, the lack of adjusted regulatory framework for peer-to-peer (P2P) lending could cause increased consumer risks due to asymmetric information. The unclear regulatory framework during this phase could have affected the trust for potential users of these alternative and digital applications. Some FinTech actors failed due to their approach toward the regulatory landscape, with too few resources spent on navigating the regulatory landscape with managing asymmetric information and preventing consumer risks. But at the same time, it was an opportunity for the startup actors to attract younger banking clients (with lower trust for traditional banks due to the financial crisis) through trust among peers, P2P offerings, and new digital interfaces and payment methods.

A noteworthy example of the failure of the regulatory framework for P2P lending, which caused a loss in trust at the time, came in 2015. News circulated that Trustbuddy, a prominent P2P lending platform, had commissioned unlawful loans on their platform by transferring existing loans on the platform to new borrowers without informing the initial lenders. Trustbuddy immediately ceased operations in October 2015, leaving SEK 44 million of the platform users' money traceless (Lundell, 2015).

Traditional banks awakening

In the middle of this phase, the traditional banks began to take notice of the FinTech movement and began to focus on meeting the challenges that the FinTech startups were facing. Two of the greater success stories for the traditional banks, which put Sweden on the map globally for its collaborative innovative environment, are Swish and BankID, which were created by the traditional banks joining forces. The true key behind the Swish innovation was the traditional banks' courage to open up their client accounts to each other and to offer real-time transactions that prior to Swish were both costly and time-intensive—taking up to a couple of days to settle transactions. BankID is a digital identification app that can be applied to banking services (issued by 12 banks) and public services. BankID has enabled new digital innovations by strengthening the issue of trust by securing identification. BankID and Swish are both strong competitive advantages and first mover advantages for traditional banks, building loyalty with free digital and real-time apps. By November 2016, Swish reached 5 million users, equaling over 50 percent of the Swedish population (Swish, 2016), and with 84 percent of all Swedes aged 20–40 using BankID (IIS, 2017). That in turn is making banks, public agencies, and FinTech startups dependent on BankID for their apps to work.

Swedish politicians starting to realize the importance of FinTech

Toward the end of this phase, in mid-2016, as the FinTech sector grew even larger, regulators and politicians in Sweden and abroad started several actions to investigate how to best regulate FinTech such that these innovative initiatives were not stifled. Also, the British Ministry of Finance identified London as a FinTech startup cluster and gave some flexibility to the regulatory framework, while the Swedish Minster for Financial Markets, Per Bolund, initiated a formal study of crowdfunding. Bolund highlighted the need to investigate the problem of asymmetric information further, as well as investigating what type of existing or adjusted regulatory framework should be applied to crowdfunding. The uncertainty about regulations remains to some extent, even though Swedish and EU legislators have given more guidance to what law should be applied.

For crowdfunding platforms, there are three concerns that are hampering the investments and innovation speed: the first is how well the crowdfunding business model stands up to increases in interest rates and a more difficult credit cycle; the second is the increase of competition and its impact on margins and risk profile of the loan book; and the third is related to the uncertainty about regulations.

According to Etienne Brunet (2017), a London-based FinTech venture capitalist, the bank-owned FinTech services Swish and BankID, albeit with their proven track record and increasing usage within their domestic markets, currently face a number of barriers to international growth that could explain the focus on partnerships that will be described in further detail in the second phase below. According to Brunet, Swish is designed based on a number of market-specific conditions in Sweden that will prove difficult to alter in the event of internationalization. Thus, a viable option for the traditional financial institutions could be to initiate partnerships with FinTechs that can enable them to access other markets more easily, or to invest in FinTech companies in targeted areas of interest. These strategies will be further explored in the second phase below.

The second phase: partnerships and client focus

In the second phase, which began around the middle of 2016, and which many consider to still be ongoing, large traditional banks and FinTech actors have been seeking to partner with each other, in the belief that they can create true win–win partnership strategies.

True win–win

FinTech actors, due to their relatively small size and lack of organizational change barriers, have the ability to move fast and be innovative, to identify cross-fertilization gains between sectors, to offer tailored and real-time solutions, and are not afraid to test existing regulatory boundaries. Yet these new actors are disadvantaged by the lack of the large banks' client databases, distribution channels, and financial infrastructure to scale their innovations, while they have limited regulatory knowledge and resources to follow and adapt to new regulatory frameworks and to ensure client security. Furthermore, they lack the credibility the larger banks have due to their societal and historical positions, for example with deposit guarantees, which offers consumers a government-issued guarantee for deposits up to SEK 950,000 (Riksgälden, 2017). Therefore, there is a true win–win in engaging in partnerships between FinTech actors and large traditional banks.

The fight for client interface due to new regulatory frameworks

In line with this focus on partnering, the traditional banking value chains are transforming from a linear and closed arrangement to a networked and open ecosystem based on partnerships. As a node in a transparent and co-created network, integrity and security for clients are identified as being crucial, as well as investing in agile IT systems interfacing partners.

During this phase, we are witnessing a transformation in the traditional banks' strategy—away from a focus on merely providing products to value creation for their clients. As a result, while these two sets of actors are developing collaborations, one area both sets of actors are fighting for is the client interface.

One significant driver of the struggle for the client interface is that the implementation of the PSD2 (Second Payment Services Directive) in the EU in 2018 is nearing. The PSD2 regulation will require banks to open up their accounts for access by third-party providers, specifically two new types of payment service providers: account aggregators and payment initiators. Account aggregators already exist and bring together information from different banks in a single place. They allow customers to access, for example, a website or app where customers can see at a glance the balances for each of their accounts—their current account, savings, cards, etc.—even if they are offered by different banks. Payment initiators go one step further and allow the third party to make a payment from the account on the customer's behalf. They are often used at website checkouts to make a bank transfer rather than pay by card. At the moment, this is unregulated, and it is the bank's decision to give access to client accounts upon a third-party provider's request. Under the PSD2, a third party will need to get permission only from the bank's client, whereupon the bank will be obliged to share the client's account information with the third party. The higher requirements on third party providers due to PSD2 indicate some key considerations around appropriate security. While one aim of the legislation is to regulate these existing businesses by requiring all payment account providers to make their online accounts accessible, PSD2 is seen as an enabler of innovation and a way for new services to emerge, as discussed further in Chapter 1 in this volume.

The ability to aggregate accounts and interrogate customer-level data is a massive opportunity for all firms in the market, with the potential to offer a significant upside for traditional banks and FinTech actors. Both banks and third-party providers need to carefully consider their strategic options. Third parties need to think about how close they'd like to be to the banks—friend, partner, competitor, or simply user. At the moment, the bank has a strong relationship with the customer, but when a third-party provider comes along, that relationship weakens as the customer's primary contact is with their third-party provider. The big fear for the traditional bank is that they become a "utility" provider, giving access to the pipes and infrastructure through which payments are made, but with new third-party providers taking the customer relationship. At its worst from a bank perspective, banks could be left with all the costs (the need to maintain a branch network, the costs of access to payment systems, etc.), but with little of the upside in terms of customer relationships. FinTech actors should be thinking about how they can interface most efficiently with the banks, and vice versa.

A variety of partnership strategies and revenue models are currently being tested, and at the moment there are no standard solutions for a partnership between traditional banks and FinTech actors. In Sweden, many of the traditional banks are implementing incubators and accelerators to attract and form a closer dialogue with FinTech actors and their innovations, potentially with the goal of partnerships and/or acquisitions.

Nordea, for instance, implemented an accelerator program called Nordea FinTech Accelerator in 2015, which runs two cohorts per year with the aim of increasing the bank's brand awareness among FinTech companies, to initiate partnerships with

FinTechs as well as to come closer to the innovations that are being spawned on the market by these companies (Nordea, 2016). Two of the other major banks, SEB and Swedbank, have both been active in supporting the Stockholm-based FinTech accelerator program STING (Stockholm Innovation, 2016).

Apart from the above-mentioned accelerator and incubator programs that banks can arrange as a way to probe the FinTech landscape for innovations and potential partnership opportunities, there are other strategies to follow in order achieve these goals. One prominent approach is through corporate venture capital, where the bank invests in FinTech startups, in many cases for strategic purposes to be able to integrate the technology into their own service offering. A case in point is SEB Venture Capital, which recently co-invested in the renowned Swedish virtual banking app Tink, and subsequently integrated parts of the technology and user interface into the native SEB mobile app (O'Hear, 2016).

We predict that we will continue to see an increase in partnerships between traditional banks and FinTech startups, but that the way in which successful partnerships and earning models are composed will depend on the strategy of the parts involved. For example, do they want to become a platform for banking and financial services, an app on another actor's platform, a commodity provider, or a platform independent in a networked society?

GDPR: stricter integrity law

At the same time as the PSD2 regulation is opening up vast opportunities for FinTech actors to "steal" the bank clients' interface, another change of rules is affecting the landscape. A new EU law on personal integrity is to be implemented in 2018—the General Data Protection Regulation (GDPR). The background to this new law is that digitalization (e.g., through the Internet, social media, big data, Internet of Things) has led to less control for EU citizens over their personal information. Currently, the laws on integrity vary between EU countries, which leads to high costs for companies to adjust to the different laws in the different countries. While PSD2 creates opportunities for FinTech actors, it is expected that the GDPR will bring additional costs for those FinTech actors handling client data to adapt to the law.

E-krona and stronger confidence in blockchain technology

An indicator that the public authorities are adopting and realizing the importance of FinTech for Sweden's competitive power and societal contract is the Swedish Central Bank's (Riksbank) initiative to analyze an e-krona. A need to solve the problem of a society with less cash and people with less access to the bank system has been identified by the Riksbank. Sweden is uniquely positioned to be the frontrunner—with a strong FinTech landscape, robust financial, economic, and political systems, and low usage of cash, as well as a high degree of institutional trust and digital maturity among Swedish citizens. Provision of money is a central bank's core business, and should remain separate and independent from private interests in a digital context. This project is in line with national priorities to secure the independence and responsibility of present and future money provision, especially in potential times of crises. The implications on financial stability and infrastructure will be analyzed during 2017.

Blockchain technology is being more analyzed, tested, and applied to both financial institutions and other sectors. The need for international cooperation regulating the blockchain in the financial sector is crucial. Due to the high complexity and dependency on other global actors, the investments in blockchain technology among Swedish traditional banks have been relatively low. Most traditional banks have a "wait and see" approach.

The government policy approach is shifting

It is true that critical voices remain, positing that a too loose regulatory framework could exaggerate issues (such as financial volatility and cybercrime). At the same time, counter voices (such as the Bank of England) are encouraging FinTech, arguing that P2P lending has no systematic risks. In Sweden, the Financial Supervisory Authority has recently been given the assignment by the government to encourage FinTech by adjusting the regulatory framework, and the Swedish FinTech Association was launched in January 2017 to strengthen the voice of Sweden's FinTech actors against regulations that may only be applicable to a large, traditional full-scale service bank.

Since Stockholm has taken the position as a leading FinTech hub, politicians must improve the landscape for innovation and partnerships in the financial sector. The dialogue must deepen between the politicians, regulators, academia, and the FinTech startup scene. From a historical perspective, Sweden has handled technological paradigm shifts relatively well. The Swedish welfare model has been a factor, but more importantly the ability to cooperate. Sweden has a world-leading position when it comes to collaboration between the government, corporations, regulators, the academy, and innovators. During the second phase, it is crucial that the regulatory framework needs to be harmonized, become more flexible, and carefully adopted to the new technologies. In addition, collaborations should be initiated with new forms of test beds.

The third phase: repositioning

While the first phase was mainly consumer- and trust-driven, the second phase is driven mainly by regulations shaping a new landscape. The third phase, starting around 2020, will be technology-driven. Even though the possibilities are enormous, the time to implement and regulate the new technologies in the value chain will take some time compared to the digital innovations in the payment segment that were consumer-driven.

During this third phase, digitalization has disrupted traditional value chains and sources of competitive advantage as networks of partnerships have been constructed, middle hands have been slashed, innovative solutions have been created by cross-fertilizing across sectors, and digitalization has left no part of the value chain untouched. Additionally, a new customer group has emerged—Millennials—who are individualists, demanding transparency and tailored, artificial intelligence-enabled services through co-creation, and at the same time collectivists, preferring social platforms and digitalized trust, where the peers on the platforms replace the traditional middle hands.

Positioning

Looking 5 to 10 years ahead, a positive scenario for the traditional banks is that their value chain has been digitalized, with new technologies incorporated. Norms and organizational structures will have been transformed to a more networked structure with partnerships with FinTech actors, while the client databases will be open and secure, enabling the co-creation of services. The regulatory framework will be harmonized and secure, spurring more innovation in the FinTech industry, while Stockholm has positioned itself as the leading FinTech startup hub.

Our future forecast in this scenario is that at least a few of the large banks will survive and take a more dominant market position based on partnerships with and acquisitions of FinTech actors, potentially protected by the high costs of compliance and difficulty in following the regulatory environment. However, another scenario that might be more of a win for FinTech actors is that they partner with cross-sector companies, such as from the fast-moving consumer goods industry, that have higher trust capital than traditional banks, thereby making client reach wider for both sets of actors. In this scenario, traditional banks may become commodity providers, with client interfaces lost to FinTech actors or cross-sector actors, enabling these actors to achieve higher margins. Thus, the challenge for traditional banks to achieve the better scenario lies in their ability to implement partnerships and new technologies. Yet the process of the regulatory framework adapting to blockchain technology and artificial intelligence will take time, and there will be risks associated with high investments in these technologies. Nevertheless, these two technologies will be crucial for staying competitive. Successful banks will be those with leaders who are adept at organizational change and can ensure the appropriate organizational structure, culture, employee talent, and IT systems while creating value through the client database and artificial intelligence. Other issues include how well the bank ensures a high degree of trust among its partners and clients through acting transparently while offering P2P platforms within the ecosystem.

FinTech positioning

In terms of the four core areas of service offerings, the question arises as to which of these may be more attractive to the FinTechs to pursue. Within lending, while consumer loans can be provided by more digitalized solutions and a faster process, the fixed costs for the accompanying regulatory burden will most likely still remain and resources spent on compliance substantial. As a result, few traditional banks see a threat to their mortgage offering from new players. While mortgages are a commodity with low margins, the challenge for traditional banks is to keep the client interface and offer other services where higher margins could be gained. As the PSD2 changes the landscape by opening access to banks' client data, third-party FinTech actors, such as Lendo, are in the process of developing a more tailored digital offering that channels individuals to the best mortgage offering. However, we believe that the probability that such third parties become banks is low, as such action would demand a bank license and a high regulatory burden. Instead, we believe third-party actors will engage in valuable strategic partnerships with traditional banks.

As for lending through crowdfunding, consumer risk will most likely remain for some time due to asymmetric information. Similar to other sharing economy platforms, there is the potential that the traditional middleman will be replaced by a platform that transfers risk from the traditional middleman (the bank) to the peers on the platform through enabling digitalized trust among peers. This can be achieved through standards and insurance offerings, along with the implementation of blockchain technology. Perfect competition could occur on the platforms, for example, if an interest rate is auctioned on a digital platform. However, it might be that the digital trust in financial services (i.e., trust among peers replacing the traditional middleman) cannot counterbalance the asymmetric information related to these offerings. As noted above, asymmetric information has been identified as a crucial aspect to investigate in order to make regulation regarding P2P and crowdfunding more explicit and transparent.

Turning to insurance, traditional banks are usually an intermediate actor between the insurance company and the client. In the future as the Internet of Things (IoT) becomes more commonplace, client data gained through PSD2 combined with IoT and other behavioral data may provide digital actors working with artificial intelligence the ability to offer tailored and user-friendly insurance solutions. For example, the digital AI insurance startup Lemonade recently set a new world record on "payment for insurance claims." It took a customer just a couple of seconds from claiming a stolen jacket through Lemonade's digital app to receiving the money in his bank account. The future is still uncertain, though, in Sweden as the Swedish Law on Integrity (PUL) will be replaced by the GDPR—the new EU law on data protection—in May 2018, and higher compliance costs may increase entry barriers in this area.

As for savings, the Swedish FinTech startup Kollektiva is a social platform for pension savings that offers smart, automated digital services based on the collective intelligence among the platform's investors. Also, the savings app Dreams is offering their clients tailored personalized saving incentives based on a partnership with Ålandsbanken. When it comes to wealth management, even as the demand for more digital tools increases, investors still value human interaction. In a survey, almost 90 percent of investors stated that face-to-face communication is important for them in wealth management; however, in addition to physical meetings, younger investors expressed a high demand for convenient digital interaction (e.g., mobile calls, video calls, chat).

Payments are an attractive market for disruptors. These payment solutions typically sit on top of the existing infrastructure, which means the FinTech disruptors do not carry the cost of onboarding, fraud, network infrastructure, or credit risk. As banks starts to launch their own payment platforms with better experience, tighter integration to the clients' financial life, and tokenization, the competition in this segment will increase.

Despite the above digitalization across the four core areas, at this moment it is difficult to see how any new competitor from within or from another sector could compete with the traditional banks on all four core business areas for both individual consumers and corporates due to numerous entry barriers in both consumer and corporate sectors.

One factor that might change this is related to the development of blockchain technology. Most experts within the financial sector are in agreement that the financial infrastructure is about to experience significant changes due to blockchain technology, primarily because it enables decentralized, digitalized trust. One potential result is that entry barriers to the corporate offering in the financial sector may be significantly reduced.

However, as mentioned, a result of digital disruption is that traditional banks may become commodity providers with the resulting lower margins. One way to avoid this is to retain the client interface, yet the entry barriers to maintaining the client interface and client flows are falling, and will continue to do so due to PSD2. This is especially the case for FinTech actors who provide an interface or a middle hand between the client and the bank, and thus are not under the burden of banking regulation. This would also pave the way the way for a sharp attack from a potential one-point-of-entry actor, or an actor that would provide a single entry point to all financial and other services demanded by clients. Such an actor would need to create strategic partnerships with a number of established and new financial actors in order to raise the credibility that its point of entry is the one that best meets the client's financial needs. Furthermore, a significant competitive edge from being a one-point-of-entry actor would depend on the ability to use the client database combined with access to other cross-sector client databases such that real-time, tailored, and cheap digital AI-enabled products could be offered. One unknown is whether the younger generation would prefer a one-point-of-entry solution for banking and financial services, or if they would be more comfortable using a variety of different apps and platforms to search for the best individual set of services.

Concluding remarks

Digitalization, regulation, and shift in trust will be the main forces driving digital disruption in the financial sector during the three phases described above. From a government policy perspective, the focus should be on balancing the gains from digitalization against the risks associated with consumer protection and asymmetric information. Increased dialogue with the FinTech ecosystem, academia, and traditional banks are crucial, as well as test beds and labs for tighter collaboration and understanding of how new technology can be applied to the banking offer and infrastructure.

Bibliography

Brunet, E., 2017. *Swish, the secret Swedish FinTech payment company created by Nordic banks and used by 50% of Swedes is challenging Swedish unicorns.* [online] Medium. Available at: https://medium.com/@etiennebr/swish-the-secret-swedish-fintech-payment-company-created-by-nordic-banks-and-used-by-50-of-swedes-cfcf06f59d6f [Accessed September 12, 2017].

Crunchbase, 2017. *Crunchbase: Discover innovative companies and the people behind them.* [online] Available at: www.crunchbase.com [Accessed August 29, 2017].

IIS, 2017. *E-handel, betaltjänster och delningsekonomi [E-commerce, payment services, and the sharing economy].* [online] Available at: www.soi2016.se/e-handel-internet-bank-och-betaltjanster/mobilt-bankid-och-swish [Accessed September 12, 2017].

iZettle, 2011. *iZettle rings up €8.2 million ($11.2 million) in Series A funding.* [online] Available at: www.izettle.com/se/press/releases/55506386480/izettle-rings-up-e8-2-million-11-2-million-in-series-a-funding [Accessed September 12, 2017].

Larsson, D., 2016. *Bankernas digitalisering – en hype? [The bank's digitalization—a hype?].* [online] Expandtalk. Available at: https://expandtalk.se/bankernas-digitalisering [Accessed September 12, 2017].

Lundell, S., 2015. *44 miljoner kronor är spårlöst borta - styrelsen går till polisen [44 million crowns gone without a trace—the board goes to the police].* [online] Breakit. Available at: www.breakit.se/artikel/1568/44-miljoner-kronor-ar-sparlost-borta-styrelsen-gar-till-polisen [Accessed September 12, 2017].

Nordea, 2016. *Nordea teams up with FinTech startups again.* [online] Nordea Press Release. Available at: www.nordea.com/en/press-and-news/news-and-press-releases/press-releases/2016/05-12-08h00-nordea-teams-up-with-fintech-startups-again.html [Accessed August 28, 2017].

O'Hear, S., 2016. *Tink scores $10M for its virtual banking app.* [online] TechCrunch. Available at: https://techcrunch.com/2016/05/19/tink-scores-10m-for-its-virtual-banking-app [Accessed September 12, 2017].

Riksgälden, 2017. *Insättningsgarantin [The deposit guarantee].* [online] Available at: www.riksgalden.se/sv/Insattningsgarantin/Om_Insattningsgarantin [Accessed September 12, 2017].

Schonfeld, E., 2011. *Michael Moritz on Klarna's $155M round: "This is the public financing of twelve years ago."* [online] TechCrunch. Available at: https://techcrunch.com/2011/12/10/moritz-klarna [Accessed September 12, 2017].

SKI, 2016. *Svenskt Kvalitetsindex Bank och Finans [Swedish Bank and Finance Quality Index].* [online] Svenskt KvalitetsIndex. Available at: http://www.kvalitetsindex.se/report/bank-och-finans-2016 [Accessed January 16, 2018].

Stockholm Innovation, 2016. *Partners.* [online] Available at: www.stockholminnovation.com/om-sting/partners [Accessed September 12, 2017].

Swedish Bankers' Association, 2014. *Bankernas betydelse för Sverige [The role of banks in Sweden].* [online] Available at: www.swedishbankers.se/media/1001/1402bankernas_betydelse.pdf [Accessed September 12, 2017].

Swish, 2016. *Fem miljoner svenskar swishar! [Five million Swedes swish!].* [online] Available at: https://www.getswish.se/oldsite/getswish/wp-content/uploads/2016/10/20161121_Pressmeddelande_5milj.pdf [Accessed January 16, 2018].

Teigland, R., Ingram, C., Wesley-James, N., Bengtsson, T., and Lamberth, J., 2015. *Stockholm – Europe's No.2 FinTech city: A dynamic hub for innovative payment, funding, banking, and transaction technologies*. [online] Invest Stockholm. Available at: www.investstockholm.com/globalassets/2.-understartsidor-investment-opportunities/fintech/stockholm_fintech_report.pdf [Accessed January 16, 2018].

Wesley-James, N., Ingram, C., Källstrand, C., and Teigland, R., 2015. *Stockholm FinTech: An overview of the FinTech sector in the greater Stockholm Region*. [online] Available at: www.hhs.se/contentassets/b5823453b8fe4290828fcc81189b6561/stockholm-fintech---june-2015.pdf [Accessed January 16, 2018].

9 Clarifying the blurry lines of FinTech

Opening the Pandora's box of FinTech categorization[1]

Michal Gromek

Introduction

When a tourist in a city center is asking about the distance to any bus stop, despite best intentions, answers will vary. To receive a more accurate response, a clarification question would have to be asked: Which particular bus stop is needed? Or where does the person intend to go? This analogy reflects an existing lack of codification in the industry summarized under the umbrella term of the financial technology (FinTech) industry.

This chapter provides a comprehensive segmentation proposal of 110 financial technology ventures operating in the Greater Stockholm Area. The first section introduces the current state of classification of FinTech. The second section focuses on the categorization attempt of FinTech companies into five main categories and 69 subcategories. For reasons of transparency, the companies have been divided into corporate and private usage of FinTech. The last section represents a visualization of featured companies by adopting a model from the area of social sciences to FinTech industry needs.

The classification specified in this chapter is the result of a joint team effort of representatives from the Stockholm FinTech Hub, Nordic Tech List, NFT Ventures, PA Consulting, and academic researchers from the Stockholm School of Economics. This team has been formed to perform a classification of regional FinTech and incorporate the results into one joined FinTech portfolio that will be kept up to date. The final result has been incorporated into a continually updated interactive map available under the following directory: http://data.stockholmfin.tech/.

Lack of a unified codification of FinTech

Despite the common belief, the idea of FinTech can be dated back to the first half of the eighteenth century (Arner, Barberis, and Buckley, 2016) with the introduction of the telegraph in 1838 and the construction of the first transatlantic cable in 1866. Before the transatlantic cable, the connection between the old continent and the United States happened only via shipping. One century after the first transatlantic cable, the Barclays Bank introduced the first ATM in Enfield in the UK (Nicoletti, 2017).

This invention allowed the bank clients to perform cash withdrawal and deposit without involving a bank clerk, and might be potentially viewed as a beginning of the modern interaction between technology and finance. After the global financial crisis of 2008, and in addition to the digitalization of trust and globalization, the development of FinTech has benefited from two additional factors.

First, trust in current financial institutions has been "consistently at or near the bottom of any survey of public trust" (Flint, 2014). Second, the entry of the Millennials customer segment into the financial markets. *Forbes* reported a 2016 netnographic US study of Facebook, conducted on 70 million users aged 21–34, which concluded that only 8 percent of users trust financial institutions, and more than half do not know where to turn to for financial guidance (McGrady, 2016). Despite growing awareness, the term "FinTech" remains ambiguous. Its usage and classification are often a source of misperception as there is no doubt that measuring something that has not yet been defined has to be difficult. The term FinTech refers mostly to startup companies that provide a service as a facilitator between financial services and technology providers. When compared with traditional financial products, the objective of FinTech products is to offer solutions including as many of the following advantages as possible: more automated, transparent, time-saving, offering better user experience and efficiency, as well as having a price advantage (Dorfleitner et al., 2017, p.5).

The growth of FinTech has become a subject of debate among researchers, practitioners, capital providers, and authorities, and it attracts growing public interest. The importance of FinTech grew with the increase of investments. Already in 2014, massive amounts of investments in FinTech ventures placed Stockholm as the third largest city in Europe by 2014 investment volume. In total, FinTech has received one-third of all of the investments made into limited liability companies (Wesley-James et al., 2015).

Growing interests in FinTech led to an unprecedented amount of industry reports describing and interpreting the phenomenon. The existence of various reports with contradictory FinTech methodology occurs not only in Sweden, but also in a global context. The lack of a commonly accepted definition has implications for robustness. While comparing two recent reports about the size of investment rounds into British FinTech ventures, two comparable industry reports display a difference of USD 80 million (Dealroom, 2016; Pitchbook, 2016). Zooming into Sweden, comparing two reports on the investments performed into the FinTech companies in the Greater Stockholm Area, the Dealroom report and the Stockholm School of Economics report 2015, displays a discrepancy of USD 50 million for the exact same location and period. This difference approaches 20 percent of the total investment values into Swedish FinTech ventures (Wesley-James et al., 2015).

The reasons for such a variety of outputs are traced back to a lack of a unified codification of FinTech. Furthermore, while reviewing the methodology sections of industry reports, it is hard to clarify what branches of business can or cannot be accounted as parts of FinTech industry.

City Bank's FinTech Report, *Digital Disruption Revised*, released in February 2017, does not define FinTech, but creates the following subcategories (Citi GPS, 2017):

- lending;
- payments;
- blockchain;
- insurance
- wealth management;
- enterprise finance; and
- RegTech.

McConnell et al.'s (2016) annual report on FinTech displays not only different investment values, but extends to the following subcategories of FinTech:

- robo-advisors;
- enterprise software;
- payments;
- online payments;
- stock and options;
- mobile lending
- lending;
- wealth management;
- personal finance; and
- asset marketplace.

Even in the previous reports on the Regional FinTech ecosystem, the fastest-growing subcategory between 2015 and 2016 was defined as "other types of FinTech" (Wesley-James et al., 2015). To display the complexity of a classification attempt, we use two examples: one from the payment and transaction, and one from the crowdfunding industry.

Toborrow.se: capital debt provider, crowdfunding company, or a wealth management tool?

Toborrow.se was founded in 2013 allowing lenders to provide loans to small enterprises and receive interest on the repayments while accepting the risk of default. Toborrow.se would qualify into three out of five main categories:

- *Lending*: From the borrower's perspective, the core revenue stream of Toborrow.se originates in the intermediary services that connect lenders willing to lend their money to companies incorporated in Sweden that need debt financing.

- *Wealth management*: From the lenders' perspective, the interest rates on Toborrow.se might result in a higher rate of return on their total financial wealth in comparison to bank deposit rates or risk-free government bond rates. From the lenders' perspective, Toborrow.se helps in managing their savings, so it is a wealth management tool.
- *Crowdfunding*: As defined in Chapter 12 in this volume, Toborrows.se collects funds from numerous capital providers and channels them to those who have financing needs.

The Stockholm-based unicorn[2] Klarna serves as a payment method for e-commerce while actually providing microcredit to consumers. Some 40 percent of the Swedish population of 10 million has used Klarna, primarily for e-commerce purchases (Milne, 2014).

Similar to Toborrow.se, the classification of Klarna depends on the particular usage of their services:

- *From the position of an e-commerce shop*: Klarna is a payment method like Visa or Mastercard. The e-commerce shop pays a setup fee and 1.5–3 percent per transaction. Using the angle of the e-commerce merchant means that Klarna would be classified as a payment and transaction FinTech venture in the subcategory of payment method.
- *Payment service provider*: One of Klarna's offerings includes not only a payment method, but an entire checkout software that allows e-commerce platforms to use a range of payment methods, including both Klarna and credit cards. Following this path, Klarna could be classified still in the payment and transfers category, but in the subcategory of payment service provider.
- *Consumer perspective*: Klarna is a microcredit provider as the user can purchase goods, services, or technology, but has to pay back to Klarna with a short time commitment. Klarna charges for late payments. Using the angle of the consumer, Klarna would be placed into the capital equity, debt provider as a consumer lending provider.

Similar output, different processes as compared to a bank

As FinTech represents an umbrella term for business models and products, it is impossible to define the term FinTech using a foundation legislation or legal documents. In order to be able to classify Swedish financial technology ventures correctly, it is important to underline how the services, technology, and products differ from traditional financial intermediaries such as banks.

The differences in the business process of financial products can be described in the examples of Wikipedia and Britannica. Both Wikipedia and the publishing house Britannica had the same goal statement: to deliver the most accurate source of knowledge to both consumers and legal entities. Britannica was reaching this statement with a pipe drive business model that was based on a team of carefully selected experts, who edited, delivered, and provided content to its encyclopedias. Wikipedia, on the other hand, relies on a platform-based business model, the internal motivation of its users, and the wisdom of crowds. Despite a common misperception, in a study conducted by Harvard Business School, Britannica and Wikipedia display a similar level of political bias toward particular keywords (Greenstein and Zhu, 2016).

Given the differences between Wikipedia and Britannica, their services are being used for the same purpose—to reinsure the end user about a meaning of a particular keyword. FinTech allows customers, both physical and legal entities, to receive a similar service to the one they acquired in the past from banks. Such services allow the users to deposit, withdraw, and transfer cash, pay invoices, exchange currencies, or engage in investment activity.

FinTech companies provide the same output to the end customer, but use a different process than the banks, similar to the difference between the Wikipedia and Britannica analogy.

FinTech is a tool, not a destination

For centuries, individuals desired to explore distant destinations. For around 30 years now, low-cost airlines have been making this travel affordable and possible for a larger group of individuals. In research, we refer to "transaction costs,"[3] which is a fee that has to be paid by an individual to a third-party provider to fulfill a particular desire. A flight ticket price from Stockholm to a distant country capital paid to a travel agency would be an example of such a transaction cost. Instead of paying directly to an airline, the individual needs to assume an additional cost and pay a higher price to a travel agency. In the past, to travel from Sweden to Japan, travelers had to organize every part of the trip by themselves. The complexity of finding a connection, high transaction costs, and the duration of travel discouraged many people from traveling.

The growth of FinTech—similar to that of low-cost carriers—didn't happen overnight. Availability and access to the Internet, and the digitalization of trust (Diekhöner, 2016) supported the recent acceleration of FinTech, together with the introduction of Bitcoin cryptocurrency (Skinner, 2016). How are FinTech firms using Bitcoin, blockchain, and mobile technologies to create the Internet of Value? Increased accessibility of the Internet, the global financial crisis of 2008, and digitalization are only some of the fundamental parts that allowed FinTech to reach its current position. The introduction of FinTech has increased efficiency and lowered transaction costs, and made financial transactions between different parties more accessible and user-friendly. Despite some successes, traditional financial players—such as the peer-to-business application Swish—did not yet exhaust the possibility to improve their service along the lines of the FinTech portfolio (Mackenzie, 2015).

Analogous to a low-cost airline, both cost considerations and some effort are needed before traveling. FinTech, and its underlying subcategories, is just a "tool" of how particular financial transaction are being facilitated. These new entrants to financial services propose more efficient solutions than conventionally performed by traditional providers such as banks, insurance companies, asset managers, and payments and credit card companies (Scardovi, 2016). FinTech ventures services or technologies have been, generally speaking,[4] more secure, more convenient, quicker, and can be customized or operated at a lower cost than a traditional financial product. FinTech as a facilitator that lowers the cost of transactions incorporates process improvements, and is characterized by high efficiency, flexibility, and innovation. FinTech could be viewed as a financial service that uses technology to satisfy the finance needs of tomorrow (Dapp, 2014).

Despite the difference in business processes and models of value creation, the fundamental purposes of financial transactions remain the same. Users still would like to transfer payments, manage wealth, and pay their bills. Thus, users still need the same services as provided by banks, so their classification should be performed as close to the existing banking products as possible.

Houston, what is your solution to our problem?

As the FinTech world in the greater Stockholm region "is an expanding galaxy" (Nicoletti, 2017), the goal is to create a visualization of the complexity of the FinTech industry from the perspective of an individual user as well as small and medium enterprises. As most of the FinTech companies have some particular, features in common, there will always be enough exceptions for rendering them adequately to produce a general definition. For example, despite the fact that FinTech companies are being mostly associated with startups, companies such as Klarna or iZettle are not startups, so this category cannot be an essential part of the definition (Dorfleitner et al., 2017).

A significant amount of FinTech companies remain obscure for the general user. Those companies, such as the payment service provider Mondido.com, help to process credit card payments in the background while an individual user buys e-commerce products online. Other companies exchange cryptocurrencies, allow transferring currencies, or provide back-end services for FinTech companies.[5] Despite a low visibility of the businesses that provide back-end services, those "background companies" are a vivid part of the FinTech ecosystem.

All of the companies that have been reviewed for the purpose of this segment had to fulfill the following criteria:

- ✓ Be incorporated in the form of a Swedish legal entity with a registration address in the Greater Stockholm Area by May 1, 2017.
- ✓ Enabling financial transaction on the intersection between technology and financial industry, while providing innovation via application, front-end or back-end services.
- ✓ Provide services, listed in detail in the following section of this chapter, that have been traditionally performed by traditional financial industry players.

The following types of companies have been excluded:

- Regulatory technology ventures and behavioral biometrics companies that are supporting FinTech companies, such as BankID, as they are being used for user authentication purposes, but don't have a "FIN-ancial" component. Those companies have been the subject to a report launched in Q4 2017.
- Companies performing innovation in the field of accounting, receipts, and salary payments.
- Enterprises performing services in the field of consulting.
- Enterprises that produce hardware exclusively for existing solutions, for example ATM, credit, and debit card providers.
- Traditional financial companies performing services to a broad spectrum of financial companies, for example debt collection and debt recovery services.
- Companies performing business in the Greater Stockholm Area that don't have a legal incorporation.
- Co-working spaces and business environment institutions, such as the Stockholm FinTech Hub.
- Companies that perform their businesses in Sweden but do not have a legal entity in Sweden, for example the Swedish crowdfunding platform Invesdor.com.

The following data sources have been used for this exploratory study:

- ✓ Data from members of the Stockholm FinTech Hub.
- ✓ Companies monitored by the Nordic Tech List.
- ✓ Companies that have been mapped by researchers from the Stockholm School of Economics, Center of Strategy and Competitiveness, during the preparation of previous reports, such as the Stockholm FinTech Report 2015 and the Stockholm FinTech Report 2016.
- ✓ Netnographic review via social media groups, Facebook groups, and LinkedIn groups.
- ✓ Press landscape mapping, including major international and Swedish media.
- ✓ Qualitative studies during interviews for this publication and the Stockholm FinTech Report 2018

User-facing FinTech circles

> We cannot solve problems with the same thinking we used to create them.
>
> —Albert Einstein

As the "focus group" members found it unreasonable to find an existing matrix that would incorporate the objective of this study, it was decided to incorporate and adopt two models from the field of psychology. Using an airplane analogy, every passenger on a plane from Stockholm to Tokyo might have a different reason to travel to Japan, but they still use the same type of transport on a scheduled flight. According to the airline's division, the passengers are being grouped into two classes of travel, economy and business, despite their travel purpose being work or leisure—similar to the economy and business class. As stated in the previous section, FinTech companies can be perceived differently, conditional on the angle of the observer. Two circles of Stockholm FinTech have been grouped in a user-centric view. The first circle is reserved for individual users, who would like to use the services of FinTech ventures for personal purposes. The second circle has been reserved for corporations and legal entities that would use the services for corporate purposes, including traditional financial industry players.

The initial visualization has been built upon the model of the zone of proximal development (see Figure 9.1), which was popularized by the psychologist Lev Vygotsky (1896–1934) (Daniels, Cole, and Wertsch, 2007). This model has attracted attention from psychologists and educators, which has directed their education work toward new ground.

Vygotsky's main idea was to place the "learner" (in his example, a child) at the center of the circle. In the visualization used for FinTech, the learner has been replaced with the "user."

He argued that the learner can't reach the outskirts of the circle without the support of a teacher or a guide. In his assumption, some tasks were too difficult to reach for the user alone, but could be mastered with the guidance and assistance of adults or more skilled, usually older, children (Hook, Watts, and Cockcroft, 2002).

In the adoption of his model, it is argued that FinTech companies that perform back-end services are only visible with the support of companies that are facing the customer with the front-end services. Companies that face the customer are the "guide" that helps the user to reach the outskirts of FinTech services, which are in the zone of proximal development between the user and back-end companies.

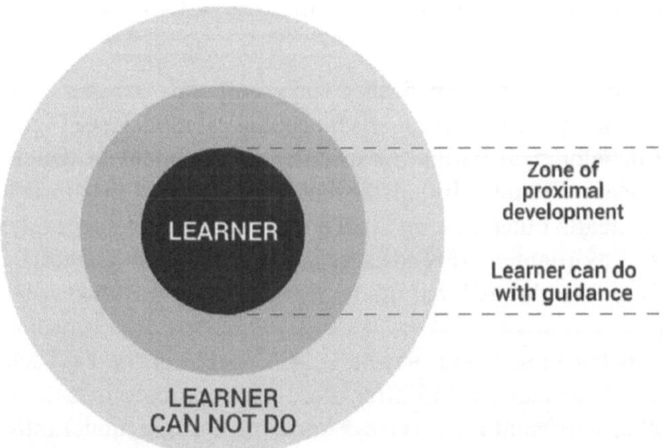

Figure 9.1 Zone of proximal development (ZPD)

Source: Adapted from Lev Vygostsky, design by Adam Strandberg.

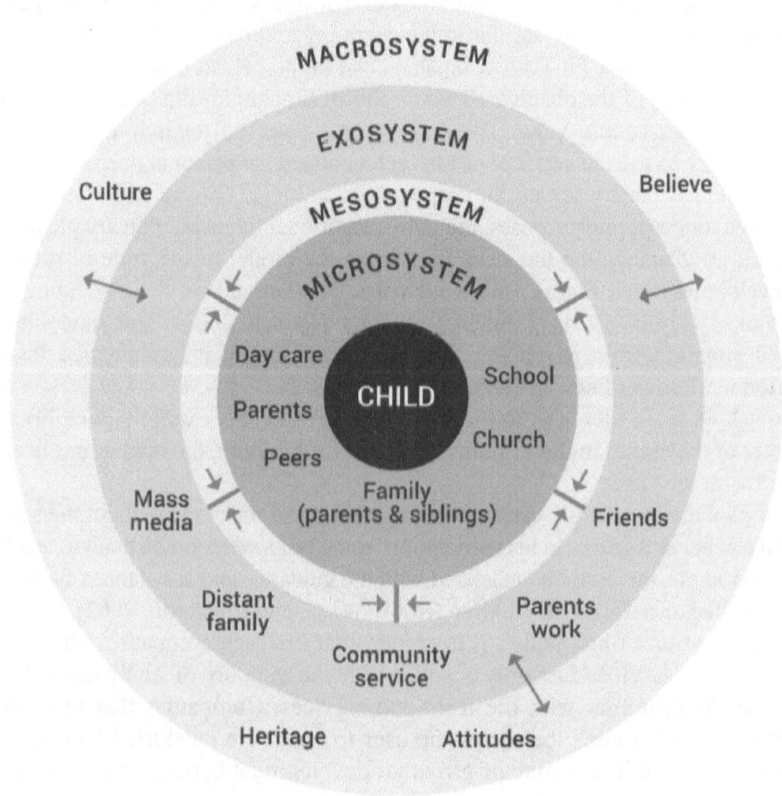

Figure 9.2 Bronfenbrenner's bioecological model

Source: Adapted from Bronfenbrenner's bioecological model, design by Adam Stranberg.

It was decided to move one step further and incorporate aspects of another model used in psychology, Bronfenbrenner's bioecological model (see Figure 9.2), which studied a development within a particular environment in which users (in his example, again children) live. Bronfenbrenner argued that interactions determine specific health outcomes, and that a well-established cooperation can benefit the entire environment (Freudenberg, Klitzman, and Saegert, 2009). Bronfenbrenner's model claimed that the borders between different parties are relatively blurry.

The blurriness between different players is also visible in the FinTech environment, as many companies tend to offer more than one type of solution and influence each other with multiple services. Additionally, this model introduces the proximal process to the structure.

Bronfenbrenner names four layers that are surrounding the environment of each user:

- *The center of the circle*: The placement of the child or, in the FinTech model, the user.
- *Microsystem*: The closest surrounding to a family/user. Translated in the FinTech model to companies that interact with the user directly.
- *Mesosystem*: More distant aspects of the user—in Bronfenbrenner's model, families' friends, mass media, extended family. Translated to companies that perform mostly background services, rarely visible to the user.
- *Exosystem*: Bronfenbrenner identified this layer as a broad ideology that includes laws and customers of one's culture, as well as a social class. Translated into our model as FinTech enterprises that perform back-end services or supply the infrastructure but are not visible to the user.[6]

As argued previously, FinTech companies do not necessarily provide new services, but rather focus on providing them more efficiently. The subcategories of FinTech have been kept as close as possible to the services provided by banks.

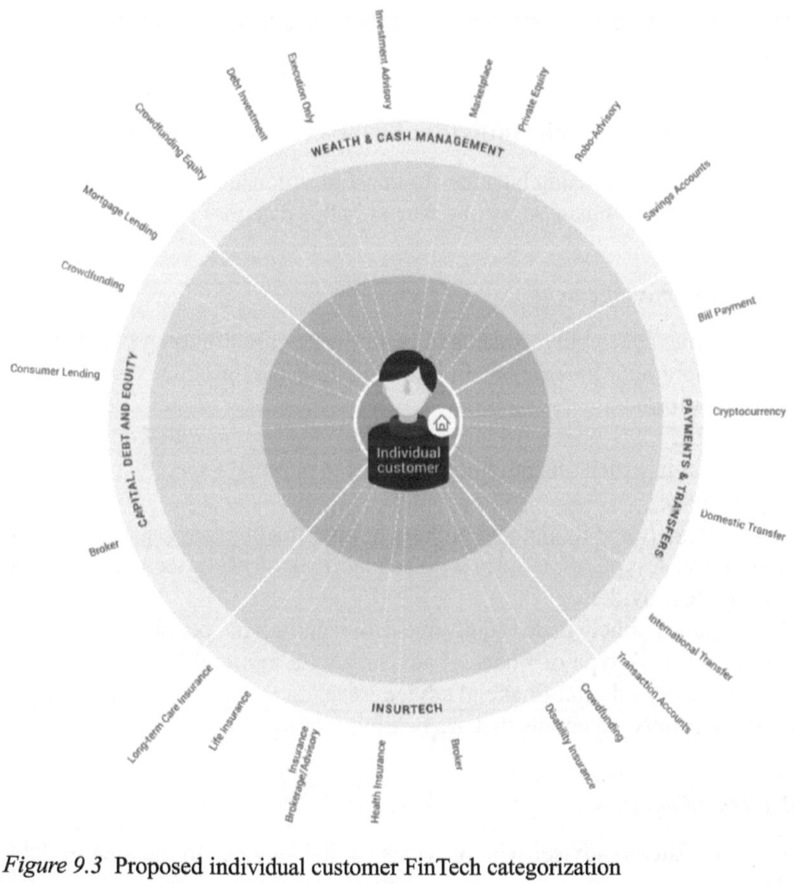

Figure 9.3 Proposed individual customer FinTech categorization

Source: Own creation, design by Adam Strandberg.

The categorization mostly overlaps in both the corporate and individual circles. Similar to traditional banking, some categories (such as clearing technology or hedging) have been reserved for corporate customers only.

Furthermore, on the matrix, the companies have been organized according to five additional classes:

- Business-to-business (B2B) companies that serve explicitly legal entities, for example payment service providers such as Mondido.
- Business-to-consumer (B2C) businesses that deliver services to individual users, for example the cryptocurrency exchange platform Safello.com.
- Consumer-to-consumer (C2C) companies that perform services between individual users, such as the peer-to-peer application Swish.
- Consumer-to-business (C2B) enterprises that empower the consumer to perform a transaction for companies, for example the real estate crowdfunding platform Tessin.se, which enables users to invest in real estate projects.

Companies performing their services using blockchain technology have been marked specially.

Individual-facing FinTech: individual user-centric visualization

FinTech companies conducting business-to-consumer, consumer-to-business, and consumer-to-consumer business will be placed in this category (see Figure 9.3).

Wealth and cash management

- ✓ *Crowdfunding equity*: Investments in equity via a crowdfunding platform.
- ✓ *Crowdfunding debt investment*: Investments in a loan product via a crowdfunding platform.
- ✓ *Execution only*: Services introduced by a financial regulator that describe the sales process in which the individual chooses to purpose a specific instrument without advice.
- ✓ *Investment advisory*: Registered brokers in investment products.
- ✓ *Marketplace*: A type of platform with products, services, or technology from third service providers.
- ✓ *Private equity*: Publicly traded equity and debt securities in operating enterprises.
- ✓ *Robo-advisory*: A type of financial advisory with minimal human intervention that provides digital financial advice based on mathematical algorithms.
- ✓ *Savings accounts*: Accounts that are bearing interest.

Capital debt and equity

- ✓ *Broker*: Registered adviser who provides capital services in the area of debt and equity.
- ✓ *Consumer lending*: Debt capital seeking products for individuals.

- ✓ *Crowdfunding*: Individuals might use donation, reward and lending products for individuals.
- ✓ *Mortgage lending*: Products supporting or facilitating real estate lending.

Payments and transfers

- ✓ *Bill payment*: Support in payments of liabilities such as bills or invoices.
- ✓ *Cryptocurrency*: Exchange, storage, and transfers of cryptocurrencies.
- ✓ *Domestic transfer*: Domestic monetary transfers in various currencies.
- ✓ *International transfer*: International monetary transfers and remittances in various currencies.
- ✓ *Transaction accounts*: Escrow, checking, transaction accounts, similar to a bank account.

InsurTech

- ✓ *Crowdfunding*: Allows a crowd to join in an insurance project and insure each other.
- ✓ *Customer acquisition*: Services as an additional sales channel.
- ✓ *Disability insurance*: Protecting from a physical or mental condition that limits a person's movement, senses, or activities.
- ✓ *Health insurance*: Covers costs of medical care.
- ✓ *Insurance brokerage/advisory*: Advises users on offers from insurance providers.
- ✓ *Life insurance*: Protects against financial loss that results from premature death.
- ✓ *Property and casualty insurance*: Covers legal liability costs of property and casualty, such as car and home insurance.
- ✓ *Long-term care insurance*: Covers costs of long-term care not covered by health insurance or public insurance.

The following categories have been suggested for corporate-centric FinTech (see Figure 9.4).

Those services performed by FinTech companies serve legal entities and corporations in one of the following subsegments:

Wealth and cash management

- ✓ *Debt collection*: Services in the field of collecting and purchasing accounts receivable.
- ✓ *Factoring/invoice trading*: Manages debt owned by others.
- ✓ *Forex (FX)*: Currency trading services.
- ✓ *Investment management*: Services to archive a particular investment goal, connected with the buying or selling of investments in a particular portfolio.
- ✓ *Liquidity management*: Services to limit risks between the cash on hand and outstanding accounts payable.

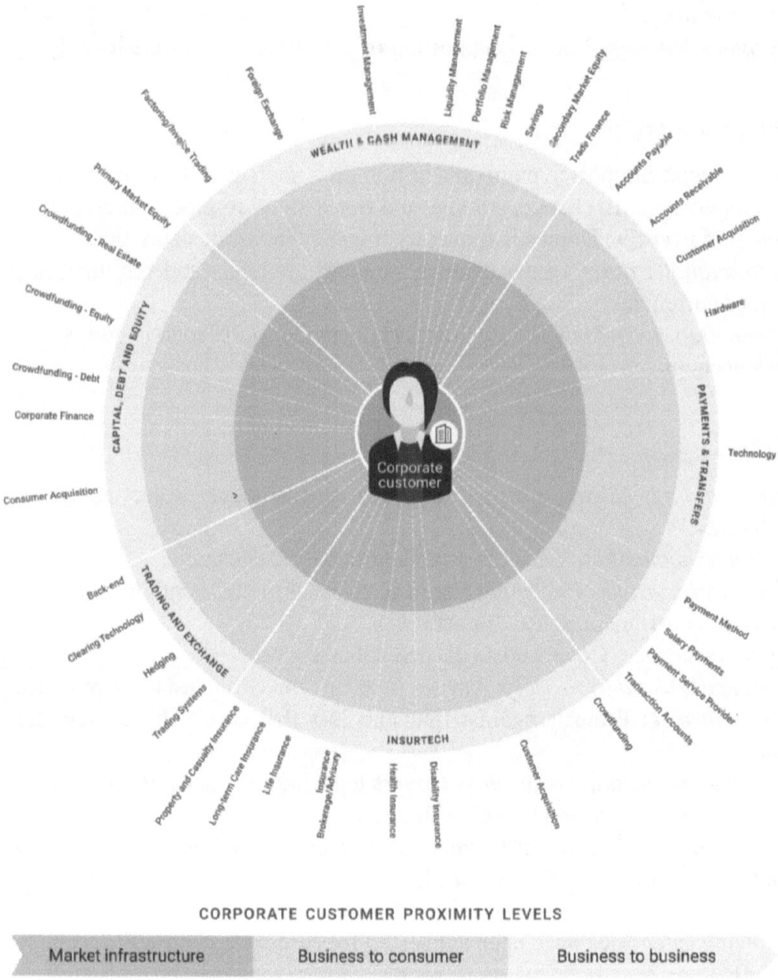

Figure 9.4 Proposed corporate customer FinTech categorization

Source: Own creation, design by Adam Strandberg.

- ✓ *Portfolio management*: Passive investments into an umbrella of securities in a portfolio with the goal to receive a rate of return.
- ✓ *Risk management*: Services that identify, manage, and control threats to earnings.
- ✓ *Savings*: Allows corporate partners to optimize savings accounts.
- ✓ *Secondary market equity*: Buying and selling established investments in equity.
- ✓ *Trade finance*: Process to perform investments into specific investments such as debt and issuing letters of credit.

Capital, debt, and equity

- ✓ *Consumer acquisition*: Offers additional channels to acquire new customers.
- ✓ *Corporate finance*: Increases the value for the shareholder and supports the improvement of the capital structure.
- ✓ *Crowdfunding real estate*: Allows financing real estate projects with the support of the crowd.
- ✓ *Crowdfunding debt*: Funding with a debt investment from the crowd.
- ✓ *Crowdfunding equity*: Funding with an equity investment from the crowd.
- ✓ *Primary market equity*: Funding into primary equity of companies.

Payments and transfers

- ✓ *Accounts payable*: Provides services in the areas of outstanding liabilities to the clients.
- ✓ *Accounts receivable*: Provides services in the fields of outstanding liabilities by clients.
- ✓ *Customer acquisition*: Offers additional channels to acquire new customers.
- ✓ *Payment method*: Type of compensation that is accepted by the buyer and seller.
- ✓ *Payment service provider*: Provides services for accepting a range of payment methods.
- ✓ *Technology*: Services in the field of payment and transfers technology.
- ✓ *Transaction accounts*: Escrow, checking, transaction accounts, similar to a bank account.

InsurTech

- ✓ *Crowdfunding*: Allows customers to join in an insurance project and insure each other.
- ✓ *Customer acquisition*: Services as an additional sales channel.
- ✓ *Disability insurance*: Protecting users from a physical or mental condition that limits a person's movement, senses, or activities.
- ✓ *Health insurance*: Covers costs of medical care.
- ✓ *Insurance brokerage/advisory*: Advises users on offers from insurance providers.
- ✓ *Life insurance*: Protects against financial loss that results from premature death.
- ✓ *Property and casualty insurance*: Covers legal liability costs of property and casualty, such as car and home insurance.
- ✓ *Long-term care insurance*: Covers costs of long-term care not covered by health insurance or public insurance.

Trading and exchange

- ✓ *Back end*: Technology services performed in the background, such as servers and CRM systems.
- ✓ *Clearing technology*: Services between payers' account and payees' account.

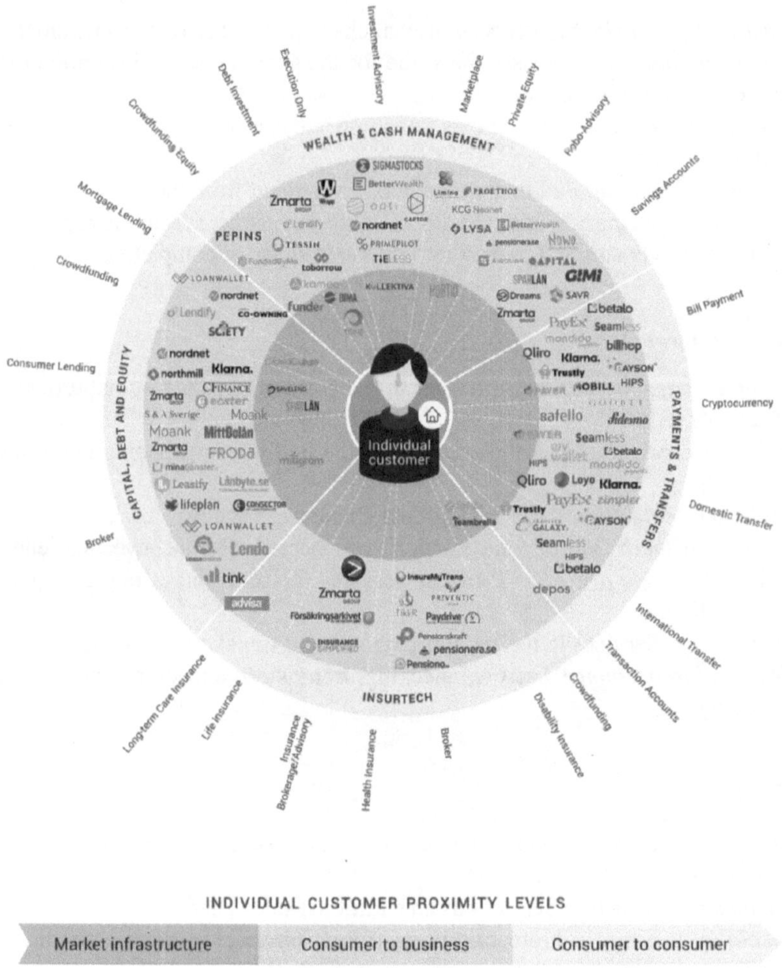

Figure 9.5 Proposed allocation of FinTech companies from the Greater Stockholm Area that serve individual clients

Source: Own creation, design by Adam Strandberg.

- ✓ *Hedging*: Services in the field of risk management strategy to limit probability of loss.
- ✓ *Trading systems*: Specifies entry and exit rules for participation in equity projects.

Individual-facing circle

This displays a fairly distributed spread of FinTech companies' throughout different sub-segments of different subsections (see Figure 9.5).

The distribution of the companies clearly demonstrates that larger amounts of businesses are active mostly in the consumer-to-business field, and less in the consumer-to-consumer areas:

- *Payments and transfers*: FinTech enterprises in this area exclusively focus on the interaction between business and consumers, primarily in the fields of bill payment and domestic transfers. The field of international transfers and the level of consumer-to-consumer payments have not reached their potentials yet.

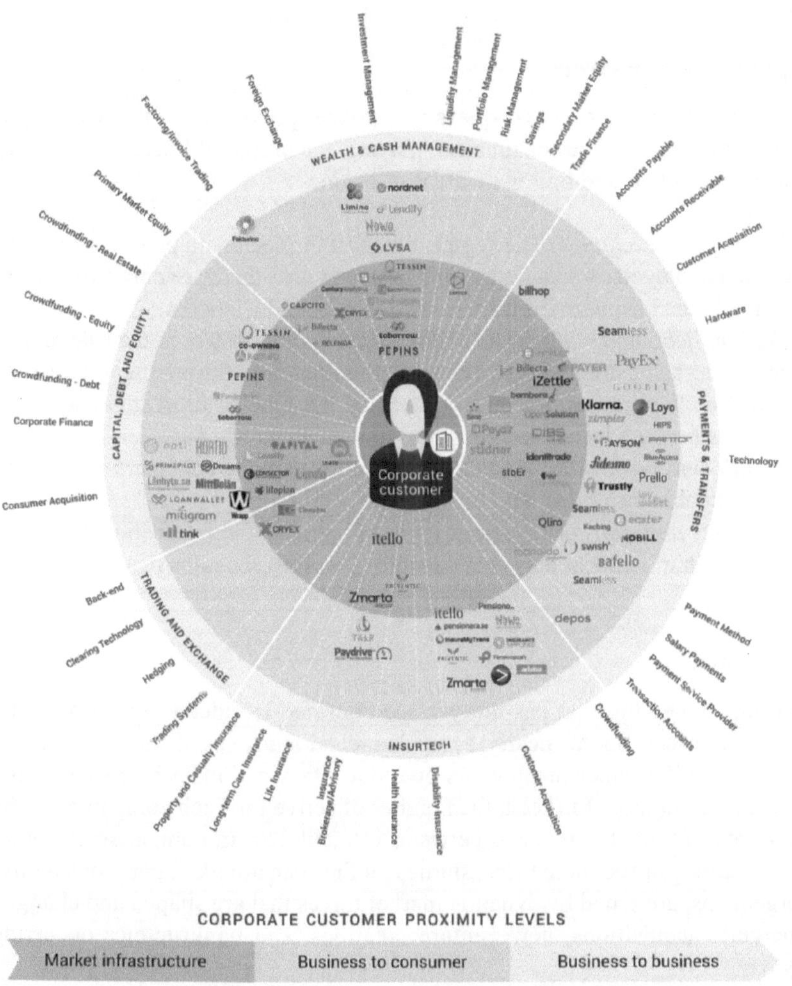

Figure 9.6 Proposed allocation of FinTech companies from the Greater Stockholm Area that serve small and medium enterprises

Source: Own creation, design by Adam Strandberg.

- *InsurTech*: Still remains a novel phenomenon. Companies in this subsection of FinTech taxonomy have concentrated around the brokerage and insurance advisory. One company, Teambrella, offers blockchain-based insurance crowdfunding services, which are relatively difficult to categorize.
- *Capital debt and equity*: This field remains dominated by companies that are active in the field of consumer lending and brokerage.
- *Wealth and cash management*: Both areas defined as "execution only" and "marketspaces" have been less exposed to FinTech involvement. The concentration of FinTech remains most potent in the area of savings accounts, with equity crowdfunding remaining the most active subsection.

Corporate-facing circle

As this circle (see Figure 9.6) displays the services provided by FinTech companies for other legal entities or financial players, the proposed FinTech taxonomy has been concentrated to four main areas of business:

- *Trading and exchange*: The segmentation of FinTech with precisely the fewest active players. According to this initial review, there are only two players active in the business-to-business field, Cryex and Cinnober.
- *Capital, debt, and equity*: The contraction remains clearly in the category of consumer acquisition and sections of crowdfunding. Surprisingly, all of the crowdfunding companies, independent of the type of crowdfunding, offer services for both business-to-business and business-to-consumer.
- *Wealth and cash management*: Reviews an explicit concentration on the investment management level.
- *Payments and transfers*: Various types of national and international transactions, both in terms of accounts payable as well as accounts receivable.

Conclusions

Measuring something that has not yet been defined is indeed very "difficult." Since the FinTech boom, nearly every launched study, published report, and released scientific paper displays its own definition of FinTech. Based on the different definitions of FinTech, the number of active FinTech companies in the greater area of Stockholm varies between 110 and 220. In comparison to other academic areas, say econometrics, studies on FinTech are like operations on living organisms, governed by dynamic market forces that are shaped and changed by mergers, acquisitions, new venture creations, and bankruptcies occurring every day.

Regulators have not always been cheerleaders of new financial products as their responsibility is to ensure investor protections, well-functioning markets, and efficient capital allocation. The development of FinTech has modified the cooperation between regulators and startups. In the same realm as the financial market regulators, finding unknown paths to new challenges has led to the incorporation of two models from psychology—the zone of proximal development and Bronfenbrenner's bioecological model—to modify them to two FinTech user-centric circles. User circles have been dedicated to the individual user and others to legal entities and corporations. These models can help display the clear usability of FinTech for those two different user groups and show clustering of companies.

This chapter displays a bold attempt to classify FinTech companies by members of the Stockholm FinTech Hub, Nordic Tech List, and NFT Ventures, with support from members of the PA Consulting team. It not only incorporates two models from psychology into FinTech, but also displays two aspects of FinTech:

- A customer-centric circle, with consumer-to-consumer and consumer-to-business services facing individual clients.
- A corporate-centric circle, with business-to-consumer and business-to-business services.

Firstly, a joint session of practitioners, academics, representatives of consulting companies, venture capital firms, and a FinTech business environment intuition drafted the initial categorization criteria. Secondly, it is argued that the user receives a financial service similar to the one offered by a bank or other traditional financial providers, in the same way that Wikipedia and Britannica feature the same keywords in their search results to resolve a request. Lastly, the financial aspect didn't change; customers still receive and transfer money, pay their bills, and purchase items online. What has changed, or rather "upgraded," is the fact that FinTech allows customers to receive the same services in a more user-friendly, accessible, cheaper, and/or faster way. Ideally, one would combine all of those adjectives into one FinTech service. It is not the technology that is subject to the regulation, but the application of that particular technology to garner new users. It has been reasoned that the categorization of FinTech changes depending on the angle of the user. The different angels of legal entities collaborating with FinTech and individuals collaborating with FinTech have been the motivation to create two "user-centric circles of FinTech." With regard to companies, a particular service can be defined in a different way.

To account for the complexity, research categorization assumptions and FinTech development in the Greater Stockholm Area have different goals. Economics and business administration remain a social science, as companies have often formed a portfolio of services and products that are being offered for a different type of customers; consequently, allocating FinTech companies into particular sections remains a mix of exploration and experimentation.

Three examples of challenges in FinTech classification:

- The Stockholm-based unicorn Klarna serves as a payment method for e-commerce while actually providing microcredit to consumers while being a payment method.

- The company Teambrella offers crowdfunded insurance for individuals based on blockchain technology.
- Debt investment company Toborrow.se allows Swedish small and medium enterprises to take loans from individuals and legal entities. For businesses, it serves either as a debt capital provider or as an investment possibility, as companies and individuals can manage their investments while providing debt to those who need capital on Toborrow.se.

Nevertheless, the outcome of a particular FinTech product is similar to traditional banking. As FinTech users demand the same services, but in an "upgraded" way, it has been decided to keep the division of FinTech as close as possible to the current portfolio of banking services. This means that FinTech companies have been defined as those that are finding innovative ways to blend finance and technology within the business functions that are offered by a full-service bank. FinTech allows customers, both physical and legal entities, to receive similar services to those traditionally provided by banks. Such services allow the users to deposit, withdraw, and transfer cash, pay invoices, exchange currencies, or perform investment activities. FinTech enterprises' goal is to offer their customers solutions that are more automated, transparent, provide better user experience, are more efficient, offer a competitive price, and save time.

Additional companies offering these services or supporting FinTech ventures in their daily business have to include a financial component to the online interface or application. This requirement excludes:

- Business environment institutions, such as the Stockholm FinTech Hub or Swedfin.
- RegTech (regulatory technology) ventures, such as the Swedish authentication service BankID, as those services help to authenticate or limit fraud, but don't perform a "FIN" technology.
- Accounting innovation services, such as the receipt innovation system from Wint.se, as those services have to connect to traditional banking providers to perform this particular bookkeeping.
- Debt collection and debt recovery services, ATM producers, and card manufacturers, as both individuals and corporate customers do not tend to purchase such a service directly from a bank.

Recommendations

Two circles that feature individuals and corporations, facing circles of FinTech in the Greater Stockholm Area, displayed the current stage of businesses activity in particular subfields. Stockholm's FinTech companies tend to cluster in particular fields (such as payments), while not competing in a wider range of areas.

Those areas might indicate potential near-future scenarios for FinTechs, as well as point to possible challenges that may limit the growth of FinTech.

The free spaces with a non-FinTech presence on displayed circles might capture the attention of regulators, capital providers, and representatives of public authorities. This signals the upcoming fields of development that regulators might approach in the near future.

Intriguingly, while focusing on the visualization charts with displayed logotypes of companies, it is more compelling to concentrate on a large number of empty categories and subcategories. There are those categories that display potential future fields of development for regional FinTech companies and picture a potential market opportunity for potential founders. Alternatively, the empty field might send signals of a particular regulatory obstacle, which indicates avoiding developing a range of businesses in a particular area.

Representatives of the academic community might question the assumptions and demand restructuring of this division to increase methodological robustness. Representatives of companies that have not been included in this categorization might contact the team at innovative.internet@hhs.se or add their businesses using the website http://data.stockholmfin.tech.

Notes

1 This chapter includes data collected and processed in the 2018 Stockholm FinTech Report. Reprinted with full permission from Stockholm School of Economics (SSE).

2 Unicorn remains as an industry term defining a high-tech startup company that reaches a valuation of at least USD 1 billion within 10 years.

3 The term "transaction costs" refers mostly to financial transactions. For example, when buying an apartment, real estate suppliers and real estate buyers have to pay a fee to the real estate agents, as well as tax to the state. Both these types of fees are transaction costs.

4 Not all FinTech companies have been successful. More on the challenges and failures is found in Chapter 19 in this volume.

5 Front end involves every aspect that a user can see on an online platform, such as the icons, the colors, and the login process. Back end includes everything that the user can not see, such as data storage, databases, and servers.

6 Bronfenbrenner specifies in his modeling one more layer, called "chronosystem," that underlines the changes in personal environment over time. Translated in the FinTech model as business environment institutions or regulatory technology ventures, which will be a part of the next report, launched by Q1 2018.

Bibliography

Arner, D.W., Barberis, J., and Buckley, R.P., 2016. *The evolution of FinTech: A new post-crisis paradigm?* [online] Available at: https://papers.ssrn.com/sol3/papers.cfm?abstract_id=2676553 [Accessed December 12, 2017].

Citi GPS, 2017. *Citi GPS: digital disruption revisited—what FinTech VC investments tell us about a changing industry*. [online] Available at: www.privatebank.citibank.com/

home/fresh-insight/citi-gps-digital-disruption-revisited.html [Accessed December 11, 2017].

Daniels, H., Cole, M., and Wertsch, J.V., 2007. *The Cambridge companion to Vygotsky*. Cambridge: Cambridge University Press.

Dapp, T., 2014. FinTech: The digital (r)evolution in the financial sector. *DB Research*, [online] p.39. Available at: www.dbresearch.com [Accessed August 26, 2017].

Dealroom, 2016. *FinTech in Europe: Early signs of Brexit impact?* [online] Available at: https://blog.dealroom.co/wp-content/uploads/2017/03/FinTech-Report-FINAL.pdf [Accessed August 26, 2017].

Diekhöner, P.K., 2016. *The trust economy building strong networks and realising exponential value in the digital age*. Singapore: Marshall Cavendish International.

Dorfleitner, G., Hornuf, L., Schmitt, M., and Weber, M., 2017. *FinTech in Germany*. Cham: Springer.

Flint, D., 2014. *Business ethics in banking*. [online] Available at: www.hsbc.com/news-and-insight/media-resources/speeches/2014/business-ethics-in-banking [Accessed August 26, 2017].

Freudenberg, N., Klitzman, S., and Saegert, S., 2009. *Urban health and society: Interdisciplinary approaches to research and practice*. San Francisco, CA: Jossey-Bass.

Greenstein, S. and Zhu, F., 2016. *Do experts or collective intelligence write with more bias? Evidence from Encyclopaedia Britannica and Wikipedia*. [online] Available at: www.hbs.edu/faculty/Publication Files/15-023_e044cf50-f621-4759-a827-e9a3bf8920c0.pdf [Accessed August 26, 2017].

Hook, D., Watts, J., and Cockcroft, K., 2002. *Developmental psychology*. Lansdowne, South Africa: UCT Press.

Mackenzie, A., 2015. The FinTech revolution. *London Business School Review*, 3(3), pp.50–53.

McConnell, J., Kaufman, M., Teare, G., Glasner, J., and Mack, A., 2016. Global innovation investment report: 2016 year in review. [online] Crunchbase. Available at: http://static.crunchbase.com/reports/annual_2016_yf42a/crunchbase_annual_2016.pdf [Accessed December 12, 2017].

McGrady, V., 2016. Facebook eavesdropped on millennials to learn their money mindset. *Forbes*. [online] Available at: www.forbes.com/sites/vanessamcgrady/2016/02/02/facebook/#862a3757350b [Accessed August 26, 2017].

Milne, R., 2014. Klarna expands online payments business. *Financial Times*. [online] Available at: www.ft.com/content/ed7edc20-89c2-11e4-9dbf-00144feabdc0 [Accessed August 26, 2017].

Nicoletti, B., 2017. *The future of FinTech: Integrating finance and technology in financial services*. Cham: Springer.

Pitchbook, 2016. *2016 Pitchbook FinTech analyst report part 1: Online lending*. [online] Available at: https://pitchbook.com/news/reports/2016-pitchbook-fintech-analyst-report-part-1-online-lending [Accessed August 26, 2017].

Scardovi, C., 2016. *Restructuring and innovation in banking*. Cham: Springer International Publishing.

Skinner, C., 2016. *ValueWeb: How FinTech firms are using mobile and blockchain technologies to create the Internet of Value*. Singapore: Marshall Cavendish.

Wesley-James, N., Ingram, C., Källstrand, C., and Teigland, R., 2015a. *Stockholm FinTech: An overview of the FinTech sector in the greater Stockholm region*. [online] Stockholm School of Economics. Available at: www.hhs.se/contentassets/b5823453b8fe4290828fcc81189b6561/stockholm-fintech---june-2015.pdf [Accessed January 16, 2018].

10 The Internet as an enabler of FinTech

Mats Lewan

Introduction and method

In order to gather information for this chapter, interviews were conducted with a group of people, chosen for their understanding and experience of various functions with regard to the Swedish FinTech industry—regulation, startups, funding, and infrastructure.

Interviews were semi-structured, and focused on a limited number of questions: the importance of Internet infrastructure, of the mobile Internet, and of Internet-related technologies such as mobile banking and the BankID system, weighing these factors against other less Internet-related enablers that the interviewees chose to highlight. Another question regarded whether emergent Internet technologies such as blockchain could enable a second wave of FinTech companies, providing their services through a new independent infrastructure, separate from the one operated by the traditional financial industry.

The following individuals were interviewed during March through April 2017:

Cecilia Skingsley, Deputy Governor of Sweden's Central Bank, the Riksbank

Henrik Rosvall, CEO of the savings app Dreams

Johan Lundberg, co-founder at the FinTech-focused VC firm NFT Ventures

Daniel Kjellén, CEO at the integrated bank information app Tink

Ulf Ahrner, CEO at the investment digital advising company Primepilot

Danny Aerts, CEO at Internetstiftelsen (IIS)

Lan-Ling Fredell, Head of Operations at Stockholm FinTech Hub

Sofie Blakstad, CEO and founder at the financial trust platform Hiveonline

Frank Schuil, CEO and co-founder at the Bitcoin-focused startup Safello

Peter Garner, Product Owner of BankID at Handelsbanken

Most interviews were recorded, but two of them, with Kjellén and with Lundberg, were not. In those cases, uncertain quotations were controlled by the interviewees at a later occasion.

The Internet is important, but not the main driving force

The Internet is a fundamental enabler

There is no doubt that the Internet as such is an important enabler for the FinTech industry (Teigland et al., 2015). Several of the interviewees confirmed this, mentioning different aspects of the Swedish growth of Internet technologies that we described in our first report of this research project, *Chasing the Tale of the Unicorn: A Study of Sweden's Misty Meadows* (Skog et al., 2016).

Among these aspects were an early introduction of Internet connections in Sweden, an effective deregulation of the telecom market, an insightful public provision of fiber infrastructure in the Stockholm region, the home PC reform in 1998, with 850,000 PCs delivered on convenient economic terms to Swedish households within three years, a high penetration of fixed Internet only a few years later, and a massive national coverage of mobile 3G networks through the spectrum licensing model chosen by the Swedish regulator PTS, with a strong uptake in mobile Internet a few years later (Skog et al., 2016).

Cecilia Skingsley, Deputy Governor of the Riksbank, noted that Sweden ranks high on lists of Internet penetration, together with Finland and Singapore, and that Sweden historically has been quick to implement new technologies. Henrik Rosvall, CEO of the savings app Dreams, pointed out that Swedish people had an early usage of PCs at home, and they also started to create web pages at an early stage. Johan Lundberg, co-founder of the FinTech-focused VC firm NFT Ventures, also mentioned the high Internet penetration and the importance of the home PC reform that quickly contributed to Swedish people becoming Internet-savvy.

Frank Schuil, CEO and co-founder at the Bitcoin-focused startup Safello, noted that while the Internet has entailed the opportunity for businesses not to be geographically limited, but to go global through the Internet's reach, its connectivity, and its network effect,[1] FinTech startups are still geographically limited by local requirements on compliance.

The mobile Internet has a particular importance

In particular, several underlined a stable high-speed mobile Internet, which is almost being taken for granted by a large majority of the Swedish population, as a significant driver. Daniel Kjellén, CEO at the integrated bank information app Tink, brought up an experience of mobile Internet when traveling:

> I was in Great Britain two years ago and the Internet connection was terribly bad and slow. It was an eye-opener to me. Just the fact that it's slower, that it takes a longer time to load a page, and that you're not even sure of having a connection is a huge obstacle. Fewer apps will be offered and the general user experience is worse. So I thought about how that could influence FinTech. It probably means that you're not willing to use new technology solutions and that you will remain with your existing bank.

A readiness to try new solutions that seem to work well favors our industry. And I realized that we are used to high-speed connections, and that's why people are used to trying and using advanced services on the phone.

But what's also important was the development of an ecosystem for the distribution of apps—Apple's App Store and Google Play. We launched the first version of Tink as a web-based service in 2013, and at that time it wasn't obvious that an app would be interesting. Personally, working at an investment bank, I had been using a Blackberry until 2012, and I hadn't used apps until then. The trend at that time was more toward mobile web pages rather than native apps.

So the Internet was clearly important, but we hadn't realized how dependent we would be on the distribution network. At first, we launched a web version, but the retention was bad. Then we launched a native app and we got a huge response, adding 100,000 users. The difference? Basically, it was the distribution, and the fact that people always bring their mobiles. Instead of competing with some other usage of desktop computers and with family time, we were competing with bathroom time and waiting for the bus time. We got access to pockets of boredom.

We could also have launched a web-based app [essentially a web-based interface adapted for a mobile web browser/screen]. It wasn't obvious that native apps would conquer the world. But we made a bet that we are happy with today. What has happened since then is that the web has got so much better, but app technology has evolved incredibly much.

Henrik Rosvall from Dreams agreed with Kjellén:

> The deployment of the mobile network is important for the user experience. You want to have as much real-time data in the app as possible; otherwise, you have to fake the real-time experience. With 4G networks, everything goes really fast and you get new data from the server continuously. The coverage of the 3G networks is extensive and the connection is high-speed and stable, which has created good conditions for being at the forefront. This creates a certain culture in Sweden—you want to be at the edge. The coverage is so good that you get annoyed when you don't have a connection.
>
> We are in the experience industry, with digital experiences. There's so much information coming continuously and customers are starting to change their behavior. They like products with a good experience that they can share. That's the new thing. Before, we were a product company. Now we're a customer experience company. And when everything gets connected really tight, that's when you can achieve a good experience.
>
> You can manage updates, you've got good coverage, things go fast, and all your friends have the same conditions. This creates an integrated entity that few countries can achieve, with experiences that happen to be banking experiences. Taiwan is another country that has also reached [that] far.

Also, Johan Lundberg from NFT Ventures highlighted the added value of access to the Internet through mobile phones: "The usage of smartphones has been revolutionary. The devices and the fact that they're always near us has been a more important driving force than Internet in itself."

Henrik Rosvall from Dreams referred to a similar situation regarding the focus on mobile phones, as expressed by Kjellén, stating:

> When we started in 2013, I think the ratio between mobile and desktop usage had just reached 50/50, and it wasn't very common to focus on mobile usage—very few were building apps for mobile phones. Instead, most people built for the web and made adapted versions for mobile phones. But thinking about a limited screen size and a well-defined framework such as iOS or Android is very different.

Rosvall noted:

> For us, focusing on a young target group, Millennials, mobile was an obvious choice. The younger you are, the more you use mobile phones. It also felt future-proof, and since we couldn't afford to be present on all platforms, we chose iOS, which we expected to go well with our audience—people with high requirements and a quality awareness from other apps. We had to show that a banking app could have the same level of quality of user experience as a gaming or a social media app.

Rosvall's view on Apple's iOS was also reflected by a comment by Kjellén from Tink:

> Another aspect of choosing a mobile platform is that design has become more important. Tink is more beautiful on iOS than on Android, and many Swedish app developers have a particular focus on design. A high market share for iOS in Sweden has favored this—Android apps are often not so good, with less attention on design.

Rosvall also highlighted another perspective on choosing native apps instead of using the browser in mobile phones—security. He explained that if you want to attack an app, you first need to attack Apple or Google's operating system on the phone, which is difficult. And if the service is not accessible via the browser, as a web page, it cannot be targeted by so-called DDOS attacks, when the server is intentionally drowned by massive amounts of server requests. "This is an important advantage with apps. I haven't heard anyone discuss it, which surprises me," Rosvall said.

As for mobile phones and for what might be the next step, Frank Schuil from Safello noted that it is not necessarily the form factor of the mobile that is important, but the fact that it allows more people to access Internet more often and more efficiently:

> Whatever the next form factor be, it might be that we will be interacting directly with physical services, where every material, everything we touch becomes an Internet connected device. So I would say that the core is the Internet and the way that information is shared, and whatever physical form it takes, it's just allowing it to grow, almost like a living organism, if you will.

Other Internet-related aspects, including BankID

While smartphones and mobile Internet clearly make it easy to distribute a service and reach customers, the interviewees brought up a few other enablers of FinTech offerings, among them a few that are also Internet-dependent: well-developed mobile banking, usage of platforms such as Facebook, and BankID for identifying users remotely.

Kjellén from Tink expressed his view on this:

> To find an addressable market, you need an indication of where you can go next, and you can look at usage of mobile banking and of mobile Facebook. Typically, Facebook is the largest mobile Internet platform in every country—it has always been the ceiling at every given moment. If you don't have Facebook, there's not a chance that you will use Tink. The second indication—if you don't have a banking app, you will not use Tink either. It's a three-step process—start with Facebook, use a banking app, then you will be ready to try to replace the banking app. The force of habit makes it impossible to skip that step.
>
> Then there's Mobile BankID, which is a result of the fact that everyone in Sweden wants to use banking apps. You cannot underestimate the value of the ecosystem. Rather, the risk is that when you have such a fantastic ecosystem, with excellent bank services compared to the rest of Europe, it's difficult to understand the challenges in other markets. We are so divorced from reality.

Rosvall from Dreams had a similar view:

> What was important to us was definitely the usage of mobile and Internet banking in Sweden. Almost no one who was born in the 1990s or the 2000s goes to the bank branch. They make their banking errands on the mobile. We are ahead and we have set a standard for how you build banking services on the Internet. Many other countries are looking to Sweden. We still have a very long lead compared to Germany, for example. And [at Dreams] we had a few requirements, such as a system for electronic signatures, which was important to us. We didn't want to use paper. And when we started, BankID was already launched. Not on the mobile yet, but it existed.

Ulf Ahrner, CEO at Primepilot, had another perspective on BankID as an enabler. Primepilot offers automated advice on savings and fund investments, aiming at providing high-quality advice at a significantly lower cost than with traditional personal advisers, and in that way potentially increasing the overall return on investments:

> What made it impossible earlier was that you couldn't identify people remotely. That changed when Mobile BankID arrived. Now about 90 percent of the population has a BankID, so that obstacle doesn't exist anymore. Now you can identify most people in the Nordics without meeting them. And the customer's true identity is fundamental if you want to offer automated services.

Ahrner added a time perspective:

> As governmental agencies started to be accessible via the Internet, acceptance for using increasingly advanced services grew. Internet banking was the first really complex service on the web, where you could pay bills and manage your accounts. It arrived quite early I think, about 1997 or 1998. Now 20 years have passed since then, so I wouldn't say that it has been a quick process going from paying the bills online to getting advice. Rather slow in fact. I think that the Internet infrastructure has been good enough for a long time, but what was missing was a way to identify people remotely. You have to identify people, primarily to prevent money laundering. The requirement has always been there, but it has become increasingly tougher every year. BankID was the missing piece of the puzzle.

Criticism of BankID

There is, however, also some criticism of the BankID system. The electronic identification and signature system BankID was developed and is owned and managed by Finansiell ID-Teknik BID AB, which in turn is owned by six Swedish banks and one Danish bank—Danske Bank, Handelsbanken, Ikano Bank, Länsförsäkringar Bank, SEB, Skandiabanken, and Swedbank. The first BankID was issued in 2003, and the app-based Mobile BankID was introduced in 2011.

About 7.5 million people hold an issued BankID, and according to Peter Garner, Product Owner of BankID at Handelsbanken, about 1,000 web- or app-based services use the system. Eleven banks can issue BankIDs on the Swedish market, and five of them offer sales and integration of the system into web- or app-based Internet services. These five banks can offer any payment model to organizations using the system, but according to Peter Garner, most often a small fee of a few tens of *öre* is charged at each ID or signature transaction. During 2017, the expected number of such transactions is expected to total about 2.5 billion. About 60 percent of these are transactions with the owning banks (Wemnell, 2017; Finansiell ID-Teknik BID AB, n.d.).

One of the criticisms regards the traditional banks' ownership and control of the system, which is not a monopoly since other systems are also used, but with its overwhelming dominance it has become a de facto standard.

Kjellén from Tink said:

> The cost doesn't bother the banks who own the system. But suppose the [Swedish Data Protection Authority] Datainspektionen rules that platforms such as Facebook need to use two-factor authentication with electronic ID. Paying a fee for every transaction would push Facebook toward bankruptcy. Another example is that Klarna was blocked from the system for using BankID in a way that was not accepted. Yet Nordea used BankID in the same way. It's complicated. At the moment, it works, but the day it gets abused, it will become problematic.

Schuil from Safello expressed a similar concern:

> It is an issue that it's owned by the banks. We are not getting direct access to Mobile BankID as a company, but we are using a third-party supplier and we are sort of lucky with that. But our competitors are not able to get Mobile BankID. Every single initiative in the Nordics is owned by the banks, and they're already getting their hands into the new stuff that's coming. They set up Försäkringsgirot, they own the Bankomat, they own the Bankgiro, Swish, Mobile BankID, and through their investment vehicles they've got a major ownership in [FinTech startups] Tink, Coinify, and Minatjänster.se. So the dominance of the traditional financial system goes into everything. And having experience firsthand as a cryptocurrency business, they can make your life very hard.

Danny Aerts, CEO at Internetstiftelsen (IIS), agreed with the criticism, also referring to years of failed attempts by the Swedish government to develop a Swedish national electronic ID:

> Sweden is lagging hopelessly. In 20 years, it hasn't been able to provide a decent service for electronic ID. Estonia has made it. It has a beautifully designed electronic ID solution. I wouldn't be surprised if we end up buying an Estonian electronic ID. And the reason the Swedish government hasn't succeeded is that the banks have done their best to defeat alternatives to BankID. They want that BankID, which they own, will remain a de facto standard. And they have succeeded. But what we need is a neutral solution. If I were an old traditional bank and I saw a newcomer becoming dangerous, then I would find out something to make it hard or expensive for them.

Aerts also referred to repeated criticism regarding the security of the BankID system, stating that the security level is not good enough. "What's important for a good evolution of FinTech in general terms, but also for Sweden, is that there are good solutions for customers both for identifying themselves and for logging in, and being able to trust it," Aerts added.

Peter Garner, Product Owner of BankID at Handelsbanken, discussed the criticism. He first explained some serious weaknesses in the now abandoned government-backed proposal for an open national system for electronic identification and signatures (a new proposal is expected from the Swedish E-identification Board, "E-legitimationsnämnden"). He then gave a description of the main elements of the system from a security perspective, indicating a high security level, but he also admitted that one possible use case of Mobile BankID has raised some concern—that person A can convince person B to confirm a remote login with Mobile BankID, allowing person A to use an Internet-based service as person B. One solution is for users to only initiate a Mobile BankID login on their own, and never if anyone else unexpectedly would prompt them to do so. Services that use BankID should also use the signing feature at the conclusion of agreements, once a user is logged in.

Regarding the risk that the banks owning BankID would use their position to stop potentially threatening competitors, Garner said, "I'm pushing hard a standpoint that we cannot use our position for stopping competitors, otherwise we will quickly be in trouble with the Competition Authority."

He also explained that Handelsbanken had sold BankID integration to several large competitors, but he admitted that he could understand the worry from some players, especially if they had been denied using BankID.

While no bank has the right to deny anyone opening a bank account, there is no obligation for the banks owning BankID to sell integration of the system to every customer. However, as Garner pointed out, competition law should to some extent protect competitors from being unfairly denied a BankID connection. But he also explained that banks, for regulatory reasons, would look more carefully at companies offering financial services when considering them as BankID customers, adding that if any player is denied BankID, it is most likely due to conditions other than that they are competitors.

Less Internet-related enablers for FinTech

Although the role of Internet-based technologies for the emergence of the FinTech industry is apparent, the interviewees described its importance as a component in a bigger perspective with other enabling aspects. Cecilia Skingsley from Riksbanken mentioned a few of these:

> We had four major banks with a structure on the Swedish banking market that had been fairly stable for many years. There was also significant collaboration regarding common interest, such as in the case of Bankgiro, [the cash-managing entity] BDB Bankernas Depå AB, and now lately [the mobile peer-to-peer payment system] Swish where you can send money in real-time, 24/7, even if you have accounts in different banks, and where, in fact, also the Riksbank participates. I had been talking at World Economic Forum meetings about that we in Sweden are trying to "walk the talk" and support innovation as long as it's not in conflict with our statutory mandate, and so we're contributing with a credit in order to make sure Swish works 24/7.

> We're also an open economy, we have been making a living on manufacturing and selling products to others for generations, we are good at English and open to the Anglo-Saxon culture and to technological progress, and if you combine that with a fairly high level of trust in the society and with a supply side—a finance industry that is collaborating on strategic matters—then things really start to happen.
>
> Then we have reasonable social security systems making it possible (e.g., maybe to build a startup while also working, and you might also meet others who have tried and succeeded). And we're also ahead in technology, which means that we encounter problems early, and so the interest to solve them increases. So, if you're far ahead with card payments, for example, as we are in Sweden, then someone will start thinking about the fact that it's expensive with payment card terminals, trying to find a way to offer terminals at a lower cost, and there you have the ground for iZettle.

Kjellén from Tink added to this:

> While the Internet is a facilitator, the main driving force is the opportunity to improve the banking market. In our case, we needed distribution, but the former model with physical branches wouldn't have worked for us, and therefore we needed the Internet. But the trigger has been the ambition to offer better banking services. It doesn't start with the Internet. It starts with the aim to solve problems on the market.

Yet Kjellén thought Swedish banks were fairly good at this:

> If you compare with the problems our colleagues are trying to solve in Europe—making a nice payment app, or a peer-to-peer payment system, or making it possible for everyone to have a payment card. Those are things every Swedish bank customer has already, paying SEK 200 a year [in their annual fee]. It feels like a non-issue. And then you have to remember that those are old companies.

However, Kjellén also thought Swedish banks have not seen the worst yet:

> I believe this market will change completely, just like the music industry or video rental industry. We're just not there yet, but at that point some Swedish banks will get challenges since they haven't really acquired real crisis awareness. Compare with the Dutch bank ING, which had to lay off a third of all managers, who then had to reapply for their jobs.

Lundberg from NFT Ventures also regarded the ambition to make banking more effective as an important driving force, and he commended the Swedish banks for their effectivity efforts:

> Many of our companies complain about banks being slow and sluggish, but we say that the Nordic banks are the most effective banks in the world. They have such few branches, such high cost-efficiency, such competitive pricing—there's no country beating us. US banks have three to five as many branches per capita. Europe twice.

Lundberg continued:

> It's not the Internet. The Internet just happens to be the rails you drive on. It's the ambition among banks, and the requirement from the market, to push efficiency. The cost-to-income ratio in the Nordics is fantastic—Swedbank has almost 39 [average cost-to-income ratio in Western European countries varied from 41 percent (Norway) to 77 percent (UK) in 2015, and worldwide from 28 percent (Egypt) to 98 percent (Brazil) (Bratton and Garrido, 2016)]. To arrive at that level, you have to eliminate cash and paper documents. Digitalization is the only way. On top of that, you have a stable banking system where it feels fairly safe to develop and try new things. FinTech startups have benefited a lot from the trust there is in the financial system, which has forced us to become more digital.

Lan-Ling Fredell, Head of Operations at Stockholm FinTech Hub, noted another FinTech enabler in Sweden—easy online access to personal data:

> Sweden is like a case study for the future. What Sweden has managed to achieve because of its rapid adoption of Internet and the government support of the Internet is that you kind of have the digital society like others would like to see. I think it's what makes it so attractive as a place to start. In the case of Europe Loan [an online mortgage bank where Fredell was part of the founding team], 15 years ago, we could do in Sweden online application, income verification, property verification, property valuation, credit scoring—all online, because we could plug in to different databases. It was due to Swedish infrastructure, with this one ID number, and you can ask people for it, not like the US social security number that you're not really allowed to use, for identification. But in Sweden you are, and that makes things really, really easy.

Fredell continued:

> But the double-edged sword of that is if you have a Swedish entrepreneur who is maybe not as aware of how special Sweden is, and they build a global business plan on the ease of access that you have here in Sweden, then clearly it doesn't work that way around. Once you've done everything here in Sweden, you cannot go to the US and just use your business idea in the same way because you just don't have access to that kind of data.

Fredell also brought up Italy as an example since the country early on had a high mobile phone penetration, but other aspects turned out to be more important:

> With Europe Loan, we elected not to go into Italy because Italy had a terrible legal process when it comes to mortgages. If someone doesn't pay his/her mortgage, it can take a hundred years for the case to be solved. One thing that's good about Sweden is that the regulations tend to be relatively clear.

Sofie Blakstad, CEO and founder at the financial trust platform Hiveonline, agreed with Kjellén about Swedish banks' lack of crisis awareness:

> The mistake that is made by a lot of banks, which is the thing that I think will ultimately lead to their demise, is they think they are still operating in the same competitive landscape. And they're not. And I think that it's especially true in the Nordics. Because the Nordic banks didn't suffer as badly in 2008 as everyone else did. When your share price has already hit the floor or gone through it, when you've been bailed out by the UK government or the US government, when people throw things at you on the bus because you're wearing a security pass belonging to a bank, then your attitude to change is significantly different from what I see here in the Nordics. Although there have been difficulties, the level of trust in the banks here is significantly higher than in other places. And my observation is that the level of cultural inertia in the Nordic banks is significantly higher than it is elsewhere, and that's precisely because they were very risk-averse, and they managed to survive the crisis better than most of the other banks in the world did. But there is nothing like a burning platform to draw your attention to how much you need to change, and the Nordic banks haven't hit that yet. They will, but they haven't yet.
>
> I have seen so many industries; I've been through this level of disruption in other areas. I'll use Facebook as an example. Fifteen years ago, we would send emails, now my main communication channel is WhatsApp. The level of interaction and the sort of information we are willing to give away is completely different. It's a communication revolution. Now if we apply that level of revolution to financial services, which I think is starting to happen, then we are talking about a very different world.
>
> I don't think that banks are going to disappear completely in the next three to five years. I think it's going to take some time before people change their habits completely. But it depends. If you look at societies [such] as Sweden for example, where people are very comfortable with digital cash, where the central bank is talking seriously about issuing a cryptocurrency—I think that will happen in the next two years—and that for me is a tipping point for banks becoming obsolete or not.
>
> Banks as we know them are unlikely to be around for much longer than seven or eight years. General purpose retail and business banking is going to be augmented by alternative players in the financial ecosystem, as financial

> services move outside of traditional banks thanks to PSD2, to the rise of wallet systems and to central bank issued digital currencies. This will leave the traditional banking system as we know it unrecognizable.

Aerts from IIS also expressed concern about traditional banks:

> One of the reasons there are so many new companies on this market is that many banks have such large legacy systems that they are pinioned when developing services. No bank dares to kill its whole investment and start all over from scratch. I advised several high-level managers to forget their existing business, to put 10 persons in Västerås and build a bank. And close your old Pascal or Cobol [old programming languages] systems, or whatever you have that still runs your invoicing system.

On the other hand, Aerts also questioned the reported success of Swedish FinTech companies:

> Fairly early, Sweden had certain enablers in place—a high broadband penetration and a high penetration of smartphones, which facilitated the building of certain services. But what I noted in Sweden was that in Biblioteksgatan [downtown Stockholm], everyone is wearing the same jacket and the same hat. And this was visible also on the startup scene—when one company stands out, it becomes a star and everyone says that they are good, which helps them getting venture capital. People here move in herds when praising a company. It's a "we are proud effect." As for Ikea, Abba, Björn Borg, and also for Klarna. It's a positive effect that you won't see in the Netherlands [Aerts' country of origin], where you will be fiercely criticized until you earn a lot of money.
>
> We say, "We are good; we are the best in FinTech." Then someone says iZettle is a good company. I don't think so. iZettle will soon succumb. It doesn't have any market opportunity.
>
> With the herd behavior, Swedish people choose one star that gets a privileged possibility. You get a very focused investment climate. It's fairly favorable. It's a small country and the money goes to the same kind of players. But no one says, "No, they're not good." I would say that at the moment, Swedish FinTech is not more exciting than in other countries.

Aerts added that he expects Swedish FinTech companies to get into trouble, partly because of the lack of what he regards as a good and neutral system for electronic identity. However, he also mentioned a difficulty that he thought both Swedish and other European FinTech companies would struggle with—the lack of large digital social platforms in Europe, a well-known issue that was also highlighted in March 2017 at the annual meeting of Brussels-based EIT Digital—an EU and industry-funded organization focusing on strengthening innovation and entrepreneurship in Europe.

Aerts suggested that the most interesting FinTech companies are not those that run traditional banking activities, but those integrating payment functionality in global platforms with lots of traffic and lots of users (e.g., messaging services such as WhatsApp and WeChat). "The question is whether Swedish FinTech companies are those best positioned to perform payments in large US services. I doubt that. Maybe rather some similar American FinTech companies are better positioned," Aerts said.

Blockchain as an enabler for the next generation of FinTechs

Schuil from Safello discussed the importance of large platforms further, noting that among social platforms where the network effect is an advantage, the largest platforms dominate—Facebook effectively pushed out all competitors from local markets, at least in the Western world. He noted:

> Most traditional financial institutions, like banks, they really don't have any particular network effect since they don't have the social glue—your company has to be social one way or another to take advantage of the network effect. Even in the FinTech scene, there are very few companies that have tried to capitalize on that social aspect of finance, and I think the only good example in developed countries is [US-based] Venmo, where you see a retention rate of the application that is very high, like people opening up the Venmo app four times a week.
>
> That allows them to have a network effect. So in my view, when it comes to finance, I think that those kinds of social interactions will work better on blockchain technology where it's more open and global from day one, where you have no silos that you have to break through with traditional finance. So I think there could be a Venmo for the world in the long run, but so far I think that it can happen at least in geographies like the US, where they have been able to take advantage of the network effect.

Schuil then referred to successful local peer-to-peer payment solutions, such as Swish in Sweden, and said that you had to conclude that in the long run, it would not be safe to remain a winner in your own geography. From this perspective, Schuil's thoughts were in line with those of Aerts, although Schuil saw a viable global and neutral alternative to existing dominant platforms in the blockchain.

Blakstad from Hiveonline expected blockchain-based applications to also challenge established financial institutions:

> With the Internet, large banks didn't really have to change their business models. They could just put an Internet front on the existing back end. However, with blockchain, the business model changes. What I'm seeing is banks beginning reluctantly to acknowledge this, and some will be successful and some won't. And where those banks are early enough to change, and have the resources to change, I think they are likely to end up being successful.

Some of them, like Dutch ING, have focused on developing business and technology architecture that can support different ways of working. An infrastructure provider like that has a much better chance of succeeding than pretty much anyone else.

And of course, the obvious infrastructure providers are Amazon, Google, etc., and they will certainly be in this space. Alipay is hugely interesting and already has a large market share in China. They are claimed to be a universal bank, but I'm still not entirely convinced whether it would work in the West because our regulations are so very different, but they have an incredibly impressive share of the Chinese market already. And give them five minutes and they will be the core infrastructure provider for Chinese banks, if they're not already.

Visa and Mastercard and Swift are all rightly very scared at the moment. Not officially—they will talk the big talk, but they are all busily researching other types of technology. And I know that Swift is looking at a completely alternative technology to blockchain.

Blockchain obviously has its challenges itself—it's not scalable to the Visa or Mastercard or Swift scale yet.

I think that we're really almost at a tipping point where very respectable central governments are telling their central banks to think about this seriously. Sweden is obviously on the cusp of doing something about it. Singapore certainly will in the next couple of years. Even the Bank of England has got a lot of research papers about crypto. It's about issuing cryptocurrency based on local currency. And once you start doing that, you won't need a bank account to hold local currency. And that's going to be a game changer.

Conclusions

The interviewees agreed that the Internet, and in particular the mobile Internet, was an important enabler for the emergence of FinTech. Specifically, the wide use of mobile banking and mobile apps such as Facebook were considered to be necessary precursors to FinTech services. However, the interviewees also pointed out that the main driving force behind FinTech ventures was the ambition to increase efficiency and solve problems in the existing banking and financial markets.

They also mentioned several other important enablers for the FinTech industry, such as a good collaboration between existing banks and an interest among them for increased efficiency through digitalization.

The widespread electronic identification system BankID was considered to be important for FinTech, but it was also criticized for lacking security and for being owned and controlled by the major banks, and thus potentially used by the incumbent banks to hinder new competition. This was also discussed by a representative from BankID.

On the other hand, some of the interviewees expected major banks, particularly in the Nordics, to run into severe challenges in the upcoming years, not being prepared for this. Also, the Nordic FinTech industry was criticized and described as not so competitive as many seem to believe.

Finally, some of the interviewees mentioned blockchain technology as a possible enabler for a next generation of truly global FinTech companies, presenting a significant challenge to the traditional financial industry.[2]

Notes

1 Network effect—a phenomenon whereby a product or service gains additional value as more people use it.

2 BankID and blockchain are discussed further in Chapter 6 in this volume.

Bibliography

Bratton, E. and Garrido, F., 2016. *Cost-to-income ratios of banks worldwide*. [online] Available at: www.snl.com/web/client?auth=inherit#news/article?id=35864188&KeyProductLinkType=0&cdid=A-35864188-10284 [Accessed September 6, 2017].

Finansiell ID-Teknik BID AB, n.d. *Finansiell ID-Teknik in brief*. [online] Available at: www.bankid.com/en/om-oss/about-finansiell-id-teknik [Accessed May 21, 2017].

Skog, A., Lewan, M., Karlström, M., Morgulis-Yakushev, S., Lu, Y., and Teigland, R., 2016. *Chasing the tale of the unicorn: A study of Sweden's misty meadows*. [online] Available at: https://www.hhs.se/en/about-us/news/2016/new-research-explores-the-success-of-swedish-high-tech-startup-companies [Accessed January 6, 2018].

Teigland, R., Ingram, C., Wesley-James, N., Bengtsson, T., and Lamberth, J., 2015. *Stockholm: Europe's no.2 FinTech city: A dynamic hub for innovative payment, funding, banking, and transaction technologies*. [online] Invest Stockholm. Available at: www.investstockholm.com/globalassets/2.-understartsidor-investment-opportunities/fintech/stockholm_fintech_report.pdf [Accessed January 16, 2018].

Wemnell, M., 2017. *Statistik BankID – användning och innehav - fördjupning [Statistics for BankID—usage and possession—in-depth study]*. [online] Available at: www.bankid.com/assets/bankid/stats/2017/statistik-2017-03.pdf [Accessed January 6, 2018].

Part 3

New norms enabled by new technologies and standards

11 Digital traces, ethics, and insight

Data-driven services in FinTech

Claire Ingram Bogusz

FinTech and digital traces

FinTech has widely been lauded as a wave of technology-enabled entrepreneurship[1] that has democratized finance, for instance by connecting willing lenders and willing borrowers in peer-to-peer lending, or by allowing "the crowd" to support nascent entrepreneurship through crowdfunding (Bruton et al., 2015). This democratization is driven by digitally delivered services; these allow new actors to offer new services, or offer old services quickly and more cheaply. Indeed, individuals' online presence creates digital trace data that FinTech service providers can use to tailor bespoke financial solutions and screen would-be customers, for instance through improved credit scoring. This abundance of online data, both from FinTech services themselves and from online activities more generally, is often seen as a boon for online service providers—and their customers.

The vast majority of today's FinTech firms rely on data that customers know about, understand, and explicitly consent to sharing: for instance, data pertaining to individuals' employments, their names, and cities of residence. Consumers not only willingly give this data, they understand the content of—and often the implications of sharing—the data that they share with the firm. Where firms today make use of customers' data, they often do so with consumers' consent. However, vast commodification of individual data, both online and offline, sometimes with consent (although consumers often do not understand what they are consenting to) and sometimes without, is underway. For instance, we readily accept that websites collect data about our activities on their sites through "cookies." Despite this, many do not understand what information is collected, and what the data are used for. More broadly, some sites collect behavioral data that are more fine-grained than cookies—for instance, what we hover our mouse over—and take consent as being implied by continued use of the website (and include this in the fine print).

The very nature of digital data is double-edged: FinTech firms and other firms can use them to improve their services and offer customers tailored deals. However, the fact that such trace data are typically unintentionally left behind by users, and that the volumes of data involved are vast, means that consumers may not fully be aware of what it is that they are sharing—and what the implications of this sharing are, even when done consensually.

This chapter examines the various kinds of data that can be—and are being—shared online, before discussing how they are being used by FinTech firms, and examining the implications of their use for consumers and policymakers. Its intention is to connect existing understandings of different kinds of online data with their use by FinTech firms, before highlighting how different kinds of digital trace data might need special protection or explicit consent.

What are digital trace data?

Big data, a popular term for very large volumes of data, can come from any one of a number of places: from data collected about the earth done by satellites, to interaction data from so-called "Internet of Things" devices connected to one another, to information about online activities (McAfee et al., 2012). Such data are often used to run automated pattern recognition. When it comes to FinTech, the more gritty "digital trace data" are of the most interest. Individuals typically unintentionally leave digital traces as they browse, shop, and transact online. These data can be used to supplement data already willingly given by individuals in order to build a clearer picture of their online activities.

Most of us are at least peripherally aware that we generate data when we interact online. Most websites that collect data on our online interactions display, for instance, a "cookie request": they ask for permission to store small amounts of data on the user's computer. These small files are linked to a particular website, and the files can in turn be accessed both from the user's computer and from the website owner's server. As such, the files carry information that is used to fine-tune the user's online experience by remembering preferences or providing targeted advertising. Often, web pages contain scripts that allow data to be carried from one visit (or page) to the next, for instance to optimize advertising. Whether we are aware of them or not, this forms the backbone of some of the largest Internet firms. Google, for instance, makes much of its revenue from advertising: in mid-2016, Google's parent company Alphabet made USD 21.5 billion in revenue, of which 89 percent (or USD 19.1 billion) came from advertising (Johnson, 2016). Facebook made USD 8.81 billion profit in 2016, exclusively from advertising—with 84 percent of that from mobile advertising (Constine, 2017).

While the best known, cookies are just the tip of the iceberg: not only are we mostly aware of them, there are limits on what can be shared, and they are regulated by bodies such as the European Union (European Parliament and European Council, 2002). Other traces left online are not as tightly controlled. However, to understand why (and how) this is so, we need to explore what it is that we are talking about when discussing digital traces.

Do we know how much we leave behind?

Consider, by comparison, physical traces left at a crime scene. A perpetrator may leave a strand of hair or fingerprints on a doorknob. These traces are typically not left deliberately, nor are they exclusively left by criminals with ill intent; anyone in the vicinity could have left their fingerprints or hair. Some of these physical traces are visible to the naked eye, such as the aforementioned fingerprints and/or hair. Others, such as DNA found in the hair sample, are invisible to the naked eye, but can become visible with the right skills and tools. Avoiding leaving all of these traces, while possible, is tricky. A perpetrator could wear gloves to avoid leaving fingerprints, or a hat to avoid leaving hair, but what about footprints or skin cells? It would take considerable effort, if possible, to avoid leaving any traces at all.

These traces, in the digital realm, are similarly difficult to avoid leaving. Moreover, we describe digital data as being one of two kinds: (1) data that have content, for instance a user's name and address; or (2) metadata, for instance a user's IP address and the dates and time he/she was last online. Data with content are substantial and personal in nature; they say something about an individual, and can easily be identified as being linked to that person.

Data with content include not only that which we explicitly share with a firm, but also include other kinds of trace online data, notably content shared on social media and on forums. When it comes to social media, for instance, photographs on Facebook are data with content, as are the links to news articles that we share.

In contrast, metadata are data about data. For instance, metadata around a Facebook photo might include the size of the photograph, the time it was shared, and the IP address from which it was shared. While the metadata from a single photograph cannot be used to say much about an individual, the metadata about all of the photographs of you shared on Facebook can. For instance, if you consistently share large files from the same IP address in Stockholm at the same time on a Friday night, algorithms might determine that you have a high-quality camera, and therefore are a photography enthusiast who lives in Stockholm and prefers not to go club-hopping.

Many companies treat the collection of this metadata as unproblematic. Indeed, metadata are often central to, for instance, a telecommunication firm, making sure that their Internet service provision is working as it should. However, depending on the patterns searched for in the data, it could show much more than intended, while giving the firm, and anyone else who can access this information, an unprecedentedly detailed picture of any number of online habits. This is especially problematic when we consider that metadata may reveal things that we might not want to reveal. For instance, the presence of a mobile phone at an anti-government protest in an autocratic country might reveal the identities of individual protestors.

Taxonomy of online data

We constantly generate data while online. Everything from how our mouse moves when interacting with a website, to sites that we visit, to the data that we enter into online forms—even if we never send the form—can be, and often are, collected.

Data typically are one of two kinds: data with content, and metadata. Data with content are data that may directly identify individuals, for instance a photograph or online activity. Metadata describes these data, for instance the size of the photograph and the IP address from which it was uploaded. Moreover, these data can come from different sources. Although we often talk about the data that we, whether intentionally or unintentionally, leave ourselves, in the age of social media it is unavoidable that third parties also leave digital traces that describe us.

Schneider (2015) details a number of important sources of data, adapted in Table 11.1.

These include the following:

> *Service data*, which include the information that one provides in order to receive a service. Some examples include your name, your age, your address, or your credit card number. For instance, in most countries, to open a bank account, you need to disclose your name, identity number, and address, and perhaps even provide proof of your income.
>
> *Disclosed data* include content such as photos, messages, and comments that we post on a web page, blog, or website that we control, own, and host. While the data are publicly available, we can decide what to share, for how long, and can typically limit access to the underlying infrastructure, limiting the collecting of digital trace data by third parties.
>
> *Entrusted data* include similar content to disclosed data, but they are data posted on a platform we do not control, such as Facebook, LinkedIn, or our employer's website. As such, someone else decides what happens to that data, and how easy it is to use and collect it. We can decide whether, and what, to post on these platforms, but we cannot control what firms subsequently do with our trace data.
>
> *Incidental data* are also things such as comments and photographs, but shared by others. Some examples might be when we are tagged in a picture on Facebook or quoted in a blog or an article. We did not decide what to share, do not control the platform in question, and therefore can neither influence what is shared or how those digital traces are used.

Table 11.1 The characteristics and kinds of digital trace data

	Deliberately left	*Unintentionally left*	*Left by a third party*
Data with content	Service data Disclosed data Entrusted data		Entrusted data Incidental data
Metadata		Entrusted data Behavioral data Derived data	Incidental data Derived data

Source: Adapted from Schneider (2015).

> *Behavioral data* are data created while interacting with our computer, mobile phone, or tablet. Some examples include how long you spend looking at a particular website, where you click, who you communicate with (via phone call or SMS), and the dates and times at which your device is active. These kinds of data give insight into what we do, with whom, how often, and where.
>
> Both behavioral and incidental data might be unintentionally (or, more accurately, unknowingly) shared. This occurs when we allow services access to data contained in other services—for instance, when we allow the Facebook mobile app to access our contacts, we share our friends' phone numbers with them. The fact that data are unintentionally shared, however, does not affect who has control over when, and to whom, data are released.
>
> *Derived data* are data about us inferred from other data. For instance, brokering companies create group profiles that group people according to their shared demographic traits, social media networks, device locations, and online activity. We are then linked to these profiles, and have no influence over whether we should be categorized as a member of a particular group, or how group-level data are used by the brokering company or other third parties.

All of these kinds of data could be either data with content, or metadata (i.e., data about data). We generate this metadata unknowingly, in an organized format, and over the long term.

These different data types are increasingly used by data analysts and data scientists, not least in the area of FinTech. However, the distinctions between different data types are important to note when it comes to how we address problematic areas around the use and collection of digital trace data.

Digital traces in action

These kinds of data have extensive uses when it comes to FinTech service provision. While using a customer's service data is commonplace, use of the other layers of digital trace data allows service providers to provide new and improved services.

Larger volumes of data, and digital trace data in particular, allow FinTech firms to build more fine-grained pictures of their customers in one of a number of ways. First, by having meta-level information about multiple customers' online activities, they can categorize individuals based on these data. Such aggregate-level categorization allows firms to calculate probabilities and preferences for those included in the category.

Second, digital trace data on the individual level allow FinTech firms to make more accurate assessments of, and thus tailor information and services to, individual behaviors and preferences. These individual-level assessments rely partly on meta-level data, but also on data with content, irrespective of whether that content is left deliberately or otherwise.

A recent analysis of artificial intelligence (AI) in FinTech by digital insights firm CB Insights grouped the use of data into five areas, as described in Table 11.2.

Table 11.2 Use of artificial intelligence in FinTech

	Description and examples of firms	*Examples*
Credit scoring and direct lending	AI used to create more accurate credit scores by nontraditional actors, facilitating peer-to-peer lending.	Upstart, Avant, Zest Finance
Regulatory, compliance, and fraud detection	AI used to detect patterns that amount to fraud, as well as test for regulatory compliance.	Trifacta, Digital Reasoning, Data Robot
Assistants/personal finance	AI used to detect patterns and allow customers to automate—or avoid—those patterns in future personal finance transactions.	Dreams, Qapital, Homebot
Quantitative and asset management	AI used to create investment portfolios optimized based on patterns in individual user behavior and market movements.	Wealthfront, Clone Algo, Sentient
Insurance	AI used in risk assessment for insurance purposes, creating group and individual profiles.	Risk Genius, Shift Technology, Lemonade

Source: Adapted from CB Insights (2017).

Taking existing services beyond service data

Many financial services today involve extensive assessments of risk and reward: obtaining a home loan relies on a bank's ability to assess a consumer's ability and willingness to pay back a loan, offset against the value of the asset. Obtaining a credit card similarly relies on a consumer's ability to pay back a line of credit, although there are assets involved.

In most developed countries today, individuals build up credit scores by borrowing and repaying progressively larger amounts of money, by consistently having their salaries paid into a single account, and by paying bills on time. Based on these and other consumer-disclosed or service data, financial institutions can lend a consumer money at an interest rate, with higher interest rates correlating to high-risk lending.

In the pre-FinTech world, decisions about creditworthiness also relied on grouping individuals based on their income, age, employment, and payment history. However, these data points provide only the broadest frame for assessing an individual's creditworthiness. While these time-honored benchmarks of creditworthiness paint a decent picture of how likely a person is to pay back a line of credit, two problems remain. First, having a credit score based on these sources of service data takes time. Implicit in this is the fact that young people and newcomers to a country will struggle to get credit, or pay disproportionately high interest rates, because they have not had the time or opportunity to build up a credit score. This is due to a lack of *data* upon which a credit assessor can make an assessment, not necessarily because an individual is high-risk. Second, from the perspective of a FinTech firm, the ability to screen potential borrowers more accurately, and possibly more quickly, than competitors is a source of competitive advantage. In China, for instance, the use of digital traces has meant that people who were once ineligible began to get credit, which served to the benefit of the economy at large (Bateman, 2017).

Debt collectors and those making credit assessments routinely collect as much data about consumers as is possible (Deville, 2012). Using additional data, including from sources over and above the conventional service data, allows FinTech firms to better assess with whom, and on what terms, they wish to do business. More fine-grained data, such as the relationship between someone's current account balance and their credit limit, or their preference for paying by credit card rather than by direct debit, may have particular "predictive power." These behavioral data help credit assessors weed out risky debtors, without risking weeding out low-risk ones.

The use of different sources of data, however, varies quite widely. Digital trace data that are deliberately left, for instance disclosed and distrusted data, have been of significant interest for FinTech firms. Until Facebook tightened up its third-party data access policies in 2016, many FinTech firms were hoping to use Facebook data, both data that were deliberately left and data provided by third parties, to generate credit scores (Lorenzetti, 2016). One of the biggest problems with the commodification of disclosed, entrusted, and derived data typically controlled by a platform such as Facebook is that consumers share their data with such platforms without intending such data to be used for serious purposes. Consequently, they may not be as careful with sharing these data as they would be with safeguarding their credit score; it is this quality that is thought to make third-party platform data more accurate than deliberately shared service data. However, it also prevents consumers from limiting how much a credit agency—or other FinTech agent—can see about their lives.

WeCash, a Chinese FinTech data analytics firm, uses algorithms to scrape and analyze individuals' mobile phone usage history, allowing them to both categorize individuals and make individual credit assessments. However, these assessments are not for their own use: they have collaborated with banks, insurance and rental service providers, and also job search websites and P2P lending platforms, showing how the data can be collected by one firm and commoditized and sold on to other firms, for better or for worse.

While consumers are often told that their data are being collected, it is not always clear for what purpose—or exactly which data—they are giving their consent. In fact, the use of machine learning may even mean that corporate data scientists are not always sure themselves what it is that their algorithms are prioritizing.

Example: Wonga and credit assessment

One application of the use of digital trace data lies in using users' online behavior to judge their creditworthiness, as payday lender Wonga in the UK does (Deville, 2012). Wonga claims that its algorithms are so reliable (and quick) that decisions are made within six minutes, and money is transferred to user accounts in 15.

While Wonga also buys traditional third-party credit scores (Deville, 2012), they make extensive use of online data collection to fine-tune their credit assessment and default prediction models. This departs from the conventional wisdom that professional credit rating agencies have access to the largest volume of individual-level data, and can therefore make the most accurate credit assessments.

Wonga emerged from the online beta experiment that was SameDayCash (Shaw, 2011). SameDayCash was a short-term loan site with the first fully automated decision-making process. In the beginning, its ability to distinguish high-risk and low-risk individuals was no better than any other credit-granting agency. However, SameDayCash gathered detailed information about each applicant and refined the underlying algorithm used to judge creditworthiness with every loan granted—and then those that were repaid and/or defaulted upon.

This algorithm is thought to rely on more than just historical behavioral data. Deville, in a close examination of the site, suggests that Wonga makes use not only of data available in public databases and through search engines, but also social media data, IP addresses, device data, and even data around how an individual interacts with Wonga's online sliders (Deville, 2012). Deville, for instance, notes that Wonga seems to offer individuals higher initial loan amounts based on the device from which they access the site:

> The loan amounts users are initially presented with currently tend to be either GBP 111 or GBP 265, although I have also achieved figures of GBP 350 and GBP 361. In my informal survey, those using Apple products (a Safari browser, or say an iPhone or an iPad) seemed to be most consistently offered GBP 265. Although tests with some obscure browsers suggest that it is likely that it is less that you are "uprated" by using Apple products, than you are "downrated" by using less niche browsers like Firefox and Internet explorer.

Deville further observes that mobile device data, a form of derived metadata, are easy to obtain:

> As those familiar with this area well know, when you visit a website, it is extremely difficult not to leak lots of information about precisely how you are accessing the site. Mobile devices are particularly leaky. Even this website routinely collects such information. As an example, here, via Google Analytics, are the top five mobile devices known to access the site:
>
> 1 Apple iPad
> 2 Apple iPhone
> 3 Samsung GT-I9100 Galaxy S II
> 4 Samsung GT-P5110 Galaxy Tab 2 10.1
> 5 RIM BlackBerry 9300 Curve 3G

Wonga further collects data about exactly how an individual interacts with the site: when a user interacts with the slider on Wonga's home page, data are collected. As BBC News reported: "The firm has found that people who immediately shove the slider up to the maximum amount on offer, currently £400 for 30 days for a first-time applicant for a personal loan, are more likely than others to default" (Pollock, 2012).

Creditworthiness is the area that, thus far, has been the most dramatically altered by digital trace data. However, identity verification and fraud detection, something that financial firms are legally obliged to do anyway, has also begun to be revolutionized. While this is not technically a new function, the use of digital trace data has meant that these services are increasingly done by specialist third parties, rather than by traditional financial actors.

New services

Other areas in which existing services can, and have, been improved by the use of digital trace data—and analytics—include detecting fraud and verifying individuals' identities. Socure, an American IT company, uses both online and offline data, including social media data, to create two platforms: one for "Certified Social Biometrics," essentially a digital biometric signature for an individual based, among other things, on his/her digital traces, and an ID+ API. These two platforms are the front end of a back-end process whereby the firm creates digital signatures of an individual based on derived metadata such as email, phone, address, and IP/geolocation data, as well as entrusted data from social media and other sites. The platform services are then sold to other parties for identity verification and fraud prevention.

Another possible way to avoid identity theft and prevent fraud is through using online behavioral data. The online university course site Coursera, for instance, tracks a user's typing patterns, and uses this behavioral data to verify if the individual completing their online exam is the same person who registered for the course (Creagh, 2013). To my knowledge, this technology has not yet been used by FinTech firms, but I imagine it is only a matter of time until it is.

Behavioral data can be a gold mine when it comes to building services that preempt consumer needs. One notable example is the use of these kinds of data to nudge consumers into certain kinds of behaviors. For instance, the Swedish FinTech app Dreams (covered in Chapter 20 in this volume) makes use of consumers' transaction data to encourage (and automate) saving. In the case of Dreams, users are offered a number of suggestions for ways in which they can save money; the app alerts them when they buy takeaway coffee, for instance, and suggests that they save the money and make coffee at home instead.

Reaching underserved consumers

Ultimately, the use of digital traces can mean that those with limited records of service data can rely on other forms of digital trace data, for instance disclosed or entrusted data. What this means in practice is that one's "digital footprint" (i.e., the digital traces left behind) can become a repository from which FinTech actors can draw to assess risks, confirm identities, and ultimately provide services to those without the extensive financial histories or formal identification relied upon today.

This access to the global unbanked has both social and financial benefits; in 2015, the World Bank estimated that 2 billion adults globally remained unbanked (World Bank, 2015). Giving these individuals access to financial services will help them gain credit through mainstream financial services providers instead of small-scale moneylenders who often charge exorbitant rates (Chaia et al., 2009). Take, for instance, the Indian digital identity system Aadhaar, which comprises 1.2 billion people of the country's population of 1.3 billion people. This identity system has allowed many people to open bank accounts for the first time, and has eliminated fraud in regard to social benefit payments (The Economist, 2016). While the Aadhaar system itself does not rely on digital traces, the digital identity system could be combined with digital trace data to provide new and more accessible financial services to formerly underserved communities. In fact, a 2016 article in *The Economist* indicated that government and private firms have shown a considerable increase in interest in doing exactly this.

The wave of new FinTech solutions has often been described as democratizing finance (see e.g. Schulman and Kirkland, 2017), and the use of digital traces is one of the features of the new digital world that facilitates this. A large number of startups have already made inroads into these spaces. However, making use of these traces should be done cautiously; while the data are readily available, there are not yet industry standards for the collection, storage, and commodification of data. Moreover, consumers' understanding of their own data, and the implications of their use, lags behind.

Downside to the commodification of data

In essence, the advent of digital trace data age means that individuals' online data (everything from photographs and devices, to interactions with key websites) can be collected. While the collection and use of digital trace data is, in many ways, a boon for FinTech firms, it raises a number of issues that deserve consideration. These issues stem largely from public safety and privacy concerns; however, large volumes of anonymized digital trace data present their own problems.

Issues around consent

The "cookies notice" is so ubiquitous online that most of us barely give it a second glance as we click to close it. Given the importance and value of online data, the fact that most of us barely acknowledge (and seldom read) notices around how our data are collected online is problematic. In fact, the norm when using a website is often just to "accept" the terms and conditions of its use, without reading what they entail. This means that users often do not know that their digital traces are being collected, and do not know what the data are being used for, or to whom they might be sold.

This problem is compounded by the fact that using most websites and digital services is contingent on accepting their terms, while there is no option to accept some terms and not others. That is to say, there is no option to make use of, for instance, Google's services without permitting them to analyze and sell the data they collect.[2]

This means that users typically make use of services without being able to limit the extent to which data are collected and used, even if they were aware of it, which many are not. Moreover, even if individuals were aware that their data was being used, they would be hard-pressed to understand how its use would affect the financial (and other) services they receive.

No privacy, and no context

Metadata have often been treated as comprising the best of both worlds; they have been said to provide insight without violating individual rights to privacy. For this reason, the use of metadata has been largely treated as being separate from the use of data with content across the globe. However, as more and more data describing a single data point are gathered, their ability to strip the privacy of the individual in question increases. A recent study, for instance, using only the metadata from phone calls and text messages identified that a small sample of individuals were suffering from sensitive medical conditions (Mayer, Mutchler, and Mitchell, 2016). The amount of data that is currently available about us, combined with advances in data analysis, have significantly increased the likelihood that an individual can be reidentified from anonymized data, whether metadata or otherwise. In fact, removing personal data from digital traces (for instance, by making it illegal to collect personal data) is therefore insufficient: identifying an individual depends on the number of data traces available, and what other data a data set can be linked to.

Metadata therefore can no longer be seen as benign when it comes to privacy. Moreover, while the volumes of metadata available today cannot only be used to violate the privacy of individuals, the decontextualization of metadata can have further negative implications for individuals. In particular, the context leading to the creation of metadata may influence how the patterns they describe should be interpreted. Without this context, inaccurate conclusions may be drawn. This is to the detriment of both the individuals in question and actors acting on that information.

Payment over quality

While some actors, such as Wonga and Dreams, conduct their own experiments and collect their own data, in principle the data that they or other FinTech actors collect could be developed into a database and sold onwards. This sale could be to other FinTech actors, to advertisers, to governments, or even to untrusted third parties. This is the business model used by actors such as Socure and WeCash: to collect individuals' data, analyze them, and provide services—including the data themselves—to third parties.

This emergent set of business models presents two potential problems: first, there is a sense that it is unfair for firms to make money off individuals' data, especially, as discussed in the previous section, because of concerns around privacy. Second, the financial value of such data and resulting analyses may create adverse incentives. As previously discussed, data without context (or insufficient data) may result in models that are so removed from the data that they are incomplete or of poor quality.

Who owns the data?

As the taxonomy of digital traces discussed earlier highlights, not only are there different types of online digital traces, but control over, and (typically) ownership of, these traces varies too. Entrusted data hosted on a third-party site, for instance, are more likely to be owned by that third party than by the person that those data describe. Incidental data submitted to a third-party site by a friend or colleague are controlled by that person and owned by the third-party site.

Some solutions to this problem have been suggested. For instance, the European Court of Justice's 2014 ruling on the "Right to be Forgotten" (Eur-Lex, 2014) points to a belief that individuals should have control over digital traces about themselves online. In the UK, one proposal has been to create a registry of data used by firms (Downey, 2016). In Australia, draft legislation has proposed a National Data Custodian body to allow individuals to have greater control of the data collected about them by both public and private sector actors (Bindi, 2016). Germany, known for the importance it places on privacy, treats data protection as a consumer protection issue, with breaches offenses under the law.

Pentland (2013) suggests that our digital trace data should be managed by data controllers in a way akin to how our banks manage our money. He highlights the tenets of possession, use, and disposal, arguing that these are the three areas of digital trace data leverage that should be regulated and overseen. He describes these tenets as follows:

> You have the right to possess data about you. Regardless of what entity collects the data, the data belong to you, and you can access the data at any time. Data collectors thus play a role akin to a bank, managing the data on behalf of their "customers."
>
> You have the right to full control over the use of your data. The terms of use must be opt-in and clearly explained in plain language. If you are not happy with the way a company uses your data, you can remove the data—just as you would close your account with a bank that is not providing satisfactory service.
>
> You have the right to dispose of or distribute your data. You have the option to have data about you destroyed or redeployed elsewhere.
>
> (Pentland, 2013)

This approach to data regulation and oversight has been well received in a number of forums, notably in the World Economic Forum.

Conclusion and recommendations for FinTech

The collection and use of digital trace data have allowed firms to optimize existing services, create new services, and reach new customers. Both firms and consumers have benefited from these advances. However, as digital trace data are used more extensively, and as consumers come to better understand how little control they have over their own data, a backlash seems likely. In both the short term and the long term, the problems identified in this chapter affect both consumers and firms who rely on data collected and analyzed by other firms.

The long-term sustainability of business models based on digital trace data requires that firms consider both privacy concerns and quality concerns when building their services. Given the potentially invasive nature of data collection, and the implications of possible backlash, FinTech firms need to be careful when designing—and obtaining consent for—their services.

Quality control

While a large number of beneficial services have been created off the back of digital trace data, as highlighted previously, some problems remain. The ones with immediate implications for FinTech firms are those around quality; when trace data are aggregated and collected in a haphazard way, much of their analytical worth is undermined.

In order to make sure that the services currently—and in the future—reliant on these trace data are reliable, FinTech firms need to scrutinize the source of trace data, how they are collected, and how they are analyzed. In a time when many firms have taken to outsourcing this data collection and analysis, this need calls on those firms to get more closely involved in the nitty-gritty of the process. This is not for principle reasons: the efficiencies and new markets created by these analyses depend on them being conducted reliably and with data that do not conceal, obscure, or exaggerate findings.

Education and self-regulation by FinTech firms

The voluntary submission of service data has meant that consumers understand the implications of sharing their service data with financial services firms. The same cannot be said of other kinds of digital trace data, especially behavioral data and data that individuals do not themselves control (notably, entrusted, incidental, and derived data). While the evidence thus far suggests that the use of these forms of data has facilitated the creation of new—and the improvement of old—financial services, this may not always be the case. Nor will consumers necessarily agree with decisions made based on these kinds of data, especially when the norm in financial services has been to use tightly controlled and well-regulated service data.

FinTech firms therefore need to be clear about what data they collect, and how they will use them. This includes where automated tools are used; the rise of artificial intelligence and smart algorithms cannot absolve FinTech firms from informing their customers about the implications of different kinds of data usage. Individual-level education by FinTech firms would also be particularly effective if firms chose to hold larger community-level education events. This would not only build trust, but also ensure that FinTech firms reach as many people as possible, helping individual consumers to make informed decisions, and thus avoid problems down the line.

Failure to be circumspect and transparent about what data are collected, and what they are used for, is likely to mean that FinTech firms lose the opportunity to self regulate. Failure to self regulate in these areas will likely lead to one or both of two things: first, onerous regulation by national or regional governance structures; and second, consumers will begin to move their data (and online activity) onto parts of the Internet that are more private, for instance through Tor networks or using IP-concealing tools.

Clear rules around ownership from governments

Both the providers of FinTech services and policymakers need to respond to the rise in digital trace data analytics in a nuanced way. As many commentators have noted, it is not just the fact that digital trace data are out there that is problematic—it is the fact that it is unclear who owns certain data. Intuitively, one would think that one would have rights to one's own photographs or other disclosed data, and perhaps a right to see what kind of behavioral data are being collected. However, this is not currently the case. Instead, ownership of data is a complex and opaque affair, governed by the small print in terms and conditions that consumers typically do not bother to read. Clear rules from governments—ideally, ones that give individuals rights and responsibilities when it comes to their own data—would go a long way toward creating a level playing field for today's and future FinTech entrepreneurs.

In closing, as has been shown above, the rise in the availability of digital trace data, and the tools with which to analyze them, has been a boon for FinTech firms, among others. However, dealing with both moral and practical issues remains imperative. Indeed, different types of data, their ownership, and their control all raise a number of issues for consideration. In the long term, vigilance by FinTech firms, education, and self-regulation will go a long way toward ensuring that the new services and markets created using digital trace data are sustainable and reliable.

Notes

1 Or, sometimes, intrapreneurship.
2 Some uses of the data can be limited, but users seldom know that these limitations exist—or how to make use of them.

Bibliography

Bateman, J., 2017. *FinTech is stimulating Chinese consumption and capital flow.* [online] TechCrunch. Available at: https://techcrunch.com/2017/02/06/fintech-is-stimulating-chinese-consumption-and-capital-flow [Accessed August 25, 2017].

Bindi, T., 2016. *Risk vs. opportunity: Data use and availability in Australia.* [online] ZDNet. Available at: www.zdnet.com/article/risk-vs-opportunity-data-use-and-availability-in-australia [Accessed August 25, 2017].

Bruton, G., Khavul, S., Siegel, D., and Wright, M., 2015. *New financial alternatives in seeding entrepreneurship: Microfinance, crowdfunding, and peer-to-peer Innovations.* [online] Available at: www.worldcat.org/title/new-financial-alternatives-in-seeding-entrepreneurship-microfinance-crowdfunding-and-peer-to-peer-innovations/oclc/5718372534&referer=brief_results [Accessed August 25, 2017].

CB Insights, 2017. *The AI in FinTech market map: 100+ companies using AI algorithms to improve the Fin Services industry.* [online] CB Insights. Available at: www.cbinsights.com/research/ai-fintech-startup-market-map [Accessed December 5, 2017].

Chaia, A., Dalal, A., Goland, T., Gonzalez, M.J., Morduch, J., and Schiff, R., 2009. *Half the World Is Unbanked.* [online] McKinsey & Company Report. Available at: http://mckinseyonsociety.com/half-the-world-is-unbanked [Accessed August 25, 2017].

Constine, J., 2017. *Facebook beats in Q4 with $8.81B revenue, slower growth to 1.86B users.* [online] TechCrunch. Available at: https://techcrunch.com/2017/02/01/facebook-q4-2016-earnings [Accessed August 25, 2017].

Creagh, S., 2013. *Online course host Coursera to ID students using typing style.* [online] The Conversation. Available at: https://theconversation.com/online-course-host-coursera-to-id-students-using-typing-style-11562 [Accessed August 26, 2017].

Deville, J., 2012. Regenerating market attachments. *Journal of Cultural Economy*, 5(4), pp.423–439.

Downey, P., 2016. *Registers in a digital ecosystem.* [online] Data in Government. Available at: https://data.blog.gov.uk/2016/09/12/registers-in-a-digital-ecosystem [Accessed August 25, 2017].

Eur-Lex, 2014. Google Spain SL v. Agencia Espanola de Protección de Datos (AEPD). 108. *American Society of International Law.* [online] Available at: http://eur-lex.europa.eu/legal-content/EN/TXT/?uri=CELEX%3A62012CJ0131 [Accessed January, 16, 2018].

European Parliament and European Council, 2002. Council Directive 2002/58/EC of the European Parliament and of the Council of 12 July 2002 concerning the processing of personal data and the protection of privacy in the electronic communications sector of 12 July 2002 concerning the processing of personal data and the protection of privacy in the electronic communications sector. *Official Journal of the European Communities.* [online] Available at: http://eur-lex.europa.eu/legal-content/EN/TXT/HTML/?uri=CELEX:32002L0058&from=EN [Accessed August 26, 2017].

Johnson, L., 2016. Google's ad revenue hits $19 Billion, even as mobile continues to pose challenges. *Adweek.* [online] Available at: www.adweek.com/digital/googles-ad-revenue-hits-19-billion-even-mobile-continues-pose-challenges-172722 [Accessed August 25, 2017].

Lorenzetti, L., 2016. Facebook no longer lets third-party online lenders access dull data. *Fortune.* [online] Available at: http://fortune.com/2016/02/24/facebook-credit-score [Accessed August 25, 2017].

Mayer, J., Mutchler, P., and Mitchell, J., 2016. Evaluating the privacy properties of telephone metadata. *PNAS*, 113(20), pp.5536–5541.

McAfee, A., Brynjolfsson, E., Davenport, T.H., Patil, D., and Barton, D., 2012. Big data: The management revolution. *Harvard Business Review*, 90(10), pp.61–67.

Pentland, A., 2013. The data-driven society. *Scientific American*. [online] Available at: www.popline.org/journal-title/scientific-american [Accessed August 25, 2017].

Pollock, I., 2012. *Wonga: What makes money lender tick?* [online] BBC News. Available at: www.bbc.com/news/business-18019272 [Accessed August 25, 2017].

Schneider, B., 2015. *Data and Goliath: The hidden battles to collect your data and control your world*, New York: W.W. Norton & Company.

Schulman, D. and Kirkland, R., 2017. *Using FinTech to democratize financial services*. [online] *McKinsey & Company*. Available at: www.mckinsey.com/industries/financial-services/our-insights/using-fintech-to-democratize-financial-services [Accessed August 25, 2017].

Shaw, W., 2011. Could Wonga transform personal finance? The facts behind payday loans cash service Wonga. *Wired UK*. [online] Available at: www.wired.co.uk/article/wonga [Accessed August 25, 2017].

The Economist, 2016. *The digit era: Indian business prepares to tap into Aadhaar, a state-owned fingerprint-identification system*. [online] Available at: www.economist.com/news/business/21712160-nearly-all-indias-13bn-citizens-are-now-enrolled-indian-business-prepares-tap [Accessed August 25, 2017].

World Bank, 2015. Massive drop in number of unbanked, says new report. *Press Release No. 2015/364/DEC*, [online] pp.13–16. Available at: www.worldbank.org/en/news/press-release/2015/04/15/massive-drop-in-number-of-unbanked-says-new-report [Accessed August 25, 2017].

12 Digital meetings

Real growth, better funding? An introduction to Swedish crowdfunding

Michal Gromek and Alexandre Dubois

Introduction

The traditional view of crowdfunding, as a collective effort to accumulate relatively insignificant amounts of funding to finance small ideas and early-stage ventures, has changed in 2016. The Swedish crowdfunding landscape in 2017 allows not only the finance of charities and early-stage ventures, but to raise up to EUR 1 million, buy real estate, take loans, and buy shares of companies. Crowdfunding represents an ancient phenomenon, during which kings or religious leaders were collecting funding offline (e.g., for places of worship or crusades). The modern version of crowdfunding is characterized by an intense concentration of Internet users that join for a common monetary purpose. Crowdfunding symbolizes an umbrella term being used to define an increasingly growing form of fundraising, typically via the Internet, where both individuals and legal entities contribute to support a particular goal (Ahlers et al., 2015). A recently published study by the University of Pennsylvania (Mollick, 2016) concluded that just the projects successfully funded on one US-based platform, Kickstarter.com, have created 300,000 new full- and part-time jobs, and had a global economic impact of USD 5.3 billion, which is equal to the yearly revenue of the government budget of the Democratic Republic of Congo, or five times the size of the annual revenue of the budget in Monaco (CIA, 2017a, 2017b).

This chapter explores the current development of the crowdfunding landscape with a focus on Sweden. It reviews the types of crowdfunding, the non-financial benefits, the types of platforms, introduces aspects of regulation, and projects potential development scenarios.

Roads toward modern crowdfunding

The precise factors leading to the rise of crowdfunding are still not completely understood. Researchers argue that the crowdfunding model did benefit from a variety of factors, such as the growing accessibility of the Internet, the digitization of trust, the creation of new legislation, which increased risk aversion by traditional financial providers, and the decline of bank funding for companies after the 2009 financial crisis.

Following a study conducted by the US Small Business Administration, 99.95 percent of entrepreneurs at an early stage of development will not receive venture capital (VC) funding to sufficiently fulfill their financial needs (Rao, 2013). The study revealed the average age of a company funded by VC funds is around four years old, which excludes early-stage ventures from funding. A study in Switzerland concluded that since the international financial crisis in 2009, many VC companies that were providing funding for early-stage companies, called "pre-seed" and "seed funding," leveraged their investments toward potentially less risky investments of entrepreneurs with more presence on the market (Salomon, 2016). The shift to more mature companies by VCs, and the decrease of loan availability from traditional financial providers such as banks, left a vacuum in the startup financing cycle and increased the so-called "funding gap"[1] in the startup financing cycle, which has been fairly filled with different crowdfunding services.

Today, crowdfunding finances, nearly exclusively, small and medium enterprises (SMEs). Swedish SMEs account for 65.69 percent of all full-time employment positions, so its development and well-being is crucial for macroeconomic stability. Swedish small and medium-size companies have recovered well after the financial crisis, as their value added increased by 30 percent between 2010 and 2015. Employment grew in this period by 8 percent. The 2016 and 2017 outlook expected SMEs to grow by 7 percent and 6 percent, respectively. Employment is expected to increase by 3 percent in 2017, which translates into 120,000 new jobs. A positive outlook will lead to a growing funding gap that might result in an increasing market of potential clients for both the national and international crowdfunding industry (European Commission, 2016a). The growth of crowdfunding might support business owners to close, or at least diminish, their capital needs. A recent staff working document of the European Commission underlined crowdfunding as a vital part of empowering entrepreneurs in the face of the downside of a global economy (Buysere et al., 2012). Crowdfunding was named a job creator that helps to jump-start economic activity (European Commission, 2016b).

Genome of crowdfunding

Crowdfunding companies have several subcategories of products, targeting entrepreneurs at different developmental stages, and investors with various investment potential. Platforms such as Kickstarter.com raise nearly SEK 700 (EUR 72) per backer, per project (Kickstarter, 2017). Companies such as FundedByMe.com report an average investment of SEK 52,500 (EUR 5,400) per investor, per project. The target market of those two companies remains very different. The recent growth of crowdfunding toward new fields such as real estate, by platforms such as Tessin.se, has increased the average investment amount to SEK 100,500 (EUR 10,400) per capital provider, per project. Nevertheless, Kickstarter.com and FundedByMe.com, as well as platforms such as Tessin.se, are part of one industry defined as "crowdfunding."

Despite a lack of commonly accepted classification, on both the national and European level, on types of crowdfunding, listed below are the most common types of crowdfunding platforms (Baeck, Collins, and Zhang, 2014).

Donation-based crowdfunding

- Purpose: Capital providers back a donation-based initiative and expect nothing in return.
- Recipients: Individuals, early-stage funding for founders, nongovernmental organizations.
- What is being offered in return from the entrepreneurs: No reward.
- Examples of platforms that operate on the Swedish market, both national and foreign: AGreatDay.com,[2] Crowdculture.se, Takespace.se.

Reward-based crowdfunding

- Purpose: Capital providers back a project with the expectation of receiving a tangible (but non-financial) reward or product later in exchange for their contribution.
- Recipients: Individuals, founders at early stages of projects, a test of market fit, companies.
- What is being offered in return from the entrepreneurs: Physical reward, such as an actual product. Examples: books, apps, vouchers for food or beverages.
- Examples of platforms that operate on the Swedish market, both national and foreign: Kickstarter.com (foreign), Indiegogo.com (foreign).

Equity-based crowdfunding

- Purpose: Sale of a stake in the business to some investors in return for investment.
- Recipients: Limited liability companies, both private and public.
- What is being offered in return from the entrepreneurs: Stake in the company. The capital provider can purchase a certain number of shares.
- Examples of platforms that operate on the Swedish market, both national and foreign: Peppins.se, FundedByMe.se, Crowdcube.com (foreign), Invesdor.com (foreign), Sciety.se (life science projects only).

Lending-based crowdfunding (also called P2P lending or crowdlending)

- Purpose: Debt-based transactions between individuals and existing businesses, mostly SMEs, with many lenders contributing to one loan.
- Recipients: Companies incorporated for at least 12–18 months, individuals with positive credit score data.
- What is being offered in return from the entrepreneurs: Lender is purchasing secured, unsecured, or convertible debt.

- Examples of platforms that operate on the Swedish market, both national and foreign: Lendify.se (C2C), Saveland.se (C2C), Toborrow.se (C2B, B2B), FundedByMe.com (C2B).

Real estate crowdfunding

- Purpose: Debt- or equity-based transactions between individuals and existing or future real estate owners.
- Recipients: Real estate owners.
- What is being offered in return from the entrepreneurs: Investor can purchase an equity or debt in a real estate project.
- Examples of platforms that operate on the Swedish market, both national and foreign: Tessin.se, Kameo.se, Co-owning.com.
- It could be argued that real estate crowdfunding is a part of equity- or debt-based crowdfunding, depending on the type of return for the investor.

Growth of crowdfunding

Since 2009, the compound annual growth rate (CAGR) of the crowdfunding industry has been doubling yearly. By the end of 2015, a crowdfunding industry report announced that all crowdfunding platforms combined had collected USD 34 billion globally per annum (Massolution, 2015). This investment amount represents USD 4 billion more than all global venture capitalist investments that have been provided to entrepreneurs within a year. In a special report by the World Bank on crowdfunding, the bank predicts crowdfunding has the ability to triple its current market size globally and reach up to USD 96 billion by 2025 (World Bank, 2013). The growth of user bases around 100 percent CAGR has been stated by all crowdfunding companies that agreed to an interview in Sweden. For example, FundedByMe.com, one of the equity-based crowdfunding platforms in Sweden, has reported a growth of 100 percent during 2016. According to the platform representatives, the average investment per investor, per project is SEK 52,500 (EUR 5,400) (Daboczy, 2016). This growth has been exceeded by Tessin.se, which grew by 340 percent in terms of capital growth, and 452 percent in terms of revenue (Tessin, 2017, p.10).

Alina Lundqvist, Head of Business Development from FundedByMe.com, stated in an interview that campaign sizes of SEK 5–6 million (EUR 500,000–600,000) were quite easy to finance at the end of 2016. This is a significant change in comparison with 2013, where the biggest funded campaigns in equity-based crowdfunding did not exceed SEK 100,000 (EUR 9,500).

Focus on non-financial benefits

Receiving funding via crowdfunding allows a range of additional benefits compared to traditional loans or government grants. Entrepreneurs receive not only funding, but additionally can utilize the support of an extensive informal network of capital providers.

Entrepreneurs that seek funding are launching campaigns on the platform of their choice, specifying how the funds will be used, and which type of investors they are looking for. Besides closing the funding needs, crowdfunding offers significant marketing opportunities. The launch of a campaign might leverage the informal network of the crowdfunding platform and its user base for entrepreneurs.

Besides providing an alternative source of financing directly, crowdfunding can offer other benefits to capital seekers and provide the entrepreneur with insights and information crowdsourced during the campaign, which is an invaluable marketing tool if a campaign succeeds. Crowdfunding creates opportunities to turn large groups of people, who otherwise would not have access to traditional channels of finance, into small-scale entrepreneurs. It introduces competition to other sources of finance, and as it is often used by innovative, artistic, and social SMEs, the projects funded by crowdfunding often promote innovation, cultural development, and social entrepreneurship (European Commission, 2013).

> We have been seeking funds via two types of crowdfunding: equity crowdfunding and crowdlending. We decided to use these options due to the lack of support from other state-based banking/funding forms when we needed them most. The benefit of "the crowd" supporting and endorsing us was a significant non-financial benefit in that it gave a vindication that we had something the market liked! During our campaigns, we specified in our "pitch" that we would like to develop our business internationally, specifically toward Germany, the UK, and the US. The investors that invested in us apparently wanted to support us in the internalization process we had outlined in our campaign. On a regional level, we have attracted attention from local journalists that were writing about us during the campaign, and also about our contribution to creating welcome jobs in the region. The cost of crowdlending is not cheap, but at least it was available, even if having to give a personal guarantee.
>
> —Mike Redford, CEO, AddMovement.com

The current state of crowdfunding research points out additional benefits of using crowdfunding:

- *Co-creation*: Crowdfunding allows potential customers and capital providers to develop a relationship with the project owner to influence a particular product or development within a company.
- *Fundraising*: Collecting funding for particular projects remains at the core of goals of crowdfunding for capital seekers.
- *Marketing*: The online presence of crowdfunding projects has simplified the sharing of information across geographical borders (Agrawal, Catalini, and Goldfarb, 2011). The presence of a crowdfunding project allows entrepreneurs to create awareness for potential capital providers, media, and potential clients. Nevertheless, the process of sharing information across geographic borders has particular limits that will be explored in the next chapter.

- *Market research*: Due to the high accessibility of crowdfunding campaigns online (Mollick, 2014), crowdfunding allows entrepreneurs to find the most efficient market–product fit. Overfunded projects in, for example, reward-based crowdfunding send a strong signal as an acceptance test. Such a positive signal will help attract other sources of funding such as VC or business angels at a later stage of an SME's development (Riedl et al., 2013).
- *Presales*: Allows entrepreneurs to collect funding for products in advance that will be delivered at a later point in time (Hemer et al., 2011). This particular type of benefit within crowdfunding has mostly been used for reward and real estate crowdfunding, where capital seekers collect funding before their engagement into the production or construction process.

Crowdfunding in practice for entrepreneurs

Crowdfunding platforms that operate in Sweden allow entrepreneurs, companies, and individuals to create, upload, and describe their funding needs on a multisided platform,[3] depending on the desired type of crowdfunding.

Submitted projects are being mostly reviewed by platform employees and pushed to "go live" for a limited time period of around 40 to 90 days. During this time period, the capital seekers undertake a substantial marketing effort to attract new capital providers, or entice investors who have invested in other projects on the same crowdfunding platform.

Platforms differ strongly in their activity to attract their existing user base to particular projects. Some platforms have been organizing offline investor meetings where capital seekers pitch their ideas; some perform an offline introduction by a platform's management; others distribute emails to their current user base, or contact the biggest capital providers personally.

Swedish crowdfunding platforms are different from traditional financial providers such as banks, VCs, or business angels, as they do not borrow, lend, or invest money by themselves. The funding mechanism is based on the facilitation of a digital meeting in which the capital seeker can meet the capital providers with the help of a particular platform. The platform's goal is to reduce the transaction costs and lower the uncertainty, while providing structured information about a particular campaign (Gierczak et al., 2016).

If the desired amount of funds has been collected on the platform, the campaign is considered "successfully closed" and the funds are paid out to the capital seekers. In case the capital seekers have not been able to collect the entire desired amount of funds, the payout process depends on each platform's terms of service.

Platforms' payout policies

Platforms make money on a small initial fee, and a larger success fee deducted before the payout of collected funds. It is in both the capital seekers' and platforms' interest to keep the raised funding amount as high as possible, to receive the highest possible commission. Nevertheless, as entrepreneurs specify an explicit goal in their online campaign, some of their goals are not reachable in cases where the funding amount has not been collected fully. This fact differentiates platforms' payout policies, which are split into one of the following subcategories:

- *All or nothing policy*: Capital seekers receive the pledged amount only when their project reaches a predefined funding goal. Platform representatives of crowdfunding platforms that follow this policy argue that only this policy allows the entrepreneur to deliver on the promises specified in their campaign (Cumming, Leboeuf, and Schwienbacher, 2014). If the anticipated volume of funds has not been collected with the help of the platform, the funds are returned to the funders via bank wire or credit card transfer.
- *Keep it all*: Capital seekers receive any collected pledges. This policy structure is mostly being executed while using donation-based platforms that finance NGO and charity payments (Gierczak, Bretschneider, and Leimeister, 2014).

Additionally, crowdfunding platforms differ in internal policies on how to process projects that collect more funding than what was initially desired by the capital seekers:

- *Overfunding*: Capital seekers can collect more funding than what was indicated as the "funding goal." This is a common industry practice for all types of crowdfunding except debt-based crowdfunding. Crowdlending companies tend to limit the amount of collected funding to the funding goal.[4]

Furthermore, funds should only be paid out when both the capital providers' and campaign owners' identity have been verified, in a procedure known as know your customer (KYC) and know your business (KYB), to diminish potential criminal activities such as money laundering.

Security of crowdfunding

The level of security strongly depends on the business models chosen by each crowdfunding platform. Most platforms act only as an intermediary between the investors and entrepreneur, or borrowers and lenders. This means the contracts are being facilitated between those different parties, and outside of the platform. In such a business model setup, if a platform might go into bankruptcy, the agreements between the users who supported a project and send in a project remain in place.

All types of crowdfunding share the following risks for the users:

- *Advertising risks*: The advertised companies, projects, development, and technology might not reflect the real situation within a company as the disclosure required by entrepreneurial firms is lower than by the prospectus regulation.

- *The cost of capital*: Compared with other sources of financing, crowdfunding represents usually a more expensive cost of capital (Agrawal, Catalini, and Goldfarb, 2015), averaging at around 10 percent of the raised capital and frequency charge.
- *Dilution of ownership*: Entrepreneurs might squander the proceeds of funding rounds with equity-based crowdfunding, and then subsequently issue more shares to them, which would cause diluting the equity values being held by the investors (Cumming et al., 2016).
- *Intellectual property protection*: Entrepreneurs might face imitation-based competitors while sharing their business ideas with the public over the Internet, as their ideas are exposed to competitors that specialize in imitation-based business models (European Commission, 2013).
- *Lack or insufficient size of the secondary market*: Purchased investment might not be transferrable to other investors, or this transfer might be difficult as the secondary market might not exist or experience low liquidity.
- *Losses*: General project or product failures may lead to high losses. The company might face reconstruction or bankruptcy, advertised technology might not be launched or delivered on time, or a loan might default.
- *Payments*: The way platforms facilitate payments, calculate interest rates, and issue refunds often relies on external payment service providers.
- *The risk of fraud*: The risk that funds collected might be misused, or used in another way than stated by the project's campaign page, can constitute fraud, but is not illegal because the money was freely given.

Potential examples of challenges within the Swedish crowdfunding scene are as follows:

- *Lack of unified risk assessment methodology*: In crowdlending, platforms act as a broker, where companies or individuals are applying for a loan as they would to a bank. The platforms are evaluating the risk level using a "scoring model," and present a certain risk analysis to the potential lenders. The lenders, based on their own assessment, and scoring provided by the platform, make their own decision if they would like to lend money to a potential borrower. As risk analysis methodology is performed by each crowdfunding platform separately, it is not unified, and differs from platform to platform. The lenders might have to compare the risk analysis models between the platforms, which might be time-consuming and difficult for investors with a limited financial background.
- *A default of a platform*: In 2015, the new management of a prominent Swedish-funded high-yield C2C debt-based crowdlending platform called Trustbuddy.se, reported "misconduct of activities" (Busch and Mak, 2016) as the new management team uncovered SEK 44 million of shortage on accounts containing the lenders' funds. Lindahl[5] informed lenders that it was uncertain if all borrowers could repay their loans. Trustbuddy.se's lenders received the information that the loans might not be repaid in full, or repaid at

all (Lindahl, 2017). A former lender into Trustbuddy.se loans reported in an interview for this chapter that as of March 2017, he had received 10 percent of his investments, and had been informed an additional 10 percent might be released shortly.

- *Lack of commonly accepted industry standards in corporate valuation*: In equity crowdfunding, the investors buy a certain amount of equity (stake) in a potential company. As there are different ways to estimate the value of a company, investors with a more limited financial background might find it difficult to review the foundation of a corporate valuation published by an entrepreneur. Investors that invested in equity crowdfunding usually await an initial public offering (IPO) on a stock exchange of the company to perform an investment exit. The IPOs of enterprises that have been funded with equity crowdfunding in Sweden can be counted on one hand.[6]

> A self-regulation might be needed as different equity crowdfunding use various valuation methods. Additionally, all of the crowdlending platforms perform risk analyses in a different way and call various risk classes in the same way as "A." This mixed approach has resulted in blurring the lines and might confuse potential lenders.
>
> —Erik Durhan, Head of Corporate Governance
> Nordea, EMBA Alumni

Regulation of crowdfunding in Sweden

Crowdfunding has not yet been fully codified in Swedish regulations. Its regulation is allocated in different sections of the legislation, created a long time before the FinTech age. On July 30, 2015, the Swedish government commissioned the Swedish financial authorities (Finansinspektionen) to investigate and extend their knowledge about the two types of crowdfunding, lending- and equity-based, with an expectation of a financial yield and their conditions for growth and sustainable development (Crowdfunding Hub, 2016a).

> We at Tessin.se[7] are currently in a stage that I would call a Swedish regulation hole. As the Swedish government is currently working on a new regulatory framework for some areas of crowdfunding, we don't know if we will not have to apply for other licenses in Sweden shortly. This lack of regulatory framework has created some uncertainty on our side, and we decided to wait for the application for a MiFID license until we receive clarify from the public body. Unfortunately, it is unclear when this new regulation will be announced and implemented by the government.
>
> —Johan, CEO Tessin.se.

The Swedish Financial Supervision, published in December 2015, is the result of the analysis on crowdfunding. The review states under certain circumstances, for example if the platform is judged to require authorization pursuant to the Payment

Service Act (2010:751), it is not clear if the responsibility for the supervision falls to the Swedish Financial Supervisory Authority or the Swedish Consumer Agency (Finansinspektionen, 2015).

In case an equity crowdfunding platform specifies to act as an intermediary and does not trade transferable securities in Sweden, the law[8] does not require the platform to apply for a license or registrations, and is not supervised by financial supervision authorities (Crowdfunding Hub, 2016a).

This is important for equity crowdfunding companies, because the Swedish Private Limited Liability Company, called Privat Aktiebolag (Privat AB), is the most common SME company type for legal entities in Sweden. Privat AB companies cannot advertise their desire to sell shares to the public, and can't take in over 200 new shareholders in one share issue.

For potential investors to view financial information, business plans, or financial forecasts of a Privat AB during an equity-based crowdfunding campaign on a Swedish platform without a MiFID[9] license, the platform requires the user to become an "exclusive member" while signing up, even going so far as to require social media accounts.

After logging in as an "exclusive member," the investor has access to full information provided by the company that is seeking funding. The platform advertises no offerings from Privat AB companies—it "informs" the project is seeking funds (being informed about a share issue process is not considered advertisement). One of the leading platforms blocks the share issue process once the 200-investor limit is reached. If the company would like to continue to raise funds, the Privat AB board must decide to issue shares for a second or third time. In this way, regulating an intake of 200 investors can be enforced (Crowdfunding Hub, 2016b).

It is unclear where the number of "200 new shareholders" originated; the Swedish Financial Supervision has considered the offering of a presale share purchase possibility, while sign-up for an issuance by up to 200 investors is regarded as a potential violation of the prohibition (Crowdfunding Hub, 2016a).

Until now, there has not been an extensive study on crowdfunding platform investors, backers, and lenders to review who is actually participating and financing companies and individuals on crowdfunding platforms. If the result of such a study concludes that professional investors[10] participate mostly in equity-based crowdfunding and crowdlending, their level of investor protection must be significantly lower than with consumers' investments.

Potential future scenarios of the national crowdfunding landscape in Sweden

Assuming the Swedish crowdfunding market will follow the European trend and double yearly, it might continue to offer numerous benefits to Swedish small or medium enterprises, helping to close the capital gap in their funding needs (Massolution, 2015). Swedish crowdfunding remains relatively decentralized, as many players offer services in their niches. We have seen a range of companies enter the crowdfunding market in both 2016 and 2017, for example Co-owning.

com, Peppins.se, and Tessin.se. This development has increased the public awareness of crowdfunding, but additionally increased the competition within the market. The crowdfunding market benefits from accessibility, but relies on the quality of the Internet infrastructure, and the digitalization of trust:

- *Synergy*: In this scenario, the Swedish crowdfunding platforms might form an organization that would facilitate self-regulation on the platforms. Such an organization could enforce "coercive isomorphic change"[11] in the industry (DiMaggio and Powell, 1983). Platforms would agree on types of valuation methods used for equity-based crowdfunding, scoring, and risk analysis models used for crowdlending. Such a development would bring a stronger transparency into the market and allow investors to directly compare different campaigns offered on various platforms.
- *Winner-takes-all market*: In this scenario, crowdfunding platforms, both national and foreign, that have undergone the complex regulatory process of receiving an MiFID license or a banking license might attract significant institutional capital. This increase of capital might result in a merge and acquisition of platforms with complementary assets. Such a strategic alliance would increase the rate of new features and product development, and crystallize recognizable market leaders in crowdfunding. The scenario would work by the theory of network effects,[12] as those merged platforms would have a bigger user base, and these users would attract a more significant number of new users in a snowball effect.
- *Participation of public funding*: In this scenario, public authorities in Sweden would allocate funding alongside crowdfunding. This process would recognize crowdfunding as a tool to diminish the so-called market failures[13] resulting from funding gap for entrepreneurs. This model is being executed in the UK. At the beginning of January 2017, Funding Circle, a crowdlending platform that allows entrepreneurs to seek funding, received GBP 40 million. The UK government, in the form of the British Business Bank, previously injected GBP 60 million into the platform. This funding has been distributed to around 10,000 businesses in the UK and allowed the bank to earn GBP 5 million in net interests over the past four years. Such cooperation allows the government to use the peer-to-peer side as a channel through which small businesses might be supported (Dunkley, 2016). The participation of public funding might be available to small businesses via the platform. Such a development might benefit the platforms, entrepreneurs, and the governmental institutions.
- *Active Financial Supervision (FI) 2.0 as a catalyst for growth and facilitator*: In this scenario, the Financial Supervision would increase its position from the regulator to a moderator and facilitator. There would be an increase of the budget and active incorporation of new employees with a FinTech background. The goal of the FI 2.0 would be not only to regulate, but to promote, alternative finance. Financial Supervision 2.0 would take a membership seat in the Swedish FinTech associations, and provide guidelines for high industry standards. The regulator as "moderator of the market model"

is being executed by the Securities Commission Malaysia in Kuala Lumpur. The Malaysian regulator is not only responsible for regulating the equity- and lending-based platforms, but additionally ensures that any imposed regulation is developing the market. The Securities Commission is facilitating roundtables with all platforms two times a year, and it hosts and promotes alternative finance conferences. It issues best practice guides and meets with representatives of platforms regularly (Securities Commission Malaysia, 2015).

- *Partnerships with traditional financial providers*: In this scenario, facilitated in the US and the UK, banks would partner with crowdfunding platforms (Dunkley, 2016). In such a partnership, banks could use the platforms as deal generators and co-finance loans of the entrepreneurs that would fulfill the scoring criteria from banks. The platforms and entrepreneurs would benefit, as their campaign needs would be reached quicker, which will increase the cash flow liquidity in the market.
- *Provide other funding options to declined loan applications*: This process has been initiated in the UK after the government issued a law that forces banks to ask small business owners to pass on their details to alternative finance providers (HM Treasury, 2014). According to a survey, only 3 percent of entrepreneurs were seeking alternative funding sources after being declined by a bank (Bank Referral Scheme, Small Business, Enterprise and Employment Act 2015).[14] This non-financial intervention aimed to reduce the funding gaps of entrepreneurs. Banks that inform entrepreneurs about alternative sources of funding might potentially receive a commission from alternative financial providers.

Notes

1 Funding gap—defines the amount of funding needed to continue to finance ongoing operations, which are not provided by entrepreneurs' own cash, equity, or debt sources.
2 This platform is still operational but has no active projects online. An interview request remains without a response (accessed, March 1, 2017).
3 Multisided platform—serves as an intermediary for two or more groups of customers who are linked to indirect network effects (Evans and Noel, 2008).
4 As capital seekers have to repay the loan, their "working capital," or "free capacity."
5 Lindahl.se—Swedish-based law firm that facilitated the bankruptcy of Trustbuddy.se.
6 Low amount of IPO might be connected with the novelty of the market as equity crowdfunding investments have been possible in Sweden since 2013.
7 Tessin.se is a Swedish real estate crowdfunding platform.
8 According to the Securities Market Act (2007:528).
9 MiFID—the Markets in Financial Instruments Directive 2004/39/EC.
10 Professional investors are being defined as individuals who earn a significant amount of their income with earnings from their investments.
11 Coercive isomorphic change—involves the pressure that is being executed by the society on particular organizations, groups, or companies (DiMaggio and Powell, 1983). Such a development can lead to coercive isomorphism, where organizations might like to copy behavior. A crowdfunding industry organization in Sweden

could agree on professional standards that would be imitated by players in the market without government intervention.

12 Network effect—a phenomenon in which a good service or a product increases its value with an increasing number of users. Airbnb or Uber might be a good example of the network effect. Platform services became more attractive while adding new hosts and travelers for Airbnb or drivers to the Uber network. As new users join the platforms, the services become more and more appealing, and still generate more new users, comparable to a snowball effect.

13 Market failures occur in the free market, when an allocation of resources shows signs of inefficient distribution in a particular market.

14 Bank Referral Scheme, Small Business, Enterprise and Employment Act 2015 available here: www.legislation.gov.uk/ukpga/2015/26/section/5/enacted [Accessed March 15, 2017].

Bibliography

Agrawal, A., Catalini, C., and Goldfarb, A., 2011. *The geography of crowdfunding*. Cambridge, MA: National Bureau of Economic Research.

Agrawal, A., Catalini, C., and Goldfarb, A., 2015. Crowdfunding: Geography, social networks, and the timing of investment decisions. *Journal of Economics & Management Strategy*, 24(2), pp.253–274.

Ahlers, G.K.C., Cumming, D., Günther, C., and Schweizer, D., 2015. Signaling in equity crowdfunding. *Entrepreneurship Theory and Practice*, 39(4), pp.955–980.

Baeck, P., Collins, L., and Zhang, B., 2014. *The UK alternative finance industry report 2014*. [online] Available at: www.nesta.org.uk [Accessed August 25, 2017].

Busch, C. and Mak, V., 2016. Peer-to-peer lending in the European Union. *Journal of European Consumer and Market*, 5(4), pp.181–181.

Buysere, D.K., Gajda, O., Kleverlaan, R., and Marom, D., 2012. *A framework for european crowdfunding*. [online] Available at: http://www.academia.edu/11377521/FRAMEWORK_EU_CROWDFUNDING [Accessed January 6, 2018].

CIA, 2017a. *World Factbook: Congo*. [online] Available at: https://www.cia.gov/library/publications/resources/the-world-factbook/geos/cf.html [Accessed January 6, 2018].

CIA, 2017b. *World Factbook: Monaco*. [online] Available at: https://www.cia.gov/library/publications/resources/the-world-factbook/geos/mn.html [Accessed January 6, 2018].

Crowdfunding Hub, 2016a. *Crowdfunding crossing borders*. [online] Available at: www.fglawyersamsterdam.com/wp content/uploads/2016/03/20160331-Crowdfunding-Crossing-Borders-Report.pdf [Accessed August 25, 2017].

Crowdfunding Hub, 2016b. *Current state of crowdfunding in Europe*. [online] Available at: www.sbs.ox.ac.uk/sites/default/files/Entrepreneurship_Centre/Docs/OxEPR2/current-state-crowdfunding-europe-2016.pdf [Accessed August 25, 2017].

Cumming, D., Leboeuf, G., and Schwienbacher, A., 2014. Crowdfunding models: Keep-it-all vs. all-or-nothing. *EUROFIDAI-AFFI paper (Vol.10)*. [online] Available at: http://leeds-faculty.colorado.edu/Bhagat/CrowdfundingModels-KeppItAll-AllorNothing.pdf [Accessed August 25, 2017].

Cumming, D., Hornuf, L., Karami, M., and Schweizer, D., 2016. *Disentangling crowdfunding from fraudfunding*. [online] Max Planck Institute for Innovation & Competition. Available at: https://papers.ssrn.com/sol3/papers.cfm?abstract_id=2828919 [Accessed August 25, 2017].

Daboczy, D., 2016. *Crowdfunding overview: FundedByMe doubles total money raised.* [online] FundedByMe. Available at: http://blog.fundedbyme.com/ [Accessed August 25, 2017].

DiMaggio, P.J. and Powell, W.W., 1983. The iron cage revisited: Institutional isomorphism and collective rationality in organizational fields. *American Sociological Review*, 48(2), pp.147–160.

Dunkley, E., 2016. Santander UK enters partnership with crowdfunder. *Financial Times*. [online] Available at: www.ft.com/content/5ee92158-8945-11e6-8cb7-e7ada1d123b1 [Accessed August 25, 2017].

European Commission, 2013. *Crowdfunding in the EU: Exploring the added value of potential EU action*. Consultation Document. [online] Available at: http://ec.europa.eu/finance/consultations/2013/Crowdfunding/docs/consultation-document_en.pdf [Accessed August 25, 2017].

European Commission, 2016a. *SME performance review*. [online] Available at: http://ec.europa.eu/growth/smes/business-friendly-environment/performance-review-2016_pl [Accessed August 25, 2017].

European Commission, 2016b. *Commission staff working document: Report on crowdfunding in the EU capital markets union*. [online] Available at: https://ec.europa.eu/info/system/files/crowdfunding-report-03052016_en.pdf [Accessed September 13, 2017].

Evans, D.S. and Noel, M.D., 2008. The analysis of mergers that involve multisided platform businesses. *Journal of Competition Law & Economics*, 4(3), pp.663–695.

Finansinspektionen, 2015. *Crowdfunding in Sweden: An overview*. [online] Available at: www.fi.se/en/published/reports/reports/2015/crowdfunding-in-sweden [Accessed December 6, 2017].

Gierczak, M., Bretschneider, U., and Leimeister, J., 2014. *Is all that glitters gold? Exploring the effects of perceived risk on backing behavior in reward-based crowdfunding*. [online] Available at: http://aisel.aisnet.org/icis2014/proceedings/EBusiness/43/ [Accessed August 25, 2017].

Gierczak, M., Bretschneider, U., Haas, P., Blohm, I., and Leimeister, J.M., 2016. Crowdfunding: Outlining the new era of fundraising. In: D. Brüntje and O. Gadja, eds. *Crowdfunding in Europe: FGF studies in small business and entrepreneurship*. Cham: Springer, pp.7–23.

Hemer, J., Schneider, U., Dornbusch, F., and Frey, S., 2011. *Crowdfunding und andere Formen informeller Mikrofinanzierung in der Projekt- und Innovationsfinanzierung [Crowdfunding and other types of informal Microfinance possibilities in project and innovation finance]*. Stuttgart: Fraunhofer Verlag.

HM Treasury, 2014. *Consultation outcome, SME finance: Help to match SMEs rejected for finance with alternative lenders*. [online] Available at: www.gov.uk/government/consultations/sme-finance-help-to-match-smes-rejected-for-finance-with-alternative-lenders/sme-finance-help-to-match-smes-rejected-for-finance-with-alternative-lenders [Accessed September 13, 2017].

Kickstarter, 2017. *Kickstarter stats*. [online] Available at: www.kickstarter.com/help/stats [Accessed September 13, 2017].

Lindahl, 2017. *Questions about TrustBuddy's bankruptcy*. [online] Available at: https://www.lindahl.se/en/latest-news/cases-and-transactions/2015/lindahl-manages-the-bankruptcy-in-trustbuddy [Accessed January 6, 2018].

Massolution, 2015. *The Crowdfunding Industry Report 2015*. [online] Available at: http://reports.crowdsourcing.org/index.php?route=product/product&product_id=54 [Accessed December 6, 2017].

Mollick, E., 2014. The dynamics of crowdfunding: An exploratory study. *Journal of Business Venturing*, 29(1), pp.1–16.

Mollick, E., 2016. *Containing multitudes: The many impacts of Kickstarter funding.* [online] Available at: https://papers.ssrn.com/sol3/papers.cfm?abstract_id=2808000 [Accessed August 25, 2017].

Rao, D., 2013. Why 99.95% of entrepreneurs should stop wasting time seeking venture capital. *Forbes*. [online] Available at: www.forbes.com/sites/dileeprao/2013/07/22/why-99-95-of-entrepreneurs-should-stop-wasting-time-seeking-venture-capital/#647f840b46eb [Accessed August 25, 2017].

Riedl, C., Blohm, I., Leimeister, J.M., and Krcmar, H., 2013. The effect of rating scales on decision quality and user attitudes in online innovation communities. *International Journal of Electronic Commerce*, 17(3), pp.7–36.

Salomon, V., 2016. Emergent models of financial intermediation for innovative companies: from venture capital to crowdinvesting platforms in Switzerland. *Venture Capital*, 18(1), pp.21–41.

Securities Commission Malaysia, 2015. *Guidelines on recognized markets.* [online] Available at: www.sc.com.my/wp-content/uploads/eng/html/resources/guidelines/recognizedmkt/guidelines_recognizedMarket_160413.pdf [Accessed August 25, 2017].

Tessin, 2017. *Building the leading platform for digital real estate financing: Q1 2017.* [Unpublished Electronic Presentation]. Stockholm: Tessin.

World Bank, 2013. *Crowdfunding's potential for the developing world.* [online] pp.1–104. Available at: www.infodev.org/infodev-files/wb_crowdfundingreport-v12.pdf [Accessed September 13, 2017].

13 The payment landscape in Sweden

Niklas Arvidsson

Introduction

Sweden was one of the first countries to launch government-supported cash, and may become one of the first to stop issuing government-supported cash. The development since 2012 has been very fast in terms of a reduction of the use of cash and an increased use of mobile payment services for peer-to-peer (P2P) payments, but there has also been an increase in the number of new firms in the payment sector and the number of alternative services that are on the market. A likely next step in this development is the introduction of contactless cards—which hitherto have been absent on the Swedish market—and other mobile payment services. This is a step in the progression toward more mobile payments, which also includes person-to-business (P2B) payments. We can also foresee a continued decrease in the use of cash, which is discussed in more detail in Chapter 4 in this volume. This chapter concludes by discussing critical factors that are the most likely to affect the development of retail payments in Sweden in the coming years.

The recent history of payment services in Sweden

The twentieth century use of payment services in Sweden was deeply influenced by the strong growth of the Swedish economy after World War II as industrialization was strengthened and international trade grew. Employment was high and real wages grew, which led to a demand for banking services. In the mid-1900s, the use of cash was widespread, even though electronic payment services were established and gradually growing in popularity. In the 1960s, banks had made efforts to make transaction processing more efficient via digitalization, and influenced employers, unions, and workers to start accepting that salaries and wages were to be paid electronically directly to employees' bank accounts instead of being paid in cash at the employers' offices. It was an easy sell for the banks since employers saved costs, the banks got new customers, unions agreed as long as banks did not charge consumers for cash withdrawals, and employees liked it. This transformation laid the foundation for the electronic banking system for retail payments that we have to this day, where the bank account is the centerpiece for making and receiving payments. Another critical transformation was made in the 1980s and 1990s when card payments started to become a reality for not only the wealthy, but made available to everyone. The use of cards was low in the early stages, but grew incrementally faster in the latter parts of the 1990s (Nyberg and Guibourg, 2003) and became a dominant part of retail payments. Checks were phased out in the 1990s as banks started to charge fees for check handling (Arvidsson, 2013). There was also an attempt by banks to launch prepaid cards, so-called "cash cards," as a less costly alternative to debit and credit cards. However, these cash cards never gained popularity among merchants and consumers, and the project pulled to a halt. Although the early 2000s saw high expectations for the establishment of mobile payments, it would not be until 2014 for these services to become conventional in the market.

The landscape for retail payments had become dominated by card payments (primarily debit cards), even if cash was still quite popular, as discussed by Arvidsson (2013). However, this was about to take a sharp turn. In the mid-2000s, there was an increase in cash-related robberies of banks, merchants, cash depots, and even of the public transportation system. Hence, efforts were made seeking to reduce the use of cash in Sweden. Lobbying campaigns against cash, such as "Kontantfritt.nu," as well as action by banks and others, such as "Tryggare rörelsen," started a movement toward reducing cash. Prominent actors in these movements were unions in public transportation, banks, and merchants. Unions and merchants acted primarily from a work environment perspective, and banks both saw the work environment issue but also had a genuine business interest in reducing the use of cash. Banks did not have revenues connected to cash, and would be happy if cash payments were replaced by card payments—an area where banks showed good profitability.

The most spectacular robbery was the so-called "helicopter robbery" of a cash depot in Stockholm on September 23, 2009 (Bonnier, 2017). This was a rigorously planned and well-executed robbery of a cash depot where the robbers used a helicopter, explosives, machine guns, and other devices to steal SEK 39 million (approximately EUR 5 million at that time). The robbers used fake bombs to hinder police helicopters from taking off, various tools to stop police cars, and stolen getaway cars. The robbers then dumped the money and landed the helicopter in a remote area where they finally set it ablaze. All robbers, save one, would ultimately escape with the money.

In retrospect, it is likely that the use of cash peaked in 2007 in Sweden, when the nominal value of cash in circulation was at its highest level of around SEK 110 billion (Arvidsson, 2013). This figure has decreased rapidly since then, and the nominal value of cash in circulation in Sweden is well below SEK 50 billion in November 2017. The number has decreased by 50 percent in 10 years! Paradoxically, it was at this peak that the Swedish Central Bank, the Riksbank, decided to launch new bills and coins in Sweden during the years 2015–2017. The decision was at the time well motivated by efforts to avoid counterfeit money and to make cash handling more efficient. To this end, the development during the last 10 years was not possible to predict.

Another factor reducing the interest in cash payments from the merchant perspective was the bankruptcy and illegal activities by the cash-in-transit service company Panaxia. The company filed for bankruptcy in September 2012 due to liquidity problems, as well as the subsequent illegal use of their clients' money in order to cover their own expenses. Some merchants, such as grocery stores, petrol stations, etc., lost significant amounts of money (with some actors losing more than SEK 100 million, or around EUR 11 million at that time). The top managers of the company were later convicted to prison for fraud by a court of law (Svea Hovrätt, 2015). These events made merchants start considering stopping accepting cash payments, an act that is not illegal according to Swedish law. This, in turn, was accentuated by the increase in fees for cash-handling services as competition decreased and the market became dominated by two players.

Mobile payment services were anticipated to start growing already in the early 2000s, but given problems related to learning processes (Arvidsson, 2014b) and a lack of interoperable service platforms (Apanasevic, Markendahl and Arvidsson, 2016), they did not start to make a strong appearance until 2012. The growth of new payment services after 2012 has been remarkable. This is attributed to several factors, such as the advancement of new technologies and new competition, along with the growth of an e-commerce industry. Furthermore, there has been a need for new payment services while interest by consumers has increased (especially so among younger consumers), aided by the strong use of apps and smartphones, as well as a general trend toward digitalization in Sweden. One essential new mobile payment service, Swish, was launched by banks on December 12 at 00:12 in 2012 (Arvidsson, 2015). Swish enabled real-time transactions between consumers (person-to-person payments) without fees and became a natural and efficient substitute to cash for payments between consumers. Another important service that has led to a reduction of cash payments in Sweden is that of iZettle, which is a card payment service based on mobile point-of-sale terminals that are connected to smartphones or tablets. It made it possible to relatively easily start accepting card payments in situations where cash payments had been dominating previously, such as in sports arenas, flea markets, temporary stands, and smaller merchants.

Another factor that influenced Swedish society to start moving toward the reduction of cash usage was identified in macroeconomic studies showing that the social costs of cash are higher than the social costs of card payments. In a study by the Riksbank (Segendorf and Jansson, 2012), it was shown that the social costs of a card payment were estimated to be SEK 5.55, while the social costs of a cash payment in 2013 were estimated to be SEK 8.32. The study concluded that it would be good for the society as a whole if Sweden reduced its use of cash payments and replaced them by primarily debit card payments. Even if politicians in Sweden were not actively engaged in this issue, these studies are likely to have strengthened the idea that reduction of cash usage is advantageous from a macroeconomic perspective. It should be noted, however, that Swedish politicians have emphasized that the actual use of cash is to be decided by the demand for cash from banks, merchants, and ultimately consumers. The responsibility for the Riksbank to make sure cash services are provided is limited to cases and situations where the market does not provide such services. It is consequently primarily a reduction of demand for cash by consumers, merchants, and banks that explains the decreased use of cash.

In recent years, we have seen an intensified debate about the need to ensure cash does not disappear. In 2014, there was an attempt to promote an entirely cash-free music festival (the Bråvalla festival), which failed and led many to doubt the benefits of an entirely cash-free society. The festival later succeeded in becoming cash-free but was cancelled for other reasons. A strong move toward keeping cash in Sweden has instead been made by the so-called "cash uprising" led by the former chief of police Björn Eriksson, who argues that cash payments must be protected and kept as a well-functioning payment service in Sweden (Kontantupproret, 2015). The national organizations for senior citizens, PRO[1] and SPF,[2] also support this initiative. In 2016, the initiative led to a hearing on cash in the Swedish parliament, and one of the political opposition parties, the Center Party, made a statement saying they should act in the political arena to make sure cash services will be provided in Sweden in the future.

The actual introduction of new bills and coins in Sweden in 2015–2017, which was decided in 2008, has led to a paradoxical development. Instead of these new bills and coins being welcomed by consumers, merchants, and banks, it has led to a situation where many have stopped using cash. Banks have reduced their number of retail offices that offer cash-handling services, and less than 50 percent of bank offices provide cash handling today (Ehrenberg and Jansson, 2016). More and more merchants have stopped accepting cash payments since the new bills and coins necessitate investments in new cash registers and other equipment, which, together with other factors such as fees for cash handling and risk of robberies, has led many merchants to say no to cash. This is also facilitated by new, alternative services. Consumers have continued to reduce their use of cash during recent years, and the launch of new cash in Sweden did not change this downward trend.

The Swedish payment system today

There is a long tradition of increasing digitalization of payments in Sweden that started as early as the middle of the twentieth century but has been increasing significantly in speed and coverage in the last decade. The success of substitutes to cash, such as Swish and iZettle, combined with other drivers of change, such as smartphones, bank strategies, the rise of FinTech, new regulations, and other factors, has meant that the last non-digital part of the system, cash, is facing a rapid decline and is potentially becoming marginalized. The introduction of Swedish cash supported by the state in 1668 (see Chapter 4 in this volume) was a successful initiative that is likely to have reached its peak at the end of 2007, when the value of cash in circulation reached its highest level. The decrease in the use of cash has been substantial throughout the past 10 years, and appears to be steadily decreasing in a consistent pattern.

As for actors providing payment services, there have been notable developments in the last 10 years. According to data from the Swedish Companies Registration Office (Bolagsverket), there has been a decline in the number of banks operating in Sweden, which should also be weighed against the increase in other types of payment service providers (see Arvidsson, 2016). The total number of banks in Sweden was 119 in 2015. This is a reduction by more than 10 percent since 2002, which is almost entirely related to a drastic reduction of savings banks. At the same time, we have seen an explosion of companies and services in the field of payments. Based on data from Sweden's Financial Supervisory Authority, Finansinspektionen, there were, for the first half of 2016, 98[3] companies that were licensed to operate as payment institutes, e-money institutes, or payment service providers. In early 2016, there were a total of around 217 companies in Sweden that had licenses to compete in the payment service markets. It should be noted that this number is likely to increase even further when the Second Payment Service Directive (PSD2) is implemented. This directive will provide opportunities for new actors—possibly from FinTech—to get relatively light licenses from the financial authorities to sell payment services that will compete with traditional services such as cash, cards, and current mobile payment services. Notable examples besides iZettle include Kivra, Betalo, Billhop, Seamless, Klarna, and Payair (Arvidsson, 2016).

The payment system is nowadays characterized by new services, businesses, technologies, laws, regulations, systems for the processing of payments, payment situations, customer behavior, and an increasing international competition (Arvidsson, 2016). The incumbent actors, primarily the big retail banks, are facing stronger competition, but have also succeeded in launching innovative services, while the new actors from FinTech and other areas are exploring ways to build services on top of the strongest solutions, such as iZettle building upon the card system, or to challenge the banks head-on, much like the endeavors of Seamless or Klarna. There are, of course, also those that seek collaboration with the banks to innovate and produce new services, much like the collaboration between SEB and Tink, where SEB invested in the FinTech company Tink, which led to a collaboration on developing new services that complement SEB's other banking services.

Arvidsson (2016) summarized the situation by arguing that the payment system is in a situation characterized by:

- increasingly specialized service providers;
- a reduced use of traditional services (including cash currency);
- the introduction of new bills and coins, in combination with new services, which seems to have contributed to an accelerated reduction of cash usage;
- a rapid growth of new mobile services such as Swish and iZettle;
- changing regulations that are likely to increase competition in the form of both new services and new companies (e.g., Payment Services Directives 1 and 2, as well as the Payment Accounts Directive); and
- an increase in e-commerce that will lead to an increasing demand for new mobile payment services.

The number of new companies in the payment service industry is also likely to increase even further as PSD2 is implemented, since it allows new services and actors such as payment initiation service providers (PISPs) and account information service providers (AISPs). Payment initiation services can be a payment service provided by a non-bank to a consumer where the consumer gives permission to the provider to use the consumer's bank account for certain transactions. This could mean that services competing with card payments, Swish payments, or other forms of bank-provided electronic transactions meet new competition. Account information services can be consumer services that rely on the information residing in a bank account and given consumers. It should be noted that there are lot of challenges related to risks, responsibilities, fees, and other concerns that still need to be considered before it is possible to know the exact format of this new regulation, but it is clear that it aims to strengthen the competitive pressure in the payment industry.

Table 13.1 Average value of card payments in Sweden (SEK)

	2005	*2006*	*2007*	*2008*	*2009*	*2010*	*2011*	*2012*	*2013*	*2014*	*2015*
Average value of card payments in Sweden (SEK)	554	505	464	435	420	403	411	388	375	374	322

Source: Sveriges Riksbank (2015, 2016).

Table 13.2 Share of payments initiated electronically (%)

	2005	*2006*	*2007*	*2008*	*2009*	*2010*	*2011*	*2012*	*2013*	*2014*	*2015*[1]
Share of transaction value	94.4	95.4	96.5	97.2	97.6	98.2	98.6	98.8	98.9	99.0	98.3
Share of transaction volume	83.2	84.2	85.2	86.6	87.9	89.3	91.0	91.9	92.5	92.7	96.6

Source: Sveriges Riksbank (2015, 2016).

Note: (1) One part of why the number is lower in 2015 is due to a change in how the numbers are calculated.

Table 13.3 Growth of Swish

	September 26, 2014	*May 12, 2015*	*January 14, 2016*	*May 17, 2016*	*August 31, 2016*	*August 31, 2017*
Registered users (millions)	1.6	2.6	3.8	4.3	4.7	5.7
Value of transactions per month (billion SEK)	1.1	2.6	5.2	6.4	8.2	12.5

Source: Swish (2017).

Table 13.4 Overview of the largest providers of payment services in Sweden

Company	*Type of business*
Bankgirocentralen BGC AB	Clearing
Telenor Sverige AB	E-money
DIBS Payment Services AB	E-money
Paynova AB	Payment institution
Hi3G Access AB	Payment service provider
Money Exchange Skandinavien AB	Payment service provider
Easycash Svenska AB	Payment service provider
Payson AB	Payment institution
Marginalen Financial Services AB	Payment service provider
Svea Exchange AB	Payment institution
Payer Financial Services AB	Payment service provider
Trustly Group AB	Payment institution
iZettle AB	E-money
Trygga Pengar i Mobilen Sverige AB	Payment service provider
Kivra AB	Payment service provider
Betalo AB	Payment institution
4T Sverige AB	E-money
Billhop AB	Payment service provider
Seamless Remittance AB	Payment institution
24Money Payments AB	E-money
Kortaccept Nordic AB	Payment institution
Getswish AB	*Not licensed*
Visa Sweden För. ek.för.	*Not licensed*
Payair Technologies AB	*Not licensed*
Payex Holding AB	*Not licensed*

Source: Based on Arvidsson (2016).

A note on the role of technological systems for innovation

It is important to note that if we are to understand innovation and development of new services related to payments, we must start by understanding the underlying technology as well as the business systems. Arvidsson (2016) points out three important parts of the payment system. The first is the basic structure for process management and settlement, the second is infrastructure that aims to create the conditions for effective and secure payments, and the third is services and applications as well as foundations for standardization and security. When we analyze how new services, such as Swish and iZettle, are developed, we can base the understanding on which underlying technological systems they are built on. Swish is built so that it is directly connected to bank accounts and generates account-to-account transfers in real time via mobile phones, while iZettle is built directly on the infrastructure for card payments and allows acceptance of card payments in mobile devices connected to mobile phones and tablets. This means that there are different actors involved in the transactions, and also that revenues and costs, as well as system properties, are very different.

The actors behind a Swish transaction are primarily the Riksbank, Bankgirot, banks, and providers of software and hardware, while the actors behind a card payment essentially include card operators such as Visa and Mastercard, card issuers, card acquirers, merchants, and providers of software and hardware. Swish transactions between consumers (P2P) have thus far not involved transaction fees, while iZettle transactions involve a fee structure that is similar to a traditional card payment. All in all, one must therefore exercise caution when analyzing and comparing different types of payment services.

The essence of the retail payment system are the accounts to which consumers receive their wages and salaries, since all types of payment services—cash, card payments, and mobile payments—in one way or another lead to a transfer of money between these accounts that predominantly are provided by banks. Starting from the bank account, each type of service has built its own infrastructure and services that enable them to offer certain types of transactions. Cash payments build on cash provided by the Riksbank, cash depots, cash-in-transit services, ATMs for both withdrawals and deposits, banks, merchants, electronic systems for handling cash, and others. Card payments build on electronic systems for storing money, systems for processing and clearing transactions, card system operators, card issuers, card acquirers, card providers, terminal system providers, software providers, merchants, and others. Mobile payments can then, as discussed above, connect to a card system, directly to bank accounts, or to other systems.

We should also note that the types of payment services discussed in this chapter are provided by companies regulated by the financial authorities, while there are other payment services that are not regulated but still very important. The most well known of such services or cryptocurrencies are Bitcoin and Ethereum. These are based on different versions of blockchain technology, and have great potential to radically change the payment system, even if it is still difficult to foresee to which extent and speed this may happen.

Table 13.5 provides an overview of critical technological and business-oriented parts of the retail payment system. The first part is the basic infrastructure of the RIX system, which is handled by the Riksbank and provides final clearing and settlement of retail payments, as well as other forms of payments and financial transactions in the Swedish financial system. The second part is directly connected to processing, clearing, and settlement of retail payments, and handled by Bankgirot—a clearinghouse for mass payments—which is owned by Swedish banks. Bankgirot operates two systems (Bankgirot, 2017): Bankgirot, which is the traditional system for mass payments, and payments in real time, which is a newer system enabling clearing and settlement in real time and used for Swish transactions. This means that these services and this part of the system is directly connected to all other parts of the technological system, including bank accounts and other accounts, cash payments, card payments, direct debits, Swish payments, and so on. Our model then points to the third part, electronic accounts, where money is stored and via which payments are made. This is mainly constituted by bank accounts or other accounts into which consumers' wages and salaries are paid, as well as accounts via which organizations make and receive payments.

Table 13.5 Overview of the technological system for retail payments

First part: basic infrastructure for financial transactions	*Interbank clearing and settlement* of all financial transactions in RIX provided by Riksbanken.		
Second part: infrastructure for retail payments	*Interbank clearing and settlement* of payment services provided by Bankgirot.		
Third part: backbone service	*Electronic accounts* to which wages and salaries are paid provided by banks and other financial actors (e.g., Swedbank, SEB, Nordea, and Handelsbanken).		
Fourth part: payment services	System for *cash*-handling services provided by the Riksbank, banks, cash-in-transit service companies, cash depot providers, providers of ATMs, and cash-handling technologies for cash payments (e.g., cash (SEK), Loomis, and Kontanten).	System for *card* payments provided by card schemes, card issuers, card acquirers, banks, and software, as well as hardware suppliers (e.g., Visa and Mastercard).	
Fifth part: mobile payment services		*Mobile payments based on card payments* provided by card schemes, card issuers, card acquirers, banks, FinTech, telecom operators, and software as well as hardware suppliers (e.g., iZettle, SEQR, and Masterpass).	Systems for *mobile payment services based directly on accounts* provided by banks, payment service institutions, e-money institutions, telecom operators, FinTech, and others (e.g., Swish).

Source: Based on Arvidsson (2016).

This is the backbone of the system for retail—or mass—payments since the other services—cash, cards, Internet banking, mobile payments, etc.—all connect to these accounts. The fourth part is then more directly focused on the type of payment service used, which, in the case of retail payment, chiefly counts as cash, cards, and mobile payments. It is important to note that a fifth part can be outlined when we discuss mobile payment services. One type of mobile payment services builds directly on the card system—here exemplified by iZettle—and another builds directly on bank accounts—here exemplified by Swish. Even if both are mobile payment services as such, they connect to different parts of the technological system, and therefore involve different characteristics related to, for example, competitive edges, capabilities, actors, business models, and degrees of interoperability.

The immediate future of the Swedish payment system: critical drivers of change

There are several factors that are likely to change the payment system in Sweden in the coming years. Some have been discussed above, while others will be discussed in this section. One process that will be happening in Sweden in the near future is the rollout of contactless cards. The current plan for launching contactless cards in Sweden has been done by the Contactless Forum, which is a forum for collaboration between card companies, banks, and technology providers with the aim to realize a system for contactless card payments in Sweden. This is driven by a need to build a shared platform for all concerned actors if the launch is to become successful. By the end of 2016, 15 percent of cards were prepared for contactless payments and 19 percent of terminals were able to receive contactless payments (Contactless Forum, 2017). The aim of the forum was that 54 percent of consumers and 46 percent of card terminals would be able to perform contactless card payments by the end of 2017. Contactless card payments are intriguing for two reasons. First, they will change the use of cards as such by making these payments faster and possibly even more convenient in more payment situations. Second, they will start a more profound transformation toward mobile payment services as such. It is likely that contactless cards in Sweden will not be seen as a long-lived payment service as such, but instead as a "transitional object"[4] (Litt, 1986) in the ongoing move toward mobile payment services.

A technologically oriented issue relates to ambitions to realize real-time clearing and settlement of retail payments. Sweden is at the forefront of this through the creation of platforms such as payments in real time (Betalningar i realtid)[5] by Bankgirot, Mobile BankID for identification, text messaging for information,[6] and apps such as Swish (Swish, 2017), which in combination makes it possible to make a payment—including clearing and settlement—in one or two seconds. This makes the electronic payment, which is done via a mobile phone, a direct substitute to a cash payment, since the basic characteristics of quickness and reliability are there. Similar ambitions are pursued in the UK under the name "faster payments," and in Denmark, the European Central Bank, and other countries under the name "instant payments" (Andersen and Gladov, 2015; ECB, 2015; Bank of England, 2017). There have also been a number of seminars on these issues, for instance related to work by SEPA on instant payments (EPC, 2017).

Another critical factor for changes in the near future is the combined effect of national and international regulatory changes related to payment services. There are several regulatory changes that are likely to change the payment system in the coming years. Much of this comes from the European Union, where the Commission (European Commission, 2003) already in 2003 articulated their ambition to create an inner market for payment services in the EU. They had concluded that there were too many obstacles for a common market, and thus aimed to reduce these obstacles through regulation. It should at the same time be noted that the Swedish market was at the forefront of many of these areas of concern. One important first action was the Payment Services Directive that was implemented in Sweden in 2010 (Finansdepartementet, 2010), which aimed to stimulate competition by introducing new legal entities for payment service provisions that would make it easier to start competing with the traditional providers. This is also what we have seen happen in Sweden.

The Second Payment Services Directive and its complementary parts, which is yet to be fully implemented in Sweden, continues the efforts to create a common market characterized by more intense competition and lower fees for payment services. The second directive intends to cover aspects that the first did not, as well as cover new aspects that has risen due to technological developments and other changes in the business system around payment services. The overall regulatory work where the second PSD is one part focuses on issues such as interchange fee regulation (i.e., caps on multilateral interchange fees for card transactions), payment accounts directive (i.e., the rights to accounts as well as responsibilities and protection when using payment accounts), and surcharging (i.e., the possibility for merchants to add payments fees to consumers when they use certain types of cards when making a payment) (Arvidsson, 2016). The new regulation also involves a stronger consumer protection provision than before.

One additional and integral part in the new payment regulations focuses on new actors and legal entities in the area of payments. The directive makes it easier for companies to start new legal entities and services such as payment initiation service providers (PISPs) and account information services providers (AISPs) with the aim that these will lead to increased competition and better value for customers. A PISP could be a service where the provider has an agreement with a consumer that the provider can withdraw money from the consumer's bank account for certain types of payments, and where the bank must allow this to happen. As discussed above, the bank account is the backbone of the payment system, and banks therefore have a unique access to consumers that other payment service providers do not. Through PISP services, the benefit and uncompetitive aspects of this unique access by banks will be reduced. One example in Sweden of such a provider is Trustly, which offers a service where a consumer may allow Trustly to access their bank account for payments related to e-commerce. The other service—AISP—builds on a similar setup, but is focused on access to information about the consumer's bank account. The overall aim is to reduce the banks' unique position in the payment system related to the fact that they manage the backbone of the system—the bank accounts. It should be noted that there are challenges arising from implementing these changes, since it must be made clear who takes the risks and responsibilities if the system and its services are misused or even abused. Is the risk then to be taken by banks, service providers, or consumers? The ambition builds on prerequisites that the overall system as such has clear specifications of risk and responsibilities; that all providers have the needed licenses, as well as the needed capabilities, intentions, and systems to provide services; and that all users are knowledgeable and in demand of these services.

It should also be noted that there will be additional regulatory changes related to cash handling as well as a likely revision of the Central Bank Law in the near future. Implications from these changes are most likely a stronger and clearer definition of responsibilities around cash-in-transit services, but also an intensified debate on the role of cash in Sweden. Even if the focus in the study of the Central Bank Law (Finansdepartementet, 2016) concerns financial and monetary policies, there will also be a discussion of the role of cash as legal tender in Sweden due to increasing social problems related to the decline in cash-handling services in Sweden (Ehrenberg and Jansson, 2016).

Concluding remarks and summary

To sum up this chapter becomes a task that is simple in one way, but difficult in another. One conclusion is that the payment system in Sweden is characterized by high degrees of change, where a combination of simultaneous change in a number of factors—social, economic, technological, political, and legal—makes it difficult to foresee what may happen in the future. The main challenge is to make sure this situation does not end up in inertia (Arvidsson, 2014a), but instead becomes a process characterized by energetic startups, new competition, and demanding users.

In the near future, we will likely witness contactless cards becoming more prevalent, even if their main role is to primarily transform the system into using mobile payments to a larger extent. The contactless card may become the factor that pushes merchants to invest in point-of-sale terminals, as well as educating their employees to use these technologies, while at the same time educating consumers to start paying without inserting their cards, and using chip and PIN[7] identification and verification. Contactless cards are likely to become important transitional objects on the road to contactless payments based on phone apps (even if still based on the technological systems for card payments). This will of course also be a way for card operators (e.g., Visa and Mastercard), as well as large retail banks, to continue being dominating players in the payment industry.

Another and more drastic—as well as unpredictable—pattern of change relates to the new payment regulations in combination with new technologies. The relative reduction of legal difficulties to start selling payment services[8] will most likely mean that new actors from the FinTech industry will launch their services and subsequently start competing with banks. It is not unlikely, of course, that we will see more cooperation between banks and FinTech firms, as well as FinTech firms becoming/transforming into banks, one example being Klarna (TT News Agency, 2017). We will see more services—some that compete directly with banks' payment services and some that complement them—and ultimately more actors. Merchants and consumers are then likely to meet lower fees, while at the same time facing the challenge of knowing which service and which service provider to select and use. In the end, it will be these choices by merchants and consumers that determine the effects of the new regulations. The challenges are many, but the opportunities are likely to outweigh them. Many attempts to revolutionize the payment industry will presumably be made where, as always, some will fail and be forgotten, while others may become front-running firms in an era of a fully digitalized payment system. On a final note, it is likely that some of the winners will come from Sweden!

Notes

1 www.pro.se.
2 www.spfseniorerna.se.
3 Based on data from the company register of Finansinspektionen. It should be noted that there were, in addition, 20 companies licensed as payment service providers that operated as cooperative real estate providers, and therefore not active on the payment service markets. The number also excludes Bankgirocentralen, which is licensed as a clearing organization.
4 This is a term used in psychological studies to explain the role an object may have for changed behaviors by humans.
5 This is a digital platform enabling real-time clearing and settlement of peer-to-peer payments done via the service Swish provided by the banks.
6 PMB—payment message broker service.
7 Chip and PIN is an abbreviation for cards where a computer chip stores all information around the transaction, the payer, and the payee, and where verification of the transaction is done by a PIN code known by the payer.
8 Both PSD1 and PSD2, with the launch of payment institutions, payment initiation service providers, and account information service providers, will make it easier to start competing with the traditional banks. It can also be mentioned that other directives such as the e-money directive and work aiming to make it easier to switch banks, lead in this direction.

Bibliography

Andersen, A.T. and Gladov, T.M., 2015. *Initial experience with instant payments*. [online] Available at: www.nationalbanken.dk/en/publications/Documents/2015/03/Initial%20Experience%20with%20Instant%20Payments_Mon1-15_UK.pdf#search=Initial%20experience%20with%20instant%20payments [Accessed January 9, 2018].

Apanasevic, T., Markendahl, J., and Arvidsson, N., 2016. Stakeholders' expectations of mobile payment in retail: Lessons from Sweden. *International Journal of Bank Marketing*, 34(1), pp.37–61.

Arvidsson, N., 2013. *Det kontantlösa samhället: rapport från ett forskningsprojekt [The cashless society: Report from a research project]*. [online] Available at: www.worldcat.org/title/det-kontantlosa-samhallet-rapport-fran-ett-forskningsprojekt/oclc/834900208&referer=brief_results [Accessed August 26, 2017].

Arvidsson, N., 2014a. A study of turbulence in the Swedish payment system: Is there a way forward? *Foresight*, 16(5), pp.462–482.

Arvidsson, N., 2014b. Consumer attitudes on mobile payment services: Results from a proof of concept test. *International Journal of Bank Marketing*, 32(2), pp.150–170.

Arvidsson, N., 2015. Emergence of an ICT-based disruptive mobile payment service. In: E. Giertz, A. Rickne, and P. Rouvinen, eds. *Small and beautiful: The ICT success of Finland & Sweden*. [online] VINNOVA, pp.200–208. Available at: https://www.vinnova.se/publikationer/small-and-beautiful [Accessed January 9, 2018].

Arvidsson, N., 2016. *Framväxten av mobila, elektroniska betalningstjänster i Sverige*. [online] Available at: www.konkurrensverket.se/globalassets/publikationer/uppdragsforskning/forsk-rapport_2016-4.pdf [Accessed August 27, 2017].

Bank of England, 2017. *Bank of England*. [online] Available at: https://www.bankofengland.co.uk/research [Accessed January 9, 2018].

Bankgirot, 2017. *Bankgirot's two payment systems*. [online] Available at: www.bankgirot.se/en/about-bankgirot/our-offer/payment-systems/ [Accessed August 27, 2017].

Bonnier, J., 2017. *Helikopterrånet [The helicopter robbery]*. Stockholm, Sweden: Albert Bonniers Förlag.

European Commission, 2003. *Communication from the commission to the council and the European Parliament concerning a New Legal Framework for Payments in the Internal Market (Consultative Document). 2*. Consultive Document. [online] Available at: http://eur-lex.europa.eu/legal-content/EN/TXT/PDF/?uri=CELEX:52003DC0718&from=SV [Accessed January 9, 2018].

Contactless Forum, 2017. *Antal kort och terminaler med kontaktlös funktion [Number of cards and terminals with contactless technology]*. [online] Available at: http://contactless.se/bild-ett/ [Accessed August 27, 2017].

ECB, 2015. *Instant payments*. [online] Available at: www.ecb.europa.eu/paym/retpaym/instant/html/index.en.html [Accessed August 27, 2017].

Ehrenberg, S. and Jansson, J., 2016. *Bevakning av grundläggande betaltjänster 2016 [Monitoring the basic payment solutions 2016]*. [online] Available at: www.lansstyrelsen.se/Dalarna/SiteCollectionDocuments/Sv/Publikationer/Rapporter-2016/Betaltjanster-2016.pdf [Accessed August 27, 2017].

EPC, 2017. *SEPA instant payments*. [online] Available at: https://www.europeanpaymentscouncil.eu [Accessed January 9, 2018].

Finansdepartementet [Swedish Ministry of Finance], 2010. *Lag (2010:751) om betaltjänster [Legal act (2010:751) on payment services]*. [online] Available at: www.riksdagen.se/sv/dokument-lagar/dokument/svensk-forfattningssamling/lag-2010751-om-betaltjanster_sfs-2010-751 [Accessed August 27, 2017].

Finansdepartementet [Swedish Ministry of Finance], 2016. *Översyn av det penningpolitiska ramverket och riksbankslagen Dir. 2016:114 [Review of the monetary framework and the Riksbank act Dir:114]*. [online] Available at: www.regeringen.se/4b02ef/contentassets/0f4c260cae774a999ae0e5b280fd6926/oversyn-av-det-penningpolitiska-ramverket-och-riksbankslagen-dir.-2016114 [Accessed August 27, 2017].

Kontantupproret, 2015. *Kontantupproret*. [online] Available at: www.kontantupproret.se/wp-content/uploads/2014/11/Skrivelse-till-Riksbanksfullmäktige-från-Kontantupproret-dec-2015.pdf [Accessed August 27, 2017].

Litt, C.J., 1986. Theories of transitional object attachment: An overview. *International Journal of Behavioral Development*, 9(3), pp.383–399.

Nyberg, L. and Guibourg, G., 2003. Card payments in Sweden. *Sveriges Riksbank Economic Review*, [online] (2), pp.29–40. Available at: www.riksbank.se/Upload/Dokument_riks bank/Kat_publicerat/Artiklar_PV/er03_2_artikel2.pdf [Accessed August 27, 2017].

Segendorf, B. and Jansson, T., 2012. The cost of consumer payments in Sweden. *Sveriges Riksbank Working Paper Series*, [online] 262, p.58. Available at: www.riksbank.se/documents/rapporter/working_papers/2012/rap_wp262_120619.pdf [Accessed August 27, 2017].

Svea Hovrätt [Svea Court of Appeal], 2015. *Dom i det s.k. Panaxiamålet [Verdict in the so-called Panaxia case]*. [online] Available at: www.svea.se/Om-Svea-hovratt/Nyheter-fran-Svea-hovratt/Dom-i-det-sk-Panaxiamalet/ [Accessed August 27, 2017].

Sveriges Riksbank [The Riksbank], 2015. *Den svenska finansmarknaden 2015 [The Swedish financial market 2015]*. [online] Available at: www.riksbank.se/Documents/Rapporter/Finansmarknaden/2015/rap_finansm_150813_sve.pdf [Accessed November 28, 2017].

Sveriges Riksbank [The Riksbank], 2016. *Den svenska finansmarknaden 2016 [The Swedish financial market 2016]*. [online] Available at: www.riksbank.se/Documents/Rapporter/Finansmarknaden/2016/rap_finansm_160831_sve.pdf [Accessed November 28, 2017].

Swish, 2017. *Swish*. [online] Available at: www.getswish.se [Accessed August 27, 2017].

TT News Agency, 2017. *Klarna – Europas största bolag inom fintech [Klarna—Europe's largest FinTech company]*. [online] SvD. Available at: www.svd.se/klarna--europas-storsta-bolag-inom-fintech [Accessed November 28, 2017].

14 Introduction to the robo-advisory industry in Sweden

Agnė Mačijauskaitė

Introduction to robo-advisory

With the advent of the Internet and computers, organizations throughout the financial industry have been forced to partly adjust or even completely change their work practices to stay competitive. The new robo-advisory industry was born in the US in 2008 as a complement to the traditional global SEK 650 trillion wealth management industry, in what one today might consider an inflection point for "business as usual" (Kocianski, 2016). According to the Swedish Financial Supervisory Authority (FSA), robo-advisors are defined as companies that provide personal advice on financial instruments with limited human involvement (Olivendahl and Thorsbrink, 2016). As of 2017, the robo-advisory companies mainly provide automated and algorithm-based asset allocation and securities, rebalancing services in accordance with an investor's risk profile and preferences (Sironi, 2016). In addition to algorithm-based platforms, robo-advisors are usually characterized by being low-cost, available to a large share of the population, and easy to use. In the global market, the robo-advisory industry is just starting to take off and, with further development of more powerful computers and artificial intelligence, it is expected to significantly impact the remaining areas of wealth management (Sironi, 2016).

This chapter provides an overall assessment of the even younger robo-advisory industry in Sweden. In the first part, I will describe the general trends in the overall market that create the vacuum for robo-advisors to enter. I reflect on the key drivers of the industry, focusing on three main factors: investor behavior, technological development, and the current structure of the financial and regulatory environment. I then take a closer look at how robo-advisory companies work and describe the most common business models currently found in the market. I then discuss the already visible directions and implications of the automated advisory market in Sweden, which are supported by case examples of four selected companies. The chapter ends with an assessment of expected future developments in the industry and subsequent effects on traditional wealth management.

Mixed environment surrounding robo-advisory

In general, FinTech companies specialize in targeting one or a few traditional financial industry areas (Sironi, 2016). As mentioned before, robo-advisors focus on traditional wealth management. Traditional wealth management services are provided by banks or other investment advisory companies that try to help clients decide on how to invest their assets and manage their wealth. The industry started a long time ago, and it has survived numerous transformations. The post-World War II period witnessed the rise of middle-class families, and the investment advisory sector expanded its target customer base from primarily ultra-high-net-worth households (families and individuals) to simply highly affluent individuals. Despite an initial broadening of the customer base, investment advisors in 2017 focus primarily on affluent households, and do not (yet) provide their services to middle-income individuals. In addition to changes in wealth distribution of households, the wealth management industry was affected by the invention of mutual funds, index funds, and exchange traded funds (ETFs). A mutual fund is an investment fund that combines the capital invested by different individual investors and invests it in selected securities. An index fund is a sub-set mutual fund that pools and tracks underlying securities according to pre-specified rules (i.e., a market index), while ETFs are investment funds, such as mutual funds, that are traded on a stock exchange. These changes in the financial security markets increased the supply of investment options, put downward pressure on the prices of traditional wealth management services, and provided higher liquidity to the market. Technological changes, such as the introduction of online trading and cloud systems, pushed automation of the industry, especially in the back office and security trading areas (Sironi, 2016). The decision-making process, however, was still primarily run by human advisors. This area of the traditional wealth management industry is now being targeted by robo-advisors. We can see that historically, the change in the wealth management industry was driven by developments in technology and the change in the behavior of the average investor. These and a few additional factors are currently driving the emergence of robo-advisors.

Technological advances create possibilities

The last 30 years of technological advances have changed a number of traditional industries. Increases in computer processing capacity and accompanying advances in data analysis have, for instance, enabled the automation of some knowledge-based work. Advances in machine learning and artificial intelligence further increase the automation of tasks that were previously performed by humans. In addition, it has become significantly easier and cheaper to launch a financial technology startup. According to Cognizant's head of banking and financial services in the Nordics, Arun Sankaranarayanan, it cost around SEK 50 million to launch a new FinTech startup in 2000, while in 2015 it cost on average SEK 50,000 (Sankaranarayanan, 2015). Robo-advisory initial costs are higher than the average FinTech startup costs because of the early stage of the industry and lack of cost-efficiencies in the unclear development process. However, there is a clear trend: entry costs have fallen, and continue to do so. In addition to the platform development, access to the financial services became easier with online banking and online signatures, such as BankID. This reduced the problem of inertia in an individual's behavior, which is discussed later in the chapter.

Trends in households lead to change

The general idea of a product or service is to serve consumer needs, and a market emerges for said products and services when consumers begin to demand them. Changes in individuals' preferences, and household characteristics, therefore drive changes in demand, whether incumbent actors offer the services demanded or not.

Financially illiterate households

One of the common reasons for slow transformation in the financial industry is the complexity of the industry itself. The complexity of the products and services that they manage has meant that many individuals opt to let wealth managers manage their financial affairs. The industry is seen as complex since it is hard to understand definitions, numerous abbreviations, and the slang used by financial advisors and experts, in addition to how the markets function. This leads to the perception that in order to correctly manage their wealth, individuals need to get advice from the experts in the industry. This has led to the perception that most people do not understand some of the basics of financial decision-making, for instance compounding, inflation, and diversification. Compounding refers to generating returns on reinvested capital gains, dividends, or interests received on the initial investment. Inflation refers to an increase in prices of the general products and services over time, which results in lower purchasing power for the consumer. Diversification is the underlying principle in finance that a portfolio with many assets in the long run will reduce the risks of investing in comparison to a portfolio with only one or a few securities. Almenberg and Säve-Söderbergh (2011) studied the Swedish understanding of these three concepts by presenting three descriptions of specific situations that apply interest rate compounding, diversification, and inflation principles. The respondents needed to choose the correct answers from multiple-choice alternatives. The concept of interest rate compounding was understood by 35 percent of Swedish respondents, inflation by 60 percent, and diversification by 68 percent. Only 21 percent of Swedes managed to answer all three questions correctly. Financial knowledge is, however, increasing due to digitalization and an increase in the overall education level (Lusardi and Mitchell, 2014); however, there is still a long way to go. Traditional wealth managers still make significant returns by providing complex services to consumers who likely do not understand them, but with further growth in education and digitalization, the pressure for firms offering traditional wealth management to transform increases.

Changing households' wealth and characteristics

Older generations remain the main customers of traditional wealth management firms. This is because younger individuals have lower incomes, meaning that they represent a small market, with low margins—and therefore are not of interest for banks (Sironi, 2016). These older generations are generally less technology-savvy, late adopters, and the ones that put higher importance on a human connection in any business situation. However, as younger generations establish themselves in the market, start to earn high salaries, and become customers, their influence is likely to be felt. These include Millennials (or Generation Y), i.e. those born between 1980 and 2000, who are thought to be more comfortable with technology, and appreciate innovation. These individuals start to demand returns on their currently held wealth, and the low interest rate environment encourages them to enter equity and bond markets (including indexes, mutual funds, etc.). The old methods that worked for baby boomers (the post-World War II generation) and Generation X customers might not work for Millennials. This generational shift will most likely change the behavior of the average retail investor, with people requiring more efficiency and consistency with the same level of advice. In addition, Millennials are becoming richer as baby boomers age and pass on their wealth to their children. If the incumbent wealth management firms fail to meet the demands of these new generations, they might disappear within a few decades, as Generation Y is expected to accumulate more wealth than previous generations within the next 10 years (PwC, 2015).

In Sweden, in addition to Millennials becoming richer, the overall wealth per capita is growing. Sweden's average wealth per adult tripled from 2000 until 2016 to SEK 2.5 million, and Sweden is now in 17th place out of 173 countries in terms of average wealth (Davies, Lluberas, and Shorrocks, 2016). This enables financial advisors to achieve higher profitability as their business models earn fees from assets under management (AUM). I discuss the business models of robo-advisors in more detail later in the chapter.

The generational shift and Millennials becoming the main customer base also poses problems. Swedish Millennials are thought to be very early adopters. This is a good thing for startup companies since it provides a fast market reaction to their products and services. However, in the long run, Millennials are thought to be less loyal customers, as they prioritize technology advances over existing relationships. The companies should have higher capital expenditures and time the market correctly in order to stay in the business in the long run. In addition, even with a higher early adoption rate and dissatisfaction with banking service (the EPSI Rating Group's report shows that consumer satisfaction with the banking services in Sweden 2016 is the lowest in 20 years), the banking services still see high customer inertia: people rarely change their banks or financial providers, even if they do not like them. Only 7 percent of banking customers in Sweden say that they are willing to switch banks (EPSI Rating Group, 2016).

Encouraging a regulatory ecosystem

With the appearance of the first robo-advisors in Europe, the regulatory authorities started to give their opinion about the market. In 2015, the Joint Committee of

European Supervisory Authorities (ESAs), comprising of the European Banking Authority (EBA), the European Securities and Markets Authority (ESMA), and the European Insurance and Occupational Pensions Authority (EIOPA), published a discussion paper concerning the automated financial advice (Joint Committee of European Supervisory Authorities, 2015). They analyzed what, if any, supervisory actions were needed in response to the growing robo-advisory market in Europe. The ESAs concluded that since the robo-advisory market in Europe is very young and it is hard to evaluate the consequences of possible problems, no specific regulations for this particular sector were needed at the time, but further monitoring of the development of the sector will be conducted (Joint Committee of European Supervisory Authorities, 2016). It could therefore be argued that EU bodies view robo-advisory positively, probably because it makes markets more efficient. Indeed, they have not taken big steps to ease the development of robo-advisors; they appear to have taken a spectator role, and will intervene in the market only if necessary.

Sweden's Financial Supervisory Authority (FSA) is taking a similar position, where they deal with ongoing issues rather than trying to act proactively. The FSA is positively disposed toward robo-advisory, since it should lead to higher objectivity in giving financial advice, better documentation, and could serve a greater customer base. The FSA requires robo-advisors to give financial advice in accordance with the law (Act 2007:528; Finansinspektionen, FFFS 2007:16). The FSA also provides two ways to give advice: general or personal. General advice does not require a financial license, while personal does. This gives the possibility of different robo-advisory business models to appear. If the company already has a financial license, they can provide financial advice both in a traditional and in an automated way, since the license is the same for both business models. The FSA, however, struggles to assess whether traditional financial advisors have complied with regulations when it comes to insuring that consumers make informed choices. This problem might be solved with automated advice. The FSA does not provide specific regulations toward technological platforms, and only mentions that internal control tools should monitor whether automated advice is calibrated correctly so as not to give an advantage to the company over the customer (Olivendahl and Thorsbrink, 2016). Future requirements by the FSA are planned to include stricter requirements for the CEO and the board of the company: to have knowledge in financial activities, understand the risks, and have relevant technical skills (Olivendahl and Thorsbrink, 2016).

In addition to direct regulators' opinions toward robo-advisors, other new regulations provide opportunities for the industry. The EU is currently promoting capital mobility among member states and is drafting regulations that provide a better ecosystem for robo-advisory companies. The Markets in Financial Instruments Directive (MiFID) is already enforced, and MiFID2 is expected to be enforced in 2017 or in early 2018. MiFID1 (Directive 2004/39/EC) tried to harmonize the financial markets in the EU by eliminating obstacles for cross-border activities, equalizing the authorization requirements and regulations. These changes should lead to lower costs for market participants since the process is simplified and bureaucratic power is lower. This helps to reach economies of scale easier, since advisors can provide the same services throughout the EU member states. MiFID2 expands the first MiFID by incorporating transparency measures and further increasing the access to the markets and promoting higher competition. It also restricts kickbacks—in the financial advisory industry, kickbacks refer to the discount received (i.e., lower commission fees) for performing specific services (i.e., frequent trading), which is popular in many countries, including Sweden. The FSA finds that issues with conflict of interest in financial advice are mainly due to commission-based product sales. MiFID2 provides stricter regulations concerning commissions: companies can receive or pay commission only if they prove that the payment increases the quality of service and that it does not negatively affect customers' interests. According to the FSA, the advice should not be considered independent if the company sells its own products. These additional regulations on the EU level will force the financial advisory sector to adjust its fee structure.

A lot of money in pension systems

Traditionally, robo-advisors appeared to serve as a substitute for human financial advisors directly for retail investors. However, in Sweden, the pension system provides the opportunity to reach a high volume of AUM by providing financial advisory services to companies and pension-related actors. The pension system is comprised of three main pillars: national pension, occupational pension, and private pension (OECD, 2008). Part of the national pension—the premium pension (2.5 percent of salary and other taxable benefits)—can be invested by selected funds, or if not selected would automatically be invested by the AP7 fund (the National Generation Management Option). In order to invest their premium pension (PPM), individuals need to choose out of 850 available funds themselves, and robo-advisors might be of help in the selection process. The occupational pension is slightly different from the national pension. The occupational pension depends on your employer's contribution and whether it has signed a collective bargaining agreement (CBA). If it has signed the collective agreement or chosen to voluntarily provide an occupational pension, employees are entitled to it (Anderson, 2015). Some 90 percent of employees in Sweden have an occupational pension, which contributes a significant amount of funds to the total pension that individuals receive at retirement (Anderson, 2015). The possibility for robo-advisors to enter this part of the market is restricted due to non-standardized user contracts, diverse tax deductions, and license restrictions. Due to these market entry restrictions, the robo-advisors might need to enter the market through partnerships with traditional players to reach the occupational pension funds.

Lessons from the US

The Swedish robo-advisory market is young. However, lessons can be learned from the more mature US market. In the US market, the drivers for robo-advisors were even stronger. In addition to the similar drivers that were previously mentioned for the robo-advisory industry to appear in Sweden, the US post-financial crisis led to a lack of trust toward the traditional wealth management companies on Wall Street, as well as stricter regulations regarding compensation, incentives, and new tax codes (Sironi, 2016). Also, information asymmetry between costs and returns among different traditional market leaders decreased as the media started to cover their performance more closely. This trend put further pressure on the market to strengthen its objective performance measures (actual costs/prices). In an opportunistic environment, robo-advisors first appeared in 2008 but gained larger publicity and scope only in 2011. In the US, the leading robo-advisors, Betterment and Wealthfront, already serve 400,000 subscribers and had accumulated a combined SEK 115 billion in AUM in 2016 (SEC, 2017). However, even with better drivers in the US, the industry still lacks profitability, and traditional banks are catching up. The trend shows that robo-advisors' move toward more affluent individuals in order to collect relatively higher-margin customers, start to provide services business-to-business-to-consumer (B2B2C) compared to business-to-consumer (B2C), and add additional customization properties to attract wealthier individuals (Sironi, 2016). The fact that robo-advisors started to tap into traditional wealth management's more affluent customer base gained attention from the big banks. Charles Schwab, Vanguard, Fidelity, Deutsche Bank, UBS, BlackRock, Invesco, and others have started to incorporate technological developments in their business models. Charles Schwab, Vanguard, Fidelity, and Deutsche Bank invested in the development of their own robo-advisory platform, while UBS, BlackRock, and Invesco acquired startups: SigFig, Future Advisor, and Jemstep, respectively. With these developments, the key factors leading to the development of the robo-advisory industry, such as full independence, passive investment strategies, an underserved low-margin customer base, and low costs, are becoming blurry. However, the entry of traditional players was celebrated as the sign of validation that robo-advisory was wishing to show—the market needs transformation. Similar future developments in Sweden could therefore arguably be expected.

Comments about robo-advisory development from Paolo Sodini

The Stockholm School of Economics professor and co-founder of robo-advisory company Advinans—Paolo Sodini—has examined the traditional wealth management industry for many years, and agrees that it needs transformation. However, he thinks that robo-advisors focus too much on the "robo" part and forget the key problem—"advisory." The "robo" part is important, since with digitalization the costs are reduced and the work becomes more efficient. But he believes the "advisory" part needs a big transformation. Much of the academic research that has been conducted has not been implemented in industry. For example, we already know that a lack of diversification is bad in the long run, active management in most of the cases gives worse results, and higher fees do not correlate with higher returns. However, these problems are still very present in practice. In addition to that, the mapping between available securities and households' needs is poorly done. The issue arises from a lack of (good) advice rather than from the lack of product supply. The households are not fully informed and cannot make the best decision for themselves. For example, the introduction of PPM was problematic, since individual investors did not know which funds out of the 850 available to invest in, and it is still hard to get proper advice in the industry without incurring significant costs.

Sodini suggests that the main drivers for the robo-advisory industry are technological development and the right timing. Today's technology provides possibilities that were not available several years ago, and the timing for the robo-advisory industry to appear is perfect. People usually equate higher quality with higher prices, and this perception has been present in the financial industry for a long time. Only recently have people started to understand that the fees are too high in wealth management and the industry needs to transform. While robo-advisory offers transformation, it suffers from the "law of inertia" and a dearth of trust. The "law of inertia" refers to people's tendency to avoid changes that would require at least a little bit of their effort. Signing one form to move the funds is already too much. The trust challenge refers to the problem that it is hard for the consumer to identify which service supplier provides better results. The financial advisor service is built on trust, and to gain it from the clients takes a long time since the consequences of their choices can be seen only after a long period of time. With the proliferation of FinTech wealth management services, consumers might be even more confused. However, Sodini believes that sooner or later, the wealth management industry will transform; if not now, it will transform with generational shift because the new generation prefers to perform most of their tasks and communicate online.

Sodini also believes that the FSA could do more to help the industry develop. There are a lot of old regulations that limit the activities of robo-advisors, especially in the pension system. Some institutions require "original" signed contracts to move the money, which adds to the inertia problem discussed before. In addition to that, some accounts are more tax-efficient within private pension or occupational pension programs, but restrictive insurance license requirements, closed system of collective agreements, and the power of employer limit the possibility to use them and make the market more efficient. Robo-advisory not only deals with some of these problems, the transparency it offers could provide the FSA the possibility to prohibit bad practices. Sodini is optimistic that even if robo-advisors will not stay for long, it will initiate the move to a more efficient wealth management industry.

Robo-advisory inside out

Currently, the most common robo-advisors in the global market take the customer through a number of steps to provide the most appropriate service. The first step is a personal assessment of the customer in order to give individualized advice. The algorithm-based systems then generate the optimal portfolio for the customer. The third step is the execution of the trades, and fourth is the monitoring and rebalancing of the investments. The customer can see the returns of the portfolio and how their choices affect their investment through an easy-to-understand reporting interface. Below, I discuss these steps in more detail.

Customer personalization

In order to give appropriate financial advice to each individual customer, a robo-advisor needs to know the individual's investment needs and preferences. An individual's investment strategy is usually based on his/her degree of risk aversion, age, expected returns, prior financial knowledge, preferred investment form (single or periodic payments), and investment time period. According to the Securities Market Act (2007:528), financial advisors in Sweden are required to collect information about a customer's financial knowledge and experience, their financial situation, and investment goals prior giving personal financial advice. This is required for both forms of financial advice: traditional human advice as well as automated advice. Within the pension industry, the age of the investor is the most important determinant of their investment strategy. In the traditional wealth management sector, customer personalization is done through an extensive questionnaire. The robo-advisors extended the traditional process by making it more involving, with graphs and easy-to-understand explanations. This marginal change in the personalization process helps the consumer feel more empowered in the decision-making process (Sironi, 2016).

The advisors are also required by law to ensure that the suggested investment meets the customer's objectives, including their willingness to take risk and the financial ability to bear risk (Olivendahl and Thorsbrink, 2016). Advisors have to be certain that customers have enough knowledge to understand the risk they are taking and that the information provided by the customer is reliable. In traditional financial advice, the company can ask subsequent questions to check whether the customer meets all the requirements and to ensure the correctness of the data; however, with automated advice, problems can arise. While human advisors can follow up on key details, robo-advisors are limited to the content of questionnaires, which may limit its ability to classify an investor, especially with regards to specific (idiosyncratic) risks. It is also hard to provide more customized services, for example to discuss future plans and investment strategies, which are usually demanded by higher-net-worth households.

Both the robo-advisory and traditional wealth management industries have predefined defaults when personalizing investments; investors are rational and do not like risk, and they should want to take a higher risk only if it is compensated with higher returns. These assumptions are present in almost all financial models. These assumptions, as well as traditional questionnaires, fail to understand the real levels of risk aversion and real desires of the investor (Kahneman and Tversky, 1979; Burns and Slovic, 2012), and can lead to advice based on incomplete information. Thus, current robo-advisors do not provide an overall better personalization of the customer, but it is safe to say that they do the job just as well as traditional wealth managers.

Investment selection

Robo-advisors base their decisions on predefined algorithms and a preselected variety of assets. These algorithms are written using traditional textbook models. This method of choosing the investment portfolio provides objectivity and eliminates human behavioral biases, such as security selection bias, sentiments, and misconceptions. The most common model used to select the portfolio is based on modern portfolio theory (MPT), also known as mean variance optimization (MVO). This model chooses the portfolio of assets by matching the expected returns for an investor with the smallest available risk in the market, or vice versa. Some platforms use different additional models or the extensions of MPT, for example the Black-Litterman model, which allows incorporating the subjective views of advisors in the portfolio selection process.

For customers to feel comfortable in investing using automated platforms, they need reassurance. For this reason, robo-advisors try to clearly promote that they use passive indexing and tax optimization techniques (Sironi, 2016). Overall, robo-advisors mainly use passive investment strategies that invest in indexes or ETFs and thus benefit from diversification (Sironi, 2016). The concept of diversification enables an investor to maximize the returns by minimizing asset-specific risk. This is done by combining assets with less than perfect correlations with the market. Thus, a passive investment helps the investor to have a higher diversification and exposure to broader sectors and geographies. According to several studies (Sharpe, 1966; Treynor and Mazuy, 1966; Arnott, Berkin, and Ye, 2000; Fama and French, 2010), passive investments generally outperform active investments. Active investors involve the personal views and expertise in making their decisions. This requires a high effort and does not provide higher after-cost returns, and usually leads to tax inefficiencies by triggering capital gains more often than advisable (Arnott, Berkin, and Ye, 2000).

In the US, robo-advisors mainly trade in ETFs and limit their trading to passive mutual funds—this leads to lower transaction costs and follows the US regulations to ban the inducements (Sironi, 2016). ETFs also allow trades throughout the day, which leads to better rebalancing and tax-efficiency. According to Morningstar, the average expense ratio of ETFs was 12 times smaller than index mutual funds (Cook, 2013). In Sweden, this trend is not that common since other alternatives are relatively inexpensive, and thus investors prefer investing directly in index funds.

Investment execution

There are two forms of traditional wealth management: discretionary and advisory. Under the discretionary investment management form, the advisors have the full right to decide how to invest an investor's funds, while the advisory form requires an approval from the investor every time. The advisory form costs more since the process becomes cumbersome and good investments can be lost due to an inefficient management of funds. Since the goal of robo-advisors is to increase efficiency in traditional markets globally, they usually choose the discretionary form. In Sweden, the most common way is to start with an advisory form since it permits more freedom in attracting the initial customer base, and then to move toward the discretionary form. In addition, there are also differences within robo-advisors in trade execution; some companies outsource, some trade in-house (Sironi, 2016). As discussed before, the regulations permit the differentiating between financial investment advice that requires licenses and that which does not. Thus, the companies that do not have licenses usually do not provide execution of the trade.

Portfolio management

After the investment is executed, market-influencing events, such as companies investing in new projects, management changes, macroeconomic factors improve or worsen, earnings are released, and so forth. Due to new information, the expected returns and perceived risk by an individual investor may change. In order to continue to meet the needs and preferences of the customer and to sustain the optimal portfolio, the individual investment weights need to be rebalanced. In essence, portfolio rebalancing ensures the risk management to the portfolio. There are different methods used: rebalances on a pre-specified schedule, a personal decision of the manager, statistical techniques that check in relation to a predefined benchmark, and rebalancing when new securities are added to the pool, to name a few. Companies that do not execute trades only advise clients on how to rebalance their portfolios, which individuals then have to do themselves. As discussed before, people do not like to be involved in the savings process, and thus many prefer that the long-term management of their portfolios be done by their advisors. Finally, throughout the whole process, investors can see the expected results, changes in performance, and new advice in an easy-to-use interface. This experience adds to customer satisfaction (Sironi, 2016).

Diverse business models

There are numerous business models in the robo-advisory business. Two big groups can be separated in the business-to-consumer (B2C) and business-to-business-to-consumer (B2B2C) segments. B2C is the original model and the most well-known model where robo-advisor services are provided to retail investors. However, in Sweden, the biggest wealth is managed through pension funds, and due to the previously discussed pension structure in Sweden, robo-advisors try to tap in to the B2B2C business model. Because of insurance license requirements and restricted access to management of pension money, robo-advisory companies need to partner up and provide their services to businesses instead of directly to customers. In the US, there is a trend towards offering B2C services, and these are expected to transform to the B2B2C model (Sironi, 2016).

Another important factor affecting business model choice in Sweden is that the financial industry is primarily based on trust. Robo-advisors are not well known in Sweden, and it will take time to build trust and recognition. Due to this fact, a lot of robo-advisory companies start their ventures with different products and business models that are dedicated mainly to customer acquisition (some of the business models are discussed later in the chapter). The business models will start to cluster in the future when the awareness of the industry will be higher. This will happen either due to generic developments and better media coverage in Sweden as well as globally, or due to a single event that will signal the validation of the industry (e.g., a strong FSA statement or traditional wealth management player's entry into robo-advisory).

An underserved customer base

Robo-advisors usually focus on low-margin, underserved younger customers. The industry appeared to provide access to financial advice that was not previously available due to large initial capital requirements. The former CEO of Wealthfront said that more than half of its clients are under 35 years old and the average account size is SEK 900,000, an amount that would be unprofitable for the traditional wealth management companies (The Economist, 2015). In addition, the digital business model and easy access attract Millennials, who, as discussed before, are becoming richer and more involved in the investment industry. However, in the US, even the high-net-worth individuals are becoming interested in the automated advice. Even 49 percent of wealthy investors would consider putting part of their wealth into automated investments (Kocianski, 2016).

Challenging revenue structure

This business model relies on using low fees, passive investment strategies, easy-to-use platforms, limited human interaction, and economies of scale. Globally, the most common revenue model is to take a percentage of AUM. However, in Sweden, flat fees are also very common. Companies with flat fees usually require fewer customers to break even; however, this restricts the upside potential to increase revenues per customer as the customers' assets grow. Also, since a percentage of AUM is dependent on the wealth of the customer, robo-advisors with this model usually change their customer base to focus more on affluent individuals in order to break even. This trend is visible in the US, which is leading to higher competition from traditional wealth management companies since robo-advisors are starting to tap into their customer base. Some companies provide advisory services without any fees. These companies expect to earn money from additional customization services or sales of their own products. The initial permission to try out the advisory services at zero costs allows uncertain individuals to get started and build their confidence. However, a disadvantage of this is that the independence principle might disappear.

A typical annual fund management fee is 1.45 percent in Sweden, while robo-advisors focus on a 0.5 percent fee. They can cut the prices since they can save on the variable costs of the business by improving efficiency in the business model and eliminating unnecessary "legacy costs." The lower the fees, the better profit the households receive in the long run because of compounding assets (i.e., the money saved on unnecessarily large fees is invested in the securities, thereby providing additional returns).

Another general characteristic of robo-advisors is their dependence on economies of scale. To break even and start making profit, robo-advisory businesses need significant levels of AUM or a large paying customer base, which takes time and high marketing efforts to reach. Since the robo-advisory startups are not well known, they need extensive marketing expenses to attract customers. Business Insider analysts estimate that the costs in the US can range from SEK 2,600 to 9,000 (Wadhwa, 2016). The analysts predict that worldwide robo-advisors break-even only after 11 years (Wadhwa, 2016). In Sweden, the cost of acquiring a new customer is expected to be lower since Swedish customers are highly digital and known to be early adopters. However, since the industry focuses on low-margin customers, the paying customers have to be very large for economies of scale to materialize. One of the venture capital companies, Anthemis, which invested in one of the biggest robo-advisors worldwide—Betterment—said, "To be successful [a robo-advisory firm] needs to manage tens of billions [AUM]; to be really successful they need to manage hundreds of billions" (The Economist, 2015). In Sweden, the scale is lower—the usual customer base to break even is estimated to be around 20,000 paying customers.

Large costs in the short run

The costs of robo-advisory companies are estimated to be, on average, 70 percent lower compared to traditional wealth management firms (Sironi, 2016). The drop comes from eliminating inefficiencies in operations and the lack of legacy costs. It is a low-margin business model, so the algorithms must be efficient and the back office kept to the minimum. In the US, the largest portion of operating costs is marketing. Because the robo-advisory business model depends on economies of scale, high consumer awareness is critical. In Sweden, the industry is arguably too young to advertise. The companies are still in the closed beta version stages and the marketing expenses will likely come later. Nowadays, the biggest costs in Sweden are labor costs and costs related to regulatory approvals. The fact that the FSA is just getting to know the industry suggests that it will likely take a lot of time and resources to get the necessary permits. The entry costs in the robo-advisory industry will decrease significantly over upcoming years.

The robo-advisory market in Sweden

In Sweden, the market for robo-advisors is very young. The first traditional robo-advisory company was started in 2013 and in 2017, was only just establishing a foothold in the market, as it only launched the product in 2015. There is no clear industry leader or clear direction. In the upcoming sections, I discuss the Swedish robo-advisory market and its players in more detail.

How big is the market?

The usage of robo-advisors is currently limited in the EU, but based on the US market and overall trends, automated advice is expected to grow significantly in the upcoming years (Joint Committee of European Supervisory Authorities, 2015). Business Insider predicts that the global market for robo-advisory will reach 10 percent of that of the wealth management industry in 2020. AUM are expected to reach SEK 70 trillion (in contrast to the wealth management market in 2014 that was valued at SEK 650 trillion) (Kocianski, 2016). According to Statista, in 2016, the AUM for robo-advisors in Sweden amounts to approximately SEK 750 million with 60,000 paying customers. These numbers are far from break-even. AUM are expected to grow annually at a 69.1 percent growth rate (CAGR), which is expected to result in SEK 10.5 billion in 2021 (Statista, 2016). It is fair to say that macro-statistics concerning the robo-advisory industry in Sweden are not objective and should be taken carefully. A lot of companies are still developing their beta versions or are in very early stages of development. Some companies are providing initial services to inform the customer base rather than to collect AUM. In addition, some companies do not provide trade execution and do not hold AUM, which undervalues the Swedish robo-advisors market. Furthermore, some companies focus on pension funds and are not calculated in AUM, which further undervalues the Swedish robo-advisors market. It is hard for the market to grow if it is not known by the customers or even experts in the industry. A CFA Institute survey showed that around 50 percent of financial industry experts know what robo-advisory is; however, the main push was from the US (CFA Institute, 2016).

Main players

The main Swedish players and their characteristics are summarized in Figure 14.1.

Competitors

Competition for robo-advisors may come from traditional wealth management players, such as banks and financial advisory companies, as well as inexpensive trading systems. International banks are already adjusting their practices, as mentioned before, and the trend is expected to be similar in Sweden. Nordea, SEB, Handelsbanken, and Swedbank are the banks that dominate the Swedish wealth management industry. Overall, banks in Sweden have a long tradition of innovation and they have digitalized a big part of their processes. However, they still have legacy costs and an independence problem, as defined previously. In the wealth management area, they sell their own products and do not want to transform their

Robo-advisors	Tieless	Primepilot	Simgastocks	Opti	Lifeplan	Kollektiva	Pensionera
Location	Stockholm	Stockholm	Gothenburg	Stockholm	Gothenburg	Malmo	Stockholm
Date of product release	Mid-2016	Beta version	Beginning 2015	Beginning 2017	2010	Mid 2016	Late 2015
Current or pension savings	Current savings	Current savings	Current savings	Current savings	Pension	Pension	Pension
The size	3,000 customers		2700 paying customers	a few billion SEK under advice	SEK 20 billion under advice	SEK 7 billion under management, 30000 customers	5,500 paying customers
Business model	Traditional robo advisory model using Black-Litterman regression model and CVaR Portfolio Optimization Model and ETFs		Advise on investments in stocks based on their own analysis. Use MPT model and Fama French strategy.	Compare clients' funds with better alternatives (using MPT) and provide transfer to better funds for a single fee.	B2B2C, provide the summary of all different pensions and provide advice	Provide advise on PPM funds based on peer to peer comparison of historic returns of the users	Overview of all pensions and provide advice or premium advice (human consultation)
Licenses	Yes	No	No	Yes	Yes	No	Yes
Revenue structure	0.5% of AUM plus fund fees (on average 0.19%)		Monthly flat fee for investments in Nordics for 19SEK, global - 49SEK. Index investment for free.	Single fee for transfer of funds - 149SEK	Receives money from licensing out the system to companies	Receive money for providing data to partners	Overview is free, but advice cost 150SEK/ month and premium service 299SEK/ month
Raised funding		SEK 2.2 million from Vinnova	SEK 1.5 million from Chalmers and 2 angel investors; SEK 1 million from Almi as a loan; SEK 8 million from 4 private investors	Funded by founders with small convertible from Almi	Linnealex AB bought the company in 2012	SEK 15 million seed fund; SEK 13 million led by Dan Olofsson; SEK 12 million local investors; SEK 28 million individual investors	Several million SEK from Gunilla von Platen; undisclosed amount from Alexander Pärleros; SEK 12.8 million from Optimizer Invest

Figure 14.1 Robo-advisory companies in Sweden

business model to more automated advice since this would lead to cannibalization of current products. Additional costs, such as compliance, risk requirements, and legacy costs, restrict banks' ability to move fast and allow robo-advisors to gain market share. In addition, robo-advisors are currently not targeting traditional wealth management companies' primary consumer base, which fails to trigger their interest to compete with robo-advisory. However, the entry of big banks might be a problem for robo-advisors since they already have an established customer base and capital. At the same time, traditional banks are facing customer trust issues and do not invest a lot in attracting young clients.

Cheap digital trading platforms, such as Avanza and Nordnet, provide low-cost access investments. They currently have a significant number of users and large capital reserves. These companies provide an outlet for investors who want to invest passively or actively, but they need to know where to invest. They already have a large trusting customer base, but it is far from the size that banks have. Currently, they do not provide personal financial advice. Avanza launched the Avanza Portfolio Generator, which helps investors to choose which funds to invest in; however, it is barely personalized and not very extensive. It is similar to robo-advisor services; however, it is hard to imagine that they would move their business to full financial advisory services, mostly because they would then need to eliminate their currently used revenue model with hidden fees. In pension systems, the main competition comes from financial advice providers such as Max Matthiessen and Söderberg & Partners. They could automate their business quite easily and provide big competition to the new robo-advisors.

Case studies

The robo-advisory industry in Sweden is, as mentioned previously, young and fragmented. In this section, I will present case studies of a few selected companies in the industry and highlight their different focuses within robo-advisory. The qualitative research method was chosen due to the comparatively young age of the industry and lack of reliable quantitative data. The interview form was chosen to be unstructured due to the highly fragmented Swedish market, with the aim to deeper understand the motivation for choosing specific business models. I conducted interviews with the co-founder of Tieless, Gustaf Haag, the CEO of Opti, Jonas Hombert, the co-founder of Sigamstocks, Nanna Stranne, and the co-founder and current CEO of Kollektiva, Nicklas Larsson, in order to paint a clearer picture of some of the current market participants.

Company A: Tieless

Tieless is the robo-advisory company in Sweden that uses the traditional robo-advisory business model described in the section titled "Robo-Advisory Inside Out" in this chapter. In 2015, Tieless started to research the financial advisory market and tried to find what could be improved. They discovered that robo-advisors in the US cut a few steps in the wealth management process and made it more cost-efficient. Traditional wealth management still had an inefficient process: the client had to call, book a meeting, and submit questionnaires to access the services. These can be replicated using digital tools. After looking in Sweden, they found similar problems in the advisory industry. In Sweden, most financial services are marketed as free or close to free, but when you look inside companies' revenue structure it is far from true. However, with new regulations, the system might need to transform. For example, in mutual funds, half of the money is received as kickbacks. With the application of MiFID2 regulations, these kickbacks will no longer be allowed, and the current distribution system will need to transform. Tieless saw this as a good time to try to make the market more transparent and efficient.

Tieless was launched to external clients in mid-2016, and in half a year advised 3,000 customers. The service starts with personalization, signing the documents with a digital signature (BankID), setting up the portfolio in an ISK, an investment account (for tax reasons), and then investing in ETFs and managing the portfolio. Tieless follows the discretionary portfolio management strategy, which allows them to make investment decisions based on an investment mandate without asking the client for continuous permission to move funds. This allows them to act on opportunities faster. They chose to use ETFs to have high liquidity and keep costs as low as possible (internationally, ETFs are significantly cheaper than mutual funds). Tieless focuses on global exposure rather than the Swedish or broader Nordic markets. They have only one Swedish ETF out of 21. This is well-advised: Swedes regard investing in foreign securities favorably. Swedish high-net-worth individuals (HNWIs) hold 40 percent of their wealth outside Sweden, while the global average is 20–30 percent (Wealth Insight, 2014). Tieless is constantly looking for ETFs to put in the selection and improve their services. Tieless chose to have a wholly automated robo-advisory service where only customer support is left non-digitalized. The optimal portfolio is selected using traditional textbook models: Black-Litterman regression model and CVaR portfolio optimization model. The revenue structure is based on one fixed fee—half a percentage point.

Tieless sees collaboration as the most important factor to success. As Haag puts it, "it is the key not only to reach short-term success, but actually transform the market." But it is necessary to keep the integrity of suppliers as the key factor when selecting partners. In the future, people will need to identify which ones are providing independent advice and can be trusted. Currently, Tieless has collaboration with Saxo Bank, which is their trading partner, through which they settle the orders. The collaboration with Saxo Bank is beneficial for clients, because Tieless has institutional agreements with them, which means that commission is close to zero. If the investor wants to trade the same portfolio that they suggest, it would cost significantly more. Stellum Asset Management provides the required licenses to operate in the business, and acts like a holding company. Stellum operated a traditional financial advisory service, but in 2014 was dissolved.

Tieless focuses on serving low capital individuals, and they therefore set their goals in number of clients rather than AUM. They aim to have 20,000 clients in two to three years, while break-even is estimated around 10,000 clients. But their bigger goal is to have more competitors and partners, provide better services to the clients, and have more efficient and transparent markets. Haag believes that traditional banks entering the robo-advisory industry in the US confirms that a change is underway in the market. In Europe, he believes this change will be realized in three years. The change will be partly triggered by the generational shift. Haag believes that banks do not invest enough to attract Millennials, and 60 percent of Millennials said that they believe there will be no banks in 10 years. Banks rank at the bottom of the trust brand index in Sweden compared to other industries. There is not a lot of trust in this industry, and trust is very important to Millennials: they look at services and promotions very skeptically and are able to quickly understand conflicts of interest and hidden fees. In addition, the possibility to compare the performance of market players will help to improve trust. Tieless will be happy if they can be part of changing the old inefficient industry.

Company B: Opti

Another startup—Opti—decided to enter the Swedish robo-advisory market in a slightly different way to Tieless. The co-founder and CEO of the company, Jonas Hombert, previously founded and managed the video editing software company JayCut, which was sold to BlackBerry. He noticed firsthand the existing issues in the traditional wealth management industry. The main problem that triggered his interest was the lack of independence among traditional service providers: they advise their clients to buy their own products instead of the best products. Therefore, at the core of Opti's message to the public is its independence.

The company was founded in mid-2014 in Stockholm. Opti was the first company that approached the FSA and applied for a financial advisor license for a company that primarily gives advice using automated algorithms. It took around 15 months to convince the regulatory authority that automated advice was sound, and thankfully the process became easier and more efficient for the other newcomers in the robo-advisory industry. In the beginning of 2017, they launched their initial product to the public. They decided to first build customer trust by providing fund comparison services instead of providing traditional financial advice. The users in the current version can compare their owned funds with other alternatives, and check whether they overpay in management fees. On average, Opti is able to find the fund that has 95 percent similarity but half the fee. Opti also allows its customers to transfer their funds to more cost-efficient ones for a fixed fee. They decided to start with the fund comparison service because they think that robo-advisors are ignoring the conversion problem (site visitors becoming paying customers): people are expected to pay for something that they did not pay for before without even fully understanding if they are getting a better product. In its first few months of trading, Opti performed health checks on a few billion SEK in funds and had a few thousand app downloads per month.

In Opti's business model, building trust is the primary focus. In addition to providing the initial comparison tool and introducing themselves to the public, they try to educate customers and make the market more efficient. In their current model, the highest-ranking funds have a beta close to 1.0 (the funds closely follow market index). They explain to the users that the funds that outperform the market will do worse in recessions and that higher return comes from higher risk. Opti follows the traditional financial theory and does not believe in long-term sustainable alphas (abnormal returns in excess of what would be expected given market conditions). Opti is also expecting that competition from traditional banks will come soon, possibly even as early as 2018, and it will be a positive thing for the market because it will show more visibly to the public that the traditional industry has problems and needs to transform.

In the long run, the goal of Opti is to provide automated portfolio selection services. They are already building the wealth management platform with personalization, a traditional revenue structure (percentage of AUM), and lower fees. The company will still keep human supervision in the advice process, and thus provide a hybrid robo-advisory model to ensure sound financial advice. This version is expected to be released to the public at the end of 2017. In 10 years, the goal of Opti is to be the biggest non-bank wealth advisory company in the Nordics with SEK 100 billion in AUM. They believe that financial advisory is a trust-based business, and that it takes time to build one. Thus, the real transformation of the market will be seen only after a decade.

Company C: Sigmastocks

Sigmastocks decided to take yet another different approach. Management fees for mutual funds exceeded SEK 32 billion in Sweden in 2013, and the founders of Sigmastocks believe it can be done much cheaper. According to Nanna Stranne, Sigmastocks wanted to do something new within finance: a business model created for the customer instead of for the money manager. They believe that the future is within automatization and digitalization, and this will lead toward higher competition in the market. Sigmastocks already has more than 2,700 paying customers and sees a growth rate of 20 percent per month. In order to break even, the company needs around 20,000 customers. Currently, the biggest costs are marketing and remunerations. Their revenue model is clear and built on fixed fees (not related to AUM), where the customer pays a monthly fee depending on his/her chosen geographical market to invest in. The customer can also choose to invest in an index fund that does not have a fee. The execution of the fund can be done using the Avanza, Nordnet, or Nordea platforms. Sigmastocks did not apply for advisory licenses from the FSA, and view their service as general advice rather than personal. In 5–10 years, Sigmastocks wants to be one of the largest companies in Europe within portfolio management.

Sigmastocks decided not to follow traditional financial textbook models, which advise to invest in diversified index funds or ETFs. Sigmastocks analyzes stocks and provide the chosen equity portfolio of selected companies to invest in. They decided not to use index funds or ETFs because they believe that investing in stocks without a middleman is the end station of the FinTech revolution.

According to Stranne, Sigmastocks is different from other robo-advisors because it replaces funds, while others try to eliminate fees within existing structures. The company believes that using currently available funds is too expensive since the client pays double fees: for the product and for the service. Sigmastocks believes that the availability to invest directly in stocks eliminates the need to use indexes or ETFs. They base their portfolio selection model on a strategy highlighted by the "Fama French three factor model": small companies outperform large ones and value companies outperform growth. This business model provides lower diversification, since it focuses on specific geographical markets and only a small selection of companies. This model decreases the ability to reduce risk by rebalancing and it bets on specific situations. In addition, the Fama French-based investing strategy provides higher returns due to higher risks (higher cost of capital and higher business risk). In the bad times, this model might have problems.

Company D: Kollektiva

Compared to other selected companies, Kollektiva decided to focus on the pension system. The co-founders of Kollektiva have a broad IT entrepreneurial background and saw the increasing automatization of the financial sector as a possibility to transform the old rigid pension system. The key problem that they saw was a misaligned business model where clients' objectives are different from the advisors'. Kollektiva decided to challenge the financial pension industry by building its business on smart technology and shared economy: they think that there should be a social platform where clients can make decisions based on collective intelligence of different clusters.

Kollektiva launched its first service in mid-2016 focusing on PPM. Instead of listening to individual advisors, Kollektiva decided to focus on shared intelligence by comparing the age-clustered data of the best performers. They take the data of all their users and look at the net returns over the total period that they have been in the PPM pension system (most of them have been in the system up to 16 years). Kollektiva takes 15 percent of best performers, converts the information in the asset classes, and provides advice based on promising portfolios. The specific funds are selected based on weighted popularity, and further rebalancing of the information is performed every month. The company decided not to provide risk-adjusted measures because they believe that taking the data points of longer periods from a lot of investors eliminates outliers and diversifies unnecessary risk. Kollektiva already has 30,000 users with SEK 7 billion in PPM capital.

After launching the first service, the company received feedback from clients that wanted to reduce their involvement in rebalancing of the portfolio: they wanted to have a product that rebalances itself. Kollektiva decided to partner up with FCG Fonder, which created the funds in the PPM system, so that investors can invest directly based on the data from Kollektiva. The funds are currently available to buy. Kollektiva decided to provide fund comparison services for free to the public and to have the main revenue source from providing data to the partners. In addition to these funds, Kollektiva focuses on creating engagement and raising the knowledge of the users by creating a competition platform, and by launching data-mining services to other companies.

Kollektiva in the future will expand its focus to include the other components of the pension system: occupational and private pensions. The company will keep the social peer-to-peer model in the other services too. The key to success will be cooperation. Kollektiva wants to remain the data and general advice provider to the partners that will have licenses to act on the information. Another factor to success will be the reaction from regulatory authorities. Nicklas Larsson believes that the current infrastructure of the pension system has problems that limit the clients and favor big corporations. For example, the user agreements from some of the insurance companies in the occupational pension system limit the automatization of data analysis by third parties, and thus restrict individuals from getting the needed information to make informed decisions. However, with a positive outlook toward regulatory change from Swedish regulatory authorities and new regulations from the EU, Kollektiva believes that change is coming.

The future impact of robo-advisory

Disruptive innovations are only successful if people can understand them. Globally, the experts think that robo-advisors will have the biggest effect on financial services in one and five years among all FinTech companies. However, the optimism mainly comes from the US (CFA Institute, 2016). Maybe with growing knowledge about the industry, it will catch up in Europe too. Currently, robo-advisory is not well known in Sweden, and it will likely not be known in the short term. In the short term, the companies will continue to focus on improving their products and raising customer awareness, rather than making big moves in transforming the wealth management industry. In the medium term, when awareness of robo-advisors may be higher, the entry from big traditional players can be expected. Their entry into the industry will express the validation of robo-advisors in Sweden, but at the same time the banks will become competitors to robo-advisors. The robo-advisory business models will start to converge. The pressure on fees and better documentation of performance might lead to price wars and increased efficiency in the market.

If the overall market will experience a downturn in the future, the robo-advisors might start to understand that they undervalue the importance of customer support. In bad times, customers tend to act irrationally and need higher reassurance (Sironi, 2016). Experts' biggest concern is that there might be flaws in the financial algorithms (CFA Institute, 2016), which might lead to significant negative consequences, especially visible in recessions. If robo-advisors are programmed correctly and they use models that are financially sound, robo-advisors should prove the advantages of automated advice since they can better limit the downside.

In the long run, the traditional wealth management industry is likely to transform. The robo-advisors will start to cluster and provide their services across geographical borders. The less profitable companies will start to provide more customized advice to attract higher-margin customers. This trend is already visible in the US; however, in Sweden, it will not be as strong since the break-even point is much lower. The profitable companies will provide more personalized new products or start to consolidate with other FinTech companies. One thing is clear: in the future, the wealth management industry will become more efficient, to the benefit of end customers.

Conclusions

The Swedish robo-advisory market is just emerging, but can be expected to make an impact on the traditional wealth management industry. The emergence of the Swedish robo-advisory market is driven by an inefficient traditional wealth management industry, advances in technology, Millennials becoming an important customer base, and a changing regulatory system with regard to fees structure. Compared to global trends, in Sweden there is no clear one business model structure for robo-advisors, since the companies are still young and mainly focus on attracting an initial customer base with innovative solutions. The robo-advisors that focus on retail investors are mainly in closed beta stages. The companies that focus on pension systems are implementing different business models that are mainly based on partnerships due to the rigid old regulatory system. A fragmented market is expected to converge to the current US robo-advisory model in the future after gaining initial recognition. Due to the lower break-even points, the robo-advisory market will have better incentives to stay independent compared to global trends; however, law of inertia will be the key barrier for fast robo-advisory expansion. Despite that, one thing that certainly will be reached, due to the emergence of robo-advisors, is higher efficiency in the wealth management market in the long run.

Bibliography

Act (2007:528) on the Securities Markets.

Almenberg, J. and Säve-Söderbergh, J., 2011. *Financial literacy and retirement planning in Sweden.* [online] Available at: https://ssrn.com/abstract=1809736 [Accessed November 29, 2017].

Anderson, K.M., 2015. *Occupational pensions in Sweden.* Berlin: Friedrich-Ebert-Stiftung.

Arnott, R.D., Berkin, A.L., and Ye, J., 2000. How well have taxable investors been served in the 1980s and 1990s? *The Journal of Portfolio Management*, 26(4), pp.84–93.

Burns, W.J. and Slovic, P., 2012. Risk perception and behaviors: Anticipating and responding to crises. *Risk Analysis*, 32(4), April 15, pp. 579–582.

CFA Institute, 2016. *FinTech survey report.* [online] Available at: www.cfainstitute.org/Survey/fintech_survey.PDF [Accessed November 29, 2017].

Cook, H., 2013. *ETFs are cheaper than tracker funds.* [online] Available at: www.morningstar.co.uk/uk/news/112325/etfs-are-cheaper-than-tracker-funds.aspx [Accessed November 29, 2017].

Davies, J., Lluberas, R., and Shorrocks, A., 2016. *Credit Suisse global wealth databook.* Zürich: Credit Suisse.

EPSI Rating Group, 2016. *Nordic banking report 2016.* Stockholm: SKI.

Fama, E.F. and French, K.R., 2010. Luck versus skill in the cross-section of mutual fund returns. *The Journal of Finance*, 65(5), October, pp.1915–1947.

Finansinspektionen, 2007. Finansinspektionen's regulations regarding securities business, FFFS 2007:16.

Joint Committee of European Supervisory Authorities, 2015. *Joint committee discussion paper on automation in financial advice.* [online] Available at: www.eba.europa.eu/documents/10180/1299866/JC+2015+080+Discussion+Paper+on+automation+in+financial+advice.pdf [Accessed December 2, 2017].

Joint Committee of European Supervisory Authorities, 2016. *Report on automation in financial advice.* [online] Available at: https://esas-joint-committee.europa.eu/Publications/Reports/EBA%20BS%202016%20422%20(JC%20SC%20CPFI%20Final%20Report%20on%20automated%20advice%20tools).pdf [Accessed December 2, 2017].

Kahneman, D. and Tversky, A., 1979. Prospect theory: An analysis of decision under risk. *Econometrica*, 47(2), March, pp.263–291.

Kocianski, S., 2016. *The robo-advising report: Market forecasts, key growth drivers, and how automated asset management will change the advisory industry.* [online] Available at: http://nordic.businessinsider.com/the-robo-advising-report-market-forecasts-key-growth-drivers-and-how-automated-asset-management-will-change-the-advisory-industry-2016-6?r=US&IR=T [Accessed November 29, 2017].

Lusardi, A. and Mitchell, O.S., 2014. The economic importance of financial literacy: Theory and evidence. *Journal of Economic Literature*, 52(1), pp.5–44.

OECD, 2008. *Pension country profile: Sweden*. Paris: OECD.

Olivendahl, C. and Thorsbrink, M., 2016. *Promemoria [Memorandum]*. Stockholm: Finansinspektionen.

PwC, 2015. *Rebooting wealth management.* [online] Available at: www.pwc.com/us/en/asset-management/investment-management/publications/rebooting-wealth-management.html [Accessed November 29, 2017].

Sankaranarayanan, A., 2015. *Vem vinner framtidens bankkund? [Who will win the future's bank customers?]* [Online] Available at: https://www.youtube.com/watch?v=dT_TkYEE23o [Accessed January 17, 2018].

SEC, 2017a. *Form ADV: Uniform application for investment adviser registration and report by exempt reporting advisers—Wealthfront.* [online] Available at: www.adviserinfo.sec.gov/IAPD/content/ViewForm/crd_iapd_stream_pdf.aspx?ORG_PK=148456 [Accessed December 2, 2017].

SEC, 2017b. *Form ADV: Uniform application for investment adviser registration and report by exempt reporting advisers—Betterment.* [online] Available at: www.adviserinfo.sec.gov/IAPD/content/ViewForm/crd_iapd_stream_pdf.aspx?ORG_PK=149117 [Accessed December 2, 2017].

Sharpe, W., 1966. Mutual fund performance. *The Journal of Business*, 39, pp.119–138.

Sironi, P., 2016. *FinTech innovation: From robo-advisors to goal based investing and gamification.* West Sussex: John Wiley & Sons.

Statista, 2016. *Robo-advisors in Sweden.* [online] Available at: www.statista.com/outlook/337/154/robo-advisors/sweden# [Accessed December 2, 2017].

The Economist, 2015. Ask the algorithm: Human wealth advisers are going out of fashion. *Special report: International banking: Money management*, May 9.

Treynor, J. and Mazuy, K., 1966. Can mutual funds outguess the market? *Harvard Business Review*, 44(4), pp. 131–136.

Wadhwa, T., 2016. *One of the hottest investment styles might be "financially unviable."* [online] Available at: http://nordic.businessinsider.com/robo-advisors-may-be-financially-unviable-2016-7 [Accessed November 29, 2017].

Wealth Insight, 2014. *Sweden 2014 wealth book, Report no. WI0157MR*, Sweden: Wealth Insight.

15 Blockchain

The Internet of Value

Alejandro Moreno Puertas and Robin Teigland

Introduction: the origins

The term "blockchain" was first introduced separately in the Bitcoin white paper in October 2008 (Nakamoto, 2008). As of 2017, the Bitcoin blockchain has been operating successfully for eight years without a single hacking incident (Baldwin, 2017). Through a set of incentives, it has managed to create a bulletproof transaction system that deals with over USD 1 billion in transactions per day without a clear centralized oversight. Its popularity has led it to become a cryptocurrency with a market capitalization of over USD 30 billion (Blockchain.info, 2017c). These figures are extremely impressive when compared to those of any other company that provides similar services, such as central banks, commercial banks, and clearinghouses. The incentives embedded in the blockchain have substituted the need for employees to keep the system secure. Bitcoin's software code and the blockchain are transparent and accessible to everybody, which makes the zero-hacking phenomenon even more remarkable. After the success of Bitcoin, the word "blockchain" became a mainstream definition for the infrastructure behind the Bitcoin electronic cash system (Gupta, 2017).

How did it all start?

In October 2008, Satoshi Nakamoto, still today an unknown entity, proposed *Bitcoin: A Peer-to-Peer Electronic Cash System* in a white paper published on the Internet (Nakamoto, 2008). Five months after the official release, Nakamoto issued a statement in the peer-to-peer (P2P) foundation explaining the reasoning behind Bitcoin. Nakamoto denounced that in order for fiat currencies to work, we must have central banks, yet they have broken the trust required for currencies to work effectively by lending massive amounts of funds, thus creating credit bubbles. He proposed bitcoin as a substitute for fiat currencies, a currency based on a peer-to-peer network with a clear, predefined path and no point of failure (Nakamoto, 2009).

In short, this electronic cash system eliminates the need for a third party to verify a transaction through a distributed network. Every transaction is irreversible and published in a public ledger on the Internet with a timestamp. A set of incentives is placed to ensure that the public ledger cannot be changed. Since every transaction is made public, the network can verify how much each user has and only approve transactions that are lower than what the user holds in their account. The system then creates an irreversible "notarized" chain of events where everyone can see every transaction ever made. The public ledger is stored by everyone running the Bitcoin software and is also published online (https://blockchain.info).

In November 2008, the Bitcoin project was registered on Sourceforge.net, a community platform focused on developing open software projects (History of Bitcoin, 2013). In January 2009, the kernel of the Bitcoin software was released on Sourceforge.net, and a year later the first Bitcoin exchange was established, the Bitcoin market. Laszlo Hanyeck, a Florida programmer, made the first real transaction in May 2010, buying two pizzas from Papa John's for 10,000 bitcoins (BTC), which corresponded to USD 25 at that time (and to USD 22 million as of May 2017) (CoinDesk, 2017a). In October, a user spotted a security flaw in the Bitcoin network and created BTC 184 billion. The problem was an integer overflow bug. The Bitcoin software could only process 2^64 Satoshi,[1] which corresponds approximately to BTC 184 billion, and the user exploited the bug by registering a transaction that exceeded the limit (Buterin, 2013a). The software wrongly identified it as a smaller amount and approved the transaction. Nonetheless, the community responded quickly, and within five hours Nakamoto published a patch solving the problem (BitcoinTalk, 2010).

In June 2011, a user table was leaked with usernames, email addresses, and password hashes of Mt. Gox, the largest Bitcoin exchange at the time. As a consequence, 600 users had their balances stolen, and Mt. Gox halted trading for seven days and reversed the trades. Bitcoin price dropped from USD 17.01 to USD 0.01. In the next year, Bitcoin slowly recovered and started to be accepted by a wider audience (e.g., tax services and the music and medical industries), and in 2013 it became acknowledged in the mainstream media (Desjardins, 2014). One of the drivers of Bitcoin's growth in 2013 was the financial crises in Cyprus and Greece. As the financial situation in these countries worsened, investors started to look for alternative investments and found in Bitcoin a possible safe haven. As a result, the currency experienced a significant hike from USD 13 in early 2013 to USD 266 in April 2013. Soon after, it experienced a small setback due to a hacker attack on a European Bitcoin exchange named Bitcoin Central and the "stabilization" of the economic situation in Cyprus and Greece (Forbes.com, 2013). However, in the fall of 2013, the Chinese public started to invest in Bitcoin due to a lack of attractive alternatives in their homeland, as both the Chinese stock market and the real estate sector were believed to be overpriced. Bitcoin's price spiked again, peaking at USD 1,242 in December 2013, only USD 8 below the price of gold (Rooney, 2013). The Chinese Central Bank then announced that it would stop handling bitcoin transactions and the price temporally dropped to USD 500. After an initial recovery in January 2014, a leaked document from Mt. Gox revealed that they had lost BTC 744,408 due to a malleability-related theft driving the price down and stabilizing at the range of USD 200–300 in 2015 (Morris, 2014; CoinDesk, 2017a).

By this time, the combination of high volatility, hacking of Bitcoin exchanges, money laundering practices, and illegal uses (such as using the currency for extortion, drugs, and hiring hitmen) gave the cryptocurrency a negative connotation (Bello Perez, 2015; Weiser, 2015). Venture capital (VC) funding of Bitcoin startups started to drop and the currency seemed to lose attractiveness. Nonetheless, proponents of Bitcoin understood its benefits and the potentially massive future implications of the underlying technology. The need to commercialize the opportunities offered by Bitcoin led entrepreneurs to create a new name, a separation of the cryptocurrency's underlying technology from the currency itself. Thus, the term *blockchain* was born.

In reality, Bitcoin is the first application to be written for the blockchain. The original white paper emphasizes the system *Bitcoin: A Peer-to-Peer Electronic Cash System* (Nakamoto, 2008), not the currency itself. However, the differentiation between Bitcoin and the blockchain allowed entrepreneurs to seek funding focusing on the advantages of the technology without carrying the negative connotation associated with Bitcoin.

In 2015, venture capital investment in blockchain technology increased by 36 percent, and the startup R3 managed to gather a consortium of 42 banks, with a combined market capitalization of USD 600 billion, to back them up financially (Hileman, 2016). In 2016, venture capital funding in blockchain reached USD 496 million. By the end of 2016, 28 of the 30 largest banks were already researching blockchain feasibility (CoinDesk, 2017b). In February 2017, a conglomerate of Fortune 500 companies formed the Ethereum Enterprise Alliance to enhance the Ethereum blockchain, which will be discussed later in the chapter. The overall investment from venture firms of USD 1.4 billion in 2016 shows that they have acknowledged the potential of this new system and are investing heavily in it (Kennedy, 2016).

The vast majority of Bitcoin and blockchain investments come from Silicon Valley and go to Silicon Valley companies. In Sweden, two prominent venture capitalists, Creandum and Northzone, invested in two Bitcoin ventures, KNC Miner and Cryex (Aronsson, 2015). KNC Miner filed for bankruptcy in 2016, and as of March 2017 Cryex had not yet launched its platform (Higgins, 2016). After those two ventures, the climate for cryptocurrencies in the Nordics cooled down. However, the situation seems to be changing as cryptocurrencies are rising in value and the blockchain is gaining again in popularity

How does the Bitcoin blockchain work?

Before diving into blockchain applications, it is important to understand how the Bitcoin blockchain works in order to fully appreciate its benefits. The original Bitcoin white paper provides the following step-by-step guide that summarizes a transaction:

1 New transactions are broadcast to all nodes.
2 Each node collects new transactions into a block.
3 Each node works on finding a difficult proof-of-work for its block.

4 When a node finds a proof of work, it broadcasts the block to all nodes.
5 Nodes accept the block only if all transactions in it are valid and not already spent.
6 Nodes express their acceptance of the block by working on creating the next block in the chain, using the hash of the previous block as the accepted hash.

(Nakamoto, 2008)

Below, we explain in more detail how a transaction is made through the blockchain. We present four concepts that are illustrated through a transaction between two imaginary individuals, Bob and Jane, to give an overview of the primary concepts within the blockchain technology.

The first concept is *public key cryptography*. Public key cryptography ensures that a user can encrypt a transaction with their own private key, and then the network can verify this transaction through the individual's public key. The public key also provides pseudonymity.[2] The system works as follows.

Bob and Jane each have a unique personal *public* key and a unique personal *private* key. The public key is available to the public while the private key is secret. If Bob wants to make a transaction with Jane, he first encrypts the transaction with both his own private key and Jane's public key and uploads the transactions file to the network. The network then verifies that the transaction was signed with Bob's private key by looking at his public key since the public key is tied to the private key. Although both the public and private keys are related, it is impossible to decipher the private key through its public key.

The second concept is the distributed ledger, or a record book that is decentralized and distributed across a network such that each node—a computer connected to the Bitcoin network—has a copy of the ledger and the records therein. The purpose of a distributed ledger is to ensure that a person transferring money has enough funds to make the transaction. In the case of Bitcoin, the distributed ledger is an open ledger (i.e., it is open to the public for anyone to see). Bitcoin's open ledger has a recording of every transaction ever made within the system since its inception, and this ledger is distributed across a decentralized network of nodes across the globe. Each Bitcoin transaction is published together with the transferor's and the recipient's public keys, and can be found on the Internet (e.g., https://blockchain.info/).

As an example, Bob has 1 bitcoin (BTC) and he wants to transfer it to Jane. Before the transaction can be conducted, Bitcoin's decentralized network will have to verify that Bob has enough BTCs to make the transaction. The network verifies the amount of Bob's funds in BTC by looking through the ledger at every transaction that Bob has ever made in the network to determine the net amount of BTC that Bob possesses. The amount of BTC at Bob's disposal is calculated through subtracting the total amount of BTC Bob has spent from the total amount of BTC Bob has received. The BTC amount that Bob wants to send is then subtracted from the net BTC amount Bob possesses. If the resulting amount is bigger or equal than 1 BTC, the network approves the transaction. If the amount is lower, it is rejected.

The third concept is the chain of blocks, which has been designed to ensure that the system cannot be cheated. A set of nodes is in charge of putting together a number of transactions into a block (with a maximum size of 1 MB). The block is then timestamped and linked to the previous block in a chronological order. This process is done through a hash function. A hash function can convert almost any type of data into a unique fixed length hash, which is not reversible (it cannot be inverted).

For instance, if we enter “A sends B 50 bitcoins” in the SHA-256[3] hash function, the SHA-256 produces a corresponding unique 256-bit output:

40911b33cc28e08a66af3a5ee3c3880f78232ae4358d8a48893ab168bf12344f

The miner—a node that participates in the verification process—gathers a set of transactions amounting to a maximum of 1 MB and enters each of them in the hash function SHA-256, producing a hash output for every transaction in the block. The miner then pairs different hash outputs together, reducing the total number by half. The process is repeated until there is only one hash output, which is a product of all the hash outputs of the transactions. This process is called a Merkel tree, and the resulting hash output is the Merkle root. In Figure 15.1 we can see the whole process where Y_1, Y_2. . .Y_8 are the transactions, and $H(1,8,Y)$ is the Merkle root.

A Merkle tree is especially useful for verifying past transactions. For instance, if a node would like to verify transaction Y_8, it only needs three hash outputs $H(5,6,Y)$, $H(7,7,Y)$, and H(1,4,Y) to reproduce the Merkle root $H(1,8,Y)$. Since $H(1,4,Y)$ includes the information about transactions Y_1–Y_4, $H(5,6,Y)$ includes the information about transactions Y_5 and Y_6, and $H(7,7,Y)$ includes the information about transaction Y_7; inputting transaction Y_8 will give the full Merkle root for all the transactions, Y_1–Y_8.

As seen in Figure 15.2, the Bitcoin software enters as input the Merkle root of the transactions in the current block, the timestamp, and the hash output of the previous block, creating a new unique hash output.

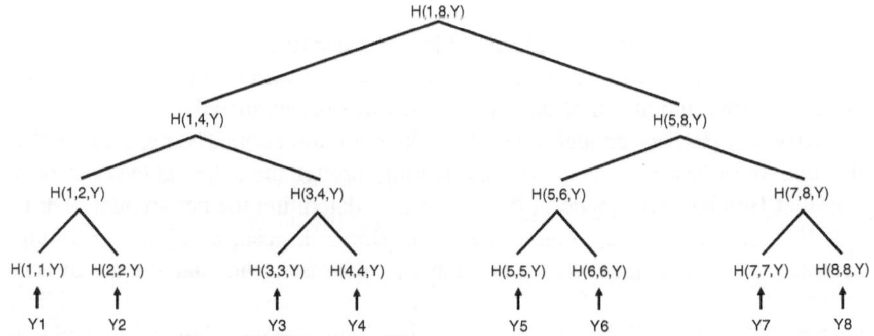

Figure 15.1 A certified digital signature

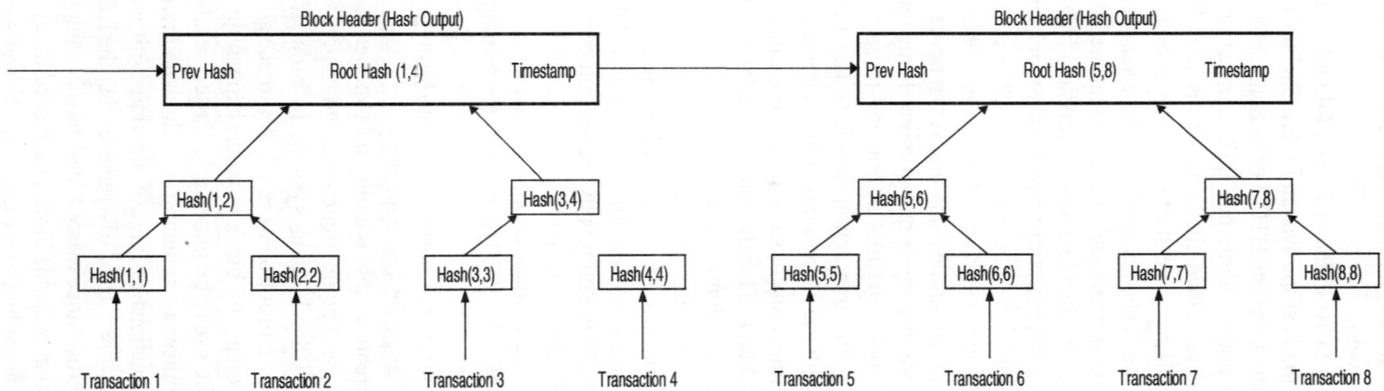

Figure 15.2 How blocks are formed

Since every hash is unique to the input text, a single modification in a transaction made in the past will alter the hash of every subsequent block and will be noticed by the whole network.

The timestamp serves to avoid the problem of double-spending. In the case of Bitcoin, Bob could try to cheat the system by sending at the same time two payment transactions with the same one BTC. For example, one to himself and another to Jane, using different nodes. While one BTC transaction may be approved by the distributed ledger as described above, the distributed ledger per se does not prevent this BTC from being spent if the two transactions are conducted at the same time. This is because the nodes approving the transaction are independent of each other and would confirm that Bob has not spent the BTC.

The blockchain solves the double-spending problem by chronologically ordering all the blocks of Bitcoin transactions through the blockchain and timestamping them. If Bob has sent two transactions of 1 BTC while only having 1 BTC in his account, the transactions can be either put in the same block or in two different blocks. If the transactions are in the same block, the nodes will acknowledge the two transactions and randomly reject one of them. If the transactions are instead processed in different blocks, the first transaction to be recorded in a block on Bitcoin's open ledger is the transaction that becomes verified by the system. When the other block with the second transaction attempts to be recorded on the ledger, the system will reject this block since the BTC has already been recorded on the ledger in the first block. Thereby, the second transaction is prevented from taking place, preventing the "double-spending problem."

The last concept is the incentive scheme, Since nodes are run by people, the blockchain needs to provide some kind of incentive for individuals to ensure that they verify each transaction and form the blocks. The incentives are provided through kickbacks to the miners by the system creating new bitcoins and depositing them in the miner's account. Initially, the Bitcoin software generated BTC 50 for every new block approved; however, this amount is cut by half every 210,000 blocks. As of 2017, a miner (or mining pool) receives BTC 12.5 for every new block that is verified. In spite of this, due to the increasing demand for verification of transactions, transferors pay miners additional transaction fees in exchange for fast approvals.

Bitcoin will cease creating new bitcoins on October 8, 2140, when a maximum of BTC 21 million will be in circulation, and miners will then only receive transaction fees through the bidding system. In order to limit inflation, the Bitcoin network requires a proof of work (PoW) to accept the block. The PoW is the mechanism that keeps the block creation happening every 10 minutes on average. Without it, BTCs may be mined a lot faster, resulting in a fast increase in the supply of cryptocurrency, reducing its value and therefore the trust in it.

The proof of work functions as follows. Previously, it was explained how the SHA-256 hash function works. The PoW requires that the hash output starts with a predefined number of zeros. Since every added zero is computationally expensive, the network can ensure that only one block is accepted every 10 minutes by adjusting the number of zeros according to the total CPU power spent by the miners.

Table 15.1 "Hello, world!"

"Hello, world!0":	1312af178c253f84028d480a6adc1e25e81caa44c749ec81976192e2ec934c64
"Hello, world!1":	e9afc424b79e4f6ab42d99c81156d3a17228d6e1eef4139be78e948a9332a7d8
…	………………………………………………
"*Hello, world!* 4250": (Input Data; Nonce)	**0000**c3af42fc31103f1fdc0151fa747ff87349a4714df7cc52ea464e12dcd4e9

Source: Nielsen (2013).

For instance, Bob wants to send the message "Hello, world!" to Jane and, for example, the PoW requires the message to have four zeros before accepting it (see Table 15.1). Since there is only one unique hash for the message "Hello, world!", the likelihood that the four zeros required by PoW will be generated with the first attempt is miniscule. Therefore, to make the system run the hash for the same message repeatedly, Bob then needs to add some random characters to the input. These added characters are called a "nonce," which is added in order to obtain the desired hash output. In the table below, it is shown how the nonce gets to 4,250 before generating four zeros at the beginning of hash output, and therefore being accepted by the PoW.

Once Bob obtains a hash value with four zeros, others can verify it by entering the message "Hello, world!4250" in the hash function SHA-256, confirming the miner's effort. The exact same concept is applied to verify every block.

If more than one block is solved at the same time, which is very uncommon (0.3 percent of all instances), the following block of the chain will be attached to one of the blocks that was solved simultaneously. The other block will then be disregarded from the chain, and the transactions of that block will have no effect on the actual money position. The blockchain quickly stabilizes as it is highly unlikely for subsequent blocks to be solved at the same time.

For instance, both Bob and Jane are miners and obtain the desired hash value (B:000bcd . . . and J:000cds) at the same time. The network forks into two different blockchains: one that rewards Bob and another one that rewards Jane. A portion of miners will include Bob's hash output in their hash function for mining the next block and the rest will include Jane's hash output. If the miners who included Jane's hash solve the next block before those who included Bob's, the blockchain continues using Jane's block and the transactions approved by Bob are considered null. In Bitcoin, after your transaction has been approved, it is common to wait for 5–10 blocks being added before considering it completed.

Blockchain applications

The main benefit of blockchain technology is to provide a "notarized" chain of events through a decentralized network. Initially, the blockchain was designed to avoid the traditional transaction fees of the financial system. In this system, each time a digital payment is made between two parties, one of them (or both) pays an interchange fee to account for the possible mediation costs that the financial institution (e.g., the bank) may incur.

Entrepreneurs and large corporations have understood the potential implications of having a "free" notarized chain and are currently developing numerous different applications. These can be categorized in general within two application areas:

1 "Cash" transfers, such as digital payment systems, money transfers, remittances, etc.
2 Complex transactions of non-cash value, such as stocks, bonds, loans, titles, smart contracts, smart properties, etc.

Cash transfers

Blockchain technology can be applied for international money transfers and domestic payments.

International money transfers are ineffective, slow, and complex, while domestic payments are rather efficient. For that reason, in the short term, the blockchain is expected to have a significant impact on international transfers by offering quick net gains through cost savings, whereas it will take longer to impact domestic payments (Crosby et al., 2016).

International money transactions

Imagine Bob, who lives in Sweden, wants to make a payment to Jane in Costa Rica. Both Bob and Jane must have a bank account in their respective countries, and Bob's bank will need to have signed a bilateral agreement with Jane's bank. The process will require administration from both banks and extra fees to cover for possible mediation costs. If the bank does not hold a bilateral agreement, it will use an intermediary to settle the transaction, adding more parties in the operation, and thus further delaying the transaction time, increasing the costs and the likelihood of encountering problems. While payments within the European Union can be made quite effortlessly through Internet banking, sending payments outside the EU can require a telephone call to the bank. In this case, Bob has to call his bank and provide all the details of the payment to the bank in Costa Rica, paying a considerable transaction fee as well as waiting around five days before the payment has been received by Jane, unless Bob would like to pay an additional fee to expedite the transaction.

The Bitcoin blockchain offers the opportunity to bypass the middlemen as there is no need for a bilateral agreement in the first place. The transaction occurs directly between Bob and Jane, with only a micro-fee attached. The transaction is irrevocable and is published in the public ledger, effectively showing a "notarized" chain of events. As a result, the transaction is faster, more transparent, and cheaper than traditional international payments. However, the downside of this is that there is no monitoring of the payment in terms of money laundering or other illegal activities.

Currently, USD 150–200 billion are spent annually on international transaction fees, and it is expected that blockchain technology will disrupt this market. However, as noted above, the main concern is the scalability, privacy, and security of the Bitcoin blockchain network (Crosby et al., 2016).

To counter this, Banco Santander has developed an app that uses blockchain technology developed by the company Ripple in California. It "offers a real-time cross-currency settlement solution that is flexible enough to comply with the risk policy, privacy and compliance needs of banks." The application is currently used for small transactions only (converting GBP 10–10,000 to EUR and USD) (Prisco, 2016).

Ripple: a public blockchain with a centralized money supply

Ryan Furger, a Canadian developer, introduced the Ripple credit network in 2004. The network consisted of credit transactions between trusted parties where the currency represented debt claims (Buterin, 2013b).

Imagine that Bob and Jane went for a trip. Jane decided to bring her friend Alice. Before the trip, Jane owed Bob USD 50 and Alice owed Jane USD 20. On the trip, Alice paid USD 10 for Bob's dinner. Since he may never see her again, he agreed to owe Jane USD 10 and Jane agreed to owe that amount to Alice. Instead of each person paying the amount owed in USD, the Ripple network provides an IOU-based currency. As seen in Figure 15.3, the network automatically adjusts the debt levels among Bob, Jane, and Alice.

The currency would expand by increasing the debt level, and vice versa. The goal was to create a global chain of trust for debt through the Ripple network. However, the system failed to expand, and by 2010 it was only used in small dispersed communities (Buterin, 2013b).

Chris Larsen, a FinTech entrepreneur, Jeb McCaleb, the founder of Mt. Gox, David Schwarz, an expert on cryptography and computer security, and Arthur

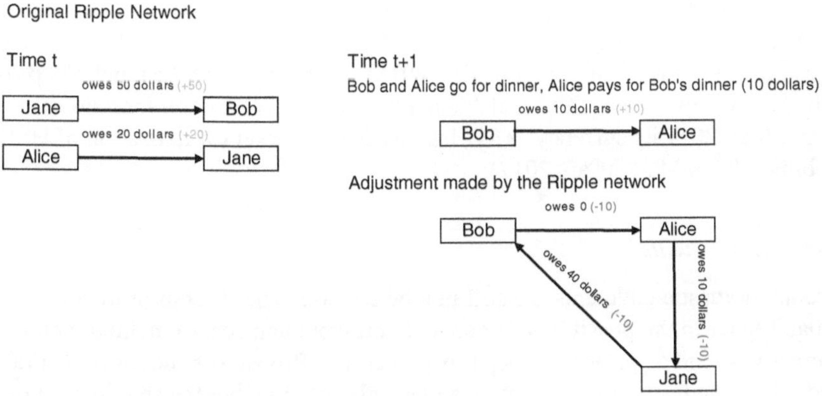

Figure 15.3 Original Ripple network

Britto partnered with Ryan Furger through the company OpenCoin in 2012 to add blockchain features to the Ripple network (Laurence, 2017).

In 2014, they announced a completely new redesigned system called the Ripple Protocol Consensus algorithm.

The new system is composed of a public blockchain that depends on a set of trusted nodes to reach consensus. Each of the trusted nodes has its own Unique Node List (UNL) composed of other nodes and only votes on their proposals. Since the UNL differs from each node, a proposal quickly propagates through the network. A plausible analogy of the UNL is the Facebook network. Imagine you only vote on the transactions proposed by your friends and each of your friends proposes the transaction to their own friends. Soon, the proposed transaction will reach every person in the network. The Ripple system acts similarly and requires 80 percent of the server to agree before approving the transaction. The nodes approve or reject the transaction by looking at Ripple's ledger. Ripple's ledger is divided into two:

- A common ledger that contains the amount of Ripple's currency in each account.
- A last-closed ledger that contains the most recent transactions ratified by the network.

This reduces the amount of information that every node in the network needs to have for approving transactions.

Since Ripple uses a voting-style consensus algorithm, it does not need to offer monetary incentives in exchange for validating transactions. Instead, Ripple started with a total money supply of XRP 100 billion, Ripple currency, owned by OpenCoin, which was renamed Ripple in 2015, and sells it at a predefined rate. As of 2017, Ripple has sold XRP 40 billion. In May 2017, Ripple announced that they would place XRP 55 billion in an escrow account with a precise schedule to eliminate the fear of an unexpected shock in the money supply. The escrow account contains 55 contracts of XRP 1 billion that expire on the first day of every month. The amount that is not sold is returned to the escrow account and offered after the original 55 contracts have expired (Garlinghouse, 2017).

By September 2016, Ripple has raised over USD 150 million, including investments from Google Ventures, IDG Capital Partners, Standard Chartered, Accenture, and SBI Holdings (Castillo, 2015). Ripple has found its niche in providing a low-cost, secure, and scalable network for cross-border transactions, and in mid-May 2017 its currency, XRP, has reached a market capitalization of USD 13 billion (CoinMarketCap, 2017).

Domestic payments

Overall, domestic payments are still in a beta phase. The Bitcoin problems with scalability harm the possibility to create an efficient and secure method, and the alternatives tend to prioritize speed over security. Private (or modestly centralized) blockchain systems seem to be a plausible solution, but the smaller number of miners increases the vulnerabilities. The Lightning Network, which may be implemented in the Bitcoin blockchain and is a decentralized network that uses smart contract functionality in the blockchain to enable instant payments, also raises security concerns among blockchain enthusiasts.

Financial institutions are currently investigating the possibility of pledging digital coins to a fiat currency (EUR, USD, etc.) to facilitate domestic payments. The resulting coin is referred to as a "colored coin" or a digital token, and it acts as a liability.

By using colored coins, it would be possible to implement blockchain technology in everyday transactions. For instance, a digital token can represent a euro and can be transferred between banks, which can be compared to a gift card backed by a fiat currency.

Alex Mizhrazi, the co-founder of the Swedish startup Chromaway, was the first person to develop colored coins, and he led the open-source project from 2012 to 2014. Chromaway's first customer was the LHV Bank in Estonia, with which they introduced the Cuber Wallet app. The app was a payment system that used colored coins pegged to euros to enable transactions free of charge (Higgins, 2015). However, due to the current scalability problems (delays on transactions), the company has shifted its focus from payment solutions to smart contracts, described in more detail below.

Some central banks and investment banks are also investigating the possibility to directly issue a state-backed cryptocurrency. The Bank of England, Royal Bank of Canada, and People's Bank of China are the main players in this field. Among them, the Bank of England has made the most substantial effort supporting a research project that has introduced RSCoin, a central bank cryptocurrency (Danezis and Meiklejohn, 2015; Evans-Pritchard, 2016).

RSCoin uses a modest centralized network to validate transactions and to avoid double-spending. Its main objective is to solve the scalability problem of Bitcoin while offering irrevocable, transparent transactions. RSCoin also changes the incentives of miners by focusing them on validating transactions instead of keeping up with the PoW requirement of creating a block every 10 minutes (although it could be done a lot faster).

The central bank (or other entity) delegates the authority to validate transactions to a specific set of trusted miners called "mintettes." Since mintettes are known, they are also accountable for misbehavior. The transaction is made through a two-phase commit. The central bank has complete power over the money supply, while the mintettes are responsible for the maintenance of the transaction ledger.

Mintettes are in charge of collecting the transactions and putting them together in blocks, but instead of approving them through a "proof of work," the mintettes are authorized by the central bank to directly validate the transactions. At first, a user requests to make a transaction and the mintettes verify whether the user has enough coins. If the majority of mintettes approve it, they send a bundle of evidence (signed with their keys provided by the central bank) to the user. The user then sends the transaction together with the bundle of evidence to the desired destination. The system then verifies the bundle of evidence, adds the transactions, seals them into the public blockchain, and confirms the transactions.

RSCoin has proved to be efficient, and processes over 2,000 transactions per second (compared to Bitcoin's two to seven transactions per second).

Safello: a Bitcoin exchange for European customers

Frank Schuil, a Dutch entrepreneur living in Sweden, envisions a cryptocurrency bank that also has connections to the regular economy. Under PSD2, the new banking regulation approved by the European Commission discussed elsewhere in this book, people will be able to have both their regular fiat currency and cryptocurrency accounts in the same app. This will allow a person to switch money directly between euros and cryptocurrencies with a single click. Safello's goal is to establish a safe brokerage exchange between fiat currencies and cryptocurrencies. Currently, most transfers are done through exchange houses. Exchange houses hold the client's currency and allow the client to trade on their platform. However, a brokerage acts as a vehicle, connecting the client directly to the buyer/seller without holding the money.

Schuil also explains that their first funding round was made during the price hike in the winter of 2013 where they raised over USD 600,000 from an angel round. Later, they raised a convertible of USD 250,000 from the Digital Currency Group, followed up by two crowdfunding campaigns, the first one backed by the Digital Currency Group and the second one on its own, raising USD 630,000 (FundedByMe, 2015).

Safello's advantage is that the client's funds will be safe even if Safello goes bankrupt or is hacked. Only the money that is being exchanged at that moment is at risk. If the same happens to an exchange, the clients may lose all their funds stored in cryptocurrencies. Discussed above, in 2014, Mt. Gox, the biggest Bitcoin exchange, was hacked and lost 850,000 of its clients' bitcoins, corresponding to over USD 1 billion in today's exchange rate. Most Bitcoin exchanges have already updated their security, and it has become extremely uncommon that they get hacked. However, there is still a risk, and Safello's goal is to mitigate this risk. Safello also stands out for its deep commitment to cooperate with the current regulations and to provide a safe environment. For example, Safello has registered with the Financial Supervisory Authority, partnered with major banks such as Barclays, and cooperated with the police to sell confiscated bitcoins.

Safello is also working on implementing its own interface for the wallet. The prototype is 80 percent completed, and it works through a multi-signature protocol. Their multi-signature setup requires two out of the three keys to move the funds. The keys are divided between a third party, Safello, and the user. If Safello or the third party disappears, the user will still have full control of their own funds.

Schuil argues that in order to have a cryptocurrency as the underlying framework for banking, the Lightning Network is needed.[4] Safello also partnered with Barclays for creating a white label version to raise funds for charities through Bitcoin. Safello and Barclays also discussed further opportunities to use Bitcoin in banking.

Complex transactions

> The design supports a tremendous variety of possible transaction types that I designed years ago. Escrow transactions, bonded contracts, third party arbitration, multi-party signature, etc. If Bitcoin catches on in a big way, these are things we'll want to explore in the future, but they all had to be designed at the beginning to make sure they would be possible later.
>
> (Nakamoto, 2010)

Since Bitcoin's conception, Satoshi Nakamoto already had in mind the boundless opportunities that blockchain can offer beyond cryptocurrencies. Blockchain was designed as an infrastructure that allows people to build their own projects on top of it. Smart contracts are one of blockchain technology's most promising applications.

The smart contract term was coined in 1995 in an *Extropy* magazine article written by a computer scientist and legal scholar, Nick Szabo, in which he explained the potential of using a combination of cryptographic elements and the Internet to automate contracts (Szabo, 1996; Gord, 2016). Although the blockchain was not yet invented, his article foresaw the recent practical developments of blockchain technology.

The similarities between his original paper, the Bitcoin proposal, and the recent developments in blockchain are striking. For that reason, many argue that he is in fact Satoshi Nakamoto (Price, 2015). A study at Aston University investigated the linguistic similarities between the Bitcoin white paper and a set of researchers who are believed to have participated in it. The study concluded that Nick Szabo's writing had the most linguistic similarities to the Bitcoin white paper (ScienceDaily, 2014). While the similarities were striking between both works, Szabo refuted this claim (Popper, 2015). Nevertheless, as the man who invented the idea of smart contracts, Nick Szabo remains one of the most influential figures of blockchain technology.

Smart contracts

The role of a contract is to formalize an agreement between different parties, and it has been essential for the advances made by the modern economy. Contracts have enabled us to form large organizations and undertake large projects by establishing trust. In order to ensure the performance of a contract, it is necessary to create a system of rules together with third parties that perform auditing and monitoring.

A smart contract is a programmable contract that is self-executed and self-enforced through a distributed network. Once a contract is signed with the correspondent's private key, the software code carries out the terms of the contract directly (Szabo, 1996). For instance, imagine the process of renting a car. You pay a certain amount in cryptocurrency in exchange for using a car tomorrow through a predefined contract. The next day, a digital key that gives you access to the car must arrive to you. If it does not, you receive a refund. This whole process happens without the need for an intermediary to ensure the contract is executed.

It also provides anonymity. The network only sees a set of predefined "if/then" statements, but it does not show the underlying information being passed, thanks to the aforementioned secret key cryptography.

Chromaway: pioneers of blockchain technology

Ludvig Öberg became involved in Bitcoin in 2011. After downloading the Bitcoin software and mining his first block, his online wallet got hacked. Öberg then decided to learn more about Bitcoin technology and the politics behind it by joining a Bitcoin exchange. Soon after, he quit his job at the exchange and joined Frank Schuil as a co-founder of Safello. After working actively at Safello for two years, Öberg reduced his participation to board membership and joined Chromaway as a business developer.

Chromaway partnered with Funderbeam, a platform using blockchain technology to facilitate equity crowdfunding for startups, allowing the investors to automatically transfer shares between each other. To comply with regulations, a holding company owns the shares of the startups and the investors trade the shares of the holding company. In early 2015, Chromaway started to specialize in complex transactions, creating its own blockchain platform and partnering with Telia and the Swedish Land Registry Bureau to facilitate the land registry process.

Blockchain technology offers two main benefits for the land registry process. The first is to facilitate the process of buying a house. The process requires many steps, such as signing documents, paying instalments, and asserting the completion of each process. Chromaway facilitates the process by using digital signatures and "state-driven" programming. "State-driven" means that each action brings the state of the contract to the next level. Figure 15.4 provides an example of all the steps required to buy a house.

As we can infer, the process is time-consuming. It requires a large amount of administrative "paperwork" and a third party (notary) to verify most processes.

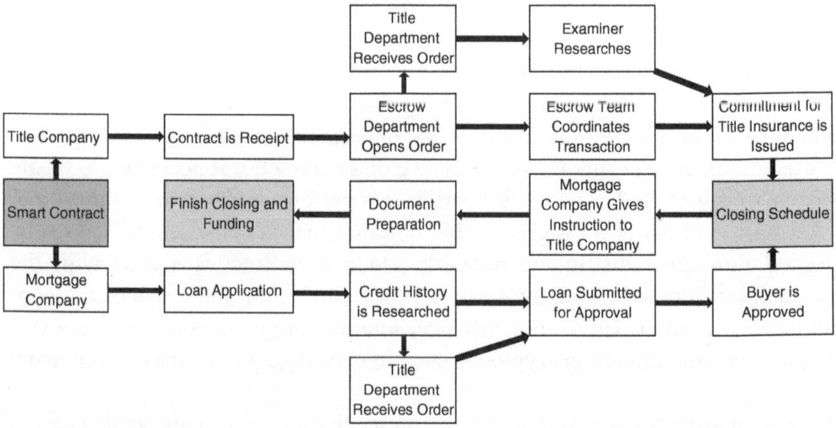

Figure 15.4 House buying procedure

Chromaway can simplify each step while offering a verified chain of events. Every time a step of the process is completed, users input their own private key to confirm in the blockchain that the step is completed. Once a process has been signed, the blockchain is updated automatically and moves toward the next state. Since the blockchain cannot be modified, it provides a secure chain of evidence. The whole idea is to offer a transparent and secure system recording processes and workflows without the need for a third party.

According to Öberg, the reason behind building their own blockchain instead of using others was due to the lack of alternatives. Bitcoin currently has a scalability problem, and other blockchains are either in a beta stage (e.g., IBM Fabrics, Ethereum) or badly programmed. Alex Mizhrazi had a unique idea on how to build a special-purpose blockchain. Instead of modeling it directly on Bitcoin, he looked at how to turn a database into a private blockchain. The Chromaway blockchain has a set of trusted parties such as banks, the land registry bureau, and governmental agencies (national and/or international) that validate the information transferred.

Another benefit is to offer the transparent allocation of mortgage deeds. For instance, imagine that Jane decides to buy a house securing the loan against her property. Years later, she decides to go to another bank to borrow more money against the same property. The mortgage deed is then split in two parts, but that transaction is not necessarily registered by the land registry. This causes a situation where the banks do not have a clear idea of who owns what, delaying the transactions and increasing the paperwork. If instead a blockchain is used, a chain of evidence is created, showing in a transparent and secure manner how the mortgage deed has evolved over time.

As of 2017, Chromaway is developing its platform with the Swedish Land Registry Bureau, and it is already in contact with foreign governments and planning to expand. Chromaway's innovative solutions can have a clear impact on how properties are registered around the world. Developing countries tend to have large problems with land registry services. This problem arises partially due to the costly process of registering the properties and the lack of trust in the governmental institutions. Through a blockchain, it would be possible to offer poor citizens the opportunity to register their properties in an easy, accessible way without the need to trust the government. This does not imply that the land registry process will always be secure; as Öberg says, "It doesn't matter what the blockchain says if there is an army outside your house." Nevertheless, the blockchain will make it easier to collect evidence for one's claims.

Ethereum: a blockchain-based distributed computing platform

> Bitcoin was designed to be a [Simple Mail Transfer Protocol] SMTP. It's a protocol that is very good at one particular task. It is good for transferring money, but it was not designed as a foundational layer for any kind of protocols to be built on top.
>
> (Buterin, 2014)

The shared vision of blockchain technology is to provide an "Internet of Value." The aim is to create a new layer on top of the Internet that allows transactions without the need for a third party to establish trust among the participants.

Vitalik Buterin, a Russian-Canadian prodigy, shared the same vision and argued that the Bitcoin scripting language is not appropriate to fully enhance the blockchain's potential. He claimed that Bitcoin's scripting language was designed with the purpose of transferring money, and not for the wider purpose of building applications on top of it. He then proposed a platform with a new Turing-complete scripting language and the blockchain. The Turing-complete scripting language allows any application readable by a computer to be built on top of the blockchain, potentially disrupting the third-party arbitrator ecosystem as we know it.

The Ethereum blockchain differs from Bitcoin in several aspects:

1. It has two types of accounts instead of one: externally owned accounts, which are similar to those in Bitcoin, and contract accounts. Contract accounts are "stateful." They have different transition states that are activated through Ether, Ethereum's cryptocurrency, which acts as "digital oil." The currency had an initial public offering in July 2014, and the rest is provided through mining blocks. If we return to our example, if Jane wants to buy a computer from Bob through the Internet, they would first create a contract account with a predefined set of instructions. The instructions require Jane to deposit the money before Bob sends the computer and to release the funds after she has received it. The transition of the contract to the next stage (releasing the funds) is done through Ether. Once Jane receives the computer, she sends Ether to the contract (signed with her private key), and the contract releases the funds to Bob. Another possibility is to use an oracle. An oracle is a system that can activate the contract based on external data. In the case above, the oracle can act as a third party. Once the mailing company updates the website with the information that Jane has received the goods, the oracle "orders" the contract to release the funds.
2. It has its own programming language called "Solidity" that defines the contract accounts. Solidity is a compiled language similar to JavaScript. The key difference is that it is contract-oriented instead of object-oriented, and understands concepts such as identity, ownership, and protection forms. Solidity compiles the instructions given by the developers, transforms them into bytecode, and sends them to the Ethereum Virtual Machine (EVM). The Ethereum Virtual Machine is Turing-complete and is in charge of enforcing the code.
3. Transactions are currently made through proof of work (PoW). Ethereum tries to avoid the consolidation of the miners by providing a system that encourages light clients. The mining is conducted through graphic processing units (GPUs) instead of CPU power. It also provides a "light implementation" that does not require the downloading of the whole blockchain. In the future, Ethereum plans to use proof of stake (PoS) instead of PoW. Proof of stake calculates the weight of the node by the amount of currency holdings instead of computational power as in PoW. However, it is still in the development phase.

4 It does not limit its block size. Instead, it includes a penalty for larger sizes called gas. The larger the size of the block, the larger the penalty is. The timing is also different. Bitcoin aims to produce a block every 10 minutes, while Ethereum aims for 12 seconds (although the average is 14.56 seconds).

Overall, Ethereum has been a success since its origin. The biggest sign of its success is the recent creation of the Enterprise Ethereum Alliance in early 2017. The organization is backed by Microsoft, J.P. Morgan, ING, Accenture, CME Group, and many other Fortune 500 companies. The goal is to develop blockchain technology through the Ethereum platform by connecting industry experts with companies to learn from each other and build smart contracts (Enterprise Ethereum Alliance, 2016; Popper, 2017b).

Ethereum has also been a success in the development of "decentralized applications" (Dapps). Developers are already flooding the market with applications such as payment systems (TheCoin), option trading (EtherOpt), forecasting "competitions" (Augur), and crowdfunding (WeiFund).[5]

Nonetheless, the power of Ethereum's scripting language also means that there are more opportunities for hacking attacks. The largest Ethereum project so far, the decentralized autonomous organization (DAO), was "hacked" in July 2016, resulting in losses of over USD 50 million (Finley, 2016; Popper, 2017a). As a result, Ethereum forced a hard fork in October 2016 to update its security and return the hacked funds to the investors (Jameson, 2016). The hard fork was approved by the majority, with 85 percent of the miners upgrading their software to the proposed version. The rest of the miners carried on with the old blockchain, and Ethereum was divided into two cryptocurrencies: Ether (ETH) and Ethereum Classic (ETC). As of mid-2017, the market capitalization of ETH and ETC were USD 16 billion and USD 1 billion, respectively (CoinMarketCap, 2017).

The main argument behind the resistance to switch to the new forked blockchain was their perception of the basic principles that a blockchain should represent immutability and decentralization. By keeping the initial currency intact, it provides the investors the security that the "laws" (code) governing the currency will never be changed (Ethereum Classic, 2016b). The ETC followers then published the Ethereum Classic Declaration of Independence and the Crypto-Decentralist Manifesto with the key arguments being that openness, neutrality, and immutability are necessary (Ethereum Classic , 2016a, 2016c).

It is important to acknowledge that Ethereum is still in a beta phase. It is expected to have many bugs and problems before it fully realizes its potential. However, the response of the market is clear—most are convinced of the opportunities that Ethereum could bring, and it is at the center of the FinTech revolution.

R3 and Corda: financial consortia

R3

In 2015, a consortium of the largest banks, including J.P. Morgan, Barclays, UBS, Deutsche Bank, and Goldman Sachs, joined forces with the FinTech company

R3 to create a framework for blockchain technology. Initially, R3 worked in a membership-style business model where financial companies paid a member fee every year in exchange for collaborating to build a new blockchain platform. Under this model, the group grew and gained support from over 80 different financial institutions. However, in 2016, R3 decided to change their business model and seek USD 150–200 million in funding in exchange for 60 percent of their equity. According to Fortune, the fundraising raised concern over the control of R3, and soon after the new business model was proposed, Goldman Sachs, J.P. Morgan, and Santander departed the consortium (Hackett, 2016).

Nonetheless, R3 is still supported by most of the largest financial institutions and has created a new platform named Corda, which is influenced by blockchain technology and acts as a global ledger facilitating the implementation of smart contracts.

Corda

The Corda platform aims to create a global ledger that is able to adjust to firm-specific needs and regulations. In the current environment, if two firms engage in a transaction, each would record it in their own private ledger and then reconcile it ("bilateral/reconciliation") or directly delegate that authority to a third party ("third party/market infrastructure"). Corda proposes a platform in which both firms can collaborate to keep a shared record of the events ("shared ledger vision"). Corda introduces the state object (see Figure 15.5), which records the current state of an agreement and contains contract code, legal prose, and a timestamp. The legal prose, which is a traditionally written contract, is referenced by a hash function facilitating the bridge between a smart and traditional contract.

The transition of a state object is achieved through a consensus mechanism that is only performed by the parties involved. The platform uses a "uniqueness service" that only serves to attest whether a state has transitioned; however, they

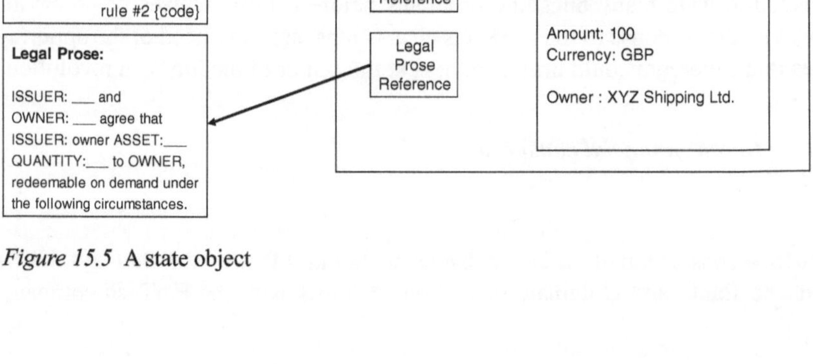

Figure 15.5 A state object

do not see any of the contents of the transactions. This is used in order to maintain privacy and scalability (fewer data to confirm) (Brown et al., 2016).

The platform was released at the end of 2016, and it is still very much in its early stage. The Mizuho Financial Group, a banking-holding company with USD 1.7 trillion in assets (MHFG, 2016), has partnered with Cognizant, a US company specialized in technology services, to use Corda for digitalizing documents such as letter of credits and bill of ladings (Prnewswire, 2017).

Hyperledger: the Linux consortium

In 2015, the Linux Foundation, a nonprofit organization, gathered a consortium of companies to create a free, open-source distributed ledger framework to support business transactions.

The project is funded by membership fees ranging from USD 5,000 to USD 250,000, and includes over 100 companies, such as J.P. Morgan, CME Group, Airbus, Cisco, Nokia, and American Express. The most renowned Hyperledger project is Hyperledger Fabric, developed by Digital Assets and IBM (Hyperledger, 2017).

Hyperledger Fabric aims to build a blockchain adapted for businesses taking into account confidentiality, transparency, flexibility, and scalability. The Hyperledger Fabric's blockchain is based on the standard blockchain concept with the key characteristic that all users/nodes have to be authenticated. This incentivizes the nodes to act in an honest manner without the need for proof of stake or proof of work. The nodes can also form their own private blockchains and only publish the reference data in the public blockchain. For instance, if Bob wants to buy a computer from Jane, she may not want others to know the price. They can instead sign a contract with each private key confirming the good is sold, insert it into a hash function, and add it to the ledger. If Jane does not deliver the computer after getting paid, Bob can claim that Jane has breached the contract by inserting the contract, which has been signed with both private keys, in the hash function and pointing it to the reference in the public blockchain. The authentication also ensures that Jane is liable for her actions (Hyperledger Fabric, 2017).

Swift, the platform used by the global interbanking system, has announced that it will use the Hyperledger Fabric as its core technology for the proof of concept, the demonstration that blockchain technology can be viable for real-world applications. The trial includes BNP Paribas, BNY Mellon, and Wells Fargo. Wim Raymaeker, the head of Swift global payment innovation initiative, said that it could save up to 30 percent of reconciliation costs in cross-border payments (Castillo, 2017; Das, 2017).

Overall, the Hyperledger is still in its maturing phase, but it is gaining ground in both the financial world and the blockchain community.

Corporate governance

Finally, David Yermack, a professor of NYU Stern School of Business, has made a substantial contribution on the potential role of blockchain in corporate governance.

In his paper "Corporate Governance and Blockchain" (Yermack, 2017), he offers insights on how the blockchain can benefit financial markets by providing transparency, liquidity, and real-time accounting.

He discusses the possibility to crowdsource, through blockchain, the role of auditing and verifying share transactions. Assuming that the blockchain accurately identifies share ownership, issuing companies could identify hostile positions by activist shareholders and corporate raiders. The shareholders would acknowledge the hostile positions and hold their shares as they expect the price to increase. As a result, the profits of a hostile takeover would be shared among shareholders instead of by the raiders.

The transparency of the ownership would also help investors to monitor the stock positions and trades by management (i.e., whether managers only sold the stock of their company or they sold other stock as well, the reasons being either possible inside information or liquidity problems, respectively).

The use of the blockchain in equity exchanges would also provide greater liquidity by reducing transaction fees and shortening the time spent on formalizing a share transaction. In the US, it takes three days to formally transfer share ownership from a buyer to a seller. Hence, the blockchain would close the bid–ask price gap and impact investors' behavior. Investors could benefit from greater liquidity by threatening to sell their shares during negotiations and affect management decisions to a greater extent.

The voting process in corporate governance could also be greatly improved. For instance, investors could use a private key that is assigned to their share to vote in the public ledger. The process would be more secure, easier to verify, and transparent. A study made by Listokin (2008) shows how the final result of corporate closed elections depends on the preferences of the management, and not on the preferences of the simple majority. This problem could be greatly diminished by introducing a blockchain voting system.

Finally, the blockchain could be used to offer real-time accounting. Investors would be able to monitor everyday transactions directly without solely relying on the company's financial reporting. It would also reduce the incentives for accountants to "manipulate" earnings as investors would have a clear view of the company.

Although it seems far away, stock exchanges are already implementing blockchain technology. The Australian Stock Exchange (ASX) partnered with Digital Asset Holdings, a FinTech company, to upgrade its system using blockchain technology (Range, 2016; Wells, 2016). Nasdaq successfully launched Nasdaq Linq, a private blockchain platform, to record private security transaction among a specific set of pre-IPO companies and its Estonian branch, Nasdaq Talinn, partnered with LHV Group, to provide a blockchain platform that facilitates voting among shareholders (Nasdaq, 2015, 2016, 2017). In the next upcoming years, blockchain technology will most likely impact corporate governance. It is not clear yet where it will be more successful, but financial institutions have acknowledged the potential and are actively investing in it (Harty, 2016; Higgins, 2017).

War of principles

Bitcoin "civil war"

Bitcoin's blockchain is the largest blockchain at the moment; its public ledger amounts to 115 GB and processes more than 250,000 transactions per day (Blockchain.info, 2017a, 2017d). The fast adoption of Bitcoin has led to an increasing challenge of the system's scalability. As noted above, blocks have a limit size of 1 MB and are accepted every 10 minutes. As a result, the Bitcoin network can only accept from two to seven transactions per second (Blockchain.info, 2017e). The low rate of confirmed transactions, compared to other cash transaction systems such as Visa, with 1,736 transactions per second, represents a problem, as many transactions stay unconfirmed for long periods of time (Visa, 2017).

Originally, Satoshi Nakamoto limited the size to 1 MB in order to keep the blockchain small until SPV or simplified payment verification wallets, which allow lightweight clients to verify transactions, were created (Hearn, 2015b). However, by the time SPV wallets were developed, Satoshi Nakamoto had disappeared, and has not communicated with the Bitcoin community since 2011. Before leaving, he gave Gavin Andressen, a software developer, access to the Bitcoin Core, the mainstream Bitcoin software. However, Andressen did not want this responsibility (Hearn, 2016). Hence, he invited four other Bitcoin developers to join the team and quickly phased himself out. The disappearance of Satoshi Nakamoto left the Bitcoin community in a difficult position since without the strong leadership of Nakamoto, it was not clear to them how to proceed. The four Bitcoin Core developers invited by Andressen, known as the Bitcoin Core or "the Establishment," were supposed to listen to those individuals running the nodes and act accordingly. Yet initially, the Core showed little interest in addressing the concerns of scalability.

In August 2015, Mike Hearn, a past contributor to the Bitcoin Core, proposed to fork the Bitcoin software. In his manifesto, Hearn complained about the lack of action within the Bitcoin Core and argued for increasing the block size from 1 MB to 8 MB. Hearn commented, "This state of affairs cannot go on. The Bitcoin Core project has shown it cannot reform so it must be abandoned. This is why Bitcoin has forked" (Hearn, 2015b).

To test the support for his idea, Hearn proposed an upgrade to the Bitcoin network, which was named Bitcoin XT. Bitcoin XT was developed together with the former head of the Bitcoin Core, Gavin Andressen. The Bitcoin system allows the nodes to vote on changes to the Core, such as Bitcoin XT, by downloading and upgrading their software to Bitcoin XT. If the overwhelming majority of the nodes upgraded the software and accepted blocks larger than 1 MB, the network would fork into two separate blockchains. After the fork, it was expected that the rest of the nodes would accept the fork and upgrade their software to Bitcoin XT, joining the rest of the network.

The outcome did not proceed as expected. Only a handful of miners followed Hearn, and the Core embarked on a fight to censor and diminish his message

(Blocke, 2016). "The Establishment" defined Bitcoin XT as an altcoin (a cryptocurrency other than Bitcoin), and used that concept to prevent any information concerning the software update from being posted in Bitcoin forums. For instance, Coinbase, one of the largest Bitcoin exchanges, was erased from the Bitcoin section of Reddit and the official Bitcoin website after showing support for Bitcoin XT (GitHub, 2015; Reddit, 2016). The Core, led by Gregory Maxwell, argued that larger blocks would increase the size of the blockchain to a point that a normal user could not participate in it (Maxwell, 2015). This would most likely result in only large corporations having the resources required for the huge storage needs, diminishing Bitcoin's core principle of security through decentralization. In the following months, the community grew further apart, with key individuals even receiving death threats and hacking attacks from other members of the community (Popper, 2016). The backlash was so strong that Mike Hearn decided to quit the Bitcoin community in 2016 (Hearn, 2016).

Since then, the Bitcoin community has evolved, and it is currently divided in two different groups: Bitcoin Unlimited and SegWit. The Bitcoin Unlimited group proposes two main arguments in their manifest *Bitcoin Unlimited: Articles of Federation*: (1) an unlimited Bitcoin block size that is regulated directly by market forces; and (2) the democratization of the Bitcoin software development (Bitcoin Unlimited, 2016a). The second point uses the original Bitcoin white paper to argue for the democratization of the Bitcoin network through CPU power:

> They [miners] vote with their CPU power, expressing their acceptance of valid blocks by working on extending them and rejecting invalid blocks by refusing to work on them. Any needed rules and incentives can be enforced with this consensus mechanism.
>
> (Nakamoto, 2008)

Bitcoin Unlimited aims to eliminate any specific guidelines on what software to use for mining bitcoins. The system would regulate itself based on the majority consensus as non-majority blocks would just not be followed up by other miners. This group also established the Bitcoin Unlimited Federation in 2016, where individuals are invited and have the right to vote for the president and participate in other decision-making activities.

SegWit was proposed by the Bitcoin Core in December 2015. SegWit stands for Segregation Witnesses, and aims to separate the signatures from the transaction data. The signatures (e.g., Bob's private key and Jane's public key) are stored instead on an extended block, reducing the size of each transaction. SegWit has also proposed an increase on the block size to 4MB for new nodes while allowing old nodes to keep mining on 1 MB blocks (Bitcoin Core, 2017).

In February 2016, the largest Bitcoin miners, which represented 80 percent of the total blocks mined at that time, and the Bitcoin Core met in Hong Kong to discuss the future of Bitcoin. In the meeting, they agreed on a timetable for implementing SegWit (Bitcoin Roundtable, 2016):

- In July 2016, the developer core team will release the code for a SegWit hard fork.
- In July 2017, the hard fork will be activated if there is enough community support.

The first release was delayed until October 2016, and by then many of the miners had started to withdraw their support for SegWit (Wirdum, 2016). The main concern with SegWit is that the proposed solution does not address the long-term scalability problem of Bitcoin. Although it reduces the size of every transaction, if the block size is not increased, the network cannot process transactions on time.

At the moment, Bitcoin Unlimited is gathering more support than SegWit, with 44 percent supporting the former and 30 percent supporting the latter. Miners are able to signal their support by updating their mining software according to their preference. Their updated software only signals the support, but still mines 1 MB blocks. Once enough miners signal their support, a hard fork will occur. The mining pool ViaBTC suggested enforcing the hard fork if 75 percent of the hash rate (mining power) supports Bitcoin Unlimited, but there is still no consensus (Bitcoin Unlimited, 2016b).

As seen in Figure 15.6, in May 2017, the mining power is distributed in the following companies (Blockchain.info, 2017b).

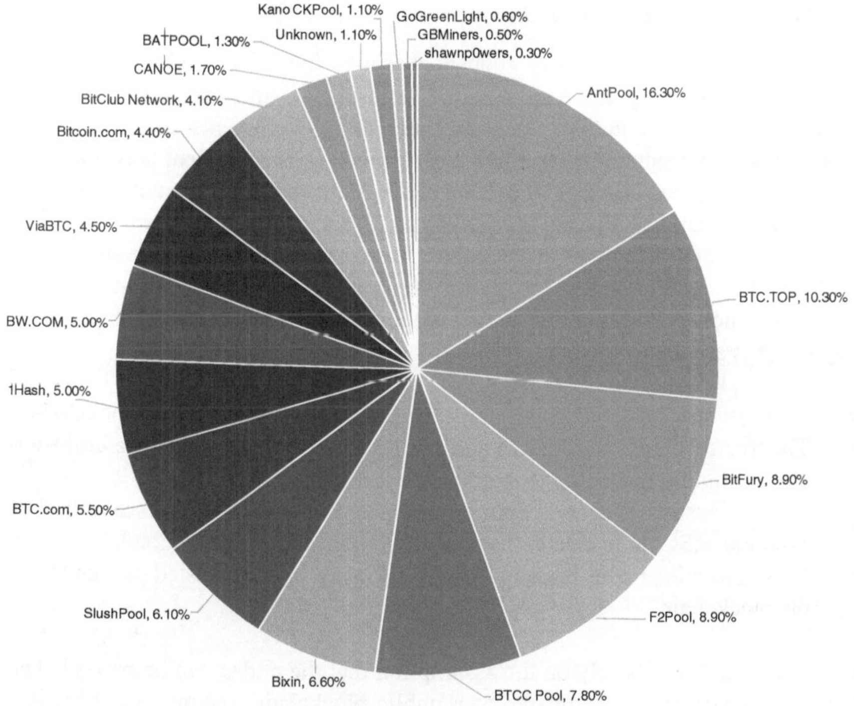

Figure 15.6 Distribution of mining power in the Bitcoin network

Bitcoin has shifted from the initial decentralized network to a set of mining pools that use specialized hardware (ASIC) designed to mine bitcoins. As explained earlier, the Bitcoin network adjusts the difficulty (number of zeros in the hash output) according to the total mining power (hash rate). As a result, electricity plays an important role in defining the equilibrium point for staying profitable. If the price of electricity is higher than the Bitcoin rewards, it is not profitable to mine. As a result, the largest mining pools are located in China due to its cheap and subsidized electricity. Antpool, BTC.TOP, F2Fool, BTCC Pool, BiXin, BTC.com, and ViaBTC are all located in China, and amount to a total mining power of 60.4 percent of the total network. The centralization of mining power in China has created a concern among Bitcoin enthusiasts as much of the motivation behind Bitcoin is to have a decentralized network. If wanted, the government could easily appropriate the mining hardware, which accounts for over 60 percent of the network, and make the Bitcoin blockchain effectively inoperative.

Bitcoin is in a tough situation right now; the hard fork and the concentration of mining power are the main challenges that it faces, and overcoming them will be essential to succeed as a cryptocurrency. The positive sign is that it is operated by a consensus mechanism, and the monetary incentives are encouraging the system to achieve an agreement.

Public versus private blockchain

Blockchain is an extraordinary concept that uses incentives and cryptographic proof for transferring value in a secure, transparent, and irrevocable manner. However, certain institutions, such as banks and governments, are reluctant to use a system that cannot be modified and relies on an independent network. As a result, there has been a surge of private blockchains that offer greater maneuverability and scalability. Private blockchains are partially decentralized; instead of offering financial incentives to the public, they provide trusted keys to a diversified set of nodes that are in charge for verifying transactions. Chromaway and RSCoin, which were explained above, are examples of private blockchains. The key benefits are the following:

- If the diversified set of nodes agree, it is possible to modify the blockchain.
- The trusted parties are known and can be audited. This prevents a collusion among miners that could jeopardize the blockchain.
- Lower transaction costs do not require proof of work and are scalable. For example, RSCoin is able to manage 2,000 transactions per second.
- It can provide greater privacy by only allowing a set of trusted parties to see the blockchain.

However, the benefits rely on the assumption that the nodes can be trusted. The lack of diversification, compared to a public blockchain, means that there is a greater likelihood for collusion between the trusted nodes. Governments and banks have colluded in the past to falsify accounts, and it is not far-fetched to think that it could happen again. Users will also acknowledge the possibility to modify the blockchain, and in the case of negative events they may engage in time-consuming negotiations with the developers (Balzli, 2010; Buterin, 2015). It is important to remember that in the original Bitcoin white paper, Satoshi Nakamoto explicitly mentioned that the key benefit of an irrevocable transaction system was to avoid mediating disputes, and thus lowering transaction costs. Besides proof of work, companies are currently investigating different methods to validate transactions through a distributed network, potentially solving the scalability issue of public blockchains. If the scalability problem is solved, the private blockchain main benefits will be maneuverability and privacy.

In our opinion, the most likely scenario will be a set of private blockchains connected to large public blockchains. On the one side, private blockchains benefit from collaborating with public blockchains by using their tested protocols and publishing their internal transactions in the public blockchains. For instance, Ethereum DAO proved that is extremely hard to program a smart contract without potential vulnerabilities. A smart contract made in the Ethereum platform is tested on the public, and a company wishing to implement similar functional smart contracts can implement the same protocol in their own private blockchain. An example is the quorum platform developed by J.P. Morgan, which is a private blockchain built on the Ethereum blockchain. Quorum uses a voting-based consensus algorithm and introduces a private transaction identifier to protect the security of its users while augmenting scalability and maintaining security (J.P. Morgan, 2017; Quorum, 2017). Another example is Chromaway, mentioned earlier, which is planning to publish a Merkle tree of their state transitions in the Bitcoin network every 24 hours, thereby adding to the transparency and security of a public blockchain. The connection ensures that companies cannot modify their private blockchains without being acknowledged by their users.

On the other side, public blockchains benefit from collaborating with private blockchains by augmenting their reach, thereby gaining network effects and testing their software on a wider range of business cases. For instance, many of the applications developed in the Quorum platform could never be tested if there was not a bridge between the Ethereum platform and the Quorum blockchain (due to privacy and scalability concerns).

Overall, both private and public blockchains gain from collaboration with each other, and we should expect a hybrid ecosystem with different public and private blockchains and cryptocurrencies interacting between each other (Smith, 2017).

Conclusion

> Is the blockchain technology going to be fundamental? I think the answer is overwhelmingly likely to be yes.
>
> Former US Secretary of the Treasury,
> Larry Summers (CoinDesk, 2016)

The excitement and developments related to Bitcoin and the blockchain can be compared to what we experienced in the 1990s with the Internet. Before the world wide web, the exchange of information from cable networks to printed papers carried large transaction costs. Initially, it was thought that the Internet's main functionality was to lower these transaction costs. For instance, in 1998, Paul Krugman famously underestimated the Internet by comparing it to the fax machine (Krugman, 1998). His opinion was not unique; people understood its short-term benefits—which are lower transaction costs—but missed the long-term impact. The main benefit of the Internet, in fact, was to create a platform that allowed entrepreneurs to enter markets more easily and facilitate innovation, not only in products and services, but also in business models, thereby increasing competition. In turn, we are now experiencing what many refer to as the new Industrial Revolution, which is characterized by platform-based business models. Companies such as Facebook, Google, Alibaba, and Amazon, which originate from an idea on how to organize a platform that establishes connections between users, businesses, and information, went on to threaten and eventually change the retail, media, and advertising industries.

Blockchain has the potential to disrupt the current society to an even greater extent as it provides a decentralized platform for the transfer of value. In this chapter, we have started by introducing Bitcoin's origins and its underlying blockchain technology. Bitcoin proved to be revolutionary, and it is still the largest cryptocurrency in terms of market capitalization in 2017. However, the system has evolved past Bitcoin, with entrepreneurs and established players presenting their own blockchains and cryptocurrencies. RSCoin and Ethereum are a private and a public blockchain, respectively, with each having their own niche. While RSCoin is a theoretically scalable blockchain that could be useful for a central bank, Ethereum aims to create a platform such as the Internet (or Android) that offers the possibility to build applications on top of it. The Ethereum platform is especially innovative because it further expands the opportunity for entrepreneurs to create new organizations and business models. The decentralized autonomous organization (DAO) based on Ethereum was the first example of a large automated organization. Although unsuccessful due to a substantial hacker attack that caused a temporary substantial financial loss for its investors, the same idea will most likely be developed in the upcoming years, and could even substitute the concept of a company with a decentralized automated organization.

Furthermore, an effectively notarized chain of events will also have a deep impact on facilitating the registration process. We have shown the example of Chromaway with the land registry bureau, and that same concept could be applied to other financial and governmental procedures, such as voting.

Finally, we acknowledge that blockchain technology is still in development. As of 2017, there are still many disagreements on the optimal blockchain, and a newly formed wave of startups and established players are aiming to improve the system. However, it is clear that the decentralized network has proven to be successful for the transfer of value.

Taking everything into account, we believe that the importance of blockchain technology lies in the opportunity for entrepreneurs to build their ideas on top of the system. The Internet has lowered the barrier for the entrance of new ideas to compete with the established systems. However, it was never able to allow the same disruption to happen in the financial world. The blockchain might be able to represent the missing link as its main potential is to become the Internet of Value, fostering innovation and helping to overtake established industries that have not yet been severely impacted by the Internet.

Notes

1 1 Satoshi = 0.00000001BTC.
2 Pseudonymity means that the identity is disguised.
3 SHA stands for Secure Hash Algorithm, and the number after it determines the size of the output in bits.
4 The Lighting Network is a controversial prototype that allows Bitcoin to do instant payments, but it has many security concerns.
5 More information can be found on the website http://dapps.ethercasts.com/.

Bibliography

Aronsson, O., 2015. Svenska Cryex tar in 84 miljoner från Northzone med flera – bygger vidare på bitcointeknik [Swedish Cryex takes in 84 million from Northzone and others – continues building on bitcoin technology]. [online] Available at: https://www.breakit.se/artikel/498/svenska-cryex-tar-in-84-miljoner-fran-northzone-med-flera-bygger-vidare-pa-bitcointeknik [Accessed January 9, 2018].

Baldwin, J., 2017. *Can Bitcoin be hacked?* [online] Available at: www.investopedia.com/articles/investing/032615/can-bitcoin-be-hacked.asp [Accessed May 16, 2017].

Balzli, B., 2010. *Greek debt crisis: How Goldman Sachs helped Greece to mask its true debt.* [online] Available at: www.spiegel.de/international/europe/greek-debt-crisis-how-goldman-sachs-helped-greece-to-mask-its-true-debt-a-676634.html [Accessed January 16, 2018].

Bello Perez, Y., 2015. *Bitcoin in the headlines: Blockchain good, Bitcoin bad.* [online] Available at: www.coindesk.com/bitcoin-in-the-headlines-blockchain-good-bitcoin-bad [Accessed May 15, 2017].

Bitcoin Core, 2017. *Segregated Witness benefits.* [online] Available at: https://bitcoincore.org/en/2016/01/26/segwit-benefits [Accessed May 16, 2017].

Bitcoin Roundtable, 2016. *Bitcoin Roundtable consensus.* [online] Available at: https://medium.com/@bitcoinroundtable/bitcoin-roundtable-consensus-266d475a61ff [Accessed May 20, 2017].

BitcoinTalk, 2010. *Overflow bug SERIOUS.* [online] Available at: https://bitcointalk.org/index.php?topic=823.0 [Accessed May 16, 2017].

Bitcoin Unlimited, 2016a. *Bitcoin Unlimited: Articles of federation.* [online] Available at: www.bitcoinunlimited.info/resources/BUarticles.pdf [Accessed April 20, 2017].

Bitcoin Unlimited, 2016b. *Bitcoinunlimited.info.* [online] Available at: www.bitcoinunlimited.info/faq [Accessed May 17, 2017].

Blockchain.info, 2017a. *Blockchain size.* [online] Available at: https://blockchain.info/charts/blocks-size [Accessed May 16, 2017].

Blockchain.info, 2017b. *Hashrate distribution*. [online] Available at: http://blockchain.info/pools [Accessed April 17, 2017].

Blockchain.info, 2017c. *Market capitalization*. [online] Available at: https://blockchain.info/charts/market-cap [Accessed May 17, 2017].

Blockchain.info, 2017d. *Statistics*. [online] Available at: https://blockchain.info/stats [Accessed May 16, 2017].

Blockchain.info, 2017e. *Transaction rate*. [online] Available at: https://blockchain.info/charts/transactions-per-second [Accessed May 17, 2017].

Blocke, J., 2016. *A (brief and incomplete) history of censorship in /r/Bitcoin*. [online] Available at: https://medium.com/@johnblocke/a-brief-and-incomplete-history-of-censorship-in-r-bitcoin-c85a290fe43 [Accessed January 16, 2018].

Brown, R.G., Carlyle, J., Grigg, I. and Hearn, M., 2016. *Corda: An introduction*. [online] Available at: http://r3cev.com/s/corda-introductory-whitepaper-final.pdf [Accessed January 16, 2018].

Buterin, V., 2013a. Bitcoin network shaken by blockchain fork. *Bitcoin Magazine*. [online] Available at: https://bitcoinmagazine.com/articles/bitcoin-network-shaken-by-blockchain-fork-1363144448 [Accessed May 16, 2017].

Buterin, V., 2013b. Introducing Ripple. *Bitcoin Magazine*. [online] Available at: https://bitcoinmagazine.com/articles/introducing-ripple [Accessed May 22, 2017].

Buterin, V., 2014. *Vitalik Buterin reveals Ethereum at Bitcoin Miami 2014*. [online] Available at: www.youtube.com/watch?v=l9dpjN3Mwps [Accessed January 16, 2018].

Buterin, V., 2015. *On public and private blockchains*. [online] Ethereum Blog. Available at: https://blog.ethereum.org/2015/08/07/on-public-and-private-blockchains [Accessed January 16, 2018].

Castillo, M.D., 2015. *CoinDesk*. [online] Available at: www.coindesk.com/ripple-blockchain-55-million-series-b [Accessed May 22, 2017].

Castillo, M.D., 2017. *Swift selects hyperledger tech for cross-border blockchain test*. [online] Available at: www.coindesk.com/swift-selects-hyperledger-tech-cross-border-blockchain-test [Accessed May 20, 2017].

CoinDesk, 2016. *Lawrence H. Summers—blockchain in a global context*. [online] Available at: www.youtube.com/watch?v=nWmF-GlH68o [Accessed January 16, 2018].

CoinDesk, 2017a. *Bitcoin USD price*. [online] Available at: www.coindesk.com/price [Accessed May 23, 2017].

CoinDesk, 2017b. *State of blockchain 2017*. [online] Available at: www.coindesk.com/research/state-of-blockchain-q4-2016 [Accessed May 20, 2017].

CoinMarketCap, 2017. *CoinMarket*. [online] Available at: https://coinmarketcap.com/currencies/ripple [Accessed May 22, 2017].

Crosby, M., Pattanayak, P., Verma, S., and Kalyanaraman, V., 2016. Blockchain technology: Beyond Bitcoin. *Applied Innovation*, 2, pp.6–10.

Danezis, G. and Meiklejohn, S., 2015. Centrally banked cryptocurrencies. *arXiv*, arXiv:(1505.06895).

Das, S., 2017. *Global banks join SWIFT for blockchain cross-border payments trial using Hyperledger tech*. [online] Available at: https://www.ccn.com/global-banks-join-swift-blockchain-cross-border-payments-trial-using-hyperledger-tech [Accessed January 22, 2018].

Deadalnix, 2017. *SegWit and technologies built on it are grossly oversold*. [online] Available at: www.deadalnix.me/2017/02/27/segwit-and-technologies-built-on-it-are-grossly-oversold [Accessed January 16, 2018].

Desjardins, J., 2014. *The definitive history of Bitcoin*. [online] Available at: www.visualcapitalist.com/the-definitive-history-of-bitcoin [Accessed January 16, 2018].

Enterprise Ethereum Alliance., 2016. *Enterprise Ethereum Alliance*. [online] Available at: http://entethalliance.org [Accessed May 20, 2017].

Ethereum Classic, 2016a. *The Ethereum Classic Declaration of Independence*. [online] Available at: https://ethereumclassic.github.io/assets/ETC_Declaration_of_Independence.pdf [Accessed January 16, 2018].

Ethereum Classic, 2016b. *A Crypto-Decentralist Manifesto*. [online] Available at: https://ethereumclassic.github.io/blog/2016-07-11-manifesto [Accessed January 16, 2018].

Ethereum Classic, 2016c. *Ethereum Classic*. [online] Available at: https://ethereumclassic.github.io [Accessed May 16, 2017].

Evans-Pritchard, A., 2016. Central banks beat Bitcoin at own game with rival supercurrency. *The Telegraph*. [online] Available at: www.telegraph.co.uk/business/2016/03/13/central-banks-beat-bitcoin-at-own-game-with-rival-supercurrency [Accessed January 16, 2018].

Finley, K., 2016. A $50 million hack just showed that the DAO was all too human. *Wired*. [online] Available at: www.wired.com/2016/06/50-million-hack-just-showed-dao-human [Accessed January 16, 2018].

Forbes.com, 2013. 2013: Year of the Bitcoin. *Forbes*. [online] Available at: www.forbes.com/sites/kitconews/2013/12/10/2013-year-of-the-bitcoin/#93c51f8303cf [Accessed January 16, 2018].

FundedByMe, 2015. *Safello*. [online] Available at: www.fundedbyme.com/en/campaign/5478/safello [Accessed May 20, 2017].

Garlinghouse, B., 2017. *Ripple to place 55 billion XRP in escrow to ensure certainty into total XRP supply*. [online] Available at: https://ripple.com/insights/ripple-to-place-55-billion-xrp-in-escrow-to-ensure-certainty-into-total-xrp-supply [Accessed January 16, 2018].

GitHub, 2015. *Remove Coinbase from the "Choose your Wallet" page by Cobra-Bitcoin*. [online] Available at: https://github.com/bitcoin-dot-org/bitcoin.org/pull/1178 [Accessed May 16, 2017].

Gord, M., 2016. Smart contracts described by Nick Szabo 20 years ago now becoming reality. *Bitcoin Magazine*. [online] Available at: https://bitcoinmagazine.com/articles/smart-contracts-described-by-nick-szabo-years-ago-now-becoming-reality-1461693751 [Accessed January 16, 2018].

Gupta, V., 2017. A brief history of blockchain. *Harvard Business Review*. [online] Available at: https://hbr.org/2017/02/a-brief-history-of-blockchain [Accessed January 16, 2018].

Hackett, R., 2016. Why Goldman Sachs and Santander are bailing on R3's blockchain group. *Fortune*. [online] Available at: http://fortune.com/2016/11/21/goldman-sachs-r3-blockchain-consortium [Accessed January 16, 2018].

Harty, D., 2016. *Finance firms seen investing $1 billion in blockchain this year*. [online] Available at: https://www.bloomberg.com/news/articles/2016-06-23/finance-firms-seen-investing-1-billion-in-blockchain-this-year [Accessed January 16, 2018].

Hearn, M., 2015a. *The capacity cliff*. [online] Available at: https://medium.com/@octskyward/the-capacity-cliff-586d1bf7715e [Accessed January 16, 2018].

Hearn, M., 2015b. *Why is Bitcoin forking?* [online] Available at: https://medium.com/faith-and-future/why-is-bitcoin-forking-d647312d22c1 [Accessed January 16, 2018].

Hearn, M., 2016. *The resolution of the Bitcoin experiment: Mike's blog*. [online] Available at: https://blog.plan99.net/the-resolution-of-the-bitcoin-experiment-dabb30201f7 [Accessed May 16, 2017].

Higgins, S., 2015. *LHV bank develops wallet app built on Bitcoin's blockchain*. [online] Available at: www.coindesk.com/lhv-bank-backs-wallet-app-built-on-bitcoins-blockchain [Accessed May 16, 2017].

Higgins, S., 2016. *Bitcoin mining firm KnCMiner declares bankruptcy*. [online] Available at: www.coindesk.com/kncminer-declares-bankruptcy-cites-upcoming-bitcoin-subsidy-halving [Accessed May 22, 2017].

Higgins, S., 2017. *Nasdaq wants to invest in more blockchain startups*. [online] Available at: www.coindesk.com/nasdaq-wants-invest-blockchain-startups [Accessed January 16, 2018].

Hileman, G., 2016. *State of Bitcoin and blockchain 2016: Blockchain hits critical mass*. [online] Available at: www.coindesk.com/state-of-bitcoin-blockchain-2016 [Accessed May 16, 2017].

History of Bitcoin, 2013. *Bitcoin history: The complete history of Bitcoin*. [online] Available at: http://historyofbitcoin.org [Accessed January 9, 2018].

Hjelte, H., 2014. *Blockchain, smart contracts, land registry, real estate*. [online] Available at: www.eurocadastre.org/pdf/sk_2016/ChromaWay%20-%20Bratislava%20Conference.pdf [Accessed December 3, 2017].

Hyperledger, 2017. *Hyperledger*. [online] Available at: www.hyperledger.org/about/join [Accessed May 20, 2017].

Hyperledger Fabric, 2017. *Welcome to Hyperledger Fabric* [online] Available at: http://hyperledger-fabric.readthedocs.io/en/latest [Accessed May 22, 2017].

Jameson, H., 2016. *FAQ: Upcoming Ethereum hard fork*. [online] Ethereum Blog. Available at: https://blog.ethereum.org/2016/10/18/faq-upcoming-ethereum-hard-fork [Accessed May 16, 2017].

J.P. Morgan, 2017. *Quorum*. [online] Available at: www.jpmorgan.com/global/Quorum [Accessed May 17, 2017].

Kennedy, J., 2016. *Silicon Republic*. [online] Available at: www.siliconrepublic.com/start-ups/blockchain-pwc-investment [Accessed May 22, 2017].

Krugman, P., 1998. *Economics: Why most economists' predictions are wrong*. [online] Available at: https://web.archive.org/web/19980610100009/www.redherring.com/mag/issue55/economics.html [Accessed December 4, 2017].

Laurence, T., 2017. *Blockchain for dummies*. Hoboken, NJ: John Wiley & Sons.

Listokin, Y., 2008. Management always wins the close ones. *American Law and Economics Review*, 10(2), pp.159–184.

Maxwell, G., 2015. *[Bitcoin-development] Block size increase*. [online] Available at: www.mail-archive.com/bitcoin-development@lists.sourceforge.net/msg07462.html [Accessed January 16, 2018].

Merkle, R., 1990. A certified digital signature. In Advances in Cryptology. *CRYPTO'89 Proceedings*, pp.218–238.

MHFG, 2016. *Financial statement for fiscal 2016*. [online] Available at: www.mizuho-fg.com/investors/financial/fin_statements/data16/pdf/fy.pdf [Accessed December 2, 2017].

Morris, D. Z., 2014. Mt. Gox shuts down: Leaked document states 744,408 bitcoin lost. *Fortune*. [online] Available at: http://fortune.com/2014/02/25/mt-gox-shuts-down-leaked-document-states-744408-bitcoin-lost [Accessed May 15, 2017].

Nakamoto, S., 2008. *Bitcoin: A peer-to-peer electronic cash system*. [online] Available at: https://bitcoin.org/bitcoin.pdf [Accessed December 2, 2017].

Nakamoto, S., 2009. *Satoshi Nakamoto Institute*. [online] Available at: http://satoshi.nakamotoinstitute.org/posts/p2pfoundation/1 [Accessed April 12, 2017].

Nakamoto, S., 2010. *BitcoinTalks*. [online] Available at: https://bitcointalk.org/index.php?topic=195.msg1611#msg1611 [Accessed May 20, 2017]

Nasdaq, 2015. *Nasdaq Linq enables first-ever private securities issuance documented with blockchain technology*. [online] Available at: http://ir.nasdaq.com/releasedetail.cfm?releaseid=948326 [Accessed May 17, 2017].

Nasdaq, 2016. *Building on the blockchain, Nasdaq's vision of innovation*. [online] Available at: http://business.nasdaq.com/Docs/Blockchain%20Report%20March%202016_tcm5044-26461.pdf [Accessed May 20, 2017].

Nasdaq, 2017. *Is blockchain the answer to e-voting? Nasdaq believes so*. [online] Available at: http://business.nasdaq.com/marketinsite/2017/Is-Blockchain-the-Answer-to-E-voting-Nasdaq-Believes-So.html [Accessed May 22, 2017].

Nielsen, M., 2013. *How the Bitcoin protocol actually works*. [online] Available at: www.michaelnielsen.org/ddi/how-the-bitcoin-protocol-actually-works [Accessed May 20, 2017].

Popper, N., 2015. Decoding the enigma of Satoshi Nakamoto and the birth of Bitcoin. *The New York Times*. [online] Available at: www.nytimes.com/2015/05/17/business/decoding-the-enigma-of-satoshinakamoto-and-the-birth-of-bitcoin.html?_r=0 [Accessed May 16, 2017].

Popper, N., 2016. A Bitcoin believer's crisis of faith. *The New York Times*. [online] Available at: www.nytimes.com/2016/01/17/business/dealbook/the-bitcoin-believer-who-gave-up.html?_r=0 [Accessed May 20, 2017].

Popper, N., 2017a. A hacking of more than $50 million dashes hopes in the world of virtual currency. *The New York Times*. [online] Available at: www.nytimes.com/2016/06/18/business/dealbook/hacker-may-have-removed-more-than-50-million-from-experimental-cybercurrency-project.html [Accessed May 16, 2017].

Popper, N., 2017b. Business giants to announce creation of a computing system based on Ethereum. *The New York Times*. [online] Available at: www.nytimes.com/2017/02/27/business/dealbook/ethereum-alliance-business-banking-security.html [Accessed May 20, 2017].

Price, R., 2015. *The man everyone thinks is the creator of Bitcoin gave a speech discussing the history of the technology*. [online] Business Insider. Available at: www.businessinsider.com/nick-szabo-ethereum-bitcoin-blockchain-history-satoshi-nakamoto-2015-11?r=UK&IR=T&IR=T [Accessed May 16, 2017].

Prisco, G., 2016. Santander becomes first U.K. bank to introduce blockchain technology for international payments. *Bitcoin Magazine*. [online] Available at: https://bitcoinmagazine.com/articles/santander-becomes-first-u-k-bank-to-introduce-blockchain-technology-for-international-payments-1464795902 [Accessed May 16, 2017].

Prnewswire, 2017. *Mizuho Financial Group partners with Cognizant to develop a distributed ledger solution for more efficient and secure trade finance*. [online] Available at: http://www.prnewswire.com/news-releases/mizuho-financial-group-partners-with-cognizant-to-develop-a-distributed-ledger-solution-for-more-efficient-and-secure-trade-finance-300445106.html [Accessed May 16, 2017].

Quorum, 2017. *Quorum whitepaper*. [online] Available at: https://github.com/jpmorganchase/quorum-docs/blob/master/Quorum%20Whitepaper%20v0.1.pdf [Accessed May 16, 2017].

Range, J., 2016. New Australian Securities Exchange chief defends blockchain plans. *Financial Times*. [online] Available at: www.ft.com/content/45851b58-62d1-11e6-8310-ecf0bddad227 [Accessed May 20, 2017].

Reddit, 2016. *Coinbase CEO Brian Armstrong: BIP 101 is the best proposal we've seen so far*. [online] Available at: www.reddit.com/r/Bitcoin/comments/3rejl9/coinbase_ceo_brian_armstrong_bip_101_is_the_best/cwpglh6 [Accessed May 17, 2017].

Rooney, B., 2013. *Bitcoin worth almost as much as gold.* [online] Available at: http://money.cnn.com/2013/11/29/investing/bitcoin-gold [Accessed May 20, 2017].

ScienceDaily, 2014. *Likely author of original bitcoin paper? Researchers uncover linguistic evidence.* [online] Available at: www.sciencedaily.com/releases/2014/04/140417090547.html [Accessed May 16, 2017].

Smith, T., 2017. *Public and private blockchains: Enemies or allies?* [online] Available at: https://medium.com/@rtylersmith/public-and-private-blockchains-enemies-or-allies-45f050c38fc0 [Accessed May 17, 2017].

Szabo, N., 1996. *Smart contracts: Building blocks for digital markets.* [online] Available at: www.fon.hum.uva.nl/rob/Courses/InformationInSpeech/CDROM/Literature/LOTwinterschool2006/szabo.best.vwh.net/smart_contracts_2.html [Accessed December 2, 2017].

Visa, 2017. *Visa.* [online] Available at: https://usa.visa.com/run-your-business/small-business-tools/retail.html [Accessed May 16, 2017].

Weiser, B., 2015. Man behind Silk Road website is convicted on all counts. *The New York Times*. [online] Available at: www.nytimes.com/2015/02/05/nyregion/man-behind-silk-road-website-is-convicted-on-all-counts.html [Accessed May 20, 2017].

Wells, P., 2016. ASX to test blockchain for trade settlement. *Financial Times*. [online] Available at: www.ft.com/content/9def626f-8c11-3ea9-9e76-612f494e04b7 [Accessed May 22, 2017].

Wirdum, A., 2016. Where Bitcoin mining pools stand on Segregated Witness. *Bitcoin Magazine*. [online] Available at: https://bitcoinmagazine.com/articles/where-bitcoin-mining-pools-stand-on-segregated-witness-1480086424 [Accessed May 17, 2017].

Yermack, D., 2017. Corporate governance and blockchain. *Review of Finance*, 21(1), March, pp.7–31.

16 How to scale Bitcoin

A payment network that no one controls

Håkan Holmberg

Introduction

Bitcoin is a software that allows its users to perform monetary transactions without the need of intermediaries. As of March 2017, the Bitcoin software was running on 6,331 different devices, also called nodes (Coin Dance, 2017), distributed throughout all continents (Bitnodes, 2017). It has, on average, a daily transaction volume of USD 300 million distributed across more than 280,000 transactions per day (Quandl, 2017). Over 16 million bitcoins were in circulation, and the network had a transaction history of more than 900 million transactions (Blockchain.info, 2017).

However, this is not much if you compare it to one of the more common payment systems in use today. For example, from March 2015 to March 2016, Visa had a payment volume of USD 7.4 trillion distributed across a total of 74 billion transactions. This boils down to an average daily payment volume of over USD 20 billion distributed across more than 200 million daily transactions. Furthermore, Visa processed, on average, over 2,300 transactions per second (txps) (Visa, 2017a), and the payment network is able to handle up to 56,000 txps (Visa, 2017b). Bitcoin, as of March 2017, can currently handle only a maximum of 7 txps. Even if Bitcoin does not need the capacity of Visa, the network needs to increase its capacity in order to scale.

As of March 2017, two major solutions have been presented by the community to scale Bitcoin: the first solution, called Bitcoin Unlimited, turns a network security measure into a market mechanism that theoretically would put no limit to Bitcoin's capacity, as long as the network is kept safe. The second solution, called Segregated Witness (SegWit), is conservative in its capacity increase. However, it comes with a new software called the Lightning Network, which enables nodes to make secure off-chain transactions that, in case of a disagreement, can be brought to the main Bitcoin network for resolution. Treating the Bitcoin blockchain as a "court" that only settles disputed transactions could greatly increase Bitcoin's capacity. The Lightning Network uses smart contracts, a more advanced form of Bitcoin transactions that can carry more information about what is being transacted, as well as more instructions for how the transaction can be spent. As such, smart contracts enable much more advanced settlements to occur over the Bitcoin network, and the Lightning Network is a great example of how this technological innovation is put into practice.

The Lightning Network is a continuation of a process that treats Bitcoin more as a settlement network than as a payment system. Limiting the block size creates a scarcity of Bitcoin transactions. This scarcity could lead to a development that favors Bitcoin as a form of digital gold. Bitcoin Unlimited, on the other hand, would prefer a future where Bitcoin becomes a form of digital cash, wherein the main Bitcoin network is capable of running an economy of microtransactions.

In the next section, we will present the inner workings of the Bitcoin network, while in the third section we will study the parameters that need to be addressed in order to scale Bitcoin. The fourth and fifth sections describe the two major options that have been developed to scale Bitcoin, and in the sixth section we look into how a decentralized peer-to-peer network is upgraded in practice. Finally, in the seventh section, we conclude the discussion by presenting possible future scenarios.

Bitcoin

Bitcoin is a peer-to-peer payment system (Nakamoto, 2008). This means that it is a network of computers that can communicate financial transactions with each other without the need of either private or central banks. This is possible since Bitcoin has its own currency called bitcoins and its own secure way of recording ownership called the blockchain. In order to join the network, you download and install the Bitcoin software. The software can be downloaded by anyone, but it is recommended that users have a good understanding of computer security as well as access to decent computer equipment. As of July 2016 (Zander, 2016), downloading had been reported to take approximately 6 hours and 50 minutes on computer equipment costing USD 1,650. However, by using cloud services, the installation process has been reported to take over four days with the much lower cost of USD 28 (Croman et al., 2016; Amazon Web Services, 2017).

During the installation, the entire transaction history of the network is downloaded on the computer. As of July 2016, this meant that you had to download 75 GB and, as of March 2017, the transaction history had already grown to a size of almost 110 GB (Blockchain.info, 2017). During the installation process, the software also identifies the ownership of all unspent bitcoins. When the installation is complete and the software is turned on, it will try to connect to other nodes in the network, with the default number being eight nodes. After you have successfully connected to other nodes, you can start to broadcast your own transactions, as well as transactions originating from other nodes. You will also start to update your copy of the transaction history based on what is being broadcast on the network.

When you download the entire transaction history, you become a full node in the Bitcoin network. Full nodes play an important role in securing and maintaining the network. However, many devices, such as smartphones, are neither able to download 110+ GB of data nor are they able to always be online. An alternative to becoming a full node is to download simplified payment verification (SPV) software. SPV software does not verify the entire transaction history; instead, it relies on other full nodes for its verification. SPV software can be installed on smartphones, and is the most common way to use Bitcoin.

After your full node or SPV client is up and running, you can start to receive and spend bitcoins. To receive bitcoins, you need a Bitcoin address, and to spend bitcoins you need to prove that you are their rightful owner. The software you installed will generate Bitcoin addresses for you and will also generate a private key to every Bitcoin address that is used to prove ownership. However, to prove ownership by simply broadcasting the private key would make it easy to steal your bitcoins. To be able to prove ownership without revealing the private key, Bitcoin uses an algorithm called Elliptic Curve Digital Signature Algorithm (ECDSA). Conceptually, the algorithm works as follows. The first part of ECDSA generates a signature from your private key. The signature is the result of applying multiple mathematical operations to your private key. This is done in such a way that is near impossible to retrieve the private key from the signature. This construction enables the network to verify that you own a specific Bitcoin address since they can ask you to generate the signature. If you can, you are almost certain to be in possession of the private key that was generated together with the specific Bitcoin address. The second part of ECDSA is a mathematical problem that can only be solved using your signature together with your Bitcoin address. Since you are the only one that can generate the signature, providing the signature to the network enables it to connect you to your Bitcoin address by solving this mathematical problem. This proves to the network that you are the rightful owner of the bitcoins that you want to spend. The first part is performed by you before you broadcast your transaction, and the second part is performed by other nodes after you sign and broadcast your transaction.

ECDSA enables you to be sure that only you can spend your bitcoins, but it is still possible for you to spend your own bitcoins twice. For example, you can broadcast two transactions, one to Alice and one to Bob, who spend the same bitcoin. Alice and Bob, not knowing that the bitcoin is being spent twice, will accept your bitcoin, believing that they are the sole owner. However, it is now unclear who has the right to spend it in the future. To solve this dilemma, called the double-spending problem, we need to understand how transactions are being submitted to the Bitcoin network.

When you turn on your Bitcoin node, it will connect to other nodes in the network, the default being eight for a full node. It is to these nodes that you broadcast your transactions. After a neighboring node receives a transaction from you, it will validate that it does not contradict their copy of the network's transaction history. If your transaction passes this test, the node will include it in its copy of the network's transaction history and continue to broadcast it to its connecting nodes. This process repeats itself until your transaction has been transmitted to the entire network. However, if you were to double-spend a bitcoin, you would be able to create two versions of the network's transaction history, which would split the network in two parts: one part that believes Alice received your bitcoin and another part that believes Bob received your bitcoin. Bitcoin solves this problem by the use of a certain kind of node called a mining node.

If you decide to become a mining node, you will continue to validate the transactions broadcasted to you by other nodes, but you will also try to impose your view of the transaction history on the entire network. In order to export your view of the transaction history, you first need to create an ordered package of the transactions that you want to broadcast. This package is called a block. After you have created your block, you need to connect it to the part of the transaction history that the entire network has already accepted as valid. You do this by finding the longest chain of accepted blocks, starting from the first block ever created. This enables you to create a reference to the last block of the longest chain, a reference that you include in your block. It is the last block of the longest chain that is the network's current point of consensus.

Finally, you need to find a solution to a difficult mathematical problem called a proof of work. A solution can only be found by pure guesswork, which in turn consumes a lot of energy through the use of expensive computer equipment. A solution to the proof of work problem enables you to broadcast your block to the network. When nodes receive your block, they will check that your block includes a reference to the current point of consensus, that its content does not contradict the transaction history already accepted as valid by the network, and that you have found a solution to the proof of work problem. Meeting these requirements will turn your block into the network's new point of consensus. However, as a block creator, you cannot forge any transactions as long as the underlying ECDSA system is secure. You may only decide in which order transactions arrived and whether to include transactions in the block. When a node accepts your block as the true transaction history, it removes all transactions from its local copy that contradict the transactions in your block. This prolongs the chain of blocks that the entire network accepts as valid, and it is this chain of blocks that has given rise to the name blockchain.

The proof of work problem is what protects the system from users who try to double-spend bitcoins. Hence, it is what maintains consensus over who owns what within the network. Without a proof of work problem, it would cost nothing to broadcast multiple blocks, all of which would contain transactions that try to spend the same bitcoin. This would lead to a split of the network along the lines of the different transaction histories. However, with a proof of work problem, you need to take on a cost in the form of energy consumption and computer equipment to broadcast a block. Furthermore, since the network compensates mining nodes in bitcoins, the cost of tampering with the transaction history is further increased due to its negative effect on the Bitcoin prize.

Two mining nodes could succeed in solving the proof of work problem at roughly the same time, leading to two blocks being simultaneously broadcast over the network. However, when two blocks are broadcast at roughly the same time, they will both reference the longest chain that their respective mining nodes were aware of and other nodes will accept the block that they see as the continuation of the longest chain. This can effectively split the network, once again, into two parts based on what different nodes consider to be the continuation of the longest chain of already accepted blocks. Mining nodes belonging to one part of the network will continue to mine blocks referencing what they see as the longest chain of blocks. The same holds for the mining nodes in the other part of the network. However, if mining nodes belonging to one part of the network are able to create a longer blockchain than the other part of the network, they are able to broadcast this longer chain, and the split is resolved. The resolution occurs when nodes receive information about the existence of a longer chain, and once again the longest chain rule makes the nodes view the new longer chain as the true transaction history instead of the older, shorter chain.

Blocks that are abandoned when a split is resolved are called orphan blocks. Orphan blocks occur naturally when two blocks happen to be mined at similar times. However, an orphan block is also a result of double-spend attacks. A node can decide to broadcast a transaction in one block, and if the transaction value is high enough, it can try to broadcast another transaction spending the same bitcoins in another block. To invalidate the first transaction, it needs to create a chain of blocks that is longer than the chain that already contains the first transaction. This in turn creates an increase in orphaned blocks independent of the success of the attack. Furthermore, a system that naturally has a high rate of orphan blocks is more vulnerable to double-spend attacks. This is due to the fact that a forked chain reduces the number of blocks that the attacker needs to create in order to invalidate one of its own transactions. For these reasons, the rate of orphan blocks, also called the stale rate, is a good overall measure of system security, and it has been shown in simulation studies that an increase in the rate of orphan blocks lowers the transaction amount that makes a double-spend attack profitable (Gervais et al., 2016).

Mining nodes are a cornerstone in the Bitcoin network since they maintain consensus concerning the transaction history. Mining power is measured in hashes per second, which correspond to the number of guesses per second a miner is able to make in order to find a solution to the proof of work problem. As of March 2017, the combined mining power of the network was 3.55 exa (1018) hashes per second (Bitcoinity.org, 2017). This means that if you want be sure to be able to tamper with Bitcoin's transaction history, you have to have a capacity of more than 3.55 exa hashes per second. Assuming that you would buy AntMiner S9 mining hardware, which has a hash rate of 0.1 joule per gigahashes, the highest hash rate per dollar for hobbyist equipment according to a comparison as of March 2017 (BuyBitcoinWorldwide, 2017), a capacity of 3.55 exa hashes per second would amount to an energy consumption of 35,500 megawatts, which is equivalent to an average nuclear power plant.

As of 2017, the reward, excluding transaction fees, was 12.5 bitcoins per block. The reward is halved every 210,000 blocks, and Bitcoin also adjusts the difficulty of the proof of work problem in such a way that the expected time to mine a block is always 10 minutes. This means that if the total computational power of the network increases, so does the difficulty of the proof of work problem. Mining nodes will be rewarded until 21 million bitcoins have been created, something that is expected to take place around the year 2140. After the 21 million bitcoin mark, mining nodes will only earn transaction fees for solving the proof of work problem.

The smallest unit in the Bitcoin economy is called a satoshi after pseudonymous Satoshi Nakamoto, the inventor of Bitcoin. One bitcoin equals 100 million satoshis, and 21 million bitcoins equals 21 thousand trillion satoshis, which is close to what a computer can store in a 64-bit floating-point number. The fact that the money supply in Bitcoin is limited turns Bitcoin into a deflationary currency—that is to say that there will be a decrease in the general price level of goods and services denominated in bitcoin. The value of Bitcoin will then increase in the sense that it will allow you to buy more goods and services than before with the same amount of bitcoins.

Even if the Bitcoin network never reaches the size of Visa, it still needs to scale. After all, a cryptocurrency is only as valuable as the economy it serves. As of March 2017, the median time a user needed to wait until they were informed that their transaction was included in a block was 10.43 minutes (Quandl, 2017). This waiting time is the sum of: (1) the time it takes for the transaction to reach a mining node; (2) the time it takes for the mining node to create a block; and (3) the time it takes for this block to reach the user with information about the validity of the transaction. This waiting time is one of the largest challenges that Bitcoin faces in order to grow as a payment network.

To better understand the different solutions that have been presented to increase the capacity of Bitcoin, we need to better understand the present design of the Bitcoin network and where we can locate its bottlenecks.

Scaling Bitcoin

Simply put, a Bitcoin transaction is a data file that as of March 2017, on average, has a size of 560 bytes (Quandl, 2017). To get your transaction verified, you need to broadcast it. Then the network needs to verify and continue to broadcast it until it ends up at a mining node. Furthermore, the mining node needs to include the transaction in a block, find a solution to the proof of work problem, and then broadcast the block onto the network. Nodes that receive information about the existence of the block will once again verify it and continue to broadcast it until you are informed about the validity of your transaction. As you can imagine, there are many steps on this path, all of which are potential bottlenecks making it harder for Bitcoin to grow as a payment network. The time from broadcasting your transaction until it reaches a mining node has proven to be stable with a median time of less than 1 second and a 90th percentile of 3.47 seconds (Decker and Wattenhofer, 2013; BitcoinStats, 2017). The time it takes for a block to be mined is fixed to an average of 10 minutes. It is fixed both because it controls the number of new bitcoins that reach the network and because it determines how hard it is to tamper with the network's transaction history. The time it takes for a mined block to reach you is a function of the block size; the larger the block, the longer it takes. In a recent article, Croman et al. (2016) estimated the median time for Bitcoin nodes to receive a block. At their time of measurement, the median time was 8.7 seconds and the average block size was roughly 540 KB. They also projected their measurements to an average block size of 1 MB and arrived at a new projected median time of 15.7 seconds.

The fact that larger blocks take a longer time is a result of the underlying equipment that the network is using. Bitcoin is a decentralized network of volunteers and it is the owners of the nodes who decide what hardware they will run. Furthermore, some parts of the world have slower broadband connection than others, which can further decrease the speed with which blocks can be propagated through the network. This means that scaling Bitcoin becomes a question of changing the software, potentially in such a way that some nodes are unable to meet the new hardware specification that is needed in order to run the upgraded software. The Bitcoin software has primarily two parameters that it can adjust in order to scale: (1) its block interval time; and (2) its block size limit.

Reducing the block interval time would increase Bitcoin's capacity. However, it could also increase the number of orphan blocks due to the fact that more blocks would be created during a shorter time period. Furthermore, it has been shown that reducing the block interval time makes double-spending attacks more profitable (Gervais et al., 2016), thus reducing network security. Croman et al. (2016) estimated that given the network infrastructure at their time of measurement, 10 percent of the network would fall behind with a block interval of 12 seconds, assuming a 1 MB block size. Partly because of these reasons, the discussion has focused on how to increase the block size limit.

An increased block size would make the transaction history take up more space on the user's computer, and hence demand a larger investment from those who want to run a node. Furthermore, nodes would need a better Internet connection in order to not fall behind. If mining nodes were falling behind, it would increase the number of orphan blocks. Nodes that are falling behind would effectively no longer perform validation since they would always accept the longer chain of blocks broadcasted to them. This would also increase the risk for double-spend attacks. For these reasons, it has been argued that an increase in block size could reduce system security through an increase in the orphan block rate. The level of centralization could also increase since it would be harder for users to run independent nodes. Croman et al. (2016) estimated that given the network infrastructure at their time of measurement, 10 percent of the network would fall behind with a block interval of 4 MB, assuming a 10-minute block interval. A 4 MB block size corresponds to a maximum throughput of, at most, 27 transactions per second.

The block size debate has primarily focused on two solutions. The first solution, called Bitcoin Unlimited, turns the problem of orphan blocks into a market mechanism. This means that the theoretical limit to the block size is removed, and instead the actual limit is set by the user's need for validation versus the miner's fear of losing the block reward due to an orphaned block. This could drastically increase capacity as well as remove the need for future block size debates. The second solution, called Segregated Witness, proposes a conservative block size increase. However, it comes with an innovation called the Lightning Network that turns Bitcoin into a type of court in charge of settling disputed smart contracts, a form of programmable Bitcoin transactions. These smart contracts enable much more advanced settlements to occur, and the Lightning Network is a great example of this new technology.

Bitcoin Unlimited

Bitcoin Unlimited (Rizun, 2015) wants to remove this block size limit and allow mining nodes to decide the block size for each mined block. To understand this proposal, we need to have a better understanding of how Bitcoin's transaction fee market is constructed. As of March 2017, a Bitcoin transaction is a data file with an average size of 540 KB, and since the block size limit is 1 MB, only a finite number of transactions can end up in each block. Because of this size limit, Bitcoin transaction fees are based on the size of its corresponding data file and not on the size of the transaction value, as is common in systems such as Visa. Broadcasted transactions that arrive to a mining node end up in something called a memory pool. A mining node can include any transaction from the memory pool as long as the total block size is less than 1 MB. A mining node that is successful in solving the proof of work problem broadcasts the block onto the network. The block includes all chosen transactions from the memory pool, as well as the corresponding transaction fees that users are paying for having their transactions included in the block. The block also includes a special transaction called the coinbase transaction that consists of bitcoins that were created by the software itself as a further reward to the mining node. The coinbase transaction, also called the block reward, enables the system to pay for its security and, at the same time, increases the number of bitcoins in circulation. However, if a block is orphaned, the mining node that created the block will lose both its transaction fees and its block rewards.

A main concern with an unlimited block size has been that it could lead to such a decrease in transaction fees that the network would become vulnerable to transaction spamming attacks (Nicolas, 2014). Furthermore, an increased block size could once again increase the cost of running a node. This could further reduce the total number of nodes that in turn would reduce the network's level of decentralization. Increased entry barriers could also lead to a less independent network, since there is a risk that the remaining nodes are more similar to each other due to the selection process.

Bitcoin Unlimited contests these concerns by exploring the economic effect of an increase in the orphan block rate. The idea that an unlimited block size would lead to a rapid decrease in transaction fees does not take into account the fact that larger blocks have a higher probability of being orphaned due to constraints in network capacity. This means that mining nodes producing bigger blocks will be at a higher risk of losing both their transaction fees and block rewards. (Rizun, 2015) shows that a rational miner would always adjust its block size with respect to the network block propagation time. This would create a dynamic fee market that takes into account both the network's need of validating transactions and its capacity to communicate these transactions to other network nodes. The fact that the model takes block propagation time into account does not guarantee that Bitcoin will maintain its decentralization. The longest chain rule dictates that an orphan block is created when two blockchain forks are resolved. This, however, is a process fully controlled by the mining nodes. The orphan block rate can thus be kept low as long as the mining nodes secure fast Internet connection with each other. This fact is already exploited in the FIBRE protocol, a network protocol that enables fast communication of blocks between different mining nodes (BitcoinFibre, 2017). However, this possibility for mining nodes to both increase the block size and keep the orphan block rate low could lead to a centralization of the network where nodes that simply validate the transaction history would fall behind. Furthermore, challengers of Bitcoin Unlimited argue that this would make Bitcoin lose its value as a peer-to-peer payment system (Vorick, 2016).

The other main alternative in the Bitcoin scaling debate is a conservative solution under the name of Segregated Witness that comes bundled with a completely novel approach called the Lightning Network.

The Lightning Network

Segregated Witness is an upgrade to the Bitcoin software that enables a more efficient way to store data inside the block, and it would increase the block size limit to approximately 1.6–2 MB (Towns, 2015). The upgrade also includes a set of new features that would enable on-chain resolution of off-chain transactions (i.e., transactions that are broadcast only among the nodes involved in the transaction). This new payment network of off-chain transactions is called the Lightning Network (Poon and Dryja, 2015).

The majority of a user's transactions do not have to be broadcast to the entire world. In fact, it would make more sense to only broadcast those transactions that resulted in some form of disagreement between the involved parties. This means that Bitcoin could become more of a settlement network instead of a payment network, a capacity that the Lightning Network tries to exploit. The Lightning Network starts by creating a bidirectional payment channel that enables two users to make secure transactions between each other without broadcasting them onto the Bitcoin network.

Assume that you want to create a bidirectional payment channel with Alice. The first step is to agree to open a shared account on the Bitcoin blockchain, where both you and Alice will deposit 0.5 bitcoins. Bitcoins deposited in the shared account can only be spent using transactions that have been signed by both you and Alice. However, you do not broadcast the shared account contract. Instead, both you and Alice create two new contracts called commitment contracts. Your commitment contract states that you will receive 0.5 bitcoins from the shared account and Alice will receive 0.5 bitcoins from the shared account. You sign your commitment contract and give it to Alice. Alice's commitment contracts looks just like yours, and Alice signs it and gives it to you. At this point, you can broadcast the shared account contract and a bidirectional payment channel has been created. The need for writing the commitment contract before broadcasting the shared account contract comes from the fact that Alice could become uncooperative and block you from ever recuperating your 0.5 bitcoins. However, by broadcasting a signed commitment contract from Alice, you are able to redeem your funds even if Alice decides to become uncooperative.

Assume now that Alice wants to send you 0.1 bitcoins. To do this, both you and Alice write two new commitment contracts. Your commitment contract states that you will receive 0.6 bitcoins from the shared account and that Alice will receive 0.4 bitcoins from the shared account. You sign your contract and give it to Alice. Alice creates an identical commitment contract, signs it, and gives it to you. At this point, you could sign the commitment contract given to you by Alice and broadcast it to the network, which would in turn give you 0.6 bitcoins. Alice would get 0.4 bitcoins and the shared account would be closed. You can also keep the payment channel open for future transactions between you and Alice by not broadcasting your commitment contracts. However, if you decide to not broadcast the last commitment contract, Alice could decide to sign the old commitment contract (the one that you already signed and gave Alice) and that would give you 0.5 bitcoins and Alice 0.5 bitcoins. To block this possibility of broadcasting old contracts, we need to implement some further modifications.

To block the possibility of broadcasting old commitment contracts, we will start to include a timestamp in our commitment contracts. Adding a timestamp will enable you to prove that Alice did, in fact, broadcast an older commitment contract, since you can show that latest commitment contract that was signed by Alice and given to you in order to update that balance of your shared account. However, this new feature enables you to prove that you were cheated on the latest agreement, but Alice can still steal your bitcoins. To solve this problem, we add another functionality to the contract. The commitment contract will include a new rule that says that the user who broadcasts their contract onto the network needs to wait until 1,000 blocks have been mined before the user receives their funds, while the other user that did not broadcast the contract will receive their funds immediately. Furthermore, if the user that did not broadcast the contract is able to broadcast a contract with a later timestamp that is signed by both parties, that user will gain access to all funds deposited in the shared account. At this point, the only thing a user needs to do in order to not be a victim of fraud is to monitor the transactions broadcast onto the network.

However, a bidirectional payment channel is a very small payment network since it only has two users. To connect multiple bidirectional payment channels with each other, we need to understand another cryptographic operation called hashing. Hashing consists of three parts: the secret, the hash function, and the secret's hash. The secret is a string of numbers and letters that are fed to the hash function in order to generate the secret's hash. The key with a hash function is that it is a one-way street. In other words, it is easy to generate a secret's hash if you know the secret, but it is almost impossible to generate a secret if you only know the secret's hash.

Assume now that you want to send 0.1 bitcoins to Bob. However, you and Bob will not open a bidirectional payment channel. Instead, you will use Alice as an intermediary since she already has two open payment channels with both you and Bob. In order to send 0.1 bitcoins, you start with generating a secret and its corresponding hash. First, you give the secret to Bob and the secret's hash to

Alice. Second, you and Alice sign a contract that states that if Alice can give you the secret, then you will give her 0.1 bitcoins. Furthermore, Bob and Alice sign a contract that states that if Bob can give Alice the secret, he will get 0.1 bitcoins from Alice. Since Alice has the secret's hash, she can verify that she gets the correct secret from Bob. In order for funds not to be locked up indefinitely, due to connection problems or uncooperative nodes, all contracts are invalidated after a specified time period.

The possibility to connect bidirectional payment channels with each other will enable an off-chain payment network, and estimates show that if users broadcast three transactions per year onto the main Bitcoin network, then the Bitcoin ecosystem would be able to serve 35 million users with a 1 MB block size (Poon and Dryja, 2015).

Organizing a network no one controls

The community organizes themselves through the use of online forums such as Bitcointalk, Reddit, and Github, as well as real-life conferences and meetups. The Bitcoin community can roughly be divided into miners, developers, merchants, and ordinary users. Any upgrade to the Bitcoin network that is not supported by a majority of mining nodes is doomed to fail, since they have a final say as to which transactions should be considered valid. However, in order to present an upgrade, you need to be able to develop cryptocurrency software, which puts the developers at the front row. Furthermore, any upgrade that is not supported by the major merchants could drastically reduce the utility of Bitcoin as a payment system. Finally, in order to become an accepted currency, Bitcoin needs to acquire a large user base. This makes the ordinary user central to the success of Bitcoin.

In order to update Bitcoin, nodes download and install their choice of upgrade. In the case of Segregated Witness and its enabling of the Lightning Network, nodes will install the Bitcoin Core version of the software. However, to be sure that the mining community supports an upgrade, Bitcoin uses a signaling system. Nodes are able to signal which version of the software they support.

To measure mining node support, the network uses the fact that the difficulty target of the proof of work algorithm is readjusted every 2,016th block in order to keep the block interval time to an average of 10 minutes. The Segregated Witness update will be activated when 95 percent of hash power (1,916 blocks) within a single difficulty period (2,016 blocks) originates from miners that support the update. One difficulty period later, the soft fork is activated, meaning the remaining 5 percent of miners have about two weeks to upgrade. If they do not upgrade, they will remain part of the Bitcoin network, but as they automatically consider all transactions generated by the updated nodes as valid they could have their blocks orphaned by other miners if they include now-invalid transactions (van Wirdum, 2016). Segregated Witness is a so-called soft fork—that is to say, it is designed in such way that non-upgraded nodes still accept the transaction that upgraded nodes create.

Bitcoin Unlimited, on the other hand, can be activated directly by the user. As soon as Bitcoin Unlimited is activated and a mining node produces a block that is larger than 1 MB, all nodes that are not running Bitcoin Unlimited will treat that block as invalid. This makes it important for Bitcoin Unlimited nodes to make sure that they have the support of at least 51 percent of the miners to succeed. An upgrade that generates blocks that are not compatible with non-upgraded software is called a hard fork.

Finally, an upgrade can be implemented through a user-activated soft fork (USAF). In a USAF, nodes that favor the upgrade start to refuse bitcoins that originate from block rewards given to non-upgraded mining nodes. This, in turn, makes it harder for non-upgraded mining nodes to spend their block reward, which creates pressure to upgrade their software.

Conclusion

Bitcoin is a remarkable technology that has already created a new paradigm in the way humans are able to organize everything from day-to-day business contracts to international trade deals. The possibility to create a more efficient administration of the economy could lower the barriers for business. This could, in the long run, increase independence among its participants.

All nodes in the Bitcoin network are autonomous in the sense that they decide which software to run. This autonomy separates Bitcoin from other banking systems that are in use as of today. However, the nature of this autonomy needs further investigation. The choice of software as well as the possibility to develop it will depend upon what software other nodes choose to use and how interconnected nodes are with each other through already existing technology. Furthermore, different software implementations could increase the cost of running a node, and smart contracts could also create unforseen lock-in effects, which in turn could reduce the autonomy of the network.

The Lightning Network is a continuation of a process that treats Bitcoin more and more as a settlement network than as a payment system. This is a very promising path; however, it could be argued that it is not enough if Bitcoin wants to be a realistic alternative to the systems that are in use as of today. This means that Bitcoin will need to make further adjustments in order to enable future growth. The proponents of the Lightning Network argue that it maintains Bitcoin's decentralization. Critics, however, argue that these off-chain payment networks can easily be turned into an IOU system, backed by a kind of Bitcoin standard (David, 2016). This would favor those in control of large Bitcoin assets, since they would become the ideal nodes in the new off-chain networks.

Bitcoin Unlimited favors a future where bitcoins are able to administrate an economy capable of handling microtransactions. This scenario would favor those who are in charge of the transaction processing as well as high-frequency users. Critics, however, argue that Bitcoin could become more centralized since mining nodes could maintain consensus within the mining community in order to preserve a low orphan block rate. Mining nodes could collectively invest in better infrastructure without taking the remaining nodes into account. Finally, since mining capacity is directly linked to electricity consumption, those with access to low electricity prices would benefit further from a network with a large transaction capacity. Access to low electricity prices has already led to a centralization of bitcoin mining, and as of 2016, Chinese miners control around 60–75 percent of Bitcoin's mining power due to China's low electricity prizes (De Filippi and Loveluck, 2016; bitcoinmining, 2017).

Furthermore, Bitcoin's electricity consumption could also become a competitive disadvantage if other networks were able to create more energy-efficient consensus technologies. The advent of quantum computing will also pose new challenges to Bitcoin since ECDSA can be compromised through the implementation of Shor's algorithm. This could once again lead to a need to upgrade the network in order to maintain network security. Finally, the impact of both deflation and inflation on user acquisition and user experience needs to be further investigated. It is obvious that deflation favors using a currency as a store of value. However, it could be argued that inflation favors the act of price-setting, and hence the capacity to act as a medium of exchange.

As a success story, it is natural that Bitcoin has to make some design choices in order to continue to grow. This in turn changes the focal point to the governance of decentralized networks. Bitcoin is governed by an intricate set of relations between miners, developers, major merchants, and ordinary users. Mining nodes do have a unique position, since without their support any major upgrade is doomed to fail. However, since mining nodes are paid in bitcoins, they are directly dependent on the well-being of the Bitcoin economy. Furthermore, as the USAF shows, strong organization among the economically active part of the community could act as a counterweight against the mining community. Developers also play an important role since they are by definition those who create any future upgrade. The fact that every node decides on which upgrade they support turns Bitcoin into a form of direct democracy. However, since most upgrades will need a large majority (up to 95 percent at certain times) in order to work, Bitcoin is maybe best described as consensus-driven network. Assuming that there would be a split in the network on the lines of a controversial upgrade, a majority cannot force a minority to continue participating in the network, and nodes can always sell their bitcoins and activate themselves in a different network. However, this will exclude them from the economic environment that Bitcoin offers. This form of passive exclusion needs further investigation, both from a technical and economic point of view. At what point should a minority leave a network and at what point should they be excluded? The strong consensus that Bitcoin needs in order to implement upgrades could become a hindrance for technological development. This merits further investigation in decision-making strategies for both individual nodes and networks as a whole.

Finally, given the innovative strength of the Bitcoin community, it should come as no surprise if all these problems are solved in ways that are currently considered impossible.

Bibliography

Amazon Web Services, 2017. *Cloud computing services*. [online] Available at: https://aws.amazon.com [Accessed September 10, 2017].

BitcoinFibre, 2017. *FIBRE Fast Internet Bitcoin Relay Engine*. [online] Available at: http://bitcoinfibre.org [Accessed September 10, 2017].

Bitcoinity.org, 2017. *Bitcoin trading volume*. [online] Available at: http://data.bitcoinity.org/markets/volume/30d?c=e&t=b [Accessed September 10, 2017].

bitcoinmining, 2017. *Everything you need to know about bitcoin mining*. [online] Available at: www.bitcoinmining.com [Accessed September 10, 2017].

BitcoinStats, 2017. *BitcoinStats*. [online] Available at: http://bitcoinstats.com/irc/bitcoin-dev/logs/2017/05 [Accessed September 10, 2017].

Bitnodes, 2017. *Global Bitcoin nodes distribution*. [online] Available at: https://bitnodes.21.co [Accessed September 10, 2017].

Blockchain.info, 2017. *Blockchain*. [online] Available at: http://blockchain.info [Accessed November 29, 2017].

BuyBitcoinWorldwide, 2017. *101+ best ways to buy bitcoins online in 2017*. [online] Available at: www.buybitcoinworldwide.com [Accessed September 10, 2017].

Coin Dance, 2017. *Bitcoin nodes summary*. [online] Available at: https://coin.dance/nodes [Accessed September 10, 2017].

Croman, K. et al., 2016. On scaling decentralized blockchains. *Financial Cryptography and Data Security. FC 2016. Lecture Notes in Computer Science*, [online] 9604, pp.106–25. Available at: http://link.springer.com/10.1007/978-3-662-53357-4_8 [Accessed August 28, 2017].

David, J., 2016. Lightning Network: Will it save Bitcoin? Or break it? *Wall Street Technologist*. [online] Available at: https://medium.com/@digitsu/lightning-network-will-it-save-or-break-bitcoin-5c8645924cb6 [Accessed August 28, 2017].

Decker, C. and Wattenhofer, R., 2013. Information propagation in the Bitcoin network. In: *13th IEEE international conference on peer-to-peer computing, IEEE P2P 2013—proceedings*, [online] IEEE, pp.1–10. Available at: http://ieeexplore.ieee.org/document/6688704 [Accessed August 28, 2017].

De Filippi, P. and Loveluck, B., 2016. The invisible politics of Bitcoin: Governance crisis of a decentralized infrastructure. *Internet Policy Review*, [online] 5(4), p.32. Available at: https://ssrn.com/abstract=2852691 [Accessed August 28, 2017].

Gervais, A., Karame, G.O., Wüst, K., and Glykantzis, V., 2016. On the security and performance of proof of work blockchains. In: *2016 ACM SIGSAC conference on computer and communications security*, [online], ACM, pp.3–16. Available at: http://dl.acm.org/citation.cfm?id=2978341 [Accessed August 28, 2017].

Nakamoto, S., 2008. *Bitcoin: A peer-to-peer electronic cash system*. [online] Available at: https://bitcoin.org/bitcoin.pdf [Accessed November 29, 2017].

Nicolas, H., 2014. The economics of Bitcoin transaction fees. *SSRN Electronic Journal*. [online] Available at: www.ssrn.com/abstract=2400519 [Accessed August 28, 2017].

Poon, J. and Dryja, T., 2015. *The Bitcoin Lightning Network*. [online] Available at: www.lightning.network/lightning-network-paper-DRAFT-0.5.pdf [Accessed August 28, 2017].

Quandl, 2017. *Financial, economic and alternative data*. [online] Available at: www.quandl.com [Accessed September 10, 2017].

Rizun, P., 2015. Block size limit debate working paper: A transaction fee market exists without a block size limit. *bitcoinunlimited.info*, [online] pp.1–16. Available at: www.bitcoinunlimited.info/resources/feemarket.pdf [Accessed August 28, 2017].

Towns, A., 2015. *[Bitcoin-Dev] capacity increases for the Bitcoin system.* [online] Available at: https://lists.linuxfoundation.org/pipermail/bitcoin-dev/2015-December/011869.html [Accessed August 28, 2017].

Visa, 2017a. *VISA*. [online] Available at: http://investor.visa.com [Accessed September 10, 2017].

Visa, 2017b. *VISA USA*. [online] Available at: https://usa.visa.com [Accessed September 10, 2017].

Vorick, D., 2016. A future led by Bitcoin Unlimited is a centralized future. *Sia Blog*. [online] Available at: https://blog.sia.tech/a-future-led-by-bitcoin-unlimited-is-a-centralized-future-e48ab52c817a [Accessed August 28, 2017].

van Wirdum, A., 2016. The segregated witness timeline: From idea to adoption in six steps. *Bitcoin Magazine*. [online] Available at: https://bitcoinmagazine.com/articles/the-segregated-witness-timeline-from-idea-to-adoption-in-six-steps-1461255570 [Accessed August 28, 2017].

Zander, T., 2016. *Tom's blog*. [online] Available at: http://zander.github.io [Accessed September 10, 2017].

Part 4

A view of the actors

17 Banks and digitalization

Jochem van der Zande

Introduction

The financial industry is currently experiencing a transformation, as disruptive financial technologies and newly founded financial startups are taking hold and challenging the current way of working. Whereas these technologies and startups are increasing in size and influence, the incumbent players, such as the banks, still play a central role in the industry. Facing these upcoming threats, banks will need to adapt to remain relevant and competitive in the future. To understand their position in relation to the situation, this chapter explores financial technology from the banks' perspective. For clarity, the concept of financial technology has been split into two parts: the internal exploration and adoption of new technologies, business models, and culture under the umbrella of digitalization, and technologies and business models that are developed externally, mainly by startups, under the umbrella of FinTech.

The chapter will start by exploring the general relation between banks and digitalization, as well as banks and FinTech, based on available literature, after which the situation in Sweden is assessed by investigating the four largest Swedish banks and their approach to digitalization and FinTech. The current standings of the four banks is largely based on publicly available information in the form of publications, articles, interviews, and the banks' websites. The chapter will conclude with a discussion on the future of the banks in Sweden, looking at the influence of the implementation of the upcoming PSD2 regulation, the entry of new competitors from the tech sector, and the potential usage of artificial intelligence. This section is based on expert interviews held with Olov Brandt, Strategic Partner at Nordea, David Sonnek, Head of SEB Venture Capital, and Emma Heimonen, Head of Digital Innovation at Swedbank.

Banks and digitalization

Confronted by a rapidly changing and increasingly challenging environment, a transformation of the banking industry is required, and needs to happen fast for the current players to survive. Most banks have already embarked on a so-called "digital journey," which is intended to transform their organizations into fully fledged digital entities (Broeders and Khanna, 2015; Buss, Freeborn, and Silva, 2016). However, while the transformation has started, many banks are still in the early stages of this evolution, operating reactively rather than proactively, and lacking an organization-wide approach, according to IDC (Buss, Freeborn, and Silva, 2016). As a result, the gap between winners and laggers is wide (BCG, 2016; Grebe et al., 2016b). The next section discusses the aforementioned threat that the banking industry is facing and explores ways in which banks can adapt to cope with the situation.

Several trends are visible that increase pressure on the incumbent players. First, inspired by developments in other industries and enabled by technological innovations, customer demand for digital experiences has increased, and a seamless combination of physical and digital offerings is expected (Grebe et al., 2016a, 2016b; Ketterer, Himmelreich, and Schmid, 2016). Meanwhile, competition is tightening as a host of FinTech startups have emerged to compete with incumbent players on almost every product offering (EFMA and Backbase, 2016; Grebe et al., 2016a, 2016b; Ketterer, Himmelreich, and Schmid, 2016). Moreover, major tech companies such as GAFAA (Google, Amazon, Facebook, Apple, and Alibaba), harnessing advanced digital capabilities, capital, and strong brand names, are also entering the field of financial services (Broeders and Khanna, 2015; EFMA and Backbase, 2016; Grebe et al., 2016a; Schmidt, Drews, and Schirmer, 2016). By offering financial services on their platforms, these players could take over the customer interface (Broeders and Khanna, 2015; EFMA and Backbase, 2016). The low brand advocacy of the banks in comparison to the tech firms stimulates this process (Grebe et al., 2016a).

Overall, digital transformation has become a must. Without action, the banks' relationship with their customers will potentially be disintermediated, and banks will be downgraded to little more than utility providers in charge of the infrastructure (Grebe et al., 2016b; Mead, 2016). Customers will be lost to (new) competitors, while pressure on margins will increasingly erode profits (Broeders and Khanna, 2015; Grebe et al., 2016b). Consequently, laggers will be punished by the financial markets limiting the supply of capital. Noncompliance with new regulation might even result in penalties from regulators (Broeders and Khanna, 2015).

On the other hand, if applied properly, digital capabilities can dramatically improve customer experience and optimize the banks' internal processes in several ways. First, by opening new (digital) channels and enhancing old ones (Schmidt, Drews, and Schirmer, 2016), banks will foster connectivity with customers, suppliers, and employees. Second, new technologies, such as AI, will significantly improve decision-making by increasing the amount and quality of data (Broeders and Khanna, 2015). Third, radically improved and digitalized internal processes, structures, and IT systems will allow for automation and optimization of the banks' workflows (Broeders and Khanna, 2015; Grebe et al., 2016b). Lastly, the culture change accompanying the transformation will ensure the banks' future performance by fostering innovation and flexibility (Broeders and Khanna, 2015).

To achieve this level of digitalization, it is essential to have the right people and skills, the right organization, and above all the right culture.

Culture

Banks will need to start thinking like tech companies and adopt matching cultures (Broeders and Khanna, 2015; Kaufman et al., 2015; Grebe et al., 2016b). Becoming a customer-centric organization is fundamental (Grebe et al., 2016b); the customer should come first in every department, and every decision should be made with the customer journey in mind (EFMA and Backbase, 2016). This also ensures that the technology and process sides of the organization are focused on creating a better customer experience (Broeders and Khanna, 2015). In addition, an atmosphere of continuous innovation is required to keep up with and profit from evolving (digital) trends, for example by organizing in-house hackathons or establishing innovation labs (Broeders and Khanna, 2015; Kaufman et al., 2015; EFMA and Backbase, 2016). Collaboration is essential, not only via cross-functional teams, but also by partnering with startups and involving the customer (Broeders and Khanna, 2015; Dany et al., 2016). Lastly, to deliver new products and services as fast as possible, an agile way of working that facilitates experimentation and rapid prototyping and stimulates cross-functional collaboration needs to be embraced throughout the entire organization (Broeders and Khanna, 2015; Kaufman et al., 2015; Grebe et al., 2016b; Ketterer, Himmelreich, and Schmid, 2016).

Leadership and people

At the core of transformation lies the organization's people, who need to have the right skills and mindset to fit into the aforementioned culture. To lead the organization through this journey, a strong and digitally capable leadership is required that can develop and realize a company-wide vision (Olanrewaju, 2014; Baumgärtner et al., 2016; Buss, Freeborn, and Silva, 2016; Dany et al., 2016). Existing leaders should be trained in digital skills and new digital leadership should be attracted. A great example of this is BBVA, where many C-suite employees have been recruited to drive the bank's transformation because of their digital experience. To leverage digital capabilities, building internal competencies and infusing the right talent is essential on all levels. However, due to scarcity, talent acquisition is not always possible, and banks might need to use other methods to satisfy their needs, such as borrowing talent through contingent labor (Kaufman et al., 2015). Moreover, proper organizational, evaluation, and compensation structures are required to stimulate cross-functional collaboration and ensure employee alignment with the company's vision and strategy (Olanrewaju, 2014; Broeders and Khanna, 2015). A focus on business outcomes rather than digital activity is important (Olanrewaju, 2014).

Front end and back end

Digitalization touches upon every aspect of the bank, and transformation is required across the entire organization to create a seamless experience for the customer (Broeders and Khanna, 2015; Buss, Freeborn, and Silva, 2016; Ketterer, Himmelreich, and Schmid, 2016). On the front end, an omnichannel strategy needs to be pursued that promotes convenience and simplicity and combines superior digital offerings with human interaction (BBA and EY, 2016; Buss, Freeborn, and Silva, 2016; EFMA and Backbase, 2016; Grebe et al., 2016a; Ketterer, Himmelreich, and Schmid, 2016). Moreover, in order to attract and retain customers, the customer experience needs to be highly compelling, differentiated, and personalized, and the journey needs to be as efficient as possible (Broeders and Khanna, 2015; EFMA and Backbase, 2016; Grebe et al., 2016b; KPMG and CB Insights, 2016).

On the back end, incorporation of new technologies and simplification of the IT landscape is required for several reasons (Grebe et al., 2016b; Ketterer, Himmelreich, and Schmid, 2016). To increase the infrastructures' flexibility and decrease interdependency, processes should be standardized and applications should be decoupled by applying decentralized interfaces, such as APIs. Moreover, processes should be digitized and automated to increase speed and efficiency (Broeders and Khanna, 2015; Ketterer, Himmelreich, and Schmid, 2016). Incorporation of advanced data analytics and AI will create possibilities to improve decision-making (Broeders and Khanna, 2015). Lastly, to be able to leverage digital applications and offer a seamless customer experience across all channels, a consistent view of the organization's data is vital (Ketterer, Himmelreich, and Schmid, 2016). This can, for example, be achieved by developing multidimensional master data management capabilities and by using shared data clusters or data lakes.

According to a McKinsey study (Broeders and Khanna, 2015), digital winners could potentially increase their net profit with 45 percent, while banks that miss out stand to lose as much as 35 percent. The main contributor to this will be a drastic decrease in operational costs due to the digitalization, automation, and simplification of organizational structures and processes. Digitalization of the front end will lead to a smaller increase of revenue, but is vital for protecting the bank against a potential loss of customers.

Banks and FinTech

Up until a few years ago, the relationship between banks and FinTech startups was largely viewed as hostile, and FinTech startups were seen as replacements for banks (Barba and Macheel, 2016). Over the last two years, the tone of this debate has shifted from competition to cooperation, as the industry has come to the understanding that banks and FinTech startups are mutually dependent on each other (Bauer, Obwegeser, and Avdagic, 2016; Dietz, Moon, and Radnai, 2016; Rohner, 2016). While direct competition will continue to exist, both banks and FinTech startups are increasingly looking at each other as potential and necessary partners. This section explores the potential benefits and different methods of collaboration between banks and FinTech startups.

Collaboration potential

FinTech startups have much to gain from banks. As innovative organizations, startups often focus on solving a single, narrow customer problem, which prohibits them from developing a comprehensive understanding of a customer's full financial situation. A multiservice provider, such as a universal bank, can more easily reach such an informed understanding, as well as offer a broad range of products to serve all the customer needs (Roberts, 2016; Rohner, 2016). Another challenge FinTech startups face is the highly complex regulatory environment. Since banks have extensive experience in this field, cooperation can help startups with legislation compliance (Deutsche Bank, 2016; Rohner, 2016). In addition, by partnering with a bank, a startup can attain scale by leveraging the bank's existing customer base (Deutsche Bank, 2016), established brand, and market reach (Schaus, 2015; ING, 2016). This will also enable a startup to expand its target audience to include less FinTech-oriented customer segments and markets, such as older, less tech-savvy banking customers. Another reason for a startup to seek collaboration rather than competition is gaining access to the banks' lower cost of capital (Roberts, 2016) and global infrastructure (Deutsche Bank, 2016). Besides, being acquired by an incumbent player is, in general, an attractive exit strategy for startups, also in the FinTech industry (Rohner, 2016).

Banks have also started to wake up and acknowledge the importance of FinTech. Bogged down by regulation, legacy systems, sheer size, and inflexible cultures that favor the status quo, banks themselves are unable to evolve fast enough to cope with the situation (Mead, 2016; Roberts, 2016). FinTech startups, on the other hand, are equipped with technology-savvy talent and agile organizational structures (Schaus, 2015; Bauer, Obwegeser, and Avdagic, 2016; Roberts, 2016). This allows them to leverage rapid testing and prototyping of new technologies to create new business ideas and concepts that smoothen and differentiate the customer experience (Deutsche Bank, 2016; ING, 2016) and decrease cost (Dany et al., 2016). Hence, startups form ideal partners for banks to drive digitalization and speed up the innovation processes. Moreover, incorporating financial technology enables the banks to better serve previously unprofitable customer segments, such as the SME sector, as FinTech offerings often work more efficiently and effectively on a small scale, whereas the banks' old offerings did not (World Economic Forum, 2015; Dany et al., 2016).

Collaboration methods

Due to scarce time and resources, banks can only target a limited number of startups and innovations. Therefore, developing a clear strategic focus is essential for picking the right targets (ING, 2016; KPMG and CB Insights, 2016). Banks should focus on the innovations that deliver the greatest impact (Dany et al., 2016) and are complementary to their core competencies (Accenture, 2016). Moreover, given the distinctiveness between banks and startups, successful collaboration is a challenge (Bauer, Obwegeser, and Avdagic, 2016) and identifying the right method of cooperation is of significant importance.

There are several ways in which banks can cooperate with startups. The simplest and cheapest methods are reward-based competitions open to internal and external individuals and teams, such as hackathons. These can create brand awareness and establish relationships for the banks in the startup community, while exposing the organization to new ideas and solutions (Briscoe and Mulligan, 2014; Schaus, 2015; ING, 2016). Hackathons are widespread in the banking community.

A more extensive type of collaboration is the incubator, an umbrella for a variety of incubation models. Though distinct, most incubation models provide startups with access to physical resources, office support services, access to capital, process support, and networking services in a variety of ways. Incubators can be run by universities, corporations, and governments, or can be stand-alone entities (Pauwels et al., 2016). Banks can establish their own incubator programs to assist new startups, source ideas, and establish relationships. However, due to the cost and complexity of these programs (Schaus, 2015), partnering up or sponsoring an independent incubator is often the preferred option (Linklaw, 2015).

A relatively new form of incubator is known as the accelerator. These type of incubation models focus heavily on mentoring and training services, and aim at keeping close and active relationships with alumni. They differ from other incubation models by their short duration, focus on early-stage tech startups, and lack of focus on physical resources (Pauwels et al., 2016). Often there is a small seed-investment, which is exchanged for equity (Bauer, Obwegeser, and Avdagic, 2016; Pauwels et al., 2016). Like the other types of incubators, corporate accelerators help bridge the gap between corporations and startups (Bauer, Obwegeser, and Avdagic, 2016) by integrating external knowledge to speed up innovation and increase the quality of the companies' offerings (Kohler, 2016). Several banks (e.g., Barclays) operate corporate accelerators, but partnerships are generally more common due to the costs associated with running the programs (Linklaw, 2015; Schaus, 2015).

Banks can opt for a more thorough form of collaboration by investing financial resources through corporate venture capital (CVC) (Schaus, 2015). This form of investing often has strategic objectives, rather than solely financial goals. Examples of strategic objectives are exploration of new technologies, importing innovation, and identification of potential acquisition partners (Anokhin, Peck, and Wincent, 2016). Many banks operate CVC arms, and corporate participation in venture capital in the financial sector has strongly increased over the past years. In the second and third quarter of 2016, CVC funds participated in 30 percent of global deals (KPMG and CB Insights, 2016). Yet, compared to other industries, the banking sector is lagging in this field, as only two CVC funds run by banks appeared in the top 100 most active CVCs of the world in 2015

(CB Insights, 2016). As the FinTech hype slowly subsides, VC funds have tightened their scrutiny on FinTech startups by increasing their focus on execution plans and proof (Barba and Macheel, 2016; Williams-Grut, 2016). Meanwhile, VC competition is mounting, especially because tech giants are becoming more active in the financial sector and deploying their own CVC funds to acquire FinTech startups (Schaus, 2015).

The last two methods for collaboration are mergers and acquisitions (M&As) and partnerships. The first provides a quick way to access and secure technology and capabilities, but finding and incorporating the right target is a challenge (Kohler, 2016). The latter also provides access to new technologies, but does not secure them from competitors. As a complete alternative to collaboration with startups, banks could also perform the innovation process internally, but, as mentioned before, this is hard to do due to the traditional characteristics of a banking organization (Mead, 2016; Roberts, 2016). One possibility to stimulate internal innovation is an innovation lab, an internal entity for exploring and testing innovations with its own innovative culture (Grebe et al., 2016a).

An option that combines both internal and external innovation without partnerships is known as open banking, a method that brings open innovation and co-creation to the banks. This could entail the use of open platforms on which APIs are offered to the banks' customers, suppliers, and third-party developers, which allows them to build new applications and products on top of the banks' technology and data or share their own technology with the banks (BBVA, 2016; Mead, 2016).

The situation in Sweden

The Swedish culture and financial landscape

Innovation has played an integral role in the Swedish culture (Alström et al., 2013; Schofield, 2016), and Swedes have been keen to adopt new technologies, which shows in the country's prime position on BCG's e-intensity index (Alström et al., 2013) and the high Internet and smartphone penetration (Andreasson, Lind, and Lundmark, 2015; Wesley-James et al., 2015). This culture, combined with the comparatively deregulated financial markets, has transformed Stockholm into an advantageous environment for tech startups and digitalization (Wesley-James et al., 2015), and the city has the highest number of unicorns per capital after Silicon Valley (Schofield, 2016). Comprising 60 percent of the country's production value, small businesses form the cornerstone of the Swedish economy (Andreasson, Lind, and Lundmark, 2015).

As one of Europe's largest financial systems relative to the size of its domestic economy, the Swedish financial system holds an important role as a regional financial hub for the Nordics and Baltics (IMF, 2016). In 2016, 159 financial institutions were active in Sweden, of which 68 were banks (Thebanks.eu, 2017). The four largest banks, Nordea, SEB, Swedbank, and Handelsbanken, account for over 75 percent of the market and hold strong positions in the other Nordic countries and the Baltics (IMF, 2016). The largest bank, Nordea, is considered as one of the 25 *global systematically important* banks according to the IMF (2016). The others are classified as *other systematically important* institutions. In the following, a brief overview of the four banks is provided.

Nordea Bank AB was founded in 2001 as a result of a merger between a Finnish, Danish, Swedish, and Norwegian bank. The bank is headquartered in Stockholm, and also sees Poland and the Baltics as home countries. Nordea serves 10 million private customers and 540,000 corporate and institutional customers, and has 31,596 employees (Nordea, 2017a).

Skandinaviska Enskilda Banken (SEB) AB was founded in 1856, and has its main activities in eight countries around the Baltic Sea. Headquartered in Stockholm, SEB serves around 2,300 large corporations, 700 financial institutions, 267,000 SMEs, and 1.4 million private customers. The bank has 15,300 employees (SEB, 2017a).

Swedbank AB was formed by a series of mergers and acquisitions, with its roots dating back to 1820. The bank's home markets are Sweden and the Baltics and its headquarters is based in Sundbyberg, Stockholm. Swedbank serves 7.3 million private customers and 650,000 corporate customers (Swedbank, 2016) with 14,061 employees (Swedbank, 2017).

Svenska Handelsbanken AB was founded in 1871. Its home markets are the Nordics, the UK, and the Netherlands, and its headquarters is based in Stockholm. The bank has 11,803 employees.

The Swedish banks and digitalization

Following its innovative culture, Sweden has been at the forefront of digitalization. Examples of this are, as mentioned previously, the country's high Internet and smartphone penetration (Wesley-James et al., 2015), the large size of the Internet economy (8.2 percent of GDP in 2015) (Andreasson, Lind, and Lundmark, 2015), and the country's high use of digital payment systems (Breman and Felländer, 2014). However, according to BCG (Andreasson, Lind, and Lundmark, 2015; Fæste et al., 2016), the digital competitiveness of the Swedish economy is expected to fall in the next years, and the private sector will need to leverage technology and digitalization to a larger extent (Andreasson, Lind, and Lundmark, 2015). The next section discusses the initiatives and approaches of the four major banks to digitalization by looking at their overarching strategy, the digital skills of their management boards, their cultural focus on innovation, and developments at the front and back end of the organization. This should serve as a general overview and indicator of the digital initiatives and readiness of the banks, and is by no means an exhaustive list or assessment.

Digitalization as part of the overarching strategy

This section on overarching strategy discusses what place digitalization or digitization takes in the strategy, organization, and plans of the four banks.

Nordea: Digitalization is a top priority at Nordea, and is seen as an important tool for scaling its relationship bank model (Bornfeld, 2014). In order to become a truly digital bank, Nordea is executing a transformation agenda for 2016–2018 (Nordea, 2016a). To drive this digital agenda, Nordea has established a dedicated division, Group Digital, in 2016.

SEB: Digitization is one of the three focus areas of SEB's three-year business plan 2016–2018 (SEB, 2017a). With this plan, the bank aims at transforming both its customer channels as well as its internal processes (SEB, 2017a).

Swedbank: Digitalization is a top priority for Swedbank (Interview Heimonen, 2017), and speeding up of the digitalization process is at the top of the agenda (Swedbank, 2016). To highlight this importance and to lead the digitalization initiatives, the digital banking unit, a new dedicated group function, was established in 2016 (Swedbank, 2017).

Handelsbanken: Digital is an important focus area of Handelsbanken as it is an enabler of its decentralized working method. The center of activity is positioned at the branch, which consists of both physical and digital channels (Handelsbanken, 2015, 2016).

Digital skills of the board of directors

As mentioned before, a digitally equipped leadership team is essential to successfully drive the digital transformation of a company. The digital savviness of the different boards is discussed by looking at the academic background, professional experience, and relevant other functions of the individual board members.

Nordea: Out of nine board members, two have an academic background in computer science (both appointed in 2015) and one in engineering. Moreover, five board members have potentially relevant digital experience, having worked as board members or managers at companies such as TeliaSonera, Nokia Corporation, and Microsoft (Nordea, 2017b).

SEB: Out of 17 members, no one has an academic background in digital-related fields; two directors have a background in engineering. Three members have potentially relevant experience, one being a director at a telecommunication company, one having a background in systems management and IT development within SEB, and one currently leading a consultancy network for digital transformation (SEB, 2017b).

Swedbank: Out of eight board members, no one has an academic background in a digital-related field. One director has potentially relevant experience as an executive at Ericsson and NXP-Semiconductors. The bank does organize relevant study trips for its board. For example, in 2016, the entire board went on a study trip to get a better insight on digitization and IT security (Swedbank, 2017).

Handelsbanken: Out of the nine board members, one holds a PhD in technology and two directors have degrees in engineering. One director has potentially relevant experience, having held various positions at Telenor (Handelsbanken, 2015).

Employees, culture, and innovation

This section discusses the role of innovation and digitalization within the culture at the four banks and their hiring and training efforts.

Nordea: As part of its transformation, Nordea is pursuing a cultural change, according to its 2016 annual report (Nordea, 2016a). Core elements of the new culture are collaboration (both externally and internally) and learning. Moreover, diversity, including the attraction of different academic backgrounds, is promoted. To encourage internal innovation, Nordea has established the Innovation LAB, where employees can explore and test new ideas, solutions, and emerging technologies. The Nordea Startup Accelerator also contributes to the atmosphere of innovation at the firm. In 2016, Nordea launched the Digital Hub, an online blog on innovation and digital transformation, to keep its employees and other stakeholders up to date with the progress.

SEB: SEB encourages a culture of change and innovation. To stimulate this, it has established SEB's Innovation Lab, a setting were employees can bring, test, and prototype ideas (SEB, 2017a). To improve employees' abilities to work together and manage change, SEB has adopted an agile way of working for which 2,000 employees received training in 2016 (SEB, 2017a). In addition, SEB has broadened its recruitment search to ensure future procurement of competencies in the areas of digital design, data analysis, and IT (SEB, 2017a).

Swedbank: Swedbank aspires a culture of simplicity, openness, and caring, and encourages learning through internal mobility and collaboration (Swedbank, 2017). Swedbank hires people with backgrounds in technology to champion digitalization throughout the firm, and has established agile ways of working with IT and digital development (Interview Heimonen, 2017). Moreover, the bank encourages everyone to get a digital mentor (e.g., employees' children) to help them in becoming more digitalized. As part of its internal innovation program, Swedbank has implemented a five-day sprint method of working and is encouraging its employees to come up with and develop ideas (Interview Heimonen, 2017). For example, three Swedbank teams joined the Test Drive program of the STING startup incubator in 2016 (Ström, 2016d).

Handelsbanken: Handelsbanken has a strongly decentralized culture. The bank strives for continuous development of its employees, and enables this by focusing on internal mobility (Handelsbanken, 2015). More information was not available through public sources.

Front end

These are the developments that affect the customer experience and the channels through which the bank offers its products. One major combined initiative has been the successful launch of the mobile payment system Swish in 2012 by a coalition of Swedish banks, including the four banks discussed in this chapter. The app allows consumers to make payments with their smartphones, both to other individuals and to online shops.

> *Nordea*: As part of its transformation agenda, Nordea is shifting its distribution from physical to digital channels (Nordea, 2016a), for example by launching online meetings and e-branches in 2015 to offer online advice to customers (Nordea, 2015).
>
> *SEB*: SEB's goal is to provide a completely remote offering by using digital customer intelligence to develop customized advisory tools, interfaces, and client portals (SEB, 2017a). In 2015, the business banking app and Internet bank were redesigned and expanded with new functionalities. Moreover, in 2016, a screen-sharing functionality for SMEs was launched to increase accessibility and the quality of online advice (SEB, 2015a), and Aida, an AI-powered virtual assistant, was introduced (Andreasyan, 2016c).
>
> *Swedbank*: Swedbank pursues an omnichannel strategy and plans to digitize all its routine banking services (Swedbank, 2017). Examples are the Swedbank Payment Portal, which allows retailers to receive payments from various payment methods through a single administrative process (Swedbank, 2016), and MasterPass, an online paying system for the mobile phone (Swedbank, 2016). In 2016, a beta version of its new digital bank was launched, containing new services and standardizing use across different devices (Swedbank, 2017). Swedbank has implemented Nina, an intelligent virtual assistant, in 2015 (Interview Heimonen, 2017).
>
> *Handelsbanken*: At Handelsbanken, digital channels are at the core of the branch strategy and serve to increase branches' availability. Most services are available through online channels, which are constantly being updated and include the latest technology (Handelsbanken, 2015). Handelsbanken also utilizes video technology to connect its customers in the local branch with experts in the regional office (Furseth, 2015). In addition, Handelsbanken launched Ecster in 2016, a subsidiary of the bank, which will provide payment solutions for e-commerce and retail organizations (Ström, 2016b).

Back end

This section discusses the initiatives that are implemented to improve the banks' organizational and IT infrastructures.

Nordea: Nordea has introduced an extensive simplification program to make its organization more agile and responsive (Nordea, 2016b). As part of the program, the number of products and processes will be decreased (Interview Brandt, 2017) and all the bank's platforms will be integrated and replaced by the core banking platform (Wikander, 2016). Moreover, a payment platform will be developed and the existing data warehouses will be merged into a group common data warehouse (Nordea, 2016a). Nordea is developing APIs, which will be opened to all registered payment providers and account information providers. The exact launch date is unknown (Interview Brandt, 2017).

SEB: Digitalization and automation of internal processes to increase the bank's efficiency is one of the core aspects of SEB's digital transformation (SEB, 2017a). As part of the program, several key processes will be completely redesigned to harness the full potential of technological developments and automation (SEB, 2017a). Moreover, SEB is introducing layers and APIs to its IT environment to increase the flexibility and availability of its infrastructure, and is exploring the application of machine learning and blockchain technologies (Interview Sonnek, 2017). SEB already has fundamental APIs, but they are still being prepared to be opened to external parties.

Swedbank: Swedbank aims to be the market leader in cost-efficiency and sees digitalization as one of the means to achieve this (Swedbank, 2017). Several projects and programs are running in parallel to improve the back end infrastructure of the bank (Interview Heimonen, 2017), and simplification and automation of internal processes is mentioned several times in its 2015 annual report (Swedbank, 2016). Swedbank is further expanding its application of artificial intelligence (Interview Heimonen, 2017).

Handelsbanken: Handelsbanken is constantly working to develop and improve its technical solutions. It utilizes technical advances to increase efficiency and decrease cost (Handelsbanken, 2015).

Swedish banks and FinTech

As highlighted in this book, Sweden, and especially Stockholm, have developed fruitful ecosystems for the development of tech startups. FinTech has led the capital investments in the tech sector in Sweden in the past years, attracting about one-fifth of all FinTech investments in Europe (Stockholm FinTech Hub, 2017), and Stockholm has been the birthplace of several internationally renowned unicorns such as Klarna and iZettle. The surge of FinTech is likely to continue in 2017, driven by the recent establishment of the Stockholm FinTech Hub, the upcoming PSD2 regulation, and increased interest of incumbent players. The following section will describe the collaboration the banks have established with FinTech startups in Sweden.

Reward-based competitions

Nordea: In 2014, Nordea hosted the Nordea Innovation Challenge for individuals, universities, and tech startups together with IBM and Apple. The challenge focused on banking in the future and aimed at creating inspiration and ideas for new innovative digital banking solutions to improve Nordea's offerings to its customers (Nordea, 2015). There is no evidence of similar programs being run in 2015 or 2016.

Swedbank: For these types of initiatives, Swedbank usually collaborates with other parties, for example with the STING incubator in 2016 (Interview Heimonen, 2017).

SEB and Handelsbanken: No information was found on the organization of reward-based competitions.

Incubators and corporate accelerators

Nordea: In 2015, Nordea established its own corporate accelerator together with Nestholma Venture Capital. The Nordea Startup Accelerator is a 12-week program for FinTech startups that ran successfully in Helsinki and Stockholm in 2015 and 2016 (Nordea, 2016c). The accelerator ensures the bank's presence in the FinTech ecosystem and helps the bank find FinTech startups with offerings valuable for improving its own products, services, and customer experience (Interview Brandt, 2017). The accelerator also enables experimentation with startups and different forms of collaboration and contributes to the bank's cultural transformation. So far, the experience with the accelerator has been positive; over 200 startups applied for the 2016 program and pilots have been started with several ex-participants to explore opportunities for collaboration. The program is expected to continue in 2017 and 2018.

SEB: SEB does not have an internal incubator or corporate accelerator. However, it does have relationships with over 15 organizations that support entrepreneurship (SEB, 2015a). For example, it has a partnership with the Stockholm-based STING incubator (SEB, 2015b), where it, among others, provided sponsorship and coaches for the FinTech accelerator program. The primary goal of these partnerships is to build brand awareness in the entrepreneurial world (Interview Sonnek, 2017).

Swedbank: Swedbank does not have an internal incubator or corporate accelerator. To get involved in the FinTech ecosystem, it has commenced a partnership with the Stockholm-based STING incubator in 2016 (Ström, 2016d). Swedbank has a similar relation with Tehnopol in Tallinn.

Handelsbanken: There is no evidence that Handelsbanken operates an internal incubator, accelerator, or has partnerships with an external organization.

Corporate venture capital, investments, and acquisitions

Nordea: Nordea does not have a dedicated venture capital arm. However, it does occasionally invest in startups. For example, in 2016, Nordea invested in Wrapp, a coupon and discount app linked to your bank card (Nordea, 2017c; Ström, 2016c). Moreover, in 2016, Nordea launched an equity-based crowdfunding service to connect its customers with entrepreneurs that are seeking capital investments (Nordea, 2016d). This service is expected to be launched in Nordea's other markets in the next two years (Interview Brandt, 2017).

SEB: SEB has its own corporate venture capital fund focusing on technology and FinTech startups. SEB Venture Capital was established in 1995, and supports startups with capital, competence, and clients (SEB, 2017c). The fund has a mixture of financial and strategic goals, and focuses on startups that provide technological breakthroughs or fundamental insights (Interview Sonnek, 2017). Investments include technologies that fit into the bank's current digitalization plan and emerging technologies of which the future application within the bank is uncertain (Interview Sonnek, 2017). Currently, the fund holds equity in five FinTech startups (SEB, 2015a, 2017c). In the past, SEB private equity, another equity investment branch of SEB, has also invested in FinTech startups, for example in iZettle (Leijonhufvud, 2016).

Swedbank: Swedbank has no dedicated venture capital arm for FinTech, but the bank is open for investments and acquisitions (Interview Heimonen, 2017). Investment decisions are made on a case-by-case basis. No acquisitions have been performed to date.

Handelsbanken: Handelsbanken has no dedicated venture capital arm focusing on FinTech and does not publically mention investments in FinTech startups. Instead, it has invested in establishing its own innovative subsidiary, Ecster (Ström, 2016b).

Partnerships

Nordea: Nordea is actively looking for partnerships with startups that can provide value to the company and expects an increasing amount of collaborations in the future (Andreasyan, 2016a; Interview Heimonen, 2017). Current examples are the partnership with Wrapp, established in 2016, and the pilots with former participants of its accelerator program (Ström, 2016c; Nordea, 2017c). Another initiative is Nordea's roundtables, meetings in which members of eight to ten startups and Nordea's management discuss structures of collaboration and market trends (Nordea, 2017a).

SEB: SEB sees startups as a great opportunity for partnerships to invest in common infrastructure and enhance customer services, and has frequently spoken about collaboration (SEB, 2015a). For example, it partnered with Ripple to develop a blockchain-based, real-time payment system (Andreasyan, 2016b).

SEB often also collaborates with its VC investments, although this is not an investment requirement.

Swedbank: Swedbank aims at collaborating with others instead of developing everything in-house. Exploration of third-party collaborations was one of the focus areas of the group executive committee in 2016 (Swedbank, 2017) and the bank meets with startups regularly (Interview Heimonen, 2017). In 2016, the bank commenced a partnership with Sprinklebit, a social investing platform that will be rolled out to the bank's customers in 2017 (Swedbank, 2017). More partnerships are expected to be announced in 2017 (Interview Heimonen, 2017).

Handelsbanken: In 2016, Handelsbanken's subsidiary Ecster has entered a partnership with the startup Betalo to expand its service offering (Ström, 2016a).

The future of banks in Sweden

A lot is happening within the financial sector in Sweden. Over the next years, there are several events that will potentially have a significant impact on the position and operations of the banks. Three of these events are the implementation of the PSD2 directive, the entrance of new competitors, and the application of artificial intelligence. To explore the future of the banks in Sweden and the potential impact of these three events, interviews were held with experts at Nordea, SEB, and Swedbank. The experts in question are Emma Heimonen, Head of Digital Innovation at Swedbank, Olov Brandt, Strategic Partner at Nordea and Site Manager of the Nordea Startup Accelerator, and David Sonnek, Head of SEB Venture Capital.

The future of banks and their relationship with FinTech startups

This section describes the experts' view on the future of banks in general, and the future relationship between banks and FinTech startups.

Olov Brandt believes that banks are currently in the middle of a transformation. In this process, he sees FinTech startups, if wisely handled, as a great opportunity. He expects much more business and collaboration between banks and FinTech startups in the future. In his opinion, a bank should use FinTech services to improve its own offerings to its customers. Startups need banks to reach the next level of maturity and gain trust from the customers and other organizations in the financial landscape. In particular, he sees a large role for private financial managers (PFMs), and is convinced that all major banks will offer PFMs in the future.

According to David Sonnek, banks will maintain their position as aggregators of trust and of services for people's and companies' economies, as he doubts that consumers will accept too many individual providers of vertical services. Nevertheless, he does expect some banks to shift their focus toward infrastructure and economies of scale. In his opinion, FinTech startups form both an opportunity and a threat to banks; a threat because FinTech will replace, standardize, and marginalize certain verticals of the bank; an opportunity because startups can serve as vehicles for innovation and rapid prototyping of new products and technologies. He holds a conservative view on the profitability potential of the startup market and believes that there has been a startup hype over the past years.

Emma Heimonen believes the financial industry is changing and that banks will look different in the future. She highlights two major drivers for this transformation: first, the implementation of new technologies, which affects customer behavior and expectations and increases the demand for digital services in the financial sector; and second, upcoming regulations, such as PSD2 and GDPR, which will have a strong impact on the way the industry functions. However, since these regulations are still under development, the exact implications are yet uncertain. Emma believes FinTech startups are a consequence of these factors, rather than a driver. She sees the startups as a great opportunity for the banks, because they can develop new products and services faster and cheaper. Banks, on the other hand, can provide startups with marketing and distribution power and help them gain the customers' trust.

PSD2

The revised Payment Services Directive (PSD2), which will be launched by the European Commission in 2018, will force banks to open up their customer data to third-party software and app providers (BBVA, 2016). As a result, banks will most likely open their internal APIs to third parties. The exact impact of the implementation of PSD2 on the financial industry is uncertain; it might enable the creation of cutting-edge banking services or it might not evoke any significant change.

Olov Brandt is convinced that the implementation of PSD2 will change the way business is done and will affect everyone in the industry. He thinks it might have some negative effects for Nordea, but that in the end, it will enable and stimulate collaboration, and thereby increase the quality of the customer experience. He links PSD2 directly to the use of open APIs.

David Sonnek is not sure whether the implementation of PSD2 itself will trigger significant new customer behavior. He does not see who the new actor will be that will repackage the information in a new way.

Emma Heimonen is convinced that the implementation of PSD2 will have significant impact on the industry. Its exact influence will be determined by the regulatory details of the directive, which have not been publicized yet.

New entrants: GAFAA

Tech companies have started to enter the industry by expanding their own services and platforms with financial offerings. These players leverage vast amounts of capital, technological expertise, data analytics, and AI, and are able to disintermediate a bank's client contact by offering financial services through their huge consumer ecosystems (Broeders and Khanna, 2015; EFMA and Backbase, 2016;

Grebe et al., 2016a). Consequently, they could become influential competitors and affect traditional banks.

Olov Brandt believes that empowering financial services with other tech services might improve the services considerably. In his opinion, the threat of GAFAA relates more to the US system and market. The entry barriers in Europe are higher, as European banks are technically more advanced than their US counterparts, especially regarding security. In general, he believes that the competition of the tech companies will be met by the major banks in Sweden.

David Sonnek sees tech companies as a major threat when it comes to a bank's customer interface. For B2C, he highlights hardware providers of voice agents, who hold a strong grip over the customer relation, and app builders such as Apple and Google, who could aspire to build interfaces that manage every aspect of our lives, including people's economies. On the corporate side, he sees providers of enterprise resource planning (ERP) software, such as SAP, as a potential threat, as they could incorporate financial services into their systems. According to David, SEB venture capital has not faced much competition from the venture funds of tech companies, as their investment activities are mainly targeted at the US.

According to Emma Heimonen, the entrance of tech companies in the industry is a very interesting development. She expects these companies to be part of the industry's transformation. For example, for startups, Emma believes conversations with the tech companies are essential to explore future collaboration.

Artificial intelligence and machine learning

Artificial intelligence and machine learning are both very broad concepts. According to Accenture (Knight, 2017), artificial intelligence is a group of multiple technologies that provide machines with the ability to sense, enable, and act, while learning from experience and adapting over time. This ability to self-learn and adapt is also known as machine learning or reinforced learning. In recent years, there has been vast progress in this field, and AI has already been applied in several industries, including banking.

According to David Sonnek, AI-powered advisory processes are one of the hypes of 2017. He sees artificial intelligence and machine learning as integral parts of the digitalization path, but believes that they will only be applied to very narrow niches within banking organizations, because of the considerable costs. On the front end, one of the main applications of AI will be in the customer interface, where voice recognition software can be used for customer interaction and advisory processes, such as SEB's Aida. On the back end, he sees opportunities for applying enhanced learning platforms to scan text, such as legal documents, and to generate leads for the corporate finance department. Another potential application is to use AI to drive customer segmentation of the banks' customers by integrating data and identifying weak patterns. He believes the application of AI and machine learning within banking will continue gradually in the future.

Emma Heimonen sees artificial intelligence as one of the most interesting technological developments of the moment. According to Emma, Swedbank is improving and expanding its use of artificial intelligence through a step-by-step process. She envisions that in the future, people will be able to have real conversations with their bank accounts to receive information and advice.

Conclusion

As this chapter has shown, the financial ecosystem is transforming as new technologies and regulations are being implemented and new players are entering the industry. Though the situation threatens the incumbent firms, the potential benefits of digitalization are considerable; it enables banks to strengthen external relations and improve the customer experience, while it simultaneously empowers banks to automate and optimize internal processes. However, to capture these benefits, banks will need to adopt new cultures, train and attract digital capabilities, and transform their front and back end processes. Moreover, banks should embrace collaboration with new players rather than seek competition.

The four largest banks of Sweden have clearly started the journey; digitalization has become a top priority and, although in different ways, all four banks are seeking collaboration with startups. Nevertheless, major steps are still required to complete the digital transformation, especially regarding the digital skills of the board, the attraction of new talent, and the digitalization and integration of the back end processes. In addition, while all four banks are actively looking to collaborate with startups, 2016 has not seen many official partnerships being announced. Based on the expert interviews, more collaboration can be expected in 2017.

The transformation of the financial industry has arguably just started, and the introduction of the PSD2 regulation, the entrance of tech firms, and further implementation of AI and machine learning (and many other events) will likely transform the industry even further. The exact impact of these events is uncertain. To ensure future competitiveness, banks should monitor the developments carefully and approach changes proactively rather than reactively. If they do so and manage to complete their transformation in time, a bright future might lay ahead.

Bibliography

Accenture, 2016. *FinTech and the evolving landscape: Landing points in the industry.* [online] Accenture. Available at: www.accenture.com/t20160427T053810__w__/us-en/_acnmedia/PDF-15/Accenture-FinTech-Evolving-Landscape.pdf#zoom=50 [Accessed August 28, 2017].

Alström, A., Gander, S., Haraldsson, A., and Lind, F., 2013. *Digital Sweden: How consumers are setting the pace and creating opportunities for business.* [online] BCG Perspectives. Available at: http://image-src.bcg.com/BCG_COM/Digital-Sweden-May-2013-Nordics_tcm22-29085.pdf [Accessed August 28, 2017].

Andreasson, P., Lind, F., and Lundmark, A., 2015. *Launching a New Digital Agenda, how Sweden can become the global leader in digitization and technology.* [online] BCG Perspectives. Available at: http://image-src.bcg.com/BCG_COM/Launching-New-Digital-Agenda-Jun-2015-Nordics_tcm22-29057.pdf [Accessed August 28, 2017].

Andreasyan, T., 2016a. Nordea's chief digital officer calls on FinTechs to get in touch. *Banking Technology*. [online] Available at: www.bankingtech.com/528132/nordeas-new-chief-digital-officer-calls-on-fintechs-to-get-in-touch/ [Accessed August 28, 2017].

Andreasyan, T., 2016b. SEB and Ripple to build real-time payments system on blockchain. *Banking Technology*. [online] Available at: www.bankingtech.com/634562/seb-and-ripple-to-build-real-time-payments-system-on-blockchain/ [Accessed August 28, 2017].

Andreasyan, T., 2016c. SEB deploys IPsoft's virtual agent, Amelia, for customer facing ops. *Banking Technology*. [online] Available at: www.bankingtech.com/602071/seb-deploys-ipsofts-virtual-agent-amelia-for-customer-facing-ops/ [Accessed August 28, 2017].

Anokhin, S., Peck, S., and Wincent, J., 2016. Corporate venture capital: The role of governance factors. *Journal of Business Research*, 69(11), pp.4744–4749.

Barba, R. and Macheel, T., 2016. Banks play growing role in funding FinTech. *American Banker*. [online] Available at: www.americanbanker.com/news/banks-play-growing-role-in-funding-fintech [Accessed August 28, 2017].

Bauer, S., Obwegeser, N., and Avdagic, Z., 2016. Corporate accelerators: Transferring technology innovation to incumbent companies. In: *MCIS 2016 Proceedings*, 57. [online] Paphos, Cyprus: University of Nicosia, pp.1–12. Available at: http://aisel.aisnet.org/mcis2016/57 [Accessed August 28, 2017].

Baumgärtner, C., van den Berg, P., Dany, O., Goyal, R., Halliday, K., and Schwarz, J., 2016. *Global corporate banking 2016: The next-generation corporate bank*. [online] BCG Perspectives. Available at: www.bcgperspectives.com/content/articles/financial-institutions-technology-digital-global-corporate-banking-2016/ [Accessed August 28, 2017].

BBA and EY, 2016. *The way we bank now: Help at hand*. [online] BBA. Available at: www.ey.com/Publication/vwLUAssets/ey-pdf-the-way-we-bank-now/$FILE/ey-the-way-we-bank-now.pdf [Accessed August 28, 2017].

BBVA, 2016. *Open banking or how banks are transformed with APIs*. [online] BBVA API Market. Available at: https://bbvaopen4u.com/en/actualidad/open-banking-or-how-banks-are-transformed-apis [Accessed August 28, 2017].

BCG, 2016. *Digital disruption will force retail banks to "radically simplify."* [online] Press Release. Available at: www.bcg.com/d/press/10may2016-banking-on-digital-simplicity-35193 [Accessed August 28, 2017].

Bornfeld, C., 2014. *Digital banking*. [online] Nordea. Available at: www.nordea.com/Images/33-41728/2014-11-08_141108-Digital-Banking-Christian-Bornfeld_EN.pdf [Accessed August 28, 2017].

Breman, A. and Felländer, A., 2014. *Diginomics: New economic drivers [Translation of "Diginomics—nya ekonomiska drivkrafter" in Ekonomisk Debatt October 8, 2014]*. [online] Swedbank. Available at: www.swedbank.se/idc/groups/public/@i/@sc/@all/@lci/documents/publication/cid_1621507.pdf [Accessed August 28, 2017].

Briscoe, G. and Mulligan, C., 2014. *Digital innovation: The hackathon phenomenon*. [online] Queen Mary, University of London. Available at: http://qmro.qmul.ac.uk/xmlui/handle/123456789/11418 [Accessed August 28, 2017].

Broeders, H. and Khanna, S., 2015. *Strategic choices for banks in the digital age*. [online] McKinsey & Company: Our Insights. Available at: www.mckinsey.com/industries/financial-services/our-insights/strategic-choices-for-banks-in-the-digital-age [Accessed August 28, 2017].

Buss, A., Freeborn, L., and Silva, J., 2016. *The digital-ready bank: How ready are European banks for a digital world.* [online] IDC Financial Insights. Available at: http://news.sap.com/wp-content/blogs.dir/1/files/IDC-WP-Digital-Transformation-in-Banking-Final.pdf [Accessed August 28, 2017].

CB Insights, 2016. *The 100 most active corporate VC firms*. [online] Research Briefs. Available at: www.cbinsights.com/research/corporate-venture-capital-active-2015 [Accessed January 16, 2018].

Dany, O., Goyal, R., Schwarz, J., van den Berg, P., Scortecci, A., and to Baben, S., 2016. *FinTechs may be corporate banks' best "frenemies."* [online] BCG Perspectives. Available at: www.bcgperspectives.com/content/articles/financial-institutions-technology-digital-fintechs-may-be-corporate-banks-best-frenemies [Accessed August 28, 2017].

Deutsche Bank, 2016. *FinTech 2.0: Creating new strategies through strategic alliance.* [online] Global Transaction Banking. Available at: http://cib.db.com/insights-and-initiatives/white-papers/FinTech_2_0_Creating_new_opportunities_through_strategic_alliance.htm#gsc.tab=0 [Accessed January 6, 2018].

Dietz, M., Moon, J., and Radnai, M., 2016. *FinTechs can help incumbents, not just disrupt them.* [online] McKinsey & Company. Available at: www.mckinsey.com/industries/financial-services/our-insights/fintechs-can-help-incumbents-not-just-disrupt-them [Accessed August 28, 2017].

EFMA and Backbase, 2016. *Omni-channel banking: The digital transformation roadmap.* [online] Available at: https://backbase.com/wp-content/uploads/2017/04/Backbase_Omni-Channel-Banking-Report.pdf [Accessed January 6, 2018].

Fæste, L., Gjerstad, K., Kunnas, P., Lind, F., Poulsen, M.-B., Ruska, T., et al., 2016. *As their lead slips, Nordics look to revitalize growth: Nordic agenda 2017.* [online] BCG Perspectives. Available at: www.bcgperspectives.com/content/articles/transformation-growth-as-lead-slips-nordics-look-revitalize-growth/ [Accessed August 28, 2017].

Furseth, J., 2015. *All change: How digital is changing the high street bank branch.* [online] *FusionWire*. Available at: https://jessicafurseth.com/2015/10/22/all-change-how-digital-is-changing-the-high-street-bank-branch/ [Accessed August 28, 2017].

Grebe, M., Mönter, N., Noakes, B., de T'Serclaes, J.-W., Wade, B., and Walsh, I., 2016a. *Customers steer digital trends driving retail bank transformation.* [online] *BCG Perspectives*. Available at: www.bcgperspectives.com/content/articles/financial-institutions-technology-digital-customers-steer-digital-trends-driving-retail-bank-transformation/ [Accessed August 28, 2017].

Grebe, M., Mönter, N., Noakes, B., de T'Serclaes, J.-W., Wade, B., and Walsh, I., 2016b. *Global retail banking 2016: Banking on digital simplicity*. [online] BCG Perspectives. Available at: www.bcgperspectives.com/content/articles/financial-institutions-technology-digital-banking-digital-simplicity-global-retail-banking-2016/ [Accessed August 28, 2017].

Handelsbanken, 2015. *Highlights of annual report: January–December 2015.* [online] Available at: www.handelsbanken.co.uk/shb/inet/icentrb.nsf/vlookuppics/investor_relations_en_q-reports_hb_2015_q4_eng_report/$file/hb_2015_q4_eng_report.pdf [Accessed August 28, 2017].

Handelsbanken, 2016. *Interim report: January–September 2016.* [online] Available at: www.handelsbanken.com/shb/inet/icentsv.nsf/vlookuppics/investor_relations_en_q-reports_hb_2016_q3_eng_report/$file/hb_2016_q3_eng_report.pdf [Accessed August 28, 2017].

IMF, 2016. *Sweden financial stability assessment.* [online] Available at: www.imf.org [Accessed August 28, 2017].

ING, 2016. *The future of banking outlined in Copenhagen*. [online] All News. Available at: www.ing.com/Newsroom/All-news/Features/The-future-of-banking-outlined-in-Copenhagen.htm [Accessed August 28, 2017].

Kaufman, E., Bailey, A., Berz, K., Choo, S., Danoesastro, M., Duthoit, C., et al., 2015. *The power of people in digital banking transformation*. [online] BCG Perspectives. Available at: www.bcgperspectives.com/content/articles/financial-institutions-people-organization-power-people-digital-banking-transformation/?chapter=3 [Accessed August 28, 2017].

Ketterer, H., Himmelreich, H., and Schmid, C.N., 2016. *Ensuring digital readiness in financial services*. [online] BCG Perspectives. Available at: www.bcgperspectives.com/content/articles/technology-digital-transformation-ensuring-digital-readiness-financial-services/?chapter=2 [Accessed August 28, 2017].

Knight, W., 2017. 5 big predictions for artificial intelligence in 2017. *MIT Technology Review*. [online] Available at: www.technologyreview.com/s/603216/5-big-predictions-for-artificial-intelligence-in-2017/ [Accessed August 28, 2017].

Kohler, T., 2016. Corporate accelerators: Building bridges between corporations and start-ups. *Business Horizons*, 59(3), pp.347–357.

KPMG and CB Insights, 2016. *The pulse of FinTech, Q3 2016: Global analysis of FinTech venture funding*. [online] KPMG. Available at: https://assets.kpmg.com/content/dam/kpmg/xx/pdf/2016/11/the-pulse-of-fintech-q3-report.pdf [Accessed August 28, 2017].

Leijonhufvud, J., 2016. Kommentar: "Nu börjar fintech-kampen" [Comment: "Now the FinTech battle begins"]. *Dagens Industri*. [online] Available at: http://digital.di.se/artikel/kommentar-nu-borjar-fintech-kampen [Accessed August 28, 2017].

Linklaw, 2015. *Startup incubators launched by banks: The ups and downs*. [online] Available at: http://linkilaw.com/banks-incubators-startup-incubators-launched-by-banks/ [Accessed August 28, 2017].

Mead, W., 2016. Banking and the e-book moment. In: S. Chishti and J. Barberis, eds. *The FinTech book: The financial technology handbook for investors, entrepreneurs and visionaries*. Chichester: John Wiley & Sons, pp.70–85.

Nordea, 2015. *Annual report 2015*. [online] Available at: www.nordea.com/Images/33-102773/2015-12-31_Annual-Report-2015-Nordea-Bank-AB_EN.pdf [Accessed August 28, 2017].

Nordea, 2016a. *Annual report 2016*. [online] Available at: www.nordea.com/Images/33-169612/AnnualReport2016NordeaBankAB.pdf [Accessed August 28, 2017].

Nordea, 2016b. *Nordea establishes new Group Digital unit*. [online] Available at: www.nordea.com/en/press-and-news/news-and-press-releases/press-releases/2016/06-30-09h00-nordea-establishes-new-group-digital-unit.html [Accessed August 28, 2017].

Nordea, 2016c. *Nordea teams up with FinTech startups again*. [online] Available at: www.nordea.com/en/press-and-news/news-and-press-releases/press-releases/2016/05-12-08h00-nordea-teams-up-with-fintech-startups-again.html [Accessed August 28, 2017].

Nordea, 2016d. *Nordea to introduce crowdfunding service to the market*. [online] Available at: www.nordea.com/en/press-and-news/news-and-press-releases/news-en/2016/2016-04-27-nordea-to-introduce-crowdfunding-service-to-the-market.html [Accessed August 28, 2017].

Nordea, 2017a. *Innovation at Nordea*. [online] Available at: www.nordea.com/Images/34-154228/Innovation-for-vendor-seminarV4_4_4.pdf [Accessed August 28, 2017].

Nordea, 2017b. *Members of the board*. [online] Available at: www.nordea.com/en/about-nordea/corporate-governance/board-of-directors/members-of-the-board/#Wahlroos [Accessed August 28, 2017].

Nordea, 2017c. *Wrapp*. [online] Available at: www.nordea.se/privat/vardagstjanster/kort/wrapp.html [Accessed August 28, 2017].

Olanrewaju, T., 2014. *The rise of the digital bank*. [online] McKinsey & Company: Our Insights. Available at: www.mckinsey.com/business-functions/digital-mckinsey/our-insights/the-rise-of-the-digital-bank [Accessed August 28, 2017].

Pauwels, C., Clarysse, B., Wright, M., and Van Hove, J., 2016. Understanding a new generation incubation model: The accelerator. *Technovation*, 50–51, pp.13–24.

Roberts, C., 2016. *Frameworks for banks to work with FinTech companies*. [online] Silicon Valley Innovation Center. Available at: https://svicenter.com/frameworks-for-banks-to-work-with-fintech-companies/ [Accessed August 28, 2017].

Rohner, U., 2016. Why partnerships are appealing. *McKinsey Quarterly*, [online] 2, pp.45–49. Available at: www.mckinsey.com/industries/financial-services/our-insights/why-partnerships-are-appealing [Accessed August 28, 2017].

Schaus, P., 2015. *4 ways banks can engage with FinTech startups*. [online] Bank Innovation. Available at: http://bankinnovation.net/2015/11/4-ways-banks-can-engage-with-fintech-startups/ [Accessed August 28, 2017].

Schmidt, J., Drews, P., and Schirmer, I., 2016. End-users' perspective on digitalization: A study on work order processing in the German banking industry. In: *22nd AMCIS 2016 proceedings*. [online] Available at: http://aisel.aisnet.org/amcis2016/EndUser/Presentations/13 [Accessed August 28, 2017].

Schofield, J., 2016. *Swedish leaders need to be prepared for tech challenges*. [online] The Local. Available at: www.thelocal.se/20160927/swedish-leaders-must-get-a-grip-on-tech-challenges [Accessed August 28, 2017].

SEB, 2015a. *Annual report 2015*. [online] Available at: https://sebgroup.com/siteassets/investor_relations1/annual_reports/annual_report_2015.pdf [Accessed August 28, 2017].

SEB, 2015b. *FinTech-program ger skjuts åt startups [FinTech program gives boost to startups]*. [online] Available at: https://sebgroup.com/sv/press/nyheter/fintech-program-ger-skjuts-at-startups [Accessed August 28, 2017].

SEB, 2017a. *Annual report 2016*. [online] Available at: https://sebgroup.com/siteassets/investor_relations1/annual_reports/annual_report_2016.pdf [Accessed August 28, 2017].

SEB, 2017b. *Board of directors*. [online] Available at: https://sebgroup.com/about-seb/who-we-are/organisation/board-of-directors [Accessed August 28, 2017].

SEB, 2017c. *FinTech investments*. [online] Available at: https://sebgroup.com/large-corporates-and-institutions/our-services/seb-venture-capital/investments/fintech-investments [Accessed August 28, 2017].

Stockholm FinTech Hub, 2017. *Investors*. [online] Available at: https://stockholmfin.tech/join-us/investors [Accessed August 28, 2017].

Ström, V., 2016a. Betalo tecknar avtal med Handelsbanken [Betalo signs agreement with Handelsbanken]. *Dagens Industri*. [online] Available at: http://digital.di.se/artikel/betalo-tecknar-avtal-med-handelsbanken [Accessed August 28, 2017].

Ström, V., 2016b. Handelsbanken lanserar Klarna-konkurrent [Handelsbanken launches Klarna competition]. *Dagens Industri*. [online] Available at: http://digital.di.se/artikel/handelsbanken-lanserar-klarna-konkurrent [Accessed August 28, 2017].

Ström, V., 2016c. Nordea investerar i Wrapp [Nordea invests in Wrapp]. *Dagens Industri*. [online] Available at: http://digital.di.se/artikel/nordea-investerar-i-wrapp [Accessed August 28, 2017].

Ström, V., 2016d. Swedbank tar Sting till hjälp för att hitta fintech-stjärnor [Swedbank enlists the aid of Sting to find fintech stars]. *Dagens Industri*. [online] Available at:

http://digital.di.se/artikel/swedbank-tar-sting-till-hjalp-for-att-hitta-fintech-stjarnor [Accessed August 28, 2017].

Swedbank, 2016. *Annual report 2015*. [online] Available at: www.swedbank.com/idc/groups/public/@i/@sbg/@gs/@ir/documents/financial/cid_1972619.pdf [Accessed August 28, 2017].

Swedbank, 2017. *Annual report 2016*. [online] Available at: www.swedbank.com/idc/groups/public/@i/@sbg/@gs/@ir/documents/financial/cid_2238210.pdf [Accessed August 28, 2017].

Thebanks.eu, 2017. *Economy and banking sector of Sweden*. [online] Thebanks.eu: Country Profiles. Available at: https://thebanks.eu/countries/Sweden [Accessed August 28, 2017].

Wesley-James, N., Ingram, C., Källstrand, C., and Teigland, R., 2015. *Stockholm FinTech: An overview of the FinTech sector in the greater Stockholm region*. [online] Stockholm School of Economics. Available at: www.hhs.se/contentassets/b5823453b8fe4290828f-cc81189b6561/stockholm-fintech---june-2015.pdf [Accessed January 16, 2018].

Wikander, S., 2016. *Everything is changing, except one thing*. [online] Nordea: The Digital Hub. Available at: www.nordea.com/en/press-and-news/news-and-press-releases/the-digital-hub/2016/2016-12-06-everything-is-hanging-except-one-thing.html [Accessed August 28, 2017].

Williams-Grut, O., 2016. *3,000 bankers, techies, and investors held a summit in Europe this week—here's what everyone is talking about*. [online] Business Insider. Available at: www.businessinsider.com/money2020-europe-fintech-buzz-2016-4?r=UK&IR=T [Accessed August 28, 2017].

World Economic Forum, 2015. *The future of FinTech: A paradigm shift in small business finance*. [online] Global Agenda Council on the Future of Financing & Capital. Available at: www3.weforum.org/docs/IP/2015/FS/GAC15_The_Future_of_FinTech_Paradigm_Shift_Small_Business_Finance_report_2015.pdf [Accessed August 28, 2017].

Interviews

Olov Brandt, Strategic Partner at Nordea and Site Manager of the Nordea Startup Accelerator. Interviews held on January 23 and 24, 2017.

David Sonnek, Head of SEB Venture Capital. Interview held on February 10, 2017.

Emma Heimonen, Head of Digital Innovation at Swedbank. Interview held on March 23, 2017.

18 The role of venture capital in the success of the Swedish FinTech industry

Elizabeth Press

Introduction

In 2015, *The Financial Times* referred to Stockholm as a "unicorn factory" (Ahmed, 2015), and FinTech is an important driver in the Swedish innovation ecosystem. A small country relative to other European markets, Sweden has been punching above its weight in the FinTech arena. Between 2010 and 2015, Stockholm-based companies received 18 percent of all private placements in FinTech companies across Europe (Invest Stockholm, 2015). Furthermore, Sweden has over eight FinTech investments for every million inhabitants. This compares with 5.2 investments for every million inhabitants in the UK, which had the highest total investment during the corresponding period, according to Atomico (De Lange, 2016). Clearly, venture capital (VC) is an integral factor in Sweden's FinTech success. This chapter contains an introduction to VC and a discussion of factors that in general make a successful venture capitalist, as well as a more specific discussion on VC in the Nordics and Sweden. The chapter will also provide some detail on which segments are being financed, average deal sizes, and notable FinTech deals, as well as some important sector trends.

Although Sweden has experienced some large wins in the past years, there is increasing competition coming from other regions, such as London, Berlin, Frankfurt, Paris, Amsterdam, and Tel Aviv. An analysis of Sweden's strengths, weaknesses, opportunities, and threats regarding investments in FinTech will be explored in the chapter, as well as a discussion of which trends are industry hype and which are part of longer-term growth. The chapter will culminate in a discussion about the future of FinTech in Sweden and recommendations from a VC perspective.

The insights from the chapter are based on both primary and secondary research. The primary research consisted of interviews with the following seven venture capitalists active in the Swedish VC industry:

- Oscar C.A. Anderson, Head of Research & Analytics at NFT Ventures.
- Henrik Aspén, Partner at Verdane Capital Advisors

- Joakim Dal, Investment Manager at GP Bullhound.
- Sofia Ericsson Holm, Investor at Industrifonden.
- Dan Ouchterlony, Investment Manager at Schibsted Growth.
- Ashley Lundström, Venture Lead at EQT Ventures.
- Pär-Jörgen Pärson, Partner at Northzone, currently residing in New York.

Secondary research consisted of a review of academic literature, reports from consulting and research firms, reports from a venture capitalist firm, and articles from the media, as well as profiles and publications from business angels and business angel networks on social media.

Introduction to venture capital

VC is a type of financing provided to startups and small businesses with perceived long-term-growth potential. VC is a high-risk business due to the high rate of failure inherent in businesses based on technological and/or business innovations Venture capitalists earn money through exits, when they sell their portfolio companies to other investors or industrial buyers. In some cases, exits take the form of an initial public offering (IPO), which means the shares of the formerly private startup are offered to the public (Koba, 2012). Most VCs have the goal of exiting an investment, and thereby earning a multiple of the money they invested in the portfolio company. Harvard Business School research found that 75 percent of venture-backed start-ups in the US failed (Gage, 2012). Because venture capitalists lose money when a startup fails, the survival of a VC firm is dependent on being able to earn high multiples on investment on a small number of surviving companies in their portfolios.

The VC process starts when the entrepreneurial team, which is usually the team that founded the company, submits their business plan to the VC. If the VC thinks the business plan has potential, they will perform due diligence, which is a detailed audit of the potential investment object. After the due diligence is completed, which means the VC firm has confirmed all the important facts and believes that the startup will not only survive, but can earn the desired multiple upon exit, the VC firm will pledge an investment, receive a portion of the firm's equity, and usually representation on the firm's board (Roth, 2012). At this point, the VC becomes a part owner of the firm, and thus has a say in the management decisions of the startup. The investment horizon for VC investments is generally three to seven years (Venture-Capital-Investment.co.uk, 2011), after which they exit. It is only at this point, if the portfolio firm survives, that most VC firms earn their money.

VC is important to any innovation ecosystem because this source of funding is provided by investors who understand emerging technologies. Venture capitalists also possess know-how to identify good entrepreneurs, and networks with customers, service providers, and potential partners, as well as extensive go-to-market knowledge, that help entrepreneurs succeed.

Types of venture capital

The classification of risk capital is based on Isaksson's (2006) paper *Studies on Venture Capital* (see Figure 18.1). Risk capital is equity that is invested either in public equity, such as equity that is available on a stock market, or private equity. Private equity is in turn divided up into three major subcategories, two of which encompass venture capital: formal and informal (Isaksson, 2006, p.16).

Informal VC usually consists of private individuals investing their own money (Isaksson, 2006, p.16), which can take the form of angel investors. Angel investors are generally high-net-worth individuals who use their own wealth or a pool of individual investors' wealth to invest in early-stage investments. Angel investors can organize themselves into business angel networks, angel funds, or invest as individuals.

Formal VC consists of investments made by professional firms, usually a VC firm focused on early-stage investments (Isaksson, 2006, p.16). The type of legal entity the VC firm takes can depend on the geography, legal environment, and other factors. Usually, they are set up as a partnership.

VC firms generally employ a small team of experts who focus on early-stage investments and rely on their formal and informal networks of mentors and service providers to help them with the investment process, industry knowledge, and support the growth of their portfolio companies. Corporations have entered the VC market as well, setting up funds referred to in this chapter as corporate VCs, which are often funded from assets that are on the company's balance sheet with the goal of investing in new technologies.

Accelerators are another vehicle through which startups get funding and/or mentoring. Accelerators generally have a structured program for a cohort of startups who apply and often take equity, making them a form of formal VC. However, accelerators often take fees and other types of non-equity remuneration.

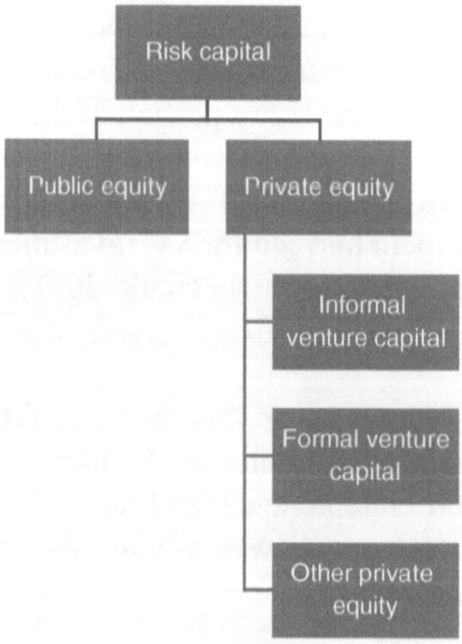

Figure 18.1 A classification of risk capital, private equity, and venture capital

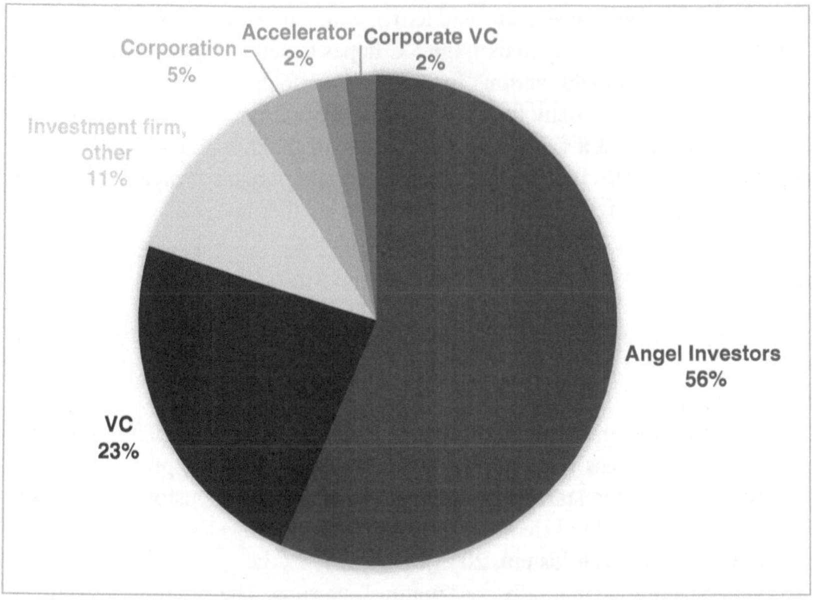

Figure 18.2 Investor type by % of deals, 2015 and 2016

There are other types of private equity as well, such as management buyouts and other forms of private equity that focus on later-stage investments (Isaksson, 2006, p.16).

Public equity consists of investments in public companies that typically are traded on stock exchanges (Isaksson, 2006, p.16).

According to Industrifonden's recent report on investor activity in Sweden, angels and VCs fund the highest number of tech startups, providing more investment in terms of number of deals than all the other actors combined (Bergström, 2016).

The investment process

Raising capital is the first step VC firms need to take to enable their investment activities. Raising capital is the process by which VC firms secure the money for their funds that they will use to invest in the portfolio companies. VC firms often turn to pension funds, banks, and insurance companies for funding.

Informal forms of VC, such as business angels, can rely on their own private wealth or pooled private wealth.

After the funds have been raised, the VCs scout for startups to invest in. The ability to identify and attract the best investment objects is core to the success of a VC. As described above, the VC must identify and conduct due diligence on their investment object.

Through funding and active management, the VC aims to enable the portfolio company to grow. VCs not only position themselves to the providers of capital, but to the entrepreneurs as well. Each VC brings their offering of expert service providers, mentor networks, management style, and terms, with which they need to both attract and manage entrepreneurs. Upon exit, the VC hopes to sell its equity for a multiple. The equity invested can take various forms, such as stocks, warrants, options, and convertible notes. After usually four to six years, the VC hopes that this equity can be converted into cash at a value that is a multiple of the investment. Although the initial public offering (IPO) is the most prestigious and publicized means of exiting, most exits take the form of sale to a company or to another investor.

Funding rounds

Seed investing is the initial round for startups. Seed funding is usually small and aimed at research and development of the initial product (Goldstein, 2015). This is the riskiest round of funding.

Startup capital generally goes to startups once they have completed the market analysis and business plan, as well as developing a sample product. At this stage, companies want to start marketing activities to acquire customers. The VC funding can also be used to hire more personnel, further develop the product, and conduct more research (Goldstein, 2015).

Early-stage capital is generally for "mature" startups. The funding here can be significant, and generally goes toward manufacturing and production, sales, and further marketing activities (Goldstein, 2015).

The expansion stage is about perfecting the competitive advantage and scaling the business on a global and/or industry-wide level. The startups generally have a commercially viable product and need funding to diversify and expand into new markets (Goldstein, 2015).

Startups can also raise further rounds of funding as they develop their business (Goldstein, 2015).

What makes a good venture capitalist?

Managing VC investments is different from managing other types of investments because of the high risk and degree of soft skills needed to succeed. Because markets for emerging technology come with inherent unknowns, qualitative abilities to assess markets, business ideas, teams, and individuals are key ingredients for good venture capitalists, and consequently a healthy innovation ecosystem.

Success in the VC business is largely reliant on the ability to identify good teams of entrepreneurs who are able to bring disruption to the market. The VCs are an integral player in identifying the right people and entrepreneurial ability.

A good VC is able "to identify driven and fantastic entrepreneurs, individuals who are strong enough to navigate the journey that being in a startup is," states Ashley Lundström, Venture Lead, EQT Ventures.

Venture capitalists are in the business of choosing the investment objects that will create a high rate of return. Finding and investing in startups is what they refer to as "deals." Dan Ouchterlony, Investment Manager at Schibsted Growth, explains that "Access to the best deals and making sure your value proposition to entrepreneurs is unique" are important for the success of a VC.

Ashley Lundström, Venture Lead at EQT Ventures, mentions that a large part of what makes a VC in Sweden is finding the best entrepreneurs in the context of the Swedish culture:

> The best entrepreneurs have humility but have something extra about them . . . The Swedish way is humble, and culturally people aren't driven to stand out from the crowd. VCs invest in trying to build a moonshot and companies that very much want to stand out. Swedish entrepreneurs have built a number of fantastic companies, and there's starting to be more of a desire among Swedish entrepreneurs to build those standout companies.

The small size of the Swedish market also impacts the selection of companies, according to Oscar C.A. Anderson from NFT Ventures. "The Swedish market is so small that if you want to make the big returns you need as a VC firm, you have to pick companies that can eventually scale internationally."

What makes a good VC in FinTech?

Because of the breadth of technology and complexity of the industry it is trying to disrupt, FinTech is a domain that requires more industry knowledge on the part of the VC as compared to other domains. An investment in the category "FinTech" can refer to a broad spectrum of technologies and services, from front-end applications to full-stack back-end solutions. FinTech is an area that entails significant capital requirements, as well as a deep knowledge of the current regulatory environment. Many of the respondents pointed to the need for deeper knowledge in the FinTech industry compared to that in other domains.

"You need to have the ability to see through the complexities in a complex industry . . . try to disrupt with simplicity", states Pär-Jörgen Pärson, Partner at Northzone.

Oscar C.A. Anderson, Head of Research & Analytics at NFT Ventures, notes that the business model needs to be much more compelling in FinTech than in other industries due to the lack of perceived "fun" inherent in FinTech from a general consumer's point of view. He states, "Consumers don't think FinTech is fun. Therefore, the business model needs to be very good to make consumers switch from what they were using before."

The success of the startup is reliant on their ability to convince people to adopt the innovation that the startup is trying to bring to market. For this reason, Oscar C.A. Anderson notes that the business-to-business (B2B) space in FinTech can offer deeper opportunity than the consumer market. He explains, "We found that many of the most profitable companies are B2B. It might be easier to get businesses to switch to new solutions."

The industry knowledge necessary to be successful in FinTech also increases the importance of the VC brand to the success of a startup. "The VC brand is very important not only to entrepreneurs and co-investors, but also to partners and clients (primarily B2B and B2B2C), to bring credibility, goodwill and exclusivity," states Sofia Ericsson Holm, Investor at Industrifonden.

Overview of VC investments in the FinTech industry in the Nordics and in Sweden

The number of deals is increasing in the Nordics, but the deals are smaller

As a region, the Nordics have become a FinTech innovation hotspot. In April 2016, TechCrunch reported that nearly one in every 10 investments in the Nordics was made in FinTech (Mitzner, 2016).

Looking at Sweden, Denmark, Finland, Norway, and Iceland, the number of VC FinTech investments has been increasing in recent years in the Nordic region (see Figure 18.3). In 2016, 67 deals were projected to be made, up from 19 deals in 2014. In 2014, EUR 232 million was invested; 2014 is the year of Sweden's two blockbuster investments. The value of the EUR 106 million investments made into Klarna and EUR 46.6 million investments made into iZettle together surpassed the combined value of the other 17 investments, which totaled EUR 53.7 million, almost threefold (Jonsdottir et al., 2017, pp.20–22). Investment volume in subsequent years did not top the volume experienced in 2014.

Because the increase in the number of investments has been happening at an earlier stage of the FinTech startup, deal sizes have been decreasing. In 2014, the average deal size was EUR 12 million, while in 2016 it had fallen to EUR 2 million (see Figure 18.3).

Neil S.W. Murray, the founder of the Nordic Web, told TechCrunch that according to an analysis of the Nordic Web's data, a majority of Nordic FinTech investments are in the USD 1–3 million size range:

> indicating that a high number of healthy-sized seed rounds are being raised, and showing that despite the increasing amount of investment, the ecosystem is still at a fairly early-stage and the Nordics potential to be a FinTech hub is still in its infancy.
>
> (Mitzner, 2016)

Sweden has dominated the Nordic FinTech investment landscape. Out of the total investments made in the Nordic region, 57 percent have been in Sweden (Jonsdottir et al., 2017, p.24).

"This is quite the achievement for a region that has long been associated with gaming, enterprise SaaS, and health and wellness as the dominant verticals," Neil S.W. Murray, the founder of the Nordic Web, told TechCrunch (Mitzner, 2016).

Despite the high level of activity in FinTech in the Nordic region, the European private equity market is still dominated by the UK when it comes to large deals (Go4Venture, 2017, p.12).

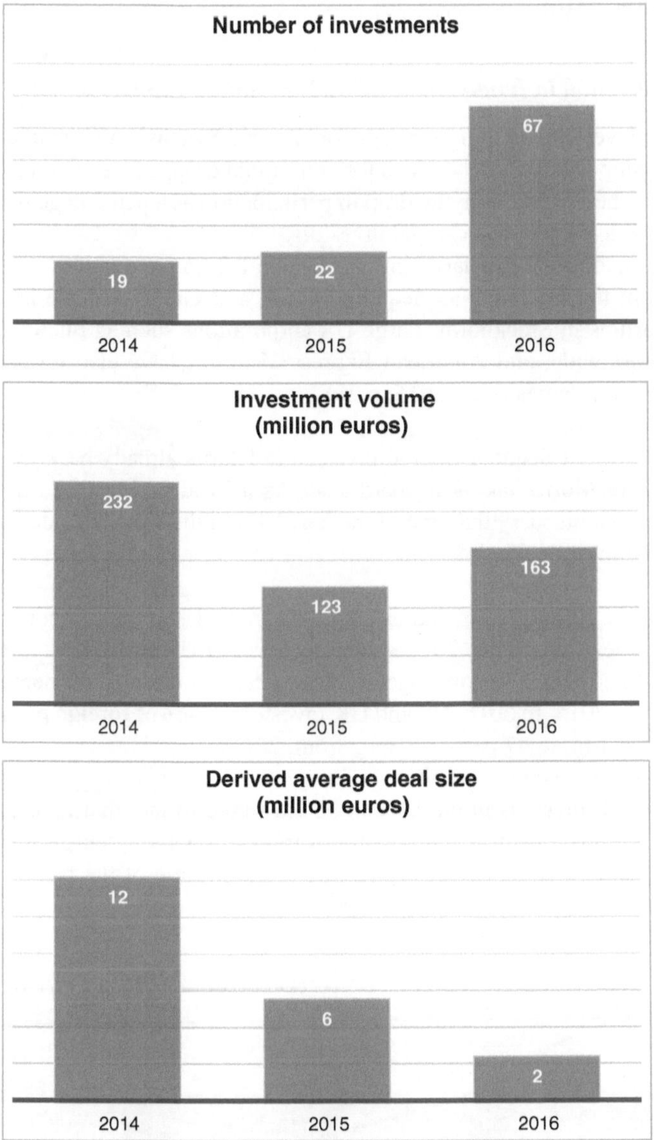

Figure 18.3 Overview of Nordic FinTech investments

Scandinavia has seen fewer large deals on a year-to-year basis. Deals above EUR 7.5 million were 15 percent of all deals in 2015 and 7 percent of all deals in 2016. Year-on-year, Sweden has seen fewer deals at a significantly lower value, with the average deal size going down by EUR 56 million (Go4Venture, 2017, p.12). As discussed later, this decrease in average deal size, overall, could be at least in part attributed to the growing amount of seed funding seen in FinTech in 2016 (Bergström, 2016).

Foreign participation in funding in the Swedish venture capital market

Although the level of foreign participation in the Swedish VC market has increased, the proportion of rounds with foreign capital dropped (see Figure 18.4). As discussed in the next section, the drop in participation as a percentage of deals is due to an increase in domestic angel investors.

The past decade has seen a large influx of capital from prestigious VC firms. Big names from the US, such as Sequoia, Accel, and Greylock have invested in FinTech startups in Stockholm. Large US corporations such as Intel Capital, Mastercard Worldwide, and American Express Ventures have also invested in Stockholm (Wesley-James et al., 2015, p.20).

> I remember when Sequoia Capital invested in Klarna already back in 2010, with Michael Moritz taking a board seat. As a local investor, it was both inspiring and a bit scary that one of the best VCs in the world decided to put their capital into Stockholm.

Foreign capital is coming from increasingly diversified sources. According to Industrifonden, year over year, 2016 saw a decrease in US and UK dominance from 2015. US and UK investors together accounted for close to 60 percent of foreign activity in 2015. In 2016, US and UK investors' share of foreign participation dropped by a fifth to 47 percent (Bergström, 2016).

According to the venture capitalists interviewed in this chapter, foreign interest in Swedish investment targets can be attributed to fact that investing in technology is a global business, the quality of innovation and talent in Sweden, and the overall strong economy of the Nordic region. Some of the respondents

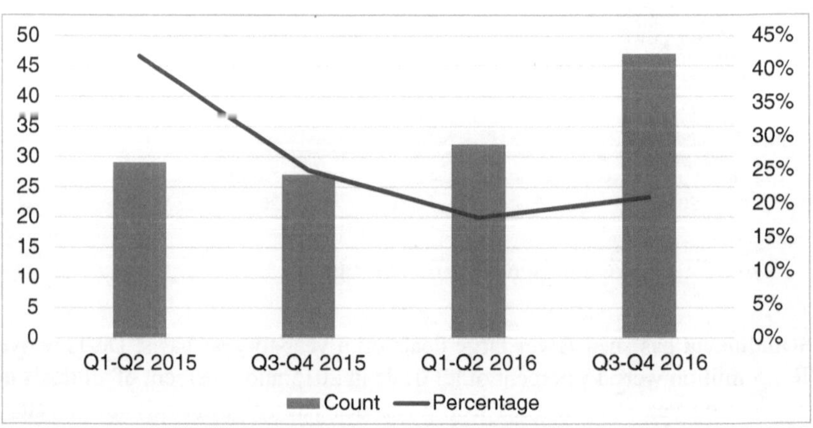

Figure 18.4 Funding rounds with foreign participation

also mentioned the fact that valuations in Sweden have been lower than those in the UK. This last reason might become less compelling, however. As discussed in the following section, due to the attention Swedish FinTech has been getting, valuations in the Swedish FinTech sector are now rising.

History of FinTech investments in Sweden

Swedes have a history of innovating in the financial services industry (see Figure 18.5). In 1959, the four major Swedish banks established the Bankgiro, a proprietary clearing system. The Bankgiro was operated by the Bankgirocentralen, which was owned by the large Swedish banks (Bankgirot, 2017). In 1984, Optionsmäklarna, the first exchange to enable remote trading and one of the first electronic exchanges, was created. The marriage of innovation in the IT and financial services industries was exemplified in 2008 when OM and Nasdaq merged to become the OMX Group (Wesley-James et al., 2015, p.10).

Handelsbanken pioneered digital banking in 1997 when they were the second bank in the world and the first bank in Europe to launch Internet banking services (Jonsdottir et al., 2017, p.27). Early adoption of technology in the financial services sector from a broad base of consumers in the Nordic region continued with subsequent innovations. According to the Deloitte Global Mobile Consumer Survey 2016, 57 percent of Nordic citizens are using mobile banking, when the European average is just 44 percent (Jonsdottir et al., 2017, p.27).

With a goal of becoming a cashless society, only about 20 percent of all payments in Sweden are done with cash. The worldwide average for cash payments is 75 percent (Jonsdottir et al., 2017, p.27).

The combination of a history of innovations in financial services, a high-quality public education system, and government subsidies in programs availing personal computers (PCs) and Internet connectivity to the entire population has created the right recipe for a tech innovation hotspot.

"In the 1990s, the government subsidised home PC purchases so that all households could be equipped with a computer. The young people now creating startups grew up with that culture," Marta Sjögren from Northzone told *The Technologist* (Gaitzsch, 2016).

The fact that Sweden is a small economy contributes to the global thinking many entrepreneurs have from an early stage. If a startup wants to succeed, it needs to be present in markets other than Sweden.

"We think globally from the outset," Niklas Zennström, co-founder of Skype, told *The Telegraph* (Davidson, 2015). Stockholm's successful startups "all realized the domestic market is not big enough," (Davidson, 2015). According to Jessica Stark, director of the Incubator SUP46, Sweden's social system is a factor driving entrepreneurship. "Sweden's social model also plays an important role," says Stark in *The Technologist*. "The entrepreneurs starting out know they'll never wind up on the street. They can take risks and dare to be creative" (Gaitzsch, 2016).

The triumph of the emergence of Stockholm as a global technology hub can be exemplified by five major unicorns, including Klarna. Unicorn is a term for

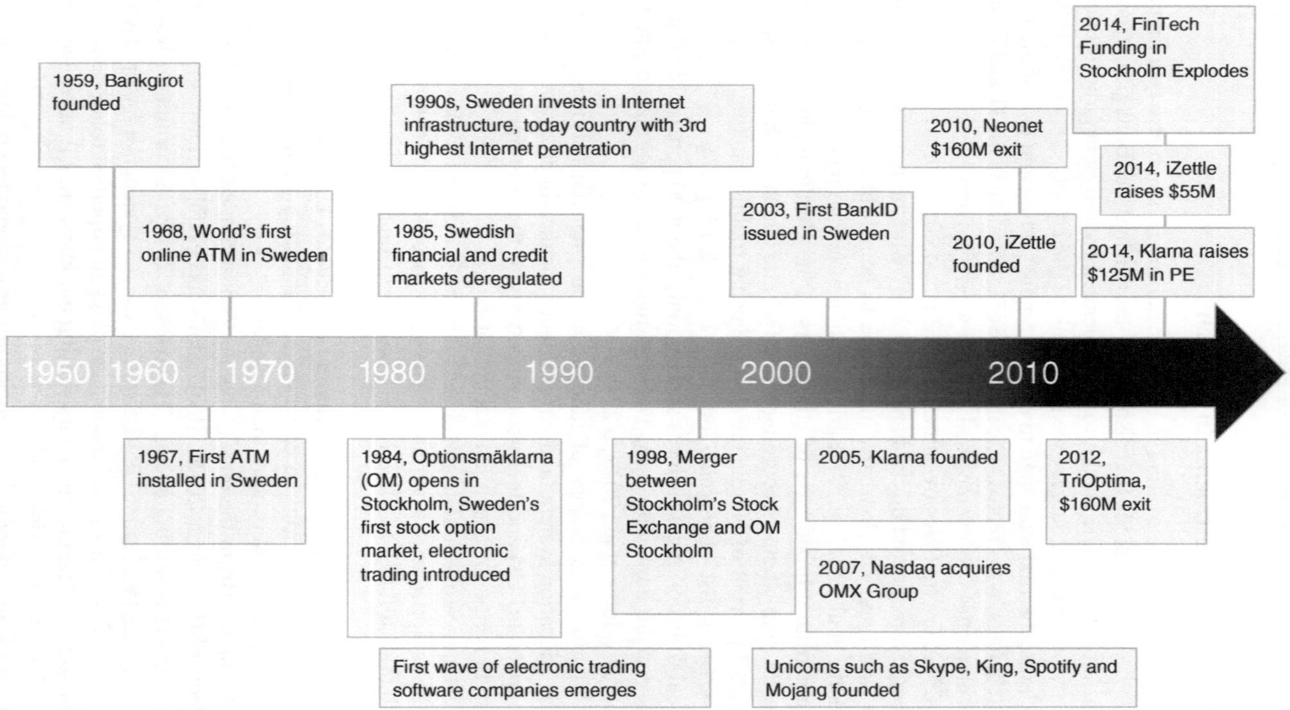

Figure 18.5 Important historical events related to FinTech in Stockholm

Source: Reproduced from Wesley-James et al. (2015, p.10).

a startup whose valuation is worth more than 1 billion dollars (Gaitzsch, 2016). These blockbuster startups are: Spotify, Skype, Mojang, King and Klarna:

- *Spotify*: A leading music-streaming service launched in 2008. In June 2015, Spotify raised USD 526 million, bringing its valuation to USD 8.53 billion.
- *Mojang*: A video game developer founded in 2009. Microsoft bought Mojang for USD 2.5 billion.
- *Skype*: Swedish entrepreneur Niklas Zennström co-founded the online voice call and video chat service with Estonian programmer Jaan Tallinn. After first being purchased by eBay, Skype was eventually acquired by Microsoft in 2011 for USD 8.5 billion.
- *King*: A video-game company founded in 2003 that has created more than 200 games. The firm is listed on the New York Stock Exchange with a market capitalization of USD 5.5 billion.
- *Klarna*: Outlined in further detail below.

Success stories such as the ones listed above proved that entrepreneurship is a valid career path for many Swedes. Broader acceptance of entrepreneurship, together with a culture that embraces technology, great technological infrastructure, and one of the best education systems in the world, were all important factors for the success of Stockholm as a startup hub and leadership in the FinTech industry.

Two big names in the Swedish FinTech ecosystem are Klarna and iZettle.

- Klarna is a startup that provides e-commerce payment solutions for merchants and shoppers that has raised USD 125 million from investment funds such as Sequoia Capital and General Atlantic. In April 2016, Klarna was valued at over USD 2.25 billion and had raised USD 291.33 million in six rounds from 12 investors (Mitzner, 2016).
- iZettle, a mobile payments company, has raised more than USD 55 million from investment funds such as Greylock Partners, Santander Innoventures, and Northzone (Techfoliance Team, 2016). In April 2016, iZettle had raised USD 244.04 million in nine rounds from 16 investors (Mitzner, 2016).

FinTech is an area of innovation that has huge potential, both in terms of financial returns and the power to transform how people all over the world do business and conduct their personal finances. The next section will take a deeper look at how Sweden is positioning itself within the FinTech industry from a VC's perspective.

Development of VCs investing in FinTech in Sweden

As discussed in the first section of this chapter, the most common types of VCs that operate in Sweden are angel investors and VC firms. In terms of deal volumes, angel investors are the most active, having been responsible for 56 percent of Sweden's deal volume in number of deals in 2016. VC firms made up 23 percent (Bergström, 2016, p.6). Other investors include corporations, accelerators and corporate VCs (Bergström, 2016, p.6). Angel investors have been the segment of early-stage investors that has seen the most growth. The number of angel investments in FinTech was less than 200 in 2015. In 2016 that number more than doubled to 400 according to Sofia Ericsson Holm from Industrifonden.

According to Industrifonden, one of the most active venture capital investors in Sweden, FinTech comprised 12 percent of all VC deals in Sweden in 2016 (Bergström, 2016). At a sectorial level, FinTech remained the most popular vertical by number of deals, followed by e-commerce, gaming, and digital health/telehealth (Bergström, 2016, p.10). The Nordic Tech List reports that FinTech has been the most active segment for tech investments, with 20 investments in the Nordics for the first quarter of 2017 (Riminton, 2017). The number of angel investments in FinTech was less than 200 in 2015. In 2016, that number more than doubled to 400, according to Sofia Ericsson Holm from Industrifonden.

On a European level, Swedish VC has been catching up to German and UK VC in terms of participation in investments in FinTech deals in 2016. NFT Ventures was ranked number six in a study by KPMG and CB Insights regarding the most active VC investors in European FinTech companies Q3 2015 to Q3 2016. Northzone was ranked as number 10 (KPMG and CB Insights, 2016, p.67).

Out of the 89 individual FinTech investments that Deloitte tracked between 2014 and 2016, payments were the largest segment by number of deals. Payments were also the sector of Sweden's two famous FinTech players, iZettle and Klarna. Personal financial management and investment management/robo-advisory were also important areas of investment activity (see Figure 18.6).

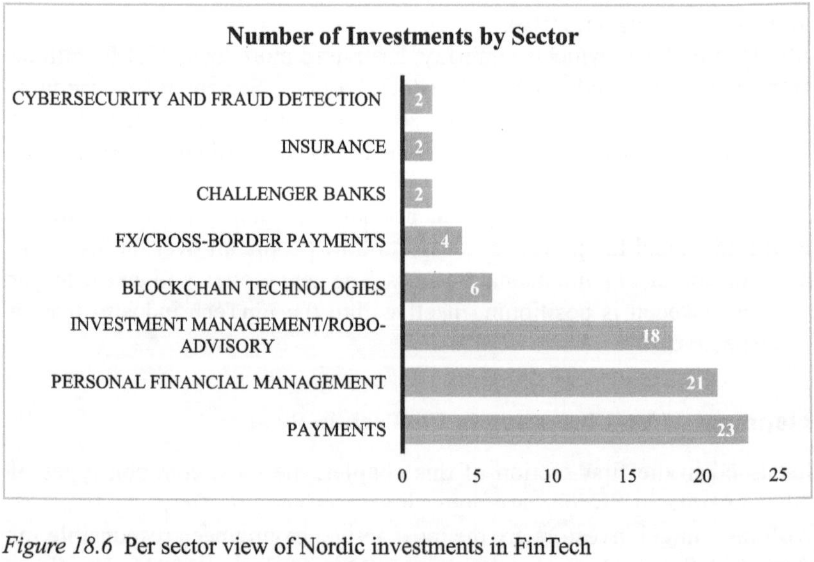

Figure 18.6 Per sector view of Nordic investments in FinTech

"For FinTech companies coming out of Sweden, most investors would expect it to be a well-designed consumer product," says Ashley Lundström from EQT Ventures.

Although there have been impressive deals being made in the blockchain space, some of the respondents pointed out that other regions in Europe have at least caught up with Sweden. According to Outlier Ventures, the UK is the most important base for blockchain startups in Europe, and Berlin is catching up (Lundy, 2016). The many angel investors in Sweden come from diverse backgrounds. As the profile of the startup scene and FinTech grow, industry veterans and celebrities alike want to get involved. Here are a few examples:

Jane Walerud is a serial entrepreneur, and was one of the first angel investors in Klarna (Startup Angels, 2017).

Hampus Jakobsson is another entrepreneur who has been an angel investor for multiple Scandinavian startups, including Holvi, which was acquired by BBVA (AngelList, 2017).

Table 18.1 Examples of VCs important for the FinTech industry in Sweden who were not interviewed for this study

Name	*Description*	*Headquarters*	*Funds raised*	*Investments*
Almi Invest	A VC that does seed investments	Stockholm	Unknown	63 investments in 52 companies
Collector Ventures	The investment vehicle of Collector Bank	Gothenburg	Unknown	6 investments in 6 companies
Creandum	An early-stage VC firm investing in innovative and fast-growing technology companies	Stockholm	USD 535 million	79 investments in 52 companies
SEB Private Equity	A private equity firm that does early-stage venture and later-stage venture investments	Stockholm	Unknown	9 investments in 6 companies
SEB Venture Capital	VC that does early-stage venture and later-stage venture investments	Stockholm	Invested over SEK 3 billion since 1995 (SEB, 2017)	44 investments in 29 companies
Spintop Ventures	An investment firm investing in early-stage Nordic technology companies	Stockholm	USD 30 million	12 investments in 8 companies

Table 18.2 VCs who participated in the interviews for this study

Name	*Description*	*Headquarters*	*Offices*	*Funds raised*	*Investments*
NFT Ventures	A VC focused on FinTech and loyalty products	Stockholm	Stockholm	Unknown	15 investments in 12 companies
GP Bullhound	A technology-focused merchant bank	London	London, San Francisco, Stockholm, Berlin, Manchester and Paris	Unknown	49 investments in 42 companies
Industrifonden	A Nordic-based evergreen VC firm	Stockholm	Stockholm	USD 500 million	97 investments in 71 companies
EQT Ventures	Part of EQT, the global private equity group	Stockholm	Stockholm, London, Amsterdam, and Luxembourg	USD 633.3 million	18 investments in 15 companies
Northzone	A VC that performs seed, early-stage venture, later-stage venture, and private equity investments	Stockholm	London, Stockholm, Oslo, and New York	USD 1.15 billion	118 investments in 81 companies
Verdane Capital Advisors	A lower mid-market growth	Oslo	Oslo, Norway, Stockholm, and Helsinki	USD 355.57 million	41 investments in 37 companies
Schibsted Growth	A corporate-backed VC that invests in digital companies	Stockholm	Stockholm, Oslo, and Paris	Unknown	3 investments in 3 companies

Mattias Weinhandl is a former professional ice hockey player who was an angel investor invested in Betalo in 2016 (Nordic 9, 2017).

> Many successful entrepreneurs return to the ecosystem as angels, playing an important role as investors, mentors and advisors. They are effectively paying it forward to a new generation of entrepreneurs. There are many examples such as Jane Walerud and Hampus Jacobsson.

The following are formal VCs that are not included in the interviews in this report. They are, however, important investors in the Swedish FinTech industry. The information in Table 18.1 was sourced from Crunchbase (2017) in May 2017.

The following is a list of VC firms and corporate VCs that participated in this report. Branch offices are important here, as the report will explore cross-ecosystem pollination based on the VCs in this study's responses. Funds raised and investments were sourced from Crunchbase (2017).

A VC perspective of the Swedish FinTech industry

Motivations for investing in FinTech

The primary motivation driving investments in FinTech is financial return. Other motivations can be strategic in nature, such as entry into new business areas and access to new technologies.

As noted above, the number of angel investors in Sweden more than doubled from 2015 to 2016 as this group of investors began to notice the potential of high return in the industry. Sofia Ericsson Holm, Investor at Industrifonden, explains this in the following way:

> I expect they [the Angel Investors] see a window of opportunity with the digitalization of banking and financial services and want to find the next Klarna. Many of the angels have professional experience from the traditional financial services industry and look to find disruptors.

While there are a large number of angel investors, the largest amount of investments in terms of capital invested in FinTech comes from institutional investments, again with the goal to reap financial returns. "Most capital is invested with a view to get a return. There are second-order priorities like strategic learning for corporate VCs and giving back to young founders from angel investors, but mostly it is to get a return," states Dan Ouchterlony, Investment Manager at Schibsted Growth.

Incumbent VCs, such as the investment arms of SEB and Citibank, have been cited as investing in FinTech ventures in order to develop their businesses and better understand the disruptive forces in their industries. SEB venture capital, which is the VC arm of SEB, has a focus on FinTech, specifically investments in products and services that "offer competitive advantages that are sustainable over time" (Crunchbase, 2017). Pär-Jörgen Pärson, a partner at Northzone, explains about incumbents that invest in FinTech, "They want to understand what is going on and what can disrupt their core business." NFT Ventures, which is the only VC that is focused on FinTech in our study, points to investments being made for strategic purposes as a way for large companies to access disruptive technology. Two of their investors are Bonnier, a Swedish media group, and Collector Bank, which is a challenger in the retail banking industry. "The investment is more strategic; they (large companies who invest in disruptive technology) don't only invest for immediate return," says Oscar C.A. Anderson, Head of Research & Analytics at NFT Ventures.

The role of foreign funding

The share of Nordic capital going into FinTech startups in the Nordic region has gone up from 32 percent in 2014 to 80 percent in 2016 (Jonsdottir et al., 2017, p.17). This might be attributed to the maturing innovation ecosystem as more domestic investors emerge with the confidence to invest in FinTech ventures. Deloitte points out that these investments are largely focused on earlier-stage ventures.

Even though domestic capital tends to be present in the early stages, VC funding from foreign investors has been very important for companies as they enter their expansion phase. Pär-Jörgen Pärson, Partner at Northzone, says:

> iZettle got access to much bigger capital pools thanks to (them reaching out to) international capital . . . This enabled much larger growth potential than if they only received local capital. A key success factor is to get access to international capital early and in building the business.

Sofia Ericsson Holm from Industrifonden points to the importance of having both foreign and local capital. She states:

> For Swedish-founded startups with an international agenda, like our portfolio company Qapital, it is equally important to attract local top tier VCs early on and add US venture capital for later rounds. It's a growth financing recipe. In these companies, local VCs add the most value in earlier stages (pre-A/A rounds) because they can be more active and patient than most US investors. If small early rounds drive up the valuation too much, it will increase the failure risk in raising later rounds.

Cross-ecosystem pollination

The VC industry is global and relies on international networks. Many VC firms are active in multiple markets, and their investment portfolio companies may be global as well, especially those in Europe. All of the VCs included in our study

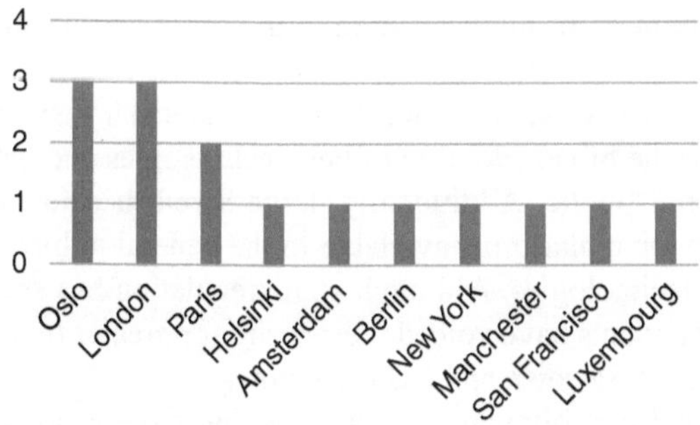

Figure 18.7 Presence of VCs in our study as measured by geographic presence of branch offices

had offices in Stockholm. The second most common cities were Oslo and London, followed by Paris.

The presence of offices roughly corresponds to the insights the respondents gave regarding cross-ecosystem pollination (see Figure 18.7). Similar to any other innovation ecosystem, the Stockholm ecosystem looks elsewhere for inspiration and ideas. The London ecosystem was the most commonly mentioned source of inspiration, followed by the US ecosystems in New York and the West Coast, then by Berlin. Norway is another regional hub. Some of the respondents said that professionals in the Oslo startup hub often look to Stockholm, which respondents described as larger, for inspiration.

Pär-Jörgen Pärson from Northzone talked about the necessity of cross-pollination and looking at what is happening in other markets. He notes, "A success criterion is to look at how things are done outside your market. You don't have the luxury of just addressing your local market, especially in the digital space." Pär-Jörgen Pärson reflected on his own cross-pollination that he brings to the New York ecosystem as a European venture capitalist, having funded non-FinTech companies such as Spotify. He explains, "The best FinTech hub in the world is London. People want to talk to us because we know iZettle and the big successes in Europe."

Exposure to different ecosystems leads to the need for more transparency and subsequent added pressure for quick growth. Oscar C.A. Anderson at NFT Ventures states:

> Entrepreneurs copy each other . . . Sometimes a business takes off in the US, and there are clones popping up in different markets . . . A secondary effect is that if they (startups) don't scale fast enough, somebody will steal their idea.

Key innovations and environmental factors

This section will discuss the innovations and environmental factors that enable future growth and innovation. These factors are important because they are conducive to the development of an ecosystem with attractive investment opportunities for VCs.

Several innovations have been key enablers for the FinTech industry insofar as they have been important for the broad adoption of new technologies and behaviors on the part of the general public. Additionally, large Swedish banks have collaboratively created innovative platforms available to the general public, thus promoting usage of mobile technologies. Although some regulation has spurred innovation, a few of the respondents have voiced their desire for greater transparency and dialogue on the part of Swedish and EU regulators.

The respondents mentioned the following innovations that have enabled the Swedish FinTech industry.

- *BankID*: There is a nationwide two-factor ID system. That means that in Sweden, there is a system that allows people to identify themselves with a two-step verification process, as opposed to a one-step verification process with, for example, only a password. Around 80 percent of people online have access to this technology, according to Dan Ouchterlony. BankID is an enabler for startups to launch secure mobile products with low friction. Security can be a double-edged sword for FinTechs. On one hand, customers will shy away from products and services they perceive as lacking in security. On the other hand, authentication processes are often hard to use and can deter usage. With a nationwide two-factor ID system, Swedish FinTech startups do not have to develop their unique authentication method, nor do they have to train their potential customers to use a new authentication system. In other markets, such as Germany, security concerns have been a large obstacle to wide-scale adoption of mobile platforms for financial products.
- *Swish*: Swish is a payment platform developed through a collaborative effort among Sweden's largest banks that has gained broad usage in Sweden. According to several respondents, Swish has had a large impact on banks, VCs, and entrepreneurs. Swish has a broad user base among the population. Because of this broad adoption, Swedish consumers are generally used to mobile banking and peer-to-peer payments. Because Swish has already driven an important change in consumer behavior, some of the respondents were positive about the Swedish consumers being open to further innovations in these spaces and perhaps other areas as well.
- *Blockchain*: Blockchain and Bitcoin had a mixed response among the respondents. Some VCs have shown enthusiasm for the technology, especially beyond its application as a cryptocurrency. Others have said that the investment required for a rollout of the infrastructure sufficient to make the blockchain a standard was too large for them to fund and that the banks would be more likely to fund an internal application.
- *Peer-to-peer (P2P) lending*: This area has also received mixed response. Some VCs mentioned that P2P lending addresses inefficiencies in the market and opens lending to new participants. Others have pointed to skepticism in the market due to fraud cases.

Key environmental factors

The Swedish banking and insurance industries are highly concentrated. Concentration is usually a disadvantage to consumers due to oligarchic powers of a few large companies in one space. In the case of the Swedish FinTech industry, their existence can have positive effects. Henrik Aspén, Partner at Verdane Capital Advisors, explains, "If four banks agree it is a good solution, they can launch it. It is easy for them to have standards." Swish, mentioned above, is a recent example of such collaboration, as was the establishment of the Bankgiro back in the 1950s.

Even if ideas are global, regulations are local. Several of the respondents have pointed to the US and UK as important geographies that are influencing the FinTech industry in Sweden. In a regulation-driven industry, even global ideas need to be translated into local products. VCs and the entrepreneurs they invest in are reliant on the regulators. PSD2 is a directive that, among other factors, forces banks to open up their APIs, enabling other providers to offer services on top of the bank's infrastructure. As PSD2 will come into effect in January 2018, Deloitte forecasted in its report *FinTech in the Nordics: A Deloitte Review* (Jonsdottir et al., 2017) that this directive will increase the collaboration between big banks and FinTechs, since the banks will be forced to open up their platforms to third parties. These third parties will very likely be FinTech companies (Jonsdottir et al., 2017, p.31).

Oscar C.A. Anderson from NFT Ventures explained that understanding how to be compliant is important when working with the regulators; however, navigating the regulations can often be a challenge in Sweden. He says:

> The Swedish financial supervisory authority, Finansinspektionen, is a black box. You submit an application, and up to three months later it gives you a yes or a no without support during the process. By contrast, the British Financial Conduct Authority provides continuous feedback and is able to assist during the application process to ensure compliance with its rules. All our portfolio companies want to follow the rules, but sometimes it is not entirely clear, even to people trained in corporate law, what the rules are until the financial supervisory authority explains them.

The EU level of regulation can add additional complexities for FinTech investors and their portfolio companies. Using PSD2 as an example, Oscar C.A. Anderson at NFT Ventures notes:

> The EU, through the European Banking Authority (EBA), is currently preparing its technical specifications for implementing the PSD2 directive. The most recent suggestion from March 2017 on regulatory technical standards involves banning the use of direct access via online bank interface, sometimes called screen scraping. This would be highly detrimental to the FinTech industry as innovation in the banking segment is based primarily on direct

access. Instead, the EBA wants to allow other technologies—but none of these have been extensively tested to date. This new uncertainty hurts the industry and is entirely manufactured by regulators.

Hype in FinTech?

Some of the respondents mentioned that FinTech itself was being hyped following high profiles such as Klarna. One VC mentioned that some entrepreneurs opportunistically classify their companies as FinTech with the hope of attaining a higher valuation.

P2P lending, as well as the blockchain and decentralized ledger technologies, were areas where some of the respondents saw hype but equally long-term potential in Sweden.

Innovative lending is an area where Sweden has seen a large amount of entrepreneurial activity. P2P lending and P2P payments are also areas that are becoming mainstream in mature markets. Gartner placed P2P payments as a technology that is climbing the slope of enlightenment in mature markets in their 2016 *Hype Cycle for Digital Banking Transformation* (Newton, 2016). The overall sentiment around P2P lending was positive despite a recent case of fraud by the Swedish FinTech TrustBuddy. Dan Ouchterlony at Schibsted Growth notes, "There has been concern about P2P lenders. They are in a bit of a tough place due to fraud with TrustBuddy. P2P has had a rough start." He did state, however, that he sees a long-term potential in the P2P lending space, while Joakim Dal, Investment Manager at GP Bullhound, notes, "P2P lending has the power to change how we think about banks and financial institutions. There are a lot of regulations that are being circumvented with that. It is taking away a lot of inefficiency."

Blockchains, decentralized ledgers, and artificial intelligence (AI) were also mentioned technologies that are currently hyped yet have long-term value. Gartner mentioned the blockchain as being at the peak of inflated expectations in their Hype Cycle for Digital Banking Transformation (Newton, 2016). This signifies that there mounting excitement around the technology and the possibilities, yet the exact business models that will monetize and scale these technologies have not yet been formed. Sofia Ericsson Holm at Industrifonden states,

> The decentralized ledger and AI technologies may also be hyped right now, but I still expect them to offer huge long-term value, but maybe in companies that are not born yet. I see that AI will become a commodity, undergoing the shift that software has done: from something unique to a commodity.

Strengths, weaknesses, opportunities, and threats of FinTech in Sweden

For this part, the VCs in our study were asked to evaluate the Swedish FinTech industry from a VC perspective, as opposed to a consumer or entrepreneur's perspective. The overall sentiment was positive, mostly pointing to a good economy and a skilled ecosystem. Worries did arise regarding regulation and the high level of recent buzz surrounding the Swedish FinTech ecosystem, and consequently higher valuations. Many of the VCs saw market and innovative opportunities in collaboration between FinTech startups and large Swedish banks. The below is a summary of their responses:

Strengths

- The overall strength of the Swedish economy.
- Local talent, including the high caliber of technical ability on the Swedish market, as well as the Swedish way of running and growing a company.
- The small market as a means of forcing entrepreneurs to internationalize early.
- Open-mindedness of Swedes to try new technologies and products, especially in the digital and mobile spaces.
- Bringing well-designed consumer products to market.
- Low-cost, compared to the London ecosystem.
- Lower valuations in Stockholm compared to London or New York.

Weaknesses

- A small market with a limited amount of growth a startup could achieve domestically.
- Limited talent as successful startups tend to take a large part of the available talent pool, especially those in technology and compliance jobs.
- High regulations and taxes, although some VCs mentioned that Swedish regulators have been open to FinTech innovations.
- Tight housing market as a potential hindrance to attracting and moving talent to the Stockholm ecosystem, similar to that of other larger cities.

Opportunities

- Banks as innovation partners, investors, and customers due to the oligarchical structure of the Swedish finance industry.
- Business development in the B2B space.
- Rolling out a standard in Sweden is easier compared with other, more fragmented financial services markets.
- Ability to engage with regulators and increased transparency and dialogue regarding compliance.
- PSD2 regulation leading to the opening of Swedish banking to third parties.

Threats

- Regulation unable to keep up on this new frontier, potentially hindering developments.
- Some potentially overvalued startups due to recent successes, as well as others inflating their valuations before being able to prove customer acquisition and retention and market success.

- Overestimation of the number of FinTech startups due to some companies classifying themselves as FinTechs to achieve higher valuations.
- Competition from other FinTech hubs in continental Europe, such as Frankfurt, Berlin, Paris, and Tel Aviv.

Conclusions and recommendations

In conclusion, the overall sentiment on the part of the VCs in the study was positive toward the Swedish FinTech ecosystem, pointing to strong fundamentals in the Swedish economy and good-quality entrepreneurs and professionals residing in Sweden. There was a level of concern about increased valuations in the Swedish FinTech industry, coupled with the possibility of a looming cyclical downturn in the economy, and that this might trickle down and lead to a downturn for FinTech. The impact of these two factors in the near to midterm future for startups who have not yet proven their ability to attract customers and generate returns is an area of concern for some of the VCs.

Despite much attention in the press regarding a possible advantage for Stockholm in the wake of Brexit, most VCs said it is too early to make predictions about the impact, or they did not believe that there would be a large impact. Some talked about other FinTech hubs in continental Europe, such as Paris and Frankfurt, benefiting from London's departure from the EU. Others pointed to London's prowess in the FinTech area/industry and its close relationship with the United States as a stabilizing factor that would not change with the Brexit decision.

Payments and innovative lending were areas that were mentioned as providing the most growth in the future. Swedish entrepreneurs know how to bring well-designed products to the market and disrupt markets that experience infrastructural and regulatory inefficiencies, according to many of the respondents. Robo-advisors were also mentioned as being a nascent sector with disruptive potential. In terms of regulation, PSD2 was mentioned as an area that would open up opportunities for new players while putting pressure on fees that banks have been charging customers.

Blockchain had mixed responses. Most of the VCs said that they see disruptive potential in the technology itself. However, some were not certain that Swedish FinTech startups would be the players who would bring blockchain to the mainstream. The large cost of actually making blockchain a standard infrastructure for the banking industry is one factor. Another factor is that other ecosystems are hard at work innovating in the blockchain space, and that Sweden has been losing its edge in this area.

Pär-Jörgen Pärson at Northzone took inspiration from his VC experience in New York, and encourages local government to be more active and confident in reaching out to the entrepreneurs. He notes, "Politicians in New York were proactive in reaching out. In Sweden, there is a passive role that local government plays."

As discussed above, some of the VCs expressed a desire for more transparency and less complexity from the regulator. Because FinTech and financial services companies in general are regulation-driven businesses, the ability to bring a product to market is contingent on compliance; thus, some of the respondents pointed toward improved dialogue with the regulators on both a Swedish and EU level.

"Ideas from the US have traveled across the Atlantic, but you still have to adapt to local regulations," says Joakim Dal from GP Bullhound. Many of the respondents also recommended that the incumbent banks increase their engagement with the Swedish FinTech ecosystem. For example, Dan Ouchterlony at Schibsted Growth suggested the following:

> There is opportunity for the banks to come online in terms of venture and FinTech. Banks such as SEB are making active investments. Nordea and Swedbank are also taking notice. Swedbank announced their first investment in FinTech in April 2017.

As for the entrepreneurs, many of the respondents pointed not only to the need for VC investment, but to the need for startups to offer new solutions that will attract customers, and that ultimately banks themselves could be great partners for startups:

> I think B2Bank offers a very compelling investment opportunity—there is an imminent need for improved internal efficiency and customer experience all over, plus a high ability and willingness to pay and a realization that they can't build it themselves.

Furthermore, Henrik Aspén at Verdane Capital Advisors recommends the following: "The ones [startups] that will be successful are the ones that will achieve reference infrastructure projects at a local bank."

Bibliography

Ahmed, M., 2015. Stockholm: The unicorn factory. *Financial Times*. [online] Available at: www.ft.com/content/e3c15066-cd77-11e4-9144-00144feab7de [Accessed August 29, 2017].

AngelList, 2017. *Hampus Jakobsson AngelList profile*. [online] AngelList. Available at: https://angel.co/hajak [Accessed August 30, 2017].

Bankgirot, 2017. *Bankgirot's history*. [online] Available at: www.bankgirot.se/en/about-bankgirot/about-us/bankgirots-history [Accessed August 29, 2017].

Bergström, B., 2016. *Swedish tech funding report 2016*. [online] Available at: http://industrifonden.com/wp-content/uploads/2017/01/Swedish-Tech-Funding-Report-2016.pdf [Accessed August 29, 2017].

Crunchbase, 2017. *Crunchbase: Discover innovative companies and the people behind them*. [online] Available at: www.crunchbase.com [Accessed August 29, 2017].

Davidson, L., 2015. How Sweden became the startup capital of Europe. *The Telegraph*, [online] June 28. Available at: www.telegraph.co.uk/finance/newsbysector/mediatechnologyandtelecoms/11689464/How-Sweden-became-the-startup-capital-of-Europe.html [Accessed August 29, 2017].

De Lange, J., 2016. *Sverige är bäst i Europa på FinTech – visar färsk rapport [Sweden is best in Europe at FinTech – shows fresh report]*. [online] Breakit. Available at: www.breakit.se/artikel/5665/sverige-ar-bast-i-europa-pa-fintech-visar-farsk-rapport [Accessed August 29, 2017].

Gage, D., 2012. The venture capital secret: 3 out of 4 start-ups fail. *The Wall Street Journal*, [online] September 20. Available at: www.wsj.com/articles/SB10000872396390443720204578004980476429190 [Accessed August 29, 2017].

Gaitzsch, S., 2016. Sweden: The land of the unicorns. *The Technologist*. [online] Available at: www.technologist.eu/sweden-the-land-of-unicorns/ [Accessed August 29, 2017].

Go4Venture, 2017. *HTI Investments report year end review*. [online] Go4Venture. Available at: http://go4venture.com/wp-content/uploads/2017/02/2016-year-end-review.compressed.pdf [Accessed August 29, 2017].

Goldstein, M., 2015. *The five stages of VC funding explained*. [online] Cox Blue. Available at: www.coxblue.com/vc-funding-stages-explained/ [Accessed August 29, 2017].

Invest Stockholm, 2015. *Stockholm is the second largest FinTech hub in Europe*. [online] Stockholm FinTech Report. Available at: www.investstockholm.com/news/fintech [Accessed August 30, 2017].

Isaksson, A., 2006. *Studies on the venture capital process [doctoral thesis]*. [online] Umeå University. Available at: http://umu.diva-portal.org/smash/record.jsf?pid=diva2%3A144734&dswid=-9968 [Accessed August 29, 2017].

Jonsdottir, F., Toivonen, O., Jaatinen, V., Utti, A., and Lindqvist, R., 2017. *FinTech in the Nordics: A Deloitte review* [online] Available at: www2.deloitte.com/content/dam/Deloitte/se/Documents/financial-services/FinTech_Publikation_A4_WEB_FINAL.PDF [Accessed August 30, 2017].

Koba, M., 2012. *Initial public offering: CNBC explains*. [online] CNBC. Available at: www.cnbc.com/id/47099278 [Accessed August 30, 2017].

KPMG and CB Insights, 2016. *The pulse of FinTech, Q3 2016: Global analysis of FinTech venture funding*. [online] KPMG. Available at: https://assets.kpmg.com/content/dam/kpmg/xx/pdf/2016/11/the-pulse-of-fintech-q3-report.pdf [Accessed August 28, 2017].

Lundy, L., 2016. *5 things we learned from analysing the location of 950+ blockchain startups*. [online] Medium: The Outlier Ventures Research Team. Available at: https://medium.com/outlier-ventures-io/5-things-we-learned-from-analysing-the-location-of-950-blockchain-startups-96daa788560c [Accessed August 30, 2017].

Mitzner, D., 2016. *FinTech dominates Nordic startup investments*. [online] TechCrunch. Available at: https://techcrunch.com/2016/04/08/fintech-dominates-nordic-startup-investments/ [Accessed August 30, 2017].

Newton, A., 2016. *Hype cycle for digital banking, 2016*. [online] Gartner. Available at: www.gartner.com/doc/3381818/hype-cycle-digital-banking-transformation [Accessed August 30, 2017].

Nordic 9, 2017. *Mattias Weinhandl (investor – angel investor)*. [online] Available at: http://nordic9.com/companies/mattias-weinhandl-investor9260722825 [Accessed August 30, 2017].

Riminton, H., 2017. *Q1 2017: The Nordic tech funding report*. [online] Available at: http://www.nordictechlist.com/assets/ntl_report_q1_17.5a05d87b56362ea9ba5087c1d55cd7ed.pdf [Accessed January 6, 2018].

Roth, D., 2012. The ABCs of VC funding and building your board. *Forbes*. [online] Available at: www.forbes.com/sites/davidroth/2012/08/22/the-abcs-of-vc-funding-and-building-your-board/#ec3802a32501 [Accessed August 30, 2017].

SEB, 2017. *SEB venture capital.* [online] SEB Group. Available at: https://sebgroup.com/large-corporates-and-institutions/our-services/seb-venture-capital [Accessed August 30, 2017].

Startup Angels, 2017. *Startup Angels: Stockholm.* [online] Available at: https://startupangels.com/market/stockholm/ [Accessed August 30, 2017].

Techfoliance Team, 2016. *#Sweden: Overview of the top 6 VC funds involved in FinTech.* [online] Techfoliance. Available at: http://techfoliance.com/fintech-corner/sweden-overview-of-the-top-6-vc-funds-involved-in-fintech/ [Accessed August 30, 2017].

Venture-Capital-Investment.co.uk, 2011. *Venture capital investment process.* [online] Available at: www.venture-capital-investment.co.uk/venture-capital-investment-process.php [Accessed August 30, 2017].

Wesley-James, N., Ingram, C., Källstrand, C., and Teigland, R., 2015. *Stockholm FinTech: An overview of the FinTech sector in the greater Stockholm region.* [online] Stockholm School of Economics. Available at: www.hhs.se/contentassets/b5823453b8fe4290828fcc81189b6561/stockholm-fintech---june-2015.pdf [Accessed January 16, 2018].

19 How distance comes into play in equity crowdfunding

Alexandre Dubois and Michal Gromek

Introduction

Humans are neither the fastest nor the largest species on this planet. We are remarkable because of our ability to cooperate to reach common purposes. A textbook example of such cooperation is the modern version of crowdfunding, which leverages the collaboration between entrepreneurs and investors using the Internet. As defined in Chapter 12 in this volume, the term "crowdfunding" represents an umbrella expression that is used to identify an increasingly growing form of fundraising, typically via the Internet, where groups of people, as both individuals and legal entities, contribute to support a particular goal (Ahlers et al., 2015). As our technological development has progressed, we have been able to communicate with each other over growing geographical distances – first in the form of letters, then landline phones, mobile phones, and recently, the Internet. The technological aspect of how we facilitate communication might have changed over time, but trust, as a glue of any cooperation, has remained relatively unaffected.

In this chapter, we explore the relationship between geographic proximity and investments performed across Sweden on FundedByMe.com, a Swedish-based equity-based crowdfunding platform. We seek to explore the importance of network economies, the digitalization of trust, and the role of physical distance between capital seekers and capital providers in the implementation of equity crowdfunding ventures.

Network economies

The advantages linked to agglomeration are reasonably known: an increased potential for face-to-face exchange leads to more opportunities for the sharing of tacit knowledge (Gertler, 2003). Some researchers have introduced the idea that network economies could act as a substitute for agglomeration economies (Johansson and Quigley, 2004). The concept of network economies suggests "that a network (and any node on a network) is more valuable the greater the number of users (or other nodes) on the network" (Malecki, 2002). Companies that cannot benefit from a central position due to their particular location may be able to compensate, through the mobilization of different networks and relations, particularly for those online[1] (i.e., those that do not require a priori co-localization).

Nowadays, geography holds a prominent place in understanding the impact of geographical proximity in finance. Indeed, finance ought to be considered a fundamental spatial industry, "which creates and organizes hyper-mobility of capital in space" (Corpataux and Crevoisier, 2016).

In the wake of globalization, finance has become increasingly spatially concentrated in a few prominent locations. These command-and-control locations tend to increase the length of financial circuits (Corpataux and Crevoisier, 2016), meaning that there are more intermediaries between actors taking part in these processes, even locally.[2] One question that has especially interested economic geographers is whether Internet and Communication Technologies (ICT) have impacted the geographical localization of economic activities, for example in different parts of Sweden.

Perhaps the growing usage of ICT and virtual networks have allowed companies to finance their funding gaps and decrease the disadvantages associated with not being located in urbanized agglomerations such as Stockholm or Gothenburg. In these particular circumstances, the accessibility of the Internet would lead to a certain "space-opening" potential inherent to modern ICT (Nijkamp and Geenhuizen, 2005).

Research has revealed that the possibility of repeated online interaction has given rise to "virtual communities" that "are communities within which interaction is mainly mediated by communication tools provided by the Internet and in publicly accessible online environments" (Grabher and Ibert, 2014). Equity-based crowdfunding, where capital seekers meet capital providers on a repeated basis, is an example of such a "virtual community."

Trust and the digital society

Investment decisions in the online world, as in the case of equity-based crowdfunding, are clearly not only based on geographic proximity, but also on the entire portfolio of invisible processes connected to judgment in decision-making, such as trust or internal and external motivation of each particular investor.[3] This transformation from analogue channels into a digital society has had a range of significant implication (e.g., the attitude toward how online trust is perceived, how the crowd evaluates potential projects, how investment decisions are made). Individuals started to connect their belongings to a more open network than to a single organization, and they developed their own "relational identity" (Donati, 2002) of each development inside, for example, an online network.

Given the possibility for entrepreneurs to upload their projects, known as campaigns, online and seek investors that are willing to buy their companies' shares online is an example of a digital society and how trust has become digitalized within the last decade. Globally, 92 percent of consumers state that they trust another consumer opinion online (Nielsen, 2012).

Trust is based on illusions of actuality; we have less information than necessary to guarantee a successful end to an action (Padua, 2012). Trust is an essential ingredient in our social relationships and is a bond between the past and future as it helps to leverage experience (Padua, 2012). There are different key aspects regarding how trust is constructed, including the management of information, expectations, reputation, and security.[4]

Buying shares online from entrepreneurs is mostly a long-term commitment, which involves not only trust, but the investment also displays a significant amount of risk. Regardless of the intrinsic or extrinsic motivation[5] of investors to participate in an equity crowdfunding campaign, their goal will be to diminish the amount of risk connected with such an investment as the entrepreneur's company can default while going into reconstruction or bankruptcy. The sociologist Giddens (1990) argued that trust is a transformer of the uncertainty, risk, and danger produced within a society. Luhmann (1989) argued that trust is a reducer of risk, while acting as a filter displaying an understandable code between different circumstances within a society.

Geography matters: the home bias in crowdfunding

The way we incorporate and use technology has an impact primarily on factors such as trust and reputation. These factors might lead to a final decision on whether an investor buys shares offered by an entrepreneur on the crowdfunding platform. Usage of technology, trust, and the desire to lower uncertainty before conducting a purchase within equity crowdfunding are, by far, not all of the factors influencing investment decisions.

Geographical proximity online has a distinctive role, while conducting business offline

In the offline world, entrepreneurs who have been seeking credit from a local bank or investors from a local community had a greater chance of receiving funding than from a distant branch office. Professional investors, investing in stocks that have been geographically closer, have outperformed their colleagues investing into shares of distant companies. This well-researched phenomenon has been defined as "home bias."

The general conclusion of the literature is that the willingness to invest decreases with the increase in the physical distance between the parties. Venture capital (VC), providing pre- and post-seed capital to early-stage ventures, prefers to invest in local entrepreneurs as well (Florida and Smith, 1993; Zook, 2002). It has been established that home bias impacts different types of investors, public equity offerings (Coval and Moskowitz, 1999, 2001; Ivkovic and Weisbenner, 2005), and bonds, as well as other financial products (Tesar and Werner, 1995).

Lowering the uncertainty while increasing familiarity of business activity is the leading reason for local investment. Investors' direct or indirect connections to an entrepreneur seeking funding leads to a home bias (Harrison, Mason, and Robson, 2010). Furthermore, as VC teams typically conduct an investigation prior to investment, the cost of such due diligence processes and monitoring services increases proportionally with the geographic distance. As the transaction costs increase over geographical distance, the investment likelihood decreases (Sorenson and Stuart, 2001).

There might be a range of indications as to why equity crowdfunding investors might respond to geographic distance differently than VC investors. Crowdfunding, a collaborative community, is characterized by a drive to build a shared sense (in the meaning attributed by Weber) (Weber, Roth, and Wittich, 1978) and to create new meanings. "Collective intelligence" is a form of synergetic process to exchange and accumulate information among peers. An example of such an exchange might be a review of the video presentation, considering that investors have already invested in the equity campaign, or the way entrepreneurs are responding to the questions asked by the "investor community." Additionally, while examining screening methods of investors, research has confirmed in a qualitative study that retail investors, who represent a majority in equity crowdfunding, are less attracted to offline physical meetings with potential investors (Moritz, Block, and Lutz, 2015). Collaborative intelligence represents a unique replacement to a structured due diligence process performed by a VC.

As the modern version of equity crowdfunding is facilitated with the help of the Internet, it is regarded as a multilayered network of relationships (Cofta, 2007). While the access to verified information is complex, investors might have to rely on their own peers, or other factors, to make an investment decision.

The physical distance separating investors from entrepreneurs tends to be short (Agrawal, Catalini, and Goldfarb, 2011). However, beyond this "local" sphere, the distance effect tends to disappear. Studies performed on the platform Sellaband.com have shown that local backers exhibit stronger support for their local music band than for distant performers. Nonetheless, this situation could be unique, considering that the music band's supporter community may consist mostly of family and friends (Agrawal, Catalini, and Goldfarb, 2011, 2015).

Similar studies were conducted while reviewing personal unsecured loans on the American website Prosper.com (Lin and Viswanathan, 2016). Both of the studies examined geographic proximity within types of crowdfunding where the invested amount often remains way below USD 100. Such a small investment might reflect philanthropy as the main reason for participation, rather than the expectation of a sizeable return on investment.

A recent paper by Guenther, Johan, and Schweizer (2017) further investigated the home bias aspects in equity-based crowdfunding using the platform Australian Small Scale Offerings Board (ASSOB). The results of that particular study pointed out a possibility for "home bias" in equity crowdfunding. This study was one of the sparks to conduct this review, to test if "home bias" also exists in Sweden, which is geographically distant to Australia.

Methods

Our review includes data exported from the back end of FundedByMe.com. The platform has facilitated equity-based crowdfunding since 2013, and it has hitherto helped raise around EUR 33 million by April 2017. We exported the data from

40+ projects that were facilitated via this platform in Sweden. The export of these data included both the data from investors as well as entrepreneurs. Both groups had to provide their personal data when pre-registering for a share issue process performed on the platform.

Data have been extracted and anonymized. The investors' place of residence and companies' registration addresses have been used in order to calculate the physical distance "as the crow flies," separating the investor from the entrepreneur. Each investment made in our sampled campaigns (i.e., each investor–entrepreneur pairing) has been mapped as a point located at the investor's address. We have included both the time of the investment while the company has been seeking funding as well as the size of the investment. We have used the free geographic information system software QGIS to map and analyze the collected material.

Results

In this section, we provide some results based on the analysis of our data set with regard to the geography of equity-based crowdfunded campaigns. First, we illustrate the geographical distribution of these campaigns across Sweden. We then map the locations and number of investments for all sampled campaigns. Finally, we use the example of the campaign launched by FundedByMe itself for expanding and consolidating their future activities to discuss the importance of physical distance in the investor–entrepreneur pairing.

Where have these equity-based campaigns been launched?

One piece of information that we could gather from the data set is the address of the company that has registered the campaign. Based on the address, we were able to map the registration address of each campaign, and thus visualize companies home quarters, defined as "home."

As seen in Figure 19.1, the process of mapping the campaigns revealed that the majority of the equity-based campaigns in Sweden have been launched by companies registered in the Stockholm area. Indeed, about 25 of them are located in and around the municipality of Stockholm. In comparison, campaigns launched from Gothenburg and Malmö, the two other large urban regions of Sweden, are scarce, with four in Gothenburg and two in Malmö.

The mapping displayed that capital-seeking entrepreneurs in less densely populated parts of the country, while few, have been able to successfully launch campaigns, and thus mobilize financial capital, despite their non-central location. For instance, three campaigns have been successfully funded around Östersund in the county of Jämtland.

However, these are, to date, the exceptions rather than the rule as there are only a handful of campaigns that have been launched from non-metropolitan regions in Sweden. In that respect, it is a fair assessment to say that in its current development phase, the geography of crowdfunding reproduces that of the "regular" finance sector in Sweden, with a significant polarization toward Stockholm.

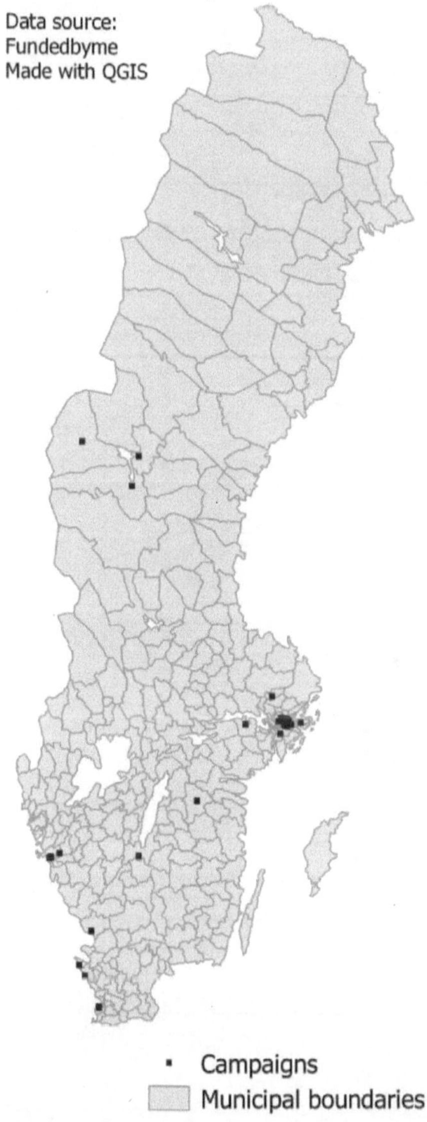

Figure 19.1 Location of sampled equity-based campaigns
Source: Own creation.

Where does the invested capital come from?

As a second step, we wanted to get a better understanding of the geographical distribution of the capital invested in equity-based campaigns. To do that, we mapped each investment by the location of its investor and then aggregated the data at the level of a grid cell for Sweden and by countries for a worldwide view.

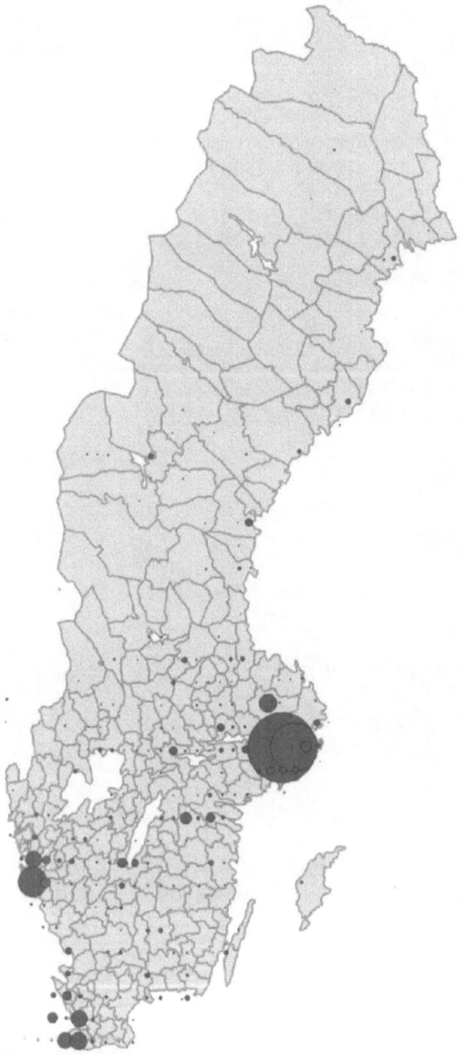

Figure 19.2 Aggregated number of investments for sampled equity-based campaigns by grid cell

Source: Own creation.

We aggregated the data because one investor, corresponding to one individual address and point data, may have contributed to several campaigns.

Figure 19.2 displays the aggregated number of investments made by Swedish investors for our entire sample of equity-based campaigns. The region where the largest number of single investments has been made is the Stockholm area.

This is consistent with the fact that Stockholm is the home market of the majority of the campaigns. Hence, most of the investors from the entrepreneur's social circles likely reside in the Stockholm area. It is also consistent with the fact that most "serial" investors (i.e., the ones that invest in multiple campaigns without being acquainted with the entrepreneur) are located in Stockholm. The combination of the two processes thus emphasizes the importance of the Stockholm area as the primary location for funding and sourcing investments.

What the latter map also shows us is that many investments are made from locations outside metropolitan regions, despite the fact that few campaigns originate from these areas. Seen from this angle, crowdfunding gives the opportunity for would-be investors located in rural parts of Sweden to take part in the financial sector despite their geographical remoteness. In that sense, crowdfunding may induce the inclusion of a wide range of participants and territories in financial ventures.

Another significant aspect of the geography of crowdfunding is the importance of internationalization in these capital-sourcing processes. Using our equity-based campaign data, we have aggregated the number of single investments made by investors from all countries worldwide. In Figure 19.3, we show a map of this geographical distribution. Not surprisingly, Sweden is the country from which most of the investments have been made. The domestic market is thus still the primary supplier of capital for these projects. Nordic neighbors such as Finland and Norway, which both have historically relevant economic and financial ties to Sweden, are countries from where many international investments have been made.

Additionally, the map shows the vast diversity of countries from which capital is sourced in crowdfunded campaigns. More distant countries such as Spain

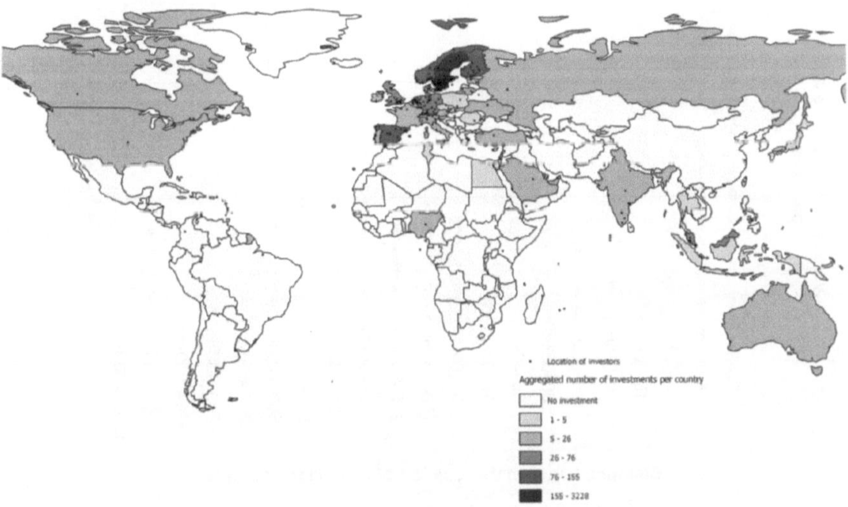

Figure 19.3 Aggregated number of investments for sampled campaigns by country
Source: Own creation; data: FundedByMe, country boundaries.

and the United Kingdom in Europe have contributed, but Malaysia, Singapore, Australia, and the United Arab Emirates are places from which investments have also been made. From these countries, the investments are made from a small number of "serial," and presumably professional, investors that seek to invest a small stake in the project with an assumed high-growth potential.

From our sample of the equity-based data set, it appears that geographical proximity is still a primary factor for sourcing capital through a digital platform, such as in the case of crowdfunding. But we have also shown that international investors are contributing to the mobilization of capital, albeit with a less philanthropic motivation. An interesting question is if these two types of contributions are substituting for one another or if they are complementary. In a nutshell, if a campaign attracts local capital, does it also attract foreign investments?

In Figure 19.4, we provide an average profile of our sampled equity-based campaigns by measuring the average number of investments that are made within different distance ranges. There are two main results that can be drawn from this figure.

First, it shows us the decay in the "home bias" effect. Indeed, the average number of investments gradually diminishes from more than 15 average investments within 5 km from the founder's location to below one investment about 40 km away. From this, we could derive that the "local" market for equity-based campaigns lies within a 40 km radius, and that within this local market, the further away one gets, the weaker the "home" effect appears to be.

Second, there seems to be a "surge" in the average number of investments between 300 km and 600 km. In this example, having in mind the geography of

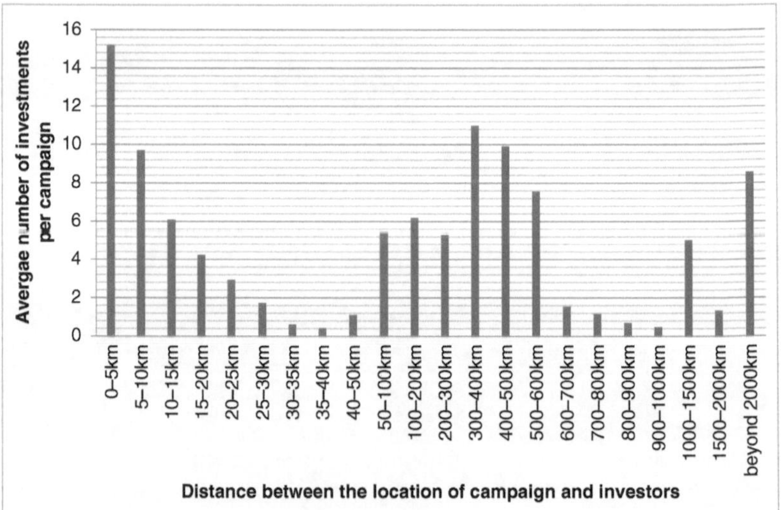

Figure 19.4 Average number of investments per campaign made within different physical distance

Sweden is necessary. We have previously shown that the majority of our campaigns have been launched from Stockholm. The other two main urban regions of Sweden, Gothenburg and Malmö, are located 450 km and 600 km, respectively, from the capital region. Hence, one reading of this "surge" is that investments are made from other main urban regions, thus stressing the important "urban" bias of crowdfunding. A second "surge" can be observed, albeit of a lesser extent, for investments made by investors located from 2,000 km and beyond of the campaign's location. Although this is certainly a statistical effect of lumping together investments originating from a very large area into one single category, it nonetheless indicates the systematic presence of international investments in Swedish equity-based crowdfunded ventures.

We finally illustrate how investments made from different locations contribute to the overall mobilization of capital in a given campaign. The example we chose to highlight this is the campaign launched by FundedByMe itself to secure more capital to consolidate and expand its operations. A total of 401 investments were made during this campaign. Figure 19.5 shows the relationship between accumulated capital and physical distance (we use the square root of the distance in order to make the graph easier to read). Take note that it does not take into consideration when each investment was made.

The results displayed in Figure 19.5 confirm the importance of the "local" market for sourcing capital through crowdfunding. Fifty percent of the capital was sourced from investors located within approximately 15 km from the campaign's launch location (in downtown Stockholm). Between around 15 km and 400 km (i.e., 20 on the horizontal axis), the steepness of the curve decreases, corresponding to a progressive weakening of the local market effect. Between 400 km and

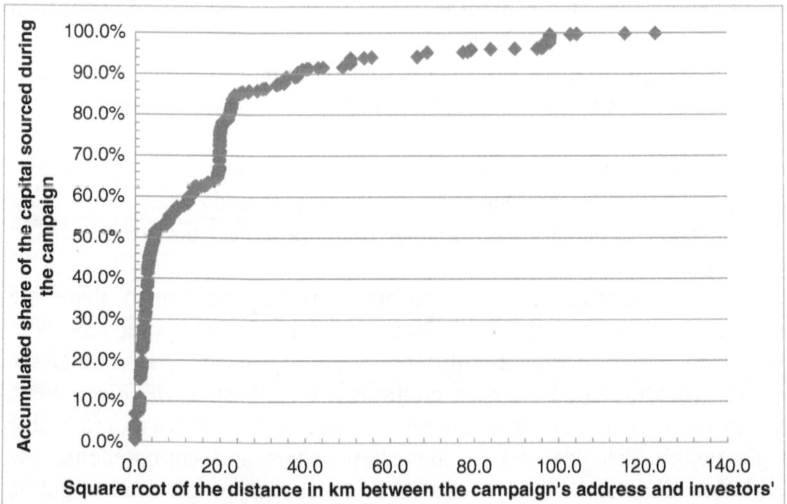

Figure 19.5 Accumulated share of capital by (square root of) the physical distance measured between founder and investors in the FundedByMe campaign

600 km (i.e., between 20 and 25 in the graph's horizontal axis), the capital accumulation curve gets steeper and the accumulated capital goes from 55 percent to about 85 percent during that span. The final 15 percent of capital is sourced from investors whose distance to the campaign's location varies widely.

Implications and conclusions

Analyzing the example of the FundedByMe campaign, as illustrated in Figure 19.5, confirms previous findings in the literature about the importance of the "home bias" in online financing. By mapping the data set corresponding to equity-based campaigns funded through the Swedish crowdfunding platform FundedByMe, we have been able to show that both the geographical distribution of campaign locations and investors' location is strongly polarized toward Stockholm, the country's financial center. In that respect, although the remotely accessible nature of the platform does not radically change the Swedish geography of finance, it certainly enables entrepreneurs outside of Stockholm to access funding and mobilize support that they would not be able to access using "regular" financing tools.

Our analysis confirms the existence of a certain home bias that appears to decay with physical distance within an approximately 15 km radius. Although our data set does not allow us to see the level of acquaintance between the campaign's founder and local investors, other studies have shown the importance of social and professional acquaintances in mobilizing local capital. Finally, our mapping exercise has shown the presence of a small number of foreign "serial" investors that invest in multiple projects. Beyond the extent of their financial contribution, these investors act as a "weak link" between different, and a priori, unrelated from the starting point of campaigns. So even if the local inertia of such networks confirms the "home bias" thesis, extra-local investors may also provide important information when consolidating the project itself.

Hereafter, we identify some practical implications that different participants engaged in crowdfunding ventures could draw from our small-scale study:

- *Entrepreneurs*: Entrepreneurs who anticipate selling shares of their companies to potential investors. Due to the home bias, their campaign marketing activities should concentrate on finding capital providers that are located in close geographical proximity.
- *Policymakers*: As traditional financial providers have confirmed, there is a home bias in startups (e.g., VCs), loan providers, and entrepreneurs, who have uneven access to capital in different areas of Sweden. As home biases in equity crowdfunding have been preliminarily confirmed with our review, it decreases the chances of crowdfunding being a cost-effective tool to bridge the geographic distance and to connect investors and entrepreneurs. As specified in Chapter 12 in this volume, this discovery might lead to public intervention while policymakers decide to support projects originating from a particular type of entrepreneur located in certain parts of the country.

- *Platform operators*: One of the goals of the crowdfunding platform is to close as many funding rounds of capital-seeking entrepreneurs as possible. Many active crowdfunding campaigns are being promoted using social media channels. A practical impact is the recommendation to reduce the geographic range of advertisement that might increase the click-through rate[6] (CTR) and reduce the marketing costs.

Future research on Swedish crowdfunding practices would need to further explore the interplay between these two main sources of investments, and especially regarding the extent to which they influence each other, that is if the "layers" composing this network are stacked one upon the other, or if there are contact interfaces between them that make the funded project "gel." Further analysis of this data set involving more advanced statistical and spatial analyses would allow a better understanding of how the physical distance separating founders and funders influences the sequencing of the investments (i.e., the chronological order at which investments are made and capital seeker–capital provider relations realized).

Notes

1 Internet-based connections that utilize social media channels are examples of an informal network.
2 In this system, physical proximity does not engender automatically direct and reciprocal interactions among local actors.
3 Please review Chapter 12 in this volume for more information on motivation of capital seekers into equity crowdfunding.
4 The traditional construct of trust is extremely complex, with several separate definitions in sociology, cognitive sociology, psychology, economics, and philosophy.
5 Intrinsic motivation refers to participation in equity crowdfunding because it is inherently interesting, philanthropic, or enjoyable. Extrinsic motivation refers to investing into crowdfunding because it leads to a separable outcome (e.g., a return on investment).
6 Click-through rate (CTR) is an indicator in online marketing that users interacted with the displayed advertisement. The higher the CTR rate, the better rate of return for the advertising companies. CTR is a component of quality score, which affects the costs of the position of online advertisement.

Bibliography

Agrawal, A., Catalini, C., and Goldfarb, A., 2011. *The geography of crowdfunding*. Cambridge, MA: National Bureau of Economic Research.

Agrawal, A., Catalini, C., and Goldfarb, A., 2015. Crowdfunding: Geography, social networks, and the timing of investment decisions. *Journal of Economics & Management Strategy*, 24(2), pp.253–274.

Ahlers, G.K.C., Cumming, D., Günther, C., and Schweizer, D., 2015. Signaling in equity crowdfunding. *Entrepreneurship Theory and Practice*, 39(4), pp.955–980.

Cofta, P., 2007. *Trust, complexity and control:Confidence in a convergent world.* Chichester: John Wiley & Sons.

Corpataux, J. and Crevoisier, O., 2016. Lost in space: A critical approach of ANT and the social studies of finance. *Progress in Human Geography*, 40(5), pp.610–628.

Coval, J.D. and Moskowitz, T.J., 1999. Home bias at home: Local equity preference in domestic portfolios. *The Journal of Finance*, 54(6), pp.2045–2073.

Coval, J.D. and Moskowitz, T.J., 2001. The geography of investment: Informed trading and asset prices. *Journal of Political Economy*, 109(4), pp.811–841.

Donati, P., 2002. *Introduzione alla sociologia relazionale.* 6th ed. Milano: Angeli.

Florida, R. and Smith, D.F., 1993. Venture capital formation, investment, and regional industrialization. *Annals of the Association of American Geographers*, 83(3), pp.434–451.

Gertler, M.S., 2003. Tacit knowledge and the economic geography of context, or the undefinable tacitness of being (there). *Journal of Economic Geography*, 3(1), pp.75–99.

Giddens, A., 1990. *The consequences of modernity.* Cambridge: Polity Press.

Grabher, G. and Ibert, O., 2014. Distance as asset? Knowledge collaboration in hybrid virtual communities. *Journal of Economic Geography*, 14(1), pp.97–123.

Guenther, C., Johan, S., and Schweizer, D., 2017. Is the crowd sensitive to distance? How investment decisions differ by investor type. *Small Business Economics*, pp.1–17.

Harrison, R., Mason, C., and Robson, P., 2010. Determinants of long-distance investing by business angels in the UK. *Entrepreneurship & Regional Development*, 22(2), pp.113–137.

Ivkovic, Z. and Weisbenner, S., 2005. Local does as local is: Information content of the geography of individual investors' common stock investments. *The Journal of Finance*, 60(1), pp.267–306.

Johansson, B. and Quigley, J.M., 2004. Agglomeration and networks in spatial economics. *Papers in Regional Science*, 83(1), pp.165–176.

Lin, M. and Viswanathan, S., 2016. Home bias in online investments: An empirical study of an online crowdfunding market. *Management Science*, 62(5), pp.1393–1414.

Luhmann, N., 1989. *Ecological communication.* Cambridge: Polity Press.

Malecki, E.J., 2002. The economic geography of the Internet's infrastructure. *Economic Geography*, 78(4), pp.399–424.

Moritz, A., Block, J., and Lutz, E., 2015. Investor communication in equity-based crowdfunding: A qualitative-empirical study. *Qualitative Research in Financial Markets*, 7(3), pp.309–342.

Nielsen, 2012. *Nielsen global trust in advertising report.* [online] Available at: www.slideshare.net/ecommercenews/global-trustinadvertising2012 [Accessed September 3, 2017].

Nijkamp, P. and van Geenhuizen, M., 2005. *Death of distance and agglomeration forces of firms in the urban e-economy: An artificial intelligence approach using rough set analysis.* [online] Available at: http://dare.ubvu.vu.nl/handle/1871/8941 [Accessed September 3, 2017].

Padua, 2012. *Trust, social relations and engagement: Understanding customer behaviour on the web.* Basingstoke: Palgrave Macmillan.

Sorenson, O. and Stuart, T.E., 2001. Syndication networks and the spatial distribution of venture capital investments. *American Journal of Sociology*, 106(6), pp.1546–1588.

Tesar, L.L. and Werner, I.M., 1995. U.S. equity investment in emerging stock markets. *The World Bank Economic Review*, 9(1), pp.109–129.
Weber, M., Roth, G., and Wittich, C., 1978. *Economy and society: An outline of interpretive sociology*. Berkeley, CA: University of California Press.
Zook, M.A., 2002. Grounded capital: Venture financing and the geography of the Internet industry, 1994–2000. *Journal of Economic Geography*, 2(2), pp.151–177.

20 The Stockholm FinTech Hub

Catharina Burenstam Linder

Introduction

In 2015, Stockholm was the second highest funded FinTech city in Europe (Wesley-James et al., 2015). In 2017, Stockholm was ranked at eleventh place by the online version of the British newspaper *City A.M.* and at tenth place by the Institute for Financial Services Zug of the Lucerne University of Applied

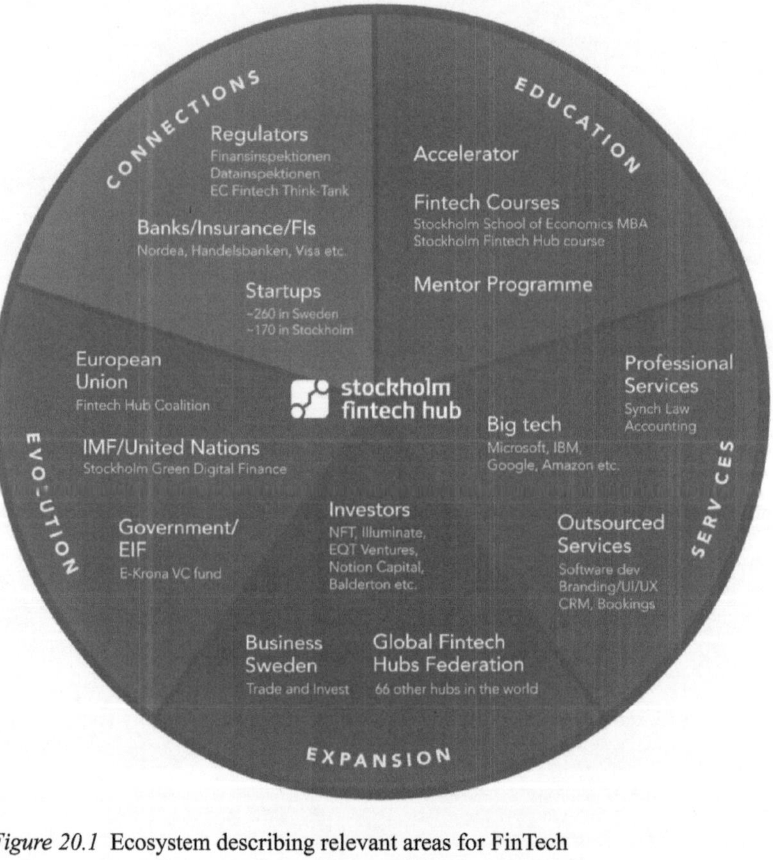

Figure 20.1 Ecosystem describing relevant areas for FinTech

Sciences. To attract top investors, talents, and partners, Stockholm needs to keep up with other European cities that are stimulating their FinTech ecosystems (see Figure 20.1). Despite being a world leader in FinTech, Stockholm needs to invest in the ecosystem to stay on top of the competition.

The social benefit from the strong FinTech community in Stockholm is significant. Successful startups such as Klarna and iZettle have created attractive jobs, increased tax revenues, facilitated commerce, and promoted Sweden globally.

Incumbent financial institutions can also gain tremendously from a vibrant FinTech community if they learn how to cooperate with startups that challenge their business model as well as the regulatory system.

Among the main challenges for FinTech startups in Sweden are regulatory issues and initiating cooperation with large financial institutions. Due to rigid regulations, the lead time in the financial sector is long, which can be a deal breaker for an early-stage startup with little or no investments.

The Stockholm FinTech Hub was launched to bring together startups, large financial institutions, and regulators in an independent physical workspace. The goal is to enable startups to launch faster with more competitive services and low regulatory risk.

This chapter aims to present a descriptive case study of the Stockholm FinTech Hub (SFH). It does not aim to analyze or evaluate the hub, its context, or its mission.

A brief background to the development of the hub

Prior to SFH, no FinTech-specific co-working spaces existed in Stockholm. Given the strength of the FinTech community in Stockholm, there existed an opportunity to create a world-leading hub. The lack of such a hub was also a risk to the FinTech community since many other cities had created their hubs in order to enable quicker regulation and speedier launches of startup companies (Wesley-James et al., 2015).

Clusters and hubs

A report by Claire Ingram (2017), *Stockholm's ICT Cluster*, explores the potential benefits of having a central information and communications technology (ICT) hub or campus in a city, with specific attention paid to whether this leads to an increase in ICT entrepreneurship—and Internet companies. A cluster is defined in the report, according to Michael Porter (Professor at Harvard Business School): "A geographic concentration of interconnected companies, specialized suppliers, service providers, firms in related industries, and associated institutions (for example, universities, standards agencies, and trade associations) in particular fields that compete but also cooperate."

Ingram concludes that the primary reason for the establishment of a central hub in a cluster is "in order to expand and deepen existing social networks, as well as create new ones and regularly revitalize a cluster with new ideas and ways of thinking." The report also gives examples of how there is a positive relationship between the strength of a country's clusters and competitiveness.

Places with established networks increase the levels of competition, learning, and trust, which are conducive to a strong entrepreneurial environment and individual startups' success. Hubs are central points for spillover of talent and information to occur, as they encourage people to interact with one another, discuss strategy, and exchange information. This exchange of information is also a source of learning. A high level of trust in network relationships can lower transaction costs among entrepreneurs and in startup ecosystems.

A comparison to international hubs

In comparison to other FinTech hubs in the world, Stockholm, a relatively young ecosystem, has yet to make a noteworthy impression on the global ecosystem. A study on global FinTech cities (Deloitte, 2017) has identified 44 hubs divided into "old hubs" and "new hubs" for FinTech. The study ranks FinTech hubs based on three equally weighted indices—the Global Finance Centre Index (Yeandle, 2016), Doing Business 2017 (World Bank, 2016), and the Global Innovation Index 2016 (Dutta et al., 2016)—to determine the strength of each hub globally.

In the ranking, London emerged as the leading FinTech Hub globally, with an index score of 11, followed by New York, with a score of 14, and Silicon Valley, with a score of 18. Stockholm, with a score of 55, ranks at a shared eleventh place globally together with Tokyo. Interestingly, however, Stockholm not only ranks fourth in Europe, but by looking at the division between "old hubs" and "new hubs," it ranks second globally together with Tokyo among the "new hubs."

The key to its success in the ranking comes from Sweden's high rankings on the Doing Business ranking (2nd) and the Global Innovation Index ranking (9th) (Dutta et al., 2016; World Bank, 2016).

Given Stockholm's relatively recent entry into the global FinTech ecosystem, its long-term prospects remain to be evaluated, and one could only speculate as to its standing in upcoming FinTech hub rankings.

Furthermore, the study anticipated a strong growth in the number of FinTechs spawning in Stockholm within the next 12 months, but also noted that it faces challenges with regard to regulatory barriers, skill shortages, particularly pertaining to technology skills, and the relatively small size of the domestic market.

One of the key recommendations from the 2015 *Stockholm FinTech* report (Wesley-James et al., 2015) was to launch a FinTech hub in what they described as Europe's second highest funded city within FinTech (i.e., Stockholm) as a way to strengthen the city's prospects within the global FinTech ecosystem. This inspired Matthew Argent, the founding partner at the IT consulting firm BLC Advisors, to research why no such hub had been set up. Invest in Stockholm responded that they would be willing to back the project if he were able to get additional funding and pull together a quorum of partners. On January 1, 2017, the SFH was launched with the support of KMPG, NFT Ventures, and Invest Stockholm.

About the Stockholm FinTech Hub

As of 2017, SFH is fully operational with a co-working space strategically located at the central station. It works with regulators and regularly hosts various financial institutions and FinTech startups.

The main success driver is the potential to enable deep, frequent, and serendipitous communication and collaboration among the actors in the FinTech community. When the players in FinTech understand each other's needs and potential, innovative ideas can flourish. Figure 20.2 illustrates how value is added at different stages of startups.

The following section is based on interviews with the founder and CEO Matthew Argent and COO Lan-Ling Fredell, and describes ongoing initiatives and services provided by SFH.

Regulatory support

One of SFH's key services is to offer support in the heavily regulated financial industry. Among startup entrepreneurs, one complaint is the difficulty in gaining access to the regulators and getting timely feedback. Investors that are new in the field might need guidance regarding compliance to make sound investment decisions.

SFH can reduce the consequences of regulatory barriers through the sharing of experience and by providing regulators with structured facts about challenges and needs from different categories of startups. Such feedback can provide guidance for the development of the regulatory framework.

SFH supports regulators in drafting innovation policy for the benefit of financial companies and consumers of financial services. The objective for

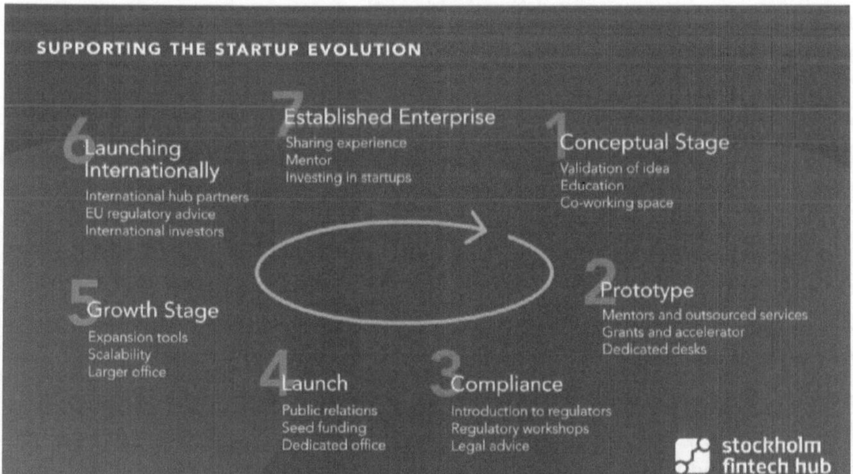

Figure 20.2 Illustration of value addition in various stages of a startup

this collaboration is for regulators to investigate how they can better handle the issues and needs that arise when financial companies offer new innovative services to ensure Sweden's position as a leading nation in the fast-growing FinTech sector.

Networking

An important feature of SFH is to enable global networking. SFH is part of the Global FinTech Hub Federation, an independent and inclusive global network of emerging and established FinTech hubs globally. The network facilitates scalability of startups by providing access to information about markets around the world, which is crucial in a market the size of Sweden for a startup to become relevant to investors.

Business Sweden is another collaboration partner to SFH, and is owned by the Swedish government and the industry. Business Sweden's purpose is to help Swedish companies reach their full international potential and foreign companies to invest and expand in Sweden.

In addition, SFH initiated a cooperation agreement between the hubs in Oslo, Helsinki, Copenhagen, and Stockholm, which links the four Nordic FinTech communities together and strengthens their influence in European and global markets.

SFH also works on collaborative projects with FinTech hubs in Paris, Frankfurt, and Brussels in order to share best practices and support European FinTechs.

Knowledge

SFH offers knowledge and expertise in different formats. There are, for instance, two-way mentorships where young innovators get advice and guidance from experienced entrepreneurs and business leaders, who in turn gain a better understanding of how young people think. SFH also offers support to startups regarding, for example, scaling issues, technology, and operations within a traditional major bank. SFH has also cooperated with SSE, with the objective to develop an executive FinTech MBA program, and a more high-level course for the startup community on how to deal with the regulators and banks. Considering that SFH has extensive access to expertise and resources, they can help startups with, for instance, IT outsourcing, for more efficient development.

Increased investments

SFH is currently working on establishing a venture capital fund. According to Argent, too few early-stage investments are made today in Swedish FinTech companies. Industries and economies are not the same any more; tech and digitalization is the future, and competing with production and manufacturing in low-wage countries such as China is useless. To this extent, Argent stated,

"To beat competition and secure the future of our children, we must invest in it and compete on a global scale."

To keep the development of FinTech startups on a high level, both in terms of quantity and quality, seed investments are needed to help more entrepreneurs into the pipeline and the opportunity to reach the market.

Sustainable development

SFH is supporting Sweden and the United Nations Environment Programme (UNEP) to pilot the UN's 2030 vision for sustainable finance. In 2015, world leaders adopted the 2030 Agenda for Sustainable Development and its 17 Sustainable Development Goals, having economic growth, social inclusion, and environmental protection as core elements (United Nations, 2015). UNEP need a supportive environment to try out the recommendations presented in their *FinTech and Sustainable Development* report (Castilla-Rubio, Zadek, and Robins, 2016). Sweden has been identified as a suitable test bed, and will become a benchmark for the rest of Europe. SFH aims to be part of the solution in using FinTech to open new opportunities for sustainable finance and new models for environmental initiatives. SFH offers a Green Digital Financial Center, where FinTech is the platform for bringing together digital finance businesses and stakeholders to accelerate FinTech innovations that address global environmental challenges to deliver against the UNEP agenda (Argent, 2017).

The perspective of startup founders and venture capitalists

To both startups and investors, the concept of operating in ecosystems is what the future of business and economies is all about. In order to better assess the impact of the establishment of a hub on the startup and venture capital ecosystems, we conducted interviews with two representatives from the Stockholm startup scene.

Startup founder Henrik Rosvall

Henrik Rosvall is the founder and CEO of a FinTech company called Dreams, launched in 2013 (Dreams, 2017). Its purpose is to facilitate savings and investment for individuals. In contrast to the way in which traditional banks operate in silos with individual KPIs for savings, investment, and lending, Dreams offers in its app instead a method and tool to easily achieve users' individual goals. The objective is to promote a change of behavior and drive society toward a long-term and sustainable economy. The core element of Dreams is the ecosystem. A service or a platform can be copied, but an ecosystem is difficult to copy. Since a product or service can have a much more dynamic development over time, you create leverage against traditional players. An ecosystem works toward a common goal and shares the same KPIs, which makes an ecosystem powerful.

Dreams is inspired by the Singularity University, a think tank in California, and their thoughts about exponential acceleration, growth, or development of an industry, such as technology or finance. The idea is that the power of the new exponential economy of companies, which build entire ecosystems instead of just offering a product or a platform, can have an enormous impact on changing culture and human behavior. Dreams' ecosystem is made up by the financial partners, academia, corporate partners, and customers. SFH is an extremely valuable supplement to this ecosystem as it provides access to other startups, regulators, and big, traditional banks. Rosvall described his interaction with SFH by saying, "Through SFH, we get into a context where we get a lot for free."

Venture capitalist Anette Nordvall

Venture capitalist Anette Nordvall, a member of Stockholm Business Angels (STOAF) and chairman for the young startup Covr Security, is a member of SFH. STOAF is an early-stage investment company, including almost 50 business angels who invest in advanced technology and future fast-growing companies in life science, industrial technology, and software. Covr is a two-way authentication tool offering users a safe way of authenticating themselves and authorizing transactions via an app on their smartphones.

To venture capitalists, the main benefits of SFH are that it becomes easier to find qualified co-investors and to get in touch with more and better startups. Simplified communication makes it easier to understand the top priorities of other ecosystem players and to figure out how to target and navigate the company they invested in. This enables venture capitalists to contribute to important infrastructural support. Nordvall elaborated by saying, "This hub will become very successful when everyone in the ecosystem realizes they should be a part of it."

Nordvall agrees that Sweden is a leader within tech and FinTech, but says there is still much work to be done. Sweden has to create smart companies and smart services, and thus knowing how to take advantage of the ecosystem is essential. An important parameter for an investor is the perseverance of the entrepreneurs. Regulations will keep changing and competition is often around the corner. With a supporting network, access to knowledge, and regulatory guidance, the young startups can hang in longer and increase their chances of success.

SFH enables budding FinTech companies to become part of the FinTech community, and they bring in the incumbent financial institutes to the infrastructure, players that can cope without the startups, but that the startups cannot cope without. Trust from a large bank, combined with a startup's high speed and ability to innovate, can create mutual opportunities and/or benefit.

Conclusion

The aim of this chapter was to present a descriptive case study of the Stockholm FinTech Hub (SFH). In conclusion, SFH's overarching ambition has been to bring stakeholders together. In doing this, SFH has sought to provide startups with an opportunity to participate in society, while giving them the perspective and knowledge to influence change. This in turn acts as a driver to ensure that Stockholm (and by extension, Sweden) remains a competitive hub in the growing FinTech industry globally.

At the time of writing, the outcome of establishing a FinTech hub in Sweden is uncertain, but the response from all directions has been good and the level of engagement from the different players involved is high.

Ideas coming out of the hub are likely to affect society in ways that we cannot yet predict, just as previous FinTech startups have done already. To follow the progress of individual initiatives, as well as the hub itself, would be very exciting since it might provide early indicators of the direction of future change and development in society within financial services.

Services for saving, consuming, investing, and transferring money not only affect the role and function of banks and financial institutions, but also the way they need to operate to adapt to the new behavioral patterns of consumers. This connection would be interesting to investigate, from both ends. On the one hand, in order to predict what societal effects are likely to expect as a result of new, disruptive financial services or products, and on the other hand, to identify what FinTech tools would be necessary in order to support a certain desired development or change in society.

Bibliography

Argent, M., 2017. *Sweden, UNEP and FinTechs collaborate for sustainable finance.* [online] Available at: www.finextra.com/pressarticle/68774/sweden-unep-and-fintechs-collaborate-for-sustainable-finance [Accessed August 28, 2017].

Castilla-Rubio, J.C., Zadek, S., and Robins, N., 2016. *FinTech and sustainable development: Assessing the implications.* [online] Available at: http://unepinquiry.org/publication/fintech-and-sustainable-development-assessing-the-implications/ [Accessed August 28, 2017].

Deloitte, 2017. *A tale of 44 cities. Connecting global FinTech: Interim hub review 2017.* [online] Available at: www2.deloitte.com/content/dam/Deloitte/uk/Documents/Innovation/deloitte-uk-connecting-global-fintech-hub-federation-innotribe-innovate-finance.pdf [Accessed December 4, 2017].

Dreams, 2017. *Om oss [About us].* [online] Available at: www.getdreams.com/sv/om-oss [Accessed December 4, 2017].

Dutta, S., Lanvin, B., Wunsch-Vincent, S., Insead, World Intellectual Property Organization, and Johnson Graduate School of Management (Cornell University), 2016. *The Global Innovation Index 2016: Winning with global innovation.* Ithaca, NY: Johnson Cornell University; Fontainebleau: INSEAD; Geneva: WIPO.

Ingram, C., 2017. *Stockholm's ICT cluster: Improving the ties that bind.* [online] Available at: www.clairebogusz.com/wp-content/uploads/2017/03/Report15.10_2.pdf [Accessed September 15, 2017].

United Nations, 2015. *Sustainable Development Goals: Seventeen goals to transform our world.* [online] Available at: www.un.org/sustainabledevelopment/ [Accessed August 28, 2017].

Wesley-James, N., Ingram, C., Källstrand, C., and Teigland, R., 2015. *Stockholm FinTech: An overview of the FinTech sector in the greater Stockholm region.* [online] Available at: www.hhs.se/contentassets/b5823453b8fe4290828fcc81189b6561/stockholm-fintech---june-2015.pdf [Accessed January 16, 2018].

World Bank, 2016. *Doing business 2017: Equal opportunity for all.* [online] Available at: www.doingbusiness.org/reports/global-reports/doing-business-2017 [Accessed January 16, 2018].

Yeandle, M., 2016. *The Global Financial Centres Index 20.* [online] Available at: www.longfinance.net/images/gfci/20/GFCI20_26Sep2016.pdf [Accessed January 16, 2018].

21 Geographic decentralization of FinTech companies in Sweden

Katarzyna Jereczek

Introduction

The extensive growth of the financial technology industry continues in 2017 as a result of new financial industry trends and numerous FinTech investments (Lavender et al., 2017). A number of strategic cooperations between new startups and well-established players such as banks or big corporations are steadily growing. Arguably therefore, it should come as no surprise that Stockholm, as a technology-based hub, is very active in fostering innovative FinTech products. Becoming an attractive center for startups and innovation requires some basics: talent, capital, hospitable policies, and domestic demand for the products and services that are being developed. However, there are some significant differences between Stockholm and other financial hubs. Undoubtedly, Stockholm is not the only hub in Sweden; there are more and more areas in Sweden that attract significant numbers of startups, such as Gothenburg and Malmö. Below, we hope to answer these questions based on interviews with companies originating from different parts of Sweden to understand what factors impacted their decision not to start their ventures in the greater Stockholm region. What are the key factors behind such a decision? This chapter aims to present the arguments for and against starting up in Gothenburg, Luleå, and Stockholm.

Most tech companies are struggling with the same challenges, such as access to talent and user acquisition (Gaskell, 2017). How can companies deal with these challenges to find the golden mean? The location in which a startup incorporates, it seems, has a significant impact on the success of the company.

Stockholm: the second largest FinTech hub in Europe

Traditional European financial centers such as Frankfurt, Zürich, or London are transforming into financial innovation centers and have a chance to further strengthen their position. Stockholm, on the other hand, has a strong track record in technology and innovation. Thanks to that, it closed up in relatively short time to a group of new-generation financial centers, not just based on capital markets, but based on hubs constructed around financial innovation.

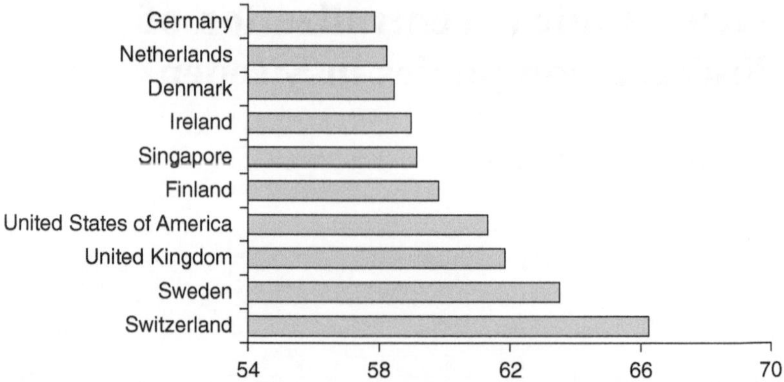

Figure 21.1 Global Innovation Index ranking (top 10) 2016

Europe is still considered the innovation hub in the world, as confirmed by the Global Innovation Index 2016, which is collaboratively published by WIPO, Cornell University, and the INSEAD Business School. As shown in Figure 21.1, the Global Innovation Index ranking rates Sweden as the second strongest innovation leader between Switzerland and the UK (Dutta et al., 2016).

But technology is just one part; the second ingredient to successful transformation is the competence to execute, and Sweden, and in particular Stockholm, has shown this extensive competence over the past decades. With the number of success stories rapidly growing, Sweden is leading the global transformation at the forefront.

According to the "Connecting Global FinTech: Hub Review 2016" published by Deloitte and supported by the Global FinTech Federation Hub, an organization of the leading FinTech hubs in the world, challenges for FinTech are connected with the local culture. The authors of the report mention "limited exit opportunities" and "risk-averse culture" as challenges that prevent the growth of FinTech. Therefore, countries willing to take more risk will encourage the development of the ecosystem until it is mature enough to support itself. Unsurprisingly, the high cost of living is a key issue in developed markets. A number of hubs reported small size of market as a challenge, suggesting that cross-border business is still problematic for FinTech firms (Deloitte, 2016).

Since technological advancements allow companies to operate globally even while being physically located in one country, it presents a great opportunity to grow revenues through global expansion. However, for FinTech companies, it is not as easy to expand globally as money is involved. When money is involved, there are a lot of regulatory and compliance issues that have to be taken into account, not to mention the licensing requirements differing between countries. As the barriers are higher for global expansion, so far very few FinTech startups have successfully managed to expand globally. Factors that contribute to or decide the success of global expansion for a FinTech startup include:

- local ecosystem;
- regulations;
- professional network;
- success in the home country;
- working with local industry bodies;
- overall market opportunity; and
- competitiveness and flexibility of business models.

Out of all these factors, regulation plays a critical role. For example, startups offering payment solutions have to devise a plan to smartly enter the foreign market, especially at a time of heightened regulatory pressure (i.e., increased levels of capital and high compliance-related costs). Thus, many FinTech startups that expand on a global scale rely on partnerships with other companies or banks (Finch et al., 2016).

Method

We conducted interviews between February and April 2017 with three successful Swedish companies from or directly related to the FinTech sector. These companies were selected based on predefined criteria:

- company with established product;
- growing number of users;
- headquartered in Sweden; and
- year of establishment before 2010.

We selected the following companies:

- Olov Renberg, co-founder and COO of BehavioSec, offering identity and access management solutions. BehavioSec focuses on a particular aspect of security; it adds a layer of behavioral analytics to an online financial service (e.g., the Internet and mobile banking). Renberg explains the advantages of founding the company in Luleå.
- Björn Elfgren, CEO of accounting software solution Wint, which was started in Gothenburg by a group of friends who decided to leave the corporate world and start their own company that successfully operates from different locations online.
- Oscar Berglund, CEO of Trustly, offering secured cross-border payments to and from consumer bank accounts at 190 banks in 29 European markets. The research team talked to Trustly's CEO to understand what brought him to Stockholm.

All interviews were recorded.

Reports from the interviews

The decision where to start a company can be one crucial aspect that determines the success of a company. In this chapter, three successful Swedish companies from or directly related to the FinTech sector share insights about the factors that played a key role when founding their businesses.

Evolution of the market

Being located in Europe, and especially in the Nordics, has a significant impact on the company's future. Our interviewees stressed the importance of geography in their businesses. One of the crucial factors is the evolution of the financial industry, and in general the market circumstances, such as Internet penetration, mobile usage, and digitalization of traditional industries in Sweden.

Olov Renberg, co-founder and COO of BehavioSec, mentioned the population distribution in Sweden and mobile penetration as two main triggers to the evolution of the industry:

> Due to our geography, Sweden has always had Internet banking, basically since the early 1990s. Some parts of Sweden are far from any bank's branch offices. That helped us to become a digital society, and especially in recent years our approach to security changed. The Nordics have always invested quite heavily into security solutions. One of them became especially prevalent, which is a security token [a physical device used to gain access to an electronically restricted resource]. Thus, we invested quite heavily into that.
>
> Second of all, what really sealed the deal is the growth in mobile banking. We saw that over the past few years, literally the whole Swedish population moved from little or no mobile identities to everyone using the same system to authenticate themselves.
>
> Sweden, Norway, Denmark, and Finland are small countries, and there are not that many people, which makes it easier to make a change.
>
> Having bank accounts in a number of countries myself, I would say that Sweden is an innovation leader, just because of the simplicity of everything. Sweden is a pretty cashless society; you can wire money to someone's phone number instantly without any fees. But, for example, when I have to transfer money in the US, I have to send a fax. Since nobody has a fax anymore, I need to send in a piece of paper. This is just hard.

Oscar Berglund, CEO of Trustly, also mentioned the digital transformation and its impact on the consumer's life:

> The digital transformation is pushing the traditional financial industry to respond to new consumer behavior and their demand for instant gratification. While the number of online consumers has increased, so have digitally enabled businesses. In Europe, there is a sophisticated finance infrastructure

with many well-established institutions, and when combining the traditional infrastructure with new FinTech innovations that simplifies life for consumers, you find a huge growth potential.

Europe has been very successful when it comes to FinTech due to a combination of factors. If we look at the Nordics, historically the region has a highly developed tech infrastructure, which has enabled early adoption and government policies that encouraged an entrepreneurial and innovative climate. In Sweden, regulators are supportive of the FinTech industry, and, for example, Mobile BankID is a good example of innovation that covers both the security and payment topic. The idea came from traditional Swedish banks, and the app is available to all consumers and provides financial authentication. FinTechs have built additional products that adapt the service, and it shows how the financial industry has created an ecosystem capable of sharing technology innovation to the benefit of both traditional players and tech startups.

Although the changes seem to be favorable to a growing number of startups offering new technologies, many banks struggle to progress in a similar way. Berglund mentioned difficulties with creating scalable solutions:

> Today, 93 percent of European citizens are using their bank accounts as their primary funding source that all other payment methods depend on. Consumers across Europe also increasingly want to shop and pay from their bank accounts. Banks cannot create a scalable solution on a European level, whereas our transaction services can be provided domestically and across borders. We have a significant growth potential and can expand our business by supporting new merchants to scale. We can grow our existing merchant base as they enter new countries, or expand to new countries ourselves. The demand for effective, affordable FinTech services along with new convenient authorization methods gives us a good momentum to roll out the best possible products across Europe.

Renberg also discussed the missing focus for the banks of user experience, where banks no longer have a couple of years to implement the changes:

> In the past few years, user experience has been moved to a whole new level. In the beginning, in 2008, when we started this company, people that worked in security were very risk-averse; they only wanted to have a really good token system. But currently, we observe that more and more innovation-focused people are hired, and they have ideas on how to change the bank and make it more modern. This relates to the problem of banks that they do not have five or more years to improve and implement innovations like it used to be. They realized that if their product is not sexy enough, they are not going to attract any customers. The user growth is what drives everyone, including banks.

Challenges of doing business in Sweden

Despite being an innovation leader that attracts a lot of startups, Stockholm, but also other regions of Sweden, struggle with similar challenges. While running the business, the interviewees pointed out that finding the right people to hire is one the most difficult challenges.

According to Oscar Berglund, the biggest challenge is to find talents and hiring the right people:

> We are always looking for people who intuitively fit into Trustly's culture and share our values. Many tech companies have experienced difficulties with hiring tech people in Sweden.
>
> Last week DI Digital reported that Migrationsverket [the Swedish Migration Agency] in 2016 denied nearly twice as many work permit extensions for people in the IT industry versus 2015 (Carlsson, 2017).
>
> To retain Sweden's top digital talent in the future, the Swedish government needs to continuously invest in digital skills and digital infrastructure, as well as address the cost of office space and rents, if it is to continue to attract tech talent to Sweden.

Björn Elfgren, CEO of accounting software solution Wint, noted that next to hiring issues, legislation is the most difficult:

> Finding the right people to hire, financing for developments, and changing people's mindset and way of doing things are the biggest challenges of doing business in Sweden. For example, our users need a different habit to be fully able to work with our product. Unfortunately, the legislation in Sweden for accounting is disadvantageous compared to the other Nordic countries.

Olov Renberg agrees with the other interviewees in regard to Swedes' attitudes toward implementing change, as well as their propensity to fight for employee rights:

> We probably did not have the best start because we are entering the security market, which is very traditional, a market where you do not want any changes. We are trying to disrupt that business, which makes it a little bit different since investments in the industry were made in early 2000. Thus, the authorities do not feel that change is needed. From that perspective, maybe it would be easier to start, for example, in the US, where the username and password are still used to authenticate people.
>
> Also, you have to remember the fight for people is much harder in Stockholm. I see my friends that I started with, how often they switch jobs from a new payment startup to another, whereas in Luleå people are more prone to stay with the same company and they really want to be there and grow. Also, they have to compare; the cost of living in Stockholm is much higher than in another part of the country.

Hometown-based startups

According to Olav Sorenson of the Yale School of Management and Michael Dahl of Aalborg University, entrepreneurs, even more than employees, tend to locate in regions in which they have deep roots ("home" regions) (Dahl and Sorenson, 2012). We asked Wint from Gothenburg, BehavioSec from Luleå, and Trustly from Stockholm why they decided to start their businesses in their respective hometowns.

Oscar Berglund confirmed that as the founders of Trustly were from Stockholm, that was also the main reason to start the business from there. Björn Elfgren agreed, and mentioned that "you start the company where you find the right people, plus the important factor is how costly the area is":

> We are free to work from anywhere. Why did we start in Gothenburg? We were actually four guys starting it; since we all lived and worked close to Gothenburg, we decided to start here. Later, we recruited people in Gothenburg and grew the team; it is actually a people-based company. The right people together can do magic stuff. Also, a side effect was that Gothenburg wasn't the tech startup area until three years ago. It was a little easier to find the people there for IT and business development, and it is a low-cost area compared to Stockholm, for example. Starting in Gothenburg was a good decision. Especially when we raised our Series A round, we directly worked with family offices in Gothenburg and didn't have to approach the VC companies in Stockholm.

Renberg, from BehavioSec, on the other hand, mentioned the proximity to talents as the reason to start the company in Luleå: "It was very good from a technological standpoint because we had the proximity to the university, so that we could attract the right staff in the fields of machine learning, artificial intelligence, and computer science."

Stockholm: the place to be

However, all of the interviewees mention how important presence in Stockholm is in their business, as it gives reputation and infrastructure.

Olov Renberg explained when the need for having a presence in Stockholm emerged for BehavioSec:

> We didn't just start with banks. First, we reached out to a broad range of customers of traditional IT security solutions, but it was just that the banks had the pressing need to solve the problem of fraud and account takeovers. They also had the willingness to pay for it because they were under attack and were losing money. That was the reason why we started traveling down to Stockholm, which is where most of the banks are, and that's why we set up the office in Stockholm. However, the IT staff is not placed in the city center because it's too small. In Sweden, if you look at the banks and their IT

> powerhouse, their IT operations are far outside. Looking from the retrospective if we could start the business again, I think it will still be the same setup actually. The IT is still in the original location. We are present in Stockholm only to have a sort of presence in the hub; operations will still be spread across the country.

Björn Elfgren argues for a similar standpoint:

> Today, we work only with the Swedish tech market since most of them are early adopters to the solution. Since a lot of these companies are Stockholm-based, we have a sales office there. If you look at the market size for the small and medium enterprises (SMEs) and regard SMEs as early adopters, there are a lot of them in Stockholm; therefore, customers are here. Not the big corporations, but tech startups are the target group for us. That is why Stockholm is important. There are 1 million SMEs in Sweden, and a whole lot of them are in Stockholm.

Oscar Berglund agrees with Renberg and Elfgren:

> Stockholm has a strong reputation and infrastructure as a tech hub where there is a very tech-savvy talent pool. Stockholm has a strong startup ecosystem and networks that inspire entrepreneurs—and on the back of that, investors. In addition, consumers in Stockholm are early adopters and have progressive payment preferences. Europe has a tradition of fostering a good regulatory framework, and because of the single market it helps businesses expand.

Nowadays, it is also not a big problem to be present in Stockholm. As Elfgren noted, the time to travel between the main cities is shrinking: "Now we host a lot of meetings in Stockholm because that is still where the cash flows, but it is not a big distance—you go there in the morning, and you go back in the evening."

Renberg also pointed out a similar observation, as today many companies have to travel to Stockholm due to their client location:

> I met with one startup last week, and they start in Gothenburg, and whenever they wanted to sell they move to Stockholm, I think that is a good example how it works in Sweden. You can run the operation from anywhere, but if you want to sell it you make yourself available in Stockholm.

On the other hand, Renberg also suggested that the best advantage of being in a hub such as Stockholm is the possibility to network, although not every startup is interested in networking:

> It depends on what you do; if you really want to be a part of the acquisition in FinTech, then you can do a lot of networking events. I attend sometimes, but not on a weekly basis. We are not a part of the startup world, but a lot of

> people are, so there are obviously a lot of ideas and collaborations. We are really into work; we focus on what we are doing instead of going out and talking to everyone else about what they are doing. Obviously, we do not get all the influence, but we can better maintain our culture and strategy.

Future outlooks: regulation, collaboration, and innovation

The interviewees agree that in the future, we will still see changes and developments in the industry based on adjusted regulation, increased collaboration, and data-driven innovation.

"I think there will be more hubs in the larger cities because people attract people and ideas attract other people with ideas," Björn Elfgren said, and spotted Malmö as a potential candidate to become a technology hub. He continued:

> I think Malmö is one of those, but many smaller cities are creating hubs. For example, if you look at Gothenburg, it took just two years to develop a hub; the big success stories are in Stockholm, but I would like to see a shining star being founded and operated in a smaller city or the countryside.

According to Oscar Berglund, the process of creating a hub is not simply a decision to "accumulate" companies in one area: "This will come as an organic process and as an effect of the market conditions. There is an entrepreneurial spirit in the FinTech sector, and a strong network with intense participants is attractive when breaking new grounds."

Elfgren added:

> Well, we are going to change even faster, but I think it is going to be a bit different since you put companies in a context, the entire FinTech industry will be more packed together, and meaning there will be a synergy of the solution.

Berglund not only sees the synergy, but also he regards the development of the industry as a step toward collaboration instead of replacement:

> As of now, there are a few big players that dominate the payment sector, and I think we will see more of a consolidation trend in this sector. There are also many smaller businesses performing well and complementing what is already available, and there are many collaborative opportunities for these companies. I think the fact that authentication procedures used to authorize bank payments are moving into the mobile phone will drive usage of bank payments.
>
> On a regulatory level, the Second Payment Services Directive will provide regulatory certainty to a service we have already provided for many years. It effectively brings an existing payment method into the scope of the regulation, but regulation does not create the payment method per se. As a consequence of regulating this payment method, providers of this kind of service

> needs to get a license, but for us that is not that big a thing as we have had a payment institution license for six years now. In five years time, things will be safer, with less fraud, and quicker, with payments being made instantly. I think online banking payments will be the payment method of choice for many more people, at least online/on the Internet.

With the ever-growing number of Internet and mobile banking users, different kinds of security and authentication methods have to be developed. According to Olov Renberg, a lot of banks sit on a great number of data:

> [The] bank basically knows everything about you. And this is opening up to a lot of different Startups. Everything is getting more global, and all services are getting more advanced, but still the banks hold most of the information, they obviously have a lot of power, and I think that they can use it in a good way, so it will be very beneficial for society as a whole.
>
> On the other hand, better security helps to lower the risk. However, many companies are struggling to provide a very secure system and a good user experience. They consider it as a trade-off. It is very hard to maintain both which makes it harder to scale.

Conclusions

This chapter is intended to shed light upon the question to what extent the geographical location of a company determines its success, and what are the underlying factors that influence the choice of location. To follow up on those questions, the co-founders of three successful, Sweden-based companies from or directly related to the FinTech industry shared their insights.

One key finding was that it does not matter where you develop your product, as long as you have access to talent and the market. Companies establish their business where they find their executives and have a constant flow of candidates. As digital products change over time, talent is the key component.

For early-stage companies, it is also extremely important to keep costs at a low level, as well as for the candidates who can't afford to live in high-cost areas. Additionally, starting your business in a traditional industry (e.g., the financial industry) involves a lot of market comprehension; you need to not only change your client's mindset, but especially closely collaborate with the local authorities and regulators.

Stockholm is regarded as the center of finance and commerce. Thus, over time, it has developed a strong reputation and infrastructure as a tech hub. Most companies agree, and consequently either directly establish their companies in Stockholm or set up a representative office. However, due to multiple factors, such as digitalization, and thereby easier access to customers from different parts of the world, and the ever-rising cost of living, Sweden, and especially Stockholm, has gone through a major change. Besides Stockholm, more and more cities have developed into hubs or centers for innovation and startups. As one of the interviewees mentioned, becoming a hub is an organic process; it comes as an effect of the market conditions. Companies are now in the situation to consider more aspects when facing the decision where to establish their business. Thus, to retain Sweden's top digital talent in the future, the Swedish government needs to continuously invest in digital skills and digital infrastructure, as well as address the cost of office space and rents, if it is to continue to attract tech talent to Stockholm.

Due to all the investment made into the FinTech industry, the ecosystem is going to change even faster, most of all thanks to the synergy of different solutions. As the interviewees point out, the development of the financial industry will be influenced and determined by collaboration of startups and banks, and a constantly improved use of data. Processes will be safer, with fewer possibilities for fraud, and quicker, with payments being made instantly. Online and especially mobile services will be the choice for many more people. Consumer habits might change, especially if FinTech innovators remove inconveniences and a more integrated global financial services system begins to develop. FinTech companies will work in a different context and will start to offer a packaged solution. We can already observe a consolidation trend in some sectors of FinTech. This relates to the problem of banks that they do not have several years to improve and implement innovations like they used to. If the product is not attractive enough, it is not going to attract any customers. The user growth is what drives everyone, including banks. Similar to the view on a rather decentralized development of the financial industry, the entire startup ecosystem is changing toward a more decentralized setup based on multiple hubs in different cities spread around Sweden.

Bibliography

Carlsson, S., 2017. Dubbelt så många kodare utvisas av Migrationsverket. *Dagens Industri*. [online] Available at: https://digital.di.se/artikel/dubbelt-sa-manga-kodare-utvisas-av-migrationsverket [Accessed September 14, 2017].

Dahl, M.S. and Sorenson, O., 2012. Home sweet home: Entrepreneurs' location choices and the performance of their ventures. *Management Science*, 58(6), pp.1059–1071.

Deloitte, 2016. Connecting global FinTech: Hub review 2016. *FSIReview*, [online] pp.1–20. Available at: www.finextra.com/finextra-downloads/newsdocs/fintech-hub-review-2016.pdf [Accessed September 14, 2017].

Dutta, S., Lanvin, B., Wunsch-Vincent, S., Insead, World Intellectual Property Organization, and Johnson Graduate School of Management (Cornell University), 2016. *The Global Innovation Index 2016: Winning with global innovation*. Ithaca, NY: Johnson Cornell University; Fontainebleau: INSEAD; Geneva: WIPO.

Finch, P., Carter, P., Hawken, B., Ina, S., Jevremovic, I., Mott, J., et al., 2016. *Q-series global banks: Is FinTech a threat or an opportunity?* [online] Available at: https://neo.ubs.com/shared/d1DAPMSiJ7/ [Accessed September 14, 2017].

Gaskell, A., 2017. Fighting the war for talent in a changing world. *Forbes*. [online] Available at: www.forbes.com/sites/adigaskell/2017/02/08/fighting-the-war-for-talent-in-a-changing-world/#65d6df5b49f8 [Accessed September 14, 2017].

Lavender, J., Pollari, I., Raisbeck, M., Hughes, B., and Speier, A., 2017. *The Pulse of FinTech Q2 2017: Global Analysis of Investment in FinTech*. [online] Available at: https://assets.kpmg.com/content/dam/kpmg/xx/pdf/2017/07/pulse-of-fintech-q2-2017.pdf [Accessed December 8, 2017].

22 When Britain leaves the EU, will FinTechs turn to the Vikings?[1]

Michal Gromek and Timotheos Mavropoulos

Introduction

For centuries, rats have penetrated the food chambers of ships, which dropped their anchors in safe harbors during turbulent seas. In the wake of the referendum on British membership in the European Union, the "remain" and the "leave" voters agreed that the UK was like a rat in a food chamber of the ship called the "EU." What had not yet been decided was whether the ship's chamber was full of food or whether the ship was about to sink (Kraus and Schwager, 2004). As the world awoke on June 24, 2016, it was rather clear that 51 percent of the UK's citizens had been convinced that the rat needed to escape the ship. This chapter will reflect on whether the current post-Brexit status of the UK as a FinTech hub could affect Stockholm's development as well. It will underline the challenges, opportunities, and uncertainty arising after Brexit.

From the harbor of FinTech and back?

Statistically speaking, while traveling on a crowded bus in a random city in the UK, you can be sure that at least one out of every 60 bus passengers is working in the financial industry (Magnus, Margerit, and Mesnard, 2016). More than 1 million employees contribute to this sector in the UK, generating a significant amount of state revenue.

When it comes to FinTech ventures in the UK, in 2015 British FinTech companies employed more than 60,000 professionals, such that one out of every 20 employees working in the financial sector was engaged in services connected to FinTech ventures. For years, the UK has been a European leader in attracting FinTech investments. In 2015, this sector generated over USD 700 million in investments and USD 9.4 billion in revenues (EY, 2016).

Sweden has chased the UK in terms of FinTech investments per capita, but the distance remained unreachable, until now at least. By the end of 2015, there were around 3,000 FinTech employees in Sweden.[2] Even accounting for the fact that the UK has 65 million inhabitants and Sweden only around 10 million, the ratio of FinTech employees to the total population is three times higher in the UK. Also, bearing in mind that Sweden has a more conservative definition of FinTech, specified in Chapter 9 in this volume, the transaction value generated by Swedish FinTech reaches just about 10 percent of that of the UK's.

Is the rat itself maybe sinking?

The Digital Market Outlook on the FinTech sector in the United Kingdom by the statistics portal for market data, Statista (2017), predicts a decline of the FinTech transaction value[3] growth in consumer and business finance by nearly two-thirds between 2016 and 2021.

Such a significant decline might have multiple origins, which do not necessarily have connections to Brexit at first glance. One such impact might be the growing impact of China on the FinTech market. FinTech investments grew from USD 19.1 billion in 2015 to USD 21.2 billion in 2016, and China's investments were responsible for a significant part of this growth. While European investments in European FinTech enterprises decreased by more than one-fourth, China's presence in this field doubled (Meola, 2016).

On a European level, London's position as a leader in FinTech might be heavily impacted by how political leadership of both the European Union and the United Kingdom decide to execute the "divorce" triggered by the so-called "Article 50" (Morales, Hutton, and Datoo, 2017). From a FinTech perspective, the "rat" may sink after jumping off the ship, depending on whether financial licenses obtained in the UK may be transferable to other EU countries.

Additionally, FinTech employees remain a rare breed because of their unique mix of skills that combine a sociological understanding of financial products with technological innovation. The current UK Prime Minister Theresa May

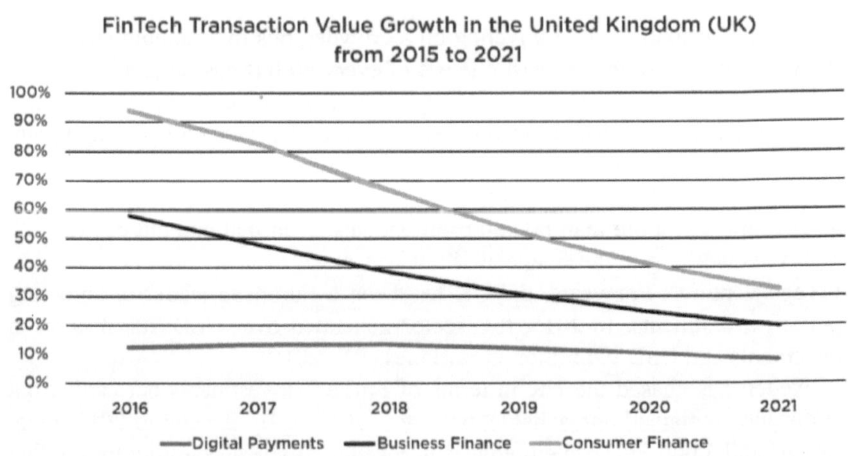

Figure 22.1 FinTech transaction value growth in the United Kingdom (UK) from 2015 to 2021, by segment

Source: Own creation; Digital Market Outlook.

underlined a desire to limit or even terminate the free movement of the labor force between different member states of the EU in relation to the UK (Financial Times, 2017). Such a limitation might trigger the diplomatic practice defined as the "reciprocity rule."[4] Such a "race to the bottom" due to a scarcity of FinTech talent in the European market and the growing presence of China could significantly decrease UK competitiveness in the field.

In every case, a soft Brexit, whereby the UK leaves the EU but remains in the single market,[5] would be a less risky option for the UK's financial services and FinTech because it would enable the financial services firms to continue to rely on certain benefits, and regulatory passporting rights (Armour, 2017) in particular.

In summary, the growing effect of China on FinTech investments and the relation between FinTech and Brexit is a blend of complex interrelations between politics, international relations, and capital flows, which cannot be analyzed as a stand-alone phenomenon.

Learning from history: Brexit versus 1997 "Hongexit"

Analytical reports by the International Monetary Fund predict that the Bank of England and Her Majesty's Treasury abandoning the EU will have overwhelming economic consequences for the UK (Bank of England, 2016; HM Treasury, 2016; IMF, 2016). In particular, a substantial proportion of the pound depreciation has been related to the Brexit referendum, yet these huge drops in the value of the pound have so far failed to yield a lasting improvement in the UK's trade deficit (Tombs, 2017). Indeed, one might be worried about these recent exchange rate movements that are resulting in the UK vying for the award for most unsuccessful currency depreciation in history almost a year after a historic Brexit vote.

As standard econometric models may miss relevant inputs, as well as not entirely account for the interaction among various effects on labor, trade, capital flows, and productivity, there is a motivation to search for historical occurrences that are analogous in key aspects to a Brexit shock. Finding such episodes is not easy as there are no fully comparable instances. Historically, there have been many instances of "sudden stops" leading to financial crises and recessions (for a more detailed explanation behind the "sudden stops," see, for example Calvo, Izquierdo, and Talvi, 2003), but such episodes are not applicable in the case of Brexit, as they are typically cases in which investor confidence evaporates as a sovereignty tries to maintain its exchange rate. However, the transfer of sovereignty of Hong Kong from the UK to China in 1997 could be comparable in nature and provide some insight.

On July 1, 1997, the sovereignty of Hong Kong was returned to China from the United Kingdom. As specified in three treaties (Tsai, 1995) between 1842 and 1998, the UK governed the territory of Hong Kong for around 150 years under something that today would be defined as a leasing agreement (Henderson, 1995). The transfer of Hong Kong's sovereignty from one country to another could be seen as a relevant historical example of transferring jurisdiction and control that led to economic and entrepreneurial uncertainty (Carroll, Feng, and Kuilman, 2014).

The transfer of sovereignty of Hong Kong did not happen overnight, and, similar to Brexit, investors had to cope with a range of uncertainty. To soften the effects of uncertainty, China introduced a policy called "one country, two systems" for a transition period of 50 years after the handover in 1997 (Surhone, Tennoe, and Henssonow, 2010). During the negotiation process before the transfer, the central government in Beijing made specific pledges connected to Hong Kong's monetary and financial systems, which are contained in official documents such as the Sino-British Joint Declaration,[6] Chen Seven Principles,[7] and Basic Law.[8] Those documents specified the free flow of currency and confirmed that the district would use its financial revenues exclusively for itself. It is important to underline that not only did Hong Kong have to pay HK 1 billion annually for the last three years to the British garrison, but it also received an exclusive privilege to be exempt from contributing to the Central People's government budget. This particular privilege of not contributing to the central budget is unique in China, and has been kept in place to date, which distresses governors of other Chinese cities that transfer a significant amount of their tax revenues for this reason (Jao, 2001).

Hong Kong's return to China not only resulted in challenges, but also an assortment of opportunities. On the one hand, while "returning" to China, Hong Kong found not only access to 1 billion potential customers at its doorstep, but also a fast-paced growing economy that has increased its GDP by double-digit growth. Such an abundance of investment opportunities might be paradoxically the seed, soil, and water for the growth of financial players that were located in Hong Kong. In absolute numbers, shortly before the handover to China, a local government report quoted the following: "From March 1996 to March 1997, finance, insurance, real estate and business services have had 8 per cent employment increase" (Economic Analysis Division, 1997). It is important to note that the period of the handover was prior to the so-called "dot-com crash"[9] and before the Asian financial crisis.[10] Thus, a Chinese diaspora and a mix of stable and predictable financial markets provided one of the explanations for Hong Kong's rise as a financial hub (Lees, 2012).

Hong Kong has been able to preserve its own currency and to avoid making significant payments to the central budget. Until recently, the political representatives of Hong Kong have been able to balance the line between stability, capitalism, and a Chinese "socialist market economy" (Yang and Dunford, 2017). This political situation has been a masterpiece of "having your cake" of advantages and "eating it too" in the market economy.

Not everything will be a bed of roses by 2047 when the transition period finishes. Similar to Brexit, everybody knows that the end of the transition period for Hong Kong will happen. What remain unknown are the implications of this transformation. However, the danger of a flight of capital and talent remains fairly real, and a contemporary version of Hong Kong might find itself in windy waters. China and Hong Kong need to be able to combine two frequently contradictory sides to the "one country, two systems" arrangement, which might carry encouragement for both the UK and the EU.

From harbor to hub . . . and back?

Recently, Article 50 was added to the pool of European treaties because it had been assumed that once a country had exerted so much effort to come into the EU, it would not be interested in leaving it.[11] If London would like to maintain the free flow of capital, it would potentially have to obey the regulatory frameworks issued by the European Securities and Markets Authority (ESMA), which governs a substantial volume of the financial regulation.

The UK would not be the only country that would benefit from the EU market while not being an EU member. In 1960, countries (Carmona, Cîrlig, and Sgueo, 2017) that wanted to benefit from the advantages of the European membership formed a European Economic Area (EEA) and its sub-organization the European Free Trade Association (EFTA). The UK was an EFTA member before the EU Accession in 1973.[12] The parliament of the UK, in one of the alternative scenarios to EU membership, expressed a potential return to EFTA (Miller, 2013). The Minister for European Affairs in Norway, which is an EFTA member, stated in an interview that the participation of the UK in EFTA could disturb the balance of this organization, which might adversely affect the Norwegian position (Wintour, 2016).

The relation between EEA, EFTA, and the EU might appear quite complex. Generally speaking, while joining the EEA and EFTA, the UK would enjoy the benefits of using a legal framework that has existed since 1994. On the one hand, the capital movement would remain unrestricted and the UK would not have to implement a range of European policies in the field of judicial affairs, foreign policies, etc. Even in a positive scenario, being an EFTA member means to accept the decision of the internal market, competition, state aid, and financial regulation. What is significant for EFTA and EEA is that none of the representatives of those organisations may participate in the meetings and cooperation between the European Parliament, the Council of Ministers, or the EU Commission. Practically speaking, if the UK wanted to receive more independence from the EU, it would have to implement regulation on the financial markets, an extremely important pillar of the economy, without having the right to contribute or veto a regulation or directive (Piris, 2016).

Challenges

Brexit adds challenges to an already turbulent industry, which currently operates under a high degree of uncertainty. The trade (re)negotiation position of the EU is much stronger than that of the UK, and there are no guarantees that the UK can achieve a position comparable to EFTA members such as Norway. Under the current definition of passporting, a company that has applied and received a banking license in Sweden (for example) does not have to apply for the same license when conducting business in other countries within the European Union. The company "only" has to notify a particular financial supervision authority that it intends to perform its services in a particular scope in another country. The complexity of such a "notification" differs from country to country within the EU, and can hardly be summarized as an effortless adjustment for the FinTech companies.

Opportunities

Similar to the case of the handover of Hong Kong to China, Brexit does not necessarily have to lead to an expensive price tag or a decrease in FinTech activity. While executed well, the gravity pole of FinTech can quickly move back toward the UK. Losing ties from common European jurisdictions might allow the UK to respond more quickly and efficiently to the changing world of FinTech. As all financial supervision regulators within the EU have to follow a mostly unified FinTech related policy framework, the post-Brexit UK regulator could use this to an advantage for the United Kingdom.

Thus, leaving the EU may position the UK not as a follower, but as an advantageous "first mover" and a smart FinTech player avoiding the "winner's curse."[13] As of May 2016 (Monerary Authority of Singapore, 2016), the UK regulator FCA[14] has established the first regulatory bridge with its Singaporean counterpart MAS.[15] Such a regulatory bridge allows the sharing of information on financial services, sharing of knowledge, and creates coherent regulation that allows FinTech companies to expand into other jurisdictions. This cooperation is just one case of how easily the UK could follow the example of Singapore, which has already established its own distinctive FinTech agenda.

Opportunities for other FinTech players, including Sweden, might also be rising. Negotiating from a *tabula rasa* FinTech perspective may lead to previously hidden synergies and establish "win–win" FinTech collaborations and projects that enhance the positions of all the collaborating parties. The FinTech game is not "the only game in town." By seemingly alienating the UK from an EU umbrella, Brexit may well create a combination of opportunities in other fields that need immediate regulatory support, such as InsurTech,[16] RegTech,[17] or its conjunction with artificial intelligence.

The sprint toward a cashless society as Stockholm's benefit from Brexit

Brexit and its effect might influence international FinTech companies looking for a door opener in Europe to reconsider their plans to open an office in the UK. German politicians have paid for billboards and letters to startups that promote Berlin as a business location; the region of Paris has sent a letter to executives; the city of Dublin launched a marketing campaign; and Milan expressed their desire to host the headquarters of the European Bank Regular (Deen and Doyle, 2017). As somebody's losses are someone else's gain, it might be argued that uncertainty connected with Brexit could result in benefits for Stockholm, which is unquestionably on the European FinTech forefront.

It should also be noted that the uncertain climate during the Brexit negotiation process will provide Stockholm FinTech with possible regulatory arbitrage opportunities: companies incorporated in London can pay salaries in Stockholm, and vice versa, with tax benefits accumulating for companies operating across jurisdictions. The EU provides access to 500 million potential consumers, while the UK alone only offers 65 million (Allen et al., 2015). Potential incoming FinTech companies might consider locations such as Berlin, Madrid, or Stockholm continuing to enable stable access to the "other" 500 million potential users with a clearer regulatory structure.

Heading toward a cashless society with a focus on digitalization, high Internet accessibility, and having an already existing strong base of FinTech companies, Stockholm can easily benefit from the uncertainty connected to Brexit to advance its image as a unicorn breeding ground (Financial Times, 2015). The Swedish capital, with its flat structures, a high level of English proficiency, a high degree of knowledge diffusion through informal networks, and a currently synergistic FinTech business environment, could provide a safe harbor for incoming FinTech talent. Additionally, nothing works as well as the firsthand internal feedback from FinTech companies from a well-functioning FinTech business environment of the city. Instead of providing funding for expensive marketing campaigns, authorities might establish some economically shrewd quick fixes that might benefit incoming or future FinTech companies.

Recommendations for Stockholm

Stockholm has the potential of offering a "safe harbor" to those British FinTech companies considering relocating to another EU country after Brexit. Some potential practical recommendations to attract UK-based companies include the following:

FinTech@Stockholm.se?

The establishment of a FinTech one-stop shop information center could operate in English and be able to support international companies considering Sweden as their future FinTech location. Companies could send in their requests connected with regulatory questions and receive practical how-to-brochures, such as: "Conduct your cryptocurrency business in Stockholm? This is how!" Such a center would not have the rights to advise FinTech companies, but could "inform" and provide guidance on which particular FinTech representatives could be consulted for a particular issue. The Stockholm FinTech Hub could facilitate this service in partnership with Invest in Stockholm and Business Sweden representative offices in London.

FinTech transparency center

It is comprehensible that information connected with FinTech changes quickly. Nevertheless, from a position of a foreign startup, the jungle of FinTech regulations remains impenetrable. A constantly updated web page, FinTech.stockholm.se, could provide one single place to draft and display case studies of companies, aggregate external reports, and provide material for FinTech@stockholm.se.

This center could leverage informal networks in Stockholm and work with existing organizations, such as the newly formed Swedish Financial Technology Association (SweFinTech).

FinTech co-living spaces

FinTech companies that establish their FinTech offices in Stockholm and successfully complete an approval process (conducted, for example, by the Stockholm FinTech Hub) could receive access to a publicly supported FinTech package. A time-limited package would include access to an accelerator office space or co-working space, as well as a place in a newly established FinTech residential apartment community. In the beginning, such support could at least provide incoming companies with solutions to a challenging housing situation in Stockholm.

However, developments in Swedish taxation policy, and tax increases in particular, could hamper these opportunities (Lind, 2016). Talent follows money, and billions of dollars in capital investment flooding into the FinTech ecosystem worldwide may urge Stockholm to position itself competitively in order to attract the FinTech stars and grow sustainably (Castilla-Rubio, Zadek, and Robins, 2016). Additionally, the idea of an extended "transition period" after Brexit is currently gaining more and more ground. If this alone will be enough to help maintain stability in the financial markets remains questionable. However, the more prolonged this period is, the more prepared Stockholm can be to receive the talent pool that can strengthen its position on the global FinTech scene.

Conclusion

One million professionals in the UK work in financial services, while FinTech companies employ 60,000 individuals—four times the amount of the Swedish railway system and SAS airline combined. In absolute numbers, the FinTech sector in the UK has 20 times the number of employees in London than Stockholm. While London has been the biggest receiver of European FinTech investments, Brexit in its complexity remains a unique phenomenon, and it is uncertain as to how it will affect London's position as a FinTech hub. As predictions about the future have been challenging for economists, the already pronounced signs of depreciation of the British pound signal some deterioration in investor trust. A peaceful change of sovereignty was conducted on July 1, 1997, with the handover of Hong Kong from the UK to China. As the year 2017 marks the 20th anniversary of this event, not everything has been a bed of roses, but the local representatives managed to align with the central government in Beijing to create a pioneering arrangement called "one country, two systems." When the Hong Kong government has been able to establish such a respected deal with China, representing a radically different political angle, hopefully the UK will be able to establish similar efficient trade ties with EU countries. As the exact terms triggered by Article 50 remain blurry, other locations such as Stockholm could benefit from this storm of uncertainty. Back in the days of the Vikings, Swedes proved themselves as reliable sailors in uncharted waters. As of today, no one argues that this fact has changed.

Notes

1 This chapter has been co-published in the *Stockholm FinTech Report 2018*.
2 Based on authors' review conducted between April 1 and May 25, 2017, on FinTech companies allocated in the greater area of Stockholm, defined in Chapter 9 in this volume.
3 Transaction value—the price paid or payable for a good or service.
4 Reciprocity is defined as a social rule in which an individual receives a repayment for what has been provided to them.
5 The European Single Market allows countries that are integrated in the EU or EFTA to trade freely. It is based on four freedoms: flow of goods, services, labor, and capital among member states.
6 The Sino–British Joint Declaration provides that the basic policies implied by the "one country, two systems" principle should be stipulated in the Hong Kong Basic Law and that the socialist system and socialist policies shall not be practiced in the Hong Kong Special Administrative Region (HKSAR).
7 Chen's Seven Principles can be summarized in one guiding principle of "one country, two currencies," which is the counterpart to the political principal of "one county, two systems."
8 The Basic Law stipulates the basic policies of China toward the Hong Kong Special Administrative Region.
9 The period when many Internet-based companies, commonly referred to as dot-coms, failed after unsustainable expansion.
10 Asian financial crisis—a series of events, including currency devaluations of up to 38 percent, that started in the beginning of 1997, also called "Asian Contagion".
11 Article 50 of the Treaty of Lisbon provides any EU member with the right to leave the EU unilaterally, and outlines the procedures for doing so.
12 The Treaty of Accession 1972 was the international agreement that gave foundation for the accession of Denmark, Ireland, Norway, and the UK to the European Communities.
13 Winner's curse describes a situation in an auction with incomplete information, where the winner tends to overpay.
14 The Financial Conduct Authority is the UK's financial regulatory body, which operates independently of the UK government and is financed by charging fees to members of the financial services industry.
15 The Monetary Authority of Singapore is Singapore's Central Bank and its financial regulator. It regulates banking, insurance, securities, and the financial sector in general, as well as currency issuance.
16 Insurance technology ventures, or InsurTechs, are companies that use technology to make insurance services more efficient and disrupt incumbent insurance corporations that rely less on technology.
17 Regulatory technology ventures, or RegTechs, are companies that use technology in the context of regulatory monitoring, reporting, and compliance to benefit the finance industry through finding solutions that address regulatory compliance challenges.

Bibliography

Allen, K., Oltermann, P., Borger, J., and Nelsen, A., 2015. Brexit: What would happen if Britain left the EU? *The Guardian*, [online] pp.1–9. Available at: www.theguardian.com/politics/2015/may/14/brexit-what-would-happen-if-britain-left-eu-european-union-referendum-uk [Accessed August 28, 2017].

Armour, J., 2017. Brexit and financial services. *Oxford Review of Economic Policy*, 33(supp. 1), pp.S54–S69.

Bank of England, 2016. *Inflation report*. [online] Available at: www.bankofengland.co.uk/publications/Documents/inflationreport/2016/may.pdf [Accessed August 28, 2017].

Calvo, G.A., Izquierdo, A., and Talvi, E., 2003. *Sudden stops, the real exchange rate, and fiscal sustainability: Argentina's lessons*. NBER Working Paper No. 9828. [online]. Available at: www.nber.org/papers/w9828 [Accessed December 13, 2017].

Carmona, J., Cîrlig, C.-C., and Sgueo, G., 2017. *UK withdrawal from the European Union: Legal and procedural issues*. [online] Available at: https://f.hypotheses.org/wp-content/blogs.dir/3671/files/2017/04/Withdrawal-from-EU.-EU-Analysis.pdf [Accessed August 28, 2017].

Carroll, G.R., Feng, M., and Kuilman, J.G., 2014. The handover in Hong Kong: Impact on business formation. *Sociological Science*, 1(22), pp.366–396.

Castilla-Rubio, J.C., Zadek, S., and Robins, N., 2016. *FinTech and sustainable development: Assessing the implications*. [online] Geneva: UNEP. Available at: http://unepinquiry.org/publication/fintech-and-sustainable-development-assessing-the-implications [Accessed December 13, 2017].

Deen, M. and Doyle, D., 2017. *Paris tries letters, Berlin billboards in London jobs quest*. [online] *Bloomberg*. Available at: www.bloomberg.com/news/articles/2016-07-06/paris-tries-letters-berlin-billboards-in-race-for-london-jobs [Accessed August 28, 2017].

Economic Analysis Division, 1997. *1997 Financial Services Bureau half-year economic report*. [online] Available at: www.info.gov.hk/isd/news/aug97/829-econ.htm [Accessed December 13, 2017].

EY, 2016. *UK FinTech: On the cutting edge—an evaluation of the international FinTech sector*. [online] Available at: www.ey.com/uk/en/industries/financial-services/banking---capital-markets/ey-uk-fintech-on-the-cutting-edge [Accessed December 13, 2017].

Financial Times, 2015. Stockholm: The unicorn factory. *Financial Times*. [online] Available at: www.ft.com/content/e3c15066-cd77-11e4-9144-00144feab7de [Accessed December 13, 2017].

Financial Times, 2017. Theresa May stands by pledge to keep cutting net migration. *Financial Times*. [online] Available at: www.ft.com/content/ae0b6066-25e9-11e7-a34a-538b4cb30025 [Accessed December 13, 2017].

Henderson, J.H., 1995. The reintegration of Hong Kong into the People's Republic of China: What it means to Hong Kong's future prosperity. *Vanderbilt Journal of Transnational Law*, 28(3), pp.503–542.

HM Treasury, 2016. *HM Treasury analysis: The long-term economic impact of EU membership and the alternatives*. [online] Available at: www.gov.uk/government/publications/hm-treasury-analysis-the-long-term-economic-impact-of-eu-membership-and-the-alternatives [Accessed December 13, 2017].

IMF, 2016. *Sweden financial stability assessment*. [online] Available at: www.imf.org [Accessed August 28, 2017].

Jao, Y.C., 2001. *The Asian financial crisis and the ordeal of Hong Kong*. Westport, CT: Quorum Books.

Kraus, M. and Schwager, R., 2004. EU enlargement and immigration. *Journal of Common Market Studies*, 42(1), pp.165–181.

Lees, F.A., 2012. *Financial exchanges: A comparative approach*. New York: Routledge.

Lind, J., 2016. Regeringen ska ändra förslag om finansskatten [The government to amend the proposal on fiscal tax]. *Dagens Nyheter*. [online] Available at: www.dn.se/ekonomi/regeringen-ska-andra-forslag-om-finansskatt/ [Accessed December 13, 2017].

Magnus, M., Margerit, A., and Mesnard, B., 2016. *Brexit: The United Kingdom and EU financial services*. [online] European Parliament. Available at: http://www.europarl.europa.eu/RegData/etudes/BRIE/2016/587384/IPOL_BRI%282016%29587384_EN.pdf [Accessed January 6, 2018].

Meola, A., 2016. *The FinTech report 2016: Financial industry trends and investment*. [online] Business Insider. Available at: www.businessinsider.com/the-fintech-report-2016-financial-industry-trends-and-investment-2016-12?r=US&IR=T&IR=T [Accessed December 13, 2017].

Miller, V., 2013. *Leaving the EU*. London: House of Commons Library.

Monerary Authority of Singapore, 2016. *First ever FinTech bridge established between Britain and Singapore*. [online] Media Release. Available at: www.mas.gov.sg/News-and-Publications/Media-Releases/2016/First-ever-FinTech-Bridge-established-between-Britain-and-Singapore.aspx [Accessed September 4, 2017].

Morales, A., Hutton, R., and Datoo, S., 2017. *What's in the Brexit white paper and what does it mean?* [online] Bloomberg. Available at: www.bloomberg.com/news/features/2017-02-02/what-s-in-the-brexit-white-paper-and-what-does-it-mean [Accessed September 4, 2017].

Piris, J.-C., 2016. If the UK votes to leave: The seven alternatives to EU membership. *Centre for European Reform*, [online] January, pp.1–14. Available at: www.cer.eu/sites/default/files/pb_piris_brexit_12jan16.pdf [Accessed September 4, 2017].

Statista, 2017. *Digital market outlook*. [online] Available at: www.statista.com/outlook/digital-markets [Accessed September 15, 2017].

Surhone, L.M., Tennoe, M.T., and Henssonow, S.F., 2010. *Transfer of sovereignty over Hong Kong*. Saarbrücken, Germany: VDM Publishing.

Tombs, S., 2017. Britain's pound depreciation isn't working. *The Wall Street Journal*. [online] Available at: www.wsj.com/articles/britains-pound-depreciation-isnt-working-1484859707 [Accessed September 4, 2017].

Tsai, J.-F., 1993. *Hong Kong in Chinese history: Community and social unrest in the British colony, 1842–1913*. New York: Columbia University Press.

Wintour, P., 2016. Norway may block UK return to European Free Trade Association. *The Guardian*. [online] Available at: www.theguardian.com/world/2016/aug/09/norway-may-block-uk-return-to-european-free-trade-association [Accessed September 4, 2017].

Yang, Z. and Dunford, M., 2017. Cluster evolution and urban industrial dynamics in the transition from a planned to a socialist market economy: The case of Beijing. *Spatial Economic Analysis*, 12(1), pp.50–71.

Conclusion

Implications for actors as institutions evolve

Robin Teigland, Shahryar Siri, Anthony Larsson, Alejandro Moreno Puertas, and Claire Ingram Bogusz

Introduction

FinTech is often described as being "disruptive"; it has begun to change how consumers—and even businesses—use financial services. However, as the chapters in this book show, progress has been uneven and is still very much emergent. For all of the actors in the field, therefore, it is important to keep abreast of the latest changes and their implications, as well as what the emergent ecosystem looks like.

The four forces described in the introduction provide the structure for this book on FinTech. First, we point to existing financial actors' loss of legitimacy, and how it made consumers in particular think differently about their financial activities (i.e., cognition in the field). Second, we point to the rise in new technologies and standards, which have created new norms for all actors in the field. Third, we point to new regulations as a source of institutional change. Lastly, we look at an unequal response to change among insiders and outsiders, and how the rise in FinTech has had different effects on different kinds of actors in different places.

This concluding chapter summarizes the main themes that this book has raised for three important actor groups, namely incumbents, newcomers, and policymakers. We find that although the changes being realized as a result of FinTech are substantial—perhaps ultimately even "disruptive"—financial services still have a long way to go before the institutionalized ecosystem is reshaped entirely.

Food for thought for incumbents

While there is no question that incumbent financial actors have been affected by the rise of FinTech newcomers, they still hold the balance of power when it comes to financial services. Indeed, particularly in the Swedish context, the fact that banks have gone out of their way to be innovative and create new digital services has meant that they have captured new markets, even as newcomers have eaten away at some of their traditional offerings.

Mark Carney, the Governor of the Bank of England, in a recent speech, spoke of the threat that FinTech innovation poses to the traditional banking sector in the UK, such as declining levels of trust and reduced "stability of funding of incumbent banks," which may force the Bank of England to step in "to ensure prudential standards and resolution regimes for the affected banks are sufficiently robust to these risks" (Burton, 2017). This statement points to the fact that incumbent actors need to remain cautious, and keep abreast of the fast changes occurring in this sector. Indeed, their failure to do so is not only likely to have implications for banks' own businesses, but also for existing financial systems.

Business as usual

Incumbents are the standard bearers when it comes to institutionalized activities in finance. Changes that affect incumbent businesses, whether banks or credit card companies or otherwise, are therefore likely to reshape the financial system as a whole. Thus far, their activities have been affected by changes in technology, loss of legitimacy, and changes in regulations, and these changes have varied across geographies and among different constellations of actors, as discussed in the introduction to this book. However, while there have been some noteworthy changes to who provides financial services to whom, and the number of FinTech newcomers has grown in the past decade, their impact on the incumbent players has not been overwhelming.

However, this does not mean that these changes are not emergent. Clayton Christensen, in his book *The Innovator's Dilemma* (1997), describes how disruptive innovations eat away at an incumbent's grip on a market: changes occur slowly, and the products involved may even be inferior to that which the incumbent offers. However, a failure to act by incumbents can lead to customers preferring the new service or product, meaning that it slowly replaces the incumbent offerings—even at the higher end of the consumer spectrum.

In the past, innovation in financial services has largely been driven by newcomers to finance, notably startups, due to their relatively small size and nimble organizational structures (Felländer et al., Chapter 8, this volume). However, as van der Zande (Chapter 17, this volume) notes, Swedish banks in particular are supporting and engaging with FinTech ecosystem newcomers, to the benefit of both their own future business and the continued development of financial technology. This marks a shift in the perception of FinTech innovation; where once innovators were seen as fringe actors with fly-by-night offerings, banks today see that their very survival may depend on learning from, collaborating with, and perhaps even mimicking newcomers' offerings.

Collaboration as a winning strategy

Collaboration has indeed become the name of the game for many incumbents. A case in point is the surge in the number of robo-advisory services in the Swedish market. These services offer a cheap (and automated) alternative to traditional wealth management and asset allocation. Where once banks might have ignored the insurgents, in this case they instead understood that they posed a long-term threat, and therefore looked for ways to collaborate with them.

For instance, Tieless, a robo-advisory firm, partnered with Saxo Bank to process and settle all their trading orders (Mačijauskaitė, Chapter 14, this volume). This collaboration allowed both firms to concentrate on their core competencies, allowing both partners to be more efficient. This ultimately leads not only to incumbent survival, but also a favorable outcome for the consumer: lower commission fees.

Many examples of incumbent–newcomer collaboration lie in the blockchain industry. Blockchain technology, which uses cryptography and distributed processing, aims to eliminate the need for a third party in financial—and other—transactions. It is therefore perceived as a threat to established financial players: banks earn USD 150–200 billion in revenues from transactions flowing through international banking networks, and blockchain technology has the potential to disrupt this source of revenues (Williams et al., 2016). Despite—or perhaps because of—this threat, banks have embraced the technology and have formed three large collaborative consortia, the Ethereum Alliance, the Linux consortium called Hyperledger, and the R3 consortium. These consortia function as loci for collaboration between startups, the financial established players, and established users of Ethereum, Linux and Corda, respectively.

The way forward

Overall, commentators have predicted that social Darwinism ("survival of the fittest") is inevitable in the financial industry (Gilberg, 2017). Given the pace, and reach, of FinTech challengers, it is reasonable to assume that the threat they pose will only increase. Financial institutions therefore would benefit from embracing innovation in order to stay competitive, whether by collaborating with startups or by developing new solutions in-house, or through collaboration with other incumbents or actors in tangential industries. The need for these new solutions, however, need not mean that today's financial institutions will lose their competitive edge, but keeping this edge will require that they adapt and focus on those areas in which they are competitive. These adaptations are necessary both at the level of service and product development, as well as on the organizational level.

Cooperation and mutual understanding between financial institutions and FinTech newcomers have the potential to produce shared benefits, as both industries gain from each other. On the one side, financial institutions have large networks, relative legitimacy, and access to financial and human capital. However, their organizational structures and regulations that govern them mean that they cannot move quickly or take substantial risks; they need to be perceived as stable companies (see Felländer et al., Chapter 8, this volume). In contrast, FinTech firms can take risks, but lack legitimacy, networks, and capital. By cooperating, financial institutions can therefore participate in innovative projects without bearing the risks associated with failing, while FinTech newcomers gain exposure and access to capital and legitimacy through association. Cooperation in this manner facilitates the creation of ecosystems that foster innovation and supports both new and incumbent players, ensuring that established firms remain relevant, and that newcomers obtain the resources that they require to build innovative new financial solutions.

Patterns among FinTech upstarts

According to CB Insights (2016), VC-backed FinTech companies raised USD 12.7 billion in 2016—five times the amount raised in 2012 (USD 2.7 billion). This acceleration in investment shows not only that there are more FinTech firms today than in 2012, but also that they are increasing their revenues and number of customers, and in so doing attracting the attention of professional investors.

In the 22 chapters of this book, we have explored different industries and looked at how the ecosystem has evolved to a point where FinTech firms can flourish. By and large, FinTech newcomers have battled a steep uphill slope to gain legitimacy and come to be perceived as genuine challengers to the status quo. Many of these firms have not only survived, but thrived. However, the ways in which they have done this have varied considerably, and they have employed both social and technological innovations to get to where they are today. The use of this two-pronged approach offers lessons to the next generation of newcomers, as well as to today's FinTech firms.

Trust is crucial

One of the biggest hurdles for a digital startup is trying to convince would-be customers to try, and ultimately adopt, their service. This hurdle is particularly tricky for FinTech newcomers, as individuals are typically risk-averse when it comes to services that involve their salaries, savings, and personal data. Today, most people trust Internet-based applications without fully understanding either their security features or the implications of possible security breaches. The main reason for this is that trust relies on a bridge—BankID, credit cards—between the application and the consumer. However, the Internet also enables security experts to voice their concerns about the applications' security, and concerns tend to propagate fast. This means that new startups are automatically trusted in their initial stages, but if their applications fail to satisfy the perceived needs of the security experts, or in the event of even a minor breach, they are likely to lose that trust. This evolving and changing role of trust online (Lewan, Chapter 6, this volume) has therefore been a boon for entrepreneurs, allowing them to try out new ideas, but has the potential to ruin newcomers that are less careful.

One nascent service area that has relied on this digital trust is robo-advisory services. Mačijauskaitė (Chapter 14, this volume) explains how the millennial generation, eager to earn returns on their newly acquired wealth, has been more willing to adopt new technologies than trust existing financial actors to manage their money. This burgeoning area of interest is, however, still emergent; while new firms are entering the space, there are few that have reached international success.

Platforms, automation, and do-it-yourself security

Another trend among digital startups—including in the FinTech space—has been the rise in peer-to-peer tools. In particular, platforms such as Uber, Airbnb, and Alibaba have come to dominate their respective industries. This rise in platforms has followed a winding road; as Moreno and Teigland (Chapter 15, this volume) point out, until recently, new platforms only provided ancillary services. For instance, Alibaba started as a platform where buyers could search for potential suppliers, without participating in any subsequent transaction. It was only after it became an established player that it started to offer payment solutions.

The reason for this lag in service provision is that value-related services require large investments to ensure the system is secure. As a result, most platform-based companies outsource their payments and other value-related services to large established players: financial institutions. However, as technologies have improved and diversified, this outsourcing has changed shape. Instead of relying on other firms, companies have begun to rely on new technologies, including blockchain technologies.

Newcomers that build upon the blockchain have also begun to offer incumbent firms—and other startups—automated security through cryptography (e.g., see Holmberg, Chapter 16, this volume). This has allowed other firms to focus on designing systems, user interfaces, and other core services. This has also generated a wave of startups offering platforms for value-related services. These kinds of platforms have attracted extensive funding from both venture capitalists and, more recently, through ICOs—a form of crowdfunding that itself uses blockchain technology. Among them, Bancor and Aragon stand out, having received USD 153 million and USD 25 million in seed investments, respectively (Chavez-Dreyfuss, 2017; Higgins, Sunnarborg, and Rizzo, 2017).

The time is now

New sets of tools, a trusting attitude toward technologies, a new generation, and the financial crisis have created a place in which startups of many stripes can thrive. Millennials, who tend to be tech-savvy, are increasing their wealth and looking for alternatives. Moreover, as newcomers have begun to win over these Millennials, they have attracted the interest of established players. They in turn, perceiving FinTech as an opportunity not to be missed, have been willing to invest in new solutions—with financial capital and collaborations. As the number of services available in FinTech markets grows, competition will hopefully drive transparency, giving an opportunity to those who will provide the best services to thrive.

Implications for policymakers

While FinTech may yet be far from mature in many respects, it is a sector that has—and is continuing to—grow rapidly. The management consulting firm

EY (2016, p.3) concluded in a report that the FinTech sector "has now grown from its disruptive roots into an industry in its own right." However, despite anecdotal recognition that FinTech is somehow different from the financial services that have come before it, it has little in the way of legislation, legal documents, or policymaking tailored specifically for it. Instead, the fact that FinTech consists of different types of business models and offers vastly diverse products and/or services has stymied policymakers (Dorfleitner et al., 2017). For this reason, it is regulated differently in different places, under different rules, and under different definitions. As such, we recommend that policymakers approach FinTech regulations cautiously, so as to avoid driving these services underground or to avoid having a chilling effect on FinTech innovation.

In search of a clear definition

On the European level, we have begun to see an increase of political awareness around FinTech. For instance, on May 17, 2017, the European Parliament's Committee on Economic and Monetary Affairs (ECON) published its final report on FinTech's influence of technology on the future of the financial sector (European Parliament, 2017). The report, however, uses a very broad definition of the word, referring to it as "finance enabled by new technologies, covering the whole range of financial services, products and infrastructure" (European Parliament, 2017, p.16). They justify this broad definition by saying that a narrower one would exclude a number of important actors. By using such a broad definition, they do fail to distinguish among the various different kinds of FinTech services, their different uses, and different challenges.

More generally, while the report lauds the work by stakeholders in areas of open banking, blockchain, and cloud computing, it raises a word of caution in terms of cybersecurity and regulation. This recognition is itself laudable; however, different areas of FinTech do require different policy responses, and clearer and more nuanced definitions in FinTech would go a long way toward achieving these aims. FinTech hubs themselves are likely to play an important role in shaping knowledge production, as well as lobbying policymakers in the future (Burenstam Linder, Chapter 20, this volume).

In the Swedish context, Olsson and Hallberg (Chapter 3, this volume) contend that Swedish policymakers have thus far not been attuned to the various trends and phenomena surrounding the financial sector in general and FinTech in particular. This lack of political interest may, in the long run, hold Sweden back, despite its expertise in science and innovations.

Flexibility from policymakers in the early days

Looking forward, it is clear that FinTech topics will take on an increasingly important role for policymakers, both on national levels as well as on a supranational level—such as in the EU. Authors in this volume have shown that there is indeed a need for a policy framework that accounts for both innovation strategies, while also introducing regulations that protect consumers and ensure good business practices, especially given the fragility of the financial system seen in recent years.

Kryparos (Chapter 2, this volume) emphasizes how the need for progress as well as the technological benefits of FinTech outweigh the potential security risks in many cases. However, he points to the importance of informed consent in the digital world. In order for this to happen, there needs to be a policy framework that both permits and requires concerned parties to be informed about the potential consequences of their decisions. Moreover, as personal data are crucial for FinTech and other digital business models, they should be examined in their own right. It is therefore vital that policymakers not only create a clear framework for transparency and personal data ownership, but also that they examine how different kinds of data should attract different kinds of responsibility from private and public actors (Ingram Bogusz, Chapter 11, this volume).

Despite the role of regulations to protect consumers and financial systems, it is important that regulations are made cautiously: while some drive business, others smother it. Moreover, multiple business models even within a single service area (as is the case with robo-advisory services— Mačijauskaitė, Chapter 14, this volume) complicates matters further. Sustainable—and careful—policymaking should therefore balance individual integrity and entrepreneurial incentives (Freij, Chapter 1, this volume).

However, new regulations can alleviate some of the restrictions incurred on new types of technological advancements, as has been the case with payment regulations (Arvidsson, Chapter 13, this volume). Clever policymaking can therefore result in innovative new FinTech services. This may lead to the decline of economic activities that we have thus far taken for granted, for instance cash; however, some social groups will nevertheless hold on to old ways of doing things (e.g., seniors, the unbanked), so their interests need to be considered by policymakers.

Respond to unequal changes

Multiple chapters in this volume have pointed to the fact that technological advancement has been irregularly distributed, with some geographic regions becoming far more digitalized than others (e.g., Arvidsson, Chapter 4, this volume; Dubois and Gromek, Chapter 19, this volume). It therefore makes sense for policymakers to explicitly consider this unequal development, and in so doing ensure that the interests of marginalized groups—whether far from large cities or without access to the latest technologies—are not left out in the cold.

This is particularly important when one considers the ramifications that digitalization and FinTech are having on the traditional banking sector—a vital service, irrespective of location or technology access. For example, the chapters by Larsson (Chapter 7, this volume), van der Zande (Chapter 17, this volume), and Felländer et al. (Chapter 8, this volume) stress the impact and disruption that digitalization has had on traditional banking sectors. These authors recommend that policymakers not only act circumspectly, but also that they collaborate, monitor, and increase dialogue with actors in business—both newcomers and incumbents.

Balancing the needs of these different groups in addition to consumers is likely to add to the challenge.

Control and cooperation across borders

Policymaking in the future, as financial services become as borderless as the Internet, is also likely to require cooperation by multiple national and supranational authorities. Discussing Bitcoin, Holmberg (Chapter 16, this volume) points to the fact that while no European country outlaws the use of cryptocurrencies, policymakers in Sweden and the EU have been (perhaps deliberately so) vague on their attitudes toward it: some countries have cautioned users of the risks, while others have not. In contrast, in the United States, bitcoins are taxed as property (IRS, 2014), while in Canada they are taxed as "intangibles" (Appel, 2014).

Both the inconsistences among European governments and the inconsistencies across the Atlantic are likely to cause problems in the future should Bitcoin use become more mainstream. Moreover, the treatment of Bitcoin points to the troubles that policymakers have had in understanding and regulating digital activities.

As these national and regional governments contemplate policies, they are also likely to try to govern new services in ways that no longer make sense—even though they worked for non-digital services. Blockchain services are one such example (Moreno Puertas and Teigland, Chapter 15, this volume). One of the key security and trust-building features of blockchain technology is the fact that no single user can change its contents. However, this decentralization may prove problematic for policymakers that want to control information or transactions occurring through it. The urgency of this desire to centralize a technology whose strength lies in its decentralization becomes apparent when one considers how blockchain technology has been presented, at least in part, as a possible enabler for the next generation of genuinely global FinTech companies (Lewan, Chapter 10, this volume). Regulating it in a digitally appropriate way is therefore vital for its continued survival, and for the creation of a new generation of financial (and other) services.

Race to the top

Another salient point for policymakers across Europe is how attractive the prospect is of being a leading FinTech nation. Gromek and Mavropoulos (Chapter 22, this volume) discuss the implications of Brexit for other nations, given that it is currently the leading European FinTech nation in the world. Press (Chapter 18, this volume) intimates that while Paris and Frankfurt may step up to the challenge, Britain may yet persevere thanks to its close ties to the United States. In which case, policymakers in the European Union must account for this possibility and decide on the direction they wish to take, whether to foster future collaboration with Britain or to set up barriers in order to promote EU countries.

When it comes to Sweden, Dubois and Gromek (Chapter 19, this volume) point to the fact that equity crowdfunding has centered on Stockholm. While this is beneficial for Stockholm, it also shows how a "home bias" in Sweden can lead to disproportionate benefits for the beneficiary of the bias. This and other biases may mean that the nation that becomes the center for FinTech activity will reap disproportionate rewards.

What is clear from the chapters of this book is that startups are moving faster than incumbents, and making inroads into areas previously dominated by incumbent firms. Both technological advances and changes in implicit rules or norms have worked to the advantage of new firms. However, as regulations start to be passed to protect consumers, they inevitably increase the costs of doing business for both startups and established firms. Incumbent firms, with their deeper pockets and robust organizational structures, are better placed to follow these regulations, while startups may face attrition owing to these regulations. As regulations become more necessary, policymakers should be mindful of the fact that firms of different sizes—and with different business models—may need to be treated differently. We therefore watch with interest at the regulatory sandboxes that some regulators (notably in the UK and Singapore) have begun to make use of.

Conclusion

The phenomenon that is FinTech has its roots in changes in technology, social changes that resulted from financial actors losing legitimacy, and from changes in regulations. However, it has been hard to define, and its effects have been diverse. This diversity is best seen in the variety of different business models that FinTech startups have pursued, and the diverse technologies that they have used. Moreover, this diversity means that there is still room for incumbent actors—whether on their own or in collaboration with newcomers—to make their mark on the FinTech space.

However, this diversity has—and continues to—pose challenges for policymakers. Given how fast it is growing, and how far it is reaching, FinTech products and services encompass a phenomenon that cannot be ignored. Policymakers therefore have a responsibility to keep abreast of changes in the phenomenon as they occur, and respond fairly and proportionately.

Bibliography

Appel, S.M., 2014. *Can you take a security interest in Bitcoin?* [online] Mondaq. Available at: www.mondaq.com/canada/x/313572/securitization+structured+finance/Can+You+Take+A+Security++Interest+In+Bitcoin [Accessed January 16, 2018].

Burton, L., 2017. Mark Carney warns of FinTech threat to traditional banks. *The Telegraph*. [online] Available at: www.telegraph.co.uk/business/2017/04/12/mark-carney-warns-fintech-threat-traditional-banks [Accessed January 16, 2018].

CB Insights, 2016. *The global FinTech report: 2016 in review*. [online] Available at: https://www.cbinsights.com/research/report/fintech-trends-2016 [Accessed January 16, 2018].

Chavez-Dreyfuss, G., 2017. *Blockchain token sale nets $25 million in under 15 minutes.* [online] Reuters. Available at: www.reuters.com/article/us-aragon-blockchain-funding/blockchain-token-sale-nets-25-million-in-under-15-minutes-idUSKCN18E32X [Accessed January 16, 2018].

Christensen, C.M., 1997. *The innovator's dilemma: When new technologies cause great firms to fail.* Boston, MA: Harvard Business School Press.

Dorfleitner, G., Hornuf, L., Schmitt, M., and Weber, M., 2017. *FinTech in Germany.* Cham: Springer.

European Parliament, 2017. *Report on FinTech: The influence of technology on the future of the financial sector (2016/2243(INI)).* [online] Available at: www.europarl.europa.eu/sides/getDoc.do?pubRef=-//EP//TEXT+REPORT+A8-2017-0176+0+DOC+XML+V0//EN [Accessed January 16, 2018].

EY, 2016. *UK FinTech: On the cutting edge—an evaluation of the international FinTech sector.* [online] Available at: www.ey.com/uk/en/industries/financial-services/banking---capital-markets/ey-uk-fintech-on-the-cutting-edge [Accessed January 16, 2018].

Gilberg, M., 2017. *Darwinism will fix the investment industry.* [online] Bloomberg Gadfly. Available at: www.bloomberg.com/gadfly/articles/2017-06-28/darwinism-will-fix-the-investment-industry [Accessed January 16, 2018].

Higgins, S., Sunnarborg, A., and Rizzo, P., 2017. *$150 million: Tim Draper-backed Bancor completes largest-ever ICO.* [online] CoinDesk. Available at: www.coindesk.com/150-million-tim-draper-backed-bancor-completes-largest-ever-ico [Accessed January 16, 2018].

IRS, 2014. *Virtual currency guidance.* [online] Available at: www.irs.gov/newsroom/irs-virtual-currency-guidance [Accessed January 16, 2018].

Williams, G., Gunn, D., Roma, E., and Bansal, B., 2016. *Distributed ledgers in payments: Beyond the Bitcoin hype.* [online] Bain & Company. Available at: www.bain.com/publications/articles/distributed-ledgers-in-payments-beyond-bitcoin-hype.aspx [Accessed January 16, 2018].

Index

Note: Italic denotes figures, bold denotes tables.